European Union

D0083978

Jeremy Richardson has succeeded in assembling an outstanding group of contributors. One distinctive merit of the book is that its focus on public policy-making encourages us to examine a variety of actors within an evolving institutional context.

Professor Jim Caporaso, *Department of Political Science, University of Washington, USA*

A number of Europe's foremost specialists on the European Union offer fascinating theoretical and empirical insights on all central aspects of the EU.

Professor Adrienne Héritier, *European University Institute, Florence, Italy*

This work is now a classic. The third edition includes contributions from some of the most interesting members of the new generation of scholars operating in the field.

Renaud Dehousse, *Jean Monnet Professor of Law and Politics, Sciences Po, Paris, France*

The third edition of this highly regarded textbook will be warmly received. It gains its considerable strength from the authority of its contributors and the comprehensiveness of its coverage.

Professor Wyn Grant, *University of Warwick, UK*

European Union continues to provide advanced undergraduate and postgraduate students with a comprehensive and accessible introduction to the European Union. The primary goal of the textbook is to advance understanding of the European integration process in terms of the EU as a maturing and ongoing policy system.

Written by a distinguished group of internationally recognised researchers, this new edition has been significantly revised to reflect the important changes that have taken place in the EU in recent years and the very latest scholarly thinking. The third edition addresses all the core components of courses on the EU such as the history of the EU, the main theoretical approaches, the role of key institutions in the policy-making process and the implications of enlargement.

The third edition has been updated throughout and includes brand new chapters on:

- theories of European integration
- Europeanisation of public policy
- the EU budgetary procedure
- the process of enlargement
- European macroeconomic governance
- implementation of EU public policy
- judicial law-making
- the European and national parliaments

Contributors: Katrin Auel, Thomas Christiansen, Henrik Enderlein, Mark Franklin, Liesbet Hooghe, Erik Jones, Michael Keating, Christoph Knill, Brigid Laffan, Andrea Lenschow, Johannes Lindner, Margaret McCown, Sonia Mazey, Mike Newman, Jeremy Richardson, Berthold Rittberger, Frank Schimmelfennig, Michael Smith, Mark Thatcher.

Jeremy Richardson is a Fellow of Nuffield College, Oxford, and Editor of the *Journal of European Public Policy*.

Routledge Research in European Public Policy
Edited by Jeremy Richardson
Nuffield College, University of Oxford

European Union

- Power and policy-making

Third edition

Edited by Jeremy Richardson

First edition published 1996
by Routledge

Second edition published 2001
by Routledge

Reprinted 2004

Third edition published 2006
by Routledge
2 Park Square, Milton Park, Abingdon,
Oxon OX14 4RN

Simultaneously published in the USA and Canada
by Routledge
270 Madison Ave, New York, NY 10016

Routledge is an imprint of the Taylor & Francis Group

© 2006 Jeremy Richardson for selection and
editorial matter; individual contributors their
contributions

Typeset in Century Old Style by
Bookcraft Ltd, Stroud, Gloucestershire

Printed and bound in Great Britain by
TJ International Ltd, Padstow, Cornwall

British Library Cataloguing in Publication Data
A catalogue record for this book is available from the
British Library

Library of Congress Cataloging in Publication Data
European Union: power and policy-making /
edited by Jeremy Richardson. – 3rd ed.
    p. cm.
    Includes bibliographical references and index.
    1. European Union. 2. European Union
    countries – Politics and government.
    I. Richardson, J. J. (Jeremy John)
JN30.E942 2005
341.242'2–dc22   2005013319

ISBN10: 0–415–35813–2 (hbk)
ISBN10: 0–415–35814–0 (pbk)

ISBN13: 9–78–0–415–35813–2 (hbk)
ISBN13: 9–78–0–415–35814–9 (pbk)

Contents

CONTENTS

CONTENTS

CONTENTS

Contributors

Katrin Auel, Department of Politics and International Relations, University of Oxford, UK

Thomas Christiansen, European Institute of Public Administration, Maastricht, Netherlands

Henrik Enderlein, Hertie School of Governance, Berlin, Germany

Mark Franklin, Trinity College, Connecticut, USA

Liesbet Hooghe, University of North Carolina, USA

Erik Jones, The Johns Hopkins University, Bologna, Italy

Michael Keating, European University Institute, Florence, Italy

Christoph Knill, University of Konstanz, Germany

Brigid Laffan, University College, Dublin, Ireland

Andrea Lenschow, University of Osnabrück, Germany

Johannes Lindner, European Central Bank, Frankfurt, Germany

Margaret McCown, Institute for National Strategic Studies, Washington DC, USA

Sonia Mazey, Keble College, Oxford, UK

Michael Newman, London Metropolitan University, UK

Jeremy Richardson, Nuffield College, Oxford, UK

Berthold Rittberger, Kaiserslautern University of Technology, Germany

Frank Schimmelfennig, Swiss Federal Institute of Technology, Zürich, Switzerland

Michael Smith, University of Loughborough, UK

Mark Thatcher, London School of Economics and Political Science, UK

Preface

The first edition of this volume was published in 1996. That year brought the start of another Intergovernmental Conference (IGC) dominated by many of the familiar debates which have dogged the European Community and the European Union since the first steps towards integration were taken in 1951. Issues on the agenda included the powers and organisational rules of the main European institutions; relationships between those institutions; the difficult problems presented by the possibility of further enlargement; the role of non-governmental actors such as interest groups and citizens in addressing the democratic deficit, and above all, the fundamental question of whether the gradual erosion of national sovereignty should continue or, indeed, whether it might actually be reversed. Most of these issues were still on the agenda of the Constitutional Convention and were (more or less) addressed in the apparently ill-fated 2004 EU Constitution.

Cries of 'Europe in crisis' and of Europe 'having lost its way' are as familiar in the year 2005 as they were in 1996, suggesting a surprising degree of agenda stability! However, the doomsters are almost certainly exaggerating the current difficulties of the EU and failing to appreciate just how resilient most political systems are. Modern, pluralistic systems are dynamic learning organisations, capable of change. The key institutions and individuals operating those systems have enough intelligence to know when to draw back, when to change tack, and when to lie low and let issues stew. Despite an apparently much more cautious approach to further integration, the ruling elites in the EU still have a keen sense of the risks of moving away from a process that has been under way for decades. Thus we should not forget that the busy 'low politics' of European integration continues in the sense that the EU remains a very 'productive' policy-making system. The pace of integration, in terms of the production of new directives and regulations, has probably slowed down, yet policy innovation continues in new ways and 'integration via policy-making' is still the norm.

If this assertion is correct, what is the main purpose of this book? It is to explain to students of European integration the ways in which power is exercised within the EU today. Our focus is on the policy-making process, as the ultimate arena of power in society. What role do institutions and other actors play in deciding what European policy is about and in determining the content of the enormous mass of European legislation? Thus, whatever labels we might attach to the EU – federal or intergovernmental for example – they are not the main focus of this volume. Suffice for our purposes that the Union still constitutes a very 'productive' and maturing system of public policy-making within which an increasing number of different types of policy actor are involved. There is a long-running 'policy-making engine' at work which seems to push along Euro-sceptics and enthusiasts alike. Our efforts should be judged by whether or not we have assisted students in developing their understanding of the institutions and processes involved in this dynamic.

As editor of this volume, I have an overriding debt. The volume could not have been produced without the enthusiasm of the individual contributors and their considerable expertise in the European policy process and its development. Their sheer professionalism made my editorial task pleasantly light. I also owe a debt to Carol Phillips of Nuffield College, for her help in preparing the manuscript for publication, to Nadia Seemungal of Routledge, for her constant patience and support, and to Matthew Brown of Bookcraft for the efficient management of the production process. Finally, I continue to owe a huge debt to my wife Sonia Mazey, who first introduced me to the importance of studying EU policy-making and who continues to teach me so much about the EU. I will need to live a *very* long time before I can match her knowledge and understanding of both the EU and comparative European politics!

As I argue in the introductory chapter, I believe that the EU is messy and ugly, yet in many ways familiar. I also believe that, warts and all, it is broadly for the good of all Europeans, especially the younger generation. I, therefore, dedicate this third edition to my four children, Rachel, Steven, Tess and Molly in the hope that they live their lives as enthusiastic Europeans.

Jeremy Richardson
Nuffield College, Oxford
April 2005

Part I

THEORETICAL AND HISTORICAL PERSPECTIVES

Chapter 1

Policy-making in the EU

Interests, ideas and garbage cans of primeval soup

JEREMY RICHARDSON

Many people have proposals they would like to see considered seriously, alternatives they would like to see become part of the set from which choices are eventually made. They try out their ideas on others in the policy community. Some proposals are rapidly discarded as somehow kooky; others are taken more seriously and survive, perhaps in some altered form. But in the policy primeval soup, quite a wide range of ideas is possible and is considered to some extent. The range at this stage is considerably more inclusive than the set of alternatives that are actually weighed during a shorter period of final decision-making. Many, many things are possible here.

(Kingdon 1984: 128)

The EU as a policy-making state: the importance of multiple policy stakeholders in the exercise of 'loose-jointed' power play

One of the main attributes of the nation state is the ability to make 'authoritative allocations' for society. In practice this means an ability to formulate and implement public policy programmes governing the operation of society. Whether the European Union (EU) can be considered a fully fledged state is debatable. For example, Hix, drawing on Almond's (1956) and Easton's (1957) characterisations of political systems, concludes that the EU is certainly a political system in that it exhibits most of the characteristics that those writers attribute to political systems. However, he concludes that it is not a state as it lacks a monopoly on the legitimate use of coercion that characterises a state (Hix 2005: 4). Even so, it is beyond dispute that the EU has acquired for itself at least the policy-making attributes of a modern state across an increasingly wide range of policy sectors. Therre is now a huge corpus of EU law affecting a wide range of policy sectors and, as Hix notes, the EU policy process remains very productive in that 'on average more than 100 pieces of legislation pass through the EU institutions every year – more than most other democracies' (Hix 2005: 4). Moreover, the EU does have a degree of 'coercive' power to enforce policy decisions due to the supremacy of EU law over national law. Also, the EU has a degree of steering capacity, via less coercive governance mechanisms, which means that 'power' can be exercised in the sense of getting other actors to change their behaviour. Thus, perhaps we need to have a more sophisticated and subtle notion of EU power, not based on old-fashioned coercion resting on the monopoly of force. (Indeed, how much of the power of the modern nation state over its citizens really rests on coercive force?)

Much of the criticism of the EU over the past decade (and part of the basis of the growing Euroscepticism) has been centred upon the alleged 'excessive' policy-making role of the EU in general and of the Commission in particular. The argument now is that the EU has become a 'nanny' state, over-regulating the economic and social life of member states. Increasing Euroscepticism appears to be causing some of the key stakeholders, particularly the member states, to apply the brakes to the seemingly inexorable extension of the EU's policy-making competence. As Radaelli (1999) suggests, things began to change in the 1990s. Not just the quantity of EU legislation has been subject to challenge, but also its quality and the processes by which it is made. As he notes, the Amsterdam Treaty contains an entire title on the quality of EU legislation. Thus, 'good legislation requires consultation, regulatory impact assessment, and systematic evaluation of the results achieved by European public policies. But it also requires transparency' (Radaelli 1999: 5). These 'process issues' were equally prominent in the Convention and are in part addressed in the 2004 Constitution (see Laffan and Mazey in this volume). In practice, the erosion of national sovereignty (which clearly has taken place, over time) means the erosion of the power of the member states exclusively to decide much of their public policy via domestic policy-making processes and institutions. Whilst retaining the traditional coercive powers of the state, such as going to war, states have in practice ceded many areas of hitherto domestic policy-making to the EU, albeit retaining a powerful role at the new transnational level at which these policies are now made. The EU level is now the level at which a significant proportion of what used to be regarded as purely domestic policy-making takes place. Hix suggests that the EU sets over 80 per cent of the rules governing the exchange of goods, services and capital in the member states' markets (Hix 2005: 4), although Moravcsik is more doubtful, citing one study which estimated that the actual percentage of EU-based legislation is probably between 10 and 20 per cent of national rule-making (Moravcsik 2005: 17). Moravcsik also argues that many policy areas are still untouched by *direct* EU policy-making, such as social welfare, health care, pensions, education, defence, active cultural policy, and most law and order (Moravcsik 2005: 17). However, other authors see a stronger European influence (albeit sometimes indirect) in at least some of these policy areas. For example, Greer's study of neofunctionalism in EU health policy concludes that 'once the European Court of Justice had decided that health systems are economic activities like any others, and therefore subject to internal market legislation, the conditions under which health systems gain and use resources changed dramatically, regardless of formal state protection or the existence of ECJ principles that limit the ability of EU law to wholly upset health systems' (Greer 2006). Whatever the true figure for the amount of legislation that now emanates from the EU, it seems reasonable to assume that the *direction* of change is steady. For many policy areas, the locus of decision-making – and therefore power – has already shifted and it seems likely that others will gradually follow this pattern, albeit along different paths. Also, as Stone Sweet argues, there appear to be no examples of rollback (Stone Sweet 2004: 236). A more complex structure of policy-making has developed at the EU level, encompassing a much wider range of public and private policy actors. All of these actors – especially national governments – are having to adjust to the reality of this situation. They have all 'lost' some power in a common pooling of policy-making sovereignty. For those European nations who are members of the EU (and for many who are not), at least two policy-making systems now cohabit – domestic and EU policy systems. As Laffan *et al.* suggest, the defining characteristic of the Union is the enmeshing of the national and the European, or the embedding of the national in the European (Laffan *et al.* 2000: 74–8). This has led to what they term a system of 'international governance', with the EU, as an arena of public policy, presenting 'a challenge to national political systems because they are confronted with the need to adapt to a normative and strategic environment that escapes total control' (Laffan *et al.* 2000: 84–7).

The EU is, of course, a complex and (like national policy systems) to some degree a unique policy-making system. Its multinational and neo-federal nature, the extreme openness of decision-making to lobbyists, and the considerable weight of national politico-administrative elites within the process, create an unpredictable and multi-level policy-making environment. Even the relationships between key institutions – such as the Commission, the European Parliament (EP), the Council of Ministers (CM) and the European Court of Justice (ECJ) – has been in a considerable state of flux for many decades, with each IGC producing a new 'institutional settlement', as many of the chapters in this volume demonstrate. Although clearly a very productive policy process, the EU political system has not been institutionally stable. The basic constitutional architecture has been a long-running cause of dispute. At best the EU policy process has exhibited some stable patterns of cross-national coalition-building; at worst some of the extreme aspects of a garbage can (Cohen *et al.* 1972) model of decision-making (for a discussion see below). It is no surprise, therefore, that the EU regulatory system has been described as a 'patchwork of different national regulatory styles' (Héritier 1996).

The EU policy process is undoubtedly 'messy' but we should be a little cautious in seeing it as especially unusual or indeed especially bad. It is certainly ugly but many aspects are perfectly familiar to policy analysts (see Mazey and Richardson, this volume, chapter 12). 'Ugly but familiar' is probably a fair description. As Zweifel suggests, when assessing the EU against measures of democracies, we should not apply higher standards of evaluation than we do for national policy systems (Zweifel 2002). The very 'messiness' of the EU as a policy system, of course, makes it difficult to formulate reliable descriptions – let alone theoretical models – which will capture more than a few aspects of the policy process as a whole or which apply to all cases. The objective of this chapter is limited, therefore, to an analysis of the possible utility of what has become the dominant 'model' for analysing the policy process in Western Europe – the so-called policy community/policy network model. One of the central features of the EU policy process, which seems to hold good for a high percentage of cases, is that it 'works' only by mobilising a large number of public and private actors, from different nations and policy domains and, somehow, persuading them to move from the status quo to a new policy settlement. Fortuitously, approaching EU policy-making via this actor-based or stakeholder perspective also enables us to utilise related approaches to the study of policy-making which emphasise the importance of ideas, knowledge and expertise, rather than pure 'interest'. It will be argued that there are inherent similarities in these two 'actor-based' approaches, even though they originate from quite different academic perspectives. Essentially they both focus on sets of actors as stakeholders in the policy process. Elsewhere in this volume, contributors analyse the roles of 'official' or 'public' stakeholders (e.g. national governments, the Commission, the EP, the ECJ). However, all of these actors are influenced by ideas, knowledge and private interests. Thus, over forty years ago E. E. Schattschneider reminded us that the supreme instrument of political power was the ability to determine what politics was about (Schattschneider 1960). Although this is a neglected aspect of the workings of the EU (for a notable exception see Peters 2001), evidence does suggest that the EU agenda-setting process is especially problematic because of its transnational nature and because of the wide range of state and non-state actors involved in the EU policy process (Mazey and Richardson 1993). Moreover, as with nation states, the EU's policy agenda is permeable to extra-territorial influences – from non-EU states such as the USA and Japan, but also from international standard-setting bodies and organisations such as the World Health Organization (WHO) (Richardson 1994), OECD (Dostal 2004), and via the EU's participation in global regulatory agencies such as the World Trade Organization (WTO). The EU is not only a form of 'supranational' policy-making in its own right, it is also part of a higher level of supranational policy-making, beyond the regional (EU) level. Such complex policy-making arrangements can, under certain circumstances, privilege the role of experts and technocrats, who are increasingly transnational in their focus and activities. Thus, analysis of the role of 'communities' of experts – so-called epistemic communities (see below) – is important in the EU because they so often transcend national boundaries. The policy community/policy network approach, in contrast, appears to have some utility in assisting our understanding of the ways in which agenda issues are translated or 'processed' into technical and workable EU legislative proposals – especially in technical areas of 'low politics' (Hoffmann 1966). Other related concepts from public policy, which attempt to integrate analyses of ideas and interests – such as Sabatier's 'advocacy coalitions' and Kingdon's 'policy streams' – may also be useful in assisting our understanding of the policy dynamics of the EU, especially if we view the EU policy process as essentially a multi-level, multi-arena game. They may enable us to better understand how all decision-makers in the EU, public or private, national or supranational, come to 'frame' public policy problems (Rein and Schön 1991). Interestingly, in terms of our earlier reference to coercion, Fischer sees the construction of 'social meanings' as a more basic strategy for generating support in a democratic system than coercion. Thus, 'while intimidation and coercion help to counter political resistance, the most basic strategy for generating support in democratic systems is the evocation of social and political interpretations that legitimize the desired course of action' (Fischer 2003: 55).

The 'level of analysis' question is, of course, important. Thus, it may be a mistake to look for only one model of the EU policy process. Within the EU, policy can be determined at a number of levels and the policy process goes through a number of stages. Also, particular policy areas may themselves be episodic, exhibiting different characteristics at different times. Different models of analysis may be useful at different levels within the EU and at different stages of the policy process. For example, if we were to conceptualise the EU policy process into four stages – agenda-setting, policy formulation, policy decision, and policy implementation – we might need to utilise rather different conceptual tools in order to understand fully the nature of the processes in each stage. The epistemic communities approach might be particularly useful in understanding stage one, the policy community/network model for stage two, institutional analysis for stage three, and inter-organisational behaviour and implementation analysis for stage four. Even then, reality is likely to be much more messy, suggesting that we need a fairly eclectic use of concepts and models. 'Grand theory' must await a much stronger empirical base, bearing in mind that there are major cross-sectoral variations in EU policy styles. For example, some policy areas may be highly pluralistic (e.g. environmental policy) and others may exhibit some corporatist tendencies (e.g. agriculture).

It is also important to note that the EU policy-making system as a whole might vary over time. Thus, just as the pace and nature of the integration process is not constant (see Laffan and Mazey, this volume, chapter 2), so the nature of the policy process within it can vary over time. It is now conventional wisdom that the EU policy style is less clearly a regulatory style, reflecting the increased resistance to further Europeanisation and the alleged weakened position of the Commission as the motor of integration (see Christiansen, this volume, chapter 5). The annual output of directives has declined; there is said to be less 'old-style' regulation; and there is an alleged shift towards new policy instruments that emphasise cooperation, voluntary action, demonstration projects, good practice, benchmarking, and so forth. The introduction of the so-called Open Method of coordination (OMC) following the Lisbon summit in 2000 can be seen as a process reform (Borrás and Jacobsson 2004: 188) designed to meet criticisms of old-style top-down and *dirigiste* legislation. Thus, it is essentially intergovernmental, there is no role for the ECJ, with the Council and the Commission 'relying to a larger extent on political rather than legal logic' (Borrás and Jacobsson 2004: 188). This more flexible approach was evident before OMC was invented of course and we should be slightly cautious in seeing OMC as some radical new dawn in EU policy-making. Also, the greater emphasis on 'softer' policy instruments may actually disguise the continuation and extension of old-style regulation (see Rittberger and Richardson 2003). The shift towards softer policy instruments has been accompanied by an intensification of consultation of stakeholders (see Mazey and Richardson, this volume, chapter 12). The more the policy-making legitimacy of the EU has been challenged, the more the Commission has mobilised stakeholder participation in the process. Interestingly the expansion of consultation also appears as a feature of OMC. Thus, 'OMC seeks to mobilize the participation of a wide range of actors, public as well as private. In terms of actor constellation, the OMC is multi-level, involves other than state actors, and is designed to foster co-operative practices and networking' (Borrás and Jacobsson 2004: 189).

In searching for useful theories and concepts, the notion of the EU as a policy-making 'state', backed by the legal authority of the ECJ, is important. Our central argument here is that the 'stuff' of European integration is as much about detailed, often technical, Euro-legislation (a mixture of Euro-regulation and softer policy instruments) as it is about high politics issues such as monetary union or the creation of a European superstate or, to take a very current example, the adoption or not of a Constitution for the EU. At the time of writing (July 2005) the new constitution appears to have little chance of being ratified after the votes against it in the French and Dutch referenda. As a British Conservative spokesman, formerly a medical doctor, put it, although he had not practised medicine for many years he could still recognise a corpse when he saw one! One should never underestimate the capacity of Europe's leaders to cobble together some patchwork of compromises that will rescue at least parts of what was supposed to be a grand (albeit foolish) constitutional settlement. Either way it is doubtful if the constitution would have very much impact, if any, on the volume (or, indeed, the nature) of the EU's policy outputs. While these big constitutional issues are, of course, important, and certainly absorb the interest of national governments, the 'European policy game' continues to be played at the detailed policy level and continues to attract the attention and efforts of a plethora of interest groups and others in the manner predicted by the neo-functionalists. Low politics this may be, in the Hoffmann terminology (Hoffmann 1966), but it is probably the nine-tenths of the EU 'policy iceberg' that is below the water line. Also, we need to remember that the EU is no longer a 'new' policy system. In terms of institutional design it has been in a state of flux, but the key point, for our purposes, is that it has been churning out public policy for a very long time. The EU policy system now fits Wildavsky's anlysis of policy-making in more 'mature' democracies as being often driven by the need to change past policies. As he put it, policy is its own cause and today's policy solutions become tomorrow's policy problems (Wildavsky 1979: 83). McGowan's recent study of the radical reform of the EU's cartel policy is a timely reminder of the maturity of much of the EU's public policy output. He notes that cartel policy was first formulated in 1962 and that the reforms which came into effect in May 2004 were sparked by three main factors: 'Firstly, a recognition that existing practices had been in place for over forty years and were becoming more problematic; secondly, changing economic circumstances and thirdly, an augmented case load after EU enlargement into Central and Eastern Europe' (McGowan 2005: 994). There is a huge amount of so-called 'low politics' activity within the EU (just as there is in any of the member states), much of it consisting of revising and reforming existing EU policies as well as extending the EU's policy remit into yet more policy areas. This policy-making activity is not simply a question of intergovernmental relations – if only because such a wide range of non-governmental actors is so obviously involved, at both the national, EU and extra-EU levels. EU policies are not simply the outcome of interstate bargaining, even if the policy process usually appears to culminate in this way in the Council of Ministers. It is a long and complex process involving many different types of actors most of whom are involved in 'nested games' (Tsebelis 1990), in serial coalition-building and a constant process of bargaining (see Farrell and Héretier 2005).

Regardless of the way that problems and issues arrive on the political agenda, it is a phenomenon of modern governance that procedural mechanisms (formal and informal institutions, formal and informal rules) are devised to bring the various stakeholders together in order to thrash out a solution which is ultimately acceptable (hence the use of the term *governance* rather than *government*). Modern government is not just characterised by ad hoc and permanent committees, but by a 'procedural logic' which brings policy actors together in some kind of relationship – hence the popularity in public policy analysis of approaches utilising variants of the 'policy network' approach which emphasise bargaining and consensus-building rather than hierarchical relationships. Even in past periods of so-called 'Euro-sclerosis' or in the current phase of Euroscepticism, the Union finds ways of 'legislating in hard times'. The very fact that it is currently more difficult to generate and pass European legislation merely intensifies the logic of actor mobilisation. For 'the European project' to move forward, the many stakeholders need to be given more incentives to participate at the Euro-level and their participation needs to be structured and institutionalised. As Laffan *et al.* suggest, 'enhanced policy responsibility has led to an expansion of policy networks and communities around the core of the Union institutions' (Laffan *et al.* 2000: 85). A central aspect of the Jacques Santer dictum 'doing less but doing it better' (European Commission 1995: 6) is even greater effort to involve the many stakeholders having a recognised interest in any given policy area. As Mazey and Richardson suggest in this volume, the trend is for more and more participation in the EU policy process such that this has become an embedded EU *policy style.*

Policy communities, policy networks and issue networks

It is worth remembering that the term 'policy community' was originally used (at least in Britain) with a quite deliberate emphasis on community, and at a time when policy stability rather than policy change seemed more common. Moreover, it was developed as a counterweight to more traditional analyses of the British policy process. For example, the subtitle of *Governing under Pressure* (first published in 1979) was provocative in claiming that Britain was a post-parliamentary democracy: the focus of the analysis was on the informal relationships between different policy actors rather than on the roles of formal institutions. Thus:

> In describing the tendency for boundaries between government and groups to become less distinct through a whole range of pragmatic developments, we see policies being made (and administered) between a myriad of interconnecting, interpenetrating organisations. It is the relationship involved in committees, the

policy community of departments and groups, the practices of cooption and the consensual style, that perhaps better account for policy outcomes than do examinations of party stances, of manifestos or of parliamentary influence.

(Richardson and Jordan 1979: 73–4)

The term policy community was meant to convey a very close and stable relationship between policy actors – somewhat close to the dictionary definition of community: 'joint ownership of goods, identity of character, fellowship (... of interest)'. Use of the word community also implied some notions regarding level of analysis. If policy actors could be brought together in a long-term and stable relationship which presented the prospect of an *exchange relationship*, then this was most likely at the sub-sectoral or even micro-level. There was also an implication of stable policies as well as stable relationships and a stable membership. Thus, it was argued that

> The logic of negotiation also suggests that policy-makers in both government and groups will share an interest in the avoidance of sudden policy change. Working together they will learn what kind of change is feasible and what would so embarrass other members of the 'system' as to be unproductive. Members of the system will begin to debate in the same language (if not with the same values), and arguments will be treated seriously only if discussed in these common criteria. There is a role diffusion in that all members – government officials, academic experts and group officials – become policy professionals.
>
> (Jordan and Richardson 1982: 93–4)

This simple picture of policy-making in which recognised stakeholders are sort of granted the franchise for public policy and strive to achieve a *negotiated environment* gets more difficult to sustain when the number and range of stakeholders expands rapidly. Within the EU (and, again, similar trends can be seen at the national level), the pattern appears to be an increase in the number of stakeholders (public and private) demanding and getting participation in EU policy-making, and an extension of the range of policy sectors from which they are drawn, for each particular example of consultation (Richardson 2000). This gradual shift in emphasis – from a world of policy-making characterised by tightly-knit policy communities, to a more loosely organised and therefore less predictable policy process – is very familiar in the US. The seminal work (on either side of the Atlantic) is still Heclo's 1978 analysis, which began to re-direct us towards policy dynamics rather than policy stability. Just as many authors (including this one!) were emphasising stable policy communities, Heclo had observed a trend which appears to be still running strongly at both the national and international levels – namely that policy problems often eventually escape the confined and exclusive 'worlds' of professionals and are resolved in a much looser configuration of participants in the policy process. Heclo argued that the nature of power in Washington had begun to change – exercising power was not as much fun as it used to be in the 'clubby' days of Washington politics (Heclo 1978: 94). Politics was less 'clubbable' because more and more groups had entered the policy process. Thus 'as proliferating groups have claimed a stake and clamoured for a place in the policy process, they have helped diffuse the focus of political and administrative leadership' (Heclo 1978: 94–5). The process had gone so far, he argued, that

With more public policies, more groups are being mobilized and there are more complex relationships among them. Since very few policies ever seem to drop off the public agenda as more are added, congestion among those interested in various issues grows, the chances for accidental collisions increase, and the interaction tends to take on a distinctive group-life of its own in the Washington community. One scene in a recent Jacques Tati film pictures a Paris traffic circle so dense with traffic that no one can get in or out; instead, drivers spend their time socialising with each other as they drive in endless circles. Group politics in Washington may be becoming such a merry-go-round.

(Heclo 1978: 97)

In the context of the EU, all we need do is substitute Brussels for Washington. Correctly, Heclo argued that we needed to rethink our notions of political power. Existing conceptions of power and control were not well suited to the 'loose-jointed' power play of influence that was emerging. In a now classic formulation, he argued that

Obviously questions of power are still important. But for a host of policy initiatives undertaken in the last twenty years it is all but impossible to identify clearly who the dominant actors are. Who is controlling those actions that go to make up our national policy on abortions, or on income redistribution, or consumer protection, or energy? Looking for the few who are powerful we tend to overlook the many whose webs of influence provoke and guide the exercise of power. These webs, or what I will call 'issue networks', are particularly relevant to the highly intricate and confusing welfare policies that have been undertaken in recent years.

(Heclo 1978: 102)

Again one is reminded of the EU policy process, where interest groups and national governments often feel that policies come from 'nowhere' (Mazey and Richardson 1993). Indeed, Dyson borrows a term from Heinz *et al.* (1993) to describe the policy processes relating to European Monetary Union (EMU). Conventional wisdom might suggest that the German state, and especially the Bundesbank, has such 'state strength' (Krasner 1978: 55) as to secure their desired pay-offs, but the policy process seems much more messy and complex. Dyson observes that 'there is little evidence that a single actor – whether the Commission or Ecofin or the Bundesbank – occupies the central policy-brokering role within the EMU process in any continuous sense, capable in a more or less autonomous way of promoting compromise or imposing settlements. In this sense, the EMU policy process has a "hollow core"' (Dyson 1994: 332). Asking 'Who runs this place?' is a singularly difficult question within the EU. The safe answer is usually 'Many people run this place'!

The primary causes of the increasing 'messiness' of the EU policy process are twofold. First, the very act of adding more countries increases complexity enormously. In formulating what he terms an 'EU law of physics', Pascal Lamoy, the EU's Trade Commissioner, has suggested that 'complexity is an exponential and not proportional function of the number of members of the EU' (*Financial Times* 3 August 2000). Second, the addition of new member states significantly adds to the number and range of interest groups who demand participation at the European level. There are simply too many players with too many diverse interests and competing policy frames for the policy community (or, indeed, corporatist) model to become the dominant paradigm within the EU.

Even Heclo, however, was reluctant to accept a total-disorder thesis, making at least two important qualifications to the model of confusion, diffuse power, and lack of accountability (all features of the EU identified as important in the Convention process leading to the 2004 Constitutions!). He pointed out a paradox of disorder *and* order when he argued that there was a second tendency cutting in the opposite direction to the widening group participation in public policy. In the midst of the emergence of the loose issue networks cited above we could also see what he called 'policy as intramural activity'. Thus:

> Expanding welfare policies and Washington's reliance on indirect administration have encouraged the development of specialized subcultures composed of highly knowledgeable policy-watchers. Some of these people have advanced professional degrees, some do not. What they all have in common is the detailed understanding of specialized issues that comes from sustained attention to a given policy debate.
>
> (Heclo 1978: 49)

In a less quoted passage, he deftly links the two apparently contradictory trends, as follows:

> Whatever the participants' motivation, it is the issue network that ties together what would otherwise be the contradictory tendencies of, on the one hand, more widespread organizational participation in public policy and, on the other, more narrow technocratic specialization in complex modern policies. Such networks need to be distinguished from three other more familiar terms used in connection with political administration. An issue network is a shared-knowledge group having to do with some aspect (or, as defined by the network, some problem) of public policy. It is therefore more well-defined than, first, a shared-attention group or 'public'; those in the networks are likely to have a common base of information and understanding of how one knows about policy and identifies its problems. But knowledge does not necessarily produce agreement. Issue networks may or may not, therefore, be mobilized into, second, a shared-action group (creating a coalition) or, third, a shared-belief group (becoming a conventional interest organization). Increasingly, it is through networks of people who regard each other as knowledgeable, or at least as needing to be answered, that public policy issues tend to be refined, evidence debated, and alternative options worked out – though rarely in any controlled, well-organized way.
>
> (Heclo 1978: 103–4)

So, how can sense be made of these contrasting images of the policy process? On the one hand, we have the policy community concept. On the other hand, there is the rather 'disorderly' issue network concept. The suggestion by Rhodes that policy communities and issue networks are part of a continuum – and that policy networks should be used as a generic term – is a sensible reminder that there is no one model of policy-making. He draws on Benson's 1982 definition of a network as 'a cluster or complex of organizations connected to each other by resource dependencies and distinguished from other clusters or complexes by breaks in the structure of resource dependencies' (Benson 1982: 148). However, he goes on to distinguish five types of networks 'ranging along a continuum from highly integrated policy communities to loosely integrated issue networks' (Rhodes 1990: 304).

Recognising the network concept as a continuum does enable us to focus on the possibility of changes in the nature of the policy process over time and from sector to sector. Thus, it may be that at any given time several types of policy networks (in the generic sense) are in operation within the EU. If so, we need to analyse the interrelationships (if any) between these and the conditions under which they emerge. Also, over time, the policy process might change its characteristics quite significantly, along the continuum; and, of course, it may often be unhelpful to use the network analogy at all for the analysis of some EU policy decisions.

Describing certain stages of the policy process in network terms can be useful and illuminating, but we must not neglect the role of institutions. For example, in the EU the role of the Council of Ministers is obviously crucial, yet it is difficult to see analysis of policy networks as being central to an analysis of the Council. No doubt ministers will to some degree reflect the power of national networks in the manner suggested by Putnam (Putnam 1988), but, clearly, they do not follow their national interest group systems slavishly. Similarly, the Commission, as an institutional actor in its own right, is enormously powerful in the EU policy process. Again it can be seen as a broker of interests, or a bourse of ideas and interests (Mazey and Richardson 1994), but it is much more than that and has its own institutional interest to protect and expand (see Christiansen, and Mazey and Richardson, in this volume). Moreover, we must not neglect the role of ideas, of ideology, or the special powers of state actors in setting the agenda for policy change at both the national and international levels; in many instances policy networks, where they exist, are responding to rather than creating policy change.

What then is the utility of the policy network approach and what is its potential for EU level analysis? Two modest but sensible claims might be made. First, by trying to identify networks of policy actors we at least focus on what might be called the stakeholders in the EU policy processes. If EU politics is about who gets what, how and when (as surely it is?), then identifying the range of actors involved and trying to see if they can realistically be described as networks is at least the starting point for understanding how the system of making EU policies works. Sensible research questions are: 'Who has an interest in this policy problem? How are they mobilised and organised? What is the timing and nature of their involvement in the policy process? How are their preferences determined, and are they really fixed? Do they develop stable relationships with each other?' We also need to ask who is likely to gain and who is likely to lose from different policy outcomes. In addressing these questions within the EU, we need to be cautious in transposing some of the (alleged) characteristics of various types of national policy networks. For example, many groups involved in the EC policy process have little or no formal involvement in policy delivery, nor are they necessarily involved in any direct resource dependencies with other decision-makers except in a very general sense. Similarly, they may have quite different value systems and often exhibit very contrasting and conflicting views of the policy problem and of possible solutions. They arrive in Brussels with competing policy frames and a process of what Schön and Rein termed 'frame reflection has to take place (Schön and Rein 1994). The basis of the relationship between these different actors is threefold: (1) recognition of each other as legitimate stake-holders in the policy area/problem; (2) a recognition that collaboration may be the best means of achieving policy gains; (3) a desire to achieve negotiated and stable policy environments in preference to instability and uncertainty. In other words, *cooperation* within various types of policy network is a sensible strategy in a policy game in which there are many veto points; there are mutual gains to be had via cooperation. This is rather different from direct resource dependency or a shared direct involvement in service delivery, or shared values. Focusing on networks of stakeholders may, therefore, help us to analyse the detailed process by which new knowledge and policy ideas (which may well originate elsewhere, see Reich 1988; Radaelli 1995; Braun and Busch 1999; Fischer 2003) are translated into specific policy proposals.

Policy-making under uncertainty: knowledge and mutual gains

The EU is faced with twenty-five different policy systems, each reflecting national power structures (and national policy networks). They bring to the Brussels table their own public policy traditions in terms of policy and regulatory styles. The EU is, therefore, a huge cauldron of policy proposals, ideas and traditions from which EU public policy must be distilled. If European integration via EU public policy is to take place, these national policy arrangements must be challenged in some way and new Euro-level policy settlements agreed. Although the processes of EU policy formulation and implementation are generally consensual, there are, of course, some aspects of an impositional policy style in the EU (Richardson 1982). Thus, QMV in the end 'imposes' decisions on the losers in any policy conflict and ECJ decisions are difficult to ignore. EU legislation is neither symbolic nor cheap talk. It matters materially to a whole host of actors, not least national governments. It is not surprising therefore that the range of potential actors in the EU policy process is enormous and the patterns of interaction are sometimes unpredictable.

Garbage can politics

With so many actors and so many ideas, how, then, does policy change take place within the EU in the absence of a European government or at least a stable 'governing' coalition? In a key passage, Adler and Haas argue that it is useful to turn the study of the political process into a question about who learns what, when, to whose benefit and why? (Adler and Haas 1992: 370). Perceiving the policy process as centrally concerned with ideas, knowledge and their use is both helpful and consistent with our concern with actor-based models of the policy process. The work by Peter Haas and his colleagues is of particular relevance to the workings of the EU. Although concerned with international cooperation (and therefore approaching the EU from an international relations perspective) Haas's comment that 'a related question/debate is the extent to which state actors fully recognise and appreciate the anarchic nature of the system and, consequently, whether rational choice, deductive-type approaches or interpretative approaches are most appropriate' is very apposite to our own task here. Acting rationally in situations of very high uncertainty and in the absence of crucial information about the policy positions and behaviour of other stakeholders is difficult. Indeed, actors may be totally unaware of other key stakeholders in the process, let alone of the policy preferences and strategies of those actors! In such situations, the term 'network' should be used with great caution. Literally, 'network' should mean that the various actors do interconnect in some way. Empirically, this is sometimes difficult to determine and, rather like the puzzle relating to the existence of life elsewhere in the universe, policy actors are often uncertain as to the identity of other actors elsewhere in the 'system'. Again, this is as true for national governments as it is true for, say, firms or associations. Actors often operate under a huge degree of uncertainty in what are often very long-running games, with uncertain pay-offs. The total 'system' is large and amorphous, with numbers of part-time participants and a range of ideas floating around in some ethereal fashion. In these situations the policy process may resemble the 'garbage can' model of decision-making developed by Cohen *et al.* in 1972 and elaborated by Kingdon (Cohen *et al.* 1972; Kingdon 1984). The central feature of the original garbage can model is that 'decision situations' (or what Cohen *et al.* termed 'organized anarchies') are characterised by three general properties. First, there are problematic preferences. The organisation operates on the basis of a variety of inconsistent and ill-defined preferences (Cohen *et al.* 1972: 1). Their description of organisational life fits well with what we already know about some aspects of the EU – namely, that 'it (the organisation) can be described better as a loose collection of ideas than as a coherent structure, it discovers preferences through action more than it acts on the basis of preferences' (Cohen *et al.* 1972: 1). The second characteristic of decision situations is unclear technology. Although the organisation manages to survive and even produce, its own processes are not understood by its members. A succession of IGCs (including the most recent, in 2004, to consider the draft Constitution) has considered demands for the simplification of the EU policy process and for greater predictability of decision pathways. The EU is just like any other decision-making organisation. Over time it changes its procedures in the light of past practice and, as we suggested earlier, it has a capacity for policy learning that leads to a continuous process of policy adjustment in the manner predicted by Wildavsky. In practice, organisations such as the national governments and the EU operate 'on the basis of simple trial-and-error procedures, the residue of learning from the incident of past experience, and pragmatic inventions of necessity' (Cohen *et al.* 1972: 1). Finally, there is fluid participation in that participants vary in the amount of time and effort they devote to different domains. In practice, it is useful to view an organisation as *a collection of choices looking for problems, issues and feelings looking for decision situations in which they might be aired, solutions looking for issues to which they might be the answer, and decision-makers looking for work'* (Cohen *et al.* 1972: 2, emphasis added).

The Haas argument is, centrally, that the politics of uncertainty lead to a certain mode of behaviour – namely that policy-makers, when faced with 'the uncertainties associated with many modern responsibilities of international governance turn to new and different channels of advice, often with the result that international policy coordination is advanced' (Haas 1992: 12).

As he argues, the concept of uncertainty is important for two reasons:

> First, in the face of uncertainty ... many of the conditions facilitating a focus on power are absent. It is difficult for leaders to identify their potential political allies and to be sure of what strategies are most likely to help them retain power. And,

second, poorly understood conditions may create enough turbulence that established operating procedures may break down, making institutions unworkable. Neither power nor institutional cues to behaviour would be available, and new patterns of action may ensue.

(Haas 1992: 14)

However, as Sebenius points out, uncertainty and *power* do go hand in hand, as uncertainty presents opportunities for power to be exercised if individuals or institutions are sufficiently alert to the opportunities. He therefore argues that we need to emphasise the interplay of power and knowledge in influencing outcomes (Sebenius 1992: 325). Alongside uncertainty in the policy process there are opportunities for mutual learning and joint problem-solving – especially when issues involve technical uncertainties in such areas as scientific, environmental, economic and security affairs. By combining the politics of uncertainty and the politics of learning, Sebenius in fact captures the core meaning of 'policy community' as a concept. Thus he states that 'beyond understanding technical uncertainties, finding joint gains also requires that each party learn about the other's priorities in order to craft mutually beneficial trades' (Sebenius 1992: 329). Cooperation, therefore, can produce what Walton and McKersie term 'integrated bargaining' as opposed to 'distributive bargaining'. In the former the effort is directed towards expanding the pie, whereas in the latter it is a more adversarial process of dividing the pie (Walton and McKersie 1965). Sebenius goes on to quote Howard Raiffa as follows:

In complicated negotiations where uncertainties loom large, there may be contracts that are far better for each negotiating party than the non-contract alternative, but it may take considerable skill and joint problem solving to discover these possibilities. Without the right atmosphere and without some reasonably trustful communication of values, such jointly acceptable contracts might never be discerned.

(Raiffa, quoted by Sebenius 1992: 329)

This is not too dissimilar to the original formulation of the policy communities concept suggested in *Governing under Pressure* in 1979. This emphasised the development of a common understanding of each other's problems and a recognition that beneficial bargains could be struck over time. Logically, this does not imply consensus on values or on outcomes – but it does imply a consensus that collaboration can produce efficiency gains all round. There may be considerable and bitter disputation, yet the game continues to be played in order to secure mutual gains or to avoid excessive individual losses. This seems to fit what we know about the EU policy process. Lax and Sebenius have emphasised that the bargaining process indeed exhibits both conflict and consensus. Thus:

the competitive and co-operative elements are inextricably entwined. In practice they cannot be separated. This bonding is fundamentally important to the analysis, structuring the conduct of negotiation. There is a central, inescapable tension between co-operative moves to create value jointly and competitive

16

moves to gain individual advantage. This tension affects virtually all tactical and strategic choice. Analysts must come to grips with it; negotiators must manage it.

(Lax and Sebenius 1986: 30)

Participating in joint policy-making activity therefore has the potential to maximise benefits to the parties involved. Using concepts from negotiation analysis, Sebenius points out that outcomes can be influenced by favourably affecting the zone of possible agreement between the parties. The 'zone of possible agreement' means 'a set of possible agreements that are better for each potential party than the non-co-operative alternatives to an agreement' (Sebenius 1992: 333).

Expertise and epistemic communities

The value of these approaches is that they remind us that policy actors, such as those participating in the EU policy process, are often operating under considerable degrees of uncertainty and are prepared to engage in a negotiative process even when there is considerable disagreement over basic goals or core beliefs. The key role of epistemic communities in this process relates directly to the principle that policy-makers are operating under conditions of uncertainty. Thus:

> Given the technical uncertainties regarding an issue and the legitimacy of claims to expertise of members of an epistemic community, especially those placed close to the decision-making process, their influence may cause the perceived interests of key players in different countries to grow closer together, along with their understanding of underlying causal relationships. In this situation, the epistemic community members may come to act as a coordinated set of common interpretative filters.

(Sebenius 1992: 354)

It is the knowledge-based (or at least perceived knowledge-based) nature of epistemic communities that provides these networks of actors with the potential to influence the policy process. Authoritativeness, and therefore legitimacy, are the key currencies of these types of networks, and they are central to the definition of epistemic communities formulated by Peter Haas, as follows:

> An epistemic community is a network of professionals with recognised expertise and competence in a particular domain and an authoritative claim to policy-relevant knowledge within that domain or issue-area. Although an epistemic community may consist of professionals from a variety of disciplines and backgrounds, they have (1) a shared set of normative and principled beliefs, which provide a value-based rationale for the social action of community members; (2) shared causal beliefs, which are derived from their analysis of practices leading or contributing to a central set of problems in their domain and which then serve as the basis for elucidating the multiple linkages between possible policy actions and desired outcomes; (3) shared notions of validity – that is, intersubjective, internally defined criteria for weighing and validating knowledge in the domain of their expertise; and (4) a common policy enterprise – that is, a set of common

practices associated with a set of problems to which their professional competence is directed, presumably out of the conviction that human welfare will be enhanced as a consequence.

(Haas 1992: 3)

As with the policy network concept, epistemic communities as a concept is also subject to refinement and redefinition. In a useful footnote, Haas reveals that other characterisations of epistemic communities were discussed during the preparation of the special issue of *International Organization* in which his seminal paper appears. Some of the additional notions used were as follows:

members of an epistemic community share intersubjective understandings; have a shared way of knowing; have shared patterns of reasoning; have a policy project drawing on shared values, share causal beliefs, and the use of shared discursive practices; and have a shared commitment to the application and production of knowledge.

(Haas 1992: 3)

Interestingly, Haas sees some kind of logic in this process of policy coordination via epistemic communities. The situation in which policy-makers find themselves leads almost naturally to the use of experts of various kinds. Just as it has been argued in Britain that there is a 'logic of negotiation' (Jordan and Richardson 1982: see also Mazey and Richardson, this volume), so the dynamics of uncertainty, interpretation and institutionalisation at the international level drive policy-makers towards the use of epistemic communities. Haas argues that 'in international policy co-ordination, the forms of uncertainty that tend to stimulate demands for information are those which arise from the strong dependence of states on each other's policy choices for success in obtaining goals and those which involve multiple and only partly estimable consequences of action' (Haas 1992: 3–54). Uncertainty gives rise to demands for information – particularly about 'social or physical processes, their interrelationship with other processes, and the likely consequences of actions that require considerable scientific or technical expertise' (Haas 1992: 4).

Haas goes on to suggest that state actors are 'uncertainty reducers' as well as power and wealth pursuers. In conditions of high uncertainty, it becomes difficult for national governments to define clearly just what the national interest is. They are not only engaged on a two-level game as suggested by Putnam, they are also involved in a multi-dimensional international game where strategies consistent with the national interest in one sector may be inconsistent with the national interest being pursued in another sector. It is not surprising that state actors look for ways of reducing uncertainty. They recognise that changing the world is going to be very difficult and that they may have to settle, therefore, for minimising their surprises. Again, this is consistent with what we know about national policy-making – many policy-makers are risk-averse and one way of reducing risk to them is to share it. For example, Henderson's now classic study of a series of British policy decisions describes risk-sharing behaviour through consultation, as follows:

making sure that, at every stage of the policy process, the right chairs have been warmed at the right committee tables by the appropriate institutions, everything possible has been done and no one could possibly be blamed if things go wrong.

(Henderson 1977: 189)

Bearing in mind just how large the EU is, it would be surprising if Commission officials, charged with the actual formulation of policy proposals, did not engage in similar behaviour. By drawing other policy actors into the policy process, the Commission may be able to build coalitions in favour of its own notions of desirable policy change. By assisting the formation of networks of 'relevant' state and non-state actors, and by 'massaging' the way that these networks operate, the Commission can maintain its position as an 'independent' policy-making institution and can increase its leverage with the Council of Ministers and the European Parliament. Information and ideas are important building blocks in this process.

In a key passage, Haas argues that epistemic communities play a central role in providing much-needed information and ideas.

> Epistemic communities are one possible provider of this sort of information and advice. As demands for such information arise, networks or communities of specialists capable of producing and providing the information emerge and proliferate. The members of a prevailing community become strong actors at the national and transnational level as decision-makers solicit their information and delegate responsibility to them. A community's advice, though, is informed by its own broader world view. To the extent to which an epistemic community consolidates bureaucratic power within national administrations and international secretariats, it stands to institutionalise its influence and insinuate its view into broader international politics.
>
> Members of transnational epistemic communities can influence state interests either by directly identifying them for decision-makers or by illuminating the salient dimensions of an issue from which the decision-makers may then deduce their interests. The decision-makers in one state may, in turn, influence the interests and behaviour of other states, thereby increasing the likelihood of convergent state behaviour and international policy coordination, informed by the causal beliefs and policy preferences of the epistemic community. Similarly, epistemic communities may contribute to the creation and maintenance of social institutions that guide international behaviour. As a consequence of the continued influence of these institutions, established patterns of cooperation in a given issue-area may persist even though systematic power concentrations may no longer be sufficient to compel countries to coordinate their behaviour.

(Haas 1992: 5)

His suggestion that 'systemic power concentrations' can also prevent policy coordination is an important qualification to the epistemic communities concept. Thus, no-one is arguing that epistemic communities explain everything about the policy process. The advocates of the concept have been notably more cautious than current 'network' supporters in making claims for its explanatory power. Haas cites Ikenberry's analysis of post-war economic management as illustrating the limitations on the effects of the consensual views of specialists. The influence of epistemic communities is over the form of policy choices – 'the extent to which state behaviour reflects the preferences of these networks remains strongly conditioned by the distribution of power internationally' (Haas 1992: 7). As Farrell and Héritier argue, epistemic communities sometimes lead to an acceleration of regional integration and sometimes not. They too see power and bargaining as very important, although also conclude that epistemic factors are a key negotiating resource in many contexts. Thus, epistemic communities 'may fundamentally reshape the parameters within which political actors bargain – and do this while bargaining is taking place' (Farrell and Héritier 2005: 288). As Haas also argues, 'knowledge can speak volumes to power … epistemic communities are transmission belts by which new knowledge is developed and transmitted to decision-makers' (Haas 2004: 587). Of particular relevance to the EU, he also argues that knowledge in conjunction with strong international institutions yields a distinctive pattern of social learning (Haas 2004: 587).

Although the (often indirect) power of epistemic communities can be considerable, it is constrained by the need for policy-makers – at both EU and national levels – to involve other forms of actors, particularly conventional interest groups. Not only are there rival epistemic communities, but there are rival interest groups. For example, telecoms are often cited as a classic example of epistemic communities at work (Cowhey 1990). The argument that much of the deregulatory trend can be traced to epistemic communities in the telecoms field looks convincing, yet national interests are directly affected, as are the interests of individual firms in the telecoms sector. One should not, therefore, go overboard in emphasising the importance of knowledge and ideas. As Jacobsen argues, the pervasive flaw in 'power of ideas' arguments is their failure to take account of the fact that ideas and interests cannot be separated (Jacobsen 1995: 309). As Campbell emphasises, 'arguing that ideational conditions affect policy-making outcomes does not mean that interests are unimportant' (Campbell 1998: 400). Like Jacobsen, he suggests that it is the interaction of ideas and interests that is crucial. For example, this is very evident in the field of EU environmental policy-making, where the environmentalists often act as a 'megaphone for science'; policy has to be mediated in some way, via these powerful political actors. It is here, perhaps, that the policy community/policy network concept comes back into its own. Thus, a Commission official may place considerable emphasis on the knowledge-based influence of an epistemic community – the threat posed to the ozone layer by CFCs for example – but practical action has to involve the close cooperation of the industries involved – such as refrigeration equipment or foam manufacturers. In practice, the Commission did indeed set up various working parties to 'process' the CFC problem, and it is at this stage that familiar policy networks – indeed policy communities in the sense defined earlier – emerged to process the CFC issue (Mazey and Richardson 1992).

The 'primeval soup' of the EU and the importance of advocacy coalitions

This later 'processing' stage in the EU policy process is possibly less problematic in terms of finding useful models – some combination of network, institutional and inter-governmental bargaining models seems reasonable. It is the emergence of problems, issues and policy proposals which seems much more problematic in terms of available models of analysis – hence the attractiveness of the epistemic communities approach. As Kingdon suggests, the phrase 'an idea whose time has come, captures a fundamental reality about an irresistible movement that sweeps over our politics and our society pushing aside everything that might stand in its path' (Kingdon 1984: 1). He identifies a number of possible actors in the agenda-setting process, including the mobilisation of relevant publics by leaders, the diffusion of ideas in professional circles among policy elites, particularly bureaucrats, changes in party control or in intra-party ideological balances brought about by elections. The processes involved in agenda-setting are identified as being of three kinds – problems, policies, politics (Kingdon 1984: 17). His objective is to move the analysis from the usual political science preoccupation with pressure and influence (possibly a criticism of network analysis) and instead to explore the world of ideas. Using a revised version of the Cohen *et al.* garbage can model (1972), he analyses three 'process streams' flowing through the system – streams of problems, policies and politics, largely independent of each other. He likens the generation of policy proposals to a process of biological natural selection. Thus:

> many ideas are possible in principle and float around in a 'policy soup' in which specialists try out their ideas in a variety of ways ... proposals are floated, come into contact with one another, are revised and combined with one another, and floated again ... the proposals that survive to the status of serious consideration meet several criteria, including their technical feasibility, their fit with dominant values and the current national mood, their budgetary workability, and the political support or opposition they might experience. Thus the selection system narrows the set of conceivable proposals and selects from that large set a short list of proposals that is actually available for serious consideration.
>
> (Kingdon 1984: 21)

He argues that the separate streams of problems, policies and politics come together at certain critical times. Solutions are joined to problems, and both of them are joined to favourable political forces. The timing of this coupling is influenced by the appearance of 'policy windows'; these windows are opened either by the appearance of compelling problems or by happenings in the political stream (Kingdon 1984: 21). Again, this seems to fit the EU rather well.

He cites one of his (US) respondents as saying that it is almost impossible to trace the origin of a proposal: 'This is not like a river. There is no point of origin' (Kingdon 1984: 77). There is an almost uncanny resemblance between this description of US policy-making and the perceptions of key actors in the EU policy process. Identifying just where a policy 'started' in the EU is extremely difficult – hence the common response that 'policies seem to come from nowhere'. It is a characterisation which is very different from that produced in the policy communities model and indeed also from the generic network model. The relationship between these two apparently opposing models of policy-making is that even the garbage can model – which does indeed seem to capture much of what we know empirically about the EU agenda-setting process – might eventually result in a more structured network of policy actors concerned with detailed policy decisions. In this sense, some kind of 'resource dependency' as suggested by Rhodes might emerge at later stages in the EU policy process because successful implementation depends on the cooperation of many stakeholders. Even Kingdon is at pains to point out that the processes he describes are not entirely random (just as Heclo, cited earlier, was not ready to accept the total disorder notion). Thus 'some degree of pattern is evident in these fundamental sources: processes within each stream, processes that structure couplings, and general constraints on the system' (Kingdon 1984: 216).

One reason why the process is not random is, of course, that policy problems and policy ideas both help determine actor preferences and attract coalitions of actors. As we have argued, the EU policy process is at least 'mature' in the sense that it has produced a mass of public policy and continues to generate yet more policy proposals and outputs. The institutional rules have been uncertain and the balance between EU institutions has been in a state of flux, but the policy game has carried on just the same. Essentially, EU policy-making is institutionalised 'repeat social interaction'. As Busch argues, situations of repeat social interactions pose special problems for game theorists and rational choice analysts (Busch 1999: 36). He quotes Hechter as arguing that game theory 'must not be judged solely by the mathematical elegance of its solutions, but by its capacity to shed light on those real world collective action problems' (Hechter 1990: 248). Busch sees ideational factors as one way out of trying to explain repeated games. He cites work by Garrett and Weingast, arguing that ideas can play a potentially pivotal role as 'shared beliefs may act as "focal points" around which the behaviour of actors converges' (Garrett and Weingast 1993: 176). Sabatier also argues that (within a policy sub-system) 'actors can be aggregated into a number of advocacy coalitions composed of people from various organisations who share a set of normative and causal beliefs and who often act in concert. At any particular point in time, each coalition adopts a strategy(s) envisaging one or more institutional innovations which it feels will further its objectives' (Sabatier 1988: 133; Sabatier 1998). An advocacy coalition can include actors from a variety of positions (elected and agency officials, interest group leaders, researchers) who share a particular belief system, i.e. a set of basic values, causal assumptions and problem perceptions, and who show a non-trivial degree of coordinated activity over time. Sabatier developed the model partly in response to the complexity of policy sub-systems. Using the US air pollution control sub-system as an example, he found that it contained a large, diverse set of actors. Normally, he argues, the number of advocacy coalitions would be quite small – in a 'quiescent sub-system' there might be only a single coalition, in others between two and four (Sabatier 1988: 140). To Sabatier, it is shared beliefs which provide the principal 'glue' of politics. Indeed, he emphasises stability of belief systems as an important characteristic of policy sub-systems. Policy change within a sub-system can be understood as the product of two processes. First, the efforts of advocacy coalitions within the sub-system to translate the policy cores and the secondary aspects of their belief systems into governmental programmes. Second, systemic events – for example, changes in socio-economic coalitions, outputs from other sub-systems, and changes in the system-wide governing coalition – affect the resources and the constraints on the sub-system actors, i.e. policy change takes place when there are significant 'perturbations' external to the sub-system (Sabatier 1988: 148). One of his hypotheses seems especially relevant to more recent developments in the EU. Thus, his 'hypothesis seven' is that: 'Policy-orientated learning across belief systems is most likely when there exists a forum which is a) prestigious enough to force professionals from different coalitions to participate and b) dominated by professional norms' (Sabatier 1988: 156). As Mazey and Richardson argue in this volume, there is some evidence that

Commission officials are moving towards institutionalised structures which do just this, i.e. bring together groups of policy actors (be they epistemic communities, advocacy coalitions or different policy communities). As Sabatier suggests, the purpose of these structures

> is to force debate among professionals from different belief systems in which their points of view must be aired before peers. Under such conditions, a desire for professional credibility and the norms of scientific debate will lead to a serious analysis of methodological assumptions, to the gradual elimination of the more improbable causal assertions and invalid data, and thus probably to a greater convergence of views over time concerning the nature of the problem and the consequences of various policy alternatives.
>
> (Sabatier 1988: 156)

Again, we see a suggestion that policy-makers are intent on securing *agreement* and *stability*, and recognise that this process must involve the participation of the various types of 'stakeholders' in the policy area or policy sub-system. (It is worth noting that, to many actors, a *stable outcome* can count as a 'win' almost as significant as gaining their own particular preference. For example it can be argued that polluters can adjust to most regulatory changes over time and that what they really abhor is constant *change* in their regulatory environment.) The concept of *stakeholder* is important as ultimately it determines who (rather than what) 'matters' in any particular case and can ultimately lead to some kind of broadly-based 'ownership' of EU policies. Identifying stakeholders also facilitates the continuation of policy-making business during implementation and the inevitable re-steering of policies as implementation problems emerge (see Knill, this volume). In fact, stakeholder is a term commonly used by the Commission when describing the consultation process. A particularly acute problem for the EU is that the number of stakeholders is very large indeed and it is a difficult managerial task to construct coherent policy communities. Also, the 'glue' holding coalitions together might be rather weak – hence the common feature of temporary, ad hoc, coalitions of actors not sharing a common intellectual base, policy frame, or belief system.

Multiple policy-making 'venues' and the erosion of national sovereignty

The very fact that EU policy-making is a collective exercise involving large numbers of participants, often in intermittent and unpredictable 'relationships', is likely to reinforce the processes by which national autonomy is being eroded, as well as the capacity for consistent EU-level political leadership. The likelihood of any one government or any one national system of policy actors (e.g. governments and interest groups combined) imposing their will on the rest is low. National governments know this. We can, therefore, expect to see the emergence of two apparently contradictory trends. First, the need to construct complex transnational coalitions of actors will force all actors to become less focused on the nation states as the 'venue' for policy-making. Just as many large firms have long since abandoned the notion of the nation state, so will other policy actors; they will seek to create and participate in a multi-layered system of transnational coalitions. Second, the 'politics of uncertainty' will lead national governments and national interest groups to try to coordinate their Euro-strategies (e.g. see DTI 1993, 1994). In that sense, Euro-policy-making may bring them closer together.

One reason for the difficulty in maintaining stable national coalitions is that membership of the EU presents all policy actors with a choice of venue for the resolution of policy conflicts. As Baumgartner and Jones argue, political actors are capable of strategic action by employing a dual strategy of controlling the prevailing image of the policy problem and also seeking out the most favourable venue for the consideration of issues (Baumgartner and Jones 1991: 1046). In this sense, the EU policy process represents a different order of multiple access points for policy actors when compared with many of the policy systems of the member states. Many of them, such as Britain and France, have traditionally operated rather centralised policy-making systems with, consequently, relatively few national 'venues' for exercising influence. The EU policy process is more akin to the US and German systems, where interests have a wide range of venues to engage in the policy process. Unified and centralised policy systems may encourage cohesion in policy communities in part because all of the players know that there are relatively few options for exercising influence elsewhere: this is not the case within the EU, where several 'venues' are available to actors who have lost out in any one of them. The tendency of the EU policy process to pass through periods of stability and periods of dramatic institutional change – in the episodic fashion suggested earlier – will also lead to instability in actor relationships. As Baumgartner and Jones suggest, changes in institutional structures (a feature of the EU) can also often lead to dramatic and long-lasting changes in policy outcomes (Baumgartner and Jones 1993: 12).

Conclusion: garbage cans and muddling through?

Fundamentally, all of these models and concepts are concerned with the policy process as a collective enterprise – whether the models are concerned with the emergence of policy problems, new knowledge, policy ideas, or the processing of these into workable policies and programmes. Policy-making and policy-implementing are collective activities, and we need models which help characterise the process of problem-solving in a collective setting where the sovereignty of a range of actors – not just of nation states – is pooled. Earlier, we suggested caution in adopting any one model for analysing the EU policy process. Clearly there is an ongoing and very 'productive' policy process, i.e. there is now an enormous mass of EU public policy in existence and a continuation of the flow of much technical and detailed EU legislation. Equally clearly there is a vast range of actors, institutions, problems and ideas from which EU policy finally emerges. It often seems like Kingdon's 'primeval soup' or the Cohen *et al.* 'garbage can'. Identifying the broad characteristics of this process is proving difficult, partly due to the disaggregated and sub-sectoral nature of much EU policy-making. In part the difficulty in making reliable generalisations is because the process is obviously exceedingly complex; in part it is because the process is changing in that the politics of the EU is also about constantly changing the 'decision-rules' of the system. And in part it is because analysing the EU tends to be approached from two rather different academic perspectives – models of national policy-making on the one hand and models of international policy-making on the other. The thrust of this chapter has been to suggest that we can make progress if we focus on policy actor behaviour – as well as on institutions and institutional relationships

– in order to begin our search for a better understanding of the EU as a policy system or series of policy sub-systems.

If we focus on actors as 'stakeholders' in the governance of the EU, we are able to survey a range of actor types and a range of relationships. Different types of actors and different types of relationship may emerge at different times. The policy process is both episodic and taking place in several venues at any one time. Actors do not always understand what they are doing and what the outcomes might be. Even when the outcome is agreed, there will be many unintended consequences in the implementation process, leading to further rounds of policy-making and so on. The multiplicity of games in which national governments are involved inevitably affects their autonomy as policy actors. Moreover, the relationship between the EU and its member states is directly affected by the extremely complex nature of the EU policy process itself – hence our advocacy of multiple models. Clearly, intergovernmentalism is important. We still have nation states; national governments try to act in either the national interest or their own political interests; and these governments are accorded a strong institutional presence via the Council of Ministers. Yet two phenomena – largely the focus of this chapter – place significant limits on intergovernmentalisation as a model of analysis. First, we do see a proliferation of various types of policy network – more usually the loose issue-networks rather than the policy community model originally suggested in Britain by Richardson and Jordan (1979). Put simply, the traditional 'clients' of national governments have become transnationally promiscuous in their relationships. Second, the 'politics of expertise' and the 'politics of ideas' have become especially important in situations of loose networks and high uncertainty. This also weakens national sovereignty because of the increasingly cross-national nature of expertise and the more open market for policy ideas and frames.

The complexity of the EU policy process means that we must learn to live with multiple models and learn to utilise concepts from a range of models in order to help us describe it as accurately as possible. In practice, the EU policy process may be closer to a garbage can model than to any 'rational' policy process. We suggest this because the EU policy system appears to be a classic case of 'bounded rationality' – that is, 'because the cognitive and computational capacities of decision-makers are limited, decision-makers consider only a very small number of alternative solutions to organizational problems' (Heimer and Stinchcombe 1999: 28). As Heimer and Stinchcombe suggest, organisations that have attempted to function with a more open agenda are particularly good cases in which to study bounded rationality at work. Clearly, the EU institutions are classic examples of open agenda-setting (see Peters 2001). Nevertheless, just as Heclo could detect the paradox of order and disorder, so, within the garbage can of the EU policy process, we can also detect a paradox. The process is not entirely random. As Heimer and Stinchcombe argue, in order to understand organisational decision-making 'we must look both at the randomness introduced by garbage can processes and the predictability introduced by participants' membership in occupational groups, the championing of solutions by professional bodies, legal constraints on choice opportunities, or outsiders' attempts to label difficulties as problems worthy of organizational attention' (Heimer and Stinchcombe 1999: 44). Translating their general analysis to the specific features of the EU we can see the emergence of something like occupational groups, in the form of interest groups, the championing of solutions by professional bodies, in the form of epistemic communities, the legal constraints on choice opportunities as exercised by the ECJ, and outsiders' attempts to pose problems as opportunities in the form of the advocacy of new ideas and policy frames.

The trajectory of European integration, and the construction of a dense European policy system, have certainly been uneven but the remarkable thing about the EU is that both phenomena have continued over time. In its own way, the Union has become adept at what Lindblom saw as a key feature of modern policy-making, the so-called 'science of muddling through' (Lindblom 1959). That this muddling through has produced a complex and inconsistent pattern of public policies and a very 'messy' institutional structure, even including opt-outs for certain member states, should occasion no surprise. In effect, the EU has become a gigantic 'frame-reflection' machine – namely, a set of rather fluid institutional arrangements for what Schön and Rein termed the 'resolution of intractable policy controversies'. As they suggest, 'when controversies are situated in messy and politically contentious policy arenas, they actually lend themselves, through design rationality [namely, policy-making as a dialectic within which policy-makers function as designers and exhibit ... a particular kind of reflective practice] to pragmatic solution' (Schön and Rein 1994: xviii). Actors come to the table with hugely different policy frames, yet more or less workable (albeit untidy) solutions emerge. The most remarkable feature of the EU is not that it is institutionally messy or that EU public policy is a 'regulatory patchwork' (Héritier 1996), but that so much EU public policy is now in place, despite the multitude of interests and policy frames in play in the EU policy game. Somehow, the EU works as a policy-making system. In part, this is because actors have usually been able to focus on specific policy issues even when deadlocked over the constitutional fundamentals of the EU and its future. High politics disputes can hide a lot of 'business as usual' for low politics. It would be a nonsense to suggest that the EU has come to a halt now (2005) because of the huge difficulties over the Constitution. As Stone Sweet notes, although the long period since the Treaty of Rome has been punctuated by discrete events registered in political, economic, and legal domains of action 'these events have been embedded in a larger flow. European integration is fundamentally about how large numbers of actors, operating in relatively separate arenas, were able to produce new forms of exchange and collective governance for themselves' (Stone Sweet 2004: 236). Börzel argues, similarly, that 'the failure to establish the political community that would have united the ECSC with a newly founded European Defence Community in the early 1950s, made once again clear that successful integration would have to follow functionalist rather than federalist logic. The focus shifted to the low politics of economic integration'(Börzel 2005; 219). As she notes, we have seen fifty years of task expansion culminating in Economic and Monetary Union, with 'political integration lagging seriously behind'. Low politics works quite effectively in contrast to high politics, in part because of the use of subterfuge as a policy style. Thus, as Héritier argues, 'subterfuge is a typical pattern of European policy making in view of an imminent deadlock' (Héritier 1999: 97). She emphasises the deep attachment to diversity in the EU and the inability of members to agree on the direction of the polity and sees the EU institutions as fragmented, with inherently ambiguous rules. As a consequence, the EU 'decisional processes are obstacle-ridden, cumbersome and ... prone to stalemate' (Héritier 1999: 97). Yet, despite this apparently unmanageable and chaotic situation, decisions do emerge. Essentially, she argues, actors find a variety of 'escape routes' with subterfuge being the only way to keep policy-making going (Héritier 1999: 97). In a sense, the EU is a rather good example, perhaps, of Hood's observation that 'elements of the garbage can model may at least in some circumstances be better viewed as a design recipe than an unintended condition' (Hood 1999: 77). In an earlier edition we concluded by borrowing the title of one of Charles Lindblom's articles on policy-making (Lindblom 1979) – namely, that the EU is 'still muddling, not yet through'! My (loose) use of the word 'through' implied that there was a specifiable destination. Yet, as Moravscik has argued recently, 'the neofunctionalist tendency to think of the EU as "becoming" rather than "being" remains at the heart of current debates on the future of the EU' (Moravcsik 2005: 2). He goes on to suggest that 'the EU's current constitutional *status quo* appears stable and normatively attractive. Beyond incremental changes in policy, it is difficult to imagine functional pressures, institutional pressures, or normative concerns upsetting the stability of the basic equilibrium in Europe today' (Moravcsik 2005: 3). His notion that policy change will be incremental and that the EU is now in a political equilibrium is seductive at this time of Euroscepticism. However, we have seen national political systems go through relatively quiescent phases, where institutions and decision rules have been rather stable, policy change slow, and politics generally pretty boring, only to see quite big shifts in policies (privatisation being an obvious example), major institutional changes (decentralisation for example), and quite major shifts in ideology (the British Labour party for example). The change process on all of these fronts is unpredictable and is not purely endogenous but is a mixture of endogenous and exogenous factors. Thus, I conclude my analysis in this edition by reverting to Lindblom. Just like its member states, the EU will continue to 'muddle through' in the sense that it will continue as a productive policy-making machine, often incrementally, as Moravcsik suggests, but sometimes more radically when circumstances force the many stakeholders to embrace new frames and ideas as a response to what Kingdon called the inexorable march of problems. This muddling through may not be purposive, in the sense of seeking some kind of 'EU promised land', but will have as its 'purpose' the solving of European societal problems via public policy-making at the European rather than the national level.

References

Adler, E. and Haas, P. (1992) 'Conclusion: Epistemic Communities, World Order and the Creation of a Reflective Research Program', *International Organization* 46/1: 367–90.

Almond, G. (1956) 'Comparing Political Systems', *Journal of Politics* 18/2: 391–409.

Baumgartner, F. R. and Jones, B. D. (1991) 'Agenda Dynamics and Policy Subsystems', *Journal of Politics* 53/4: 1044–74.

—— (1993) *Agendas and Instability in American Politics* (Chicago: Chicago University Press).

Benson, J. K. (1982) 'A Framework for Policy Analysis', in D. Rogers and D. Whitten *Interorganizational Coordination* (Ames: Iowa State University Press).

Borrás, S. and Jacobsson, K. (2004) 'The Open Method of Co-ordination and New Patterns of Governance in the EU', *Journal of European Public Policy* 11/2: 185–208.

Börzel, Tanja (2005) 'Mind the Gap! European Integration between Level and Scope', *Journal of European Public Policy* 12/2: 217–36.

Braun, D. and Busch, A. (eds) (1999) *Public Policy and Political Ideas* (Cheltenham: Edward Elgar).

Busch, A. (1999) 'From "Hooks" to "Focal Points": the Changing Role of Ideas in Rational Choice Theory', in D. Braun and A. Busch (eds) *Public Policy and Political Ideas* (Cheltenham: Edward Elgar).

Campbell, J. L. (1998) 'Institutional Analysis and the Role of Ideas in Political Economy', *Theory and Society* 27: 377–409.

Cohen, M., March, J. and Olsen, J. P. (1972) 'A Garbage Can Model of Organizational Choice', *Administrative Science Quarterly* 17: 1–25.

Cowhey, P. F. (1990) 'The International Telecommunications Regime: The Political Roots of Regimes for High Technology', *International Organization* 44/2: 169–99.

Dostal, J. M. (2004) 'Campaigning on Expertise: How the OECD Framed EU Welfare and Labour Market Policies – and Why Success Could Trigger Failure', *Journal of European Public Policy* 11/3: 440–60.

DTI (1993) *Review of the Implementation and Enforcement of EC Law in the UK* (London: DTI)

—— (1993) *Getting a Good Deal in Europe: Deregulatory Principles in Practice* (London: DTI)

Dyson, K. (1994) *Elusive Union: The Process of Economic and Monetary Union in Europe* (London: Longman).

Easton, D. (1957) 'An Approach to the Study of Political Systems', *World Politics* 9/5: 383–400.

European Commission (1995) *Commission's Work Programme for 1995*, OJC225, August, Brussels.

Farrell, H. and Héritier, A. (2005) 'A Rationalist-Institutionalist Explanation of Endogenous Regional Integration', *Journal of European Public Policy* 12/2: 273–90.

Fischer, F. (2003) *Reframing Public Policy: Discursive Politics and Deliberative Practices* (Oxford: Oxford University Press).

Garrett, G. and Weingast, G. (1993) 'Ideas, Interests and Institutions: Constructing the European Community's Internal Market', in J. Goldstein and R. Keohane (eds) *Ideas and Foreign Policy: Beliefs, Institutions and Political Change* (Ithaca, NY: Cornell University Press).

Greer, S. (2006) 'Uninvited Europeanisation: Neofunctionalism and the EU in Health Policy', *Journal of European Public Policy* 13/1.

Haas, P. (1992) 'Introduction: Epistemic Communities and International Policy Co-ordination', *International Organization* 46/1: 1–35.

—— (2004) 'When Does Power Listen to Truth? A Constructivist Approach to the Policy Process', *Journal of European Public Policy* 11/4: 569–92.

Hechter, M. (1990) 'Comment: On the Inadequacy of Game Theory for the Solution of Real-world Collective Action Problems', in K. S. Cook and M. Levi (eds) *The Limits of Rationality* (Chicago: University of Chicago Press).

Heclo, H. (1978) 'Issue Networks and the Executive Establishment', in A. King (ed.) *The New American Political System* (Washington DC: American Enterprise Institute).

Heimer, C. and Stinchcombe, A. L. (1999) 'Remodelling the Garbage Can: Implications of the Origin of Items in Decision Streams', in M. Egeberg and P. Laegreed (eds) *Organizing Political Institutions: Essays for Johan P. Olsen* (Oslo: Scandinavian University Press).

Heinz, J. P., Laumann, E. O., Nelson, R. L. and Salisbury, R. H. (1993) *The Hollow Core* (Cambridge, MA: Harvard University Press).

Henderson, P. D. (1977) 'Two British Errors: Their Probable Size and Some Possible Lessons', *Oxford Economic Papers* 29/2: 159–205.

Héritier, A. (1996) 'The Accommodation of Diversity in European Policy-Making: Regulatory Policy as Patchwork', *Journal of European Public Policy* 3/3: 149–67.

—— (1999) *Policy-Making and Diversity in Europe: Escape from Deadlock* (Cambridge: Cambridge University Press).

Hix, S. (2005) *The Political System of the European Union* (Basingstoke: Macmillan).

Hoffmann, S. (1966) 'Obstinate or Obsolete: The Fate of the Nation State and the Case of Western Europe', *Daedalus* 95/3: 862–915.

Hood, C. (1999) 'The Garbage Can Model of Organization: Describing a Condition or a Prescriptive Design Principle?' in M. Egeberg and P. Laegreed (eds), *Organizing Political Institutions: Essays for Johan P. Olsen* (Oslo: Scandinavian University Press).

Jacobsen, J. K. (1995) 'Much Ado about Ideas: The Cognitive Factor in Economic Policy', *World Politics* 47: 283–310.

Jordan, G. and Richardson, J. (1982) 'The British Policy Style or the Logic of Negotiation?' in J. Richardson (ed.), *Policy Styles in Western Europe* (London: Allen and Unwin).

Kingdon, J. W. (1984) *Agendas, Alternatives and Public Policies* (New York: HarperCollins).

Krasner, S. D. (1978) 'United States Commercial and Monetary Policy: Unravelling the Paradox of External Strength and Internal Weakness', in P. Katzenstein (ed.), *Between Power and Plenty: Foreign Economic Politics of Advanced Industrial States* (Madison: University of Wisconsin Press).

Laffan, B., O'Donnell, R. and Smith, M. (2000) *Europe's Experimental Union: Rethinking Integration* (London: Routledge).

Lax, D. and Sebenius, J. K. (1986) *The Manager as Negotiator* (New York: Free Press).

Lindblom, C. (1959) 'The Science of Muddling Through', *Public Administration Review* 19: 79–88.

—— (1979) 'Still Muddling, Not Yet Through', *Public Administration Review* 39: 517–26.

McGowan, L. (2005) 'Europeanisation Unleashed and Rebounding: Assessing the Modernisation of EU Cartel Policy', *Journal of European Public Policy* 12/6.

Mazey, S. and Richardson, J. (1992) 'Environmental Groups and the EC', *Environmental Politics* 1/4: 109–28.

—— (eds) (1993) *Lobbying in the European Community* (Oxford: Oxford University Press).

—— (1994) 'The Commission and the Lobby', in G. Edwards and D. Spence (eds), *The European Commission* (London: Longman).

Moravcsik, A. (2005) 'The European Constitutional Compromise and the Legacy of Neofunctionalism', *Journal of European Public Policy* 12/2: 349–86.

Peters, G. (2001) 'Agenda-setting in the European Union' in J. Richardson (ed.), *European Union: Power and Policy-Making* (London: Routledge).

Putnam, R. D. (1988) 'Diplomacy and Domestic Politics', *International Organization* 42/3: 427–60.

Radaelli, C. (1995) 'Knowledge Utilisation and Policy-Making', *Journal of European Public Policy* 2/2: 159–83.

—— (1999) *Technocracy in the European Union* (London: Longman).

Reich, R. B. (ed.) (1988) *The Power of Public Ideas* (Cambridge, MA: Harvard University Press).

Rein, H. and Schön, D. (1991) 'Frame-Reflective Policy Discourse', in P. Wagner, C. H. Weiss, B. Wittrock and H. Wollman (eds) *Social Sciences, Modern States: National Experiences and Theoretical Crossroads* (Cambridge: Cambridge University Press).

Rhodes, R. A. W. (1990) 'Policy Networks: A British Perspective', *Journal of Theoretical Politics* 2/3: 292–316.

Richardson, J. (ed.) (1982) *Policy Styles in Western Europe* (London: Allen and Unwin).

—— (1994) 'EU Water Policy-Making: Uncertain Agendas, Shifting Networks and Complex Coalitions', *Environmental Politics* 4/4: 139–67.

—— (2000) 'Government, Interest Groups and Policy Change', *Political Studies* 48/5: 1006–25.

Richardson, J. and Jordan, G. (1979) *Governing under Pressure: The Policy Process in a Post-Parliamentary Democracy* (Oxford: Martin Robertson).

Rittberger, B. and Richardson, J. (2003) 'Old Wine in New Bottles? The Commission and the Use of Environmental Policy Instruments', *Public Administration* 81/3: 575–606.

Sabatier, P. (1988) 'An Advocacy Coalition Framework of Policy Change and the Role of Policy-Orientated Learning Therein', *Policy Sciences* 21: 128–68.

—— (1998) 'An Advocacy Coalition Framework: Revision and Relevance for Europe', *Journal of European Public Policy* 5/1: 93–130.

Schattschneider, E. E. (1960) *The Semi-Sovereign People: A Realist's View of Democracy in America* (New York: Holt).

Schön, D. A. and Rein, M. (1994) *Frame Reflection: Toward the Resolution of Intractable Policy Controversies* (New York: Basic Books).

Sebenius, J. K. (1992) 'Challenging Conventional Explanations of International Co-operation: Negotiation Analysis and the Case of Epistemic Communities', *International Organization* 46/1: 323–65.

29

Stone Sweet, A. (2004) *The Judicial Construction of Europe* (Oxford: Oxford University Press).

Thatcher, M. (1998) 'The Development of Policy Network Analysis. From Modest Origins to Overarching Frameworks', *Journal of Theoretical Politics* 10/4: 389–46.

Tsebelis, G. (1990) *Nested Games: Rational Choice in Comparative Politics* (Berkeley: University of California Press).

Walton, R. and McKersie, R. (1965) *A Behavioral Theory of Labor Negotiations* (New York: McGraw Hill).

Wildavsky, A. (1979) *The Art and Craft of Policy Analysis* (London: Macmillan)

Zweifel, T. D. (2002) *Democratic Deficit? Institutions and Regulation in the European Union and the United States* (Oxford: Lexington Books).

Chapter 2

European integration

The European Union – reaching an equilibrium?

BRIGID LAFFAN AND SONIA MAZEY

> We believed in starting with limited achievements, establishing a *de facto* solidarity from which a federation would gradually emerge. I have never believed that one fine day Europe would be created by some great political mutation ... The pragmatic method we had adopted would ... lead to a federation validated by the people's vote, but that federation would be the culmination of an existing economic and political reality.
>
> (Jean Monnet, *Memoirs*, London: Collins, 1978)

Introduction

The 'Community method' of functional integration advocated by Jean Monnet was an ingenious device; crucially it enabled the federalist-inclined founding fathers of European integration to sidestep the politically intractable barrier of national sovereignty. Then, as now, there was no consensus over the precise form that European cooperation should take. The founding Treaties of the European Communities represented an ambiguous compromise between intergovernmentalists and European federalists involved in the post-war debate on European cooperation. The institutional arrangement created by the founding Treaties reflected this ambiguity. On the one hand, the European Commission and the European Court of Justice provided for a supranational European executive and legal authority. On the other hand, national governments, represented in the Community's Council of Ministers, enjoyed important legislative and executive powers with regard to the adoption and implementation of EC laws and policies. European integration was and remains a contested project.

In the absence of a clear blueprint and political consensus among the member states, the process of European integration has been uneven. Nevertheless, since 1957, the legal basis, institutional framework and policy competence of the EC has been incrementally extended way beyond the provisions of the original Treaties, as reflected in successive Treaty reforms during the 1980s and 1990s. Significantly, however, these reforms neither reflected nor generated widespread popular support for the European Union. On the contrary, since the early 1990s, European integration has been accompanied by increasing levels of Euroscepticism among European voters. The European Constitution was intended to democratise the EU and increase public support for European integration. Not only has this ambitious, high-profile strategy for increasing public support for European integration failed, it has actually exacerbated the problem. The resounding rejection in May and June 2005 by French and Dutch voters of the 2004 European Constitution provided irrefutable proof of the huge gulf that now exists between the democratic ideals of European political elites and the material concerns of European publics. Many commentators viewed the 2004 Treaty as heralding a new period of political and constitutional stability within the EU. Following the French and Dutch referenda results, this now seems an unlikely prospect. At the level of 'high politics' the EU is undoubtedly now in disarray. Meetings between member-state heads of government at the June European Council were characterised by mutual recrimination and conflicting visions of how to proceed. At this meeting, the member states were able to agree only on the need for a period of reflection. However, it would be unwise to exaggerate the significance of this constitutional crisis. As Moravcsik has argued, over a period of years, a de facto 'European constitutional settlement has quietly emerged, based on the single market, single currency and enlargement ... The mistake was to upset this pragmatic arrangement with an idealistic scheme for greater democratic deliberation and high profile constitutional revision' (*Financial Times* 14 June 2005). For the time being, the EU will continue to function on the basis of the existing treaties and there is no reason to suppose the *acquis communitaire* is likely to unravel. However, the meaning and ultimate objective of European integration has once again been called into question in a very visible way. Since the collapse of the fragile political consensus constructed around the European Constitution, member-state governments have been at loggerheads over two conflicting models of European integration: the 'social' model, championed by France and Germany; and the liberal 'Anglo-Saxon' model advocated by the UK government. Over the coming months, politics will be primary as member states seek to build coalitions to embed these competing visions of Europe into policies, including those on sensitive issues such as the EU budget reform, the working time directive and the services directive.

Throughout the EU transformation process, four tensions have been – and indeed remain – the key drivers of integration. First, there was a tension between the balance and boundary of national and EU competence; as the policy competence of the Union expanded, it triggered demands from some national governments and regional authorities that clearer limits be set to the policy reach of the Union. Second, there was a tension between public and market power. The resurgence of formal integration in the 1980s was driven by market creation and the political economy challenges facing Europe. The key policy instrument was regulation through law, otherwise known as negative integration. The macroeconomic power of the member states was further restricted with the arrival of the euro and the responsibility of the European Central Bank for monetary policy and inflation. Hence, the impact of the EU on the member states was to internationalise and liberalise their economies. Third, there was a tension between those who perceived the EU as a problem-solving, public policy arena and others who saw it as a polity in its own right. Opposition to the project of European integration and to EU public policies emerged during the 1990s as the integration project became more politicised. Fourth, there is a tension between the internal development of the Union and demands from outside. The impact of the Union's external environment upon its development in the 1990s was dramatic. The collapse of the Soviet Union in the late 1980s prompted demands from the countries of Central and Eastern Europe for membership, which in turn led to the largest single enlargement of the Union on May 1 2004, when ten countries joined the EU. The process of enlargement is set to continue when Romania and Bulgaria join in 2007. In December 2004, the European Council agreed to open accession negotiations with Turkey, though given the salience of this issue in both the French and Dutch referenda, Turkish accession is now more doubtful. The expansion of the Union is not, however, the only external challenge now confronting the Union. The events of 9/11 and the consequent war in Iraq have also raised serious internal and external security dilemmas for the Union and significantly altered the dynamic of transatlantic relations. The member states remain deeply divided on how to respond to the changing geopolitical landscape. The Madrid (March 2004) and London (July 2005) bombings highlight the interaction between events in the world and the cities of Europe.

The tensions outlined above have dominated the Union's agenda; they have also altered both its constitutional and institutional architecture, and its policy profile. Greater diversity among the member states and candidate countries ushered in a new era of 'flexible integration' that was consolidated in treaty provisions on closer cooperation. Enlargement engendered pressures for reform of the Union's decision rules and institutional structures. The end of the permissive consensus and the growing debate on the Union's democratic deficit prompted a sustained search for ways of bringing Europe closer to its citizens (an endeavour which ironically culminated in the European Constitution). Growing security challenges generated sustained cooperation in Justice and Home Affairs and the development of an EU competence in defence and security. Concern about the weak economic performance of a number of Europe's large economies and a growing competitiveness gap with the US and emergent China led to the 'Lisbon process' and a new, non-legislative mode of governance known as the 'open method of coordination', designed to trigger economic and welfare reform in the member states in areas where the Union has weak policy competence. Based upon the establishment of common guidelines and goals, exchange of best practice and collective evaluation, the open method of coordination is characterised by voluntarism, subsidiarity, flexibility, and multi-level integration (Borrás and Greve 2004).

This chapter highlights the historical development of the EU and seeks to explain how and why this process occurred. The central theme of the discussion is that there is no *single* dynamic of European integration and, therefore, no single theoretical framework can encapsulate the totality of European integration. Rather, it is argued that European integration has been a 'multi-faceted, multi-actor and multi-speed' process. At different times in the Union's history, different actors, institutions and pressures have been influential in either facilitating or limiting the further development of the EU. Thus, even when European integration seemed to have stalled at the so-called 'high politics' level (as appeared to be the case during the late 1970s), integration nevertheless continued to take place at the level of low politics and by means of policy implementation.

A framework for analysis

As argued by intergovernmentalist models of integration, national interests and national governments have undoubtedly played a crucial role in determining the degree, nature and pace of European integration. This dynamic is particularly apparent with regard to 'history making' decisions (Peterson 1995) such as the initial establishment of the European Communities (Stirk and Weigall 1999; Milward 1992; Moravscik 2003), subsequent renegotiation of the Treaties (Moravcsik and Nicolaïdis 1998), and the creation of European Monetary Union (Dyson and Featherstone 1999). In this context, interstate bargains conducted by national political leaders and administrative elites have been a very visible dynamic of integration. Domestic core executives remain key 'translator devices' between the Union and the member states. They are privileged actors in the Union's institutional system and retain formidable political authority and legitimacy at domestic level. The EU policy preferences of national governments are informed in part by political ideology and 'core beliefs' (Sabatier 1988) – not least with regard to the principle and practice of European integration. However, to confine our explanation of European integration to the motivations and actions of national governments would be to study the tip of the iceberg. We also need to evaluate the often less visible, but equally important, role played by other actors and institutions involved in this process. First, as Mazey and Richardson suggest in Chapter 12, organised interests have since the establishment of the

ECSC played an important role in the European decision-making process (Haas 1958; Kirchner 1980; Mazey 1992). As the policy competence of the EC expanded, increasing numbers and types of interests were drawn into the policy-making process. Thus, there is now a dense European level interest group system centred upon Brussels. The permeation of the European Commission (and, increasingly, the European Parliament) by an increasing range of interests, many of whom have become powerful, albeit discreet, Euro-lobbyists has been influential in shaping the integration process.

Second, the EU institutions themselves have by means of both their own development and their actions contributed to the process and dynamic of European integration. The incremental development of the European Parliament, for instance, highlights the way in which institutions can, under certain circumstances, acquire institutional momentum. Having begun life as a rather insignificant consultative body, the European Parliament, consciously sought to strengthen its authority and, over time, secured incremental, but sustained increases in its budgetary and legislative powers. These developments, combined with the introduction in 1979 of direct elections to the European Parliament and the increasing cohesion of the transnational party groupings within the assembly, significantly increased the democratic legitimacy of the European Parliament. The enhanced role of the Parliament is one of the most significant shifts in the Union's institutional balance since the 1970s. The Parliament is not the only EU institution which, in seeking to increase its own power, effectively strengthened the supranational character of the EU. The entrepreneurial encroachment by the European Commission into new policy sectors since 1957 and the progressive 'constitutionalisation' of the EU Treaties by the European Court of Justice also (often unobtrusively) increased the supranational authority of the EU. In principle, member states retain the authority to reverse these institutional and policy developments, but in reality 'recapturing ground in previously institutionalized fields of activity ... will often be rather difficult. Decision rules hamper reform, and extensive adaptations to existing arrangements increase the associated costs' (Pierson 1996: 146). In consequence, integration becomes 'path-dependent', characterised by piecemeal adaptation of existing arrangements.

Third, any satisfactory account of the historical development of the EC should consider the extent to which external geopolitical and economic pressures as well as ideas have been influential in determining the pace of European integration and in shaping the EU policy agenda. In the immediate post-war period the threat of Soviet communism, and the positive attitude of the US government towards European integration, persuaded European leaders of the need for some form of European cooperation. Subsequently, the dramatic collapse of the Soviet Union in 1989 was an important catalyst for further 'deepening' and 'widening' of the EU in the 1990s. More recently, the events of 9/11 prompted further Europeanisation of national security and anti-terrorist policies. Community initiatives such as the Single European Market project were prompted in large part by the need to counter the economic challenge posed to European industries by US and Japanese firms and the so-called 'tiger economies' of East Asia.

Fourth, as Kingdon (1984) argues, prevailing ideas are also important in helping to frame and shape public policy outcomes. As indicated below, federalist ideas and aspirations were undoubtedly important in shaping the immediate post-war debate on the future organisation of European cooperation. These ideals were enthusiastically promoted by the European Federalist movements and prominent individuals such as Jean Monnet who together constituted an influential 'advocacy coalition' (Sabatier 1988). In contrast, the current preference among EU member states for economic liberalisation owes much to the Anglo-Saxon fashion for market solutions to problems, espoused by an influential advocacy coalition within the EU, led by the UK government.

In similar vein, constructivist accounts of European integration capture the evolution of the Union as a 'community of values' based upon a shared conception of social reality and the dynamic interaction between this mutual understanding of reality, European institutions and agents (Checkel 2004; Risse 2004; Christiansen *et al.* 2001). The implicit values that informed the foundation of the Union in the 1950s were made more explicit as the Union's constitutional architecture (itself shaped by mutual understandings and shared norms) deepened and a sizeable enlargement beckoned. The Treaty of Amsterdam, the Charter on Fundamental Rights and Freedoms negotiated in parallel to the Nice Treaty, and the European Constitution agreed by the European Council in June 2004 are replete with references to the normative underpinnings of the integration project. The nature and degree of conditionality attached to accession to the Union, a pronounced feature of the enlargement to the east, underlined the consolidation of the Union as a 'community of values'. The evolution of the Union has had a varied impact on the national identities of the member states and their citizens. For some there is a high degree of compatibility between national identities and membership of the European Union whereas for others, the EU is an unwelcome 'other', a threat to national identities.

Interaction between these different variables makes it impossible to identify any single dynamic of European integration; rather the present constitutional and institutional arrangement of the EU is the culmination of a multi-level, multi-faceted process of change and adjustment. At times, change was incremental and ad hoc, at others it was transformative. As the policy competence of the Union expanded, so the Union's constitutional and institutional basis evolved. One aspect of the European integration process has, however, been constant throughout the period under discussion, namely the deep-seated ideological divide between the commitment (at elite levels) of the original Six to some form of political union and the more sceptical attitude of some later entrants to the Community, notably the UK, Denmark and Sweden. The significance of this cleavage – not to mention other conflicts of interest – begs the question as to how the Union has not only survived, but also continued to evolve and accommodate a sizeable enlargement in 2004. Intergovernmentalist, neo-functionalist, historical institutionalist and constructivist explanations of integration provide different, but not mutually exclusive, answers to this question. However, it would be wrong to assume that European integration is moving inevitably towards 'ever closer Union'. It is too early to know whether the abandonment of the 2004 constitutional treaty represents an end point as suggested by Moravscik. Past experience suggests that the European Union will continue to evolve incrementally, especially in those policy areas where it has already established legitimacy, but further constitutional reform on a grandiose scale now seems unlikely, at least for the time being.

Creating the European Community 1945–65: the primacy of politics

The immediate origins of European unification lie in the economic and political problems confronting European countries, notably France and Germany, in the immediate aftermath of the Second World War. Of crucial importance in this respect was the urgent need – given the onset of the Cold War – to anchor West Germany into the Western alliance system. However, before this could be achieved, French fears about the threat posed to France by an economically powerful West Germany would have to be allayed. The Schuman Plan, which formed the basis of the ECSC, was specifically designed to reassure French policy-makers on this point. The post-war debate on the future of European cooperation was thus clearly an issue of 'high politics'. As such, it was dominated by intense, intergovernmental negotiations between national politico-administrative elites, whose support for (though, in the case of the UK, non-participation in) European integration can be explained primarily in terms of perceived national interest (Stirk and Weigall 1999; Milward 1992; Devuyst 2005). However, the experience of war had also created widespread revulsion towards nationalism and given fresh impetus to federalist movements, which argued that the nation-state system was a primary cause of international conflict (Lipgens 1982). Between 1945 and 1955 European federalist movements constituted an important 'advocacy coalition' which pushed the issue of European integration to the forefront of political agendas throughout Western Europe, and whose vision of Europe inspired key policy-makers such as Jean Monnet and Robert Schuman.

The political impact of post-war European federalism

The basis of the post-war European federalist movement was the belief that the establishment of a federal European government would put an end to the long-established pattern of wars between European sovereign nation-states. (Lipgens 1982). From the outset, however, the post-war European federalist debate was ambiguous: though the general idea of European cooperation commanded widespread support, no such consensus existed regarding the precise nature of any such arrangement. There were important divisions between the plethora of 'European' movements established during this period. By far the largest and most prominent of these competing advocacy coalitions was the European Union of Federalists (UEF), which comprised some sixty, affiliated, national groups and over 100,000 members. But not all movements shared the federalist aspirations of the UEF. For example, the United Europe Movement, founded in 1947 by Winston Churchill, and the European League for Economic cooperation, presided over by the Dutch ex-prime minister, Paul van Zeeland, advocated European cooperation rather than federalism.

The momentum created by the post-war advocacy coalition in favour of some form of European integration culminated in the European Congress held in The Hague in May 1948, organised jointly by the above associations. The Congress brought together 713 delegates from thirteen countries (Vaughan 1979). On the key issue of what kind of European design should be created there emerged at the Hague Congress a clear divide between the federalist UEF and the more moderate United Europe Movement which, backed by other conservative groups, advocated a confederal association. In the event, the latter view prevailed. In October 1948, the broad-based European Movement was established to implement the recommendations of the Hague Congress. Subsequent negotiations were marked by a (now familiar) cleavage between the French, Italian and Belgian governments, who wanted to establish a supranational European organisation, and the British government (backed by the Scandinavian governments), who favoured an intergovernmental arrangement. The federalists were defeated. The Council of Europe, established in May 1949, provided a forum for voluntary cooperation between sovereign, national governments in the Committee of Ministers and between members of national parliaments in the Consultative Assembly.

Undeterred, the European federalists launched a further attempt in 1952 to establish a supranational European Political Community (EPC) as part of a proposal for a European Defence Community (EDC). Though it enjoyed the support of the West German Chancellor, Konrad Adenauer, and the US government, the EDC project collapsed in August 1954 with the refusal of the French National Assembly to ratify the so-called Pleven Plan. The failure of the EDC project was an important turning point in the post-war debate on European integration. Despite the favourable post-war conditions for European federalism, it was clear that nationalism and the nation-state system remained an insurmountable barrier to such a radical political development.

The establishment of the European Communities: the Monnet method

The founding fathers of the European Community – Jean Monnet, the French Planning Commissoner, and Robert Schuman, the French Foreign Minister – were essentially pragmatic federalists. Though they shared the ideals of radical federalists, they disagreed with their head-on approach, believing instead that the only way to achieve European integration was by small, incremental steps in sectors where the issue of national sovereignty was less contentious than in 'high politics' areas such as defence and foreign policy (Monnet 1978; Duchêne 1994). This 'Community method' of functional integration underpinned the Schuman Plan, drawn up in April 1950 by Robert Schuman, at the request of Jean Monnet. The Plan was presented to the French government as a European solution to the urgent need to find a new structure to contain the resurgent heavy industries of the Ruhr (Willis 1968). It proposed that French and German coal and steel production should be 'pooled' and placed under a common, supranational authority, the High Authority, which would be responsible for establishing a common market for coal and steel among the member states. European regulation of these industries would also facilitate economic reconstruction. Six countries – Belgium, the Netherlands, Italy, Luxemburg, West Germany and France – signed the Paris Treaty in April 1951, establishing the ECSC. The British government refused to join the ECSC. Three reasons help to explain the British aloofness from Europe during this period. First, the British wartime experience had strengthened rather than weakened national sentiments. Second, as Churchill had made clear in his 1946 Zurich speech, the primary British obligation at this time was to another 'natural grouping', the Commonwealth (Lipgens 1982). Third, Labour and Conservative politicians alike were united in their ideological opposition to a supranational European authority, which they believed would constrain national policy-makers and undermine the sovereignty of the UK Parliament.

The ECSC Treaty provided for five main institutions, which constitute the foundations of the present institutional framework of the EC: a Special Council of Ministers (subsequently, the Council of Ministers); a High Authority (prototype of the European

Commission); a 78-member Common Assembly (which developed into the European Parliament); a corporatist Consultative Committee (which later became the Economic and Social Committee); and a Court of Justice for settlement of disputes. The organisation and internal power structure of the ECSC was characterised by ambiguity and compromise. Monnet's personal commitment to European federalism and his own experience of working in international organisations had convinced him of the need for the High Authority to be a supranational executive, wholly independent of national governments. Yet the High Authority was far from being a sovereign body. It was paralleled as an executive by the Special Council of Ministers, insisted upon by the Benelux countries as a means of defending the national interests of the smaller countries (Urwin 1989). The ECSC was followed by the creation in 1957 of two new communities: the EURATOM, intended to facilitate cooperation between member states in the development of nuclear technology for peaceful purposes; and the EEC, which sought to establish both a customs union and a common market. While the customs union lay at the heart of the EEC Treaty, it also provided for a number of common policies in areas such as agriculture, transport and competition policy. Social policy was also included, in the sense of policy relating to employment. A Social Fund and an Investment Bank were established and the policies were to be financed by a Community budget, whose income would eventually come from its 'own resources' (Pinder 1995). Compared to the ECSC, the integrative impact of the EEC was potentially far-reaching. Once again, the British government remained aloof from the integration process.

Several factors facilitated the establishment of the European Communities: the pressing need to achieve Franco-German conciliation, the post-war economic situation, and the onset of the Cold War all served to focus the minds of European policy-makers upon the problem of European cooperation. The particular solution adopted reflected the influence of competing advocacy coalitions (pro- and anti-European federalism), the pivotal role played by individuals such as Jean Monnet and Robert Schuman, and the political commitment of the six member governments to European integration. Thus, in Kingdon's terms, there had existed an important 'window of opportunity'. In the early 1960s, support for the EEC (which quickly established itself as the most important of the three Communities) increased among member governments, business and agricultural interests. Rapid economic growth rates in the EEC were attributed, in part at least, to the removal of internal tariffs. Meanwhile, the CET, far from provoking protectionism in the international economy, provided the catalyst for far-reaching multilateral tariff cuts, as reflected in the Kennedy Round of GATT negotiations in the mid-1960s.

De Gaulle and the 'empty chair' crisis: towards intergovernmentalism

The founders of the EC had intended that the European Commission would become a technocratic, supranational European executive, embodying the European General Will (Featherstone 1994). Between 1957 and 1965 an assertive Commission, under the presidency of the German federalist Walter Hallstein, set about realising this aim. The Treaties, however, were ambiguous in this respect and in 1965, the Commission's authority was seriously challenged by the French President, General de Gaulle. Elected in 1958, de Gaulle had immediately made clear his opposition to European supranationalism, which contradicted his *certaine idée* of France, based upon a powerful sovereign state, nationalism and an independent foreign and defence policy. With de Gaulle's election to the French presidency, the political consensus in favour of European integration disappeared, along with agreement on the existing institutional balance of power within the Community. In 1961, de Gaulle launched his intergovernmental alternative to the EC, the so-called Fouchet Plan which sought to establish a 'union of states' to coexist with the existing Community in a number of areas, most notably foreign policy, defence and culture. When this initiative failed, de Gaulle sought to exploit the EC in defence of French national interests – a strategy reflected in the priority accorded by France to the establishment of the CAP.

De Gaulle's antagonism towards the Community culminated in the so-called 'empty chair' crisis, which lasted from July to December 1965. During this period French ministers refused to attend meetings of the Council of Ministers and the French permanent representative was withdrawn from Brussels. The crisis was triggered by French opposition to the Commission's proposals for financing the Common Agricultural Policy, the introduction of the Community's 'own resources', the granting of more extensive budgetary powers to the European Parliament and, in particular, the introduction of majority voting into the Council of Ministers. The crisis was resolved in January 1966 by the Luxemburg Compromise, which shifted the institutional balance of power away from the Commission in favour of the Council of Ministers. While the Commission's right to initiate policy was confirmed by this document, it was agreed that the Commission should, in future, consult more closely with member governments before issuing new proposals. With regard to majority voting in the Council of Ministers, the Luxemburg Compromise stated that where 'issues very important to one or more member countries are at stake ministers will seek to reach solutions with which all can be comfortable'. Thus, the Luxemburg Compromise effectively confirmed the right of member states to veto EC legislative proposals, thereby reversing the federalist ambitions of the Commission.

1965–84: European integration by other means

Conventional wisdom holds that the integration process stalled during the 1970s and early 1980s. Evidence cited in support of this view typically includes references to the Commission's increasing resort to 'package deals', recurrent 'crisis' EC summits, 'deadlocked' meetings of the Council of Ministers and the discordant relationship between the UK (which joined the EC in 1972) and the rest of the Community (George 1990). This apparent 'slowing down' of the European integration process at the high politics level is usually attributed to the Luxemburg Compromise, EC enlargement and the onset of worldwide recession in 1974. This view of the European Community during the 1970s has some validity. The Luxembourg Compromise *did* alter the European policy style: henceforth the Commission was forced to negotiate complex package-deals with the member states. EC enlargement from six to nine members inevitably increased the '*lourdeur*' (Dehousse and Majone 1994: 94) of EC decision-making, especially in the light of the Luxemburg Compromise and the opposition of two of the new member states (the UK and Denmark) to further political integration. Meanwhile, the onset of economic recession in Western Europe gave rise to protectionist temptations in some quarters as national governments struggled to control rising unemployment and domestic inflation levels.

Nevertheless, European integration continued to take place in some form or another throughout the 1970s. In terms of EC 'institution-building', for instance, the 1970s witnessed the introduction of European Political Cooperation (EPC), the establishment of regular meetings of the European Council and the introduction of direct elections to the European Parliament. The creation of EPC, which brought together the foreign ministers of the EC, was an intergovernmentalist development, but it marked the beginnings of European foreign policy coordination. The introduction of regular meetings of the EC heads of government reflected their desire – despite the differences between them – to maintain a European dialogue. The European Council, though an intergovernmentalist body, subsequently played an important agenda-setting role in the integration process. Meanwhile, the incremental development of the European Parliament's budgetary powers in 1970 and 1975 gave the EP increased leverage over the Council of Ministers. The introduction in 1979 of direct elections to the EP established the democratic legitimacy of the Parliament – another crucial step in this campaign.

Second, the capacity of the EC institutions to set and process the 'normal' policy agenda remained relatively unaffected by public clashes between the heads of government. Moreover, during the 1970s, the policy-making competence of the EC continued to expand: existing policies were extended and new policies introduced – in some areas, beyond the parameters of the founding Treaties. EC enlargement in 1974, for instance, was accompanied by the introduction of a European regional policy and European Regional Development Fund. The origins of EMU also lie in the 1971 Werner Plan and the 1979 launch of the first EMS (the snake). Less dramatically, a large corpus of EC environmental legislation was adopted during the 1970s (despite the absence of a Treaty basis for such legislation), and the scope of EC social policy was extended beyond the narrow confines of the Treaties. Two crucial consequences of the expansion of the EC's policy competence during this period were the increase in the size and complexity of the European Commission (further EC institution-building) and the progressive 'Europeanisation' of domestic policy-making. The latter development was reflected in the steady rise in the number of transnational Euro-groups and the progressive harmonisation of national legal and technical standards. ECJ rulings during this period quietly reinforced this trend.

The pace and direction of European unification during the 1970s was shaped by several interrelated dynamics. Within this process, individuals often played a key role. For example, the decision in 1978 to launch the original EMS owed much to the personal efforts of the UK Commissioner Roy Jenkins and the French President, Valéry Giscard d'Estaing. As in 1945, the EC external environment was also influential in persuading EC heads of government of the potential benefits of European cooperation. In particular, international currency fluctuations following the collapse in 1971 of the Bretton Woods system gave an important impetus to European monetary integration. Meanwhile, the development of EC social and environmental policies during the 1970s owed much to the mobilisation of interest groups – notably environmentalists and women – and the 'purposeful opportunism' (Cram 1993) of the European Commission.

Treaty reform and European integration: an iterative process

Since 1985, the EU has experienced considerable change that cumulatively transformed the salience and reach of the European Union. Successive enlargements, combined with a series of intergovernmental conferences and Treaty reforms, resulted in the simultaneous deepening and widening of the EU. These developments have been extensively analysed elsewhere and no attempt is made here to undertake such a task. Rather, the following (necessarily brief) review of the continuing process of Treaty reform is used here to highlight three central themes of this chapter: the multi-faceted nature of European integration; the increasing 'democratisation' and 'politicisation' of both the integration process and conception of the EU; and the extent to which integration has been path-dependent. The impetus for reform has generally come from recognition of the need for EU adaptation to exogenous imperatives of an economic, commercial or geo-political nature. As such, reform agendas have been to a large extent policy- and problem-driven. However, as the political salience of European integration increased, other actors and new issues became increasingly influential in the reform process. Their impact has been to broaden the reform agenda to embrace more fundamental issues relating to citizenship, human rights, democracy and the international role of the Union. In keeping with historical institutionalist models of integration, the progressive impact of incremental, institutional adjustments to the EU has also been significant. Notwithstanding the increasing resort since 1992 by member states to non-legislative forms of policy coordination, subsidiarity and flexibility as mechanisms for accommodating diversity, the cumulative impact of successive reforms has been significant. The competence of the EU has been significantly extended and the powers of the 'supranational' European institutions considerably increased. Significantly, these developments have taken place within the context of an increasingly hostile political context. Successive reforms have inevitably increased the political salience of the EU and the last twenty years have witnessed a widening divide between European elites on the one hand, and European citizens on the other, most of whom perceive the EU to be undemocratic, or a threat to national identity and sovereignty.

The 1986 Single European Act: completing the Single European Market

The 1986 SEA was a watershed in the development of the EC. It committed the twelve member states to completing the Single European Market (SEM), i.e. a Common Market, by January 1993 and to establishing EMU. The SEA also committed the signatories to EC institutional reform, designed primarily to facilitate the establishment of the SEM. More specifically, the SEA extended qualified majority voting (QMV) in the Council of Ministers and introduced the 'cooperation procedure', which further increased the legislative powers of the EP. The SEA also strengthened the legal basis for EC environmental, social and regional policies, and gave formal recognition to the European Council and EPC. Explanations of the SEA abound. Intergovernmentalist interpretations emphasise the importance of national interests and intergovernmental bargaining (Moravcsik 2003; Keohane and Hoffmann 1991). However, this explanatory model cannot wholly account for the linkage in the SEA between the SEM project and EC institutional reform, greater social and environmental protection, and economic and social cohesion – issues that seriously divided member states.

A more comprehensive explanation of the SEA has to evaluate the impact of other pressures and actors involved in the negotiation of the Act. While national governments were centrally involved in the negotiation and ratification of the SEA, there were other actors involved in setting and processing this policy agenda. Considerable evidence exists, for instance, of the agenda-setting role played in the early 1980s by transnational business and financial interest groups in favour of the SEM, EMU and European regulation (Majone 1992; Mazey and Richardson 1993; Sandholtz 1993; Cowles 1995). Within the EP, the Kangaroo Group, an all-party grouping, which had since 1980 campaigned for the removal of non-tariff barriers within the EC, was influential in laying the foundations for the 1985 Single Market programme. The EP was also influential in maintaining the momentum for EC institutional reform. Back in 1980, the federalist MEP Altiero Spinelli had formed the Crocodile Club, which drew up the Draft Treaty establishing the European Union (DTEU). Adopted by the EP in 1984, the DTEU formed the basis for the IGC discussions, which culminated in the SEA. During the 1985 IGC, the Commission, headed by the dynamic Jacques Delors, played a crucial 'brokerage' role, linking market integration (the core, substantive policy choice embodied in the SEA) to institutional reform, social regulation and economic cohesion. The SEA was therefore the product of several interlinked institutional and systemic dynamics, which converged around the SEM project. As Dehousse and Majone argue, 'once the general idea of completing the internal market was accepted, it proved possible to convince even the most reluctant member states that a shift towards more majority voting was necessary in several areas' (Dehousse and Majone 1994: 104).

The 1992 Maastricht Treaty on European Union: achieving European Monetary Union

The SEM project unleashed a fresh wave of 'low politics' integration in the form of harmonisation of national standards and regulations, and the abolition of non-tariff barriers. The dynamic for European integration was further maintained by the combined impact of the Commission and the advocacy coalition in favour of EMU. In June 1988, the Commission president, Jacques Delors, secured the European Council's support for his proposal to establish a high-level working party to draw up proposals for achieving EMU. In 1989, the committee recommended the gradual establishment of a single currency and an IGC was convened to consider the Treaty amendments required in order to establish the EMU. This pragmatic strategy was, however, suddenly blown off course by international events. The dramatic collapse of the Soviet Union after 1989 and consequent unification of Germany in 1991 thrust upon member states a much wider policy agenda. First, just as in 1945, France was again anxious to anchor a powerful Germany into the Community system. The German Chancellor, Helmut Kohl, was also anxious to demonstrate Germany's continuing commitment to European integration. Crucially, these objectives reinforced both countries' commitment to further deepening of the EU, and more specifically, to the realisation of EMU. Second, the disintegration of the Soviet system created new uncertainties about the future development of Western security. Third, Eastern enlargement of the Community – and the financial and institutional implications of such a development – was also now an unavoidable issue. At the suggestion of the French President, François Mitterrand, and Helmut Kohl, the European Council in June 1990 agreed to set up a second IGC on European political union. The outcome of the two IGCs was the TEU, adopted at the Maastricht meeting of the European Council in December 1991.

Again, there are numerous analyses of the Maastricht Treaty (see for example Duff *et al*. 1994; Laursen and Vanhoonacker 1992). The single most important achievement was the commitment by the signatories to create the EMU by 1 January 1999 at the latest. Predictably, the IGC on political union had reopened, but failed to resolve, a bitter debate on the meaning and direction of European integration. The newly named 'European Union' established by the Treaty comprised three institutional pillars: the European Community (EC), Common Foreign and Security Policy (CFSP), and Justice and Home Affairs (JHA). Of these, only the European Community had a supranational executive and legal authority. The CFSP and JHA pillars provided instead for intergovernmental cooperation in the fields of European foreign and security policy, and policing, asylum and immigration policies respectively. The Treaty also established a Franco-German defence corps and committed member states (albeit in vague terms) to the eventual establishment of a common foreign and security policy (CFSP) within the framework of the West European Union (WEU).

Within the EC pillar, member states acknowledged the need for faster decision-making. Thus, QMV was extended slightly to areas beyond the realm of the internal market. For similar reasons a new 'co-decision procedure', which gave the European Parliament a veto power in specified policy areas such as the internal market, the environment and consumer protection, was introduced. In a feeble attempt to address the problem of the 'democratic deficit' within the EC, the TEU introduced the principle that a new Commission must enjoy the support of a majority of MEPs and included symbolic references to 'European citizenship'. Finally, a new, consultative, Committee of the Regions was also established (largely in response to demands from the German *Länder*) to represent local and regional authorities in EC decision-making. The Community's competence was further extended in the fields of education, vocational training, youth, social policy, public health, consumer protection, environment, culture, research and technology, and trans-European networks. At the same time, however, the principle of subsidiarity was affirmed, restricting the actions of the Community to those matters where the objectives 'cannot be sufficiently achieved by the Member States' (Article 3b TEU). In order to resolve the intractable divide between the UK government and the other eleven member states, Protocols to the Treaty permitted the UK to opt out of the EMU and the new Social Chapter, which enhanced employees' rights in the workplace.

Viewed as part of a much longer-term process, the Maastricht agreement heralded the completion of the Union's economic constitution and the intensification of pressures for the constitutionalisation of political Europe. The establishment of an institutional framework for foreign policy and defence cooperation was a potentially significant development, as was the introduction into the discourse of the concept of European citizenship. Political Europe was striving to join economic Europe and the Maastricht agreement carried the Community over an important threshold. However, the legal and institutional patchwork created by the Treaty also heralded an important change in the *method* of European integration. The creation of the two intergovernmental pillars and the decision to allow the UK to opt out of key Treaty obligations (EMU and the Social Protocol to the Treaty) represented the first moves towards more flexible integration.

The Maastricht Treaty also marked the end of the 'permissive consensus' on the part of European publics with regard to European integration. Whereas the SEA had prompted little public debate, ratification of the Maastricht Treaty provoked an unexpected upsurge of public opposition to European integration in general and to the Community institutions in particular. Popular fears of mass immigration and strong nationalist sentiments were compounded by more specific concerns about the Community's 'democratic deficit' reflected in the unaccountability of the Commission, the weakness of the European Parliament, and the non-transparency of the EC decision-making process. Ratification of the Treaty proved problematic in several member states. In Denmark, the 1992 referendum on the TEU produced a negative vote (which was subsequently reversed in a second referendum in 1993) and the French referendum produced only a *petit oui* – 51 to 49 per cent in favour of the TEU. In the UK, the Conservative government, itself bitterly divided over Europe, was forced to make ratification of the Treaty an issue of confidence in order to obtain the necessary parliamentary majority. Several factors – some specific to individual member states – help to explain this backlash against European integration. However, one important cause of this sentiment was the increasing impact of European integration, especially after 1986. The incremental expansion of EU legislation inevitably increased the political visibility of European integration. European policies were also beginning to constrain national policy-makers. In particular, completion of the SEM and member states' determination to meet the rigorous 'convergence criteria' for entry to the EMU had, by 1992, begun to have unpleasant economic consequences in several countries. Many people who had hitherto either benefited from or been unaffected by EU policies began to worry about the potential costs of membership. Public support for European integration continued to fall throughout the 1990s. European integration became an increasingly salient political cleavage in many member states, dividing mainstream parties and spawning a host of populist, anti-European movements and parties. The emergence of a vigilant and critical public had rendered the Monnet method of integration both impractical and politically unacceptable.

The 1997 Amsterdam Treaty: towards flexible integration

Provision for another IGC to review the 1992 TEU was written into the Maastricht Treaty. (On the 1996 IGC see Edwards and Pijpers 1997.) The stated purpose of the IGC that began in March 1996 was to revise the European Treaties 'with the aim of ensuring the effectiveness of the mechanisms and the institutions of the Community'. However, the decision taken by the Madrid European Council in 1995 to proceed with eastern enlargement inevitably shifted the focus of this review. Whereas previous IGCs had taken the form of diplomatic negotiations between national officials, foreign ministers, and heads of states and governments, the changed political circumstances demanded that the 1996 IGC be conducted in a more open and more democratic manner. Throughout 1996 regional, national and European institutions, parties and interest groups were invited to insert their ideas and interests into the process. The impact of this initiative was twofold. First, participation in the IGC by large numbers of NGOs in favour of a more democratic EU meant that the discourse of the IGC was characterised by normative and political debate rather than by legal reasoning. Second, the openness of the IGC made it difficult for national- and EU-level political and administrative elites to control the agenda (Sverdrup 2000).

Analyses of the 1997 Amsterdam Treaty (see Duff 1997; Westlake 1998; Neunreither and Wiener 2000) generally emphasise the modest nature of the Amsterdam Treaty. Yet there were a number of important institutional developments – some of which reflected NGO concerns regarding human rights. The European Parliament's legislative powers were further increased through a substantial extension of the co-decision procedure. The Council also lost its right under the co-decision procedure to override the opinion of the Parliament. Thus, in many areas the EP became a co-equal legislator with the

Council. As a gesture towards those lobbying for greater Commission accountability, the EP also gained the right to approve the appointment of the Commission President. Meanwhile, the Commission's authority was strengthened by the creation of new community competences, by the (gradual) 'communitarisation' of immigration, visa and asylum policies and by the introduction of a shared right of initiative between member states and the Commission for other third-pillar (JHA) policies. Meanwhile, the European Court of Justice's jurisdiction was extended to include immigration and visa issues.

With respect to competence, the Treaty introduced a new Employment Title (VIII), which made 'a high level of employment' an EU objective and provided for non-legislative coordination and monitoring of national employment policies; this became the model for the 'open method of coordination' that was developed under the Lisbon process (Borrás and Greve 2004). Second, a new title, headed 'Visas asylum immigration and other policies related to the free movement of persons', incorporated the Schengen agreement as well as visa, immigration and asylum policies into the first pillar. Third, the Treaty reiterated the Union's commitment to liberty, democracy, respect for human rights and fundamental freedoms, strengthened the legal basis for the promotion of sex equality (Article 12) and introduced a new anti-discrimination provision (Article 13). From a constructivist perspective, these provisions were important in so far as they embedded in the Treaties, the foundations for a normative community based on liberal democratic values. Fourth, in an attempt to make CFSP more effective, the Amsterdam Treaty incorporated the so-called 'Petersberg Tasks' into the Treaty. Meanwhile, the new Article 17 extended CFSP to include the progressive framing of a common defence policy and the possible integration of the WEU into the EU. The Treaty also introduced the principle of 'constructive abstention', which enables the Council to adopt CFSP policies relating to an agreed common strategy or joint action by QMV. 'Constructive abstention' constituted one of three forms of flexibility introduced in the Amsterdam Treaty, designed to facilitate enhanced cooperation by a majority of member states in selected policy areas (see Stubb 2000; Wallace 2000; Junge 1999; Philippart and Sie Dhian Ho 2000).

Integration beyond Amsterdam: the Treaty of Nice

The IGC 2000 started on 14 February 2000 and ended with the Nice European Council in December that year (on the IGC 2000 see Best, Gray and Stubb 2000). The main purpose of this IGC was to deal with pressing issues unresolved by the Amsterdam Treaty. Key institutional issues to be resolved included the size of the European Parliament and the Commission, and the weighting of national votes within the Council. The agenda was limited but politically charged. The Nice IGC was characterised by an emerging cleavage between the large and small member states concerning representation in the Union's institutions and the system of weighted voting. Nevertheless, difficult decisions were taken.

With regard to the size of the Commission, the Nice Treaty established that from 2005 there should be one Commissioner per member state until the Union comprises 27 member states. The ceiling of 700 seats in the European Parliament established by the Amsterdam Treaty was breached – member states fixed the maximum number of MEPs at 732 and agreed that each member state should have between 99 and 5 seats. With regard to the weighting of votes in the Council, member states finally agreed to increase the number of total votes from 87 to 345 (with 27 member states) and to reallocate the number of votes allotted to each country. A new 'double' threshold for a qualifying majority was also established, based on 258 votes out of 345 and 62 per cent of the Union's population (compared to the previous informal requirement of 58 per cent). Overall, the changes to the Council's voting rules favoured the larger (and more populous) states. Though balance of power issues dominated the Nice Council, a number of other reforms were agreed by the member states, which, though incremental in nature, represented a further deepening of the Union. Such developments included the further extension of QMV and co-decision to new policy areas, further increases in the powers of the Parliament; enlargement and reform of the European Court of Justice, and the incorporation of WEU into the EU.

Parallel to the formal IGC, the Commission, the Council and the Parliament jointly proclaimed the EU Charter of Fundamental Rights at the Nice summit (Quinn and Flynn 2001; Peers and Ward 2004). The Charter had been prepared by an ad hoc 'Convention' composed of representatives of the heads of state and government, the Commission, the European Parliament and national parliaments. However, member states were unable to agree upon the incorporation of the Charter into the Treaty. Predictably, the UK, Sweden, Denmark and Ireland were bitterly opposed to this proposal. In consequence the Charter was accorded the status of a non-binding solemn declaration. Despite its weak judicial status, the Charter nevertheless represented a potentially important landmark in the incremental construction of a European polity, building upon the concept of European citizenship introduced in the TEU and the commitment to fundamental rights and freedoms provided for in the Amsterdam Treaty. In a declaration annexed to the Treaty of Nice, the member states mapped out the route to a new reforming treaty; it was on the basis of this declaration that the move towards the Constitution took on a concrete form. Meanwhile, however, the rejection of the Nice Treaty in June 2001 by the Irish electorate (which was subsequently reversed in a second referendum), underlined the continuing gap between Europe's elites and its citizens on the future of the European Union and the fragility of the integration process.

Towards a European Constitution

From Laeken to the Draft Constitutional Treaty

At its meeting in Laeken in December 2001, the European Council established the European Convention to prepare the reform proposals The choice of a Convention represented a significant departure from previous treaty revision procedures, reflecting the increasing importance of a 'constitutional discourse', and acknowledgement by member governments of the political imperative of involving civil society groups in the reform process (Magnette and Nicolaïdis 2004; Shaw 2003). The Laeken Declaration established four broad areas for deliberation by the Convention. These were:

- A better division and definition of competence in the European Union;
- Simplification of the Union's instruments;
- More democracy, transparency and efficiency in the European Union;
- Towards a Constitution for European citizens.

(Laeken Declaration, europa.eu.int/constitution/futurum)

The Laekan Declaration was sufficiently broad and non-directional to embrace the concerns of all the member states. It did not privilege either a federalist or intergovernmental agenda for the Convention/IGC, but it read more like a 'constitutional agenda than the basis for a classic treaty reform' and 'went beyond the restricted list of left-overs agreed at Nice' (Magnette and Nicolaïdis 2004: 388).

The Convention, which was chaired by former French President, Valéry Giscard d'Estaing, comprised fifteen representatives of heads of state and national governments, thirty members of the national parliaments, sixteen MEPs and two Commission representatives. Each candidate state had three representatives who took part fully in the deliberations of the Convention without being able to prevent a consensus emerging among the member states. The Convention was a multilateral exercise in deliberation and negotiation, but as Magnette and Nicolaïdis remark, the Convention was not Europe's Philadelphia: 'discussions took place under the shadow of the IGC and under a leadership extremely sensitive to the positions of big member states' (Magnette and Nicolaïdis 2004: 381). Nevertheless, the Convention was important in three respects. First, it was a market place for ideas about constitutional and institutional reform of the Union (Norman 2003). Second, its recommendations established the broad parameters for the subsequent IGC negotiations. Third, notwithstanding its shortcomings as an exercise in deliberative democracy (many groups were unrepresented and debates were dominated by two familiar cleavages: intergovernmentalists *vs* supranationalists, and big *vs* small states), the fact that the Convention agreed a single document lent considerable weight to its agenda-setting power for the IGC that succeeded it.

From Convention to IGC

The draft Treaty agreed by the Convention and submitted to the Thessaloniki European Council in June 2003 was the default document for the subsequent IGC. The task of the IGC was not to begin to draft a Constitution. Rather, its purpose was to reach agreement among the member-state governments on an acceptable version of the Convention text. Though most states felt that some changes were necessary for agreement, they were generally reluctant to unravel the entire Convention text, fearing that agreements already arrived at might come unstuck. The style of bargaining that had animated the Convention's deliberations enabled the participants to reach agreement on a series of difficult issues. Among the achievements of the Convention were:

- Agreement on a legal personality for the Union;
- Abolition of the pillar structure;
- Agreement on a constitutional treaty;
- Incorporation of the charter;
- Strengthening of the external capacity of the Union;
- Agreement on the constitutive values and objectives of the Union.

The Italian Presidency formally opened the IGC on 4 October 2003 with the intention of reaching agreement by the December European Council. Unlike previous IGCs, the 2003/2004 IGC met predominantly at political level, in meetings of foreign ministers and the European Council without formal working groups. This reflected the fact that the preparatory work and the drafting of text had already been largely achieved by the Convention. Non-institutional issues that remained sensitive during the IGC included demands for a reference to God in the preamble, and the mechanisms for incorporating the Charter on Fundamental Rights. In addition, institutional issues remained highly contentious. The key institutional issues were the composition of the Commission, the system of weighted voting in Council, and the Presidency of the European Council and the Council of Ministers.

These issues related to the nature of decision-making in the Union, the voice and representation of the member states, and member-state control over sensitive areas. Put simply, these issues were about power – the power balance between the Union and the member states on the one hand, and the power balance among the member states on the other. Three cleavages dominated the discussion of these questions. First, there was the perennial cleavage between those states (notably the UK) that favoured more inter-governmental control and member states such as France, Germany and the Benelux countries that favoured supranational outcomes. Second, there was a cleavage between large and small states about membership of the Commission, voting weights and the establishment of a permanent chair of the European Council. Unsurprisingly, small states favoured the retention of one Commissioner per member state. They also saw the establishment of a new chair of the European Council as a large-state ploy to weaken the Commission, the organisation regarded by small states as their protector in the Union. Third, there was a cleavage between large and medium-sized states about weighted voting. The Convention text proposed the introduction of a voting system based on a double majority – a majority of member states and of states representing over 60 per cent of Europe's peoples. In a significant shift from their policy preference in Nice, France accepted a double majority system of voting. The move from the traditional QMV system was, however, bitterly opposed by Poland and Spain, who issued a joint statement on 29 September 2003 rejecting the new system. In the event, the December European Council failed to conclude the negotiations.

Following the failure of the December Summit, the Irish presidency took over responsibility for the IGC with a mandate to 'listen, assess and report' back to the European Council in March 2004. In fact, by March the Irish presidency was confident that it could conclude negotiations by the end of June. Although none of the member states had actually given up their negotiating positions, all member states were keen to reach agreement: the Madrid bombings and the subsequent change of government in Spain had dramatically altered the political context within which the IGC was conducted. Hence the formal IGC was re-convened in May. It consisted of a limited number of official and ministerial meetings and the final European Council, which agreed the final text on the evening of 18 June. The key innovations of the constitutional treaty are as follows:

The founding principles of the Union

- The values and objectives of the Union are enshrined, as are the rights of European citizens, thanks to the incorporation into the Treaty of the European Charter of Fundamental Rights.
- The Union is accorded a single legal personality.
- The Competences (exclusive, shared and supporting) and their distribution between member states and the Union are clearly and permanently defined.
- The instruments of action available to the Union are simplified.

49

- The democratic underpinnings of the Union, including participatory democracy, are defined for the first time, and a right of popular legislative initiative is introduced.

The Institutions

- The seats in the EP are distributed on a degressively proportional basis.
- The European Council is formally institutionalised and the rotating Presidency of the European Council is discarded.
- The size of the Commission is to be reduced from 2014 to make the number of Commissioners equal to two-thirds of the number of member states.
- The President of the Commission is to be elected by the European Parliament based on a proposal from the European Council.
- A European Minister for Foreign Affairs is to be appointed.

Decision-making

- A new qualified majority system is established under which 55 per cent of the member states representing 65 per cent of the EU population will constitute a qualified majority. A blocking minority must comprise at least four member states. A number of Council members representing at least three-quarters of a blocking minority, whether at the level of member states or the level of the population, may demand that a vote is postponed to allow further discussions to take place in order to reach a broader basis of consensus within the Council.
- Qualified majority voting in the Council of Ministers is to be extended.
- The joint adoption of European laws by the Council and the European Parliament is to become the norm.

Union Policies

- Economic coordination between countries that have adopted the euro is to be improved and the role of the Euro-Group is to be recognised.
- The pillar structure is abolished. The second (common foreign and security policy) and third (justice and home affairs) pillars, which were hitherto subject to the inter-governmental method are brought within the Community framework.
- The common foreign and security policy is strengthened with the creation of a European Minister for Foreign Affairs and the progressive definition of a common defence policy.
- A genuine area of freedom, security and justice is to be created through the planned implementation of common policies on asylum, immigration and external border control, in the field of judicial and police cooperation, and through the creation of a European Public Prosecutor's Office.

The 'Treaty Establishing a Constitution for Europe' has a legal status similar to earlier treaties that are traced in this chapter. It is a treaty under international law, agreed by the High Contracting parties, the twenty-five member states, and must be ratified in accordance with their domestic constitutional requirements. The Constitution provides a 'values map' and a 'power map' for the Union and reduces the ambiguity about the status and purpose of European Integration. Parts I and II of the text set out the normative framework of the Union and its institutional architecture, and are thus similar to the provisions of classical statist constitutions. The values and objectives of the Union are enshrined as are the rights of European citizens and, for the first time, the demo-cratic underpinnings of the Union, including participatory democracy, are defined, and a genuine right of popular legislative initiative is introduced. Parts III and IV contain detailed provisions concerning the policies of the Union and are thus not unlike the earlier treaties. Although the Treaty represents a further deepening of the EU in several respects, it also contains important provisions intended to prevent further erosion of member states' control over future European legislation or budgetary commitments. As Devuyst points out, the safeguards sought by member states during the IGC were designed 'to ensure that the EU's supranational internal policy-making process would not create unwanted obligations that would be fiercely enforced' (Devuyst 2005: 193). National parliaments, for instance, may object to new EU legislation if they believe the proposal does not comply with the principle of subsidiarity. The qualified majority voting system introduced by the Treaty leaves intact opportunities for member states to create mutual blocking mechanisms. And the national veto is maintained in important policy fields (including foreign policy, taxation, some areas of social policy, Treaty reform, legislation relating to the EU's 'own resources' and the adoption of financial perspec-tives. The new President of the European Council also strengthens the weight of member states vis-à-vis the 'supranational' Commission (Devuyst 2005).

The Constitution is scheduled to enter into force on 1 November 2006 following ratifi-cation by the member-states. However, as indicated above, this now seems unlikely to occur. On 29 May, French voters decisively rejected the European Constitution in a referendum (55 per cent of the poll voted no). Just three days later on 1 June a vast majority of Dutch citizens (62 per cent of the ballot) also voted against ratification of the Treaty. Significantly, in both countries, the turnout was high, 69 and 63 per cent of the electorate respectively. In both countries the 'no' vote comprised disparate groups across the political spectrum, some of whom were registering opposition to the national government. However, in the French case polls indicated widespread concern among moderate left-wing voters about the impact of EU policies on the persistently high levels of unemployment in France; voters were protesting against further enlargement of the European Union and liberal economic reforms, both of which have been vociferously championed within the Union by the British government. Meanwhile, in the Nether-lands, the euro, the loss of national sovereignty and national identity, diminishing Dutch influence within an enlarging Union, Turkish accession and the Netherlands' position as the biggest per capita contributor to the EU budget were key mobilising issues in the no-campaign. Following the double rejection of the constitutional treaty by France and the Netherlands, a relieved UK government immediately postponed the UK referendum planned for 2006 – a move which irritated other member states and the EU institutions, who insisted that the ratification process should continue. At the acrimonious June Council meeting in Brussels, EU leaders agreed to extend the November 2006 deadline for ratifying the Charter, but without setting a new target date. It is unclear what will happen now. It is possible that some governments will propose a new 'slimmed-down' treaty, though in the current political context, this would be a politically difficult and lengthy exercise; others might suggest pushing ahead with lesser reforms which would not require a treaty change. Non-ratification also opens up the possibility that some member states might try to forge ahead with integration on their own to form an inner core. The outcome of this crisis is rendered more uncertain by the current political situa-tion in Europe. The UK government began its six-month presidency of the EU on 1 July

2005, determined to persuade other member states of the need for liberal economic reform. However, it may be difficult to persuade some member states – notably France and Germany – of this case, not least because all governments are now particularly aware of the need to be seen to be defending national interests within the EU.

Conclusion: the stability of instability

The European Union did not spring from a single founding moment; it is the product of over fifty years of incremental change. As Marks writes, though 'notions of federalism, intergovernmentalism and so forth, have influenced the development of the EU ... they have not determined it. In practice, the institutions of the EU have been created to achieve discrete, diverse, contested and contingent goals' (Marks 1997: 27). At each stage, the final destination or *raison d'être* of the European Union has been fudged by the member states. Nevertheless, the integration process has continued, driven by national governments, self-interested individuals and groups, European institutions such as the Parliament, the Commission and the Court, and exogenous pressures. Since the 1980s, the Union has been in a constant state of constitutional and institutional flux. Successive reforms of the founding Treaties have incrementally brought about significant deepening of the EU, a process that has been accompanied by successive enlargement of the Union, which now comprises twenty-five member states. The draft constitutional treaty represented the culmination of this increasingly difficult political process. Essentially, it sought to clarify the distribution of power between the Union and the member states and to render the EU decision-making process more accountable to European citizens. Ironically, the European Constitution was intended to increase public support for the European Union, but in practice, it seems to have fuelled Euroscepticism.

The decisive rejection of the Treaty by voters in France and the Netherlands has once again demonstrated the enduring tensions within the EU over the nature and purpose of European integration. Yet, although the European Constitution may be dead (no member state is prepared to say so publicly), the European Union is still very much alive. When the UK government took over the Council Presidency on 1 July it immediately announced an ambitious list of priorities for the next six months, including major initiatives on climate change, development and Africa, peace in the Middle East, and legislation in sensitive areas including the Services Directive, the Working Time Directive and chemicals regulation, In addition to persuading the twenty-five member states to agree on difficult legislative proposals, British diplomats and officials must also seek to finalise the EU budget for 2007–13 and initiate discussions aimed at changing the financial structure of future EU spending. None of this will be easy in the current political climate. In a sense, it's business as usual within the EU. The ties that bind the member states appear sufficiently dense to ensure that business continues even when the political climate is not auspicious.

References

Best, E., Gray, M. and Stubb, A. (eds) (2000) *Rethinking the European Union: IGC 2000 and Beyond* (Maastricht: European Institute of Public Administration).

Borrás, S. and Greve, B. 'Concluding Remarks: New Method or Just Cheap Talk?', special issue of *Journal of European Public Policy* 11/2: 329–36.

Checkel, J. T. (2004) 'Social Constructivisms in Global and European Politics', *Review of International Studies* 30/3: 229–44.

Christiansen, T., Jørgensen, K. E. and Wiener, A. (eds) (2001), *The Social Construction of Europe* (London: Sage).

Cowles, M. (1995) 'Setting the Agenda for a New Europe: The ERT and EC 1992', *Journal of Common Market Studies* 33/4: 501–26.

Cram, L. (1993) 'Calling the Tune without Paying the Piper? Social Policy Regulation: The Role of the Commission as a Multi-Organization: Social Policy and IT Regulation in the EU', *Journal of European Public Policy* 1/2: 195–217.

Dehousse, R. and Majone, G. (1994) 'The Institutional Dynamics of European Integration', in S. Martin (ed.), *The Construction of Europe: Essays in Honour of Emile Noël* (Dordrecht: Kluwer Academic Publishers).

Devuyst, Y. (2005) *The European Union Transformed: Community Method and Institutional Evolution from the Schuman Plan to the Constitution for Europe* (Brussels: Peter Lang).

Duchêne, F. (1994) *Jean Monnet: The First Statesman of Interdependence* (New York: Norton).

Duff, A. (ed.) (1997) *The Treaty of Amsterdam: Text and Commentary* (London: Federal Trust).

Duff, A., Pinder, J. and Pryce, R. (eds) (1994) *Maastricht and Beyond: Building the European Union* (London: Routledge).

Dyson, K. and Featherstone, K. (1999) *The Road to Maastricht: Negotiating Economic and Monetary Union* (Oxford: Oxford University Press).

Edwards, G. and Pijpers, A. (eds) (1997) *The Politics of European Treaty Reform* (London: Pinter).

Featherstone, K. (1994) 'Jean Monnet and the "Democratic Deficit" in the European Union', *Journal of Common Market Studies* 32/2: 149–70.

George, S. (1990) *An Awkward Partner: Britain in the European Community* (Oxford: Oxford University Press).

Haas, E. (1958) *The Uniting of Europe* (Stanford, CA: Stanford University Press).

Junge, K. (1999) *Flexibility, Enhanced Cooperation and the Treaty of Amsterdam* (European Dossier Series, London: Kogan Page).

Keohane, R. O. and Hoffmann, S. (eds) (1991) *The New European Community: Decisionmaking and Institutional Change* (Boulder, CO: Westview).

Kingdon, J. W. (1984) *Agendas, Alternatives and Public Policies* (New York: HarperCollins).

Kirchner, E. (1980) 'Interest Group Behaviour at the Community Level', in L. Hurwitz (ed.), *Contemporary Perspectives on European Integration: Attitudes, Non-governmental Behaviour and Collective Decision Making* (Westport, CT: Greenwood Press).

Laursen, F. and Vanhoonacker, S. (1992) *The Intergovernmental Conference on Political Union: Institutional Reforms, New Policies and the International Identity of the European Community* (Maastricht: European Institute of Public Administration).

Lipgens, W. (1982) *A History of European Integration 1945–1947: The Formation of the European Unity Movement* (Oxford: Clarendon).

Magnette, P. and Nicolaïdis, K. (2004) 'The European Convention: Bargaining in the Shadow of Rhetoric', *West European Politics* 27/3: 381–404.

Majone, G. (1992) 'Regulatory Federalism in the European Community', *Government and Policy* 10: 299–316.

Marks, G. (1997) 'A Third Lens: Comparing European Integration and State Building', in J. Klansen and L. Tilly (eds) *European Integration in Social and Historical Perspective* (Lanham, MD: Rowman & Littlefield).

Mazey, S. (1992) 'Conception and Evolution of the High Authority's Administrative Services (1952–1960): From Supranational Principles to Multinational Practices', in *Yearbook of European Administrative History* (Baden-Baden: Nomos Verlagsgesellschaft).

Mazey, S. and Richardson, J. (1993) *Lobbying in the European Community* (Oxford: Oxford University Press).

Milward, A. (1992) *The European Rescue of the Nation-State* (London: Routledge).

Monnet, J. (1978) *Memoirs* (London: Collins).

Moravcsik, A. (2003) *The Choice for Europe: Social Purpose and State Power from Messina to Maastricht*, 2nd edn (Ithaca, NY: Cornell University Press).

—— (2005) 'The European Constitutional Compromise and the Legacy of Neo-Functionalism', *Journal of European Public Policy* 12/2: 349–86.

Moravcsik, A. and Nicolaïdis, K. (1998) 'Federal Ideals and Constitutional Realities', *Annual Review, Journal of Common Market Studies* 36: 13–38.

Neunreither, K. and Wiener, A. (eds) (2000) *European Integration after Amsterdam: Institutional Dynamics and Prospects for Democracy* (Oxford: Oxford University Press).

Norman, P. (2003) *The Accidental Constitution: The Story of the European Convention* (Brussels: Eurocomment).

Peers, S. and Ward, A. (eds) (2004) *The EU Charter of Fundamental Rights: Politics, Law and Policy* (Oxford: Hart).

Peterson, J. (1995) 'Decision-making in the European Union: Towards a Framework for Analysis', *Journal of European Public Policy* 2/1: 69–94.

Philippart, E. and Sie Dhian Ho, M. (2000) 'From Uniformity to Flexibility: The Management of Diversity and its Impact on the EU System of Governance', in G. De Burca and J. Scott (eds), *Constitutional Change in the EU: From Uniformity to Flexibility* (Oxford: Hart).

Pierson, P. (1996) 'The Path to European Integration: A Historical Institutionalist Analysis', *Comparative Politics* 29/2: 123–63.

Pinder, J. (1995) *European Community: The Building of a Union* (Oxford: Oxford University Press).

Quinn, G. and Flynn, L. (2001) *The EU Charter on Fundamental Rights: Issues and Perspectives* (Oxford: Oxford University Press).

Risse, T. (2004), 'Social Constructivism and European Integration', in A. Wiener and T. Diez (eds), *European Integration Theory* (Oxford: Oxford University Press).

Sabatier, P. (1988) 'An Advocacy Coalition Framework of Policy Change and the Role of Policy Orientated Learning Therein', *International Organisation* 42: 1–35.

Sandholtz, W. (1993) 'Choosing Union: Monetary Politics and Maastricht', *International Organisation* 47: 1–39.

Shaw, J. (2003) 'Process, Responsibility and Inclusion in EU Constitutionalism', *European Law Journal* 9/1: 45–68

Stirk, P. M. R. and Weigall, D. (eds) (1999) *The Origins and Development of European Integration: A Reader and a Commentary* (London: Pinter).

Stubb, A. (2000) 'Negotiating Flexible Integration in the Amsterdam Treaty', in K. Neunreither and A. Wiener (eds), *European Integration after Amsterdam: Institutional Dynamics and Prospects for Democracy* (Oxford: Oxford University Press).

Sverdrup, O. (2000) 'Precedents and Present Events in the European Union: An Institutional Perspective on Treaty Reform', in K. Neunreither and A. Wiener (eds), *European Integration after Amsterdam: Institutional Dynamics and Prospects for Democracy* (Oxford: Oxford University Press).

Urwin, D. (1989) *Western Europe since 1945: A Political History*, 4th edn (London: Longman).

Vaughan, R. (1979) *Twentieth Century Europe* (London: Croom Helm).

Wallace, H. (2000) 'Flexibility: A Tool of Integration or a Restraint on Disintegration?', in K. Neunreither and A. Wiener (eds), *European Integration after Amsterdam: Institutional Dynamics and Prospects for Democracy* (Oxford: Oxford University Press).

Westlake, M. (ed.) (1998) *The European Union beyond Amsterdam: New Concepts of European Integration* (London: Routledge).

Willis, F. R. (1968) *France, Germany and the New Europe 1945–1967* (Stanford, CA: Stanford University Press).

Chapter 3

Europeanisation of public policy

ANDREA LENSCHOW

Introduction

The European Union (EU) affects national political and administrative systems, domestic politics and policies. Currently, we witness under the label of 'Europeanisation' a turn towards this research perspective which brings into focus that Europe 'matters' in the daily political life of national bureaucrats, politicians and the wider public (Jordan and Liefferink 2004: 1). Analytically, Europeanisation research has blown fresh air into older debates on European integration, policy-making and European governance.

'Classical' research on the European Community/Union has focused on economic and political integration. A core concern of this scholarship was the future of the sovereign nation state, its relative strength vis-à-vis the emerging supranational institutions of the Community and its possible 'withering away'. Europeanisation from this perspective implied the relative weakening of national state structures due to a shift of political responsibilities and possibly public loyalties to the European level (e.g. Haas 1968). Others argue, by contrast, that European-level arrangements have strengthened the territorial state, and especially national governments (e.g. Milward 1992). A second stream of EU research moved attention from the systemic level to the dynamics of policy-making in Brussels and policy implementation in the member states. Not only national governments but also national pressure groups, national and subnational administrations, and national parliaments now came into focus and their reactions to new opportunity structures, on the one hand, and demands for adaptation, on the other hand, became subject to analysis.[1] Such mid-level investigation first hinted at important transformations in domestic politics. The concept of 'multi-level governance' (e.g. Benz 2004; Marks *et al.* 1996) signifies the end of the separate treatment of European and national politics. It treats the vertical levels of governance as interlinked and the multitude of political and societal actors as potential parts of a dynamic network (cf. Kohler-Koch and Eising 1999). From the perspective of Europeanisation, research activities became interested not only in how processes of European integration and policy-making impacted on national policy and elements of domestic political structures but also in how they produced changes in the overall nature of political systems and their politics.

Emerging from such a variety of theoretical debates, it comes as no surprise that Europeanisation research is characterised by a degree of unwieldiness which has prompted concern that we are dealing with a 'faddish' concept (Featherstone 2003: 1) with only limited utility as an organising concept (Kassim 2000: 238). Indeed, many competing definitions of the concept have been generated; it has been applied to a great variety of different phenomena; and the research community is still struggling to develop an explanatory framework, let alone theory, of Europeanisation.

This chapter offers some orientation through the thicket of recent scholarship on Europeanisation. First, it will introduce the reader to important – and contested – terminological and conceptual 'scoping' issues. What do we mean when we speak of Europeanisation? This question guides the first part of this chapter. I turn to explanations in the second part, and argue that the literature has advanced farther in identifying potentially relevant explanatory factors than in defining the scope conditions under which one or more factors assume an explanatory role. In the light of persisting knowledge gaps, the question 'What has been learned?' can be answered only in a preliminary fashion. The concluding part returns to the contributions this research has made to understanding European integration, policy-making in the EU and the nature of the EU governance system.

What is Europeanisation?

Concepts serve as a bridge between the observed 'reality' and generalising statements about this reality. In order to sort empirical material and to raise interesting theoretical or empirical questions concepts need to be clearly defined both in terms of content (what is it about) and scope (to what does it apply). 'Europeanisation' has been introduced as a new concept in EU research, presumably focusing our attention on a previously neglected set of empirical phenomena which deserve our attention from a theoretical as well as possibly from a normative standpoint. Examining the literature closely, however, we quickly note considerable confusion and disagreement about both content and scope of the concept. Such a state of affairs will hamper cumulative research and undermines any theoretical aspirations.

Definitions

So far, the concept of Europeanisation has not been given a single and precise definition. On the contrary, several authors have begun to count an impressive number of rather diverse definitions (cf. Eising 2003b; Olsen 2002; Radaelli 2000). Box 1 identifies four different ways in which Europeanisation has been defined.

   These four definitions have in common that they are all concerned with the EU. Beate Kohler-Koch (2000) suggested with some justification that Europeanisation should be renamed EU-Europeanisation or Unionisation and I will return to the issue of the territorial scope below. Also, all definitions conceive of Europeanisation as a process rather than a status. In other words, none of these definitions treats Europeanisation as a dependent variable (a 'European model') but rather as a process leading to still unspecified outcomes. The quoted statements differ widely, however, with respect to the direction of the process at work. Europeanisation has been characterised as a bottom-up (national state→EU), top-down (EU→national state), horizontal (state→state) and round-about (national state→EU→national state) process. There is no doubt that all these processes exist and may deserve close investigation. But if Europeanisation denotes all these processes at once, this raises the issue of concept stretching (Satori 1970; see Radaelli 2000 specifically on Europeanisation) where few general statements are possible that apply to all cases captured by the concept.

   Europeanisation as a bottom-up process is not distinguishable from the 'classical' concept of European integration and this definition may be discarded as introducing a synonym rather than a new concept. Somewhat curiously, it was suggested in a book that actually dealt with the top-down process of EU governance structures having an *impact* on the domestic structures of EU member states (Cowles *et al.* 2001). All other definitions have in common that they do not perceive the EU as the target but rather as the direct or indirect origin of developments on the national level. This is most clearly the case in the 'top-down' definition, which is also the one most widely used in the literature. Especially in studies focusing on the impact of EU policies on national policy goals, choices of policy instruments and policy-specific organisational structures this

---

Box 1 Definitions

- *'The emergence and development at the European level of distinct structures of governance ...'* (Risse *et al.* 2001: 2): In this definition Europeanisation is synonymous with European integration. Europeanisation is the independent variable exerting transformative effects on the national level.
- *The top-down impact of the EU on its member states:* Ladrech, for instance, defined Europeanisation as 'an incremental process re-orienting the direction and shape of politics to the degree that EU political and economic dynamics become part of the organisational logic of national politics and policy-making' (1994: 69). Héritier *et al.* (2001: 3) define it more narrowly as 'the process of influence deriving from European decisions and impacting member states' policies and political administrative structures'. Both definitions have in common that Europeanisation is considered a process that takes place in the member states, affecting institutional structures, policies and politics.
- *The horizontal transfer of concepts and policies between member states of the EU:* Several authors note the facilitating role of the EU for inter-state transfers. New modes of regulatory policy-making in the EU even specifically aim at such horizontal processes (cf. Bomberg and Peterson 2000; Radaelli 2004).
- *The circular interaction between the EU and its member state:* Dyson and Goetz speak of a 'complex interactive top-down and bottom-up process in which domestic polities, politics and public policies are shaped by European integration and in which domestic actors use European integration to shape the domestic area' (2003: 20; see also Radaelli 2000: 3–4).

---

perspective carries the advantage that 'the top', i.e. the independent variable, is typically quite clearly identifiable. Europeanisation defined as a top-down process varies both in scope and in normative connotation from the nevertheless closely related concept of implementation. Normatively, Europeanisation is concerned with national transformation processes in general; these need not necessarily imply following a European standard or adopting a prescribed European approach. Furthermore, Europeanisation explicitly widens the perspective beyond the immediate policy level and brings the impact on polity and politics structures into focus.

Horizontal, state-to-state transfer processes may take place independently of the existence of the EU; such processes are captured by the concepts of inter-state transfer or diffusion. However, the EU may facilitate such horizontal processes by providing the arena for inter-state communication or competition. On the one hand, the very existence of the internal market, guarded by measures of negative integration, sets in motion competitive dynamics and adaptations across member states (Scharpf 2003; Holzinger and Knill 2004). On the other hand, EU institutions – most notably the extensive committee structure – bring national policy-makers and opinion leaders into contact with each other, facilitating the exchange of ideas which may diffuse into national practices. Increasingly, the EU also develops formal policies intended to facilitate such horizontal transfers and learning processes. The Open Method of Coordination, for instance, is a device for the transfer of so-called 'best practice models' especially in areas where the EU lacks competency to exert top-down pressures. In policy-making practice EU-facilitated horizontal transfer supplements the top-down mechanism described above and hence may be subsumed under the Europeanisation concept.

A third way of widening the concept of Europeanisation has been suggested in several recent studies which propose looking at it from a cyclical, more dynamic point of view. Europeanisation is considered a discursive context, creating a frame of reference for domestic actors who not merely react to European impulses but anticipate such impulses by either inducing bottom-up processes changing the European level[2] or by 'using' or 'endogenising' Europe in domestic politics independent of specific pressures from Brussels (Bulmer and Radaelli 2004; Busch 2004; Thatcher 2004). This notion is compatible with the top-down model of Europeanisation in the sense that we still deal with a point of reference on the EU level which influences the behaviour of national political actors. This perspective requires that special care is taken to avoid imputing processes of Europeanisation in possibly purely domestic processes.

In sum, Europeanisation is indeed a broad – even 'stretched' – concept interested in domestic adaptations to 'EU-Europe'. The concept assumes the EU as the direct or indirect provider of a necessary impulse for domestic change. The EU represents a set of rules, an arena and a discursive framework for domestic actors, in short a point of departure for impulses that flow top-down, horizontally and 'round-about' when impacting on the domestic level (figure 3.1). It is clear from this that Europeanisation is not an explanatory concept itself; rather it subsumes several mechanisms that bring about domestic change.

Territorial scope

It was already established that Europeanisation research generally takes the EU as its reference point and may therefore properly be called EU-Europeanisation or Unionisation. Methodologically, this definition requires the isolation of EU effects on domestic developments from other – international or national – impacts. Numerous general policy developments, ranging from the liberalisation of public utilities (e.g. Levi-Faur 2004),

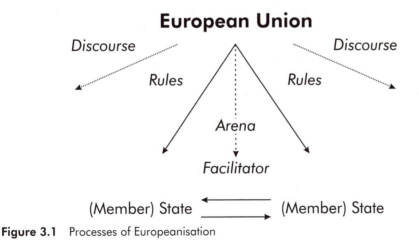

Figure 3.1 Processes of Europeanisation

Box 2   Europeanisation in Switzerland

A particularly remarkable case of Europeanisation is Switzerland, which celebrates an image of international economic involvement while keeping a distance from European political and to some extent even economic integration. Despite such prevalent EU-scepticism several authors have noted patterns of Europeanisation in public policy. Horizontal economic relations with EU members induce the country to adopt many Community rules and hence ensure market access via direct, bilateral agreements (for instance on free movement, transport policy, R&D, agriculture, public procurement and non-tariff barriers to trade) as well as indirectly via autonomous domestic reform, for instance in the field of telecommunication (Church 2000; Sciarini et al. 2004). However, not only policy in Switzerland may be affected but also the political distribution of power and processes of decision-making. Fischer (2003) notes that indirect Europeanisation, where the EU reference point is used to engage in domestic reforms but no formal bilateral agreements between Switzerland and the EU are negotiated, has resulted in the loss of veto powers for trade unions and other societal actors while strengthening the executive. Direct and formal Europeanisation, by contrast, protects the veto powers of these actors. Consequently, trade union actors – traditionally sceptical about European economic integration and the EU – have developed a friendlier attitude towards formal relations with the EU.

---

reforms of social welfare regimes (e.g. Wincott 2003), or the discourse of sustainable development effecting environmental policy (e.g. Lenschow 1999), can be traced to global or domestic factors as well as EU-induced effects, which in turn may have been triggered by global or national dynamics. In light of this multi-causality (cf. Eising 2003b: 407) Europeanisation research faces a problem in attributing unambiguous explanatory weight to the EU. Not even in policy areas of 'positive integration', i.e. in areas where the EU formulates uniformly applicable market-correcting rules such as environmental or consumer protection standards, do domestic adaptation processes tend to be 'responses' only to this one factor. Jordan and Liefferink, comparing the Europeanisation of environmental policy in nine EU member states and one non-member state (Norway), find that 'Europeanisation has probably been a weak and indirect cause of the policy convergence reported … remov[ing] the most obvious outliers … and [bringing] the environmental systems of the economically peripheral states (namely Ireland and Spain) up to the same level as the states in the more industrialized north' (2004: 232–3).

There are a number of methodological tools that may be applied to isolate Europeanisation from other drivers of domestic change. First, in a cross-country comparative design the differential impact of the EU on members and non-members may be analysed. Second, historical studies are needed to establish the temporal link between national, EU or international developments and domestic change; Europeanisation requires that the EU impulse is sent before domestic changes come under way. Third, if the analysis starts at the domestic level adaptation processes can be best traced without prejudice and with an open mind for all potential drivers. Finally, the analysis may explore counterfactuals, asking whether domestic developments would have taken place without the impact of the EU.

The issue of territorial scope applies not only to isolating the European impulse, it also relates to limiting or permitting the number of potential addressees. May the concept be applied to domestic adaptations outside the EU? Can Europeanisation be considered a process of exporting policies, political organisations and governance practices beyond the EU territory? Considering the variety of processes that may be subsumed under the concept, there are no analytical reasons why such extended territorial scope should not be permitted. Also empirically there are good reasons to extend the territorial scope of the concept in this way. Several countries hope to join the EU in the future and engage in adaptations with this perspective in mind. Applicant countries are already subject to explicit rules and conditions triggering internal reform processes (cf. Schimmelfennig *et al.* 2003) and they are allowed to participate in the EU arena (Drulák *et al.* 2003; Lippert *et al.* 2001). From the perspective of an enlarging EU the extent, speed and depth of Europeanisation process in 'not-yet member states' will hint at post-enlargement political dynamics in Europe that can be revealing to both scholars and practitioners. Other countries may not wish to join the EU but are part of the European economic area (Norway, Iceland) or are linked economically through bilateral arrangements (Switzerland). In these countries the top-down process of Europeanisation may be less direct and less formal; horizontal and discursive processes will be relatively more significant. Considering the EU-sceptical attitude of some of these countries (or their populations) it is certainly interesting to observe to what extent they may be nevertheless drawn into dynamics of Europeanisation (see Box 2).

Substantive scope

Besides the territorial scope of the concept, we need to gain some clarity with respect to the substantive scope of the concept, i.e. the domains that are being impacted upon on the domestic level and to what degree. Political scientists tend to focus on three dimensions that were already hinted at on the preceding pages: policy, politics and polity. Table 3.1 lists a range of concrete dimensions that may be subject to Europeanisation.

Table 3.1 Dimensions of domestic change

Polity	Politics	Policy
• Government– parliament relations	• Party and electoral politics	• Norms and goals
• Administrative structures	• Interest intermediation	• Policy instruments and style
• Judicial structures	• Patterns of contestation	• Standards
• Intergovernmental relations	• Public opinion	• Resources
		• Organisational structures
		• Actor networks

Analytically, these three domains form distinct categories. But empirically, the three dimensions interact and European policies, processes, institutions and discourses frequently affect more than one dimension. The Swiss example above illustrated how the Europeanisation of market policies led to some strengthening of the executive (polity dimension) and triggered a change of political strategies and attitudes toward the EU among trade union actors (politics dimension). Many EU policies even explicitly pursue objectives reaching beyond the immediate policy context. EU regional policy and the principle of partnership introduced in the 1988 reforms affects intergovernmental relations in the member states (Marks 1993: Hooghe 1996). Procedural environmental policies, ranging from certification or permitting procedures to the formulation of public rights to information, pose challenges for administrative structures and patterns of interest intermediation (Knill and Lenschow 2000). Such empirical interrelations between the three domains will pose some difficulty (a) for measuring and comparing effects of Europeanisation and (b) for developing parsimonious explanatory models (see below).

In order to study the Europeanisation of national polity, politics or policy, we need not only to identify causal pathways but also to develop a measure of the change or transformation that is taking place. But even in the seemingly easy case where the EU imposes a model (e.g. a standard) on the member state and one might 'calculate' Europeanisation by establishing the quotient between the level of actual adaptation and the level of required adaptation, this will pose serious problems of operationalisation. Few EU 'models' can be reduced to a single 'item' of change which in addition needs to be expressed as ordinal data. As we have just seen, EU 'models' may even exert impacts beyond the policy domain. But, more importantly, the EU very rarely defines unambiguous models. More common are frameworks for policy, procedural or institutional adaptation. Hence Europeanisation becomes an issue of reaching compatibility rather than congruence, providing for a range of options on the domestic level (cf. Eising 2003b). Finally, as will be further elaborated below, the EU not only 'pressures', it is also 'used' by domestic actors who follow European discourses or exploit new opportunity structures with no explicit model guiding their activities. Europeanisation under such circumstances can no longer be captured as a distance.

Most authors therefore 'measure' Europeanisation in terms of the depth of the change taking place – ranging from inertia, retrenchment, absorption, accommodation to fundamental transformation (Börzel 1999; Héritier *et al.* 2001). In the case of *inertia* member states resist adaptations; *retrenchment* implies the fortification rather than adaptation of existing structures; in the case of *absorption* member states incorporate European requirements or inputs without modifying existing structures; *accommodation* implies the adaptation of existing structures without challenging their core features; and finally, *transformation* points to a fundamental shift of national practices. This 'scale' focuses attention on the domestic dynamics of change and the level of movement rather than the 'closing in' on a target. This distinction is important as member states start from different levels. For instance, the absorption or accommodation of some new elements in domestic structures may suffice in some countries to achieve compatibility with the European framework whereas in other countries this would require a fundamental transformation.

In sum, the wide territorial and substantive scope of Europeanisation as well as the range of processes – however related – that it hopes to capture may make this concept more suitable for uncovering new empirical insights than for developing a theoretical framework and even here some serious methodological problems need to be mastered. For explanatory purposes – and the satisfaction of theoretical ambitions – Europeanisation research has turned to some general analytical approaches dealing with issues of change. The next part provides an overview of these attempts and proposes a heuristic scheme that can guide the research through the many instances of Europeanisation.

Explaining domestic change

The literature has identified several mechanisms through which 'Europe' can affect domestic policy, politics and polity structures and offered a variety of explanations why and how national structures persist or transform. The following discussion will join an emerging literature attempting to systematise these attempts at explaining the Europeanisation effects. This part will draw on three sets of authors – Radaelli (2004), Börzel and Risse (2000) and Knill and Lehmkuhl (2002) – who each contributed one particularly important insight which will be combined in one general scheme.

Radaelli (2004) pinpoints two main types of impulses from the EU level that may have an effect on domestic actors and structures – pressure and potential for 'use'. Most Europeanisation research commences with the pressure model in mind, in which certain demands are formulated on the European level with the expectation that they are being complied with or acted upon by domestic actors. But Europeanisation is a more dynamic process than this merely reactive model. Europe is also 'used' by domestic actors, who may pre-empt adaptation pressure by actively shaping European rules, who may strengthen their domestic position by exploiting new opportunity structures or who may adopt a European discourse in domestic discussions. The 'usage' dimension of Europeanisation brings to life that the EU is not merely a hierarchical rule-producing machinery, but an interwoven system of governance. At least on a general level, pressure and 'usage' function as scope conditions for different dynamics of Europeanisation as they constitute clearly distinct frameworks for political actors.

Börzel and Risse (2000), drawing on neo-institutional approaches, have identified two main corridors into which domestic adaptation processes can be grouped – a rationalist and a constructivist explanatory path. Rationalist explanations assume that actors have a fixed set of preferences and act in a calculating, goal-oriented and instrumental fashion. Actors engage in strategic interaction with others in order to maximise individual utility. Institutions are viewed as external constraints as well as potential opportunity structures. The change of institutions depends on the relation between the costs of adaptation and the benefits to be gained. Constructivists and sociological institutionalism, in turn, assume actors to be guided by collectively shared norms, values and understandings of what is the 'right thing to do'. Institutions in this perspective entail these norms, values and structures of meaning and frame actors' behaviour. Börzel and Risse introduce these explanatory models as parallel, rather than competing, pathways guiding national actors in responding to impulses from the EU. Schimmelfennig *et al.* (2003), investigating the reactions of Eastern European 'EU candidates' to EU conditions with respect to democratic reforms, explicitly test whether domestic actors tend to follow in their choices primarily a cost–benefit logic or whether they are guided by the normative resonance or dissonance of the EU requirements. They conclude that the logic of calculus dominates in the practical reactions to EU conditionality although normative resonance features strongly in the domestic justification of the choices made. In other cases where EU pressures or opportunities are vague or absent and the cost or benefits of change unclear – for instance, in their impact on identities (Risse 2001) – the constructivist pathway may be the more relevant one. However, the literature so far has failed to develop clear scope conditions under which any of the logics applies; Europeanisation research may in fact use the wealth of comparative material to contribute to this debate (see Katzenstein *et al*. 1998).

A third crucial distinction is made by Knill and Lehmkuhl (2002), who deal with the explanatory role of structure versus agency, and especially with the limits of strong institutionalist explanations that conceive of institutions primarily as constraints to change. In fact, the so-called 'goodness of fit' hypothesis features as the point of departure in many analyses including those that ultimately develop a critical stance (see Cowles *et al*.; Knill 2001; more critically, Haverland 2000, and Treib 2003). It states that, in order to trigger any effects on the domestic level, the EU policy or context must pose some challenge for domestic structures/actors. If the challenge or impulse is small it can and often will be easily neglected by domestic actors; if the misfit is very high and demands radical transformations, by contrast, domestic actors are likely to resist the adaptation. Most 'successful' effects from Europeanisation are expected in cases of moderate 'goodness of fit', where EU demands can be absorbed or accommodated without changing the fundamental existing institutional structure. This hypothesis rests on the assumption that Europeanisation operates as a top-down process, imposing concrete pressure for national adaptation. Distinguishing various modes of policy-making – positive and negative integration and policy 'frame-making' – the authors suggest that the explanatory weight will shift away from institutional to more actor-centred perspectives.

Table 3.2 combines these three important analytical distinctions into one scheme and suggests the typical 'conduct' of actors and institutions in light of different EU impulses (pressure/usage) and according to different behavioural logics.

We may now ask whether one can be more specific in defining the scoping conditions for any of the explanations to apply. As this seems not the place to join the general 'calculus versus culture' debate on behavioural logics (Hall and Taylor 1996), we might in this discussion of Europeanisation ask whether the two categories 'Europe as pressure' and 'Europe as usage' can be clearly assigned to specific cases. The following discussion focuses on EU public policy as this represents not only a major but also a (perhaps surprisingly) complex area.

Bulmer and Radaelli (2004), in part following Knill and Lehmkuhl (2002), distinguish three policy types – positive and negative integration and coordinating policies – and propose that the 'goodness of fit' hypothesis associated with the pressure pathway should be limited to the context of positive integration where an EU model (i.e. regulatory policy) descends in a commanding fashion to the member states which may then engage in the necessary reform to ensure compliance. Comparative case studies on EU environmental policy have in fact shown that a poor fit between EU policy and domestic policy patterns, legal and administrative structures or forms of interest intermediation has hampered compliance with EU directives. This was true even in countries otherwise known as environmental leaders where one might expect a generally positive attitude towards the imposed standards (Knill and Lenschow 1998).

Table 3.2 Explaining the domestic impact of the European Union

	Europe as pressure	Europe 'to use'
Rationalist explanatory framework	• Actors *calculate the costs* (and benefits) and weigh the capacities of adaptation. • National institutional misfits operate as constraining factor for adaptation (= costs).	• Actors behave in a calculating and instrumental fashion, *seeking opportunities* in pursuit of their – status quo or change-oriented – interests. • National institutions structure the opportunity space (e.g. veto points, voting rights).
Constructivist explanatory framework	• Actors *comply* with rules. • In the case of conflicting national and European rules of appropriateness and values (misfit), national structures operate as constraints for adaptation.	• Actors *learn* of alternatives within an extended frame of reference. • National institutions frame formal and informal communication and network structures.

An important caveat to this simple association, however, rests on an implicit assumption made in the model, namely the expected dominance of status-quo-preserving domestic actors. This expectation is of course grounded in the neo-institutionalist literature which emphasises the 'stickiness' of existing arrangements, since their reform may be both costly and perceived as inappropriate (see above). Nevertheless, doubts may be raised by such studies as that by Oliver Treib (2003) on the implementation of six EU employment rights directives in four countries. He shows that national governments may be quite willing to adopt even poorly fitting EU directives. Partisan identification and the respective majorities in government played a more decisive role in explaining compliance patterns than the extent of adaptation requirements. In the UK, for instance, the delay of transposing the working time directive corresponds at first sight with the expectations of the misfit hypothesis as the directive required costly reforms. The fact that the directive was rapidly transposed once the Labour party rose to power suggests that the delay was in fact due to ideological opposition within the Conservative party rather than institutional inertia.[3]

This example suggests that one needs to think more carefully about the political costs and benefits of following EU pressure as opposed to the institutional costs that are given priority in the 'goodness of fit' thesis. In this context it is also necessary to consider the nature of the addressees of EU pressure. The political circumstances (e.g. electoral demands) may make it more advantageous for governments (or individual parties) to *use*

EU pressure domestically for pushing reforms of deeply embedded structures than to stick with the status quo. On the administrative level, in turn, the effort of change may neither be compensated by political gains nor appear normatively justified. In general terms, to the extent that 'Europe as pressure' may also be 'Europe to use' in the domestic context, 'positive integration' is a plausible but not sufficient scoping condition for the goodness of fit thesis.

The leverage of the 'goodness of fit' thesis in any event decreases once the concrete pressure descending from Brussels diminishes or even disappears as there is no longer a clear model to match. Our four authors argue that this is the case in the area of 'negative integration' policies, which by limiting autonomous national regulation and protectionist measures open the playing field for competitive dynamics inside the member states and horizontal state interactions. Domestic change is being traced to actors successfully exploiting new institutional (removal of barriers) and argumentative (reference to external competition) opportunity structures. In the case of the cabotage directive within the EU's common transport policy, for instance, the position of users of transport services was strengthened vis-à-vis the supply side of the transport sector as the latter could no longer be protected by governments imposing discriminatory measures on foreign competitors. Depending on the actual shift in national actor constellations and the new power equilibrium, some countries maintained and others reformed the framework of their transport regimes (Knill and Lehmkuhl 2002).

But is it true that negative integration implies merely 'Europe to use'? Arguably, this link is premature. On the one hand, the removal of trade barriers on the member state level is often accompanied by the creation of new regulatory institutions and competencies on the European level. Grande and Eberlein (2000) show how such reorganisation of competencies in the European multi-level system implies also new mixes of bureaucratic control, self-regulatory opportunities and market mechanisms and the need to build (or dismantle) the respective capacities on the various levels. Susanne Schmidt (2002) points out how open-ended formulations in EU liberalisation policies with regard to the road haulage and insurance sectors nevertheless induced domestic actors to react to presumed demands – frequently assuming more concrete adaptation pressure than was later confirmed by the European Court of Justice. The legal uncertainty created by EU policy induced both opportunistic behaviour and precautionary compliance. In short, since negative integration typically implies a mix of de- and re-regulation, direct, though sometimes ambiguous, pressure on national structures is exerted (or felt), and hence the issue of 'fitness' will at least in part apply.

In cases of soft law (such as non-enforceable political or legal declarations) and merely coordinative policy of the EU – i.e. in the policies of the second and third pillar of the Union and areas where the Open Method of Coordination has been adopted – the explicit hierarchical pressure on domestic institutions and practices is weak. Instead of complying with rules, national actors are expected to widen their ideational horizon due to the exposure to European or neighbour country discourses and to reconsider previously held beliefs, expectations and preferences. Europeanisation may take place because the EU had provided an arena for the exchange of ideas and shaped a discourse by identifying general goals or principles, disseminating information and pointing out examples of 'best practice'. These ideas and discourses may either enter into the belief systems of domestic actors (i.e. by persuasion) or they may be used instrumentally. While learning due to the widening of the interpretative frames and persuasion processes can be held distinct from the logic of pressure, instrumental use can take several forms implying the domestic construction of pressure. EU guidelines or discourses may be construed either as the herald of hierarchical imposition calling for anticipatory measures or as a competitive setting in which the performance of other states ought to be matched in order to secure a good reputation.

In short, the direct effect of soft forms of governance in the EU is the creation of supranational and inter-state platforms for learning. Indirectly, as a consequence of the interaction, competitive and even impositional dynamics may develop if models of 'appropriate' structures or norms have emerged in the EU-facilitated but mostly horizontal inter-state discourse. Such models will resonate more or less well with domestic structures and institutional structures may frame and constrain the domestic change actually occurring. The European Employment Strategy, for instance, formulates non-binding guidelines and benchmarks on female employment rates, on measures ensuring the employability of the workforce (e.g. lifelong learning), or on rates of job creation which – if taken on board – pose significant challenges to several national employment policies as well as general conceptions of the state (e.g. how actively should it intervene in the working place?) and of societal structures (e.g. what is the appropriate role of women?) (De la Porte and Pochet 2002).

In summary, the analytically laudable attempt – since parsimonious and systematic – to link policy types to different 'default explanations' (Bulmer and Radaelli 2004: 16) of Europeanisation may underestimate the complexity of EU policies and their effects. Most EU policies are in reality 'mixed types' – with hard and soft elements, binding and discretionary content – which may trigger hierarchical, horizontal and round-about dynamics with the different mechanisms of Europeanisation. Under the assumption that the EU has arrived on the political horizon of national political actors downward pressure may be constructed and 'Europe' used on domestic politics in increasingly credible ways, cutting across policy types. Reality is further complicated by the fact that EU policies go through various loops at once – impacting on the policy, politics and polity dimension, creating multi-dimensional links of cause and effect. Therefore, the distinction between 'Europe as pressure', which may be 'real' or constructed, and 'Europe as usage', which may be instrumental or by conviction, serves as a heuristic device to disentangle complexity; it does not very easily lead us to concrete hypotheses about when and to what extent Europe affects the domestic level.

Conclusion: what did we learn?

This chapter began by stating that Europeanisation research has blown new fresh air into older debates in European Union studies rather than establishing a new 'school'. In light of the discussion so far and some evidence presented in the research conducted under the label of Europeanisation I will now – even though briefly – return to this statement.

First, although the concept of Europeanisation is distinct from the concept of European integration the process of Europeanisation and its effects on the domestic level will nevertheless be informative about the status of the integration 'project'. While we may have already suspected that the national state is not withering away, we are now gaining additional clarity that we are not facing a process of harmonisation or convergence of national policy, politics and polity structures either. National patterns in many cases have proven quite resilient to converge to a common 'European model'. However – and this may be the crucial insight of Europeanisation research – non-convergence must not be confused with the maintenance of the status quo. Besides imposing some obvious pressures to adapt to European rules or procedures on the policy level, Europe has widened the political and discursive context of national policy-makers and societal actors who may (a) adapt to new opportunity spaces themselves and (b) politicise previously unquestioned embedded national structures triggering national reform processes (usually along distinct national paths). These processes do not require a shift in political loyalty but only a shift in the attention frame.

Second, with respect to policy-making in the EU, Europeanisation research can sharpen our understanding of the interactions between bottom-up, horizontal and top-down processes by breaking with the departmentalisation between EU decision-making, national implementation of EU rules and national policy-making processes. While the dynamics between policy-making and -taking has been noted in EU policy studies (e.g. Héritier *et al.* 2001), Europeanisation may go further in framing 'national' politics and policy-making as well as facilitating inter-state policy transfers.

Finally, Europeanisation may be considered in the context of governance in the EU (e.g. Radaelli 2004; Kohler-Koch and Eising 1999), though from a distinctly national perspective. Rather than tackling questions of a transfer of power from the national to the EU level or of patterns of convergence, Europeanisation research focuses on processes (and limits) of national transformation. Such transformations affect shifts in capacity and responsibility, hence issues of effectiveness and accountability; they also affect actor and power constellations, hence issues of political voice and ultimately the legitimacy of governance in Europe and the European states. Here, the 'bundle' of research on Europeanisation shows quite clearly that EU-induced policy changes outpace comparable effects with regards to politics and polity, introducing tensions in governing European societies. This 'problem' of Europeanisation (Radaelli 2004: 1) needs to be tackled analytically by adopting a framework looking at interactions between policy, politics and polity in a multi-level system, hence using an attention-drawing concept that may appear somewhat 'stretched'.

Notes

1   On the impact on administrative structures compare Bossaert *et al.* (2001), Page and Wouters (1995); for the subnational level see Börzel (2002), Fallend (2002) and Jeffery (2003). National structures of interest intermediation are the focus of studies by Eising (2003a) and Schmidt (1999). For research on national parliaments see Maurer and Wessels (2001) and Raunio and Hix (2001).

2   This notion of trying to shape EU rules in order to minimise later adaptation cost corresponds with many empirical accounts (cf. Héritier *et al.* 1996; Jordan 2002).

3   One may of course try to rescue the 'goodness of fit' thesis by pointing out that the UK polity with its low number of veto players is generally more prone to permit political reforms and to shift even core features of previous practices than, by contrast, Germany where the large number of veto players in the federal system may block even rather moderate reforms. In short, the UK polity tends to undermine the creation of stable misfits, whereas the German polity supports their creation and maintenance. Besides some oversimplification inherent in such a statement, it points to the danger of ad hoc explanations unless one succeeds in operationalising and measuring misfit prior to hypothesis testing (see Falkner 2003) whereby

misfit needs to be seen not only from a policy but also from a polity perspective and may change over time.

References

Benz, A. (2004) 'Multilevel Governance – Governance in Mehrebenensystemen', in A. Benz (ed.), *Governance – Regieren in komplexen Regelsystemen* (Wiesbaden: VS Verlag für Sozialwissenschaften).

Börzel, T. (1999) 'Towards convergence in Europe?', *Journal of Common Market Studies* 39/4: 573–96.

—— (2002) *States and Regions in the European Union* (Cambridge: Cambridge University Press).

Börzel, T. and Risse, T. (2000) 'When Europe Hits Home: Europeanization and Domestic Change', *EIoP online working paper series* 4: 15.

Bomberg, E. and Peterson, J. (2000) 'Policy Transfer and Europeanization: passing the Heineken test?', *Queens Papers of Europeanization* 2/2000.

Bossaert, D., Demmke, C., Norden, K. and Polet, R. (2001) *Civil Services in the Europe of the Fifteen* (Maastricht: EIPA).

Bulmer, S. and Radaelli, C. M. (2004) 'The Europeanisation of National Policy?', *Queens Papers of Europeanization* 1/2004.

Busch, A. (2004) 'National Filters: Europeanisation, Institutions, and Discourse in the Case of Banking Regulation', *West European Politics* 2: 310–33.

Church, C. (2000) 'Switzerland: an Overlooked Case of Europeanization?', *Queens Papers of Europeanization* 3/2000.

Cowles, M. G., Caporaso, J. and Risse, T. (eds) (2001) *Transforming Europe* (Ithaca, NY: Cornell University Press).

Drulák, P., Česal, J. and Hampl, S. (2003) 'Interactions and Identities of Czech Civil Servants on Their Way to the EU', *Journal of European Public Policy* 10/4: 637–54.

Dyson, K. and Goetz, K. H. (2003) 'Living with Europe: Power, Constraint, and Contestation', in K. Dyson and K. H. Goetz (eds), *Germany, Europe and the Politics of Constraint* (Oxford and New York: Oxford University Press).

Eising, R. (2003a) 'Interest Groups: Opportunity Structures and Governance Capacity', in K. Dyson and K. H. Goetz (eds), *Germany, Europe and the Politics of Constraint* (Oxford and New York: Oxford University Press).

—— (2003b) 'Europäisierung und Integration. Konzepte in der EU-Forschung', in M. Jachtenfuchs and B. Kohler-Koch (eds), *Europäische Integration* (Opladen: Leske & Budrich).

Falkner, G. (2003) 'Comparing Europeanisation Effects: From Metaphor to Operationalisation', paper for the ECPR General Conference, Marburg, 18–21 September.

Fallend, Franz (2002) 'Europäisierung, Föderalismus und Regionalismus: Die Auswirkungen der EU-Mitgliedschaft auf bundesstaatliche Strukturen und regionale Politik in Österreich', in H. Neisser and S. Puntscher Riekmann (eds), *Europäisierung der österreichischen Politik: Konsequenzen der EU-Mitgliedschaft*. Schriftenreihe des Zentrums für Angewandte Politikforschung, vol. 26, Wien: 201–29.

Featherstone, K. (2003) 'Introduction: In the name of Europe', in K. Featherstone and C. Radaelli (eds), *The Politics of Europeanization* (Oxford: Oxford University Press).

Fischer, A. (2003) 'Die Schweizer Gewerkschaften und die Europäisierung helvetischer Politik', *Österreichische Zeitschrift für Politikwissenschaft* 2003/3: 303–20.

Grande, E. and Eberlein, B. (2000) 'Der Aufstieg des Regulierungsstaates im Infrastrukturbereich. Zur Transformation der politischen Ökonomie der Bundesrepublik', in R. Czada and H. Wollmann (eds), *Von der Bonner zur Berliner Republik? 10 Jahre Deutsche Einheit (Leviathan-Sonderheft* 19/1999*)* (Wiesbaden: Nomos).

Haas, E. B. (1968) *The Uniting of Europe: Political, Social and Economic Forces, 1950–1957* (Stanford, CA: Stanford University Press).

Hall, P. and Taylor, R. (1996) 'Political Science and the Three New Institutionalisms', *Political Studies* 44/5: 952–72.

Haverland, M. (2000) 'National Adaptation to European Integration: the Importance of Institutional Veto Points', *Journal of Public Policy* 20/1: 83–103.

Héritier, A., Knill, C. and Mingers, S. (1996) *Ringing the Changes in Europe: Regulatory Competition and the Transformation of the State* (Berlin: de Gruyter).

Héritier, A., Kerwer, D., Knill, C., Lehmkuhl, D., Teutsch, M. and Druillet, A.-C. (2001) *Differential Europe: New Opportunities and Restrictions for Member-State Policies* (Lanham, MD: Rowman & Littlefield).

Holzinger, K. and Knill, C. (2004) 'Regulatory Competition and Regulatory Cooperation in Environmental Policy: Individual and Interaction Effects', *Journal of Public Policy* 25/1.

Hooghe, L. (1996) *European Integration, Cohesion Policy and Subnational Mobilisation* (Oxford: Oxford University Press).

Jeffery, C. (2003) 'The German Länder: From Milieu-Shaping to Territorial Politics', in K. Dyson and K. H. Goetz (eds), *Germany, Europe and the Politics of Constraint* (Oxford and New York: Oxford University Press).

Jordan, A. (2002) *The Europeanization of British Environmental Policy: A Departmental Perspective* (Basingstoke: Palgrave).

Jordan, A. and Liefferink, D. (eds) (2004) *Environmental Policy in Europe: The Europeanization of National Environmental Policy* (London and New York: Routledge).

Kassim, H. (2000) 'Conclusion', in H. Kassim, A. Menon, B. G. Peters and V. Wright (eds), *The National Co-ordination of EU Policy* (Oxford: Oxford University Press).

Katzenstein, P., Keohane, R. and Krasner, S. (1998) 'International Organization and the Study of World Politics', *International Organization* 4: 645–85.

Knill, C. (2001) *The Europeanization of National Administrations: Patterns of Institutional Change and Persistence* (Cambridge: Cambridge University Press).

Knill, C. and Lehmkuhl, D. (2002) 'The National Impact of European Union Regulatory Policy: Three Europeanization Mechanisms', *European Journal of Political Research* 41/2: 255–80.

Knill, C. and Lenschow, A. (1998) 'Coping with Europe: The Impact of British and German Administration on the Implementation of EU Environmental Policy', *Journal of European Public Policy* 5/4: 595–614.

—— (eds) (2000) *Implementing EU Environmental Policies: New Directions and Old Problems* (Manchester: Manchester University Press).

Kohler-Koch, B. (2000) 'Europäisierung: Plädoyer für eine Horizonterweiterung', in M. Knodt and B. Kohler-Koch (eds), *Deutschland zwischen Europäisierung und Selbstbehauptung* (Frankfurt/Main: Campus).

Kohler-Koch, B. and R. Eising (eds) (1999) *The Transformation of Governance in the European Union* (London and New York: Routledge).

Ladrech, R. (1994) 'Europeanization of Domestic Politics and Institutions: The Case of France', *Journal of Common Market Studies* 32: 69–88.

Lenschow, A. (1999) 'Transformation in European Environmental Governance', in B. Kohler-Koch and R. Eising (eds), *The Transformation of Governance in the European Union* (London and New York: Routledge).

Levi-Faur, D. (2004) 'On the "Net Impact" of Europeanization. The EU's Telecoms and Electricity Regimes between the Global and the National', *Comparative Political Studies* 37: 3–29.

Lippert, B., Umbach, G. and Wessels, W. (2001) 'Europeanization of CEE Executives: EU Membership Negotiations as a Shaping Power', *Journal of European Public Policy* 8/6: 980–1012.

Marks, G. (1993) 'Structural Policy and Multilevel Governance in the EC', in A. Cafruny and G. Rosenthal (eds), *The State of the European Community: II The Maastricht Debates and Beyond* (Harlow: Longman).

Marks, G., Hooghe, L. and Blank, K. (1996) 'European Integration from the 1980s: State-Centric v. Multi-Level Governance', *Journal of Common Market Studies* 34/3: 341–78.

Maurer, A. and Wessels, W. (2001) *National Parliaments on Their Way to Europe: Losers or Latecomers?* (Baden-Baden: Nomos).

Milward, A. S. (1992) *The European Rescue of the Nation-State* (London and New York: Routledge).

Olsen, J. P. (2002) 'The Many Faces of Europeanization', *Journal of Common Market Studies* 40/5: 921–52.

Page, E. and Wouters, A. (1995) 'The Europeanization of National Bureaucracies?', in J. Pierre (ed.), *Bureaucracy in the Modern State* (Aldershot: Edward Elgar).

Porte, C. de la and Pochet, P. (eds) (2002) *Building Social Europe through the Open Method of Coordination* (Brussels: Peter Lang).

Radaelli, C. M. (2000) 'Whither Europeanization? Concept Stretching and Substantive Change', *EIoP online working paper series* 4/8.

—— (2004) 'Europeanisation: Solution or Problem?', *EIoP online working paper series* 8/16.

Raunio, T. and Hix, S. (2001) 'Backbenchers Learn to Fight Back: European Integration and Parliamentary Government', in K. H. Goetz and S. Hix (eds), *Europeanised Politics? European Integration and National Political Systems* (London and Portland: Frank Cass).

Risse, T. (2001) 'A European Identity? Europeanization and the Evolution of Nation-State Identities', in M. G. Cowles, J. Caporaso and T. Risse (eds), *Transforming Europe* (Ithaca, NY: Cornell University Press).

Risse, T., Cowles, M. G. and Caporaso, J. (2001) 'Europeanization and Domestic Change: Introduction', in M. G. Cowles, J. Caporaso and T. Risse (eds), *Transforming Europe* (Ithaca: Cornell University Press).

Satori, G. (1970) 'Concept Misformation in Comparative Politics', *American Political Science Review* 64/4: 1033–53.

Scharpf, F. W. (2003) 'Politische Optionen im vollendeten Binnenmarkt', in M. Jachtenfuchs and B. Kohler-Koch (eds), *Europäische Integration* (Opladen: Leske & Budrich).

Schimmelfennig, F., Engert, S. and Knobel, H. (2003) 'Europäisierung in Osteuropa: Reaktionen auf die demokratische Konditionalität', *Österreichische Zeitschrift für Politikwissenschaft* 2003/3: 321–38.

Schmidt, S. K. (2002) 'Die Folgen der europäischen Integration für die Bundesrepublik Deutschland: Wandel durch Verflechtung', *Max Planck Institut für Gesellschaftsforschung, Discussion Paper* 02/4, Köln.

Schmidt, V. (1999) 'National Patterns of Governance Under Siege: The Impact of European Integration', in B. Kohler-Koch and R. Eising (eds), *The Transformation of Governance in the European Union* (London and New York: Routledge).

Sciarini, P., Fischer, A. and Nicolet, S. (2004) 'How Europe Hits Home: Evidence from the Swiss Case', *Journal of European Public Policy* 11/3: 353–78.

Thatcher, M. (2004) 'Winners and Losers in Europeanisation: Reforming the National Regulation of Telecommunications', *West European Politics* 27: 284–309.

Treib, O. (2003) 'EU Governance, Misfit, and the Partisan Logic of Domestic Adaptation: An Actor-Centered Perspective on the Transposition of EU Directives', paper prepared for the EUSA 8th International Biennial Conference, Tennessee, 27–29 March.

Wincott, D. (2003) 'The Idea of the European Social Model: Limits and Paradoxes of Europeanization', in K. Featherstone and C. Radaelli (eds), *The Politics of Europeanization* (Oxford: Oxford University Press).

Chapter 4

Theories of European integration

Assumptions and hypotheses

FRANK SCHIMMELFENNIG
AND BERTHOLD RITTBERGER

Introduction

Why does the EU have a common currency, but only a rudimentary common security and defence policy? Why have the EU member states successively endowed the European Parliament with more competencies? Why do member states comply with the jurisprudence handed down by the European Court of Justice? Why has the membership base of the EU expanded from initially six member states to presently twenty-five?

In this chapter, we cannot offer answers to these questions. However, we will show how the European integration theoretic toolbox developed over the past decades can help students and scholars of European integration to go about finding systematic explanations for phenomena of European integration. The theoretical debate about the dynamics of EU integration has been dominated by two 'families' of integration theorising: intergovernmentalism and supranationalism. Within these families we further distinguish two variants: a realist and a liberal one for intergovernmentalism and a rationalist and a constructivist one for supranationalism. Rather than offering a history of the development of the theoretical debate, we will describe the core assumptions of the theories and specify their main hypotheses about the conditions for integration in three dimensions: the sectoral ('broadening'), the vertical ('deepening'), and the horizontal ('widening').

European integration: the sectoral, vertical and horizontal dimensions

We define European integration as a process whereby (a) new policy areas are regulated on the EU level partially or exclusively (sectoral integration), (b) competencies are increasingly shared across EU member states or delegated to autonomous supranational institutions (vertical integration), and (c) the EU expands territorially by accepting new members (horizontal integration). Table 4.1 provides an overview of the three different dimensions of European integration.

Sectoral integration refers to a process through which new policy areas or sectors are becoming increasingly regulated at the EU level. An increase in sectoral integration thus implies that at least one new policy sector is being (partially or exclusively) regulated by the EU. In the most recent past, sectoral integration has progressed, for instance, in security and defence policy as well as in immigration and asylum policy. In the realm of

Table 4.1 Dimensions of European integration

	Sectoral integration	Vertical integration	Horizontal integration
What is being integrated?	Policy areas/ sectors	Decision-making competencies	Territory, borders and boundaries
What is integration?	Integration of new policy areas/sectors ('broadening')	Transfer of domestic competencies ('deepening')	Extension of the territory governed by the EU *acquis* ('widening')

sectoral integration, the key research question asked by integration theories thus runs as follows: Why and under what conditions do policy sectors become regulated at the EU level (and thereby 'escape' the exclusive authority and competence of nation states)?

Vertical integration refers to the distribution of competencies between EU institutions in integrated policy sectors. As already stated, the process of sectoral integration 'extracts' policy areas from the exclusive competence of individual member states and subjects them to institutionalised cooperation at the EU level. Assessing the scope of

Table 4.2 Sectoral and vertical integration in the EU

Policy sector	1950	1958	1967	1993	2004
Regulatory policies					
Movement of goods and services	1	2	3	4	4
Movement of capital	1	1	1	4	4
Movement of persons	1	2	3	4	4
Competition policy	1	2	3	4	4
Environmental standards	1	2	2	3	3
Health and safety standards	1	2	2	3	3
Labour market standards	1	1	1	3	3
Foreign and security policy					
Foreign policy/diplomacy	1	1	1	2	3
Security and defence policy	1	1	1	1	2
Humanitarian and development aid	1	1	1	3	3
Citizen policies					
Civil rights and human rights	1	1	1	2	2
Policing	1	1	1	2	2
Immigration and asylum	1	1	1	2	3
Expenditure policies					
Agricultural price support	1	1	4	4	4
Regional development	1	1	1	3	3
Research	1	1	2	2	2
Social welfare and pensions	1	1	1	2	2
Public healthcare	1	1	1	2	2

Notes:

1950: before European integration; 1958: entry into force of EEC Treaty; 1968: entry into force of Merger Treaty; 1993: entry into force of Treaty of Maastricht; 2004: status quo.

1 = all policy decisions are taken at the national level

2 = some policy decisions are taken at the EU level

3 = policy decisions are taken at both levels

4 = most policy decisions are taken at the central level

Sources: Donahue and Pollack 2001; Hix 2005

sectoral integration in the EU, however, does not allow us to draw conclusions about the form of institutionalised coordination and cooperation which sectoral integration takes. For instance, cooperation can have a largely intergovernmental character (the 'minimum level' of vertical integration), yet it can also mean that competences in a particular policy sector have been fully delegated to the EU level as, for example, in the case of monetary policy.

Table 4.2 provides an overview of sectoral and vertical integration in the EU. It is the task of theories of European integration to help us to understand why, for instance, sectoral integration has taken off in the regulatory and expenditure policy area much earlier than in the areas of foreign and security as well as citizen policies. Furthermore, integration theorists may ask why vertical integration has progressed furthest in the area of regulatory policy whereas in the area of citizen and foreign and security policies, cooperation is still very much characterised by intergovernmental decision-making.

Horizontal integration refers to the territorial extension of sectoral and vertical integration. When we are writing about horizontal integration, we most commonly refer to 'EU enlargement', the process whereby new states subject themselves to the *acquis communautaire* (the body of primary and secondary EU law). Yet, horizontal integration also comprises instances which do not reach the level of full EU membership, such as association or trade agreements between the EU and individual states or groups of states. Even among EU member states horizontal integration is not homogeneous: for instance, some EU member states have negotiated 'opt-outs' from Economic and Monetary Union (EMU) or have not joined the Schengen regime of passport-free travel. The research questions central to the analysis of horizontal integration thus run as follows: Why does the EU extend its membership base and thus its *acquis communautaire* by inviting certain states to join (but not others)? Why do non-EU member states (but not all of them) strive to join the 'club'? Table 4.3 offers an overview of horizontal integration in the EU.

Theories of European integration

The purpose of theories of integration is to explain the scope and dynamics of European integration in its sectoral, vertical and horizontal dimension. They allow us to formulate expectations as to when and under what conditions integration will progress (or stall) across the different dimensions. Irrespective of the enormous diversity of theories of European integration (see, for example, Caporaso and Keeler 1995; Rosamond 2000; Cram 2001; Wiener and Diez 2004 for overviews), we argue that these approaches can be grouped into two broad 'schools of thought': intergovernmentalism and supranationalism.

Neofunctionalism, belonging to the supranationalist 'school of thought', was the dominant theory of integration in the early periods of integration theorising, with prominent scholars such as Ernst Haas, Leon Lindberg, Joseph Nye and Philippe Schmitter defining the neofunctionalist research agenda. The mid-sixties saw the birth of intergovernmentalism to mark a counter-point to neofunctionalism with Stanley Hoffmann being its most prominent proponent. Since the mid-eighties, both 'schools of thought' have undergone a process of internal diversification. While Andrew Moravcsik's liberal intergovernmentalism was the major new innovation within the intergovernmentalist camp, Wayne Sandholtz's and Alec Stone Sweet's supranational institutionalism marked

Table 4.3 Horizontal integration in the EU

Enlargement round	Candidate countries	Application	Accession negotiation	Accession	'Opt-outs'
Northern enlargement	Denmark, United Kingdom, Ireland	1961, 1967	1961, 1970	1973	UK (EMU/Schengen); Denmark (EMU); Ireland (Schengen)
	Norway	1962, 1967	1962, 1970		
Southern enlargement	Greece	1974	1976	1981	
	Portugal, Spain	1977	1978/79	1986	
EFTA enlargement	Austria	1989	1993 (except Switzerland)	1995 (except Norway)	Sweden (EMU)
	Sweden, Finland, Norway, Switzerland	1991/92			
Eastern enlargement	Turkey	1987			EMU and Schengen participation to be negotiated in the future
	Cyprus, Malta	1990	1998/2000	2004	
	Poland, Hungary	1994	1998		
	Czech Republic, Estonia	1995			
	Slovenia	1996			
	Latvia, Lithuania, Slovakia, Bulgaria, Romania	1995	2000	2004 (except Bulgaria and Romania)	
	Croatia	2003			

a major refinement of neofunctionalism. The recent past has also seen the rise of a constructivist research agenda in integration theorising (see, for instance, Christiansen *et al.* 2001). In this chapter, we offer a classification of integration theories in order to provide students of European integration with a menu of testable hypotheses to systematically analyse and explain instances of sectoral, vertical, and horizontal integration. We will distinguish between a *realist* and a *liberal* version of intergovernmentalism on the one hand, and a *rationalist* and a *constructivist* version of supranationalism on the other.

The key distinction between intergovernmentalism and supranationalism can be found in their different answers to the question whether or not the process of integration can be seen as a transformative, self-reinforcing process. Intergovernmentalists practise denial: for them, the process of integration is under the control of member state governments, which determine the speed and substance of any further steps of integration. Supranationalists answer this question in the affirmative: under certain conditions, the institutions created by member state governments trigger a self-reinforcing process which begets further integration and which not only escapes member state control, but which also – in the course of the process of integration – exercises a transformative impact on the identity of member states.

Within the intergovernmentalist camp, realist and liberal intergovernmentalism (RI and LI) differ with respect to the determinants of member state government's preferences, their bargaining power, and the choice of EU institutions. For LI, governmental preferences and bargaining power are sector-specific, that is, they vary from policy area to area. Furthermore, as far as institutional choices are affected, the main concern for governments is to establish institutions which monitor and control compliance of EU rules and regulations. For RI, actors' preferences and their bargaining power are determined by the geopolitical situation within which member states interact; institutional choices reflect member state government's concerns about securing autonomy and influence. Within the supranationalist camp rationalist and constructivist supranationalism (RS, CS) differ with respect to the effect of EU institutions in the integration process. For RS, the loss of member state control over the process of integration has its roots in the EU's institutional decision-making arrangement and its status quo bias, as well as in governments' short time-horizons. In contrast, CS assumes that the process of integration fundamentally affects, and is affected by, the identities and worldviews of governments and EU institutions. In the ensuing sections, we will present the four-fold classification of theories of integration in more detailed fashion.

Intergovernmentalism: realist and liberal

Intergovernmentalism is a variant of rationalist institutionalism in International Relations (IR) theory specifically tailored to explain European integration. We will therefore begin our presentation of intergovernmentalism by explicating its theoretical roots in rationalist IR theory and then move on to concrete propositions on European integration. The presentation is mainly based on Andrew Moravcsik's *Choice for Europe* (1998, above all 3–77), the most complete and theoretically sophisticated treatment of intergovernmentalist integration theory. Table 4.4 provides an overview.

Rationalist assumptions

It is the first basic assumption of intergovernmentalism that European integration is similar enough to general international politics, and the European Union is sufficiently like other international institutions, that it can be profitably studied and explained in an IR perspective. Indeed, Moravcsik maintains that the 'EC is best seen as an international regime for policy co-ordination' (1993: 480; cf. Hoffmann 1982: 33) and that European integration represents 'a subset of general tendencies among democratic states in modern world politics' (1998: 5). IR theories traditionally assume that states are the central actors in international politics and that they act in a context of anarchy, that is, in

Table 4.4 Intergovernmentalism

Level of abstraction	Dimensions of integration: Sectoral	Horizontal	Vertical
General assumptions	Rationalist institutionalism in International Relations: states interact in an anarchical international system		
Explanatory theory	Bargaining theory	Club theory	Functional theory of institutions
Factors explaining integration	Exogenous preferences and relative bargaining power of governments		Governmental interests and control
	LI: sector-specific societal preferences and issue-area power		LI: monitoring and sanctioning of compliance
	RI: geopolitical preferences and overall power		RI: state autonomy and influence

the absence of a centralised authority making and enforcing political decisions. Policy-making in international politics generally takes place in intergovernmental negotiations, and agreements require the consent of all state participants.

The second fundamental is a rationalist framework, which entails a general explanatory program and basic action-theoretic assumptions. As for the explanatory program, rationalism is an individualist or agency theory, which requires an explanation of, first, actor preferences and, second, collective outcomes as a result of aggregated individual actions based on these preferences. The core action-theoretic assumption is 'rational choice': actors calculate the utility of alternative courses of action and choose the one that maximises their utility under the circumstances. Rationalist institutionalism in IR theory then seeks to explain the establishment and design of international institutions as a collective outcome of interdependent ('strategic') rational state choices and intergovernmental negotiations in an anarchical context.

In correspondence with IR rational institutionalism, intergovernmentalism generally assumes that governmental preferences are exogenous, that is, they are not formed or changed in the course of international negotiations or by international institutions. Governments enter negotiations with predefined ('national') interests and leave them with the same interests. The international institutional or interaction context has an impact on the costs of pursuing state interests and attaining state goals but does not affect the substance of these interests and goals.

A second commonality is the bargaining theory of international cooperation and the functional theory of institutions that Moravcsik uses to explain integration. Rationalist institutionalism distinguishes several interrelated problems of international collective choice in problematic situations of international interdependence – that is, situations in which non-cooperative behaviour is the individually rational choice but in the end leaves all states worse off. The basic problem consists in overcoming such collectively suboptimal outcomes and achieving coordination or cooperation for mutual benefit. This efficiency problem, however, is connected to problems of distribution and enforcement. First, how are the mutual gains of cooperation distributed among the states? Second, how are states prevented from defecting from an agreement in order to exploit the cooperation of others?

In this context, rational-institutionalist theory argues that the outcome of international negotiations, that is, whether and on which terms cooperation comes about, depends on the relative bargaining power of the actors, on the one hand, and on the effects of international institutions, on the other. First, efficient, welfare-maximising solutions to problematic situations of international interdependence require reliable information on the state of the world, cause–effect relationships and other actors' preferences and capabilities. International institutions are better at providing this information than governments alone. They furthermore reduce transaction costs by providing a forum for multi-actor negotiations and services for effective and efficient communication.

Second, the solution to the problem of distribution depends on the actors' bargaining power. Bargaining power results from the asymmetrical distribution of (i) information and (ii) the benefits of a specific agreement (compared to those of alternative outcomes or 'outside options'). Generally, those actors that have more and better information are able to manipulate the outcome to their advantage (cf. Schneider and Cederman 1994), and those actors that are least in need of a specific agreement are best able to threaten the others with non-cooperation and thereby force them to make concessions.

Finally, compliance with international norms and rules requires effective monitoring and sanctioning. Again, international institutions are established because they fulfil these tasks more effectively and efficiently than individual states. Different institutional designs then reflect the specific problems of cooperation caused by, above all, the severity of distributional conflict and enforcement problems and by uncertainty about the preferences of other actors and the state of the world (Koremenos *et al.* 2001). Bargaining theory thus mainly explains sectoral integration whereas the functional theory of international institutions accounts for vertical integration. What about horizontal integration then?

When states integrate their markets and economies, they produce external effects for non-member countries (for instance, by diverting trade and investments). However, third countries can also produce externalities for the integrated states. For example, lower taxation or less social and environmental regulation attract business away from the integrated market and bring its rules and policies under pressure. In addition, horizontal integration might produce economies of scale and increase the budget of the international organisation. Thus, in a rationalist perspective, the question is whether a given integrated area already has optimal size or whether collective welfare may be maximised by admitting further countries. The rationalist theory that deals with the problem of organisational size is club theory. A club is a voluntary association deriving mutual benefit from producing and sharing collective goods. Membership in clubs can be limited – and needs to be because new members are not only additional contributors to the club goods but also rival consumers who restrict the old members' access to the club goods (causing so-called crowding costs). The core hypothesis of club theory therefore posits that a club will expand (only) until the marginal costs of admitting a new member equals the marginal benefits. Since clubs are voluntary associations, all old and new members must derive a positive utility from expansion lest they use their veto. Otherwise, the cooperation problems in horizontal integration are the same as in sectoral integration. The states have to find an efficient, welfare-maximising solution (an optimal size for the integrated area), to distribute the costs and benefits of enlargement among the old and new members, and to secure compliance. Correspondingly, bargaining theory and the functional theory of institutions are used to explain horizontal integration as well.

Intergovernmentalism and European integration

Which specific propositions on European integration does intergovernmentalism derive from these general rational-institutionalist assumptions? The theoretical framework still leaves the relevant actors and preferences, as well as their resources and constraints, unspecified and does not provide concrete hypotheses about the extent of sectoral and horizontal integration in European integration or the specific institutional design of the European Union.

Two main authors represent traditional, realist intergovernmentalism: Stanley Hoffmann (1966; 1982) and Alan Milward (1984; 1994). These are their core tenets:

- Member states are and will remain the dominant actors in the process of European integration: they shape European integration according to national goals and interests.
- The extent of European integration is limited by the state interest in autonomy, the interest in self-preservation of nation-state bureaucracies, the diversity of national situations and traditions, the dominance of national identities, and by external actors and influences (such as the United States or NATO).
- European integration does not undermine the nation-state but has strengthened it in the post-World War II reconstruction, in the global competition with other economic powers and emerging markets, and against domestic societal interests and pressures.
- Sectoral integration is limited to the economic sector and related 'low politics'; core functions of the state (the 'high politics' of internal and external security or foreign policy) will be prevented from being integrated by states anxious to preserve their autonomy.
- For the same reason, the supranational organisations of the EU are and will remain weak. They lack the expertise, the resources, or the popular support to expand their power at the expense of the member states.

Thus, the analysis of European integration must start with the preferences of states or governments, as well as their interdependencies and interest constellations, and must focus on negotiations among governments and between governments and the community organisations.

Andrew Moravcsik's liberal intergovernmentalism (LI) shares the intergovernmentalist thrust of these propositions in general but embeds them systematically in a liberal theory of international relations and a rationalist analysis of international institutions. In its most condensed form, it is the general argument of LI that

> EU integration can best be understood as a series of rational choices made by national leaders. These choices responded to constraints and opportunities stemming from the economic interests of powerful domestic constituents, the relative power of each state in the international system, and the role of institutions in bolstering the credibility of interstate commitments.

> (Moravcsik 1998: 18)

81

As indicated by the label 'liberal intergovernmentalism', LI follows a liberal theory of foreign policy preference formation: governmental preferences are issue-specific and reflect the interests of societal interest groups (intermediated by domestic political institutions). In agricultural policy, they reflect the cost–benefit calculations and the relative power of agricultural producers and consumers, whereas in energy policy, they reflect the interests of the dominant energy producers and consumers, and so on. Insofar as European integration has been predominantly economic, so have state preferences. While the general interest in European integration resulted from the pressure to cooperate for mutual benefit from economic gains in an expanding and 'globalising' international economy, concrete preferences emerged 'from a process of domestic conflict in which specific sectoral interests, adjustment costs and, sometimes, geopolitical concerns played an important role'. They reflected 'primarily the commercial interests of powerful economic producers' in market integration and 'secondarily the macro-economic preferences of ruling governmental coalitions' – as in monetary integration (Moravcsik 1998: 3). In other words, domestic interests, shaped mainly by the competitiveness of the national economy, acted as a filter between the structural incentives of the international economy and the national preferences in European integration. As a consequence, governments pursue integration as 'a means to secure commercial advantages for producer groups, subject to regulatory and budgetary constraints' (Moravcsik 1998: 38). To the extent, however, that European integration expands into other sectoral domains, other interests and interest groups become relevant. In contrast, realist intergovernmentalism (RI) assumes that governments have comprehensive ('geopolitical' according to Moravcsik) foreign policy goals that span and dominate specific sectors, and that they are able to define and pursue them independently of societal pressures. These goals are the maximisation of state autonomy, security, or influence.

LI describes the most relevant negotiation processes in European integration as processes of *intergovernmental* bargaining concerning the *distribution* of gains from substantive cooperation. More concretely, they have in the past consisted of *hard bargaining*,

> in which credible threats to veto proposals, to withhold financial side-payments, and to form alternative alliances excluding recalcitrant governments carried the day. The outcomes reflected the relative power of states – more precisely patterns of asymmetrical interdependence. Those who gained the most economically from integration compromised the most on the margin to realize it, whereas those who gained the least or for whom the costs of adaptation were highest imposed conditions.
>
> (Moravcsik 1998: 3)

The difference in the assumptions about state preferences between RI and LI entails differences in the explanation of negotiations and integration outcomes. First, LI assumes that just as states have issue-specific preferences, they also have issue-specific bargaining power. It is the relative intensity of issue-specific preferences that determines the bargaining power of the actors – in contrast with the overall power resources (such as territory, population, armed forces) that realism emphasises. As a consequence, small states may well stand up to big states in EU negotiations or extract concessions in specific issue-areas.

Institutional choice is again driven by governments – and by their concern about each other's future compliance with the substantive deals reached. By transferring sovereignty to international institutions, governments remove issues from the influence of domestic politics, which might build up pressure for non-compliance if costs for powerful domestic actors are high. They also remove them from decentralised intergovernmental control, which may be too weak to secure compliance, in particular if powerful member states violate the rules (Moravcsik 1998: 9, 73). The degree to which governments favour pooling (voting by procedures other than unanimity), and the delegation of sovereignty to supranational institutions, depends on the value they place on the issues and substantive outcomes in question: the higher the gains of a cooperative agreement for a government, and the higher the risk of non-compliance by other governments, the higher its readiness to cede competences to the EU to prevent potential losers from revising the policy (Moravcsik 1998: 9, 486–7).

In contrast with LI, RI assumes that states are primarily concerned about autonomy and influence in institutional choice. They only consent to transferring competencies to the European Union if they expect net gains in autonomy and influence. This, for instance, is the essence of Joseph Grieco's voice-opportunity thesis, which posits that weak states are particularly interested in European integration and willing to sacrifice formal sovereignty because they see it as a way to bind the stronger states and to enhance their influence on international outcomes (Grieco 1996). Another trade-off is captured by Klaus Dieter Wolf's 'new raison d'état' (1999). Governments agree to those transfers of national competencies, and thus to external autonomy losses, that reduce their domestic vulnerability to societal pressures. Social movements and interest groups cannot organise and influence politics at the European level as effectively as in the domestic context.

The core propositions of intergovernmentalism have three negative corollaries. First, the efficiency problem of international negotiations, the search for welfare-maximising collective solutions, is far less relevant in European integration than the distribution problem. Information and ideas are plentiful and symmetrically distributed among states, and transaction costs are generally low so that intergovernmental negotiations reliably produce efficient outcomes (Moravcsik 1998: 479–80). It follows, second, that the bargaining power of supranational actors is low because they are deprived of their main bargaining resource: scarce and asymmetrically distributed information. Finally, if they obtain competencies nevertheless, it is only because governments need them to monitor and sanction each other. But they continue to act in the interest and under the control of the member states.

Intergovernmentalism: basic assumptions

- States (governments) are the relevant actors who rationally initiate, steer and control the process of integration on the basis of exogenous, predominantly material preferences.
- The scope, form, and substance of political integration are negotiated between governments and reflect intergovernmental constellations of preferences and power.

Intergovernmentalism: hypotheses

The core hypotheses about sectoral and horizontal integration resemble each other, yet they partially differ for RI and LI:

- Sectoral and horizontal integration expands to the extent that it increases the utility of the member governments (and candidate governments).
  - —*LI*: Utility is defined by the issue-specific welfare interests of the dominant domestic interest groups.
  - —*RI*: Utility is defined by the overall interest of the state in autonomy, security, and influence.
- The substantive regulation of sectoral and horizontal integration (distribution of welfare gains) results from the distribution of bargaining power among governments.
  - —*LI*: Bargaining power decreases with the availability of outside options, and as the intensity of issue-specific societal preferences increases.
  - —*RI*: Bargaining power increases with overall power resources.

Intergovernmentalist hypotheses about vertical integration also have a realist and a liberal variant:

- *LI*: Vertical integration deepens as compliance problems increase (relative to expected welfare gains).
- *RI*: Vertical integration deepens if and as long as it increases the autonomy and influence of member governments.

Supranationalism: rationalist and constructivist

Like intergovernmentalism, supranationalism has its origins in International Relations theory. In the fifties and sixties neofunctionalism and transactionalism were the main challengers of the dominant realist approach; constructivism, on the other hand, was 'imported' from International Relations to European studies in the nineties. In contrast to intergovernmentalism, supranationalist approaches share a transformative ontology: they hold that the international system is not bound to be anarchical, but can be transformed through processes of institutionalisation and identity change. Furthermore, supranationalism assumes that the process of integration has a transformative and self-reinforcing effect: even though the beginnings of the integration project may well reflect the interests of the most powerful states, further integration has been largely the result of a self-reinforcing dynamic that was and is beyond the control of the member states. Supranationalist approaches differ, however, with respect to the mechanisms underlying this self-reinforcing process. RS is founded on a rationalist theory of international institutions and thus conceives of institutions as factors enabling or constraining actors; the self-reinforcing process of integration displays path-dependent features which prove to be enabling for some actors (supranational actors) while they are difficult to reverse for others (member state governments). In contrast, CS sees the ongoing process of integration as a product of actor socialisation and identity change. While RS shares its rationalist-institutionalist assumptions with intergovernmentalism, CS departs from a different institution theoretic perspective: sociological institutionalism. Sociological institutionalism is founded on an idealist ontology and a logic of action driven by 'appropriateness' and not by 'anticipated consequences'. According to the logic of appropriateness, actors follow what is normatively expected of them in a particular role or situation (March and Olson 1989: 160–1). From a sociological institutionalist perspective, states interact in a highly institutionalised and culturally dense environment, which is structured by collectively held ideational schemes and rules. In contrast to RS (and the intergovernmentalists), CS takes preferences not as exogenous; preferences are endogenous, the products of ideational structures and social interaction. Consequently, international institutions are not so much instruments to efficiently solve collective action problems; rather, their goals, institutional structure and procedures mirror collectively held norms and values and a common identity. Table 4.5 provides an overview of RS and CS.

Historical institutionalism and socialisation

The key task of supranationalism is to explain – both from the perspective of RS and CS – the self-reinforcing process of European integration. In the following paragraphs, we will treat RS and CS separately, pointing at the theories which underlie them, historical institutionalism in the case of RS and theories of socialisation in the case of CS, and conclude by advancing RS and CS hypotheses about European integration.

Historical institutionalism

Historical institutionalism constitutes an important counterpoint to functional theories of institution-building. Functional theories of institution-building explain institutional choices by imputing these choices from the effects which states wish these institutions to produce. Hence institutional choices are explained by their (expected) effects, and functional theorists assume that the effects of institutions correspond to what the founders had in mind when they created the institutions in the first place. Historical institutionalists

Table 4.5 Supranationalism

Level of abstraction	Dimensions of integration:		
	Sectoral:	Vertical:	Horizontal:
General assumptions	States and other actors interact in an institutionalised international environment		
	RS: rationalist institutionalism		
	CS: sociological institutionalism		
Explanatory theory	Dynamic theory of integration/institutionalisation		
	RS: historical institutionalism		
	CS: theories of socialisation		
Factors explaining integration	RS: intensity of transnational exchanges, autonomy of supranational actors, rule density, path dependence		
	CS: identity, legitimacy, resonance		

reject this conjecture (Pierson 1996, 2000). First, historical institutionalists doubt that political actors are as far-sighted as suggested by functional theorists; instead, historical institutionalists assume that political actors have rather short time-horizons, and do not always take into account the potential long-term consequences of their initial institutional choices. Second, historical institutionalists dispute that actors can foresee the exact consequences of their actions, and initial institutional choices can thus have 'unintended consequences': complex social processes that involve a large number of actors are likely to produce feedback-loops and interaction effects which cannot possibly be foreseen or understood by the most far-sighted of actors (Pierson 1998: 39). Third, historical institutionalists contend that political actors can only marginally correct certain institutional developments due to institutional path dependence (Pierson 1996) and 'joint decision traps' (Scharpf 1988) even if they realise that institutional developments contradict their initial preferences. In order to stabilise institutions, political actors often introduce high thresholds to change them (for instance, supermajority or unanimity decision rules), which can block institutional reforms even if they are desired by a majority. Over time, institutional changes may lose their attractiveness due to the existence of sunk costs: when new institutions are introduced, actors make personal investments to adapt to the new institutions. These investments are often so high that, as a consequence, actors 'stick' to these institutions even if new and more efficient alternatives appear which – absent these investments or sunk costs – appear more attractive. Unless there are major 'exogenous shocks' (such as wars, revolutions, economic crises) the institutional route once taken becomes increasingly hard to change, a state of affairs which is captured by the metaphor of path dependence.

Socialisation

Theories of international socialisation depart from the assumption that institutions only have a regulative effect by affecting actor behaviour as constraints or opportunity structures; rather, theories of international socialisation conceive of institutions as constitutive forces, i.e. they constitute and change actors' understanding of a situation and problem as well as their interests and identities. Theories of international socialisation postulate and analyse different mechanisms and conditions for the transformation of interests and identities of state and non-state actors in international institutions; furthermore, they propose mechanisms for the change of state and societal structures as a consequence of these transformations. In the context of European integration research, the effects of EU-level institutions on domestic institutions and actors are analysed by the research programme on 'Europeanisation' (see, for example, Featherstone and Radaelli 2003; Cowles, *et al.* 2001). In the constructivist theory of socialisation, the central mechanisms capturing transformative processes are social learning mechanisms, processes of imitation, persuasion and social influence. Checkel (2001: 562–3) and Johnston (2001: 498–9) have elaborated a catalogue of conditions under which these mechanisms are likely to be effective (see also Risse 2000: 19). Social learning is most likely when actors face novel situations characterised by high uncertainty: when a socialising agent possesses the authority to act on behalf of a community or collectivity which a particular actor identifies with or desires to belong to; when the social learning process affects norms and rules which enjoy a high degree of legitimacy in the community or collectivity; when the social learning process takes place in an environment corresponding to an 'ideal speech situation' which encourages deliberation and is characterised by the absence of external and political constraints; and when the domestic or societal resonance of international norms and rules is high (or, at least, when domestic/societal rules and norms do not contradict international rules and norms).

Supranationalism and European integration

How do the mechanisms of institutional path dependence and social learning feature in supranationalist theories of European integration? How do path dependence and social learning affect sectoral, vertical and horizontal integration? Neofunctionalism, the predecessor theory of supranationalism, does not establish a clear distinction between rationalist and constructivist mechanisms; both groups of mechanisms of transformative change are subsumed under the label of spill-over mechanisms. Ernst Haas saw in the logic of spill-over the central mechanism to explain the 'expansive logic' of European integration (see Haas 1968: 283–317). Later works have categorised the factors and conditions producing integration's expansive logic into functional, political, and cultivated spill-over mechanisms (see Schmitter 1969; Tranholm-Mikkelsen 1991: 15–16). In contrast to intergovernmentalism, which is founded on a theory of inter-state bargaining, supranationalism is rooted in a theory of pluralism: groups, not states, are the central actors in the integration process. In modern, economically interdependent societies, it is the competition among interest groups – striving to maximise the utility of their individual groups – which drives the political process. Policy outcomes are the result of the differential pressure exercised by different interest groups (see Haas 1961: 374, 378; 1968: xxxiii–xxxvi).

Functional spill-over

Functional spill-over results from the connectedness of different policy sectors. The functional spill-over mechanism postulates that there will be a demand for further integration if the gains resulting from integration in policy sector A remain sub-optimal, unless adjacent policy sectors B and C will also be integrated, or when integration of A has negative effects on sectors B and C unless they are all being integrated collectively (see Lindberg and Scheingold 1970: 117). To put it differently: the externalities of sectoral integration incite governments to undertake further, previously unplanned, steps of sectoral integration in order to prevent welfare losses. A similar logic is behind what Haas calls 'geographical spillover' as a trigger of horizontal integration/enlargement (Haas 1968: 313–15). States which may be initially reluctant to join the EU will feel pressured to join eventually given the negative externalities of staying outside the Community.

Political spill-over

Political spill-over occurs as a reaction to initial integrative steps once interest groups, bureaucrats and other domestic political actors direct their expectations and activities at the new, supranational level of decision-making. To the degree that integration improves the likelihood that the actors will realise their political aims at the supranational level rather than on the national level, we are likely to observe the formation of transnational coalitions and the development of common problem-solving perspectives (Haas 1968: xxxiv). Even though this process does not necessarily have to be harmonious (Schmitter 1969: 166), political actors will – in the course of time – develop new loyalties which transcend the nation state. Lindberg and Scheingold (1970: 199) characterise this process as actor socialisation, thereby underlining the proximity of political spill-over to CS (see also Haas 2001). Interest groups, bureaucrats and other domestic actors will – on the basis of these newly acquired identities, attitudes and coalitions – exercise pressure and influence on governments and press them to advance the process of integration.

Institutional spill-over

This third kind of spill-over is triggered by the activities of the EU's supranational actors, the Commission, the European Court of Justice and the European Parliament. On the one hand, these actors contribute to the processes of functional and political spill-over: they allude to connections between different policy sectors and point to the potential positive externalities of further integration and, conversely, the negative externalities and consequences of potential failures to advance sector integration (Nye 1971: 59). For the same reason, supranational actors support the formation of transnational coalitions. On the other hand, supranational actors – first and foremost the Commission – also help the governments of EU member states to discover their common interests and possibilities for efficient cooperation. Furthermore, they play a crucial role in helping the member states to 'upgrade their common interest' (see Haas 1961) in finding bargaining solutions which are considered optimal from an integration perspective. This argument, however, is founded on the condition that supranational organisations – such as the Commission – possess an information advantage vis-à-vis the member state governments which they are willing to fully exploit (a condition that runs fundamentally counter to intergovernmentalist assumptions). In this sense, the Commission seeks to 'cultivate' the ground to advance the integration process through its role as a mediator and provider of ideas, a process also referred to as *cultivated spill-over*.

The work of a 'supranationalist' group of researchers around Alec Stone Sweet, Wayne Sandholtz, and Neil Fligstein is the most prominent example of research in the tradition of Ernst Haas (Stone Sweet and Sandholtz 1997, 1998; Fligstein and Stone Sweet 2001, 2002; Stone Sweet *et al.* 2001). In their works, they have argued that European integration progresses as a result of the interplay of three developments: the expansion of transnational exchange, supranational actors' capacity to pursue an integrative agenda, and the role of European rule-making in solving policy externalities (see Stone Sweet and Sandholtz 1997: 301). Their approach, however, can be firmly located in the RS camp since they conceive of social, transnational and political actors as self-interested, utility-maximising and strategically acting actors and emphasise the regulative role of institutional arrangements which serve as incentive structures enabling or constraining actor behaviour. Stone Sweet and Sandholtz advance their argument in close correspondence with the concepts of functional and political spill-over: as transnational economic exchange expands, the costs of national rule-making increases, as does the demand of transnational actors – interest groups, transnational corporations, producer and consumer groups – for supranational rule-making and policy coordination. This demand will be stronger, the more these actors expect to profit from cross-border exchange and hence, the larger the perceived advantage of uniform EU-level rules vis-à-vis different national rules. Transnational actors direct their demands for uniform EU-level rules to facilitate cross-border exchange at their respective national governments; yet if these prove reluctant to push the agenda for more uniform EU-level rules, transnational and societal actors do also turn to supranational institutions to voice their demands. In keeping with the logic of institutional spill-over, the Commission and the European Court of Justice use the powers and information at their disposal to expand the scope of EU-level rules to facilitate cross-border exchange and thus help to increase collective transnational utility (Sandholtz and Stone Sweet 1997: 299, 306; 1998: 4).

Apart from the integrative impetus generated by transnational agents who are promoting cross-border exchange and uniform EU level rules, Stone Sweet and Sandholtz advance another factor for explaining further integration. This factor can be captured in what they call the logic of *institutionalisation* (1997: 310–12; Fligstein and Stone Sweet 2001: 31; see also Haas 1968: 283). Even though the EU's primary law laid down in the Treaties may have been created by member state governments reflecting their preferences and respective bargaining power, the application of the EU Treaty may develop in directions unforeseen or unintended by member state governments. First, actors who operate under the Treaty rules adapt to them and use the opportunities offered by them to realise their own preferences which may not be congruent with those of the member states who enacted the rules in the first place (see Lindner and Rittberger 2003: 451–55). Second, Treaty rules never represent a 'complete contract' which caters for every possible contingency. Hence, rules are open to interpretation; actors (obviously) may offer controversial interpretations, and sometimes they may not even offer clear prescriptions or proscriptions for action. In situations like these, supranational organisations such as the Court and the Commission – who have been charged by the member states with applying and interpreting these rules – may exploit this 'grey zone' for their own advantage. The process of rule-modification and rule-interpretation is a continuous one:

> As they interpret and apply the rules, courts, legislators, and administrators necessarily modify them by establishing their effective meaning. The new or changed rules then guide subsequent interactions, as the actors which act under these rules adapt their behaviours to the rules. The disputes that arise thereafter take shape in an altered rule structure and initiate the processes that will again reinterpret and modify the rules. The new rules guide actor behaviour, and so on.
> (Stone Sweet and Sandholtz 1997: 310)

Unlike early neofunctionalism, RS disputes that integration progresses automatically and in a linear fashion. However, RS expects that once a certain level of integration is reached, this will be next to impossible for governments to reverse (Fligstein and Stone Sweet 2001: 38, 55). As stated, RS takes recourse to the mechanisms of high institutional thresholds and sunk costs postulated by historical institutionalism in order to explain the (near) irreversibility of an institutional path once taken (Pierson 1998: 43–7). First, the rules to amend or change the Treaties are very restrictive since they demand unanimous agreement among the member state governments plus ratification in each member state; furthermore, policy changes within the Treaties require at least a qualified majority. When thus only a minority of states benefits from a particular rule, it will do everything it can to block change. EU policy-making thus possesses a high degree of 'policy stability' (Tsebelis 2002: 281–2). Second, over the course of the past half-century, national political systems have become increasingly penetrated by rules originating at the EU level. The sunk costs of adapting national rules and policy-making processes to the exigencies of EU politics render the mere existence of a state outside the EU increasingly unattractive. In this sense 'exit' is also becoming an ever more unlikely policy option for an existing EU member state as is the threat of leaving the EU as a credible bargaining strategy.

LI and RS converge on several issues. Both approaches are founded on a rationalist model of action. Both see the most fundamental source of integration in societal interests. RS does also not dispute that governments are central and powerful actors in the integration process and that bargaining constitutes an important mode of interaction among the member states (Pierson 1998: 29; Stone Sweet and Sandholtz 1997: 314). Yet RS claims that governments are not *the* central actors and that interstate bargaining is not the only mode of interaction through which preferences are aggregated. Obviously, there are also a number of differences between RS and LI. First, RS stipulates – unlike LI – that socio-economic pressure for integration, for instance by producer groups, is not only channelled through the state; rather, societal and transnational actors form transnational coalitions and direct their demands to supranational institutions, thus bypassing the state. Second, intergovernmental negotiations are embedded in transnational and supranational contexts: intergovernmental conferences take place in an environment which undergoes significant changes in periods between two intergovernmental conferences. In this respect, intergovernmental conferences are convened against the background of new demands by transnational actor coalitions and an institutional context shaped by the self-reinforcing dynamic of the process of institutionalisation mentioned earlier. Third, supranational organisations are not only willing but also able to make extensive use of their powers and to promote rules and policies that member states would not have agreed on during intergovernmental negotiations (see, for example, Lindner and Rittberger 2003; Rittberger and Stacey 2003). In the light of the preceding discussion, the demand for further integration is thus less the result of 'exogenous shocks' but rather of endogenous, path-dependent processes, and intergovernmental negotiations are less the generators of integration but its product (Caporaso 1998: 350; Stone Sweet and Sandholtz 1998: 12, 26).

In contrast to RS, KS has not (yet) developed a comprehensive theory of European integration. Yet, there exist a number of analyses of EU politics inspired by constructivist theorising which enable us to infer elements of a constructivist theory of integration. According to CS, the willingness of actors to further European integration depends on the degree to which they identify with 'Europe', on the perceived legitimacy of further integrative steps, and on the degree to which attempts for further integration resonate with political ideas and norms in the domestic realm. Furthermore, the process of integration can have a transformative effect: it may strengthen actors' identification with the EU and increase the legitimacy of further integrative efforts.

A crucial factor in CS theorising is *identity*. Actors' willingness to support European integration varies with the degree to which political actors in the member states identify with the EU (which does not imply that domestic actors have to 'give up' their national identity; European, national or regional identities can exist alongside each other). This stipulation affects all dimensions of European integration: the willingness of non-EU member states to opt for EU membership, as well as the willingness of EU member states to further sectoral and vertical integration. CS agrees with neofunctionalism that political actors' identification with the EU increases through direct experiences with and participation in EU affairs (socialisation). The transformative potential of European integration can precisely be traced back to these processes of socialisation (see, for example, Egeberg 1999; Risse *et al.* 1999; Risse 2003).

Actors' willingness to support European integration also depends on the perceived *legitimacy* of sectoral, vertical, and horizontal integration. Legitimacy determines to what extent attempts for integration are considered 'appropriate'. How far an integrative step is considered legitimate depends on the degree to which it resonates with domestically held political norms and ideas. Willingness to further European integration then increases with the degree to which further integration is compatible with national 'constitutional traditions' (Wagner 2002) or domestically held 'legitimacy ideas' (Jachtenfuchs *et al*. 1998). Legitimacy, however, does not necessarily have to be rooted in domestic traditions, institutions or ideas. Legitimacy can equally be generated outside of the national context. Legitimacy can be generated externally: rules and institutions which operate outside the EU context and which command a high degree of legitimacy are likely to be 'copied' onto the EU's institutional blueprint by political actors independent of the rule's or institution's 'functionality' (DiMaggio and Powell 1991; see also McNamara 1998). Legitimacy can also be generated internally, for instance, if a new integrative effort is compatible with EU-level discourses and practices, or if it provides a good 'fit' with more abstract norms and principles of 'good' or 'appropriate' governance (Rittberger 2003, 2005). The normative environment may thus provide an impetus for further integration, even though it may not be considered 'efficient' from the perspective of the member states (Schimmelfennig 2001, 2003).

Finally, CS emphasises that EU institutions and procedures encourage deliberative processes (see Joerges and Neyer 1997; Lewis 1998), which stands in stark contrast to LI's focus on hard-nosed inter-state bargaining processes. In fora such as 'comitology' or Coreper – which operate outside direct government control, are exposed to a low degree of publicity, and do not face strong external pressures – an atmosphere that facilitates processes of persuasion and socialisation is encouraged even though the participants may be national bureaucrats or government representatives.

Supranationalism: basic assumptions

- The process of European integration generates a self-reinforcing dynamic which begets further integration and which governments did not intend, which they are unable to control or to reverse.
- Transnational societal actors in conjunction with supranational actors are the relevant actors pushing the integration process. The scope, form and content of integration develop as a result of complex transnational social and institutional processes and transcend the preferences and power-constellations of national governments.

Supranationalism: hypotheses

The core hypotheses across the different dimensions of integration resemble each other, yet they differ for RS and CS:

- *RS*: Integration is likely to progress, if it increases transnational societal actors' expected utility and to the degree to which supranational actors possess and are able to make use of their capacity to further the interests of transnational actors. Variation in scope of integration reflects variation in the relative intensity of transnational activity and the capacity of supranational actors. The framework of substantial regulations and rules of integration corresponds with the constellation of transnational interests and supranational rule-making and rule-interpreting activity.

- *CS*: Integration is likely to progress, if actors' identification with the EU increases, when integrative efforts enjoy a high degree of legitimacy and resonance in the member states. Variation in the scope of integration reflects variation in the relative intensity of identification with the EU, institutional legitimacy and societal resonance. The framework of substantial regulations and rules of integration depends on the legitimacy and resonance of these regulations and rules.

Conclusion

In this chapter we have presented the most important theories that are currently employed to explain European integration in its sectoral, vertical, and horizontal dimension: realist and liberal intergovernmentalism (RI and LI) as well as rationalist and constructivist supranationalism (RS and CS). In order to explain the wealth of European integration phenomena, we have presented and classified theories of European integration as well as their central hypotheses. It is hardly a controversial claim that not one single theory of European integration can claim to possess the explanatory power to account for 'European integration' in its entirety. As existing theory-driven empirical research has amply demonstrated, a combination of the factors and conditions postulated by different theories of integration may be necessary to account for phenomena of sectoral, vertical and horizontal integration. We echo others when we claim that intergovernmentalism and supranationalism are not incommensurable, but can in principle engage in a fruitful 'theoretical dialogue' (Jupille *et al.* 2003: 19). For instance, there is no reason why LI should not be generally open to theoretical 'dialogue' with approaches which share its rationalist foundations and a positivist commitment to theory-testing, such as RS.

However, given its emphasis on states as key actors in the integration process, LI has been particularly 'strong' in accounting for the main substantive and institutional outcomes of intergovernmental conferences, while RS – with its emphasis on the autonomous influence of supranational actors and institutions – has been able to capture both processes and instances of sectoral integration (Stone Sweet *et al.* 2001; Fligstein and Stone Sweet 2002) and vertical integration (Hix 2002; Farrell and Héritier 2003; Rittberger and Stacey 2003) which occur *between* Treaty re-negotiations.

Recently, there have also been attempts to combine LI and RS in order to explain how (rational) choices made by member state governments during intergovernmental conference may lead to effects which were either unintended or even unavoidable (Lindner and Rittberger 2003) in the light of the constraints faced by member states during intergovernmental conferences. Yet we also see that theoretical dialogue can occur between approaches which do not necessarily share the same theoretical foundations. By identifying a theory's respective 'home turf', by specifying the elements of each theory that do the explaining, and 'by bringing together each home turf in some larger picture' (Jupille *et al.* 2003: 21), we can offer *additive* explanations of integration phenomena which we could otherwise only partially account for. Recent work on horizontal integration in the EU ('enlargement') has demonstrated that elements from constructivist approaches are a necessary complement to rationalist approaches such as LI in order to account for the decision of EU member states to support Eastern enlargement (Schimmelfennig 2001, 2003).

In order to reap the benefits of theoretical dialogue, it is, however, unavoidable for students of European integration to specify the elements of their theories, to deduce testable hypotheses and to be aware of the empirical domain where the theory is expected to do 'best' in explaining integration phenomena. In this chapter we have sought to offer an integration theoretic toolbox which, as we hope, proves to be user friendly while, at the same, encourages rigorous theory-driven research on European integration.

References

Caporaso, J. A. (1998) 'Regional Integration Theory: Understanding Our Past and Anticipating Our Future', in W. Sandholtz and A. Stone Sweet (eds), *European Integration and Supranational Governance* (Oxford: Oxford University Press).

Caporaso, J. A. and Keeler, J. T. S. (1995) 'The European Union and Regional Integration Theory', in C. Rhodes and S. Mazey (eds), *The State of the European Union: Building a European Polity* (Boulder, CO: Lynne Rienner).

Checkel, J. T. (2001) 'Why Comply? Social Learning and European Identity Change', *International Organization* 55: 553–88.

Christiansen, T., Jørgensen, K. E. and Wiener, A. (eds) (2001) *The Social Construction of Europe* (London: Sage).

Cowles, M. G., Caporaso, J. and Risse, T. (eds) (2001) *Transforming Europe: Europeanisation and Domestic Change* (Ithaca, NY: Cornell University Press).

Cram, L. (2001) 'Integration Theory and the Study of the European Policy Process: Towards a Synthesis of Approaches', in J. Richardson (ed.), *European Union: Power and Policy-Making*, 2nd edn (London: Routledge).

DiMaggio, P. J. and Powell, W. W. (1991) 'The Iron Cage Revisited: Institutional Isomorphism and Collective Rationality in Organizational Fields', in W. W. Powell and P. J. DiMaggio (eds) *The New Institutionalism in Organizational Analysis* (Chicago: University of Chicago Press).

Donahue, J. D. and Pollack, M. A. (2001) 'Centralization and Its Discontents: The Rhythms of Federalism in the United States and the European Union', in K. Nicolaidis and R. Howse (eds) *The Federal Vision: Legitimacy and Levels of Governance in the United States and the European Union* (Oxford: Oxford University Press).

Egeberg, M. (1999) 'Transcending Intergovernmentalism? Identity and Role Perceptions of National Officials', *Journal of European Public Policy* 6/3: 456–74

Farrell, H. and Héritier, A. (2003) 'Formal and Informal Institutions under Codecision: Continuous Constitution-Building in Europe', *Governance* 16: 577–600.

Featherstone, K. and Radaelli, C. (eds) (2003) *The Politics of Europeanisation* (Oxford: Oxford University Press).

Fligstein, N. and Stone Sweet, A. (2001) 'Institutionalizing the Treaty of Rome', in A. Stone Sweet, W. Sandholtz and N. Fligstein (eds) *The Institutionalization of Europe* (Oxford: Oxford University Press).

—— (2002) 'Constructing Polities and Markets: An Institutionalist Account of European Integration', *American Journal of Sociology* 107: 1206–43.

Grieco, J. (1996) 'State Interests and Institutional Rule Trajectories: A Neorealist Interpretation of the Maastricht Treaty and European Economic and Monetary Union', *Security Studies* 5: 261–306.

Haas, E. B. (1961) 'International Integration: The European and the Universal Process', *International Organization* 15: 366–92.

—— (1968) *The Uniting of Europe: Political, Social, and Economic Forces 1950–1957* (Stanford, CA: Stanford University Press).

Haas, E. B. (2001) 'Does Constructivism Subsume Neo-functionalism?' in T. Christiansen, K. E. Jørgensen and A. Wiener (eds), *The Social Construction of Europe* (London: Sage).

Hix, S. (2002) 'Constitutional Agenda-Setting Through Discretion in Rule Interpretation: Why the European Parliament Won at Amsterdam', *British Journal of Political Science* 32: 259–80.

—— (2005) *The Political System of the European Union*, 2nd edn (London: Palgrave).

Hoffmann, S. (1966) 'Obstinate or Obsolete? The Fate of the Nation-State and the Case of Western Europe', *Daedalus* 95: 862–915.

—— (1982) 'Reflections on the Nation-State in Western Europe Today', *Journal of Common Market Studies* 21: 21–37.

Jachtenfuchs, M., Diez, T. and Jung, S. (1998) 'Which Europe? Conflicting Models of a Legitimate European Political Order', *European Journal of International Relations* 4: 409–45.

Joerges, C. and Neyer, J. (1997) 'From Intergovernmental Bargaining to Deliberative Political Process: The Constitutionalization of Comitology', *European Law Journal* 3: 273–99.

Johnston, A. I. (2001) 'Treating International Institutions as Social Environments', *International Studies Quarterly* 45/3: 487–515.

Jupille, J., Caporaso, J. A. and Checkel, J. (2003) 'Integrating Institutions. Rationalism, Constructivism, and the Study of the European Union', *Comparative Political Studies* 36: 7–40.

Koremenos, B., Lipson, C. and Snidal, D. (2001) 'The Rational Design of International Institutions', *International Organization* 55/4: 761–99.

Lewis, J. (1998) 'Is the "Hard Bargaining" Image of the Council Misleading? The Committee of Permanent Representatives and the Local Elections Directive', *Journal of Common Market Studies* 36: 479–504.

Lindberg, L. and Scheingold, S. (1970) *Europe's Would-Be Polity* (Englewood Cliffs, NJ: Prentice-Hall).

Lindner, J. and Rittberger, B. (2003) 'The Creation, Interpretation and Contestation of Institutions – Revisiting Historical Institutionalism', *Journal of Common Market Studies* 41: 445–73.

McNamara, K. R. (1998) *The Currency of Ideas: Monetary Politics in the European Union* (Ithaca, NY: Cornell University Press).

March, J. G. and Olsen, J. P. (1989) *Rediscovering Institutions: The Organizational Basis of Politics* (New York: Free Press).

Milward, A. S. (1984) *The Reconstruction of Western Europe 1945–51* (London: Methuen).

—— (1992) *The European Rescue of the Nation-State* (London: Routledge).

Moravcsik, A. (1993) 'Preferences and Power in the European Community: A Liberal Intergovernmentalist Approach', *Journal of Common Market Studies* 31: 473–524.

—— (1998) *The Choice for Europe: Social Power and State Purpose from Messina to Maastricht* (Ithaca, NY: Cornell University Press).

Nye, J. S. (1971) *Peace in Parts: Integration and Conflict in Regional Organization* (Boston, MA: Little Brown and Company).

Pierson, P. (1996) 'The Path to European Integration: A Historical-Institutionalist Analysis', *Comparative Political Studies* 29: 123–63.

—— (1998) 'The Path to European Integration: A Historical-Institutionalist Analysis', in W. Sandholtz and A. Stone Sweet (eds), *European Integration and Supranational Governance* (Oxford: Oxford University Press).

—— (2000) 'Increasing Returns, Path Dependence, and the Study of Politics', *American Political Science Review* 94: 251–67.

Risse, T. (2000) '"Let's Argue!": Communicative Action in World Politics', *International Organization* 54: 1–39

—— (2003) 'The Euro between National and European Identity', *Journal of European Public Policy* 10/4: 487–505.

Risse, T., Engelmann, M., Knopf, H.-J. and Roscher, K. (1999) 'To Euro or Not to Euro? The EMU and Identity Politics in the European Union', *European Journal of International Relations* 5/2; 147–87.

Rittberger, B. (2003) 'The Creation and Empowerment of the European Parliament', *Journal of Common Market Studies* 41: 203–25.

—— (2005) *Building Europe's Parliament: Democratic Representation Beyond the Nation State* (Oxford: Oxford University Press).

Rittberger, B. and Stacey, J. (2003) 'Dynamics of Formal and Informal Institutional Change in the EU', special issue of *Journal of European Public Policy* 10/6.

Rosamond, B. (2000) *Theories of European Integration* (Basingstoke: Macmillan).

Scharpf, F. W. (1988) 'The Joint-Decision Trap: Lessons from German Federalism and European Integration', *Public Administration* 66: 239–78.

Schimmelfennig, F. (2001) 'The Community Trap: Liberal Norms, Rhetorical Action, and the Eastern Enlargement of the European Union', *International Organization* 55: 47–80.

—— (2003) *The EU, NATO and the Integration of Europe. Rules and Rhetoric* (Cambridge: Cambridge University Press).

Schmitter, P. C. (1969) 'Three Neofunctional Hypotheses about International Integration', *International Organization* 23: 161–6.

Schneider, G. and Cederman, L. E. (1994) 'The Change of Tide in Political Cooperation: A Limited Information Model of European Integration', *International Organization* 48: 633–62.

Stone Sweet, A. and Sandholtz, W. (1997) 'European Integration and Supranational Governance', *Journal of European Public Policy* 4: 297–317.

—— (1998) 'Integration, Supranational Governance, and the Institutionalization of the European Polity', in W. Sandholtz and A. Stone Sweet (eds) *European Integration and Supranational Governance* (Oxford: Oxford University Press).

Stone Sweet, A. and Fligstein, N. (eds) (2001) *The Institutionalization of Europe* (Oxford: Oxford University Press).

Tranholm-Mikkelsen, J. (1991) 'Neo-functionalism: Obstinate or Obsolete? A Reappraisal in the Light of the New Dynamism of the EC', *Millennium* 20: 1–22.

Tsebelis, G. (2002) *Veto Players: How Political Institutions Work* (Princeton, NJ, and New York: Princeton University Press and Russell Sage Foundation).

Wagner, W. (2002) 'The Subnational Foundations of the European Parliament', *Journal of International Relations and Development* 5: 24–36.

Wiener, A. and Diez, T. (2004) *European Integration Theory* (Oxford: Oxford University Press).

Wolf, K. D. (1999) 'The New Raison d'état as a Problem for Democracy in World Society', *European Journal of International Relations* 5: 333–63.

PART II

INSTITUTIONAL PROCESSING

Chapter 5

The European Commission

The European executive between continuity and change

THOMAS CHRISTIANSEN

Introduction

National governments like to claim that their European policies place them at the heart of the European Union, but it may be more appropriate to place the European Commission at this prime location (Nugent 2000). From the outset, when Jean Monnet became the first president of the Commission's precursor, the High Authority of the European Coal and Steel Community (ECSC), the institution has been closely linked to, even identified with, the progress of the integration project.

The Commission is central to the integration process because in most areas of EU policy-making it carries the sole responsibility for proposing new legislation. The monopoly of initiative with respect to most first-pillar matters has made the Commission a pivotal actor in the EU policy process, placing it in a privileged position in relation to national governments, organised interests and the European Parliament. It has allowed the Commission a part in framing the issues, setting the agenda and, in a wider sense, shaping the evolution of the European Union.

Beyond initiating EU legislation, the Commission's functions also include the mediation – even 'manipulation' – of member state positions during the decision-taking phase of the policy process (Schmidt 2000), and control over compliance with EU legislation once this has been passed (Mendrinou 1996; Peters 2000). Furthermore, in a range of areas, the Commission itself is either the decision-taker (for example in competition policy) (McGowan 2000; Brent 1995) or policy-manager (for example in managing pre-accession assistance to the countries of Central and Eastern Europe) (Levy 2000; Laffan 1997). Finally, the Commission also has a role in informing citizens about EU policies (Mak 2004) and representing the EU's trade interests in international fora (Woolcock 2000).

The variety of tasks it has to perform within the system of European governance make the Commission a complex institution. It has to possess technical expertise in almost every area of government activity as well as an astute awareness of the politics of these issues, if it wants to see its policy proposals and other initiatives succeed. The need to handle the often contradictory demands of administrative expertise and political preference within the same institution can exacerbate tensions within the Commission. And pressure to meet an expanding range of tasks with often limited resources can create problems with administrative 'overload', which in turn may damage the efficiency and legitimacy of Commission actions.

The identification of administrative and political logics within the Commission make it essential to stress one fundamental point at the beginning of this chapter: the term 'Commission' is being used to denote a number of different 'animals': 'Commission' stands both for the college of twenty-five individual Commissioners constituting the political, quasi-ministerial level of the institution, as well as for the body of more than 20,000 officials who make up its administrative services. In view of the tensions mentioned above, the relationship between these political and administrative levels of the Commission has been difficult.

In the early phase, Commissioners tended to be senior civil servants, but in the recent past have been recruited from among senior politicians in the member states (Donnelly and Ritchie 1994; MacMullen 2000). Commission staff are normally recruited through competitive examinations from across the European Union, but at the higher echelons of the administration appointments have traditionally involved an element of 'parachuting' –

the appointment of senior officials according to national and party political patronage rather than by promotion through the ranks (Spence 1994) as well as the growing practice of filling Commission posts through secondment of officials from national administrations (Trondal 2001).

While the need to reconcile administrative and political responsibility within the Commission can be dated back to the origins of the High Authority, the more recent phase of dynamic integration following the creation of the Single Market has brought new pressures. Given the direct or indirect relevance of Commission activities for governments, interest groups, businesses and consumers, the institution is now frequently in the spotlight of public attention. This higher profile has had two consequences which are essential to an understanding of recent developments concerning the Commission: on the one hand, there is now an often critical, if not hostile, scrutiny of Commission activity by the – predominantly national – media. In this respect, the focus is not only on potentially controversial policy proposals or decisions the Commission is preparing, say in areas of tax harmonisation or state aid control. Crucially, the focus is on the Commission itself, often with heavy emphasis on its arcane internal practices and its alleged propensity to mismanagement or even fraud (Grey 2000).

The second, related consequence is a lingering debate about the Commission's lack of public accountability. The Commissioners are nominated and appointed by national governments, and while they are not 'faceless bureaucrats', as critics sometimes claim, they can legitimately be called 'unelected'. Changes introduced in recent treaty reforms have enhanced the role of the European Parliament in the confirmation of the Commission President and the College of Commissioners but have not altered this basic fact, and the legitimacy of the Commission has been precarious as a result. Indeed, when objections from MEPs to individual candidates for Commissioner posts caused a delay in the appointment of the Barroso Commission the public reaction was one of crisis, rather than seeing this as the legitimate consequence of the democratic process.

The combination of high political profile, administrative overload, media scrutiny and questionable public accountability made for a heady brew in the 1990s. Jacques Delors, Commission President from 1984 to 1994, had invigorated the institution after decades of 'eurosclerosis' by putting it into the driving seat of the successful and dynamic Single Market programme. But the next big project, the agreements on Economic and Monetary Union and on Political Union contained in the Maastricht Treaty, already saw the Commission's star wane. Delors' successor, Jacques Santer, assumed office with the motto 'Doing less, but doing it better', but towards the end of his term he became the victim of the volatile mix of political ambition, administrative mismanagement and fragile legitimacy which the Commission had developed in the 1990s. In response to criticism from within and outside the Commission, the European Parliament first instituted a Committee of Independent Experts to investigate fraud and mismanagement. When the EP then threatened to dismiss the Commission on the basis of the Committee's report (Committee 1999), emphasising the absence of either collective or individual responsibility in the Commission, the entire Santer Commission was forced to resign in March 1999.

The events at the end of the 1990s constituted a major crisis for the Commission, but it also constituted an opportunity to approach the first substantial reform of the Commission in twenty-five years (Spence 2000). The Prodi Commission had to embark on a wide-ranging process of reform which implied significant changes for the institution, the individuals working within it, and its relations with other institutions, the member states and the wider public. For a time, the 1999 crisis and the subsequent reform process appeared to have certainly weakened, even traumatised, the Commission. In the long run, though, the 'fresh start' afforded by these events may come to be seen as invigorating, and ultimately a 'new Commission' may emerge as a stronger player in the policy process. At the end of the Prodi Commission, academic opinion on the outcome of the reforms remained divided (Rhinard and Vaccari 2005).

This chapter analyses the evolution of the European Commission against the background of these problems and opportunities. The next section charts the development of the Commission's role in the European policy process. Subsequent sections deal with the resulting pressures for the administrative and political levels of the Commission, before attention returns to the current internal and treaty-based reforms. By way of conclusion, the chapter discusses the key issues for the Commission in view of the challenges ahead.

Conflicting demands and internal tensions

The above comments have already indicated that the Commission is having to deal with internal tensions such as the political/administrative divide (Christiansen 1997). Another such contradiction is the Commission's dual role of providing both stability and dynamism for the European Union. To some extent, this balancing act between dynamism and continuity which the Commission has to perform matches a related conflict: from the beginnings of the High Authority, Jean Monnet, its first president, had been aware of what he regarded as the dangers of bureaucratisation (Mazey 1992). He had wanted the High Authority to remain an elitist body of policy-making experts, rather than risk becoming bogged down in the quagmire of parliamentary politics (Wallace and Smith 1995) or in the minutiae of sectoral integration (Mazey 1992). Walter Hallstein, the first EEC Commission President and former diplomat, chose a more explicitly political approach to conducting Commission business. When clashing with de Gaulle, he learned to his cost what the dangers of a 'political' Commission were. The '1965 crisis' – which had France withdrawing from the Council for almost a year after a dispute over the Common Agricultural Policy – was as much about the content of policy as it was about the power of the Commission. De Gaulle's concern at this juncture was not only to preserve French interests in a particular policy field. In a wider sense, the crisis was sparked by – and put an end to – Hallstein's ambition to turn the Commission into something like an internationally recognised 'European government'.

What followed the showdown between de Gaulle and Hallstein were two decades of a decidedly 'non-political' Commission: implementing treaty provisions where it was acceptable to member states, but remaining passive where there was opposition from national capitals. The initiative on institutional reform was definitely left to member states and the European Court.

But while the experience of the 1960s spelled an end to far-reaching federalist ambitions, it did not incapacitate the Commission in its more subtle policy-making role. In what remained a cumbersome institutional framework and an unfavourable overall climate, the Commission executed its assigned tasks and indeed sought to extend Community competences. The main aim of the Rome Treaty, the abolition of all custom tariffs within the Community and the creation of a Common External Tariff by 1969, was achieved ahead of schedule. But more than just the administration of agreed policies, and the successful management of two rounds of enlargement in the 1970s and early 1980s, this period also saw the Commission 'quietly' extending the limits of Community activity.

In fields such as education, research and development, and the environment, on which the treaties were silent, the Commission developed, first, a Community agenda, and, subsequently, the policy tools to facilitate Community action. In regional policy the Commission sought to go beyond the straightforward budget bargain among member states and began to design policies such as the Integrated Mediterranean Programmes that actually had a substantial regional dimension. Progress in all of these cases was gradual, cumbersome and slow-moving, and yet these early advances were the essential foundations for the Commission's more ambitious and self-confident projects of the late 1980s.

The pattern of Commission activity in this period was to circumvent potential obstruction of national governments by involving a wide range of non-governmental groups and interests in deliberation about new policy initiatives. Such groups and organisations were regularly drawn into the ambit of the Commission by its comparative openness to outside views and representation (Mazey and Richardson 1994). They would then emerge favourable to the development of a European policy in the design of which they had participated. The advantage of such a strategy was that the emerging transnational network of interest groups and non-governmental organisations, supportive of a Community role in social regulation, would eventually put pressure on national administrations and governments to 'fall into line'. At the very least, the Commission could point to 'demand' from private interests in a given Community policy, and in this way legitimise its activity in the unchartered waters outside the treaty.

Simultaneously, the Commission built up a body of 'soft law': it oversaw the growth of frameworks of rules, recommendations, decisions and practices in novel policy sectors which were strong enough to structure social and economic interests – leading them to accept that 'Europe matters' – without having to seek explicit member state approval by sending formal proposals to the Council. This construction of soft law continued to be significant even when policy-making in the wide variety of sectors become codified later (Snyder 1993). It provided valuable experience in a novel system of administration and implementation – a system in which the Commission cannot rely on hierarchy or coercion, but where its power must be based on negotiation and persuasion.

In this way, although its political ambitions had run dry, the Commission's capacity to mould social and economic interests, to construct agendas for EC action and to develop the innovative practices necessary for European governance, meant that the 1970s and early 1980s were an important phase in its 'maturation process'. It was on the basis of this experience that, with Jacques Delors taking up the presidency in 1985, there was a return to a proactive, political leadership from the Berlaymont. A number of factors – and many of them external to the Commission and even the Community itself – came together in the success of the '1992' programme. But there was also Delors' ability to invigorate and lead an administration that had in many areas shown the kind of bureaucratic fatigue Monnet had feared from the outset. At the end of Delors' ten-year tenure at the helm of the Commission its potential for political leadership (Drake 1995) had been demonstrated conclusively.

Jacques Santer may have tried to scale back the profile and politicisation of the Commission, concentrating instead on consolidation of policies and a series of modest reforms (Peterson 1999). But it was too late to return the genie to the bottle. Given the range of activities in which the Commission is now involved and the potential for any matter, however technical, to become a matter of controversy and thereby of 'high politics', the Commission can not avoid publicity and exposure to public debate. The appointment of Romano Prodi – a former prime minister from one of the larger member states – to succeed the disgraced Santer in 1999 appeared as an acknowledgement of this state of affairs among national governments. Prodi did not shy away from either limelight or political controversy, although he soon had to confront a hostile media reception (*Financial Times*, 18 January 2000). The challenge of communicating from the centre to a broad and diverse (and increasingly sceptical) European public has increased further with the enlargement to twenty-five member states, and has accordingly been elevated to one of the key tasks of the Barroso Commission.

As a result of its increasing significance and high profile, the Commission has been facing a broad range of criticisms. It is castigated for being too bureaucratic or technocratic (for which read: insensitive to the political priorities of the day) as well as for too much political activism (for which read: too involved in deciding political priorities). Such criticisms of the Commission are contradictory, but not necessarily wrong. The fact of the matter is that there is an inherent contradiction in the Commission providing both political leadership and an impartial civil service to the EU system. The tension, if not contradiction, between the organisational modes underlying 'bureaucracy' and 'politics' was recognised early on as a fundamental issue for the Commission (Coombes 1970; Scheinmann 1966). Insofar as there is a general problem of reconciling democracy and bureaucracy in liberal democratic systems (Pollit 1988), the problem for the Commission was simply the reproduction, perhaps exacerbation, of similar conflicts erupting in national administrative systems.

As already indicated at the outset, the Commission had been steering such a course between the Scylla of bureaucratisation and Charybdis of politicisation for a long time, and the resulting tension has been a persistent feature in the work and the public perception of the Commission. A recent review of the literature on the Commission reveals that this is still a dominant preoccupation of observers in the early twenty-first century (Rhinard and Vaccari 2005).

But from the mid-1990s onwards the Commission started to face more than the traditional balancing act between political bargaining and technocratic rule. The pressures on the Commission appeared as a triangular force-field, in which the 'corners' were constituted by public accountability, attention to member state interests and a measure of independent expertise. This state of affairs reflects, for the Commission, the overall 'contradictions between intergovernmental bargaining, functional administration and democracy [which are] embedded in the treaties establishing the European Communities' (Wallace and Smith 1995: 140).

Such an observation leads us to concentrate on the study of the Commission's internal tensions. Studying the internal dynamics of the Commission is analytically useful because such a perspective avoids the pitfalls of envisaging the Commission as a single, unitary organisation, without having to abandon the idea of institutional self-interest. The institutional self-interest (or 'survival') argument, often advanced when it comes to explaining Commission activity (Moravcsik 1993; Fuchs 1995), is, while useful, not in itself very profound. It does not tell us much about the precise content of that self-interest. As has been pointed out, in the making of public policy, a complex interaction is going on between individual bureaucrats' self-interest and their institutional environment (Egeberg 1995). Charting the Commission's activity in terms of the demands put on it by democratic, intergovernmental and technocratic pressures helps to fill the notion of institutional self-interest with content. Crucially, it allows us to account better for its change over time.

Second, studying its internal dynamics will lead us to an understanding of differences within the Commission. It is a complex and varied institution, where organisational logics are not always compatible with each other. The coexistence of a number of distinct administrative traditions and policy styles (Richardson 1982; Burnham and Maor 1995), the autonomy of individual administrative units (Schink 1992), the way in which sectoral policies engender differing organisational cultures (Cini 2000), the persistence of national allegiance within 'inter-national' organisations (Egeberg 1999; Macdonald 2000) – all these are important in generating a comprehensive understanding of the European Commission.

Expansion and functional specialisation of the Commission's services

The European Commission is the product of a functionalist path of integration. While often seen as the champion of a federalist cause for Europe, its organisational design has largely been determined by the tasks it has had to fulfil within the European Union. As these have grown over time, so the Commission has grown in size and administrative specialisation. Commission services are organised in some 25 Directorates-General (DGs) and a number of centralised services which the Commission provides for the EU institutions (e.g. the Publication Office or the European Personnel Selection Office). These are predominantly sectoral in nature, that is, they provide for the specialised technical and administrative know-how in the various policy sectors in which the Union is active. In addition, there are 'horizontal' DGs which are dealing with cross-cutting concerns such as the budget, personnel or financial control. (Nugent 1995, 2001). The European External Action Service, the establishment of which is foreseen by the Constitutional Treaty, may in the future constitute a new institutional form bringing together officials from the Commission, the Council Secretariat and the member states.

As a result of this process of expansion and specialisation, it is probably fair to say that the Commission is now both too large and too small. It is too large considering Monnet's initial plans were for a moderate supranational agency with limited functional responsibility. It is too large also for those who want to see European integration as an intergovernmental affair that can do without expansive bureaucratisation at the centre. Yet, at the same time, the Commission's services are small in relation to both the size of national administrations and the size of the problems it has to address. It is also for these reasons of size, and because of constrained financial and administrative resources, that the Commission now operates largely regulatory policies.

Most of the Commission's competences relate to the regulation of the internal market. Creating and maintaining the 'four freedoms' – the free movement of capital, goods, services and persons – has precedence over the regulation of individual sectors. The Commission continues to spend considerable resources managing the coal and steel, agriculture and fisheries sectors, but the balance has been steadily tilting. With the implementation of the '1992' programme, overseeing deregulation on the national level and building up a corresponding European-wide regulatory framework has taken centre-stage inside the Commission. There are essentially three aspects to this issue: facilitating the abolition of national rules, policing the emerging single market, and developing minimum standards for those areas affected by deregulation.

The main task for the Commission here is in dealing with non-tariff barriers – the vast amount of national health, safety and trading standards inhibiting free trade and the free movement of production factors. In theory, there is a distinction to be made between the distortion of trade through illegitimate practices designed to benefit national producers, and the legitimate interests in social and environmental protection that member states may continue to undertake. In practice, member states had used taxes, technical and health standards for products and services, state subsidies and public procurement policies as subtle forms of protectionism, after tariffs and customs duties had been abolished.

A key tool in approaching this issue has been the mutual recognition principle, which the Commission first spelt out in its 1985 White Paper on the Single Market. Forcing all member states to allow trade in products once they have been licensed for trade in one member state, and the resulting process of regulatory competition, the introduction of this principle has allowed the Commission to concentrate on designing the minimum requirements that all products still have to fulfil, and on policing the market that is emerging (Majone 1993).

In this way, the Commission could leave the cumbersome process of harmonisation, which had bogged down Community activity in the decades before the Single Act, to market-led competition between member states' regulatory systems. It could then concentrate on the creation of the policy tools necessary to police the emerging market, and to devise auxiliary policies to provide for minimum standards in fields affected by deregulation. Yet even this was in many cases decentralised to bodies such as CEN and CENELEC – European-wide industry-based standardisation organisations seeking to develop non-binding standards for product safety and electrical appliances, respectively. Consensus on standards emerging from these private organisations would, once endorsed by the Commission, become de facto EU standards for the single market. Essentially, the Commission developed a policy of merely overseeing what became in many sectors market self-regulation.

Policing the internal market – which for the Commission has mainly meant the definition and application of rules for merger control and state aid control – has also become increasingly important. The Commission's DG Competition is widely seen as one of the most powerful sections of the administration. The direct, wide-ranging and open-ended powers given to the Commission in this field justify the observation that this is 'the first supranational policy of the Union' (McGowan and Wilks 1995). A legal scholar even likens the Commission, combining the roles of prosecutor and of judge in this policy field, to a 'leviathan' that must be 'bound' in the future (Brent 1995).

If the policing of the internal market has not been an uncontroversial process, then the same is true for the regulatory framework the Commission is building up to ameliorate its effects and provide for minimum social, environmental and health standards. Arguably, the Commission has often used the 'free movement' argument on a tenuous legal basis to build up additional competences. A result of this, and of subsequent treaty changes, are extensive policy competences in the education, environmental and social field, and policies which constitute more than simply a combat against non-tariff barriers (Pollack 1994; Eichener 1992; Mazey 1995).

The often uncertain legal basis, its limited financial resources and the sometimes hostile attitude of member states have forced the Commission to be innovative in going about the creation of such policy competences. The presence of a 'health and safety at work' clause in the Single Act, requiring only a qualified majority vote in the Council, has resulted in the Commission basing a whole host of social policies on this article rather than facing the national veto in the Social Chapter procedures (Cram 1993).

There is, however, more to the Commission's work than just the more or less extensive definition of the internal market programme. The Single Act had introduced, next to the 'four freedoms', Community competences in environmental policy and made the achievement of economic and social cohesion a goal of the integration process. The latter, in turn led to the reform and extension of structural funds for regional policy, the development of 'Trans-European Networks' and of a 'European Spatial Development Perspective' as well as the creation of the Cohesion Fund.

The reformed structural funds and the associated process of implementation and lobbying, in particular, brought state actors in direct contact with the Commission (Marks *et al.* 1996). The Commission actively assisted this 'partnership' by establishing an advisory committee composed of local and regional decision-makers (Hooghe 2000). The combined effect of these developments was, for the EU, the establishment of the Committee of the Regions in the TEU and for the Commission an involvement in European territorial politics.

Periodically expanding framework programmes for environment and research and development policy did much the same in these fields. Here, too, the Commission established direct links with affected actors in domestic systems: national administrations, business firms, universities, research institutes, interest and pressure groups. Again, the DGs involved increased in size and significance, but also had to resort to policy innovation and indeed experimentation in order to find a way of cooperating with often hesitant or reluctant national administrations.

After Maastricht, the Commission had accumulated competences in most fields that national administrations have traditionally controlled. In some areas, such as state aid control or the management of aid for Eastern Europe, the Commission's responsibilities are, in fact, unique even by national standards. In the hangover mood following the Maastricht ratification it came as little surprise, therefore, that questions should be asked about the 'limits' (Dehousse 1994) of this 'creeping' (Pollack 1994) extension of competences. In a variety of policy areas there were demands for 'decentralisation' – often little-disguised attempts at repatriation of Commission powers back to national administrations. At the same time, the Commission has had to accept the imposition of limitations set on its role even in areas like trade where its dominance had long been established (Meunier and Nicolaides 1999). In other areas in which the Commission had begun to acquire a recognised role – in particular CFSP/external relations (Nuttall 1996; Bruter 1999) and Treaty reform (Christiansen and Jørgensen 1998; Dinan 2000; Christiansen and Gray 2004) – it has to contend with the established role of the Council Secretariat. Further challenges to the 'community method' have come from the increased use of the Open Method of Coordination which tends to marginalise the role of the Commission.

Member states had already been attempting to regain some control over policy management and implementation through increased use of 'comitology' (Chapter 7, this volume). In addition, a growing number of 'Decentralised Community Agencies' were established from the early 1990s onwards (e.g. the European Environmental Agency in Copenhagen, the European Monitoring Centre for Drugs and Drug Addiction in Lisbon, and the European Agency for the Evaluation of Medicinal Products in London) – a development that received a new impetus with the agreement to create new agencies in the areas of transport, health and food safety since 2000.

Decentralised agencies are meant to facilitate the exchange of information and to prepare the harmonisation of national provisions in areas requiring detailed technical expertise. The creation of such agencies first appeared like an intrusion into what would otherwise have been the territory of the Commission, but now looks more like a sensible 'outsourcing' of specialised knowledge, allowing the Commission to concentrate on core tasks.

With respect to the impact of institutional changes elsewhere, it is worth mentioning the way in which the Council Secretariat has increased in significance as a result of recent treaty changes. The 'triple-hatting' of the Council's Secretary-General as 'Mr CFSP' and WEU Secretary-General, the establishment of a CFSP policy unit in the Secretariat and its partial merger with the WEU secretariat have turned the Secretariat into an important institution in its own right. The next step of this evolution, as foreseen by the Constitutional Treaty, may be the fusing of the posts of EU foreign minister and External Relations Commissioner, which, together with the creation of the External Action Service, will lead to a much closer cooperation between the two institutions. (see Chapter 7 in this volume).

The need for policy coordination

But it would be misleading to look just at the conflict between the Commission and the member states without also recognising the incidence of conflicts and bureaucratic politics within the Commission. The dual aim of the Union, to provide for an internal market and for economic and social cohesion – reminiscent of the earlier distinction between negative and positive integration – has also led to conflicts between the DGs in the Commission championing different objectives. Internal disputes between the environment and the internal market DGs about the stringency of environmental protection, or between the Competition and Regional Policy DGs about the degree of public support for poorer regions (Wishlade 1993), are prime examples in this respect. The point to be made is a straightforward one: far from being a unitary actor, the Commission is an internally much-fragmented organisation. The term 'multi-organisation' has been coined to capture the way in which different logics are being followed by different parts of the administration (Cram 1994).

Consequently, there are dangers of fragmentation: inter-institutional contacts and relations proliferate in specific sectoral areas, so that ultimately each DG has regular contact with 'its' working groups in the Council, with 'its' committee in Parliament, and, indeed, with 'its' specific policy 'constituency of interests' in European society or market-place. The emergence of 'epistemic communities' – the development of and emergence of shared values among dedicated policy-makers, -recipients, -advisers, and experts in a given field – is a recognisable phenomenon (Richardson 1996). The extent to which the Commission not only participates but actively encourages such transnational policy communities is only one side of the coin. The other side is the increasing difficulty of uniting the policy-making strands of various DGs behind a formal 'Commission line'. More significantly, perhaps, in addition to inter-institutional wrangles, deadlock *within* the Commission may be becoming an obstacle to Union decision-making.

Such intra-Commission conflict is not simply an issue for technocratic coordination. It affects the cohesion among Commissioners and, given the increasingly politicised nature of their work, leads to cabinet-style instances of 'bureaucratic politics' under the motto 'where you stand depends on where you sit' (Peters 1992; Page and Wouters 1994). It might well be a sign that it is because more power and significance now go with the job that it has become difficult for the Commissioners to avoid turf-battles and polit-ical differences. But, whatever the underlying reasons, this has not made it any easier for the Commission to carry out its mission.

If the Commission has matured from a small agency to an extended bureaucracy, then individual DGs have turned from organisational sub-sections into quasi-ministries in their own right. Consequently, insofar as the Commission has been able, also on behalf of the EC/EU as a whole, to project the image of 'corporate actor' (Kenis and Schneider 1987; Fuchs 1995), and indeed to continue functioning as a unified institution, it is impor-tant to look at the institutional arrangements which bind it together. There are a variety of procedures to counter such centrifugal trends.

First of all, there are various bureaucratic mechanisms to provide for the harmonisa-tion of Commission business. Most of these involve the Secretariat-General (SG), which is designed to coordinate the work of the various DGs. Its responsibility for coordinating the drafting of legislative texts within the Commission makes the SG the nerve-centre of the institution. The increasing difficulties of such horizontal coordination have led to suggestions for the development of the SG into something like a 'clearing-house' for the Commission's legislative proposals (Dehousse *et al.* 1992). Monitoring legislation, chairing the regular meetings of Directors-General, and representing the Commission in inter-institutional negotiations, the SG is the gatekeeper between the Commission's internal activities and its relations with other institutions.

Further mechanisms for coordinations are provided by the weekly meetings of Direc-tors-General, *chefs de cabinet* and deputy *chefs de cabinet*, respectively. The *cabinets*, the personal advisory staffs of each Commissioner, are primarily responsible for relaying information back and forth between the Commissioner's desk and the Directorate-General under his or her responsibility. In this sense they play a crucial part in the vertical integration of political and administrative spheres within the Commission. But in the post-1992 phase their role in the conduct of the Commission's horizontal coordina-tion has become equally, if not more, important. In monitoring policies conducted by other Commissioners and DGs, the *cabinet* members provide their Commissioner with the ability to keep track of the whole range of business at the weekly Commission meeting (Donnelly and Ritchie 1994; Ross 1994). This function is more than merely supportive of policy coordination: each Commissioner's capacity to follow and accept the whole of the Commission agenda is the necessary basis for the principle of collegiality – the acceptance that Commission decisions will be supported and defended collectively vis-à-vis other institutions and the general public.

Thus there are elaborate efforts that the Commission undertakes, through the formal 'inter-service consulation' procedure, but also at the Director-General and *chef de cabinet* level, to coordinate its policy-making activity internally. Yet the very need for such extensive coordination indicates the ways in which the Commission is different from ordinary bureaucracies. It lacks, in this context, a full-blown hierarchical structure: while the individual DGs provide the 'chain of command' which is traditionally associated with bureaucracies, the Commission – the college of Commissioners – is essentially a non-hierarchical body. Its members are equals, with equal voting rights, and their President a *primus inter pares*, even though, since Nice, the President's hand been strengthened in that he (or she) can request the resignation of individual Commissioners. However, that possibility is likely to remain an exceptional instrument meant for crises rather than the everyday work of the institutions.

What is crucially important in understanding the nature of the Commission is the principle of collegiality: individual Commissioners, unlike national ministers in some member states, are not meant to run their portfolio autonomously. Instead, decisions by the Commission are taken *collectively*: the entire college takes the decision (though that can be delegated to individual Commissioners or even Director-Generals for routine matters). Commission decisions require a simple majority of the college, though here as elsewhere in the Union the general practice is one of searching for common ground and maintaining a consensual approach. The collegiality principle also implies that a Commission decision, once taken by the college, must be supported by all Commissioners and that, in turn, all Commissioners take an interest in every portfolio.

This coordination imperative places considerable strain on *cabinets* of the President and the Commissioners as well as on the Secretariat-General. Their work to coordinate policy is not only directed at identifying overlap, closing gaps and avoiding inconsistency, but also at bringing the principle underlying the Commission's work – that the Commissioners speak with a collective voice – closer to becoming reality. The officials involved have to look as much sideways as they have to look up and down. Procedural delays and interdepartmental differences within the Commission are a result of this basic requirement for coordination. But there is also the positive effect of a culture of compromise and bargaining, which prepares the Commission well for the interinstitutional negotiations that follow. The internal process of policy coordination will probably have brought out the sensitive issues of a policy proposal, and the result is something that is less likely to offend Council and Parliament than any directive that might be the product of a single DG acting autonomously.

Problems of accountability and legitimacy

The re-emergence of a proactive and 'political' Commission from the late 1980s onwards, together with the more general critique of the Union's 'democratic deficit', meant that there has been increasing focus on the democratic credentials of the Commissioners and of the Commission President (Haaland Matlary 1997). The most immediate response has been a redefinition of the Parliament's powers of supervision vis-à-vis the Commission. Until Maastricht, parliamentary powers over the Commission were purely negative: the EP could, with a two-thirds majority, force the entire Commission to resign – a provision potentially so damaging that the Santer Commission chose to resign voluntarily rather than face such a vote in the EP.

For a long time, the EP had no say in the more 'positive' process of appointing the Commission. A number of reforms have since changed this situation. First, the change in the Commission's term of office – extending it to five years and making it run parallel to the parliamentary term – enhanced the potential for linking the Union's party politics and the appointment for the Commission. This linkage was not very strong during the 1994 European elections, and the 1999 election was overshadowed by the wider crisis of the Commission. However, the potential for a more dynamic relationship in the future is certainly there, especially as parties become more involved in the legitimation of Union politics (Hix 1995). In 2004, the debate preceding the selection of the Commission President illustrated that this had become an appointment that was not, any more, solely about the preferences of member states, but also that the choice of the Commission President needed to reflect the parliamentary majority.

One important development in this respect has been the investiture procedure, which requires the Commissioners-designate not just to undergo lengthy hearings in front of the respective committees of the European Parliament, but also to complete extensive questionnaires about their competence and their European credentials. The new investiture procedure may, in itself, not do much about the EU's 'democratic deficit' as long as the Parliament lacks a stronger link to the electorate (Hix 2000), but it is a reform that strengthens further the hand of the Parliament vis-à-vis the Commission. The revised procedure is part of an emerging model of appointments in the EU which provides the Parliament with considerable leverage vis-à-vis the EU's 'executive' (Jacobs 1999).

This turns the discussion to the more general area of the Commission's inter-institutional relations. Above we discussed the explosion of the Commission's contacts with interest groups and other non-governmental organisations during the past ten years. During the same time, the nature of interinstitutional relations between Commission, Council and Parliament has changed fundamentally. As we have seen, the Commission's relationship with the Parliament has become more adversarial as the EP's influence and self-confidence have increased – the traditional partners in the integration project are now also rivals (Westlake 1994).

The Commission's relations with the Council of Ministers have also become more structured, despite the balance between autonomy from national interference and dependence on member state support. One aspect of this has been the allocation of executive tasks to the Council Secretariat, as mentioned above. Another feature is the growth of what is now generally referred to as 'comitology'. Council and Commission share the executive function in the Union, and the preferred method of conducting the execution of policies is through the creation of specialised committees (Docksey and Williams 1994). With the expansion of Union competences, the 'comitology' structure has been greatly expanded: there are hundreds of these committees now, and their supervision – not to mention legitimation – has become increasingly difficult (Buitendijk and van Schendelen 1995). In a wider sense, the expansive layer of committees dealing with consultation, coordination, management and implementation can be seen as a form of joint governance of EU policies by Commission officials and member states representatives (Christiansen and Kirchner 2000).

Perhaps more importantly, the Commission's relations with the other institutions have been altered through successive changes to the legislative procedure, leading to the co-decision procedure becoming the standard procedure for adopting legislation in the first pillar. Co-decision requires constant communication and frequent mediation between the two legislative institutions. The Commission's role in this context is crucial not only with respect to its efforts of shepherding legislative proposals through the various stages of the procedure, but also to actively participate in the so-called 'trialogue', the tripartite negotiations between EP, Council and Commission if and when proposals come before the Conciliation Committee. It is a demanding role for the Commission which requires not only some flexibility in responding to member state positions that emerge in the course of the legislative procedure, but also good relations with MEPs and EP officials (Burns 2004).

The challenge of continuous institutional reform

The driving forces for the recent phase of reforming the Commission are derived from a mixture of external and internal pressures on the Union. Externally, the prospect of enlargement demanded institutional changes for almost a decade. Minor changes to the Commission resulted from successive treaty reforms, but – perhaps more significantly – internal reforms outside the treaty change became necessary because of the circumstances of the Santer Commission's resignation in 1999. The following Prodi Commission took office on a platform of reform, resulting in a White Paper on Commission Reform (European Commission 2000).

In fact internal reforms had already been initiated during Santer's Presidency (Peterson 1999), and to a limited extent the current reform programme is a continuation of earlier reforms. In the light of the events in 1999, there is now much greater impetus and political will to change the workings of the Commission. But at the more technical level, there are definite signs of continuity: for example, the DECODE exercise – a kind of internal census and survey of Commission staff and their occupation – was launched in October 1997, and its results informed Kinnock's reform programme (European Commission 1999b).

Further and far-reaching changes have become necessary in response to the report into mismanagement and corruption by the Committee of Independent Experts (Committee 1999) mentioned at the outset. These concern a number of issues both at the micro-level – in terms of internal auditing and accounting – as well as at the macrolevel – in terms of the redefinition of the relationship between Commission and Parliament. The former issues have been tied into the catalogue of reforms contained in the White Paper. The latter have in part been addressed by ad hoc arrangements between the new Commission President, the Commissioners and the European Parliament, and are in part on the agenda of treaty reform. Beyond, or rather below, the treaty reform process, the Commission sought to contribute to the debate about the future of European governance with the publication of the White Paper on European Governance, by proposing a more structured relationship between civil society and EU institutions, and in the process to re-position, and to legitimise, the European Commission as the central actor at the interface between societal demands and the EU legislative process (Tsakatika 2004).

The 1999 crisis could be seen to point in two quite different directions for the Commission: it could either be used to support the argument that the Commission is too unprofessional, badly organised and mismanaged to be entrusted with the high politics tasks with which it now deals on a daily basis – a rolling back of its competences and a greater degree of oversight by the member states would have been the logical response based on this reasoning. But the opposing view seems to have won out: that the Commission needs to be fundamentally reformed in order to be equipped for the tasks assigned to it by the member states.

In looking at the direction of these ongoing changes, three trends can be identified: the search for greater public accountability, a strengthening of internal hierarchy and an enhanced institutional independence for the Commission. These are, to some extent, interrelated developments, but reforms feed into each of these individually, making distinct trends discernible. There are further reform issues not captured by these trends, but they are of lesser significance in this context. The remainder of the section will discuss the direction of the Kinnock reforms in more detail.

In line with greater accountability to the public, the Commission is heading for a more hierarchical internal organisation. In part, the latter is a result of the former: if individual action is more clearly identifiable (thanks to greater transparency) and more likely to be subject to sanction (thanks to greater accountability), then the dynamics of command and control are more likely to respond. But there are also reform trends directly aiming at making the Commission more hierarchical and strengthening the role of the Commission President.

Beyond its aim of addressing the Commission's inherent need for coordination, the above-mentioned principle of collegiality has an important consequence: providing sustained leadership and giving direction to Commission affairs are extremely difficult to achieve. Traditionally, the lack of formal powers to 'govern' the Commission have been very challenging for successive holders of this office. The Commission President has to oversee an increasingly large administration and a diverse group of Commissioners. To advance, in this context, the course of European integration against at times sceptical national governments and an uncertain public takes special qualities. In retrospect it is perhaps fair to say that some of the previous Presidents failed in their task of actively promoting European integration. Much of what the Commission does and can do depends on the willingness of national governments to proceed with European integration. But the Commission President can exercise political leadership and thereby exert significant influence on the course of integration. Jacques Delors' two and a half terms in office are the best manifestation of this potential (Drake 1995).

What is important, in this respect, is that an effective Commission President's qualities must include not only a determination to advance the course of European integration, and an awareness of what is politically feasible, but also a relatively tight control over the institution itself. As is well documented (Ross 1994; Grant 1994), Delors' success as Commission President hinged also on his ability to 'run' the Commission itself. Towards this aim, the presence of a group of dedicated staff, in particular Delors' *chef de cabinet* Lamy, and Secretary-General Williamson, was critical in allowing Delors to streamline policy-making, to promote forcefully his strategy for a 'relaunch' of the Community and, ultimately, to enhance greatly the institutional standing of the Commission. A leadership role for the Commission depends therefore much on the individual choices made by the President in office – it is a capacity for leadership that depends on the utilisation of the Commission's resources (Nugent 1995).

Successive treaty revisions agreed at Amsterdam and Nice provided for two further changes here: first, that the designated Commission President now has to agree to the nominations of the other members of the Commissioners (Art. 158) and, second, that the Commission shall work under the 'political guidance' of the President (Art. 163). The President now also has a greater say in the allocations of portfolios to individual Commissioners.

Both Prodi and Barroso made use of his new power of 'political guidance' by appointing a number of new 'Commissioners' Groups', bringing a number of Commissioners together in order to oversee developments in a particular area (Reform, Inter-institutional Relations, External Relations, etc.). As these Groups are tasked with overseeing the coordination of Commission policy in a particular area, and since the Commission President reserves the right to attend and chair these Groups, they can be seen as a means not only of improved horizontal linkage of policy, but also of greater control of the college by the President.

During the Prodi Presidency there had also been a reform of the *cabinets*, with mixed results: what was first a demand to appoint a *chef de cabinet* of a different nationality was then downgraded to *chef* or deputy *chef* and eventually became a minimum requirement of three nationalities to be represented among the members in the *cabinet*. Allowing for the nationality of the Commissioner, this has meant the appointment of at least two non-nationals – which is one more than was required previously. The size of *cabinets* was also reduced to six members.

When Prodi took over as Commission President, he also initiated a territorial shift: Commissioners had to leave the Breydel Building, where until then the entire college had been residing, and were moved to new offices close to their respective services. While this assisted the vertical integration of the work done by DGs, *cabinet* and Commissioner, it made horizontal coordination among *cabinets* and the college more difficult and may thus have contributed to a more fragmented Commission. Barroso, upon taking office, reversed this decision and brought the college back together into the same building – conveniently just as the Commission was able to move back into the Berlaymont, its historical headquarters, which has been closed for refurbishment for some thirteen years.

Changes were also made at the top of the administrative level of the Commission. While a new rule that Director-Generals may not be of the same nationality as their Commissioner has led to some movement among the top grades (Peterson 2000), Kinnock has also stated on more than one occasion that the practice of 'flags on posts' (Spence 1994) will come to an end (European Commission 1999a). Given what was said earlier about the nature of appointments in the Commission, this development can be regarded as the beginning of a 'cultural revolution' (*European Voice* 1999). The effort to maintain broad geographical representation will remain, but it will be a matter for the Commission to decide who gets which job.

The reform White Paper, while talking the language of new public management, may yet make the Commission a more traditionally bureaucratic organisation, with greater central control over the activities of its various parts. At the same time, treaty changes and secular developments promise to make the college of Commissioners more like a traditional cabinet, with the ability of the President to direct, and dismiss, individual members. The sum product would be a more hierarchical institution.

The Nice Treaty included changes with regard to both the size of the Commission and the appointment of its President and its members. The question of the size of the Commission has been resolved in the following manner: from 2005 the Commission will include only one national from each member state. Implying the loss of a second Commissioner for the larger member states, this concession contributed to their demand to increase their relative voting power in the Council and the Parliament. As such, this reform of the Commission was part of the wider confrontation between smaller and larger member states at Nice.

Finally, the Nice Treaty also contained changes in the appointment procedure of the Commission President and Commissioners. The European Council is to select the Commission President, and the Council is to adopt the list of Commissioners, by qualified majority vote – a departure from the previous provision where these decisions required unanimity. President and Commissioners will be formally appointed by the Council by QMV, after they have received the approval by the European Parliament. This is a reform that may be seen to reduce the hold of individual member states over members of the Commission; the clear link between Commissioner and member state has, however, been reinforced through the new provisions mentioned above.

Dependence on support from the European Parliament has become more significant, whereas the Commission President now has greater freedom to act independently of guidance from national governments. It is important, however, to remember that, in the main, formal changes have been outlined here, and that informal influence from the member states is, if at all, only indirectly affected. But the formal changes are already quite significant, in that member states are increasingly bound to lose control over the appointment procedures, both at the Commissioner level and at the level of senior officials. The Treaty changes giving the Commission President new powers while making him (or her) more directly accountable to the EP ought to marginalise the role of member states – *once* the President has been nominated. As regards senior officials, it will have to be seen whether, after the turmoil of the initial changes, a new modus vivendi develops, or whether member states and/or informal networks based on nationality find a way to play the new system in a fashion similar to the old one.

Conclusion

The past decade has been an extremely turbulent period for the European Commission. At the outset was the ambitious and largely successful project by Jacques Delors to reposition the Commission within the system of EU governance. But the advances the Commission had made had been bought with credit, on the assumption that the Commission would in due course deliver efficient and accountable decision-making. At the end of the decade, the bills kept coming in, and the modest reforms offered by Jacques Santer were not enough to cover the debt. The year 1999 was a nadir for the European Commission, but it has also opened the door for a unique opportunity to overhaul the institution and restructure its place within the Union's architecture.

The wide-ranging reforms implemented under Prodi and Kinnock sought to modernise and 'streamline' the institution, and had to confront bureaucratic inertia, staff unions and the vested interests of national governments. The latter are bound to lose their privileged access to Commissioners and officials, if the Commission as a whole is to operate in a more transparent, accountable and 'consumer-oriented' fashion. But while direct access for member states may be waning, cooperation and coordination between Commission and Council Secretariat is becoming more important. More important still will be the Commission's relationship with the Parliament, not only in the extraordinary circumstances of investiture or potential dismissal, but also with respect to routine decision-making.

Beyond the formal process of internal reform, which had been largely completed by the time Barroso took office, there is the anticipation of further changes and challenges ahead. Apart from the implementation of the changes that would have been required by the Constitutional Treaty, if that was ratified, the new Commission also needs to manage the institutional impact of enlargement (Christiansen and Gray 2005). This concerns inter alia the impact that officials recruited from the new member states will have on the nature of the Commission's administration. There is, for example, the likely impact on language, with much greater use of English language rather than the traditional French among the new recruits. The whole culture of language use will be affected, both in terms of fewer languages used in internal meetings and documents (these already feature almost only French and English) and in terms of pressure on Commission staff to keep documents requiring translation as short as possible. Thus the counterintuitive effect of the arrival of new nationalities among the Commission staff, and the increase in the number of official languages may actually be a rationalisation of language use inside the Commission.

Similarly, one should also expect the arrival of new administrative cultures to challenge the traditional modus operandi in the Commission. This will most likely be a gradual change, but over time there is the expectation that the Commission will be transformed by thousands of new staff from Central and Eastern Europe. However, what the medium- to long-term impact of the arrival of different administrative traditions will be is difficult to predict. On the one hand, it may exacerbate the already fragmented nature of the Commission. Thus a significant number of new staff with a very different culture of public administration may be making their mark on the institution, just as the arrival of a wave of officials from Sweden did lead to a push for greater transparency in the work of the Commission. On the other hand, the new nationalities in the Commission may 'dilute' the existing patterns of different national cultures, proving better chances of the development of a genuine European administrative culture. And, last but not least, the arrival of new Commissioners will have an impact on the nature of politics in the college, suggesting a Commission that is becoming more liberal than interventionist. This trend has already been visible in initial moves by the Commission that indicated that regulatory activity might be curbed in comparison to the previous Commission. It was also reflected by Barroso when outlining his plans to the European Parliament, where he stated his intention to do less, but to do it better – incidentally a statement that sounded uncannily like Jacques Santer when he presented his programme some ten years earlier.

The Commission continues to face numerous challenges both internally and vis-à-vis the outside world. Recent reforms which have sought to make the institution leaner have yet to demonstrate their medium- and long-term effects, and the same is true with respect to the impact on enlargement. The need to communicate policies and institutional choices at the European level effectively to the wider public is greater than ever given the problems the Constitutional Treaty has been facing in the course of ratification, and thus communication has become a key task for the Barroso Commission. And while its role as a strategic leader in the public debate and the making of policies may have been waning in the post-Delors era, the Commission remains central to the European project. The high political profile of the Commission sits uneasily next to the growing need to maintain independence and to work closer together with the European Parliament, the Council Secretariat and the member states. The longstanding tension between politicisation and bureaucratisation is as alive as ever, and after a decade of sometimes significant reforms one may be forgiven for thinking of the famous dictum from Tommasi di Lampedusa's novel that 'everything has to change so that everything can remain the same'. It is a different Commission that has to face the new challenges of the twenty-first century, but it is also a Commission that is still subject to the tensions that have been inherent in this institution from the outset, and its remarkable development will continue to be driven by the dynamics resulting from the way these tensions play out in the future.

Acknowledgements

I am grateful for helpful comments and suggestions I received from Sonia Piedrafita and Beatrice Vaccari on a previous version of this chapter. The usual disclaimer applies, of course.

References

Brent, R. (1995) 'The Binding of Leviathan: The Changing Role of the European Commission in Competition Cases', *International and Comparative Law Quarterly* 44/2: 255–79.

Bruter, M. (1999) 'Diplomacy without a State: The External Delegations of the European Commission', *Journal of European Public Policy* 6/2: 183–205.

Buitendijk, G. and van Schendelen, M. P. C. M. (1995) 'Brussels Advisory Committees: A Channel of Influence?', *European Law Review* 20/1: 37–58.

Burnham, J. and Maor, M. (1995) 'Converging Administrative Systems: Recruitment and Training in EU Member States', *Journal of European Public Policy* 2/2: 185–204.

Burns, C. (2004) 'Co-decision and the European Commission: A study of declining influence?', *Journal of European Public Policy*, 11/1: 1–18

Christiansen, T. (1997) 'Tensions of European Governance: Politicised Bureaucracy and Multiple Accountability in the European Commission', *Journal of European Public Policy* 4/1: 73–90.

Christiansen, T. and Gray, M. (2004) 'The European Commission and Treaty Reform', *Eipascope* 2004/1

—— (2005) 'The European Commission in a period of change: A new administration for the wider European Union?', *Eipascope* 2005/1.

Christiansen, T. and Jørgensen, K. E. (1998) 'Negotiating Treaty Reform in the European Union: The Role of the European Commission', *International Negotiation* 3/4: 435–52.

Christiansen, T. and Kirchner, E. (eds) (2000) *Committee Governance in the European Union* (Manchester: Manchester University Press).

Cini, M. (2000) 'Administrative Culture in the European Commission', in N. Nugent (ed.), *At the Heart of the Union: Studies of the European Commission*, 2nd edn (Basingstoke: Macmillan).

Committee of Independent Experts (1999) *First Report into Allegations regarding Fraud, Misman-agement and Nepotism in the European Commission* (Brussels).

Coombes, D. (1970) *Politics and Bureaucracy in the European Community: A Portrait of the Euro-pean Commission* (London: George Allen and Unwin).

Cram, L. (1993) 'Calling the Tune without Paying the Piper? Social Policy Regulation: The Role of the Commission in European Community Social Policy', *Politics and Policy* 21/3: 135–46.

—— (1994) 'The European Commission as a Multi-organization: Social Policy and IT Policy in the EU', *Journal of European Public Policy* 1/2: 194–217.

Dehousse, R. (1994) 'Community Competences: Are There Limits to Growth?', in R. Dehousse (ed.), *Europe After Maastricht: An Ever Closer Union?* (Munich: Law Books in Europe/C. H. Beck).

Dehousse, R., Joerges, C., Majone, G. and Snyder, F. (1992) *Europe after 1992: New Regulatory Strategies (EUI Working Paper LAW No. 92/31)* (Florence: European University Institute).

Dinan, D. (2000) 'The European Commission and the Intergovernmental Conference', in N. Nugent (ed.), *At the Heart of the Union: Studies of the European Commission*, 2nd edn (Basingstoke: Macmillan).

Docksey, C. and Williams, K. (1994) 'The Commission and the Execution of Community Policy', in D. Edwards and G. Spence (eds), *The European Commission* (London: Longman).

Donnelly, M. and Ritchie, E. (1994) 'The College of Commissioners and their Cabinets', in D. Edwards and G. Spence (eds), *The European Commission* (London: Longman).

Drake, H. (1995) 'Political Leadership and European Integration: The Case of Jacques Delors', *West European Politics* 18/1: 140–60.

Egeberg, M. (1995) 'Bureaucrats as Public Policy-Makers and their Self-Interest', *Journal of Theo-retical Politics* 7/2: 157–67.

—— (1999) 'Transcending Intergovernmentalism? Identity and Role Perceptions of National Offi-cials in EU Decision-making', *Journal of European Public Policy* 6/3: 456–74.

Eichener, V. (1992) *Social Dumping or Innovative Regulation? (EUI Working Paper SPS No. 92/28)*, paper prepared for the European University Institute, Florence.

European Commission (1999a) *Communication from Neil Kinnock to the European Commission: Some Strategic Reform Issues (SEC (99) 1917/2)* (Brussels).

—— (1999b) *Designing Tomorrow's Commission: A Review of the Commission's Organisation and Operation* (Brussels).

—— (2000) *Reforming the Commission*, White Paper (Brussels).

European Voice (1999) 'Commission Needs a "Cultural Revolution"', 29 July: 5.

Financial Times (2000) 'Prodi's Progress', 18 January: 9.

Fuchs, G. (1995) 'The European Commission as a Corporate Actor? European Telecommunica-tions Policy After Maastricht', in S. Rhodes and C. Mazey (eds), *The State of the European Union*, vol. 3 (Boulder, CO: Lynne Rienner).

Grant, C. (1994) *Delors: Inside the House that Jacques Built* (London: Brealey).

Grey, S. (2000) *Tackling Fraud and Mismanagement in the European Union*, paper prepared for the Centre for European Reform, London.

Haaland Matlary, J. (1997) 'Democratic Legitimacy and the Role of the Commission', in P. Koslowski and A. Foellesdal (eds), *Democracy and the EU* (Berlin: Springer).

Hix, S. (1995) 'Parties at the European Level as an Alternative Source of Legitimacy: The Party Federations and the EU Socio-Economic Agenda', *Journal of Common Market Studies* 33/4: 527–54.

—— (2000) 'Executive Selection in the European Union: Does the Commission President Investi-ture Procedure Reduce the Democratic Deficit', in K. Neunreithner and A. Wiener (eds), *European Integration after Amsterdam* (London: Routledge).

Hooghe, L. (2000) 'A House with Differing Views: The European Commission and Cohesion Policy', in N. Nugent (ed.), *At the Heart of the Union: Studies of the European Commission*, 2nd edn (Basingstoke: Macmillan).

Jacobs, F. (1999) *Nominations and Appointments: An Evolving EU Model*, paper prepared for the Biennial ECSA Conference, Pittsburgh.

Kenis, P. and Schneider, V. (1987) 'The EC as an International Corporate Actor: Two Case Studies in Economic Diplomacy', *European Journal of Political Research* 15/4: 437–57.

Laffan, B. (1997) 'From Policy-Entrepreneur to Policy-Manager: The Challenge Facing the European Commission', *Journal of European Public Policy* 4/3: 422–38.

Levy, R. (2000) 'Managing the Managers: The Commission's Role in the Implementation of Spending Programmes', in N. Nugent (ed.), *At the Heart of the Union: Studies of the European Commission*, 2nd edn (Basingstoke: Macmillan).

Macdonald, M. (2000) 'Identities in the European Commission', in N. Nugent (ed.), *At the Heart of the Union: Studies of the European Commission*, 2nd edn (Basingstoke: Macmillan).

McGowan, L. (2000) 'Safeguarding the Economic Constitution: The Commission and Competition Policy', in N. Nugent (ed.), *At the Heart of the Union: Studies of the European Commission*, 2nd edn (Basingstoke: Macmillan).

McGowan, L. and Wilks, S. (1995) 'The First Supranational Policy of the European Union: Competition Policy', *European Journal of Political Research* 28/2: 141–69.

MacMullen, A. (2000) 'European Commissioners: National Routes to a European Elite', in N. Nugent (ed.), *At the Heart of the Union: Studies of the European Commission*, 2nd edn (Basingstoke: Macmillan).

Majone, G. (1993) 'The European Community between Social Policy and Social Regulation', *Journal of Common Market Studies* 31/2: 153–70.

Mak, J. (2004) 'Informality as an Asset? The Case of EMU', in T. Christiansen and S.Piattoni (ed.), *Informal Governance in the European Union* (Cheltenham: Edward Elgar).

Marks, G., Nielsen, F., Ray, L. and Salk, J. E. (1996) 'Competencies, Cracks, and Conflicts: Regional Mobilization in the European Union', *Comparative Political Studies* 29/2: 164–91.

Mazey, S. (1992) 'Conception and Evolution of the High Authority's Administrative Services (1952–1956): From Supranational Principles to Multinational Practices', in E. Heyen with G. Melis, J.-L. Mestre, V. Wright and B. Wunder (eds), *Jahrbuch der Europäischen Verwaltungsgeschichte, 4: Die Anfänge der Verwaltung der Europäischen Gemeinschaft* (Baden-Baden: Nomos).

—— (1995) 'The Development of EU Equality Policies: Bureaucratic Expansion on behalf of Women?', *Public Administration* 73/4: 591–610.

Mazey, S. and Richardson, J. (1994) 'The Commission and the Lobby', in D. Edwards and G. Spence (eds), *The European Commission* (London: Longman).

Mendrinou, M. (1996) 'Non-compliance and the European Commission's Role in Integration', *Journal of European Public Policy* 3/1: 1–22.

Meunier, S. and Nicolaidis, K. (1999) 'Who Speaks for Europe? The Delegation of Trade Authority in the EU', *Journal of Common Market Studies* 37/3: 477–501.

Moravcsik, A. (1993) 'Preferences and Power in the European Community: A Liberal Intergovernmentalist Approach', *Journal of Common Market Studies* 31/4: 473–523.

Nugent, N. (1995) 'The Leadership Capacity of the European Commission', *Journal of European Public Policy* 2/4: 603–23.

—— (2000) *At the Heart of the Union: Studies of the European Commission*, 2nd edn (Basingstoke: Macmillan).

—— (2001) *The European Commission* (Basingstoke: Palgrave).

Nuttall, S. (1996) 'The Commission: The Struggle for Legitimacy', in C. Hill (ed.), *The Actors in Europe's Foreign Policy* (London: Routledge).

Page, E. and Wouters, L. (1994) 'Bureaucratic Politics and Political Leadership in Brussels', *Public Administration* 72/3: 445–59.

Peters, G. (1992) 'Bureaucratic Politics in the European Community', in A. Sbragia (ed.), *Europolitics: Institutions and Policymaking in the 'New' European Community* (Washington, DC: Brookings Institution).

119

Peters, G. (2000) 'The Commission and Implementation in the European Union', in N. Nugent (ed.), *At the Heart of the Union: Studies of the European Commission*, 2nd edn (Basingstoke: Macmillan).

Peterson, J. (1999) 'The Santer Era: The European Commission in Normative, Historical and Theoretical Perspective', *Journal of European Public Policy* 6/1: 46–65.

—— (2000) 'Romano Prodi: Another Delors?', *ECSA Review* 13/1: 1–8.

Pollack, M. (1994) 'Creeping Competence: The Expanding Agenda of the European Community', *Journal of Public Policy* 14/2: 95–145.

Pollit, C. (1988) 'Bureaucracy and Democracy', in D. Held and C. Pollit (eds), *New Forms of Democracy* (London: Sage).

Rhinard, M. and Vaccari, B., 'The Study of the European Commission', *Journal of European Public Policy* 12/2.

Richardson, J. (1982) *Policy Styles in Western Europe* (London: Allen & Unwin).

—— (1996) 'Actor Based Models of National and EC Policy-Making: Policy Communities, Issue Networks and Advocacy Coalitions', in H. Kassim and A. Menon (eds), *The EU and National Industrial Policy* (London: Routledge).

Ross, G. (1994) *Jacques Delors and European Integration* (Cambridge: Polity Press).

Scheinmann, L. (1966) 'Some Preliminary Notes on Bureaucratic Relationships in the European Economic Community', *International Organisation* 20/4: 750–73.

Schink, G. (1992) 'Kompetenzerweiterung im Handlungsystem der Europäischen Gemeinschaft: Eigendynamik und "policy-entrepreneure"', unpublished Ph.D. thesis, Florence.

Schmidt, S. (2000) 'Only an Agenda-Setter?', *European Union Politics* 1/1: 37–61.

Snyder, F. (1993) *Soft Law and Institutional Practice in the European Community (EUI Working Paper LAW No. 93/5)* (Florence: European University Institute).

Spence, D. (1994) 'Structure, Functions and Procedures in the Commission', in D. Edwards and G. Spence (eds), *The European Commission* (London: Longman).

—— (2000) 'Plus ça change, plus c'est la même chose? Attempting to reform the European Commission', *Journal of European Public Policy* 7/1: 1–25.

Trondal, J. (2001) *The 'Parallel Administration' of the European Commission*, Paper presented at the ECPR Joint Sessions of Workshops, Grenoble, April 2001.

Tsakatika, M. (2004) 'Claims to Legitimacy: The European Commission between Continuity and Change', *Journal of Common Market Studies* 43/1: 193–220

Wallace, W. and Smith, J. (1995) 'Democracy or Technocracy? European Integration and the Problem of Popular Consent', *West European Politics* 18/3: 137–57.

Westlake, M. (1994) *The Commission and the Parliament: Partners and Rivals in the European Policy-making Process* (London: Butterworth).

Wishlade, F. (1993) 'Competition Policy, Cohesion and the Coordination of Regional Aids in the European Community', *European Competition Law Review* 14/4: 143–50.

Woolcock, S. (2000) 'European Trade Policy', in H. Wallace and W. Wallace (eds), *Policy-making in the European Union*, 4th edn (Oxford: Oxford University Press).

Chapter 6

Fluctuant nec merguntur [1]

The European Parliament, national parliaments, and European integration

KATRIN AUEL AND BERTHOLD RITTBERGER

Introduction: the de-parliamentarisation of politics?

The thesis about a 'decline of legislatures' is nothing new to political scientists. As early as 1921, Bryce was claiming that the 'admiration of and confidence in the system of representative democracy' had experienced a phase of decline (Bryce 1921: 367), even though the sources of this alleged decline were of a different nature than those that fuel the contemporary debate about 'de-parliamentarisation' in advanced industrial democracies. Yet, despite an increase of public interest in political affairs in general, this growing interest does not translate into activities traditionally associated with support for representative, parliamentary democracy. Evidence of a 'spreading dissatisfaction with the institutions and processes of representative democracy' (Dalton *et al*. 2003: 1) is reflected in declining turnout at elections, a creeping erosion of the membership base of political parties and waning confidence in politicians, political parties and political institutions.[2] Underlying this growing public disaffection with the model of representative, parliamentary democracy is what might be called an expectations–capability gap from which parliamentary institutions in advanced industrial democracies suffer and which contributes to the above-mentioned crisis symptoms. While publics in democratic polities across the world (still) consider parliaments to be the 'major basis for legitimising political authority and legislation' (Burns 2000), they appear to be increasingly ill-equipped to meet public demands and expectations. Parliamentary institutions around the world are said to be increasingly marginalised and displaced from major legislative and policy-making activities as a consequence of socio-economic and political forces which continue to transform the conditions under which policy-making takes place. For instance, the growing scientification of politics and the tendency to increasingly rely on expertise, and – in a world characterised by socio-economic interdependencies – the expanding role of governmental and, more importantly, non-governmental organisations and transnational corporations, have produced a situation in which 'major legislative and policy-making activities are being substantially displaced from parliamentary bodies' (Burns 2000). Ralf Dahrendorf sums up the contemporary mood, claiming that 'representative government is no longer as compelling a proposition as it once was. Instead, a search for new institutional forms to express conflicts of interest has begun' (Dahrendorf 2000: 311). At the same time, democratic decision-making 'is moving toward new forms of more direct involvement in the political process' (Dalton *et al*. 2003: 2) with publics and political groups placing more emphasis on direct forms of citizen participation through citizen initiatives and referenda as well as on improving the possibilities for citizen consultation and public hearings.

Against this background, we will ask in this chapter whether the process of European integration affects or even exacerbates the 'de-parliamentarisation' trend. For instance, it is often argued that national executives, represented in the Council of Ministers, play the key role in EU policy-making while, at the same time, national parliaments have only limited opportunity to scrutinise and control their executives in EU matters.[3] This problem becomes ever more pressing once EU member states transfer decision-making competencies from the domestic to the EU level to cover ever more policy areas. Most regulatory policy decisions (affecting the movement of goods, services, capital and persons, competition rules, product standards etc.) and monetary policy decisions are presently taken at the EU level. Even in the realm of expenditure polices (including agriculture, regional development, research, social welfare and so forth), a significant number of policies are presently taken at the EU level (see Hix 2005). This trend towards 'centralisation' of policy-making has, as some claim, short-circuited national parliaments' ability to shape public policies. Klaus von Beyme found that about one-fifth of all legislation which passed through the German Bundestag during the 1990–1994 period had had an 'impulse' from the EU level, i.e. it was based on EU directives which national parliaments had to transpose into national law (von Beyme 1998: 25).[4] Seen in this light, European integration can be said to provide an additional impetus for the process of 'de-parliamentarisation' or *Entparlamentarisierung* (Börzel 2000).[5]

Even though we do not dispute this assessment in general, this chapter takes issue with the 'de-parliamentarisation' thesis. It does so by considering two developments, which, from the perspective of a proponent of the model of parliamentary democracy, add some brightness to an otherwise rather gloomy scene. First, we turn to the European Parliament. Even a cursory glance at the European Parliament's role in EU decision-making raises the question of how the 'de-parliamentarisation' thesis can be squared with the growing importance attributed to the European Parliament in legislative decision-making over the past two decades. Second, we ask how national parliaments have responded to the challenges of European integration and provide evidence that national parliaments are anything but moribund as a consequence of the integration process.

The European Parliament: defying the crisis of parliamentary democracy

What we have learned

In previous editions of *European Union: Power and Policy-Making* the contributions by Earnshaw and Judge (1996) and Bergman and Raunio (2001) have focused chiefly on the European Parliament's role in the EU's legislative decision-making process. Their contributions form part of a research programme that has left a firm imprint on the study of European integration in the past decade. Driving this programme was the question about the changing influence of the European Parliament relative to the other EU actors, the Commission and the Council, in the legislative decision-making process. Since the adoption of the Single European Act (SEA), the European Parliament's influence over EU legislation has increased steadily. The (then) newly introduced *cooperation* procedure, which used to be applied in most areas of single market-legislation, supplemented – from the Parliament's perspective – the rather inconsequential *consultation* procedure. The move from consultation to cooperation effectively endowed the European Parliament with what George Tsebelis has famously termed 'conditional agenda-setting power': the right for the European Parliament to propose amendments in a second reading of the legislative decision-making process, which – if supported by the Commission – can only be overturned by a unanimous Council, but can be accepted by the Council by a qualified majority (Tsebelis 1994). Legislation amended by the European Parliament, the argument runs, is thus easier for the Council to accept (it can do so by qualified majority) than to reject or amend (for which it needs unanimity).[6] It is undisputed among practitioners and scholars that the introduction of the cooperation procedure represented both a *quantitative* and a *qualitative* leap for the European Parliament as regards the *scope* and *impact* of its actions on Community legislation.[7] Empirical evidence demonstrates that the European Parliament was able to exercise considerable influence on the substance of important pieces of Community legislation, which it most likely would have not been able to exercise under the consultation procedure.[8] Following the Maastricht Treaty and the introduction of the new *co-decision* procedure, the European Parliament was given the power to unconditionally veto legislation. In the academic literature, there has been a virulent controversy whether the veto power actually marked an improvement for the European Parliament in legislative decision-making (Crombez *et al.* 2000, Garrett *et al.* 2001) since the co-decision in its Maastricht version gave the Council the right, failing successful conciliation between representatives of the Council and the European Parliament, to present the European Parliament with a 'take it or leave it'-proposal. Some scholars have argued that on average the European Parliament would be inclined to accept rather than reject a Council proposal as long as the question about the advancement of European integration remained the dominant dimension of political contention (Garrett and Tsebelis 1996, Tsebelis and Garrett 2000). Empirical findings, however, provide little support for the proposition that co-decision implied a backwards step for the European Parliament.[9] Finally, the reform of the co-decision procedure at Amsterdam, which rid co-decision of the possibility for the Council to re-introduce its common position after a break-down of the conciliation committee, put the Council and European Parliament on equal footing.

In sum, given the European Parliament's role as 'co-equal legislator' (Tsebelis and Garrett 2000: 15), its increasingly prominent role in the investiture of the Commission, as well as its role as twin-arm of the budgetary authority, it is hardly controversial to claim that – in terms of its powers and functions – the European Parliament resembles national parliaments more than its international counterparts. Consequently, comparisons between the European Parliament and *national* parliaments assume an ever more prominent place in the literature.[10] Endowed with legislative, budgetary and 'executive' control powers, comparisons between other parliamentary assemblies in international organisations – which play a merely consultative role – and the European Parliament are exercises of a distant past.

Where, then, 'does the contemporary European Parliament stand in comparison to other institutions, others in the genus "legislatures" and "parliaments"?', asks Roger Scully (2000: 229) According to Michael Mezey, parliaments are 'salient in the policy-making process to the extent that their presence and prerogatives act as a constraint on the executive' (1979: 25). The power of a parliament to constrain the executive is 'grounded primarily in an ability to exercise a veto over policy proposals, and secondarily in being able to modify them short of veto' (Scully 2000: 236). Norton has advanced a distinction between policy-*making* and policy-*influencing* legislatures to point at the differences displayed by parliaments in their capacity to constrain the executive. Policy-*making* legislatures are able to modify or reject government measures as well as to formulate and substitute a policy for that proposed by the government (see Norton 1990), whereas policy-*influencing* legislatures have more modest policy-making powers. While they possess the capacity to reject or amend measures by the government, they lack the ability to promote their own agenda vis-à-vis the executive. Since the adoption of the SEA, the formal powers of the European Parliament allow us to qualify it as a policy-making legislature, which can amend and, under certain conditions, even reject legislation. In noting the extent and nature of these formal powers, however, we may overlook the fact that the European Parliament, in contrast to most national legis-latures, actually uses its formal powers to their fullest possible extent. The separation of the European Parliament from the executive (as in a presidential system), and the absence of a dominant majority or coalition inside the European Parliament, enable the European Parliament to exploit its powers much more effectively than national legisla-tures in parliamentary systems. Scully thus concludes that 'the policy influence wielded by the EP is surely greater than that of most national chambers in the EU', and that, consequently, the European Parliament 'deserves to be ranked at least towards the upper end of the category of "policy influencer"' (2000: 238–9).

How did it get there? The legislative empowerment of the European Parliament[11]

The reasons for the European Parliament's gradual empowerment remain obscure. Scholarship on the European Parliament has taken its powers as given. The aforemen-tioned literature on EU legislative decision-making, for instance, looks at the effects of changes in the formal power distribution among Commission, Council and Parliament, yet it does not treat the changes in the European Parliament's powers as a problem to be explained. It is the task of this section to illuminate the motivations that led policy-makers from EU member states to empower the European Parliament. Table 6.1 offers an overview of the changes in the Treaties as far as they affected the European Parlia-ment's legislative powers. In the following paragraphs, we present a theoretical argu-ment which sheds some light on why the member state governments increased the European Parliament's legislative powers and offer evidence to demonstrate the plausi-bility of this argument.

With the gradual growth of the EU's policy-making powers – resulting from the ongoing transfers of sovereignty (through the delegation of powers to suprana-tional 'agents' and pooling by introducing qualified majority voting) – the EU has come to exercise functions that, traditionally, belonged to the domain of nation

Table 6.1 The European Parliament and EU legislative decision-making

	Role of the European Parliament and legal base
Single European Act (1986)	Introduction of 'cooperation' (Art. 189C EEC) and 'assent' procedures (applies, e.g., to association agreements and accession of new Member States)
Maastricht Treaty (1991)	Introduction of co-decision procedure (Art. 189B ECT), extension of other procedures
Treaty of Amsterdam (1997)	Reform and extension of co-decision procedure (Art. 251 ECT)
Treaty of Nice (2000)	Extension of co-decision procedure (Art. 251 ECT)
Treaty establishing a Constitution for Europe (2004)	Co-decision declared to be 'ordinary legislative procedure' (Art. I–34, 1 and Art. III–396)

states. Against this background, Robert Dahl has observed that the process of European integration presents the European publics and its political leaders with a 'fundamental democratic dilemma' (Dahl 1994: 23). Dahl argues that wherever and whenever democratic polities are subjected to significant socio-economic or security challenges which cannot be managed unilaterally, political elites face a trade-off. On the one hand, they could enhance the capacity of their polity to deal with these challenges effectively by increasing the size of their political unit (i.e. through inter- or supranational cooperation); on the other hand, they thereby risk that citizens' and their representatives' ability to influence the government through direct or indirect participation diminishes (with increasing unit size). In democracy theoretic terms, this 'democratic dilemma' can be translated into a *legitimacy deficit* defined as an imbalance between *output* and *input* legitimacy. What does this mean specifically? Democratic theorists agree that the maintenance of and compliance with political order can only be guaranteed by balancing input and output legitimacy. Input-oriented legitimacy emphasises that 'political choices are legitimate if and because they reflect the "will of the people" – that is, if they can be derived from the authentic preferences of the members of a community' (Scharpf 1999: 6). Output legitimacy, on the other hand, highlights that 'political choices are legitimate if and because they effectively promote the common welfare of the constituency in question' (ibid.). The ongoing transfers of sovereignty through pooling and delegation to deal with challenges of security or socio-economic interdependencies have left democratic processes, on the domestic and European level, not unchallenged. Bernhard Wessels claims that a transfer of sovereignty to the supranational level 'naturally raises the democratic question of how the system of institutions exercising this power is to be controlled and held accountable' (Wessels 1999: 2). Given the far-reaching competencies of EU institutions, the democratic legitimacy of the evolving EU polity is considered a key concern by national political elites. According to a survey conducted in 1996 and asked about their satisfaction with the workings of democracy in the EU (as opposed to the domestic level), 50 per cent of the respondents among national Members of Parliament (MPs) from eleven Community countries were 'not very satisfied' (40 per cent) or 'not satisfied at all' (10 per cent). In contrast, when asked about the workings of democracy in their own countries, only 20 per cent of the respondents among national MPs were not satisfied (Wessels 1999: Table 1; see also European Commission 1998).

The argument advanced here suggests, therefore, that during episodes of sovereignty-transfers, political elites are likely to perceive the legitimacy deficit – the looming asymmetry between output and input legitimacy – as particularly pertinent. While the EU member states are concerned with the pooling and delegation of sovereignty to manage socio-economic and security interdependencies so as to enhance the EU's problem-solving capacity (and thereby increase the polity's output legitimacy), traditional channels for citizen participation and interest representation come increasingly under stress. For instance, if member states pool sovereignty (via the adoption of qualified majority voting), concerns about input legitimacy are likely to be mirrored in the expression of the following questions which are brought before domestic political elites: How does pooling affect the channels of democratic participation and domestic parliamentary prerogatives? Who are national governments accountable to when portions of their decision-making powers are pooled?

In summary, transfers of sovereignty are likely to produce an asymmetry between input and output legitimacy ('legitimacy deficit'). The empirical question now is whether the subsequent decisions by member states to enhance the European Parliament's legislative powers since the mid-1980s have actually been caused by the concern about alleviating the legitimacy deficit once pooling and delegation loom.

The socio-economic and political forces leading to the adoption of the SEA have been well documented.[12] The literature, however, remains mute on the question of how to account for national governments' decisions to agree to a broadening of the European Parliament's legislative powers by endowing it with 'conditional agenda-setting power' (Tsebelis 1994) in the newly designed cooperation procedure. Recalling the proposition elaborated above, we expect pooling and delegation of national sovereignty to produce an asymmetry between output and input legitimacy, and, in turn, we would expect political elites to make proposals for its remedy (see Rittberger 2005: 51–7). The introduction of qualified majority voting in the Council and its application to virtually all matters relating to the creation of an internal market was one of the quintessential features of the SEA. All national governments came to the conclusion (even though it took some 'convincing' of the British government) that this large extent of pooling sovereignty was acceptable or even desirable given the objective to pass almost 300 pieces of Community legislation until the end of 1992, the target date for the completion of the internal market. Pooling was thus expected to partly fulfil the function of speeding up decision-making by making it more demanding to muster a blocking minority and also to demonstrate the member states' commitment to advance the internal market programme (see Moravcsik 1998: chapter 5). Overall, pooling had become a crucial underpinning of the EU's 're-launch' in the mid-1980s.

However, as we hypothesised, pooling 'did not come alone'. Although certain national governments, members of national parliaments and the European Parliament have, throughout the 1980s, consistently criticised that the EU suffered from a democratic legitimacy deficit (see Corbett 1998), it was the impending introduction of qualified majority voting and the ensuing prospect for a reform of the EEC Treaty, that made the prospect of an empowerment of the European Parliament in the legislative domain increasingly likely. There is ample evidence that domestic political elites were well aware of the link between the proposals for pooling and the concomitant challenges to *input* legitimacy. For example, at the European Council summit meeting in Fontainebleau in June 1984, the member states set up an ad hoc committee – the so-called 'Dooge Committee' – composed of personalities appointed by the member state governments to discuss the pressing issues of deeper cooperation and institutional reform. In its final report to the Brussels European Council in late March 1985, the committee advocated, *inter alia*, the creation of a 'fully integrated internal market' and simultaneous institutional reform in order to achieve the policy goals set out by the report. A plea was made for the provision of more 'efficient' but also for more 'democratic' institutions. A majority of member state representatives wanted the European Parliament to play a more prominent role in the EU's legislative process once the member states opted for qualified majority voting (pooling of sovereignty).[13] Domestic parliamentary debates and resolutions equally reflected the awareness that the introduction of pooling would exacerbate the 'legitimacy deficit'.[14] In France, for instance, the centre-right politician Adrien Zeller (UDF – Union pour la démocratie française) emphasised that 'the only means to re-establish democratic control of such decisions [which henceforth escape national parliamentary control] is to endow the European Parliament with the means not just to *influence* Community decisions but also to *legitimise* them by its votes'.[15] In Germany, the governing Christian Democrats (CDU/CSU) and Liberals (FDP) as well as the opposition Social Democrats (SPD) were very explicit about the challenges further pooling posed for input legitimacy. The chair of the EC Committee, Renate Hellwig (CDU), criticised the executive dominance prevalent in EU decision-making processes and concluded that in order to alleviate the perceived legitimacy deficit the legislative powers of the European Parliament had to be increased.[16] Overall, a number of national governments, pressured by the domestic political parties and the European Parliament alike, invoked the need to compensate national democratic constituencies for the prospective increase in EU level-induced legislation 'escaping' domestic parliamentary control once qualified majority voting became a reality by strengthening the legislative powers of the European Parliament. The prospect of pooling sovereignty through the introduction of qualified majority voting at the SEA thus increased the demands for alleviating the widening asymmetry between output and input legitimacy.

This logic was also at work in the negotiations leading towards the adoption of the Treaty of Maastricht. During the intergovernmental conference, member state governments agreed on the extension of qualified majority voting to new policy areas. This prospect prompted national governments and domestic political parties to activate the link between the extension of qualified majority voting (pooling) and enhancing the European Parliament's legislative role in areas where qualified majority voting was to apply. Although some member states opposed the European Parliament's demand for legislative 'co-decision' – whereby Denmark and the United Kingdom, in particular, were anxious that the relative influence of the European Parliament over the substance of legislation would be increased – there was widespread agreement on the basic principle that the European Parliament should be able to exercise influence in legislative decision-making wherever EU policies were decided by majority vote.[17] After Maastricht, the intergovernmental conferences that led to the adoption of the Amsterdam and Nice Treaties did not see serious efforts by member state governments to dispute the link between extending qualified majority voting and including the European Parliament in the legislative process.[18] Disagreement, however, continued to be pungent regarding the scope of the European Parliament's influence and the scope to which qualified majority voting should be extended to new policy areas. In Nice for instance, the extension of qualified majority voting to policy areas hitherto governed by the unanimity rule was sparse and thus was the extension of the co-decision procedure and, in consequence, the 'sectoral' extension of the European Parliament's legislative powers.[19] In the light of the imminent enlargement, the member state governments drafted Declaration No. 23, attached to the Nice Treaty, in which they called for an encompassing debate about the future of the EU as a result of which 'a simplification of the Treaties with a view to making them clearer and better understood without changing their meaning' should ensue.[20] Following the European Council meeting at Laeken in December 2001 and the establishment of the European Convention, which was endowed with the task to sketch out possibilities for a 'simplification' of the Treaties, a working group on 'simplification' (Working Group IX) was instituted which set itself the twin objectives of making the European system of governance more clear and comprehensible and thus more legitimate.[21] With respect to the simplification and reform of legislative decision-making procedures, the report issued by the working group stipulated that 'the logic of the co-decision procedure requires qualified-majority voting in the Council in all cases'[22] and that the co-decision procedure should also 'become the general rule for the adoption of legislative acts'.[23] The Draft Treaty establishing a Constitution for Europe (DTC) and the ensuing intergovernmental conference adopted the working group's recommendation: Article I–34, 1 DTC stipulates that what was hitherto known as the co-decision procedure becomes the *ordinary legislative procedure*. The logic inherent in the 'QMV equals European Parliament legislative involvement' formula had thus not only gained a largely uncontested status in the post SEA-era; this formula also offered a clear behavioural prescription regarding its implementation: 'If you extend QMV, you have to allow for parliamentary participation in the legislative process.' The subsequent intergovernmental conference, which adopted the Treaty establishing a Constitution for Europe, signed in Rome on 29 October 2004, adopted this provision unaltered (Article I–34, 1).

In this section, we have argued that the pooling of sovereignty by introducing and extending qualified majority voting at subsequent intergovernmental conferences has contributed to the de-parliamentarisation of national polities by short-circuiting democratic procedures of interest representation and procedures to ensure accountability. This challenge to input legitimacy at the level of domestic polities has, however, not gone unnoticed or uncontested by political elites. Although one might assume that, behind closed doors, national executives are unlikely to complain too loudly about the creeping de-parliamentarisation of their domestic polities, we have argued that pressure from domestic political parties as well as the intrinsic valuation of representative parliamentary democracy have produced behavioural responses on the part of national governments which – from either a purely power-maximising perspective or an efficiency-enhancing perspective – seem perplexing (see Rittberger 2003: 204–6). To remedy the perceived challenge to input legitimacy political elites in the member states have proposed remedies at the *supranational* level (by supporting the empowerment of the European Parliament), but also – more recently – at the *domestic* level (by supporting closer involvement of national parliaments in EU affairs).[24] The story about the increasing legislative powers of the European Parliament thus defies the de-parliamentarisation trend. In the following section, we turn from the European Parliament to the domestic level and demonstrate that national parliaments, even though displaying varying responses to the process of European integration, have been active in shaping and influencing their fate equally defying the odds, which see them in demise.

National parliaments: strategies of adaptation

While the decisions by member state governments to enhance the powers of the European Parliament have greatly contributed to the parliamentarisation and thus the democratic legitimacy of the EU, the European Parliament – however powerful – cannot guarantee democratic legitimacy alone, because it can neither control nor hold to account the (main) law-making body of the EU, the Council (Auel and Benz 2000). Through the strengthening of the European Parliament the relationship between both institutions has evolved into a system of checks and balances. Yet the members of the Council remain representatives of national governments and therefore accountable to their national parliaments.

In spite of their important role for legitimising European policy-making, national parliaments remained in the European Parliament's shadow for quite some time, which featured more prominently in institutional reforms determined to enhance the parliamentary legitimacy of the European Union. It was only in 1997 that the legitimising function of national parliaments was formally recognised through a legally binding 'Protocol on the Role of National Parliaments in the European Union' (PNP) that was added to the Treaty of Amsterdam.[25] The Treaty of Nice, finally, triggered an even broader debate on the role of national parliaments in the European political system; an issue the Convention on the Future of the EU then dedicated considerable effort to.[26]

Within the member states, however, many national parliaments reacted much earlier to the challenges of European integration. As we argued in the previous section, subsequent transfers of sovereignty have not only led to the loss of an increasing part of their legislative sovereignty, it also strengthened national executives considerably at the expense of other domestic actors, legislatures most notably. Due to their direct involvement in European legislation, it has been argued that governments act as gatekeepers between the national political system and the European level (see Moravcsik 1994). This position not only enables member state governments to initiate negotiations on policy issues without prior consultation with other domestic actors but also allows them to confront their legislatures with 'take-it-or-leave-it' choices after agreements at the European level have been reached and renegotiations are impossible. National executives also control the flow of information from the European to the national level, which not only weakens the ability of national parliaments to control their government, but also allows the executive to manipulate the ideological justifications for a particular policy. Yet no institution or actor can be expected to simply accept such a loss of power without resistance. And indeed, compared to the developments in domestic politics leading to the much-lamented de-parliamentarisation of politics, we can observe a remarkable resilience of national parliaments in the European context. The reason for this stronger resilience is that in the domestic context the 'decline' of parliaments is the result of incremental and informal developments, which diminish the impact of legislatures. The power shifts caused by European integration, on the other hand, are the result of political decisions that modify the formal rules of the political system. As we have seen, these formal changes not only challenged the position of national parliaments more immediately but also provoked intensive discussions about the democratic legitimacy deficit of the EU, which induced national parliaments to respond.

Institutional Europeanisation of national parliaments

The debate about the democratic legitimacy of the EU, and, in particular, their interest in maintaining their own power, has motivated national parliaments to implement institutional reforms in response to the process of European integration. Although the institutional provisions implemented in different national parliaments vary considerably,[27] this institutional Europeanisation was generally meant to achieve three basic objectives. First, it aimed at giving national parliaments the right to obtain comprehensive information on European issues from their respective governments. While this right at first applied mainly to the 'first pillar' of the EU, it was later expanded to the 'second' and 'third pillar' in most national parliaments. Second, the reforms were designed to enhance parliamentary capacities to handle and process this information. All national parliaments have reformed their infrastructure by setting up one or more special European Affairs Committees and by implementing a scrutiny procedure for European documents and decisions. Finally, the aim was to establish participation rights that parliaments hold vis-à-vis the government within the national arena for European affairs as well. This includes the right to draft resolutions on European issues before a final agreement is reached ('scrutiny reserve'). These institutional reforms were meant to counterbalance the redistribution of political resources in favour of the national executives. The aim was to obtain the same information as the government, to be able to influence European decision-making before the stage of formal ratification or implementation and to improve the 'infrastructural' preconditions for both. Yet this institutional Europeanisation did not completely make up for the structural disadvantages. Parliaments still depend on their government as the main information source, they are still not directly involved in European policy-making and – as a consequence – neither have complete control over agenda-setting at the European level, nor can they directly influence European decisions. The government still holds the position of gatekeeper.

Nevertheless, the institutional reforms have enabled national parliaments to have more control over the gatekeeper by opening up the possibility to influence and control the negotiation position of their national government. These rights, however, do not inevitably contribute to advancing parliamentary control and democratic accountability of national governments, but expose especially the majority party or parties to a dilemma (Benz 2003a; Auel and Benz 2000, 2004). In a parliamentary system majority parties are not only expected to loyally sustain the government in office, but to mediate citizens' interests and to influence and scrutinise the government's policies at the same time (Norton 1998: 194). This dual role is even more pronounced in European affairs. Although the majority can usually be expected to support their government in EU matters as well, the motivation of the majority to do so is lower compared to domestic politics since the agenda to be decided upon does not originate from a programme that has been agreed upon by the government and the majority parties. On the contrary, policies are initiated by an external institution, namely the European Commission, and decided upon by external institutions, the Council and, where applicable, the European Parliament. In contrast to domestic policies, the parliamentary majority neither has any influence on the agenda of European policy-making, nor does it ultimately decide European policies. As a consequence, parliamentary majorities can be expected to have a higher motivation to influence and scrutinise their governments in European affairs, and, therefore, by extension, so do national parliaments. The problem is, however, that the more effectively they influence and scrutinise their government, the more they bind their representatives negotiating at the European level to 'national' interests. Parliaments that strictly supervise their governments and thus tie their hands in multi-level negotiations must face the possibility that outcomes of negotiations are inferior to compromises that might have been obtained if the government had enough room for manoeuvre. This is not only true in the cases where parliaments have formal veto rights. Indeed, most national parliaments have the right to draft only non-binding resolutions on European issues. Yet the government cannot simply ignore a public parliamentary statement. A basic norm of parliamentary systems is that the government needs the support of the parliamentary majority. Therefore, governmental action is only legitimate if it is subject to parliamentary control and a potential parliamentary veto. Therefore, even a non-binding resolution can have the effect of politically binding the government. If, on the other hand, parliament tries to avoid these effects by allowing its respective government to act autonomously, parliamentary involvement is reduced to a mere symbolic use of power, which undermines the legitimacy of European policy-making. Consequently, the democratic legitimacy of the Council depends not only on the rights and the formal power of national parliaments, but also on the way parliaments handle this dilemma.

Strategic Europeanisation of national parliaments

The previous section has shown that parliamentarians face a serious dilemma in EU policy-making. Either parliamentary scrutiny and control are effective, but potentially diminish their respective government's success in European negotiations and policy-making, or they are merely symbolic measures to disguise the actual loss in parliamentary power resulting in a de-legitimisation of European policy-making. Interestingly, neither is the case, because parliamentary actors are well aware of this dilemma and try to find 'escape routes' (Héritier 1999) through the strategic use of their institutional rights. As Elinor Ostrom has argued, actors are able to learn from problematic situations and to develop 'heuristics that approach best-response strategies' (Ostrom 1998: 9).[28] And indeed, based on their practical knowledge national MPs develop strategies to cope with the disadvantages resulting from the government's gatekeeper position while at the same time avoiding getting caught in the dilemma described above. From a theoretical point of view, four potential strategies of national parliaments can be identified. First, parliamentarians can focus on holding the government publicly to account. Instead of trying to influence the government's negotiating position, they expose it to public scrutiny. In this case, the parties supporting the government leave the government sufficient room for manoeuvre in European negotiations, but force it to explain their negotiation behaviour to parliament and the general public. Second, parliaments or committees can turn into forums of public deliberation. In this case, they do try to influence the government's European policy, but not through institutionalised participation rights, which might establish veto positions and hamper the policy-making process. Public deliberation of European matters rather aims at changing decision premises or contexts through information, ideas and arguments. Third, MPs can cooperate informally with the responsible minister during European negotiations. This enables national parliaments to influence the government's position in a particular European policy issue without publicly binding the government to a specific negotiation position. At the same time, they can adjust the parliamentary position to the opportunities or constraints arising during the negotiation process. Finally, MPs may try to completely bypass the gatekeeper. By establishing direct contacts to actors at the European level or in other member states they can try to open up their own independent channels of influence in EU policy-making. Although this strategy brings parliaments in competition with their governments, it does not necessarily lead to a problematic power game in European affairs.

Although more comparative research is needed, it can be shown that the strategies, which parliamentary actors develop to cope with coordination problems resulting from the European multi-level structure, are influenced by the overall institutional context of the respective parliamentary system: 'After all, the institutions provide venues for the interactions between MPs and ministers, rules for behaviour of participants and above all, role models for the "inmates" of the parliamentary/governmental complex' (Andeweg and Nijzink 1995: 157). Above all, the strategies reflect both the type of executive–legislative relations as well as the parliamentary function that dominate parliamentary work in the respective parliamentary systems. The greater the independence of the executive and the less significant the 'transformative' power of a parliament (Polsby 1975),[29] the higher is the probability that parliamentarians choose a more public strategy to strengthen their position. More transformative legislatures, on the other hand, are able to place greater constraints on the executive's policy-making in EU affairs. In order to both avoid the traps looming in the European multi-level system and to safeguard their power, national parliaments adopt strategies that enable them to informally influence the government. We will illustrate the plausibility of these arguments by presenting evidence on the strategies developed in four national parliaments, each of which represents a distinctive types of parliamentary system: the British House of Commons, the French Assemblée Nationale, the German Bundestag and the Danish Folketing (see Table 6.2 for an overview).[30]

Public scrutiny

The British House of Commons,[31] characterised by a single-party majority as well as an almost complete fusion of government and its parliamentary majority, traditionally acts as an institution controlling the government, while policy-making is almost completely monopolised by the executive. As is typical with this type of political system, the House of Commons focuses its resources on the public scrutiny of the government's European policy, yet the possibility to effectively influence the government remains marginal.[32] Not only would the government reject a limitation of its own power, but any ex-ante vetoes by parliament would also entail a structural disruption in a parliamentary system based on the absolute loyalty of the majority party to its government. And indeed, the European Standing Committees of the House of Commons do have the right to debate a European decision and the respective governmental motion, and may decide to pass the government's motion, amend it or even reject it. However, 'at present, a motion passed by the Committee has no practical effect ... their decisions can simply be ignored' (HC 152-xxx, para. 70). As a consequence, strategies developed in the British House of Commons aim less at influencing the negotiation process but at holding the government accountable. The aim of the scrutiny process is not 'to tell the government what to do, but to see that the government explains what it is doing and follows the rules properly' (personal interview with majority MP). MPs in the House of Commons abstain from challenging the central position of the executive as the gatekeeper, but aim at preventing the government from exploiting its gatekeeper position and at making the use of this position more transparent to parliament and the electorate. In their effort to force the government to respect parliamentary rules, to explain and defend its negotiation position and the decisions taken in Brussels, a very potent strategy seems to be 'public embarrassment', where the majority decides to side with the opposition if the government neglects parliamentary rights. Not only does the European Scrutiny Committee keep a 'Black Book' where government's failures to provide the Committee with information on time are meticulously listed and published (HC 791/ 98, Annex G; HC–152-xxx/02, para. 47) but ministers are also regularly called before the Committee to be questioned in public evidence sessions on certain issues or to be held accountable for incomplete information or breaches of the scrutiny reserve : 'Our job is

Table 6.2 Institutional context and strategic Europeanisation in the UK, France, Germany and Denmark

Type of legislature (cf. N. Polsby)	Legislature	Dominant parliamentary function	Strategies in EU affairs
Arena legislatures	**House of Commons**		
	Westminster model, characterised by executive dominance	Public debate, scrutiny and control of executive policy-making	Public scrutiny, 'public embarrassment'
	Assemblée Nationale		
	'Rationalised' parliament characterised by executive dominance	Public debate, 'instrument de vigilance'	Public deliberation and weak informal cooperation
	Bundestag		
	'Working parliament', executive less dominant, strong standing committees	Legislative function	Informal cooperation and bypassing
	Folketing		
Transformative legislatures	Strong policy-influencer, minority governments highly dependent on legislature	Legislative and control function	Close internal cooperation and selective use of vetoes

to hunt them' (personal interview with majority MP). As a result, the majority party provides the responsible minister with enough leeway in European negotiations but induces him to act as a representative of the electorate and offers him no opportunity to shift the blame or disguise his responsibility.

Public deliberation

Due to the restrictive provisions of the French constitution, the 'rationalised' French parliament is neither a powerful legislator nor a fiercely scrutinising assembly such as the House of Commons. As in the 'Westminster system', the legislative process is mainly dominated by the executive, but at the same time, the French Assemblée Nationale has 'virtually no opportunities for scrutinising executive acts and making the executive give an account of them ... executive power is a little too immune from proper scrutiny' (Frears 1990: 33). Its committee structure, however, as well as the institutional provisions for the legislature's involvement in EU affairs[33] do allow for an involvement in the policy-making process. Consequently, members of the majority parties do try to influence the government informally, especially in the more 'private' committee atmosphere, but the strategies developed in the Assemblée Nationale are mainly focused on providing long-term reflections and on organising a public debate. French MPs have thus taken recourse to a combination of *informal* cooperation with the executive and parallel *public* communication of arguments through extensive *rapports d'information*. Contrary to the reports of many other national European Affairs Committees, these *rapports* frequently have paperback dimensions and are often in-depth studies of a certain European issue. By drafting these detailed and – most importantly – *public*[34] reports, not only does the French Parliament provide information on European affairs for the general public but French parliamentarians are also able to argue for their views and standpoints and formulate indirect demands without directly determining or criticising the government's negotiation position. As interviews in different French ministries revealed, the government regards these reports as important sources of information and as finely tuned seismographs of parliamentary opinion: 'L'information et la diffusion sont à la racine du pouvoir ' (Kessler 1999: 243).

Informal cooperation and bypassing

In Germany, the Bundestag is regarded as a more powerful policy-influencer than the House of Commons or the Assemblée Nationale. In the 'working parliament' with its sophisticated standing committee structure, the legislative function and the involvement in governmental policy-making clearly dominates. This is also reflected in the parliamentary participation procedure in EU affairs.[35] Article 23 of the German Basic Law speaks of 'collaboration' (*Mitwirkung*) and the respective accompanying law of 'cooperation' (*Zusammenarbeit*) of the Bundestag with the government. It is therefore not surprising that parliamentarians have the objective to be involved in policy-making in EU matters. Yet, in order to avoid the dysfunctional effects of politically binding mandates, the government's request for a broad scope of action in European negotiations is generally respected. The parliamentary majority either completely abstains from drafting parliamentary resolutions or it drafts resolutions in close cooperation with the government in order to strengthen the latter's negotiation position in Brussels.[36] At the same time, parliamentarians cooperate informally with the government via the internal parliamentary party working groups. The most important precondition for effectively influencing the government, however, is having access to independent information. For this reason, MPs seek mostly informal contacts with European actors or other national parliaments to open up independent information resources. MEPs especially, and also European Commission officials, serve as a kind of 'burglar alarm' for some German MPs by informing them of important Commission initiatives as early as possible. But contacts to the European level not only serve as information sources. A small but growing number of parliamentary 'Euro-wizards' also try to influence European drafts directly through contacts with Commission officials or MEPs. These strategies are aimed at influencing European policies without tying the government's hands in the European negotiation process, partly by informal cooperation with and partly by bypassing the government.

Cooperation in the shadow of a formal mandate

The *Folketing* in Denmark represents a parliament in a consensus democracy (Lijphart 1999; Nannestad 2003: 55). Parliament's power vis-à-vis the government is relatively strong, because Danish governments are generally formed by minority coalitions unable to act without a supporting majority (Laursen 1995). Similar to the German Bundestag, but even more powerful, the Folketing is regarded as a 'transformative' or a policy-making parliament (Norton 1990: 5), where committees and commissions play a major role in legislation (Nannestad 2003: 60). This is also true in European affairs, where the powerful European Affairs Committee has the right to mandate the government's negotiation position.[37] This procedure entitles the Committee to formal veto-rights vis-à-vis the government in European policy-making (Arter 1996; Laursen 1995), and 'a government wanting to survive politically knows it will have to listen to the Committee' (Laursen 2001: 105). As a result, the government and the European Affairs Committee cooperate very closely. For the government, fully explaining negotiation situations at the European level and its strategic options in these negotiations is a necessity, because the European Affairs Committee has the possibility to deny the mandate as long as it is not satisfied with the information and explanations by the government. In return, members of the European Affairs Committee mainly focus the deliberations of the Committee on the strategic questions of what would be in Denmark's best interests and, even more importantly, on what is achievable with what kind of coalition in the Council. Party politics, on the other hand, plays only a minor role in the European Affairs Committee's debates.[38] In addition to its rights of ex ante influence, the Committee also has the possibility of controlling ex post whether the government has stayed within the confines of the parliamentary mandate. The combination of these two features generally makes it unnecessary for the Committee to bind the government to very narrow mandates as the members are aware of the negotiation situation and the government's options and objectives. Given their powerful position, members of the Danish European Affairs Committee feel no need to develop strategies of bypassing the government by opening up independent information sources or channels of influence at the European level. On the other hand, the issues and mandates debated in the Committee are highly confidential, which rules out the development of strategies of holding the government publicly to account. Thus the only strategy observed in the Danish European Affairs Committee so far is to strategically veto the government's mandate, i.e. to refuse a mandate to a government minister, when it feels that it has not been properly informed or involved.[39] This ensures the Committee's influence on European policy-making and guarantees that the government respects parliamentary participation rights.

Summary

In this chapter we presented evidence to qualify the 'de-parliamentarisation' thesis by offering a two-pronged argument. In a first step, we argued that political elites have – since the SEA – gradually empowered the European Parliament's legislative powers and thus its capacity to influence European policy-making. Even though the decisions by member states to increase the legislative powers of the European Parliament were all but uncontroversial, the introduction and extension of qualified majority voting and the concomitant transfer of sectoral policy decisions to the European level triggered what we coined a democratic 'legitimacy deficit': European political elites came to perceive that the centralisation of policy-making tasks at the European level undermined the power of domestic parliaments to control and influence their respective governments in European policy-making. The legislative empowerment of the European Parliament was thus considered to serve as a mechanism to 'compensate' for domestic 'de-parliamentarisation'. In a second step, we demonstrated that the process of European integration does not inevitably turn national parliaments into powerless institutions as claimed by the proponents of the 'de-parliamentarisation' hypothesis. We argued that we need a more nuanced analysis of the way national parliaments adapt to the challenges of EU multi-level governance to assess parliamentary strengths and weaknesses. Undeniably, the process of European integration has weakened national parliaments as a consequence of the centralisation of policy-making competencies at the EU level, and they are further weakened by the executive's gatekeeper position between the national and the European arena. However, national parliamentarians have not simply accepted their demise but have actively counterbalanced this shift in power and searched for ways to manage the challenges of multi-level policy-making. As the comparative analysis of domestic parliaments' responses to Europeanisation has revealed, the strategic adjustment of national parliaments to European integration depends to a large degree on the respective institutional context. Legislatures with less influence on governmental policy-making appear to take recourse to strategies with a more public impact to enhance their power. Allegedly weak parliaments thus gain their relative strength by acting as an intermediary public arena between Europe and the citizens. Strategies of bypassing the government in order to gain access to independent information or to influence policy-making directly at the European level, on the other hand, are rarely developed. More 'transformative' legislatures, in contrast, cooperate more closely with their respective government, either formally or informally. Thus, they develop strategies that enhance their influencing capacities, either by bypassing the government or through the use of selective vetoes to remind the government of their power. This close cooperation, however, seems to rule out strategies of public scrutiny and deliberation.

Conclusion

At face value, both trends depicted in this chapter – the successive empowerment of the European Parliament, and the variable but successful adaptation of national parliaments to the challenge of 'executive dominance' in European decision-making, should be marked as positive entries in the democratic legitimacy account. However, the empowerment of the European Parliament – while alleviating the 'legitimacy deficit' of *perceived* political elites – does not solve a more fundamental problem of democratic governance in the EU. First, while the member states have gradually empowered the European Parliament, this is not reflected in increased voter interest in European affairs. The reverse can actually be said to be the case: turnout at European elections has steadily decreased from 63 per cent in 1979 to a mere 45.7 per cent in 2004. Those who believed that European elections and a potent European Parliament would produce Europe-wide election campaigns on European issues and European political parties must be disappointed. First, European elections are fought as 'second order national contests' and not as *European* elections (see Reif and Schmitt 1980). National political issues and domestic political parties tend to dominate European elections, and since European elections do not produce a decision about who holds executive office in government, European elections, like regional or local elections, are considered 'secondary'. As a consequence, European elections attract fewer voters than ('first order') national elections where parties compete for national executive office. Second, despite the growing influence and hence importance of the European Parliament in European policy-making, party organisation at the European level is – as yet – underdeveloped (see Hix 2005: chapter 6). Since national parties control the process for MEP candidate selection, MEPs are more likely to defect from their party group inside the European Parliament if their voting instruction from their national party differs from that of their European Parliament party group (see, for instance, Hix and Lord 1995, Hix 1997). Even though the gradual empowerment of the European Parliament has contributed to alleviate the *perceived* 'legitimacy deficit' during episodes of transfers of sovereignty, an ever more powerful European Parliament does not alleviate the underlying *structural* democratic deficit characterised by the weakness of European political parties, the absence of both campaigns on European issues and electoral contests over who holds key government offices in European decision-making.

Turning to national parliaments, the various strategies that national parliamentarians develop to deal with the challenges of European integration have implications for the democratic quality of a national parliament's involvement in EU affairs, especially if we take into account the need for transparency and public control. In the German Bundestag and the Danish Folketing, the close cooperation with the government takes place behind closed doors, either in internal parliamentary party working groups, or in non-public sessions of the European Affairs Committee, rendering the parliamentary process opaque. In Denmark, the mandating procedure also requires confidentiality among the partners and therefore rules out public scrutiny in plenary sessions of the parliament. In addition, as the opposition generally takes part in the forming of a mandate, it cannot critically scrutinise the government's policy-making in European affairs. In both parliaments, this opaqueness of the parliamentary process is not sufficiently counterbalanced by parliamentary debates in the plenary. Both parliaments therefore cannot adequately fulfil their functions of public control and deliberation. In the European multi-level system, however, with its non-transparent inter-institutional decision-making processes the functions of public control and scrutiny are ever more important (Benz 2003a). So far, the French Assemblée Nationale and, in particular, the British House of Commons, in spite of their much weaker institutional position, seem to be more important actors with regard to democratic legitimacy in European affairs by providing for public parliamentary deliberation and scrutiny of governmental policy-making, both essential in a representative democracy. Yet the strategies developed in both parliaments cannot completely compensate the shift in power towards the government. In the evaluation of European issues as well as the negotiation process and possible outcomes, French and, especially, British MPs depend mainly on their governments as the main information source. This, of course, enables governments to exploit their gatekeeper position through a strategic transfer of information (Schelling 1960). This asymmetry can only be overcome if parliaments have access to independent information about future and current developments at the European level, the negotiating position of other governments and the negotiating behaviour of their own government. Thus the quality of democracy in multi-level governance depends not only on institutional provisions for parliamentary involvement but also to a great degree on the strategic adaptation of parliamentary actors. As the case studies illustrate, none of the strategies developed in the different parliaments represents an ideal way of linking national parliamentary democracy and European policy-making. A more promising solution seems to lie in searching for a combination of different strategies with a positive effect on democratic legitimacy.

Notes

1   *Fluctuant nec merguntur* is the plural form of the inscription on the Paris coat of arms: 'Shaken by the waves, but it will not sink.'
2   See, for instance, Pharr and Putnam (1990) and Cain *et al*. (2003).
3   See, for example, Moravcsik (1994) and Marschall (2002: 379). See Raunio and Hix (2000) or Auel and Benz (2004) for an alternative perspective.
4   See also Sturm and Pehle (2001: 58).
5   See also Norton (1996a).
6   A strategically acting European Parliament will thus propose amendments which the Commission and the pivotal Council member will prefer to a unanimous Council decision. See, for example, Tsebelis (1994), Garrett and Tsebelis (1996). For a more recent contribution, see Selck (2004).
7   See, for example, Westlake (1994), Maurer (1999) and the overview in Judge and Earnshaw (2003: 246-248)
8   See, for example, the studies by Judge *et al*. (1994), Earnshaw and Judge (1996) and Hubschmid and Moser (1997).
9   See Hix (2005: chapter 3) for an overview.
10   See, for example, Scully (2000), Bergman and Raunio (2001), Judge and Earnshaw (2003).
11   This section is largely based on Rittberger (2003, 2005).
12   See, for example Corbett (1987), de Ruyt (1989), Moravcsik (1991, 1998), Budden (1994).
13   See *Agence Europe*, 16 March 1985.
14   See Corbett (1998: 185–94) for an analysis of the debates in national parliaments prior to the SEA.
15   *Journal Officiel*, Assemblée Nationale, debate of 11 June 1985: 1613 (author's translation, emphasis added).
16   Deutscher Bundestag, debate of 27 June 1985: 11111.
17   In a Danish government memorandum, it reads: 'As regards the strengthening of the European Parliament's role, the Danish government suggests extending the cooperation procedure to include all cases of internal policy decided on by qualified majority. It should not be necessary to amend the cooperation procedure itself' (Corbett 1992: 160).
18   For instance, the Benelux governments issued a memorandum in which they explicitly acknowledged the link between the application of qualified majority voting and legislative co-decision for the European Parliament (European Parliament 1996: 20). Similarly, a Spanish government document on the intergovernmental conference foresaw that 'there will be considerable scope for progress through an extension of the field of application of the co-decision procedure; this concept should ... logically be viewed in close relation to majority decision-making' (European Parliament 1996: 47).
19   During the intergovernmental conference leading to the adoption of the Nice Treaty, co-decision and parliamentary involvement was a lesser concern. The Treaty provided for six new cases of co-decision. Yet, among the new cases under qualified majority voting, three legislative ones remained outside the co-decision procedure: financial regulations, internal measures for the implementation of cooperation agreements, as well as the Structural Funds and

the Cohesion Fund. Since these policies are particularly important issues on account of their major budgetary implications, some member states resisted the call for co-decision in these areas. The European Parliament bemoaned that 'in refusing even to consider switching matters already subject to qualified-majority voting to the co-decision procedure, the [intergovernmental conference] was rejecting a basic institutional principle on which significant progress had been made at Amsterdam: as a general rule, co-decision should accompany qualified-majority voting in matters of a legislative nature' (European Parliament 2001: 28).

20 Treaty of Nice, 'Declaration on the Future of the Union' (No. 23, paragraph 5).

21 See European Convention, CONV 424/02.

22 See European Convention, CONV 424/02, p. 14.

23 See European Convention, CONV 424/02, p. 15.

24 See Rittberger (2005: chapter 6) and Raunio (2004).

25 The protocol mainly aimed at improving the national parliaments' abilities for pre-legislative scrutiny by giving them the right to receive all Commission consultation documents including green and white papers at least six weeks before the matter appears on the Council's agenda for decision. The second part of the PNP aimed at strengthening inter-parliamentary cooperation by enhancing the status of the Conference of EU Committees, the COSAC.

26 The Convention set up a working group (Working Group IV) for this issue, which discarded proposals for a direct involvement of national parliaments at the European level and instead proposed measures to make the parliamentary scrutiny of governmental policy-making in EU affairs more effective. Depending on the ratification of the Constitutional Treaty, national parliaments will be included in the implementation and observation of the EU's subsidiarity principle. See European Convention, CONV 353/02.

27 A detailed account of the reforms and the variations between member states can be found in Auel and Benz (2004); Bergman and Damgaard (2000); Laursen and Pappas (1995); Maurer (2002); Maurer and Wessels (2001); Norton (1996b); Smith (1996).

28 In the literature on multi-level governance in federal systems and in the EU, we find ample evidence for strategies actors develop to circumvent dilemma situations (e.g. Auel 2003b; Benz 2003b; Héritier 1999; Scharpf 1988; Scharpf, Reissert and Schnabel 1976). However, these studies mainly focus on executives, while strategies of members of parliament in the intricate multi-level governance structure have not yet been the subject of empirical research.

29 According to the classification by Nelson Polsby, legislatures in modern democracies can be placed on a continuum between two ideal types: 'Arena' legislatures serve as 'formalized settings for the interplay of significant political forces in the life of a political system', while 'transformative' legislatures possess 'the independent capacity, frequently exercised, to mould and transform proposals from whatever source into laws' (Polsby 1975: 277). Polsby argued that the two legislatures that stood as the best examples for both types of legislatures were the US Congress as the archetype of a transformative legislature and the House of Commons as the prime example of an arena legislature.

30 The following is based on evidence derived from 68 interviews with Members of the House of Commons, the Assemblée Nationale, the Bundestag and the Folketing. For more details on institutional reforms and developed strategies in these legislatures, see Auel (2003a), and Auel and Benz (2004).

31 The scrutiny procedure in the House of Commons is based on two basic mechanisms. First, European documents are transferred to the European Scrutiny Committee (ESC) whose task is to assess their legal and/or political importance (Standing Order 143). For this task, the Committee not only obtains information from the responsible department, but also has the right to ask for further information and to question the responsible minister. Once the ESC has determined the political and/or legal importance of a document, it can be deferred to one of the three European Standing Committees or – by a motion put down by the government – to the Committee of the Whole House. This gives the government the possibility to avoid a ple-

nary debate by not putting down the respective motion. The rights of the European Standing Committees were designed accordingly. According to Standing Order 119, the Committees, generally meeting in public, have the possibility to debate a European decision and the respective governmental motion and to move amendments to this motion. However, for the amendments to become effective the Committees again have to rely on the government, as it is the government that puts down the final motion on the Floor of the House (House of Commons 2002). To ensure that parliament has the opportunity to deal with European matters before they are agreed upon at the European level, the House of Commons adopted a resolution on the scrutiny reserve. The current scrutiny reserve is based on the resolution of 18 November 1998, see ESC 2001: Appendix III.

32   'The purpose of the scrutiny system in the Commons is [...]: to ensure that members are informed of European proposals likely to affect the UK, to provide a source of information and analysis for the public, and to ensure that the House and the European Scrutiny Committee, and through them other organisations and individuals, have opportunities to make Ministers aware of their views on EU proposals, seek to influence Ministers and hold Ministers to account' (HC 152-xxx/02, para. 25).

33   According to Art. 88-4 of the French Constitution, the government is obliged to 'lay before the National Assembly and the Senate any proposals for Community instruments which contain provisions which are matters for statute as soon as they have been transmitted to the Council of the Communities'. In addition, the article includes a right to draft explicitly non-binding resolutions on the documents. In order to be able to deal with European documents effectively and to analyse them in detail, the Delegation for European Affairs can designate one or more *rapporteurs* to draw up a detailed report (*rapport*). The outcome may be the tabling of a resolution, but the report may also remain informative in character (*rapport d'information*). For details, see Nuttens and Sicard (2000); Szukala and Rozenberg (2001).

34   The reports reach a large public as they are not only published on the internet but also distributed among European institutions including the Coreper, the ambassadors of other EU member states, the European Affairs Committees of other national parliaments as well as among the press and interested associations (Assemblée Nationale 1998: 17f.).

35   According to Article 23 of the German Basic Law (*Grundgesetz*, GG), the Bundestag cooperates with the government in affairs of the European Union. This broad definition includes not only directives and regulations, but all matters of the European Union, i.e. measures and agreements under the second and third pillar. Accordingly, parliament has to be informed by the government comprehensively and in time, i.e. receive all relevant formal and informal documents. In addition, the Bundestag has the right to draft a resolution, which the federal government has to take into account in the negotiations. The European Affairs Committee is, like the Foreign Affairs, the Defence, and the Petitions Committee, but in contrast to all other committees, established through constitutional law (Article 45 GG) and therefore not subject to the Bundestag's Parliamentary Standing Orders. According to §93a of the Bundestag's Standing Orders, the European Affairs Committee has the right to adopt a resolution on behalf of the plenary, i.e. act on behalf of the whole parliament, as long as none of the standing committees disagree. As the Committee deals with all the important institutional decisions made at the EU level it is regarded as the Bundestag's central arena for European affairs. However, all European decisions dealing with matters connected directly to a policy field are, as domestic policies, dealt with in the sectoral standing committees.

36   Only in exceptional situations does the Bundestag use its powers very effectively against the government to force it into adopting the parliamentary position. For example, a conflict erupted between the government and parliament with regard to the European Convention. While Chancellor Schröder had preferred a more executive based Convention, the MPs demanded a stronger representation of national parliaments. After the European Affairs Committee had voted a respective resolution according to § 93 a of the Bundestag's Standing Orders on behalf of the plenary (Deutscher Bundestag 2002: 241 ff.) it formed alliances with

other Member States' parliaments to enhance the pressure on the government. 'That is something we used quite deliberately. This was about forcing the government to accept the parliamentary position' (personal interview with majority MP, author's translation). The outcome of their efforts is well known.

37 The decisive provision, which lays down the competence of the Committee, is not to be found in the constitution or even a law, but in the first Report of the Market Relations Committee of 29 March 1973: 'The Government shall consult the Market Relations Committee of the Folketing in questions relating to EC policy of a major importance so that the regard for the influence of the Folketing as well as the freedom to negotiate are respected. Prior to negotiations in the EC Council of Ministers on decisions of a wider scope, the Government submits an oral mandate for negotiation to the Market Relations Committee. If there is no majority against the mandate, the Government negotiates on this basis.' The distinction between questions of 'major importance' and decisions of 'a wider scope' made in the report has become less and less important over time. Today, the Government submits negotiation mandates for practically every legal document prior to its adoption in the Council.

38 Foreign and European policy-making in Denmark is traditionally based on a broad coalition between the four 'old' parties: the Conservatives (Konservative Folkeparti), the Liberals (Venstre), the Social-liberal Democrats (Radikale Venstre) and the Social Democrats (Socialdemokratiet i Danmark). This is also true for the current Folketing, where the liberal-conservative minority government of Prime Minister Anders Fogh Rasmussen is generally supported by the Danish People's Party (DPP) in domestic politics. In European affairs, however, this 'governing coalition' changes. As the nationalistic DPP is violently anti-European, the government cannot and will not rely on its support in the European Affairs Committee but rather forms the traditional 'grand coalition' with the Social Democrats and the Social-Liberal Party, currently the main opposition parties.

39 As interviews revealed, this had been the main reason in several of the cases in which the Committee completely refused to give any mandate to a minister.

References

Andeweg, R. B. and Nijzink, L. (1995) 'Beyond the Two-Body-Image: Relations Between Ministers and MPs', in H. Döring (ed.), *Parliaments and Majority Rule in Western Europe* (Frankfurt and New York: Campus).

Arter, D. (1996) 'The Folketing and Denmark's "European Policy": The Case of an "Authorising Assembly"?', in P. Norton (ed.) *National Parliaments and the European Union* (London: Frank Cass).

Auel, K. (2003a) *Regionalisiertes Europa – Demokratisches Europa? Eine Untersuchung am Beispiel der europäischen Strukturpolitik* (Baden-Baden: Nomos).

—— (2003b) 'Strategische Anpassung nationaler Parlamente an das europäische Mehrebenensystem – Ein deutsch-britischer Vergleich', in E. Grande and R. Prätorius (eds.), *Politische Steuerung und neue Staatlichkeit* (Baden-Baden: Nomos).

Auel, K. and Benz, A. (2000) *Strength and Weakness of Parliaments in EU Multilevel Governance. Accountability in a Compounded Representative Democracy*, paper presented at the IPSA World Congress, 1–5 August 2000, Quebec.

—— (2004) 'National Parliaments in EU Multi-Level Governance – Dilemmas and Strategies of Adaptation', *polis-Arbeitspapiere* 59, Hagen: FernUniversität, Institute for Political Science, http://www.fernuni-hagen.de/POLALL/index.htm

Assemblée Nationale (1998) 'Assemblée Nationale et l'Union européenne', Rapport série 'Connaissance de l'Assemblée', No. 9, texte rédigé par Daniel Hochedez and Vannina Partriar.

Benz, A. (2003a) 'Compounded Representation in EU Multi-Level Governance', in B. Kohler-Koch (ed.), *Linking EU and National Governance* (Oxford: Oxford University Press).

—— (2003b) 'Konstruktive Vetospieler in Mehrebenensystemen', in R. Mayntz and W. Streeck (eds), *Die Reformierbarkeit der Demokratie. Innovationen und Blockaden* (Frankfurt and New York: Campus).

Bergman, T. and Damgaard, E. (eds) (2000) *Delegation and Accountability in European Integration: The Nordic Parliamentary Democracies and the European Union* (London: Frank Cass).

Bergman, T. and Raunio, T. (2001) 'Parliaments and Policy-making in the European Union', in J. Richardson (ed.), *European Union: Power and Policy-Making* (London: Routledge).

Beyme, K. von (1998) 'Niedergang der Parlamente. Internationale Politik und nationale Entscheidungshoheit', *Internationale Politik* 53: 21–30.

Börzel, T. A. (2000) 'Europäisierung und innerstaatlicher Wandel. Zentralisierung und Entparlamentarisierung?', *Politische Vierteljahresschrift* 41: 225–50.

Bryce, J. (1921) *Modern Democracies* (London: Macmillan).

Budden, P. (1994) *The United Kingdom and the European Community, 1979–1986. The Making of the Single European Act*, D.Phil. thesis, Oxford: University of Oxford.

Burns, T. R. (2000) 'The Future of Parliamentary Democracy: Transition and Challenge in European Governance', Green Paper prepared for the Conference of the Speakers of EU Parliaments, 22–24 September 2000, Rome.

Cain, B. E., Dalton, R. J., and Scarrow, S. E. (2003) (eds) *Democracy Transformed? Expanding Political Opportunities in Advanced Industrial Democracies* (Oxford: Oxford University Press).

Corbett, R. (1987) 'The 1985 Intergovernmental Conference and the Single European Act', in R. Price (ed.), *The Dynamics of European Union* (London: Croom Helm).

—— (1992) *The Treaty of Maastricht. From Conception to Ratification: A Comprehensive Reference Guide* (Essex: Longman).

—— (1998) *The European Parliament's Role in Closer Integration* (Basingstoke: Palgrave).

Crombez, C., Steunenberg, B. and Corbett, R. (2000) 'Understanding the EU Legislative Process. Political Scientists' and Practitioners' Perspectives', *European Union Politics* 1: 363–81.

Dahl, R. A. (1994) 'A Democratic Dilemma: System Effectiveness versus Citizen Participation', *Political Science Quarterly* 109: 23–34.

Dahrendorf, R. (2000). 'Afterword', in S. J. Pharr and R. D. Putnam (eds), *Disaffected Democracies. What's Troubling the Trilateral Countries?* (Princeton, NJ: Princeton University Press).

Dalton, R. J., Scarrow, S. E. and Cain, B. E. (2003a) 'New Forms of Democracy? Reform and Transformations of Democratic Institutions', in B. E. Cain, R. J. Dalton, and S. E. Scarrow (eds) *Democracy Transformed? Expanding Political Opportunities in Advanced Industrial Democracies*, (Oxford: Oxford University Press).

De Ruyt, J. (1989) *L'Acte Unique Européen* (Brussels: Institut d'Etudes Européen).

Earnshaw, D. and Judge, D. (1996) 'From Co-operation to Co-decision: The European Parliament's Path to Legislative Power', in J. Richardson (ed.) *European Union: Power and Policy-Making* (London: Routledge).

European Commission (1998) *The European Union: 'A View from the Top', Top Decision Makers and the European Union*.

European Parliament (1996) *White Paper on the 1996 Intergovernmental Conference, Vol. II*, http://europa.eu.int/en/agenda/igc-home/eu-doc/parlmentpeen2.htm.

—— (2001) *Report on the Treaty of Nice and the future of the European Union*, A5–0168/2001.

European Scrutiny Committee (2001) *The European Scrutiny System in the House of Commons – A short guide for Members of Parliament by the Staff of the European Scrutiny Committee* (London: House of Commons).

Frears, J. (1990) 'The French Parliament: Loyal Workhorse, Poor Watchdog', in P. Norton (ed.), *Parliaments in Western Europe* (London: Frank Cass).

Garrett, G. and Tsebelis, G. (1996) 'An Institutional Critique of Intergovernmentalism', *International Organization* 50: 269–99.

Garrett, G., Tsebelis, G. and Corbett, R. (2001) 'The EU Legislative Process. Academics vs. Prac-titioners – Round 2', *European Union Politics* 2: 353–66.

Héritier, A. (1999) *Policy-Making and Diversity in Europe. Escaping Deadlock* (Cambridge: Cambridge University Press).

Hix, S. (1997) 'Executive Selection in the European Union: Does the Commission President Investiture Procedure Reduce the Democratic Deficit?', *European Integration online Papers* 1 <http://eiop.or.at/eiop/texte/1997–021.htm>.

—— (2005) *The Political System of the European Union*, 2nd edn (London: Palgrave).

Hix, S. and Lord, C. (1995) 'The Making of a President: The European Parliament and the Confir-mation of Jacques Santer as President of the Commission', *Government and Opposition* 31: 62–72.

House of Commons 791/98: Select Committee on the Modernisation of the House of Commons Seventh Report on 'The Scrutiny of European Business', 17 June 1998.

—— 152-xxx/02: European Scrutiny Committee Thirtieth Report on 'European Scrutiny in the House of Commons', 22 May 2002.

—— (2002) Standing Orders of the House of Commons, Public Business, London.

Hubschmid, C. and Moser, P. (1997) 'The Co-operation Procedure in the EU: Why was the EP Influential in the Decision on Car Emission Standards?', *Journal of Common Market Studies* 35: 225–42.

Judge, D., Earnshaw, D. and Cowan, N. (1994) 'Ripples or Waves: The European Parliament in the European Community Policy Process', *Journal of European Public Policy* 1: 27–52.

Judge, D. and Earnshaw, D. (2003) *The European Parliament* (London: Palgrave).

Kessler, M.-C. (1999) *La politique étrangère de la France. Acteurs et processus* (Paris: Presses de Sciences Po).

Laursen, F. (1995) 'Parliamentary Bodies Specializing in European Union Affairs: Denmark and the European Committee of the Folketing', in F. Laursen and S. A. Pappas (eds), *The Changing Role of Parliaments in the European Union* (Maastricht: European Institute of Public Administration).

—— (2001) 'The Danish Folketing and its European Affairs Committee: Strong Players in the National Policy Cycle', in A. Maurer and W. Wessels (eds), *National Parliaments on their Ways to Europe: Losers or Latecomers?* (Baden-Baden: Nomos).

Laursen, F. and Pappas, S.A. (eds) (1995) *The Changing Role of Parliaments in the European Union* (Maastricht: European Institute of Public Administration).

Lijphart, A. (1999) *Patterns of Democracy: Government Forms and Performance in Thirty-six Coun-tries* (New Haven, CT: Yale University Press).

Marschall, S. (2002) '"Niedergang" und "Aufstieg" des Parlamentarismus im Zeitalter der De-nationalisierung', *Zeitschrift für Parlamentsfragen* 33: 377–90.

Maurer, A. (1999) '(Co-)Governing after Maastricht: The European Parliament's Institutional Performance 1994–1999. Lessons for the Implementation of the Treaty of Amsterdam', *Working Paper POLI 104*, European Parliament: DG for Research.

—— (2002) *Parlamentarische Demokratie in der Europäischen Union: Der Beitrag des Euro-päischen Parlaments und der nationalen Parlamente* (Baden-Baden: Nomos).

Maurer, A. and Wessels, W. (eds) (2001) *National Parliaments after Amsterdam: From Slow Adapters to National Players?* (Baden-Baden: Nomos).

Mezey, M. (1979) *Comparative Legislatures* (Durham, NC: Duke University Press).

Moravcsik, A. (1991) 'Negotiating the Single European Act: National Interests and Conventional Statecraft in the European Community', *International Organization* 45: 19–56.

—— (1994) 'Why the European Community Strengthens the State: Domestic Politics and Interna-tional Cooperation', Center for European Studies Working Paper Series # 52, Cambridge: Center for European Studies, Harvard University.

—— (1998) *The Choice for Europe. Social Purpose and State Power from Messina to Maastricht* (Ithaca, NY: Cornell University Press).

Nannestad, P. (2003) 'Das politische System Dänemarks', in W. Ismayr (ed.), *Die politischen Systeme Westeuropas* (Opladen: Leske und Budrich).

Norton, P. (1990) 'Parliaments: A Framework for Analysis', in P. Norton (ed.), *Parliaments in Western Europe* (London: Frank Cass).

—— (1996a) 'Conclusion: Addressing the Democratic Deficit', in P. Norton (ed.) *National Parliaments and the European Union* (London: Frank Cass).

—— (ed.) (1996b) *National Parliaments and the European Union* (London: Frank Cass).

—— (1998) 'Conclusion: Do Parliaments make a Difference?', in P. Norton (ed.) *Parliaments and Governments in Western Europe* (London: Frank Cass).

Nuttens, J.-D. and Sicard, F. (2000) *Assemblées parlementaires et organisations européennes* (Paris: La documentation Française).

Ostrom, E. (1998) 'A Behavioral Approach to the Rational Choice Theory of Collective Action', *American Political Science Review* 92: 1–22.

Pharr, S. J. and Putnam, R. D. (eds) (2000) *Disaffected Democracies. What's Troubling the Trilateral Countries?* (Princeton, NJ: Princeton University Press).

Polsby, N. W. (1975) 'Legislatures', in F. I. Greenstein and N. W. Polsby (eds), *Governmental Institutions and Processes (Handbook of Political Science, vol. 5)*, (Reading, MA: Addison-Wesley).

Raunio, T. (2004) 'Two Steps Forward, One Step Back? National Legislatures in the EU Constitution', The Federal Trust, http://www.fedtrust.co.uk/uploads/constitution/Raunio.pdf.

Raunio, T. and Hix, S. (2000) 'Backbenchers Learn to Fight Back: European Integration and Parliamentary Government', *West European Politics* 23: 142–68.

Reif, K. and Schmitt, H. (1980) 'Nine Second-Order National Elections: A Conceptual Framework for the Analysis of European Election Results', *European Journal of Political Research* 8: 3–45.

Rittberger, B. (2003) 'The Creation and Empowerment of the European Parliament', *Journal of Common Market Studies* 41: 203–25.

—— (2005) *Building Europe's Parliament. Democratic Representation Beyond the Nation State* (Oxford: Oxford University Press).

Scharpf, F. W. (1988) 'The Joint-Decision-Trap. Lessons from German Federalism and European Integration', *Public Administration* 66: 239–78.

—— (1999) *Governing in Europe. Effective and Democratic?* (Oxford: Oxford University Press).

Scharpf, F. W. , Reissert, B. and Schnabel, F. (1976) *Politikverflechtung. Theorie und Empirie des kooperativen Föderalismus in der Bundesrepublik Deutschland* (Kronberg: Scriptor).

Schelling, T. (1960) *The Strategy of Conflict* (Cambridge, MA: Harvard University Press).

Scully, R. M. (2000) 'Democracy, Legitimacy and the European Parliament', in M. Green Cowles and M. Smith (eds), *The State of the European Union*, vol. 5 (Oxford: Oxford University Press).

Selck, T. J. (2004) *The Impact of Procedure: Analyzing European Union Legislative Decision-Making* (Göttingen: Cuvillier).

Smith, E. (ed.) (1996) *National Parliaments as Cornerstones of European Integration* (London: Kluwer Law International).

Sturm, R. and Pehle, H. (2001) *Das neue deutsche Regierungssystem* (Opladen: Leske und Budrich).

Szukala, A. and Rozenberg, O. (2001) 'The French Parliament and the EU: Progressive Assertion and Strategic Investment', in A. Maurer and W. Wessels (eds), *National Parliaments on their Ways to Europe: Losers or Latecomers?* (Baden-Baden: Nomos).

Tsebelis, G. (1994) 'The Power of the European Parliament as a Conditional Agenda-Setter', *American Political Science Review* 88: 128–42.

Tsebelis, G. and Garrett, G. (2000) 'Legislative Politics in the European Union', *European Union Politics* 1: 9–36.

Wessels, B (1999) 'Political Integration in Europe: Is it Possible to Square the Circle?' *European Integration online Papers* 3, http://eiop.or.at/eiop/texte/1999-009.htm.

Westlake, M. (1994) *A Modern Guide to the European Parliament* (London: Pinter).

145

Chapter 7

The Council of Ministers

Facilitating interaction and developing actorness in the EU

THOMAS CHRISTIANSEN

Introduction

Given its prominence in the decision-making process of the European Union, the Council of Ministers is strangely elusive: it is both a permanent institution and the frequent gathering of ministers from all member states, representatives or officials. It is part of the EU's executive (with the European Commission) and part of the EU's legislature (with the European Parliament), but its work is less transparent than either of the other two institutions. The Council occupies the impressive Justus Lipsius buildings in the heart of the Brussels Euro-district, yet several times a year ministerial meetings take place in Luxemburg. All this may make it difficult to generalise about the Council, but it also makes for an interesting institution.

At the most basic level, the Council provides for the formal representation of member states in the European Union. Ministers attending Council meetings arrive with positions derived from domestic preferences regarding the issues under consideration. Yet this almost immediately leads to one fundamental tension in the work of the Council: given that member state positions on policy proposals are rarely ever identical, the Council is not simply an – or even *the* – decision-making organ of the Union, but also the main forum for negotiation in the EU.

The idea that a *single* institution should be the channel of the *multiplicity* of national interests is a subset of the wider 'unity in diversity' paradox of the European Union. The Council is generally regarded as an intergovernmental institution, making it the focus of those who regard the member states as being in ultimate control of the integration process. Yet – in part precisely because member states have sought to maintain a close hand in the running of the integration process – the Council itself has become increasingly institutionalised. In the first years of the new millennium, the Council's Secretary-General was also acting as the EU's High Representative for Foreign Policy, and the Council Secretariat was becoming the hub of the EU's foreign policy, military and internal security bodies. Thus there has been increasing emphasis on what is *common* rather than on what is *intergovernmental* in the work of the Council – reinforcing a trend that had already been identified at the beginning of the 1990s (Wessels 1991). The Council may not (yet) be a supranational institution in its own right, but it certainly has moved on from being purely a site of decision-taking and the forum for bargaining among representatives of national governments for which it was originally conceived.

This chapter will examine the institutional evolution of the Council. In doing so it will look at the variety of institutional forms that together constitute the Council. The following sections discuss the politics of the Council as a meeting place of national and sectoral interests respectively. Given the expansion of the EU's agenda and the number of sectoral Councils, a special focus here will be the concerns about coherence and coordination in the Council's work. The next section looks at the role of the Presidency – an important institutional device which was, in part, a response to the problem of coordination – before turning to the European Council, which has become an increasingly important part of any Presidency's work programme. After this excursion into the Council's 'superstructure' follows a discussion of its 'underbelly' of committees and working groups, where much of the routine matter of Council decision-making takes place. A further section charts the role of the Council Secretariat, with particular emphasis on its gradual rise to institutional prominence. The conclusion assesses the increasing institutionalisation of intergovernmentalism and the issues that this raises for the future evolution of the Council, and of the EU in general.

The Council of Ministers: institutionalising intergovernmentalism

The Council is the main formal point for the representation of national interests in the EU policy process. There are, of course, numerous ways in which member states influence EU business informally, whether this is through the lobbying of the Commission in the pre-proposal stage of the legislative process, the impact of domestic party hierarchies on voting in the European Parliament (EP) or the use of comitology committees to oversee the implementation of policies. But in a formal, constitutional sense, the Council provides for the systematic involvement of member state representatives in almost any aspect of European integration.

Before going further in discussing the nature of the politics of the Council, it may be useful to distinguish between three different levels at which this interest representation occurs:

- Ministerial: ministers from all member states meeting in the composition of different sectoral Councils
- Heads of State and Government: prime ministers and/or presidents meeting as the European Council (while this is not a formal decision-making body in the Council structure, it is so closely associated with the work of the Council that it ought to be included here)
- Administrative: national officials and/or experts meeting in committees and working groups.

While subsequent sections will look at the latter two of these categories, this section will concentrate on the role played by ministers in the Council. Nevertheless, it is important to recognise from the outset that the work of the Council is embedded within this wider institutional structure.

Ministers from all member states attend Council meetings in order to take decisions on the legislative proposals from the European Commission or amendments proposed by the EP. As implied above, they do so in a wide range of different sectoral Councils. What was initially the preserve of foreign ministers soon involved also ministers of agriculture and, with the widening of the EU's competences, an ever-wider range of ministers, which in the case of the more federal EU member states, can also include ministers from the regional level. By the mid-1990s the number of sectoral Councils had mushroomed to more than twenty, roughly matching the number and designation of Commission Directorate-Generals or EP Committees. However, as coordination of such a growing number of Council formations was getting too difficult, a reform of the Council, agreed at Seville in 2002, reduced this to nine configurations in which the Council can meet.

Member states have two rather different, even opposing, rationales for representing their interests in the Council: on the one hand, individual governments will seek to see their policy preferences realised in decisions about EU policies, if necessary (and possible) against the opposition of other governments. In this respect one

149

can distinguish between various 'cleavages' separating national governments (Hix 1999), including the left/right split, differences about the speed and reach of European integration and, with respect to the EU budget, the divide between net contributors and net recipients. In addition, there has been frequent reference to the division between small and large member states, but this has been a dividing line more in the context of intergovernmental conferences than in legislative decision-making in the Council.

On the other hand, the Council also serves the collectivity of governments to advance a common interest in the intergovernmental aspects of European integration. This refers less to the substance of policy, and more to the structure of the Union and to questions like inter-institutional relations and the use of decision-making procedures. Even in this area, though, there is scope for disagreement among national positions, since some member states, in particular some of the smaller ones, may prefer more supranational solutions (like a strengthened role of the European Commission) to the more intergovernmentalist positions of others. Much of the defence of member states' structural interests takes place in the European Council and in Intergovernmental Conferences, but it also plays a part in routine policy-making. This has contributed to some of the particularities of the EU system of governance like the decentralised implementation of policies, the creation of independent agencies or the growth of comitology.

When looking at the politics of the Council, much depends on the decision-making procedure at force in any given area. The main distinction here is between 'unanimity' and 'qualified majority vote' (QMV). Unanimity requires a decision to be taken without opposition from any member states. In other words, a single member state can block a decision, which is why unanimity is the decisional mechanism applied to policy areas or issues which are sensitive and where some member states would not accept to be overruled.

The application of QMV, on the other hand, provides opportunities for coalition-building, confrontations between different camps and decision-taking against the votes of one or more member states, as long as the required majority agrees. The majority is 'qualified', because it is more than the simple or absolute majority of member states. Instead, in areas in which QMV applies, each member state has a weighted vote recognising its relative size. In 2005, the qualified majority therefore required only the majority of member states, i.e. at least thirteen out of twenty-five states, to be in favour.

In addition, the weighted votes of these states have to constitute at least 232 votes out of a total of 321. States' voting weights range from 29 for the four larger member states to 3 for Malta (see table 7.1). This also goes to show that Council votes are hardly proportional to the population size of the member states: proportionality would give Germany 200 times – rather than 10 times – as much weight as Malta, to point just to the most obvious discrepancy.

In an effort to counter-balance this lack of proportionality, the Nice Treaty introduced a further condition for achieving QMV – the population criteria. A member state may ask for a confirmation that the member states in favour of a decision represent at least 62 per cent of the total population of the EU. This additional 'population element' to Council voting privileges larger member states over smaller ones further, but it benefits Germany, with more than a quarter of the current EU population, in particular.

QMV is of fundamental significance for the EU for a number of reasons. It constitutes the departure from the principle of 'one state, one vote' which characterises the nature of decision-making in traditional intergovernmental institutions. More important still is

Table 7.1   Votes per member state in the Council of Ministers (February 2005). When Romania and Bulgaria join the EU in 2007 they will have 14 and 10 votes respectively, raising the total number of votes to 345.

Germany, France, Italy, United Kingdom	29
Spain, Poland	27
Netherlands	13
Belgium, Czech Republic, Greece, Hungary, Portugal	12
Austria, Sweden	10
Denmark, Ireland, Lithuania, Slovakia, Finland	7
Cyprus, Estonia, Latvia, Luxembourg, Slovenia	4
Malta	3
Total	321

the acceptance of member states that legally binding decisions can be taken against their will, which is what giving up the national veto implies. That is why QMV can be seen as one of the defining features of the European Union. But it is also for this reason that the application of QMV has been highly controversial. While it had been written into the Rome Treaties, it was challenged by President de Gaulle when what he saw as core interests of France were being threatened by the integration process. Temporarily suspended by the 'Luxemburg Compromise' in 1966, the non-application of QMV has been blamed for its part in the decades of 'eurosclerosis' that followed. But QMV survived, not only in terms of a gradual return to the actual treaty provisions, but also through the expansion of its application in every instance of treaty reform since the Single European Act.

With the increased use of QMV, the weighting of votes has become more important, both in terms of member states' individual votes and in terms of the threshold for the achievement of a qualified majority. The matter is particularly thorny in the context of enlargements, as the arrival of new member states inevitably opens the issues of the relative weights not only of the new members but also of the existing ones. This had already been a bone of contention in the preparation for previous enlargements and was only resolved through the so-called Ioannina compromise, in March 1994 – just before the EFTA enlargement (Hayes-Renshaw and Wallace 1997).

The issue of Council voting weights has required a more fundamental reform in view of the eastward expansion of the EU, the pressure for re-weighting had become strong, especially from the larger member states (Best 2000). It had been on the agenda of the IGCs preparing the Amsterdam, Nice and Constitutional Treaties, and on every occasion it proved to be a highly contentious issue. Both the Nice Treaty and the negotiation of the Constitutional Treaty almost failed on this obstacle. The re-weighting of the votes for the member states was one of the issues that led to the failure of the Brussels European Council in December 2003, and a solution was only possible under the subsequent Irish Presidency in the first half of 2004. The Constitutional Treaty provided for a simplified 'double majority' system which requires the support of at least 55 per cent of member states (at least 15) representing at least 65 per cent of the total EU population, though it remains doubtful whether this provision will come into force this way, given the problems that have arisen in the course of ratification. Under the same Treaty, the use of QMV and co-decision procedure would have become the default mechanism for EU decision-making, calling it the 'ordinary legislative procedure', though unanimity would still remain for significant exceptions from this rule.

The high-profile battles among state leaders about the issue of voting weights in the Council in the last instances of treaty reform betray somewhat the limited use that member states actually make of majority voting. In fact, there is a strong tendency among states to act consensually, rather than seeking to achieve results through partisan voting. According to recent research, more than 80 per cent of Council decisions are taken consensually, and in some years the figure is as high as 97 per cent (Heisenberg 2005). Thus, the vast majority of decisions – many more than would be formally required – are taken by consensus.

In an apparent paradox, the introduction and expansion of QMV has supported this tendency. Under QMV the dynamic of decision-making is a desire by all states to be either among the winning majority or among the blocking minority. However, if it is impossible to construct a blocking minority, states, even when they have misgivings about the proposed legislation, will rather seek to join the majority, in return for amendments, rather than be 'left out in the cold' of a losing minority. And in the same vein, the states holding a qualified majority will usually continue to negotiate to reach a consensus rather than outvote a number of countries, in the knowledge that in future instances of legislative decision-making they may be at the receiving end.

Consensualism in the Council is also a reaction to the particular nature of EU policy-making more generally. In a system of decentralised implementation, with the EU institutions relying to a large extent on national parliaments to transpose EU laws, on national authorities to implement these, and on national courts to adjudicate on the basis of them, the wisdom of taking decisions *against* certain member states when their subsequent cooperation is required may be doubtful. Instead, more efficient implementation may be gained by negotiating their agreement to the legislative act, thus being more certain of compliance later. In other words, efficiency losses in decision-making are expected to be outweighed by efficiency gains in implementation.

Consensualism in Council decision-making can thus be explained in terms of the rational interests of the member states, even, and perhaps especially, under conditions of QMV. But over time it has also become part of the culture of negotiation in the Council (Heisenberg 2005). The development towards consensual decision-making is in part also a reaction to the way in which the structure of the Council forces member states to represent their interests along sectoral lines, thus creating the bureaucratic politics discussed in the following section.

Beyond interstate relations: bureaucratic politics in the Council

The debates about re-weighting of votes and the extension of QMV reflect the expectation that the politics of the Council pitch member states against member states. Given the nature of the Council as the main forum for the representation of member state interests, that is justified. But the politics of the Council go beyond the confrontation between different member state positions. Indeed, the development of the Council – the expan-

Table 7.2   The different configurations of the Council of Ministers (February 2005)

General Affairs and External Relations

Economic and Financial Affairs

Cooperation in the fields of Justice and Home Affairs (JHA)

Employment, Social Policy, Health and Consumer Affairs

Competitiveness

Transport, Telecommunications and Energy

Agriculture and Fisheries

Environment

Education, Youth and Culture

sion in the number of sectoral Councils – is a powerful illustration of the way in which the concept of 'national interest' needs to be unpacked when studying the politics of the European Union. Looking at the relationship between the various Councils reveals the differences in opinion not just between, but also within countries.

As mentioned above, the initial Council was composed of foreign ministers, whose meeting is termed the General Affairs and External Relations Council (GAERC). As the extension of Community competences has progressed, other Councils dealing with more specialised matters have been created. After the Seville reforms of 2002 there are nine Council configurations (see table 7.2). The more prominent among these are the Agriculture Council, the ECOFIN Council and the Competitiveness Council (comprising the previous Internal Market, Industry and Research Councils). While the Seville reforms have nominally reduced the number of configurations, they leave open the opportunity for member states to meet in different compositions, bringing together ministers with different portfolios on different days – a development that in itself may generate new challenges of internal coordination.

Each of these Councils brings together the ministers who have domestic competence in the respective area. The frequency of their meetings differs according to the volume of EU decision-making in that sector. For example, foreign ministers or agriculture ministers hold monthly meetings, whereas employment ministers meet only four times a year.

The sectoral Councils provide a forum for the representation of diverse national interests in their respective areas, but they also have a wider significance as an arena for the socialisation of ministers who share a common interest in the management of the sector for which they are responsible domestically. This is a major departure from domestic politics, where meetings at ministerial level – usually in the cabinet – will pitch the ministers from different departments against one another. In a domestic cabinet meeting, the positions of, say, the transport, environment and budget ministers are bound to reflect the different sectoral and bureaucratic interests at play. The emergence of such interdepartmental differences would be expected from a bureaucratic politics perspective (Peters 1992).

In the Council, sectoral ministers, who 'at home' have to fight lonely battles in cabinet meetings, will find themselves in the company of colleagues from the other member states with often similar experiences from their domestic background. In addition, they all will share the knowledge of the subject-matter, are used to the lobbying from organised interests in the field and are familiar with the political and administrative problems in the area. It is on the basis of such a common background that they meet in the context of the Council. If the right conditions are present an *esprit de corps* may grow among them – participation in, for example, the Agriculture Council will emphasise identification as the UK *Agriculture* Secretary as well as the *UK* Agriculture Secretary. In that sense, the Council fulfils a function not only in terms of the representation of national interests but also in terms of the creation of transnational policy communities at the highest political level. This 'reverse dynamic' is even stronger at lower administrative levels, where bureaucratic interaction is more frequent, and where much of the routine decision-making takes place – a subject to which we will return below.

The development of a transnational sense of community in the Council will depend on numerous factors, including the length of time individual ministers spend in their jobs, the frequency and intensity of their meetings, the contentiousness of issues under discussion and the antagonism of domestically determined positions to be represented (Egeberg 1999). Socialisation is actively encouraged through the increasingly frequent recourse to 'informal' Councils – Council meetings which are organised by, and held in, the country holding the Presidency, rather than in the usual meeting rooms in Brussels or Luxembourg. It is a practice that originated among foreign ministers, who started in the mid-1970s to hold 'Gymnich-type meetings' in the context of European Political cooperation. Foreign ministers extended this practice, first to the General Affairs Council, and subsequently to other configurations. The rationale for holding such meetings, which are limited to five per Presidency, is the expectation that a meeting conducted in an informal atmosphere and without the pressure to take routine decisions permits a more relaxed discussion of the broader strategic issues and the general direction of policy. Initially conceived as meetings without a set agenda, they now provide an opportunity to address a specific issue in greater depth (Council of the European Union 1999). Often informal Councils conclude by espousing a certain vision for the development of EU policy in a given area.

The point to be made here is that the Council has to be regarded as more than simply the meeting place of national interests. It is also the meeting place of different sectoral and bureaucratic interests and thus exposes the complexity – and potential contradictions – subsumed by the concept of a 'national interest' (Lewis 2000). But if individual Councils do develop an *esprit de corps*, dividing lines between the various Councils are likely to emerge, in line with the observation about domestic bureaucratic politics made above. In institutional terms this means that there is also the potential for internal fragmentation and that coordination across the various sectoral Councils becomes an issue (Lipsius 1995). It is in this respect that the role of the GAERC Council has been elevated, so that it stands above the sectoral Councils. If issues cannot be resolved, they can be referred to the GAERC, though the crowded agenda there means that the potential for the resolution of the often highly technical issues of other Councils may be limited (Lipsius 1995). There are other mechanisms for coordinating the activity of the sprawling complex of Councils. These include the Presidency, the European Council, the work of preparatory committees, in particular the Committee of Permanent Representatives, and the Council Secretariat. The following sections will look in more detail at the role these institutions play in the structure of the Council.

Member states as agenda-setters: the role of the Presidency

The Council's position as the key legislative institution of the Union implies a reactive role: it has to respond to the proposals made by the Commission and, increasingly, to the amendments proposed by the Parliament. That is why traditionally the Commission rather than the Council is regarded as the agenda-setter in the EU policy process. But there are a number of ways in which national governments have sought to regain control of, or at least play a part in, the setting of the Union's agenda. The most important mechanisms to be discussed here are developments linked to the Council: the EU Presidency and the European Council.

The Presidency started off as a seemingly functional innovation in the Council: to share among national administrations the task of organising Council business and chairing the various ministerial meetings and working groups (Westlake 1995). Every six months, one member state takes over this role, and ministers and officials chair any of the meetings that are convened during that period. Apart from allowing individual meetings at any level to run more smoothly, this also facilitates the continuity of negotiation and decision-making over time. The institution of the Presidency also permits a greater degree of both horizontal coordination (across the various sectoral Councils) and vertical coordination (between meetings of ministers, permanent representatives and national officials). The growing number of sectoral Councils is one reason why the Presidency has become more important over time: as more EU business is being debated and decided in a larger number of fora, there is greater potential for inconsistency and therefore greater demand for effective coordination (Wallace 1985).

Yet the Presidency is anything but an innocent functional creation. The institution of the Presidency is political not only because it affects the relationship between the individual member state, the collectivity of states and the EU institutions, but also because it is closely linked to the management of the EU's external affairs – arguably a key area of 'high politics', and one from which member states have long sought to exclude the more supranational institutions. Starting in the 1970s with the establishment of European Political coordination and now in the context of the Common Foreign and Security Policy, the Presidency is responsible for the external representation of the EU's foreign policy positions. This is a delicate task, given the increasing visibility of the EU in world politics, and considering that it requires the state in question to handle foreign policy in a manner that is different from the execution of its national foreign policy. Both the nature of the issues, and the way in which these are handled, will be different from that country's conventional national foreign policy.

The nature of European foreign policy means that there is bound to be a tension between, on the one hand, the need to respond quickly to issues or crises as they happen, and, on the other, to maintain a process of inclusive consultation with all member states. Similar demands are present in other policy areas, putting great pressure on the government holding the Presidency. Therefore the Presidency not only constitutes a substantial administrative responsibility but also involves a high political profile and carries with it the accompanying risks and opportunities.

For these reasons of political balance and administrative efficiency, changes to the Presidency system have been discussed since the Nice Treaty, in the context of both the internal Council reforms agreed at Seville in 2002, and the Convention on the Future of Europe. There had been plans in the Convention to create a Team Presidency, but in the end the 2003–4 IGC chose the more traditional method of individual member states holding the Presidency for six months on the basis of equal rotation. However, a declaration attached to the Treaty foresees a decision by the European Council that would create 'groups' of three member states that would jointly organise and coordinate their subsequent presidencies.

Thus the Constitutional Treaty, if ratified, would not formally change the current practice of the rotating Presidency. However, in addition to laying the foundations for the team presidency concept, it did provide for important changes, such as the European Council President (chairing the European Council) and the EU foreign affairs ministers (chairing the GAERC) which would have a major impact on the nature of the Presidency.

The change that *was* agreed in the Seville reforms and is currently in practice is that of the two forthcoming Presidencies coordinating their plans each December by adopting an annual operational programme. This has led the two countries who each year hold the Presidency for six months to work closely together, not only in terms of agenda-setting and legislative planning but also in organisational and logistical terms. In a way, this is a move towards informally achieving something that the idea of the Team Presidency was supposed to deliver: member states working together and sharing the administrative burden while providing the Union with greater stability and continuity in its overall direction.

The establishment of a rotating Presidency among member states also reaffirms the role of national governments in the EU structure. In fact, in terms of the distinction of different types of interest representation made earlier, it emphasises the role of the *individual* country rather than the collectivity of member states. In that sense, the Presidency has become an important, albeit limited, counterweight to the loss of national autonomy in the EU generally, and in the Council in particular. Holding the Presidency permits the respective national government to prioritise certain issues during its term and to manage the agenda accordingly. For example, if the country holding the agenda is a southern or northern member state, it may want to push a specific geographical concern such as, respectively, the Euro-Mediterranean Partnership or the Northern Dimension. On the other hand, if the country holding the Presidency is a net contributor to the EU's budget, then it has a stronger interest in privileging budget reform in the setting of the agenda. However, as the above discussion of the need for cooperation among subsequent Presidencies by adopting annual programmes demonstrates, with internal reforms and after enlargement, the constraints for any individual Presidency have grown enormously. If the cost of the Presidency has always been the administrative workload, and the gain the ability to shape EU decision-making, then in recent years the costs have increased and the gains diminished.

Shaping the EU's agenda is also difficult for any Presidency because this agenda is influenced by numerous factors outside the control of individual actors. Some of these are structurally or externally determined, especially since much of EU business is now conducted in the form of multi-annual programmes. This is true both for spending programmes like the structural funds and for regulatory programmes, for example in environmental or social policy. When such programmes need to be renegotiated, any Presidency will have to address these accordingly during its term. Developments that are 'external' to the EU, for example the need to respond to the changes in Central and Eastern Europe through an accession strategy, will also impose themselves on the agenda of any country holding the Presidency. Other member states or actors like the

Commission or foreign countries will also raise issues that the Presidency may be unable to ignore. Crucially, the Presidency is expected to act as an honest broker with regard to issues raised by other member states and will have to take these into account when constructing the agenda.

It is only within these limitations that the Presidency can emphasise – rather than impose – its own priorities in the setting of the agenda. In fact, the Presidency is very much a double-edged sword, precisely because of these limitations and the requirement to appear as an objective keeper of the common good (Wallace 1993). A Presidency which is seen to be abusing its agenda-setting role and its chairmanship in the pursuit of its own national interest will be ineffectual, and it may even be that it is easier to defend a certain position or push a specific interest when *not* holding the Presidency. In any case, holding the Presidency requires the member state in question to strike a fine balance between, on the one hand, the pursuit of a national agenda – which may have built up over a considerable period of time – and, on the other hand, the necessities of effective decision-making and agenda-management – which may override the national interest.

Beyond the rational calculation of interests, the Presidency also performs a powerful symbolic function: it confers upon the incumbent country a special role which permits the government to emphasise its specific understanding of the goals and the direction of the integration process. The Presidency unifies the European and the national identity of the state, enabling the government to pursue a discourse (and perhaps a European policy) which may at other times prove elusive. For domestic consumption, the image of a country holding the Presidency removes the potentially antagonistic perception which often regards the state as pitched against an external 'Europe'. In its place governments seek to put the image of a country that, while asserting its role and identity within the Union, works for the common good – an imagery that is accompanied by symbols, logos and slogans specifically designed for the occasion. In a wider sense, the Presidency also serves as a powerful symbol externally that European integration is driven by states, rather than being a process happening to them.

The term of the Presidency begins formally with the identification of a number of key themes at the outset of the term. These themes are part of a communication to the Council, European Parliament and the Commission – and the wider public – in the first week of the term, and form the basis of a more detailed work programme involving the various sectoral Councils over the coming six months. In addition to the prepared programme, the Presidency will be expected to lead the EU response to unexpected developments and crises, whether these are internal to the EU or part of its foreign policy. An effective Presidency therefore needs both a clear vision of what it seeks to achieve during its term and an ability to respond rapidly to the changing political circumstances of the day. Again, there is a balance to be struck between strong leadership and intensive consultation in order to ensure that all member states agree to, comply with and, if necessary, contribute to the policy that emerges from the deliberations in the Council.

In practical terms, the Presidency raises substantial resource issues for the country concerned. Setting the agenda and coordinating EU business across the range of sectoral Councils and administrative levels requires much preparation before, and constant attention during, the term. The greatest part of the pressure will be on the relevant sections in foreign ministries, prime ministers' offices and any other ministries that would usually perform a coordinating role in the domestic EU process. Staff in these

departments will now be required also to relate regularly and systematically to their counterparts in other member states. Also the EU sections in sectoral ministries will be affected by their country holding the Presidency, as they will have to coordinate the discussions or negotiations with regard to dossiers falling into their area of competence.

The member state's Permanent Representation in Brussels will probably witness the greatest change to its volume of work – Perm Reps regularly double their staff numbers in the run-up and during the period of the Presidency, given the additional workload they have to cope with. One significant resource issue is the need to chair meetings of working groups, committees of Councils in Brussels: given that these meetings number in the hundreds over the term of any Presidency and imply preparation as well as physical presence, there is much demand on staff time at both ministerial and official level as well as a greater reliance on the assistance of the Council Secretariat (see below).

The resources of any country are stretched by the demands of the Presidency, but this has been an issue particularly for the smaller member states. For them, the combination of greater political responsibility and extraordinary demands on resources is especially challenging. On the other hand, more used to compromising national positions in the context of EU negotiations, smaller countries are more likely to avoid the temptation of overlaying the formal responsibilities of the Presidency with their own political priorities – something which has been a more obvious problem for the larger member

Table 7.3 Calendar of Presidencies as agreed by the Council of Ministers on 13 December 2004

Year	January–June	July–December
2005	Luxembourg	United Kingdom
2006	Austria	Finland
2007	Germany	Portugal
2008	Slovenia	France
2009	Czech Republic	Sweden
2010	Spain	Belgium
2011	Hungary	Poland
2012	Denmark	Cyprus
2013	Ireland	Lithuania
2014	Greece	Italy
2015	Latvia	Luxembourg
2016	Netherlands	Slovakia
2017	Malta	United Kingdom
2018	Estonia	Bulgaria
2019	Austria	Romania
2020	Finland	

states. In either case, the size of a member state matters for the conduct of the Presidency, both in terms of the resources of the administration and in terms of the political weight of the incumbent. That is one reason why in the determination of the sequence of countries holding the Presidency there has been a departure from the simple alphabetical rule that was in place until the accession of Spain and Portugal. A new sequence has been specifically written into the Treaty, in order to ensure a balance between larger and smaller member states (Westlake 1995). In late 2004 the Council decided on a Presidency calendar stretching to 2020 and including not only all the new member states, but also the future member states of Bulgaria and Romania (table 7.3).

Leadership from the top? The evolution of the European Council

It is also the responsibility of the Presidency to organise regular meetings of the Heads of State and Government. Above, reference has already been made to informal Council meetings, but the Presidency is also responsible for running ministerial meetings with representatives of third countries, for example from the accession countries, or landmark conferences on topical aspects of the integration process. But the 'highlight' of any Presidency is the organisation of a summit meeting that originally was not contained in the founding treaties but has become one of the pivotal institutions of the EU: the European Council. What began in the 1970s first as extraordinary summits of prime ministers eventually became normalised as regular meetings of heads of state and government, hosted by the Presidency. With the passage of the Single European Act in 1985 the new institution, by then recognised as the European Council, was formally incorporated into the Treaty. At least twice a year, the European Council brings together the heads of state and of government – i.e. all prime ministers and the presidents of France and Finland – as well as the President of the Commission. While the European Council does not have a formal role in the legislative process (which is a change that would have come with the ratification of the Constitutional Treaty), it plays an important part in the wider decision-making process of the Union.

Each Presidency usually holds two European Council meetings throughout its term. These meetings usually take place in March (which is earmarked as a regular review of the Lisbon Strategy), in June, in October and in December. Due to the inherent significance of a meeting at the highest political level, the European Council functions as a stocktaking exercise for the Presidency – an opportunity for decision-makers as well as observers to see how much progress has been achieved with respect to the Presidency's work programme. Beyond stocktaking, the European Council has become a focal point of the decision-making process. Particularly in cases where there has been deadlock in the sectoral Council, and where the foreign ministers in the GAERC Council have been equally unable to reach agreement. In this situation, the European Council can function as the arbiter of the last resort. In order to be more proactive about future planning and giving direction to the work of the Union, the European Council has decided to adopt a 'multiannual strategic programme'. The first of these was agreed in December 2003 by the six countries holding the Presidency between 2004 and 2006 (Council 2003).

In contrast to the ministerial Council meetings, which have become routine matters in the EU policy process, the European Council remains a high profile event that can concentrate the minds of the decision-makers. The Presidency, in particular, will want to see *their* European Council meeting regarded as a success – which means prime ministers need to be seen taking decisions on the major issues. It is because of this particular dynamic of the European Council that it has on occasion given fresh impetus to specific issues or to the integration process at large. Especially with respect to the 'big issues', such as budget reform or enlargement, the European Council, rather than the Council of Ministers, has been the forum in which landmark decisions have been taken (Bulmer and Wessels 1987). Decision-making in the European Council has always required a consensus among member states.

This is an interesting reversal of roles, since critics originally expected the European Council to be the more conservative player in the integration process (Sasse 1975; Wessels 1980). The initial expectation was that the meeting of heads of state and government would reassert national interests and rein in ministers who, in the course of frequent meetings in the Council, had been socialised into compromising too quickly domestically agreed positions in the search of EU-wide agreement. This may well be the case in certain instances, but the European Council has also seen vested sectoral interests being overridden at the highest political level. After all, it is at this level that package deals and trade-offs, these quintessential features of EU policy-making, are best constructed. And as it has become more difficult to strike such deals in the fragmented world of ministerial Councils, the European Council has increasingly performed this role.

In the 1990s, there has been a marked increase in the frequency of treaty reform, with three major revisions of the founding treaties contained in the Maastricht (1992), Amsterdam (1997) and Nice (2000) Treaties. Each of these treaties takes its name from the place at which the respective European Council met in order to take the final decisions and to sign the final act. This symbolises the significance of the Presidency for running – and concluding – the negotiation of Treaty reform. IGCs are mainly conducted at the level of senior officials representing the member states in weekly meetings, with participation also from the Commission and the European Parliament. There are regular meetings also of foreign ministers in order to provide political guidance, and any European Council meeting held during an IGC constitutes a forum to review the state of the negotiations. The European Council meeting which is to conclude the IGC and agree the draft treaty will largely be taken over by the need to reach agreement on the last remaining – often most controversial – aspects of that round of treaty reform.

The Presidency and the European Council are key institutions in the European Union: they reaffirm the role of individual countries and of the highest political level in the integration progress. As such, they have proved to be an integral part of a Euro-polity that is being constructed with, and by – not against – the member states. In practical terms, they both constitute mechanisms for coordination across the various areas of EU activity and provide the political leadership that may otherwise be missing in a Union of twenty-five and more member states. And they offer opportunities for national governments, and for the collectivity of states, to influence the setting of the EU's agenda and to maintain control over the direction of EU policy. In that sense, they are aspects of the institutional structure which assists member states to balance the agenda-setting powers of the supranational institutions, in particular those of the European Commission.

The Constitutional Treaty took the actorness of the European Council one step further by introducing the post of President of the European Council. The role of this new President would be to work towards greater cohesion and dynamism in the European Council, and represent the EU internally and externally. One has to wonder to what extent this post will be more than a symbolic role, given that there may be little to do for the President between European Councils, and given also that the function of external representation should not prejudice the powers of another post to be newly created, that of the EU Foreign Minister (which is discussed below). But this position, though it may be frustrating for the individual performing it, still shows that the member states seek institutional solutions to achieve greater unity and facilitate collective decision-making among themselves – intergovernmentalism in the EU is getting ever more institutionalised.

Administrative integration: the committees and working groups of the Council

The Council's relationship with the Commission is often characterised as one of rivalry, with the Commission pushing for further integration, with the Council holding back and providing member states with a mechanism to hold the Commission in check. In reality, the situation is more complex, not only because the European Parliament is an increasingly potent player in a tripartite relationship, but also because both the Commission and the Council are internally more differentiated than these one-dimensional images suggest (Christiansen 2001). Chapter 5 in this volume demonstrates the degree to which intergovernmental dynamics impinge on the work of the Commission (Christiansen 2005). The reverse can be said of the Council, where we can witness an accelerating trend towards a greater degree of institutionalisation.

The previous sections have emphasised the fluidity of Council business, with different ministers meeting in different places, guided by a Presidency that changes hands every six months. But the Council is a central institution of the European Union, with a physical presence in Brussels, an expanding number of permanent staff and a certain capacity for independent action. The building blocks of this institutionalisation of intergovernmentalism are, on the one hand, the structure of committee and working groups which do the preparatory work for the ministerial meetings, and, on the other hand, the Council Secretariat, which provides organisational, logistical and legal backup for the meetings of ministers and officials. This section and the next will look at each of these aspects of institutionalised intergovernmentalism in turn.

The institution 'Council of Ministers' extends well beyond the regular meetings of ministers. In fact, much of the legislative decision-making of the Council is done in committees and working groups which 'prepare' the ministerial meetings. With the expansion of the number of ministerial Councils, the number of committees and working groups had also grown exponentially, as there are numerous specialised committees and working groups working for each individual Council. The number of such committees and working groups had risen to about 250 in the 1990s, but has since then been reduced in line with the reduction of Council configurations agreed in Seville.

It is at this administrative level that the bulk of the routine work of the Council is done. Council working groups are the first port of call for Commission proposals and, if applicable, EP amendments. Here, national officials who are familiar with the technical detail of the measure in question vet Commission proposals, EP amendments and the various opinions of representatives emerging in the meeting with a view to their respective domestic preferences.

At the heart of the Council's committee structure stands Coreper, the standing committee of permanent representatives. Its members are the member states' 'ambassadors' (or their deputies) to the EU, heading their countries' permanent representations in Brussels. As such, they fulfil a dual role which perfectly characterises the function of the Council's committee structure as the 'hinge' between member state and European Union more generally (Christiansen and Kirchner 2000). Permanent representatives are an important part of the individual countries' system of interest representation as well as being an integral part of the EU's decision-making process. Wearing their 'national hat', permanent representatives are gatekeepers of information and interests, working across the range of issues and regularly committing their member state to decisions in the process. Wearing their 'EU hat', they help to coordinate the work of the sectoral Councils and of more specialised working groups by preparing the agendas of Council and of European Council meetings (de Zwann 1995). Indeed, permanent representatives help to keep the agendas of ministers free for sensitive questions or the debate of politically contested issues, as Coreper itself takes decisions on matters which are considered routine business or on which member states can more easily find agreement.

Coreper stands at the top of a hierarchy of the numerous committees which form part of the Council of Ministers (Hayes-Renshaw and Wallace 1997). In fact, a distinction needs to be made between the committee of permanent representatives, who meet as Coreper II, and the meeting of their deputies, which is known as Coreper I. In addition, there are a number of specialised committees – for example, the Standing Committee on Agriculture or the Political and Security Committee –which consist of senior officials from the ministries in the member states. Like the two Corepers, these committees receive their workload from working groups made up of officials or experts from national or regional administrations, who have been evaluating and searching for agreement on the detailed policy proposals issued by the Commission. Within the allotted period, the working groups or specialised committees either reach agreement on the measure in question or else notify the permanent representatives of the need for further discussions. It is at this stage that administrative issues start to be overtaken by political considerations (Westlake 1995).

As items move up through the Council hierarchy, from working group to Coreper and eventually to ministerial meetings, they are being designated as either 'A' or 'B' points (or, in the case of Coreper, 'I' and 'II' points) on the agendas of the respective meetings. An 'A' point implies that the issue has been settled at a lower level, and it will usually be passed as a matter of course at the higher level, with no further discussion required. Ministers, when meeting in the Council, will therefore concentrate on the 'B' points of the agenda, indicating the – much smaller – number of items on which officials or permanent representatives have not been able to reach agreement in their preparatory meetings. It is worth emphasising that the bulk of Council decisions is effectively agreed here: according to estimates, some 70–80 per cent of all decisions made in the Council are already prepared in Coreper or in the Council working groups, and then only formally taken by the Ministers through the 'A' points procedure.

A look at the committee structure of the Council demonstrates the degree of 'administrative interaction' between national and European levels (Wessels 1990). Every month, Council working groups and committees bring together thousands of officials from the ministries and regulatory authorities of the member states in Brussels. Here they interact not only with representatives from other member states but also with officials from the Commission and the Council Secretariat who also participate in their meetings. In addition, they are likely to be the object of attention from lobbyists and organised interests who will seek to influence the decision-making process in one or the other direction. The volume and the intensity of these bureaucratic interactions has a number of significant consequences for European governance. First, it does establish a strong and permanent presence of member state administrations at the European level. This deserves emphasis, also because frequent references to the 'Brussels bureaucracy' in the media and in the political debate tend to imply that the corridors in Brussels are only populated by Commission officials. This is obviously misleading, as the number of national officials travelling to, or living in, Brussels in order to attend Council, committee and working group meetings is probably greater that the number of A-level officials in the Commission.

Second, in terms of the decision-making process, it is important to recognise administrative interaction in the Council as a two-way process. Interests are channelled from the national to the European level, but in the process officials are also becoming aware of the positions taken by other countries and will communicate these back to their superiors 'at home'. On the one hand, there are opportunities here for genuine problem-solving and the search for best practice, making the Council's committee structure an important site for the transnational integration of member state administrations (Lewis 2000). On the other hand, the participants in working group meetings will recognise the limits of any emerging consensus and – if politically acceptable – will adjust their negotiating position accordingly. At times, this can mean that negotiators, rather than receiving orders from the national capital as to what position they *should* take, end up telling their masters what position in a shifting debate they *can* take. Researchers have also pointed to the resistance by officials in the working groups – those who have the technical expertise in a given area – to hand over issues for decision-making to generalists such as the diplomats in Coreper. There, package deals linking issues from otherwise separate arenas – the staple diet of Coreper – may compromise the detailed technical work that has already gone into the deliberation of a particular proposal. The dynamic of this interaction between specialists and generalists contributes to proposals often spending long periods of deliberation in working groups, and a high share of them (eventually) being resolved there.

Often the nature of deliberations in Council working groups is characterised as 'technical' rather than 'political', and of course it is the case that here we have meetings of technical experts, usually attachés from the member states' permanent representations, rather than political office-holders. However, it would be simplistic to convey the impression that the issues under discussion may not be political – as the events such as the BSE crisis have demonstrated, even highly technical issues have the potential to turn into major political controversies. Instead one can look at the way in which issues are discussed, deliberated and negotiated in the working groups in terms of processes of politicisation and de-politicisation (Smith *et al.* 2005). Depending on instructions, political sensitivities and dynamics in the negotiations, issues emerge from the Council working groups as 'political' (i.e. needing be resolved at higher levels) or 'technical' (i.e. they can be resolved by technical experts).

The recognition of the nature of the Council as an arena for two-way exchange, rather than a site of one-directional representation of national interests, is related to a further point about socialisation. This was already mentioned in the context of ministerial Councils. If anything, this dynamic effect of frequent interaction in transnational meetings is even more important at the administrative level. With party politics and media attention (normally) taken out of the equation, officials can concentrate on the technical necessities of the issue at hand. They will have to work within the confines of a politically circumscribed negotiating space, but within these limits there is much potential for collegiality and group dynamics. This includes not only the potential development of a common identity or the growth of an epistemic community, but also the opportunity for individual participants to influence the proceedings based on their knowledge, the strength of their argument or negotiating skills rather than purely on the political weight of their member state (Lewis 1998). That is why it is justified to look for the supranational rather than only the intergovernmental features in the system of Council working groups (Beyers and Dierckx 1998).

Towards 'actorness': the elevation of the Council Secretariat and the Secretary-General

Administrative interaction within the structure of the Council already demonstrates the difficulty in clearly distinguishing between supranational and intergovernmental dynamics of the European institutions. The picture becomes even more blurred if the Secretariat-General of the Council is entered into the equation. Here we have an institution whose original purpose was simply the logistical assistance of regular meetings of ministers and officials from the member states, but which has gone a long way towards developing into a political institution in its own right.

The core function of the Secretariat-General remains the support of the meetings of working groups, committees and ministers in the Council. This ranges from the provision of meeting space, via the taking of minutes and dissemination of agendas, supporting papers and minutes, to assistance through legal advice and research services. The Secretariat is the institutional memory of the Council, and as such is the ultimate guide to working methods, internal procedures and past practice. It is the legal and procedural know-how, in particular, which has helped the Secretariat to become a distinct player in the Council. In advising member states on the procedures by which decisions are taken, and on legal questions arising from the drafting of legislation, the Secretariat makes an important, albeit hidden, contribution to the decision-making process (Beach 2004; Christiansen 2002).

Beyond assistance to the Council generally, the Secretariat works in particular for, and with, the Presidency. In the preparation of meetings, but in particular in the drafting of joint opinions or legal documents afterwards, the Secretariat will assist the Presidency (Sherrington 2000). It is here that demands on the administrative resources of the member states, especially of smaller countries, are being counterbalanced by administrative support from the Secretariat. In such cases, when the member state holding the Presidency relies heavily on the services of the Secretariat, the two operate closely together, with the Secretariat rather than the national capital taking on an influential role in drafting minutes, agendas and legislation.

The Secretariat's role of assisting the Presidency with legal and procedural advice before, during and after meetings of national representatives is of political significance in the context of any important decision taken in the Council, but even more so in the course of an Intergovernmental Conference (Christiansen and Jørgensen 1998). Given the legal implications of any treaty change and the complexity of the existing constitutional arrangements, the expertise present in the Secretariat's legal service provides it with an important role in the process of negotiations (Hayes-Renshaw and Wallace 1997). Crucially, though, it depends on the attitude of the Presidency whether that potential is being realised or not: a strong Presidency with clear goals and an ability to manage the demands of the role effectively may not defer to the Secretariat's opinions. A weaker Presidency, on the other hand, may leave much of the work – and the opportunity to influence the direction of negotiations – in the hands of Secretariat officials.

If the Secretariat has a role in the EU's decision-making process, it may be worth asking what its interests are. A simple answer would point to the institutional interests of the Council, as the Secretariat is bound to benefit, or suffer, from any change in the Council's institutional standing. But the Secretariat's attitude to institutional reform may differ from one issue to another, and would also depend on (the nationality of) the officials involved. In general, though, it makes most sense to look at the Secretariat in relation to the European Commission. In the past, both institutions have been keen to take over wider responsibilities as the competences of the EU were being enlarged.

Against this background, the Secretariat has been remarkably successful in gaining an executive role in the more intergovernmental policy areas of the Union, and in particular with respect to the development of the EU's common foreign, security and defence policies (Presidency of the European Union 1999). In doing so, the Secretariat has acquired new competences in representing the EU abroad. The European Commission, whose responsibilities in areas such as trade, development and humanitarian aid make it an important player in the management of the Union's external relations, is 'fully associated' with the CFSP. Through its President, the Commission also represents the EU at G8 summit meetings of major industrial powers. But the central institutions of EU diplomacy are now firmly located in the Secretariat, turning it into a new actor in the conduct of the EU's external relations.

The process began with the EPC Secretariat, which had been established outside the existing institutional framework of the Community, being integrated into the Council Secretariat through the Maastricht Treaty. After the addition of a 'Policy Planning Unit', the Secretariat also contains 'task forces' on the different geographical areas of CFSP activity as well as a Situation Centre for crisis management. Also attached to the Secretariat are the EU's observer mission in the former Yugoslavia and the growing number of Special Envoys appointed to coordinate EU policy to troubled regions like South-Eastern Europe, the Middle East and the African Central Lakes region.

Compared to the foreign policy machinery of states, this is still a very small administration, but through cooperation with the member states' diplomatic services and the Commission's network of representations in third countries there would be growing potential for effective joint action (*Financial Times* 2000). For much of its history, there has been a search for 'actorness' in the intergovernmental nature of CFSP, and the use of the Secretariat as the home of an emerging EU foreign policy bureaucracy is one answer to this aspiration. A further, far-reaching step has been the creation of the post of High Representative of the CFSP through the Amsterdam Treaty. This role of 'Mr CFSP' (or, as the case may be, 'Ms CFSP') has been added to the existing post of the Secretary-General, who heads the Secretariat.

Past Secretaries-General of the Council Secretariat were senior diplomats in one of the member states before taking up their job in Brussels, but the political significance of the post experienced a quantum leap with the appointment, in 1999, of Javier Solana. Before joining the Secretariat, Solana had been Foreign Minister in Spain and Secretary-General of NATO, and as such is regarded as a political 'heavyweight'. His responsibilities were further extended when, later in 1999, he was also appointed as Secretary-General of the Western European Union, signalling the strengthening links and the partial merger of this organisation with the Council. Solana's seniority together with his experience in foreign affairs and defence matters adds substantially to the actorness of the CFSP: now there is a central authority to communicate common positions, negotiate on the EU's behalf with third countries and oversee the growing number of EU missions and interventions in crisis regions. Nevertheless, the emphasis in judging the significance of this new post must be on the *potential* for enhancing the EU's foreign policy capabilities. Much still depends on the political will among member states – often lacking in the past – to agree to common positions and subsequently to comply with these.

Javier Solana's experience as NATO Secretary-General is significant also in the context of efforts to develop a dedicated EU role in defence matters. For decades, the 'security' aspect of CFSP had been treated sensitively in order to ensure that military issues would not appear on the agenda of the EU. This was in response both to internal constraints – the sensitivities of neutral or non-aligned member states – as well as to external relationships – the desire among most EU members to maintain a strong link with the USA in the framework of NATO. But in the late 1990s, in response to an Anglo-French initiative and in the wake of the Kosovo war, consensus was emerging among member states that the EU ought to have a military capability to conduct so-called 'Petersberg tasks' – military intervention in crisis areas for the purposes of peace-keeping, peace-enforcement or humanitarian assistance. The Helsinki Council in December 1999 spelt out the vision and the needs of such a military dimension of the EU. It implies not only the designation of up to 120,000 troops in the member states for use in EU-led operations, but also the build-up of military expertise in the EU's central institutions (Presidency of the European Union 1999).

In order to achieve this, a number of political and military bodies have been convened within the Council (Presidency of the European Union 2000). One new body, the Political and Security Committee, generally known by its French acronym COPS, is at the pinnacle of this development, bringing together the Political Directors of the national foreign ministries. Since 2001 COPS has replaced the previous Political Committee (PoCo) and now not only oversees the work of the CFSP working groups but is also the body exercising political control over the EU Military Staff and EU Military Committee (Duke 2005). A further addition to the expanding security structures has come with the appointment, in the wake of the March 2003 Madrid bombings, of an EU Counter-terrorism coordinator. The creation of a European External Action service, in effect giving the EU it's own full-blown diplomatic service by bringing together parts of the Commission and the Council Secretariat departments, strengthened through seconded officials from the member states, will be another quantum leap in this process. Even though the creation of this service is foreseen in the Constitutional Treaty, it is one aspect of it which may be realised in some form even without the ratification of the Treaty.

The emergence of the Council Secretariat as a political institution and the transformation of the Secretary-General into a significant player in the development of CFSP could be expected to exacerbate existing rivalries with the Commission, given that institution's own role in the area of external relations. In this context it is worth mentioning that the relationship between Chris Patten, the EU Commissioner for External Relations in the Prodi Commission, and Javier Solana has, on the whole, been cooperative. Clearly, in the search for a coherent and effective conduct of the EU's foreign relations, encompassing external economic relations, humanitarian aid, CFSP and military intervention, cooperation between Commission and Council – both Secretariat and foreign ministers – is more important than ever. Their mutual dependence in managing the EU's external relations is encouraging and points to a stronger foreign policy partnership between Council Secretariat and Commission in the future – not quite the result that was to be expected from the long-standing efforts of member states to keep foreign policy matters out of the hands of supranational institutions.

In some ways, the idea contained in the Constitutional Treaty to create the post of an EU Minister for Foreign Affairs is an interesting solution to this issue. It dodges the issue whether it should be *either* Commission *or* Council Secretariat that has control over the resources in the external relations field. Instead, continuing with the current practice that the Commission stays in charge of those foreign policy instruments that are more economic, trade-related and budgetary, and the Council Secretariat responsible for the more traditional diplomatic, security and military aspects, the Treaty proposes to square the circle by making a single individual – the new foreign affairs 'minister' – responsible for both. He or she (in fact it has already been decided that Javier Solana will be promoted to the job should it come into existence) will then chair the GAERC Council, head the CFSP and security bodies in the Council structure, but also be Vice-President of the Commission. Such a solution certainly provides for easier recognition of who is in charge of EU foreign policy, but it may cause difficulties in establishing how the holder of this new post relates to the Presidents of the Commission and the European Council.

Conclusions

The Council of Ministers operates on a number of different levels, and is embedded within a wider context of intergovernmental institutions. Its role remains central to European governance as the key channel for the representation of national and sectoral interests from the member states to the European Union. Interest representation has become more complex as the number of member states has grown, the range of issues has expanded and the negotiations involve questions of greater technical detail. In response to these developments, the number of sectoral Councils has multiplied and an extensive network of committees and working groups has evolved around the original meeting of foreign ministers which remains at the heart of the Council structure.

The expansion of competences and the growing number of arenas for deliberation in turn require greater coordination of Council business. In this respect, the Presidency and the European Council have become more important, but beyond coordination they have also provided welcome opportunities for member states to regain the initiative and a greater degree of control over the integration process.

But, as this chapter has sought to show, the evolution of the Council is also marked by some unexpected and arguably unintended consequences. Negotiations among ministers and officials are not just a one-way street of interest representation: frequent meetings and continuous deliberation among member state representatives also provide an environment for policy-learning, cultural exchange, socialisation and even the transformation of allegiances. As such, the Council structure constitutes an important site for the establishment or growth of policy networks and other channels of interest representation which cut across the member states.

Most recently, the Council Secretariat has witnessed a boost, as new foreign policy and military bodies have been created and its head who is already the EU's High Representative for the CFSP, is designated as the future EU Minister for Foreign Affairs. The combined effect of these developments is that the Secretariat is being recognised as the core of the EU's ambitions in the diplomatic and security field. If these ambitions are being turned into reality, the Secretariat and the High Representative stand much to gain, but, given the past record of the EU in this field, there is also a case for caution. These are still very early days in the long-term endeavour to provide the EU with effective institutions for foreign policy and military intervention. From an institutional point of view it remains to be seen, in particular, whether the relationship between the Council Secretariat and the Commission evolves as one of partnership or rivalry in the management of the Union's external relations. It is in this context that we have to see the proposal contained in the Constitutional Treaty, of a European foreign minister who would have had a crucial role in managing the external relations of *both* the Council and the Commission.

The strengthening of the Secretariat illustrates the trend towards a greater degree of institutionalisation in the Council more generally. It demonstrates the dilemma national governments face as they ask the EU to perform additional tasks while also seeking to maintain close control over their execution. It may be that, by transferring powers to the Secretariat and the committee structure, governments have prevented the Commission from gaining further powers. Yet, in the process the Council itself has become more of a supranational body and the conglomerate of institutions now involved in the making of EU policy has become ever more difficult to hold to account.

In the early years of the new century, institutionalised intergovernmentalism has found new ways of responding to the dilemmas and challenges of European governance. The reality of enlargement, which has added several new challenges to the work of the Council (Bayer 2005), and the potential implementation of the reforms foreseen in the Constitutional Treaty, should that be ratified, will interact with this long-term trend towards greater institutionalisation. Internal changes such as the reduction of the national veto and the external challenges of an enlarged European Union will test the effectiveness and the legitimacy of these institutions. There may be testing times ahead, but the experience so far shows that member states are willing and able to adapt the Council to the changing demands of its environment.

Acknowledgements

I am grateful for comments received from Manuela Alfe, Edward Best and Alain Guggenbuehl on a previous version of this chapter. The usual disclaimer applies, of course.

References

Bayer, N. (2005) 'EU 25 – Creating a New Design for the Council', *Eipascope* 2005/1: 8–13.

Beach, D. (2004) 'The unseen hand in treaty reform negotiations: the role and impact of the Council Secretariat', *Journal of European Public Policy* 11/3: 408–39

Best, E. (2000) 'The Debate about the Weighting of Votes: The Mis-Presentation of Representation?', in E. Best, M. Gray and A. Stubb (eds), *Rethinking the European Union* (Maastricht: European Institute of Public Administration).

Beyers, J. and Dierckx, G. (1998) 'The Working Groups of the Council of the European Union: Supra-national or Integovernmental Negotiations', *Journal of Common Market Studies* 36/3: 289–319.

Bulmer, S. and Wessels, W. (1987) *The European Council: Decision-making in European Politics* (Basingstoke: Macmillan).

Christiansen, T. (2001) 'Intra-Institutional politics and Inter-institutional relations: towards coherent governance?' *Journal of European Public Policy* 8/5: 747–69.

—— (2002) 'Out of the Shadows: The General Secretariat of the Council of Ministers', in M. P. van Schendelen and R. Scully (eds), *Unelected Legislators in the European Union*, special issue of the *Journal of Legislative Studies* 8/4.

—— (2005) 'The European Commission: The Role of the European executive in the EU Policy-process', in J. J. Richardson (ed.), *The European Union: Power and Policy-making*, 2nd edn (London: Routledge).

Christiansen, T. and Jørgensen, K. E. (1998) 'Negotiating Treaty Reform in the European Union: The Role of the European Commission', *International Negotiation* 3/4: 435–52.

Christiansen, T. and Kirchner, E. (eds) (2000) *Committee Governance in the European Union* (Manchester: Manchester University Press).

Council of the European Union (1999) *An Effective Council for an Enlarged Union: Guidelines for Reform and Operational Recommendations* (Brussels).

—— (2003) *Multiannual Strategic Programme of the Council 2004–2006* (Brussels).

Duke, S. (2005) 'The Linchpin COPS: Assessing the workings and institutional relations of the Political and Security Committee', paper prepared for the European Institute for Public Administration, Maastricht.

Egeberg, M. (1999) 'Transcending Intergovernmentalism: Identity and Role Perceptions of National Officials in EU Decision-making', *Journal of European Public Policy* 6/3: 456–74.

European Commission (2000) *Adapting the Institutions to Make a Success of Enlargement (COM(2000) 034)* (Brussels).

Financial Times (2000) 'EU Prepares to Streamline its Failing Diplomacy'", 4 September: 2.

Hayes-Renshaw, F. and Wallace, H. (1997) *The Council of Ministers* (London: Macmillan).

Heisenberg, D. (2005) 'The institution of "consensus" in the European Union: Formal versus informal decision-making in the Council', *European Journal of Political Research* 44/1: 65–90.

Hix, S. (1999) *The Political System of the European Union* (Basingstoke: Macmillan).

Lewis, J. (1998) 'Is the Hard Bargaining Image of the Council Misleading? The Committee of Permanent Representatives and the Local Election Directive', *Journal of Common Market Studies* 36/4: 479–504.

Lewis, J. (2000) 'The Methods of Community in EU Decision-making and Adminstrative Rivalry in the Council's Infrastructure', *Journal of European Public Policy* 7/2: 261–89.

Lipsius, J. (1995) 'The 1996 IGC', *European Law Review* 20/3: 235–57.

Peters, G. (1992) 'Bureaucratic Politics in the European Community', in A. Sbragia (ed.), *Euro-Politics* (Washington, DC: The Brookings Institution).

Presidency of the European Union (1999) *Presidency Conclusions of the Helsinki European Council* (Brussels).

—— (2000) *Presidency Report on Strengthening the Common European Security and Defence Policy to the Lisbon European Council* (Brussels).

Sasse, C. (1975) *Regierungen, Parlamente, Ministerrat: Entscheidungsprozesse in der Europäischen Gemeinschaft* (Bonn: Europa Union Verlag).

Sherrington, P. (2000) *The Council of Ministers: Political Authority in the European Union* (London: Pinter).

Smith, A., Fouilleux, E. and de Maillard, J. (2005) 'Technical Or Political? The Working Groups of the EU Council of Ministers', *Journal of European Public Policy* 12/4 .

Wallace, H. (1985) 'The Presidency of the Council of Ministers of the European Community: Tasks and Evolution', in C. O. Nuallain (ed.), *The Presidency of the European Council of Ministers: Impacts and Implications for National Governments* (London: Croom Helm).

—— (1993) 'A Critical Assessment of the Styles, Strategies and Achievements of the Two Presidencies', in E. Kirchner and A. Tsagkari (eds), *The EC Council Presidency: The Dutch and Luxembourg Presidencies* (London: UACES).

Wessels, W. (1980) *Der Europäische Rat* (Bonn: Europa Union Verlag).

—— (1990) 'Administrative Interaction', in W. Wallace (ed.), *The Dynamics of European Integration* (London: Pinter).

—— (1991) 'The EC Council: The Community's Decisionmaking Center', in R. O. Keohane and S. Hoffmann (eds), *The New European Community: Decisionmaking and Institutional Change* (Boulder, CO: Westview).

Westlake, M. (1995) *The Council of the European Union* (London: Catermill).

de Zwann, J. (1995) *The Permanent Representatives Committee: Its Role in European Union Decision-Making* (Amsterdam: Elsevier).

Chapter 8

Judicial law-making and European integration

The European Court of Justice

MARGARET MCCOWN

Introduction

The dynamic interaction between the European Court of Justice (ECJ) and its litigants generated a transformational case law, the effects of which have been far-reaching. The consequences attributed to ECJ rulings have been widespread, creating and shaping both policy and constitutional issues, although academics have extensively debated the means through which this occurred. This chapter explores these outcomes in the context of the deeply political questions of how and with the aid and despite the opposition of which actors did this happen?[1]

Amongst academics there is a great deal of consensus as to the legally important developments in the European Union (EU), which will be outlined below. A significant amount of debate remains between political scientists, however, about whether these rulings reflect the influential decisions of the ECJ in its capacity as an independent decision-maker or whether other important political actors, especially member states, have actually exercised control over the consequences of ECJ decisions by facilitating or opposing them. This chapter presents ECJ case law that has been important to the evolution of the EU political system and discusses the actors that have been central to shaping that case law.

The chapter commences with an introduction to what are considered to be the main political changes in the EU attributed to ECJ decisions: the constitutionalisation of the EU's founding treaties, the ECJ's separation of powers case law and the ECJ jurisprudence shaping public policy. It then discusses how they have been theoretically evaluated by different academics and concludes by weighing these different accounts in light of the examples introduced in the chapter.

The Constitutionalisation of the Treaties

The treaties founding the EU were international law, binding on nation states and holding those states as their objects. Individuals and their rights under and vis-à-vis the European institutions were barely mentioned and not significantly developed. Although the treaties spoke of establishing a Parliament, majoritarian bodies were a long time in coming (Rittberger 2003). Similarly, the Court was essentially created in order to adjudicate disputes between member states, rather than citizens.

The sections of the treaties establishing the ECJ did, however, include a clause allowing national courts to send references to the European Court of Justice in order to ask for clarification about how to apply EU laws in cases pending before them (Article 234, TEU). This technocratic provision for harmonising the application of EU law turned out to be of pivotal importance once the ECJ began to interpret it in its decisions. In 1962, a case was referred to the ECJ by a national court reviewing a case between the Netherlands customs agency and a Dutch import firm, Van Gend en Loos (ECJ 26/62 *Van Gend en Loos*). The firm claimed that a Dutch law adjusting customs fees on imports actually increased them and was, thus, contrary to treaty provisions in Article 23 which prohibited member states from enacting new import taxes on goods once they had entered the customs union. What was novel about the case was that a private actor claimed an EU law in their defence. The Belgian government, which along with the German government submitted observations to the case,[2] argued that the appellant, Van Gend and Loos, could not claim rights from the treaties in court – that the law in the treaties was addressed only to states. The ECJ found, however, that EU law 'not only imposes obligations on individuals but also confers upon them rights' and thereby, in a sentence, took the first step towards the 'constitutionalisation' of EU law (Weiler 1999). This was the point from which the ECJ began the transformation of the treaties into documents that, like constitutions, granted rights to individual citizens which they could claim before their national courts and request to have referred to the ECJ.

The ECJ subsequently extended this new concept of 'direct effect' to other areas of EU law. Now, not only regulations but also parts of directives[3] (ECJ 41/74 *Van Dyne v. Home Office*) create rights that individuals can claim in court. Regulations create rights that individuals may claim in disputes both against public agencies and with other private parties – so called 'horizontal direct effect' – whilst directives only create rights that can be claimed against the state. States can also be found liable for damages for failing to appropriately transpose directives into law.

The political benefits to the ECJ of its ruling are as clear as its legal consequences. The ECJ substantially increased its power when it expanded the number of potential litigants able to bring suit before it. As Craig and De Búrca note, half the then members of the EU submitted observations opposing the ECJ's interpretation (Craig and De Búrca 1998: 167). The ECJ demonstrated its authority when it successfully ruled against the stated preferences of member states. The member states, in turn, lost some sovereignty – an implication that they clearly recognised in their arguments before the Court. The government of the Netherlands forthrightly asserted, in Court proceedings, that a ruling finding for *Van Gend en Loos* would undercut member states' sovereignty and that there was a risk that member states would simply not comply with such a decision. National courts, too, have been identified as having gained power under the new interpretation as they were now able to bypass higher courts, send a reference to the ECJ and get decisions that would be binding on national courts superior to them (Alter 2001).

The second major leg of the constitutionalisation of the treaties addresses member state sovereignty even more directly: what to do when EU and national laws conflict? From the point of view of legal certainty and coherence, it is virtually unworkable to allow conflicting EU and national laws to coexist, but striking down one law in favour of another is a deeply sensitive matter. In 1964, the question finally came to a head before the ECJ when a case was referred in which there was a clash between Italian rules governing the national electricity monopoly and treaty provisions relating to free movement of goods (ECJ 6/64 *Costa v. ENEL*). The ECJ ruled that EU law always trumps national law in conflicts between the two, establishing the supremacy of EU law and a clear hierarchy of norms.

Asserting the supremacy of EU law elevated the ECJ to the position of constitutional court – as the body responsible for overseeing the application of EU law, it was also, suddenly, the arbiter of the validity of all national norms where they had to do with some aspect of European law. This cut deeply into national competences, a trend which the ECJ only accelerated in subsequent decisions when it considered the principle of supremacy relative to national constitutions.

The ECJ's first constitutional case was particularly sensitive as it was referred from a German court. Given the paramount importance assigned to the German constitution in the post-war period as a declaration and safeguard of democracy and civil liberties, the case was closely watched and of great concern. In an early supremacy reference dealing with the relative status of national constitutions to EU law, the ECJ weighed the primacy of provisions in the German constitution guaranteeing proportionality of laws and economic liberty against EU legislation setting up a deposit system for exports within the EU (ECJ 11/70 *Internationale Handelsgesellschaft*). The ECJ argued that the EU law was hardly disproportionate but also that 'the law stemming from the treaty, an independent source of law, cannot because of its very nature be overridden by national laws however framed'. Even given that the German constitution details an enormously long and not always precise list of issues potentially relevant to human rights, the ruling in favour of EU law was still extremely bold. In a later case referred by an Italian court, the ECJ asserted that when it found a national law to be incompatible with EU law, the national court must set aside that law immediately, even if the constitution, as was the case in Italy, granted the exclusive power to strike down laws to a higher court (ECJ 35/76 *Simmenthal*).

Supremacy proved to be rather more controversial over a longer period of time than direct effect and was most bitterly opposed by national constitutional courts. The French Council of State, one of the three highest courts in the land, only accepted the supremacy of ECJ rulings over its decisions in the 1980s, in its *Nicolo* decision (Conseil d'Etat 20/10/1989). The German Constitutional Court heard a series of cases addressing the question of supremacy of EU law relative to the German constitution. Following *Internationale Handelsgesellschaft*, it delivered its famous *Solange* ('so long as') decision in which it asserted that, in a conflict between EU law and constitutionally guaranteed human rights, so long as the EU didn't redress the conflict, the constitutional provisions would have to prevail. Over time, it retreated somewhat from this stark statement but its final verdict, in its *Maastricht* decision – that it would act as if EU law was supreme over all national law so long as decisions did not do violence to fundamental human rights protected in the constitution – is, at best, a rhetorical compromise (BverfG 89, 155).

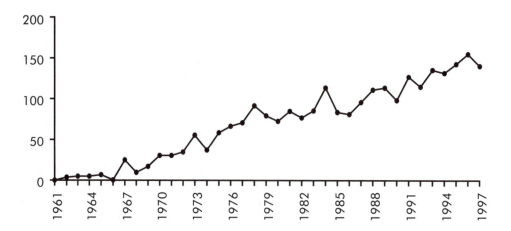

Figure 8.1 Total number of ECJ decisions pursuant to a preliminary reference

Source: *Alec Stone Sweet and Thomas Brunell Data Set on Preliminary references in EC Law, 1956–98*, Robert Schumann Centre for Advanced Studies, European University Institute (San Domenico di Fiesole, Italy: 1999)

It is unsurprising that the national constitutional courts were opposed to supremacy – it constitutes an erosion of their status as the ultimate judicial authority in their respective countries (Slaughter *et al.* 1998). They have, indeed, never referred a case to the ECJ. On this issue, however, constitutional courts are out of step with what is practised on the ground – after initial opposition in the early landmark cases, member states have not significantly engaged the issue and national courts, below the level of constitutional courts, have referred an ever-increasing volume of cases to the ECJ.

The constitutionalisation of the treaties changed the environment in which the ECJ made its decisions and other actors made their political and legal choices. The establishment of direct effect, allowing litigants to bring suit via the preliminary reference mechanism in Article 234, vastly increased the number of cases that came to the ECJ. This had the effect of greatly expanding the number of actors able to police the application of the treaties and press for changes in national law, via the ECJ – this proved to be crucial to the integration process (Stone Sweet and Brunell 1998). As is clear in the graph in figure 8.1, references to the ECJ increased quickly from the mid-1960s as the major constitutional decisions made the Court an attractive venue to litigants in which to seek legal change.

A greater caseload also increased the opportunities for the ECJ to make rulings that implemented its preferences over the shape of European law. An important feature of ECJ decision-making emerged early in this period and sustained this process: the use of precedent. Precedent does not formally exist in international law or in continental European legal systems, largely because it is viewed as enabling judicial activism and allowing the judiciary to encroach on the law-making prerogatives of the legislature (Merryman 1985). The ECJ, however, began applying its past decisions as precedents at the same time as it was delivering these constitutional rulings with precisely that

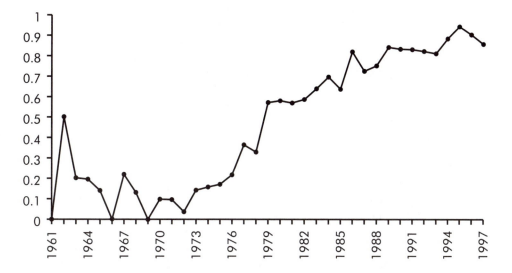

Figure 8.2 Proportion of ECJ rulings in a preliminary reference citing precedence

Source: *Margaret McCown Data Set on European Court of Justice Citation Practices in Preliminary Reference Rulings, 1961–1998*, Margaret McCown, Nuffield College, Oxford University (2002)

effect (McCown 2004). As is visible in figure 8.2, the ECJ's recourse to precedent has, like references, only increased with time.

By the 1980s, it used precedent more often than not in its decisions and it is now a firmly entrenched practice. Moreover, the complexity and sophistication of its precedent-based arguments has increased. The Court has not only cited more, with time, it constructs legal rules based on sets of precedents and invokes these same sets over many decisions, codifying them through repetition (McCown 2004).

The ECJ's 'constitutionalising' decisions set the stage for and enabled the role it was to play in the integration of the EU. Following the decisions, litigation increased, as did the efficacy of its decisions, which is quite visible in the next period of constitutional case law, discussed below.

Separation of powers

Although the basic constitutional questions of the EU had largely been resolved by the end of the 1970s, the late 1980s saw the emergence of a new and yet classically constitutional matter that was also rather more contested by member state governments: the separation of powers at the supranational level. Article 230 of the treaties gives member states and supranational actors the means to legally appeal for the annulment of legislation passed inappropriately. These claims of impropriety typically rest on an assertion that the parts of the treaty chosen as the basis or authority for legislation were incorrectly chosen and that other treaty articles, usually implying a different decision-making procedure, would have been appropriate. Although these may sound like the driest of procedural questions, they are some of the most intensely political cases resolved by the ECJ and indeed in EU politics (McCown 2001; McCown and Jun 2003; Jupille 2004), which, indeed, the legal academic literature (Emiliou 1994; Cullen and Charlesworth 1999) and the Court itself (cf. Advocate General Lenz at §38 in ECJ 45/86) acknowledge.

These disputes essentially concern two main issues: how legislation can be voted on in the Council of Ministers and how involved the European Parliament may be in the legislative process. By the late 1980s, the growing complexity of the EU legislative process and the gradual increase in the European Parliament's involvement in it began to generate more disputes about the appropriate ways in which to pass EU laws. As the ECJ delivered decisions in these cases, it slowly constructed many of the relevant rules arbitrating the separation of powers in the EU.

Laws made pursuant to different parts of the treaties require different decision-making procedures, ranging from unanimous to qualified majority voting in the Council and from the consultation to co-decision procedures. This complexity has, moreover, only increased with each treaty revision. If a piece of legislation could be based on multiple treaty provisions, there are strong incentives for member states who are outvoted under qualified majority voting rules in the Council of Ministers or for the Parliament, when its position fails to be implemented in legislation, to go to Court in order to claim that the legislation is based on inappropriate articles in the treaty and demand that it be annulled. As treaty changes have increased the complexity of decision-making and the number of such suits, the ECJ has generated a case law that has steadily constricted EU institutions' discretion to choose or change the legal basis of legislation for their political convenience.

The treaties are largely silent about how to resolve disputes over the correct legal basis of legislation, so that virtually all the rules governing these disputes have been generated in ECJ decisions. Thus, the Court is the institution that has created much of the law concerning EU separation of powers. In the decision in the first legal basis case (ECJ 45/86 *Commission* v *Council*), the Court asserts that the treaties require actors to give justification for their choice of legal basis and that these justifications are adjudicable. It thus imposes a strict obligation to state reasons on the supranational actors and member states and establishes itself as the body with the power to weigh these justifications. In two subsequent cases it creates further rules dictating this choice of reasons, specifying that they must be related to the 'aim and content' of the legislation, not other, explicitly political goals (ECJ 300/89 '*Titanium Dioxide*'). Moreover, it ruled that where a more specific and a more general provision exist in the treaties that could serve as a potential legal basis for legislation, the specific ought always be chosen (ECJ 68/86 *United Kingdom* v *Council*). The ECJ's approach to resolving these highly political disputes has been the construction of neutral legal tests but it has, thereby, itself won political power vis-à-vis the member states and other institutions: It has established itself as the creator of the authoritative rules for governing legal basis cases and significantly reduced EU actors' ability to use the selection of legal bases as a means of advancing their own political goals.

The European Parliament has quite successfully used the ECJ as a means for expanding its influence, affecting the balance of powers between the EU institutions. The ECJ's ruling in *Les Vertes* (ECJ 294/83) famously asserted that Parliament's right to be consulted could not be omitted from the legislative process. Under the consultation procedure, the Council of Ministers was not obligated to follow the results of its consultation with Parliament, but did have to ask their opinion. It has been argued that by this means, the ECJ gave the EP its first, small measure of influence: the power to delay, by requiring that it be consulted but not setting down limits about amount of time in which it had to deliver its opinion.

Academics' assessments of the importance of this delaying power differ: Tsebelis and Garrett find it to be insignificant relative to the legislative powers later acquired by the EP (Tsebelis and Garrett 2001); McCown (2003), however, shows that the EP has litigated this procedure fairly heavily even as it has acquired other, more extensive means of influence and seems, itself, to regard it as an important part of its repertoire of policy tools. The crucial part of *Les Vertes* is arguably, however, that it was the first step in a sequence of cases that gave the EP standing before the ECJ and made litigation strategies available to it.

The treaties do not list the EP amongst the institutions empowered to refer cases to the ECJ and its ability to do so is court-created. In '*Chernobyl*' (ECJ 70/88) the Court ruled that a Parliament was able to bring legal basis cases asking for the annulment of legislation if the legal basis chosen affected Parliament's role in the legislative process. Therefore, if the difference in legal basis selected implies recourse to the co-decision versus the consultation procedure, the case is admissible, whereas if the alternative legal basis proposed would not imply a difference in Parliamentary involvement, then the case is inadmissible. The EP has since brought about a third of all inter-institutional cases that come before the ECJ and gained a reputation as an aggressive litigator (McCown 2003; McCown and Jun 2003).

Member states' reaction to both the ECJ's rule-making in legal basis cases and with regard to the EP was rather hostile. It was 1993 before the EP brought a case the admissibility of which was not challenged (McCown 2003; McCown and Jun 2003) and member states have been openly hostile to ECJ jurisprudence on many occasions. Member state opposition has not been effective at rolling back the jurisprudence, however. In fact, treaty revisions following rulings have codified several ECJ precedents rules in treaty articles, even borrowing the ECJ's language. The Maastricht Treaty revision, for example, affirmed the EP's right to bring suits 'for the purposes of protecting its prerogatives' (Art. 173(3) TEU), just as the ECJ declared in *Chernobyl* and many later decisions. Other areas litigated as legal basis disputes, such as the treaty articles governing overseas aid for development were also confirmed in the same treaty revision (McCown 2004, chapter 4).

The separation of powers cases are interesting because none of the actors are present that could be argued to bolster the Court's authority; there are no national courts to refer cases, no private litigants to bring waves of cases and lobby their national governments to comply with them; and the disputes are deeply political. The ECJ has, however, established itself as the authoritative arbiter of these disputes. Again, factors such as the ECJ's recourse to precedent seem to make a difference: even litigants that strongly opposed various ECJ interpretations start using those decisions as precedents in their argumentation in later cases, knowing that it makes their arguments more effective and trading off a desire to win in individual cases against their disapproval of the general line of case law. On eight occasions (of about thirty legal basis rulings), an observer or litigant cites a case which they had, in the past, explicitly opposed, or been the losing party to. In this way, it appears that, through incremental, repeated use, they slowly accept rulings that they initially opposed.

The ECJ and policy-making

Going to court is a classic means by which both individuals and organisational actors can seek policy change. If you are a special interest that fails at or is disadvantaged by lobbying, you can always try to get a law that you dislike struck down in court (Bouwen and McCown 2004). So much the better if, in ruling against the law, you get the court to stipulate what it ought to look like in a way that more closely matches your preferences. At the same time as it was delivering rulings setting up a constitutional framework for the EU, the ECJ was deeply involved in developing the substance of EU law and inserting it into national legal systems. Policy change through litigation has shaped a considerable portion of EU law. The ECJ is credited both with advancing integration during periods in which legislative output from the Commission and Council was low and stimulating the development of entirely new policy areas. Free movement of goods will be discussed as an example of the former and gender equality policy as one of the latter.

Free movement of goods

The free movement of goods, along with the free movement of persons, services and capital, constitutes one of the core 'four freedoms' that are the foundation to the EU and EU citizens' rights. The oldest and most litigated of the four, free movement of goods cases, constitute the site of some of the court's earliest activism (Stone Sweet and McCown 2004; McCown 2004, chapter 4). Many of the classic constitutional cases such as *Van Gend en Loos* were free movement of goods disputes but the decisions of the ECJ as they pertain directly to trade are, in many instances, equally activist. During the era of the 'Luxembourg Compromise', according to which the Council of Ministers agreed to take all votes on legislation by unanimity, irrespective of the requirements set in the treaties, legislative output was extremely low (Nugent 1994). European integration did not, however, come to a complete halt in this period, in good part due to ECJ decisions that slowly proceeded with the removal of national barriers to trade and the promotion of EU endeavours to liberalise trade in goods.

The ECJ's free movement of goods decisions are good examples of the kind of policy change most often associated with courts – the elimination of rules conflicting with certain policy priorities by finding them to be incompatible with superior parts of the legal order. In the context of regional integration, this has been called 'negative integration' – the elimination of national rules that inhibit European integration (Scharpf 1996). 'Positive integration', replacing the disparate national rules with newly constructed EU level laws, is typically the province of the legislature. The ECJ, however, has also delivered some rather prescriptive rulings that also have this effect.

In order to establish a common market for goods in the EU, the treaties prohibit the member states from maintaining their own tariff regimes and from passing laws that prevent or hinder the import of goods from other member states (Articles 23–30 TEU). There are, however, numerous additional means by which countries can inhibit imports or protect domestic industries – lengthy or expensive border inspections, onerous licensing requirements that must be met before a good can be marketed, content or production requirements that favour domestic goods, are all common examples of non-tariff barriers to trade. The treaties, therefore, couple prohibitions on explicit barriers to importation (Art. 23–25 TEU) with requirements that member states not enact any of these 'measures having equivalent effect' to quantitative restrictions on trade (Art. 28). What constitutes a measure having equivalent effect and where the border lies between regulation in the public interest and trade-distorting protectionism present both an enticing litigation opportunity for EU importers wishing to gain access to other European markets and a wide space for ECJ interpretation.

A pair of ECJ rulings have been the lynchpin of the integration of the common market and litigation over Art. 28. In its *Dassonville* decision, the ECJ found that all laws governing importation 'which are capable of hindering directly or indirectly, actually or potentially, intra-Community trade are to be considered measures having equivalent to quantitative restrictions.' (ECJ 8/74 *Dassonville*). This extraordinarily expansive language – that any law that might possibly have the consequence of inhibiting an import was to be considered contrary to EU law – opened the floodgates to more litigation. National rules demanding lengthy or expensive inspections on products or licenses to sell imported goods were suddenly very vulnerable to litigation.

Soon after *Dassonville*, a case was referred to the ECJ in which a piece of German legislation was accused of creating a standard for labelling products as alcohol that, although it applied throughout Germany, had the effect of discriminating against a French liqueur, Cassis (*'Cassis de Dijon'* ECJ 120/78). In one of its most famous decisions, the Court went on to apply the *Dassonville* interpretation to all national laws, even to what EU law calls 'indistinctly applicable measures' – those rules which apply equally to domestic and imported products. This pair of cases took on such importance because they were decided during a period when relatively little legislation was occurring – the 1970s were a highly unproductive time for the Commission.

With *Cassis* and *Dassonville* as the driving force, the ECJ decided nearly 700 cases in free movement of goods by the end of the 1990s, making it one of the largest single areas of EU litigation (Stone Sweet and Brunell 1999). *Cassis* and *Dassonville* undoubtedly cleared the way for more decisions, further sweeping away national rules and, it is often argued, expanding trade in the EU (Stone Sweet and Brunell 1998). The consensus amongst legal scholars is that 'the significance of *Cassis* can hardly be overstated' (Craig and De Búrca 1998: 606). Some political scientists, stressing the importance of intergovernmental actors' decisions and their relative power as compared to the ECJ, differ, asserting that *Cassis*, in particular, made little difference to law-making over free movement of goods and emphasise the preferences of member states in explaining market integration (Moravcsik 1998: 353; Alter and Meunier-Aitsahalia 1994; Garrett 1992). It is certainly true, however, that, at the time, member states were quite vocally opposed to the case law, but were not successful in pushing the ECJ to use alternate interpretations as the basis of future decisions, which casts doubts on intergovernmentalist interpretations of ECJ authority. In fact, *Cassis* is the most cited precedent in the ECJ's case law (McCown 2004). The importance of the relentless attentiveness of private actors to litigation opportunities is very apparent in this area of law – even in the face of a complete lack of political will to promote market integration, litigants were able, through the ECJ, to promote a broadly trade liberalising agenda.

Gender equality

A remarkable aspect of ECJ jurisprudence has to do with the way in which it has stimulated the production of entirely new policy areas, a classic example of which is EU-level gender equality policy. Article 141 (TEU) asserts that, under EU law, men and women shall receive equal pay for equal work. This provision is hardly new – it was introduced with the Rome Treaty founding the European Economic Community in 1957 (then, as Art. 119) and, for over two decades, essentially ignored, used neither in legal proceedings nor as the basis of a legislative agenda. Much as in the free movement cases, litigant mobilisation, bringing suits before the ECJ in attempts to change domestic member state laws and practices, was key to the development of this area of law and the creation of new rights for EU citizens where no substantive ones existed before.

Art. 141, itself, was largely disregarded until, in the 1970s, a pair of cases were referred by the same lawyer, on behalf of the same client, complaining that Sabena airline's practice of paying male and female flight attendants different wages and providing different pensions and retirement ages was a violation of Art. 141 (*Defrenne I* and *Defrenne II*). When the ECJ found Art. 141 to be directly effective, it enabled the sophisticated and concerted litigation and mobilisation that was to follow. Moreover, its finding in *Defrenne II* that Art. 141 had horizontal direct effect, and, thus, was applicable to agreements contracted between individuals, as well as to the individual–state relationship, made it applicable to an enormous number of private employer–employee interactions.

An interesting aspect of the ECJ's sex equality case law is that, in addition to changing how litigants could challenge national level practices with regard to gender and employment, it prompted the crafting of secondary EU legislation. As Cichowski details, Art. 141 only addresses gender equality in terms of pay, but was extended over time to include maternity leave and protection against job discrimination during pregnancy (Cichowski 2004; see also Ellis 1998; Cichowski 2001). In contrast to the free movement of goods case law, where, until the Single Europe Act revived a legislative and ministerial commitment to the integration of the Common Market, ECJ decisions took the place of a legislative agenda, in the sex equality cases, there has been a more dynamic interplay between judicial decisions and legislation, each enabling more of the other.

The *Defrenne* decisions were, thus, followed by the passage of legislation such as the Equal Pay Directive, the Working Time Directive and the Equal Treatment of Work Directive (75/117/EEC, 79/7/EEC, 76/207/EEC). These were all, especially the Equal Treatment directive crafted expansively enough that they enabled further litigation, to clarify their scope and the obligations they set on member states and EU employers (Cichowski 2004; Ellis 1998).

The mobilisation of interest groups representing gender equality issues was central to the development of the new policy area. The ECJ delivered a series of rulings promoting gender equality, creating opportunities for subsequent litigation and guiding the path of the development of the area of law. The interest groups, however, did the work of finding litigants with adjudicable complaints and bringing the cases (Cichowski 2001; Alter and Vargas 2000). Following up on the *Defrenne* cases, disputes came before the ECJ in which the Court was asked whether dismissing women because of pregnancy, in *Dekker* (ECJ 177/88), or whilst on maternity leave, in *Haberman-Beltermann* (ECJ 421/92), contravened Art. 141. When the ECJ answered 'yes' to both, building on both the *Defrenne* cases and the EU legislation passed subsequent to them, it created substantively new rights for EU citizens.

Politically, these rulings did not enjoy a particularly warm reception. Member state governments complained in the course of legal proceedings that the ECJ exceeded its authority in finding Art. 141 to be directly effective. They were slow to change national legislation to come into compliance with the ECJ's rulings, often only doing so as pushed by focused interest groups (Alter and Vargas 2000; Conant 2002). In one famous instance, member states grew so concerned about the potential liability costs of an ECJ ruling – which had found that the dismissal of pregnant women from public service was a wrongful action against which litigants could claim damages (ECJ 262/88 *Barber*) – that they inserted a clause in the Maastricht Treaty to prevent the ruling from being made retroactive (the 'Barber Protocol'). They did not, however, succeed at all in preventing the ECJ's discovery of directly effective gender equality protection in the treaties or the development of an entirely new area of law.

The emergence of this new area of law, a development stimulated and underpinned by ECJ decisions is, as in other aspects of EU judicial politics, often attributed to different causes. Intergovernmentalist writers, who emphasise the continued dominance of member states over the integration process, would assert that it in no way contravened the preferences of member states who remained in firm control of the process as evidenced by their checking of the Court in the Maastricht Treaty's Barber Protocol (Garrett *et al.* 1998). Alter and Vargas (1998) show quite oppositional member states, but attribute decisive importance to interest groups' lobbying and pressing politically at both the domestic and EU level in order to make the ECJ's decisions effective. Cichowski, in contrast, shows how pieces of legislation and ECJ decisions were passed overriding the articulated preferences of powerful member states such as the UK and Italy and concludes that 'it is important to emphasize, however, that it was the Court that defined and constructed these rights … while national governments and, the UK in particular, stymied the process' (Cichowski 1991: 131). That they were rulings with real political consequences and subject to intense scrutiny and debate is, certainly, uncontested and this case law shows a Court acting decisively in the midst of such controversy.

Conclusion

Why and how courts matter to politics are classic questions and much debated issues in political science. That constitutional courts can intervene dramatically in the political process is unsurprising: having the final authority to find legislation or practice to be unconstitutional and to identify what actions are compelled by a constitution gives the judicial branch of government considerable power. How they exercise that power and how effectively they do so is, however, open to question as they have little influence over the cases that come to them and the subsequent enforcement of them. The authority of Alexander Hamilton's 'least dangerous branch' of government is equally contested in the study of EU politics.

The example of the ECJ makes fairly clear why courts matter to political science and what is political about legal decisions. Where courts decide cases by precedent, they engage in judicial law-making, and thus individuals can go to court to try to get rid of national rules they dislike by persuading a court to find them contrary to some higher legal provision. The higher the court and relevant law, the more sweeping the potential change, making courts a venue for seeking even constitutional change that is then made concrete as precedent and affirmed every time it is applied in subsequent decisions. This process of the 'judicialisation' of politics – bringing political conflicts ever more under the spotlight of courts', particularly constitutional courts', ongoing scrutiny – is a long-standing characteristic of American politics and has been one of the distinctive trends in post-war Europe (Stone Sweet 2000). The ECJ is an important part of that trend made more remarkable by its transnational nature but does not represent a fundamentally different phenomenon. Why the ECJ and courts, generally, are deeply involved in the political process and highly relevant to analyses of it is not particularly controversial in the study of the EU.

How courts in general and the ECJ in particular make their rulings matter, though, is quite another matter and much more contested. Because courts get to rule widely on issues but cannot bring cases to themselves and lack direct means of enforcing their rulings, it is difficult to assess how they affect politics. Without power to enforce or get cases, some argue that courts are quite powerless and in the study of the EU, this usually takes the form of an intergovernmentalist argument asserting that the ECJ essentially implements the wishes of the member states, the real powers in the EU, in its decisions.

The extent to which courts exercise authority can be assessed, to a degree, however, by observing other factors taken as indicative of any influence attributable to their decisions. Most generally stated, one tries to identify systematic changes in the behaviour of other actors in response to court rulings. These changes include not only compliance with individual decisions, but evidence of ways in which they shape subsequent legal behaviour in the medium term, especially in the types of cases later referred to the court and the manner in which they are argued.

When litigants bring follow-on cases that pursue the interpretations asserted by the Court, especially where precedent exists, it not only demonstrates the relevance of those decisions, it gradually solidifies their hold over that area of law. Where even litigants that previously opposed decisions refer to them and use them as the basis of other legal arguments, it inserts the language and structure of the rulings further into the framework of pertinent law and incrementally ratifies the older rulings.

Any account of the ECJ seems to highlight the significance of such developments over the long term. Litigation has enabled entire lines of successive cases, with sweeping consequences. The ECJ has even shaped the manner in which issues are contested legally: member states and the Council of Ministers are much restricted in their discretion to choose legal bases for legislation for reasons of convenience and must also present their justifications in terms of the 'aim and content' of the measures. The ECJ's *Barber* ruling was modulated by the member states during a treaty revision, but entire sets of its gender equality case law remain the governing constitutional provisions. Despite national constitutional court reservations about the doctrine of supremacy, EU-wide, the legal system functions with that principle as its operating assumption. And litigants, be they supranational actors like the European Parliament or private individuals, via Art. 234 references, continue to press for constitutional and policy change through the ECJ, bringing it an ever-increasing stream of cases.

Although scholars continue to disagree, to an extent, about how much the ECJ was the authoritative driver of this process, it is manifestly clear how substantial the changes are to the EU that have been wrought in the legal arena. The preponderance of evidence, arguably, points towards an ever more powerful court, and a vital role for litigants in that process of judicialisation. It is certainly true that ECJ interpretation and the framework of EU law, as adjudicated by the Court, have come to exercise a profound and pervasive influence over the EU to an extent quite incomparable to other international associations and very similar to national polities.

Notes

1   This chapter is based on research done whilst a research fellow at the Max Planck Institute for Research on Collective Goods in Bonn and represents my own opinions and theoretical research. It does not reflect the research or analyses of the Government of the United States, the Department of Defense or the National Defense University. I would like to thank Hae-Won Jun for her helpful comments on an earlier draft of this chapter.

2   EU law allows member states and EU institutional actors not a direct party to a pending case to submit 'observations', similar to the *amicus curiae* briefs submitted to US courts, to the ECJ, advocating their preferred interpretation of legal issues relevant to it.

3   The two principle legislative instruments in the European Union are 'regulations' and 'directives'. Regulations are binding upon all member states and immediately and directly applicable within all member states. Directives, in contrast, can be directed to individual member states and do not have to be directed to all of them and, whilst binding in terms of the goal stated in them, leave it to the member states to pass national legislation implementing them.

Cases cited

European Court of Justice

ECJ 26/62, *Van Gend en Loos / Administratie der Belastingen.* [1963] ECR: 3.

ECJ 6/64, *Costa / E.N.E.L.* [1964] ECR: 1194.

ECJ 11/70, *Internationale Handelsgesellschaft mbH / Einfuhr- und Vorratsstelle für Getreide und Futtermittel.* [1970] ECR: 1125.

ECJ 8/74, *Procureur du Roi / Benoît and Gustave Dassonville.* [1974] ECR : 837.

ECJ 41/74, *Van Duyn / Home Office.* [1974] ECR: 1337.

ECJ 35/76, *Simmenthal Spa / Ministero delle finanze.* [1976] ECR: 1871.

ECJ 120/78, *REWE-Zentral AG / Bundesmonopolverwaltung für Branntwein.* [1979] ECR: 649.

ECJ 294/83, *Partie Écologistes, 'Les Vertes' / Parliament.* [1986] ECR: 1339.

ECJ 45/86, *Commission / Council.* [1987] ECR : 1493.

ECJ 68/86, *United Kingdom / Council.* [1988] ECR : 855.

ECJ 70/88, *Parliament / Council ('Chernobyl').* [1991] ECR : 4529.

ECJ 177/88, *Dekker / Stichting Vormingscentrum voor Jong Volwassenen.* [1990] ECR: 3941.

ECJ 262/88, *Barber / Guardian Royal Exchange Assurance Group.* [1990] ECR: 1889.

ECJ 300/89, *Commission / Council ('Titanium Dioxide').* [1991] ECR: 2867.

ECJ 421/92, *Habermann-Beltermann / Arbeiterwohlfahrt Berzirksverband.* [1994] ECR: 1657.

Member State Constitutional Courts:

20/10/1989 Conseil d'Etat. *Nicolo*

BverfG 89, 155. Bundesverfassungsgericht. *Maastricht Urteil.*

References

Alter, K. (2001) *Establishing The Supremacy of European Law* (Oxford: Oxford University Press).

Alter, K. and Meunier-Aitsahalia, S. (1994) 'Judicial Politics in the European Community: European Integration and the Pathbreaking Cassis de Dijon Decision', *Comparative Political Studies* 26: 535–61.

Alter, K. and Vargas, J. (2000) 'Explaining Variation in the Use of European Litigation Strategies: European Community Law and British Gender Equality Policy', *Comparative Political Studies* 33: 452–82.

Bouwen, P. and McCown, M. (2004) 'Lobbying v. Litigation: Political and Legal Strategies of Interest Representation in the European Union', paper read at the SAIS-ECPR Pan-European Conference on EU Politics, Bologna, Italy, June.

Cichowski, R. (2001) 'Judicial Rulemaking and the Institutionalization of European Union Sex Equality Policy', in A. Stone Sweet, W. Sandholtz and N. Fligstein (eds) *The Institutionalization of Europe*, (Oxford: Oxford University Press).

—— (2004) 'Women's Rights, The European Court and Supranational Constitutionalism', *Law and Society Review* 38 :489–512.

Conant, L. (2002) *Justice Contained: On Law and Politics of the European Union* (Ithaca: Cornell University Press).

Craig, P. and De Búrca, G. (1998) *EU Law: Text, Cases, and Materials*, 2nd edn (Oxford: Oxford University Press).

Cullen, H. and Charlesworth, A. (1999) 'Diplomacy by Other Means: The Use of Legal Basis Litigation as a Political Strategy by the European Parliament and Member States', *Common Market Law Review* 36: 1243–70.

Ellis, E. (1998) *EC Sex Equality Law*, 2nd edn (Oxford: Clarendon Press; Oxford University Press).

Emiliou, N. (1994) 'Opening Pandora's Box: the Legal Basis of Community Measures Before the Court of Justice', *European Law Review* 19: 488–507.

Garrett, G. (1992) 'International Cooperation and Institutional Choice: The European Community's Internal Market', *International Organization* 46: 533–60.

Garrett, G. , Kelemen, D. and Schulz, H. (1998) 'The European Court of Justice, National Governments and Legal Integration in the European Union', *International Organization* 52: 149–76.

Jupille, J. (2004) *Procedural Politics: Issues, Influence, and Institutional Choice in the European Union* (New York: Cambridge University Press).

McCown, M. (2001) 'The Use of Judge Made Law in European Judicial Integration: Precedent Based Arguments in EU Inter-Institutional Disputes', paper read at European Community Studies Association Biennial Conference, Madison, WI.

—— (2003) 'The European Parliament Before the Bench: ECJ Precedent and EP Litigation Strategies', *Journal of European Public Policy* 10: 974–95.

—— (2004) 'Drafting the European Constitution Case by Case: Precedent and the Judicial Integration of the EU', Doctoral Dissertation, Department of Politics, Oxford University, Oxford.

McCown, M. and Hae-Won Jun (2003) 'Inter-Institutional Disputes in the European Union: The Constitutional Dimension of European Integration', paper read at European Union Studies Association Conference, Nashville, TN.

Merryman, J. H. (1985) *The Civil Law Tradition: An Introduction to the Legal Systems of Western Europe and Latin America*. 2nd edn (Stanford, CA: Stanford University Press).

Moravcsik, A. (1998) *The Choice for Europe: Social Purpose and State Power from Messina to Maastricht* (Ithaca, NY: Cornell University Press).

Nugent, N. (1994) *The Government and Politics of the European Union*, 3rd edn (Durham: Duke University Press).

Rittberger, B. (2003) 'The Creation and Empowerment of the European Parliament', *Journal of Common Market Studies* 41: 203–25.

Scharpf, F. (1996) 'Negative and Positive Integration in the Political Economy of European Welfare States', in G. Marks, F. Scharpf, P. Schmitter and W. Streeck (eds), *Governance in the European Union* (London: Sage Publications).

Slaughter, A.-M., Stone Sweet, A. and Weiler, J. (1998) *The European Court and National Courts – Doctrine and Jurisprudence: Legal Change in its Social Context* (Oxford: Hart Publishing).

Stone Sweet, A. (2000) *Governing with Judges: Constitutional Politics in Europe* (Oxford, New York: Oxford University Press).

Stone Sweet, A. and Brunell, T. (1998) 'Constructing a Supranational Constitution: Dispute Resolution and Governance in the European Community', *American Political Science Review* 92: 63–81.

—— (1999) 'Alec Stone Sweet and Thomas Brunell Dataset on Preliminary References in EC Law', ed. T. Brunell. San Domenico di Fiesole, Italy: Robert Schuman Centre, European University Institute.

Stone Sweet, A. and McCown, M. (2004) 'Free Movement of Goods in the European Union' in *The Judicial Construction of Europe* (Oxford: Oxford University Press).

Tsebelis, G, and Garrett, G. (2001) 'The Institutional Foundations of Intergovernmentalism and Supranationalism in the European Union', *International Organization* 55: 357–90.

Weiler, J. (1999) *The Constitution of Europe: 'Do the new clothes have an emperor?' and Other Essays on European Integration* (New York: Cambridge University Press).

Chapter 9

The EU budgetary procedure in the Constitutional debate

Henrik Enderlein and Johannes Lindner

Introduction

Despite widespread calls for reforms of the EU budgetary procedure, the European Convention and the Intergovernmental Conference (henceforth IGC) have generated only minor institutional adjustments in that area. This chapter explores the underlying reasons for this.[1]

On the basis of an analysis of the current budgetary procedure and a detailed assessment of the various reform proposals, the chapter contends that an important reason for keeping the institutional status quo has been the lack of a suitable alternative. It argues that the current design of the EU budgetary procedure corresponds by and large to an equilibrium between all actors involved, given the present state of political integration in the European Union. Altering that equilibrium would require a significant shift in integration, notably towards more fiscal federalism. Given that neither the European Convention nor the IGC dwelled on questions related to fiscal federalism, it is not surprising that the calls for far-reaching reforms of the EU budgetary procedure did not amount to the desired institutional change.

The chapter indirectly implies that neither the failure to reach a compromise at the June 2005 negotiations on the Financial Perspective nor the possible re-negotiation of the Constitutional Treaty are likely to result in a fundamental overhaul of the budgetary procedure, unless Europe were to resolve its crisis by making a leap forward in political integration.

The contrast between the perception of a large scope for reform and the de facto agreement on keeping the status quo in the area of the EU budget is remarkable. Calls for reform have enjoyed some prominence in the recent discussions. Both in academic and policy-making circles, it has become common to refer to the 'problem' deriving from the present framework at both the multi-annual and annual levels. The Chairman of the European Convention, President Giscard d'Estaing, commented on the present budgetary procedure by claiming that 'there is indeed a real problem in that area' (Plenary Session of the Convention on 12 September 2002). The representative of the United Kingdom (UK) in the Convention, Peter Hain, was equally bold on this issue when calling upon his colleagues to 'simplify where we can'. The Sapir Report prepared upon the request of Commission President Prodi calls upon member states to 'refocus the EU budget' (Sapir et al. 2003); while the special report of the European Parliament on the budgetary procedure stresses the 'need for reforming, updating and simplifying' (European Parliament 2003).

Against this background, this chapter seeks to provide explanations of why there have been so few institutional changes to the budgetary procedure. Over recent years, institutionalist literature has (slowly) embarked on the analysis of institutional change (Lieberman 2002; Pierson 2004; Streeck and Thelen 2005). For a long time researchers have focused largely on how rules and procedures affect policy outcomes. Now that the relevance of institutions is widely recognised, the logical next step on the research agenda is to explain the origin and development of institutions. Within EU research, two recent special issues of the *Journal of European Public Policy* provide a range of interesting explanations of institutional change and stability. In contrast to the existing literature on Treaty change (e.g. Moravcsik 1998), the articles in these two special issues combine the focus on the evolution of rules and procedures with a detailed analysis of the day-to-day functioning of institutions (Rittberger and Stacey 2003; Falkner 2002). They contend that the experience with the current set of rules and procedures conditions the emergence of institutional change and that informal changes in the way rules and procedures are applied often precede formal Treaty change.

In this context, Lindner (2003, 2005) has developed an approach specifically related to changes and stability within the EU budgetary procedure between 1970 and 2000. He has argued that by stabilising the current budgetary procedure a number of reproduction mechanisms prevent a far-reaching institutional reform. These reproduction mechanisms include (i) the bargaining power of the anti-change coalition; (ii) the interdependence between the different sub-fields within EU budgetary politics; (iii) the costs and benefits of switching to another institutional setting; and (iv) the ability to accommodate pressure for change through minor institutional adjustments.

In this chapter, we follow up on this approach by focusing in particular on the third of these aspects, namely the relevance of costs related to switching to another institutional setting ('switching costs' – see also Pierson 2000). Such switching costs were key components of institutional stability in the EU budgetary procedure before and after the reform of 1988. Formalised institutional changes in the EU budgetary procedure were largely prevented by uncertainty over the distributive impact of new institutional choices and the outcomes of negotiations, as well as the relatively low opportunity costs of maintaining the status quo (Lindner 2003, 2005).

One might argue that the European Convention could have provided a setting of considerably low switching costs, since it gave rise to an institutionalised debate aiming at constitutional reforms. If the European Convention nonetheless did not lead to an overhaul of the EU budgetary procedure, as is the case, then the switching costs argument requires further specification.

In this chapter we attempt to provide such further specification, arguing that one (if not the main) reason for the striking contrast between calls for reform and the modest result at the IGC has been the lack of a suitable alternative to the current budgetary procedure. We argue that the design of the EU budgetary procedure as it was in place before the start of the constitutional debate largely corresponds to an optimal equilibrium between all actors involved, given the present state of political integration in the European Union. Altering that equilibrium would have required a significant shift in integration: the 'embeddedness' of the budgetary field in the overall state of European integration constrained the scope of reform significantly. In this context, the switching costs argument can be upheld, given the undeniably very large costs related to the uncertainty over implications of changes to political integration and given the relatively low opportunity costs of maintaining the status quo – despite the numerous and vehement calls for reforms in the budgetary area.

After some theoretical considerations in the following section the chapter presents an overview of the EU budgetary framework in order to identify its distinctive procedural and institutional features and to illustrate the embeddedness in the overall state of integration. The chapter then reviews the main reform proposals for streamlining the EU budgetary procedure, and the outcome of the IGC, before drawing final conclusions.

HENRIK ENDERLEIN AND JOHANNES LINDNER

Some theoretical considerations

Analysing the institutional underpinnings of the EU budgetary procedure and trying to assess them in terms of their level of political integration requires a focus on two different types of approaches that are intimately related. As with all national budgets, the EU budget is rooted in a principal–agent framework. Given the specific set-up of the EU, however, this framework yields quite specific implications deriving from the two sources of EU legitimacy, which are supranational and intergovernmental decision-making. From the perspective of budgetary issues, a focus on the legitimacy-resources of the budget as an instrument of redistribution is warranted. This is best achieved in the perspective of the fiscal federalism literature.

Procedures on public finances have to be put into the context of the underlying principal–agent framework. The origins of constitutional orders and their legitimacy and efficiency are grounded in the pooling of individual citizens' sovereignty and the delegating of functions and powers to elected representatives. Citizens, as principals, allow elected representatives, as their agents, to be in charge of public institutions and to take political decisions (e.g. Buchanan and Tullock 1962).

While the principal–agent analogy allows the constitutional choice literature to explain the rationale behind the existence of states, the analogy is also used to analyse institution building at the international level and, in the specific European context, at the supranational level (Pollack 2003; see also Riker 1964, the fundamental theoretical text). Here, states are regarded as the principals. Under certain circumstances, cooperation among states is beneficial and states may decide to pool their political sovereignty in selected areas. In the context of pooled sovereignties at the international level, there are, however, two types of decision-making procedures:

- *Intergovernmental cooperation.* States agree to take decisions in the relevant policy area by unanimity, thus preserving a considerable degree of 'ultimate' sovereignty, deriving from the power of each individual member state to veto decisions. These decisions are legitimised by the direct link between citizens and their national governments and the fact that these governments cannot be outvoted. At the same time, the unanimity rule renders negotiations difficult, as decision-making is clearly hampered by national vetoes.
- *Supranational governance.* States might realise that it is beneficial to take some decisions by qualified majority and to delegate, as principals, certain functions to an (independent) agent helping them to overcome collective action problems. This move towards qualified majority voting and delegation is motivated by an interest in increasing the efficiency of international decision-making. The states sacrifice their veto-power and assign political tasks, such as the oversight of the implementation and the role of mediating between states, to a supranational agent. Yet supranational governance may, in the view of citizens, be regarded as less legitimate than intergovernmental cooperation, because national governments can be outvoted and supranational agents exercise power without a direct mandate from the citizens.[2] In order to counteract this lack of legitimisation, supranational actors may be directly elected by the citizens, thus circumventing national governments as the sole source of legitimacy. However, this increase in legitimacy comes again

190

at the cost of efficiency. The involvement of an additional directly elected agent might increase the complexity of decision-making.

Pooled sovereignty and delegation to supranational agents constitute two main dimensions of *political integration*. A political system of interstate cooperation is highly integrated when national governments have pooled large parts of their national competences at the supranational level and created strong supranational bodies that can overturn national vetoes.

However, there is also a third dimension of integration. This is the degree of political identification with, and acceptance of, interstate cooperation. Integration is well advanced when the citizens of the different states are united by a sense of belonging to the same community, when they share common values and goals, and – most relevantly from the perspective of this chapter – when they are willing to enter a system of national redistribution.[3]

Income redistribution within a nation state is a key ingredient in considerations on the optimal scale of government. As the large body of literature on 'fiscal federalism' in political science convincingly demonstrates, there is an obvious trade-off between the greater effectiveness of large units and the greater legitimacy of small units (e.g. Scharpf 1988; Oates 1972, 1999; Inman and Rubinfeld 1997). Research in economics has tried to gain objective insights on the appropriate size of nations and has developed positive theories of integration and decentralization (Alesina and Spolaore 1997; Bolton and Roland 2000). Research in political science has tried to gain insights on the original bargain that establishes a federation (Riker 1964; Stepan 1999; see Rodden 2005 for an overview).

What is relevant from this literature on the redistributive functions of federalism for the understanding of the EU budgetary procedure is the accent on the importance of (i) appropriate sources of legitimacy and (ii) appropriate protections against future exploitation either by the centre or by other states in the bargain over distributive federations.

The first two and the third dimension of integration are obviously interlinked. Political identification and willingness to enter a redistributive framework may evolve as a result of successful pooling and delegation. They are at the same time also important preconditions for further pooling and delegation.

The EU budget and European integration

Applying these theoretical considerations to the European Union, it becomes apparent that any significant reform in the area of the EU budgetary procedure would require a parallel move towards further integration in terms of institutional efficiency and legitimacy on the one hand, and willingness to redistribute income across Europe on the other. The simple presence of a framework that would reduce switching costs of institutional change (such as the drafting of an EU Constitution) is thus the necessary but not the sufficient condition of budgetary reform.

As this section argues, the present set-up of the EU budgetary procedure appears to be fully in line with the overall balance between legitimacy and efficiency in the EU institutional framework and also corresponds to EU citizens' willingness to allocate and redistribute income across Europe.

With regard to the institutional set-up, the EU level is governed by a combination of supranational and intergovernmental forms of decision-making. In the intergovernmental realm, heads of state or government set the grand lines in the European Council by consensus. Moreover, the European Council adopts Treaty changes, which are subsequently ratified according to national domestic procedures. In the Council of Ministers, representatives of national governments take detailed policy decisions upon legislative initiatives from the supranational Commission. Voting rules vary among policy fields. Where unanimity voting still applies, the Council acts as an intergovernmental body, while in the case of qualified majority voting ministers move into the supranational realm. The directly elected European Parliament introduces a link between the supranational decision-making process and the citizens. Its involvement as a strong veto-player is largely connected to qualified majority voting in the Council where, in terms of legitimacy, it compensates for the loss of member states' veto power. Moreover, it fulfils control functions vis-à-vis the Commission, which, as an independent supranational agent, is not directly legitimated. The present institutional set-up of the European Union thus combines elements of intergovernmental cooperation and supranational governance and strikes a balance between legitimacy and efficiency concerns.

This overall balance lays the foundation for the specific rules and procedures in the different policy fields of the EU. The involvement of the Commission, the European Parliament and the Council is a common feature to most policy domains. It caters for similar legitimacy and efficiency concerns regardless of the particular characteristics of the specific policy field.[4] Calls for reforming the decision-making procedure in a particular policy field should not be assessed independently of the general state of integration. On the contrary, their contents should be put under scrutiny with a view to the 'meta-level' that the state of integration constitutes. This meta-level does not only overarch but also determines decision-making in the different policy fields of the EU. The complexity or alleged inefficiency of a decision-making procedure can therefore not be exclusively attributed to the institutional provisions governing the specific policy field but they need to be linked to the characteristics of the meta-level. Moreover, the embeddedness in the meta-level constrains the scope of institutional reform in a policy field. Reform proposals that seem appropriate to increase efficiency and legitimacy of the procedure are actually incompatible with the current state of integration.

In the budgetary field, the embeddedness in the meta-level is particularly strong as budgetary decision-making cuts across the different policy fields. The EU budget reflects the range of areas in which sovereignty is pooled at the EU level. Moreover, budgetary decision-making is intertwined with the different legislative procedures, because policy decisions often have a legislative and a budgetary component. Both components need to be coordinated. The legislative and the budgetary realm cannot be viewed as separate policy fields.

Institutional reform in the budgetary area is further complicated by the difficult relationship between efficiency and legitimacy concerns in that domain. Taking into account the limited degree of European citizens' political identification with supranational decision-taking at the EU level, it can generally be argued that legitimacy concerns are mainly catered for by a strong involvement of member states' representatives. Such intergovernmental elements, however, necessarily allow for extensive bargaining thus coming at the expense of efficiency concerns. Budgetary decisions are usually regarded as an issue close to national sovereignty and at the heart of governments' powers.

Hence, member states may be reluctant to give up their authority over spending and raising taxes to the supranational level. Moreover, winners and losers of budgetary decisions are more clearly identifiable than in legislative decision-making because costs and benefits are specified in monetary terms. Therefore, the potential for conflict is probably high. At the same time, transparency of costs and losses also lends itself to judgements on the efficiency of the decision-making procedure and the resulting policy outcomes. In contrast to legislative decision-making, complaints about wasted resources and inefficient use of taxpayers' money are widespread in the budgetary field.

In the particular context of European decision-taking in the budgetary domain, we would argue that it is possible to simplify the relationship between efficiency and legitimacy concerns as a trade-off (see also Enderlein *et al.* 2004). Using a metaphor, possible solutions to this trade-off are limited by a 'Pareto frontier' that is determined by the state of integration (see figure 9.1). Similarly, the quality and nature of a policy field can be assessed in terms of their Pareto optimality and their location on the Pareto frontier. Shifts to the Pareto frontier itself are triggered by increases or decreases in political integration, i.e. citizens' willingness to enter into cross-European redistribution.

Proponents of reform assume that the budgetary procedure is currently situated at point A, while we assume that the point B is probably a more accurate description of the current procedure. This means that while the proponents of reform think reforms are possible that significantly increase efficiency and legitimacy we contend that improvements could only be marginal and would have to concentrate either on efficiency (leading to B') or legitimacy (leading to B").

Returning now to the research question of the chapter, namely why is there no significant change in the EU budgetary procedure, we hypothesise that the main reason is the lack of suitable (i.e. Pareto superior) procedural alternatives, taking into account the exogenously given state of political integration (i.e. the Pareto frontier). In line with this hypothesis, proponents of far-reaching reforms in the budgetary field would seem to have underestimated, first, the constraints that are set by the general state of integration and, second, the high degree to which current procedure is already in tune with these constraints.

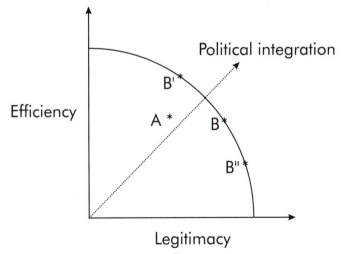

Figure 9.1 The efficiency–legitimacy trade-off.

The EU budgetary procedure

The following section outlines the main features of the present EU budgetary procedure by first presenting some overall considerations before analysing more closely the procedures at both the multi-annual and annual levels.[5]

Content of the budget

Given that welfare state policies still remain national competences, the EU budget is not the key layer of budgetary activities in the European Union. It focuses largely on two specific policy fields with a strong redistributive bent, namely agricultural and regional policies which alone account for more than 80 per cent of expenditure. While agricultural spending provides European farmers with subsidies, regional spending redistributes funds from richer to poorer memebr states. Although often presented as such (e.g. Leonardi 1999), these policies cannot be regarded as public goods benefiting the Union as a whole. They make for a system in which member states are particularly pressed to demand a *juste retour*. Amounting to less than 1 per cent of EU-GNI, the economic function of the EU budget looks disproportionate in comparison to the legislative functions of the EU (directly determining more than 50 per cent of domestic legislation in EU member states).[6] Thus, while important areas of national sovereignty are pooled at the EU level and a certain degree of political identification and acceptance has been achieved, as far as redistributive functions are concerned, the nation state still provides the most important reference point.

The EU budget is expenditure-led, so that, within a limit set by agreed spending and revenue ceilings, resources are raised to match the needs to carry out the EU policies. This creates very different incentives for the European Parliament (EP) and the Council as the two arms of the budgetary authority. For member states, efforts to reduce expenditure would imply a reduction in their direct contributions, while for the EP it may provide an incentive to suggest expenditure programmes, since the matching financing would be automatically furnished by the member states up to the overall ceiling. Members of the EP (MEPs) thus enjoy a unique position: they gain credit for expenditures agreed by the EP but are not associated with the related costs. In practice, however, differences in the incentives for member states and MEPs have been blurred, on the one hand, by a growing acceptance among MEPs of an austerity approach towards budgetary decisions and, on the other hand, by individual member states' interests in those expenditure policies, where they gain more from the budget than they contribute.

On the revenue side, the current system of 'own resources' implies – despite its label – that the EU is funded predominantly by direct transfers from the member states, which facilitates computation of net positions and does little to curb member states' pursuit of a *juste retour*. The system of own resources has become increasingly less autonomous since its creation in the 1970s when it aimed to give resources to the Community (customs duties, agricultural levies and VAT contributions) that would 'belong' to it and would not depend on decisions by national finance ministers. The introduction of 'own resources', together with the granting of the 'power of the purse' to the EP in the 1970s, was a development of a *federal* nature, aimed at enhancing the supranational element of the union.

However, as EU expenditure increased the traditional own resources proved insufficient and a fourth resource was established as part of the Delors-I package in 1988 which also introduced the multi-annual Financial Perspective (see below). This fourth resource, which now accounts for approximately two-thirds of total EU budget revenues, can be regarded as similar to the pre-1970 period in which the Community was financed entirely by contributions from the member states (Begg and Grimwade 1998). In line with the notion of an expenditure-led budget and the sovereignty concerns of member states, changes in the revenue structure of the EU have to be taken by unanimity following a procedure that is completely separate from the annual budgetary procedure.

The Financial Perspective

The Financial Perspective is a multi-annual budgetary framework (namely, seven years) which lays down the maximum amounts of both total annual expenditure and annual expenditure on specific policy headings.

The Financial Perspective was a welcome development when it was first introduced in 1988. In the late 1970s and early 1980s EU budgetary negotiations had been characterised by confrontations between the European Parliament and the Council that eventually led the EP to reject entire draft budgets (Lindner and Rittberger 2003). The early 1980s also saw vigorous complaints from the UK and a lack of sufficient resources, which was prompted by the ballooning of Common Agriculture Policy spending and aggravated when the UK rebate was agreed. In this context, the Financial Perspective was intended to significantly restrict the scope for political choice during the actual annual budgetary procedure. By linking revenue and expenditure sides, it ensured that expenditure-led budgets would not any more exceed existing resources (Shackleton 1990).

The Financial Perspective combines intergovernmental with supranational elements. It is discussed, upon a proposal by the Commission, in the European Council, where it requires unanimous agreement among member states. The involvement of heads of state or government ensures overcoming differences and stalemate between EU ministers. The Financial Perspective is finally adopted as an 'Interinstitutional Agreement' between the EP, the Council and the Commission. In contrast to indicative financial programming (which is prevalent in national budgetary procedures), the ceilings of the Financial Perspective are binding on the three parties. While the revenue ceilings are codified in legal acts that are unanimously adopted by member states in the Council, the expenditure ceilings gain their binding character from the political willingness of actors to adhere to the 'Interinstitutional Agreement' which by itself does not have the status of enforceable law (Monar 1994). The semi-voluntary character of the Financial Perspective forces actors to cooperate as otherwise the multi-annual framework would break down.

Planning stability and a reduction of conflict comes at a price: the Financial Perspective clearly limits the flexibility of budgetary actors and introduces a strong status quo bias. Annual expenditure ceilings for regional spending, for example, have the status of spending targets and thus commit annual budgetary decisions over a period of seven years. Moreover, when the Financial Perspective is renegotiated in the European Council, national governments use their veto-power in order to maximise budgetary gains. The use of veto power and the bargaining dynamics resulting from it lead to a largely incremental update of the ceilings, thus respecting the key spending interests of member states, such as the rebate for the United Kingdom, regional spending for the

Cohesion Countries, and unaltered CAP for France.[7] In such a setting, major changes and far-reaching reforms are very unlikely to occur (Begg 1999).[8]

Overall, in the EU a binding multi-annual budget plan – adopted by heads of state or government – plays a key role in reducing the conflict between budgetary actors and ensuring planning stability, while, at the same time, the flexibility of the annual procedure is curtailed and major budgetary impulses are de facto very difficult to generate. The intergovernmental level, at which legitimacy concerns clearly dominate over efficiency concerns, thus uses multi-annual planning to limit the room for supranational decision-taking in the annual procedure.

Annual budgetary procedure

The annual budgetary procedure for the EU budget, set out in detail in Article 272 of the Treaty, appears to conform with the division of labour between an executive branch that proposes the budget and a legislative branch that adopts it (see figure 9.2). The Commission prepares a 'Preliminary Draft Budget' (PDB), which is amended by the Council; this version of the budget, which at this stage of the procedure is called 'Draft Budget', is forwarded to the EP for proposals for amendments or modifications. Following two readings by each of the two institutions, the EP adopts the final budget. Yet the role of the Commission is much more limited than the division of labour suggests. Although the Commission is present at all stages of the budgetary process, its main function is fulfilled once the 'preliminary draft budget' is submitted.

The Treaty bestows each of the two arms of the EU budgetary authority, i.e. the EP and the Council, with specific powers which largely rest on the distinction between compulsory expenditure (that directly results from Treaty application or acts adopted on the basis of the Treaty) and non-compulsory expenditure. This is another particularity of the EU budget. Compulsory expenditure accounts for around 45 per cent of the EU budget and is mainly used for the CAP. While the EP can – within the limits set by the Financial Perspective[9] – overrule the Council's amendments to non-compulsory expenditure, it has to accept the Council's prerogative in the domain of compulsory expenditure. Moreover, the EP has the exclusive power to reject the overall budget.

For years, the distinction between compulsory and non-compulsory expenditure has been a bone of contention between the EP and the Council (Lindner and Rittberger 2003). It was introduced in 1970 in order to limit the budgetary powers of the EP and to ensure the exclusive control of member states in the Council over legislative decisions with financial implications. With that distinction, the Council was able to continue its practice of introducing legally binding entitlements. As the definition of compulsory expenditure in the Treaty left scope for interpretation, EP and Council fought intense battles over the classification of certain expenditure lines.

Since the introduction of the Financial Perspective and the extension of the EP's legislative powers, the distinction has gradually lost relevance and the role of the EP has strengthened. A routine of close cooperation, with different fora for formal and informal meetings during the course of the annual procedure, has emerged.[10] This gives the two arms of the budgetary authority the opportunity to confer together over both types of expenditure. Often a compromise is found at the conciliation meeting shortly before second reading in the Council, which is then endorsed by both institutions in their respective readings.

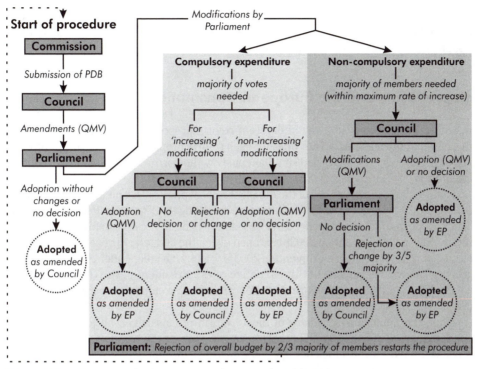

Figure 9.2   The current budgetary procedure (Article 272 TEC).

Taking up the theoretical claims presented in the second and the third section of this chapter, the main features of the current budgetary procedure clearly display a set-up that, first, balances supranational and intergovernmental forms of governance and that is, second, in line with the overall state of integration in the European Union. The largely supranational annual budgetary procedure brings together delegates of national governments in the Council taking decisions by qualified majority and directly elected MEPs. The Commission, as a representative of the executive branch, is a bureaucratic actor that sets the agenda for the budgetary decisions, but plays a limited role in the final stages of the procedure. The ceilings of the Financial Perspective provide a largely intergovernmental framework around the annual procedure and thus coordinate the supranational expenditure realm with the intergovernmental revenue realm.

Looking at the evolution of budgetary decision-making from the theoretical perspective, it seems that the introduction of multi-annual planning in 1988 corrected mismatches between political integration and the budgetary procedure (Lindner 2003). The creation of the 'own resources' and the granting of budgetary powers to the EP in the early 1970s did not fully match the state of political integration at the time. Conflict over the respective role of the EP, tensions between the majority of member states and the outvoted minority and a constant lack of resource to cover the ever-expanding expenditure signalled that budgetary decision-making was not at the Pareto frontier set by political integration. The Financial Perspective and the Interinstitutional Agreement increased the legitimacy of budgetary decision-making (by introducing a forum for unanimous decisions on medium-term budget planning) and its efficiency (by reducing the level of conflict and eliminating the problems of overshooting expenditure). Moreover, since

197

1988 the gradual strengthening of the EP in the annual budgetary procedure (through the introduction of rules on closer cooperation) reflected changes in the state of integration, namely a general shift towards a more powerful EP.

Reform proposals and the European Constitution

In political discussions an array of different reform proposals have been presented. In this context, the question arises whether such reform proposals indicate that legitimacy and efficiency could be increased simultaneously without a major step forward in political integration.

Table 9.1 gives an overview of the different reform proposals. The EP set out its ideas in a report that was initiated by the Committee on Budgets (European Parliament 2003). The European Convention focused before issuing its draft Treaty establishing a Constitution (European Convention 2003b) extensively on the budgetary procedure in a special discussion circle (European Convention 2003a). Finally, an independent high-level study group which was established at the initiative of the President of the Commission also covered the budgetary procedure in its report on the economic governance of the EU (Sapir *et al*. 2004).

While the detailed assessment of these reform proposals can be found elsewhere (Enderlein *et al*. 2004), table 9.2 presents an overview of the effects that these reform proposals have on the efficiency and legitimacy of the budgetary procedure. As the various (+) and (–) symbols indicate, most reform proposals either have a mixed effect on efficiency or the resulting increase in efficiency is offset by a decrease in legitimacy. Taking, for example, the introduction of qualified majority voting for the adoption of the Financial Perspective, this would significantly reduce the status quo bias, as individual member states would lose their power to uphold an agreement. At the same time, such a move might impede the conflict-reducing role of the Financial Perspective and undermine its acceptance as a binding framework for the annual procedure. Much of the legitimacy of the Financial Perspective stems from the fact that it is unanimously adopted. In particular on the revenue side, member states that are net contributors to the EU budget would find it extremely difficult to justify domestically significant increases of the EU revenue, if these increases result from decisions that they opposed.

Against the background of these different proposals and on the basis of the draft Constitution of the Convention, representatives at the IGC negotiated the possible institutional reforms in the budgetary field. Although the budgetary field featured prominently many of the presented proposals were soon rejected. In the end, the European Constitution that Heads of State or Government agreed upon in June 2004 did not entail major changes, but presented a budgetary procedure that remains very close to the current budgetary decision-making process. In fact, the main novelties that the 'new' budgetary procedure entails are taken from the rules and procedures that are currently laid down in the Interinstitutional Agreement. Thus, it simply institutionalises existing informal arrangements and does not enact institutional change (for a similar assessment see Laffan and Lindner 2005).

While the European Constitution does not touch upon the *content* of the budget, it does implement a reform proposal that concerns the Financial Perspective, namely the institutionalisation of the multi-annual budgetary framework. This change simply

Table 9.1 Overview of reform proposals

Reform proposals	European Parliament[1]	Convention discussion circle on budgetary procedure[2]	Sapir Group[3]	European Convention[4]
Content of the budget				
Re-focusing the expenditure side of the EU budget	—	—	Yes	—
Modifying the revenue base of the EU budget	Yes	—	Yes	—
Financial Perspective				
Adopting the Financial Perspective and/or the revenue side by qualified majority among member states	Yes	Yes (preferably with 'super-majority')	Yes	FP: Yes, but later Revenue: No
Institutionalising the Financial Perspective	Yes	Yes	—	Yes
Taking the veto power from the EP	No	No	—	No
Shortening the time frame of the Financial Perspective and synchronising it with the EP elections	Yes	No (at least five years)	—	No (at least five years)
Increasing the flexibility of the expenditure headings	Yes	No (but provisions for flexibility reserve)	Yes	No
Annual budgetary procedure				
Eliminating the distinction between compulsory and non-compulsory expenditure	Yes	Yes	—	Yes
Giving either the Council or the EP the last word	Yes (EP[5])	Yes (EP[5])	—	Yes (EP[5])

1 European Parliament (2003): 'Report on the reform of the budgetary procedure: possible options in view of the revision of the treaties', 20 February 2003, A5-0046/2003.

2 European Convention (2003a): 'Final report of the discussion circle on the budgetary procedure', 14 April 2003, CONV 679/03.

3 Sapir et al. (2004): 'An Agenda for a Growing Europe. Making the EU Economic System Deliver', July 2003.

4 European Convention (2003b): 'Draft Treaty establishing a Constitution for Europe', 18 July 2003, CONV 820/1/03 REV 1, CONV 847/03, CONV 848/03.

5 Within certain limitations.

Table 9.2 Assessment of reform proposals

Reform proposals	Efficiency	Legitimacy
Content of the budget		
(a) Re-focusing the expenditure side of the EU budget	(+) A stronger focus on public goods would reduce *juste retour* calculations.	(–) This would undermine package deal character of the current distributive order.
(b) Modifying the revenue base of the EU budget	(+) Tax would increase transparency.	(–) This would infringe fiscal sovereignty of member states; only acceptable in combination with strengthening of EP.
Financial Perspective		
(a) Adopting the Financial Perspective and/or the revenue side by qualified majority among member states	(+) This would reduce the *status quo* bias. (–) This would undermine the conflict-reducing effect on the annual procedure.	(–) In particular majority voting on revenue would infringe fiscal sovereignty of member states.
(b) Institutionalising the Financial Perspective	(+) This would adapt the Treaty to current practice. (–) Current soft law character forces actors to cooperate; this would be lost.	
(c) Taking the veto power from the EP	(+) This would marginally facilitate negotiations. (–) This would undermine the conflict-reducing effect on the annual procedure.	(–) This would reduce legitimacy of the framework gained from EP support.
(d) Shortening the time frame of the Financial Perspective and synchronising it with the EP elections	(+) This would increase flexibility. (–) This would increase bargaining costs due to more frequent renegotiations.	(+/–) This would increase legitimacy only if EP gained more power over the financial perspective.
(e) Increasing the flexibility of the expenditure headings	(+) This would make the framework more adaptable. (–) This would undermine the conflict-reducing effect on the annual procedure.	
Annual budgetary procedure		
(a) Eliminating the distinction between compulsory and non-compulsory expenditure	(+) This would marginally reduce the complexity of the procedure and eliminate traditional sources of conflict.	(–) This would affect negatively the current balance between EP and Council.
(b) Giving either the Council or the EP the last word	(+) This would reduce the complexity of the procedure and facilitate decision-making.	(–)This would affect negatively the current balance between EP and Council.

reflects the current practice. It only affects the way that the Financial Perspective is legally codified. Under the European Constitution, the binding force of the Financial Perspective will not any more be based on the political willingness of actors to cooperate, as laid down in the Interinstitutional Agreement, but on the legal force of the Constitution, which obliges the budgetary authority to adopt a multi-annual framework. Laffan and Lindner (2005: 208) correctly point out that the institutionalisation of the Financial Perspective was the minimum reform that the drafters of the Constitution were expected to enact: 'Given the objectives of the constitutional process, namely to update and to streamline the Treaty, the contrast between the Treaty provisions and current practices was simply too pronounced in this area of the budgetary decision-making for the drafters of the Constitutional Treaty to ignore'. Proposals to go beyond merely institutionalising the current Interinstitutional Agreement, in particular the introduction of qualified majority voting, were strongly disputed and, in the end, failed.

With regard to the *annual budgetary procedure*, changes appear at first glance to be more far-reaching. Figure 9.3 illustrates the new budgetary procedure. The distinction between compulsory and non-compulsory expenditure is eliminated. The Council and the European Parliament meet at a Conciliation Committee to agree on a Joint Text that is then adopted by the Council and the European Parliament in separate readings. The Constitution does not specify the order of the readings after the Conciliation Committee, but, in analogy to the co-decision procedure, figure 9.3 assumes that the Council will vote first. Parliament has the right to reject the overall budget. What looks different from the current procedure is in fact, largely an institutionalisation of the current practice. Already the Interinstitutional Agreement gives the EP some say over compulsory expenditure through the ad hoc conciliation procedure and the equivalent to a Conciliation Committee is already in place. Most of the time, the annual budget is adopted de facto in a conciliation meeting between the Council and the EP shortly before the second reading in Council. The agreement is then adopted by the two institutions in their respective readings.

The only actual change that the Constitution introduces concerns the right of the EP and the Council to veto an agreement in the Conciliation Committee. While currently the procedure continues even if the conciliation meeting fails, the Constitution stipulates that the Commission would need to present a new proposal for a 'Draft Budget'. However, the effect of this change should not be overstated. Granting the Council the right to withdraw its consent to the budget had to be introduced to keep the delicate balance of legitimacy between the power of the EP and of the Council.

Overall, the IGC seems to have settled on reform of the current budgetary procedure only to the extent that proven rules and procedures from outside the Treaty are introduced into the Constitution. This is consistent with the theoretical approach presented in the beginning of the chapter: excessive switching costs of institutional reform in the budgetary domain prevented major changes. The uncertainty of their effect and lack of suitable alternatives, which would have increased efficiency *and* legitimacy, prevented constitutional negotiators from embarking on the discussed reform proposals. Moreover, taking into account the tight link between overall state of integration of the European Union and procedural issues related to budgetary matters, it is not surprising that the IGC was risk-averse with regard to changes to the budgetary procedures that would have entailed significant consequences for the general set-up of the EU.

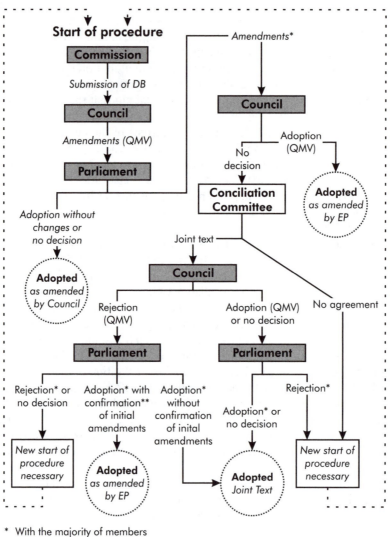

* With the majority of members
** With 3/5 of votes and majority of members

Figure 9.3 The amended annual budgetary procedure in the Constitutional Treaty (Article III-404)

Conclusion

The aim of this chapter was to shed light on the question of why – despite widespread calls for reforms of the EU budgetary procedure – the European Convention and, even more importantly, the Intergovernmental Conference seem to have generated only minor institutional adjustments. On the basis of existing institutionalist and political economy literature, we argued that that an important reason for keeping the institutional status quo was the lack of suitable alternatives. Our analysis of the EU budgetary procedure and various reform proposals revealed that the current institutional design corresponds by and large to an equilibrium between all actors involved, given the present state of political integration in the European Union. Altering that equilibrium would require a significant shift in integration. The 'embeddedness' of the budgetary field in the overall state of European integration thus constrains the scope of reform significantly. Given that neither the European Convention nor IGC have dwelled on questions related to the general state of political integration, it is not surprising that the calls for far-reaching reforms of the EU budgetary procedure did not amount to the desired institutional change.

While it is beyond the scope of this chapter to consider the pros and cons of changes in the state of political integration, a number of elements are key in demarcating the room for manoeuvre for the EU budgetary procedure. Such key elements, which we called dimensions of political integration, are (i) the assignment of tasks to the different levels of government; (ii) the balance of power between the various EU actors and the corresponding voting modalities; and (iii) the degree to which citizens identify themselves with the EU level and with the politicians that are supposed to represent them there.

These conclusions should not be read as a panglossian view of current EU budgetary procedures but rather as a cautionary tale about the limited impact that may be expected from a simplification of budgetary procedures that leaves unaltered the broader EU institutional and political set-up. To fundamentally change current EU budgetary outcomes would require the modification of the current set of broader constraints in which any EU budgetary procedure is necessarily embedded.

Notes

1 The opinions expressed in this chapter are those of the authors and do not necessarily reflect those of the European Central Bank. This chapter is part of a larger research project on the reform of the EU budgetary procedure that we conducted between 2003 and 2005 together with Oscar Calvo-Gonzalez and Raymond Ritter. We thank Theodor Martens, Hedwig Ongena, Demosthenes Ioannou, Wouter Coussens, Berthold Rittberger, and Amy Verdun for helpful comments.

2 However, it is also argued that efficient decision-making procedures yielding effective policy outcomes can also create a high degree of legitimacy (see the distinction between input- and output-legitimacy in Scharpf 1999).

3 This third dimension may also be linked to the idea that a fully integrated political system (at least in its democratic variant) would need a common public sphere that allows for discourse among citizens and creation of supranational demos (Habermas 1996).

4 This does not mean that there is no variation in the degree to which political authority is delegated to supranational agents in the different domains. Indeed, in certain policy fields, such as competition policy, the Commission is very powerful; while in others, such the Common Foreign and Security Policy, decisions are taken by unanimity in the Council. However, policy fields evolve as part of the overall institutional setting. Moreover, they reflect the general scope of pooled sovereignty and degree of political integration and acceptance.

5 The description draws on Laffan (1997), European Commission (2002), Laffan and Lindner (2005) and Lindner (2005) as the main references.

6 Although there are no comprehensive studies on the matter, most analyses converge around that level (*The Economist* 2003).

7 Renegotiations in the European Council take place in conjunction with other political issues. Hence, bargaining (and horse-trading) among member states combines budgetary issues with non-budgetary issues. In this context, it has been argued that the EU budget fulfils an impor-

tant 'compensation function'. It compensates those member states that might incur costs from the integration process and thus facilitates a consensus for further integration among member states (Folkers 1997).

8   Although the Commission and the EP have, as signatories of the International Agreement, a veto-power over the ceilings of the Financial Perspective, they rarely exercise it. Usually, the EP gets compensated for its consent to the ceilings through informal extensions of its budgetary powers.

9   The Treaty provides for a 'maximum rate of increase' as a limit for non-compulsory expenditure. With the Interinstitutional Agreement, the ceilings of the Financial Perspective replace the maximum rate of increase.

10 Successive renewals of the Interinstitutional Agreement (in 1993 and 1999) introduced rules on closer cooperation.

References

Alesina, A. and Spolaore, E. (1997) 'On the Number and Size of Nations', *Quarterly Journal of Economics* 107/4: 1027–56.

Begg, I. (1999) 'Reshaping the EU Budget: Yet another missed opportunity?', *South Bank European Paper* 5/99, South Bank University.

Begg, I. and Grimwade, N. (1998) *Paying for Europe* (Sheffield: Sheffield Academic Press).

Bolton, P. and Roland, G. (2000) 'The Breakup of Nations: A Political Economy Analysis', *Quarterly Journal of Economics* 112/4: 1057–90.

Buchanan, J. M. and G. Tullock (1962) *The Calculus of Consent* (Ann Arbor: University of Michigan Press).

Enderlein, H., Lindner, J., Calvo-Gonzalez, O. and Ritter, R. (2005) 'The EU Budget – How Much Scope for Institutional Reform', *ECB Occasional Paper Series* 27. Also in H. Berger and T. Moutos (2005) *Designing the New EU* (Boston, MA: MIT Press).

European Commission (2002) *European Union Public Finance* (Luxembourg: Office for Official Publications of the European Communities).

European Convention (2003a) 'Final Report of the Discussion Circle on the Budgetary Procedure', 14 April 2003, CONV 679/03.

—— (2003b) 'Draft Treaty Establishing a Constitution for Europe', 18 July 2003, CONV 820/1/03 REV 1, CONV 847/03, CONV 848/03.

European Parliament (2003) 'Report on the Reform of the Budgetary Procedure: Possible Options in View of the Revision of the Treaties', 20 February 2003, A5–0046/2003.

Falkner, G. (ed.) (2002) 'EU Treaty Reform as a Three-level Process: Historical Institutionalist Perspectives', special issue of *Journal of European Public Policy* 9/1.

Folkers, C. (1997) 'Finanz- und Haushaltspolitik', in P. Klemmer (ed.) *Handbuch der Europäischen Wirtschaftspolitik* (München: Verlag Franz Vahlen).

Habermas, J. (1996) *Between Facts and Norms. Contributions to a Discourse Theory of Law and Democracy* (Cambridge, MA: MIT Press).

Inman, R. P. and Rubinfeld, D. L. (1997) 'Rethinking Federalism', *Journal of Economic Perspectives*, 11/4: 43–64.

Italian Presidency (2003) *Presidency Proposal for the Intergovernmental Conference* (12–13 December 2003), Addendum 1, CIG 60/03.

Laffan, B. (1997) *The Finances of the European Union* (Basingstoke: Macmillan Press).

Laffan, B. and J. Lindner (2005) 'The EU Budget', in M. Pollack, H. Wallace and W. Wallace (eds) *Policy-Making in the European Union*, 5th edn (Oxford: Oxford University Press).

Leonardi, R. (1999) *The Socio-economic Impact of Projects Financed by the Cohesion Fund: A Modelling Approach* (3 vols), (Luxembourg: Office of Official Publications of the European Communities).

Lieberman, R. (2002) 'Ideas, Institutions, and Political Order: Explaining Political Change', *American Political Science Review* 96/4: 697–712.

Lindner, J. (2003) 'Institutional Stability and Change: Two Sides of the Same Coin', *Journal of European Public Policy* 10/6: 912–35.

—— (2005) *Conflict and Change in EU Budgetary Politics* (London: Routledge).

Lindner, J. and Rittberger, B. (2003) 'The Creation, Interpretation and Contestation of Institutions – Revisiting Historical Institutionalism', *Journal of Common Market Studies* 41/3: 445–73.

Monar, J. (1994) 'Interinstitutional agreements: The Phenomenon and its new Dynamics after Maastricht', *Common Market Law Review* 31: 693–719.

Moravcsik, A. (1998) *The Choice for Europe: Social Purpose and State Power from Messina to Maastricht* (London: Routledge/UCL Press).

Oates, W. E. (1972) *Fiscal Federalism*. (New York: Harcourt Brace Jovanovich).

—— (1999) 'An Essay on Fiscal Federalism', *Journal of Economic Literature* 36(Sept.): 1120–49.

Pierson, P. (2000) 'Increasing Returns, Path Dependence, and the Study of Politics', *American Political Science Review* 94/2: 251–67.

—— (2004) *History, Institutions and Social Analysis* (Princeton, NJ, and Oxford: Princeton University Press).

Pollack, M. A. (2003) *The Engine of European Integration – Delegation, Agency, and Agenda Setting in the EU*, (Oxford: Oxford University Press).

Riker, W. H. (1964) *Federalism: Origin, Operation, Significance* (Boston, MA: Little, Brown & Co).

Rittberger B. and Stacey, J. (eds) (2003) 'The Formal and Informal Dynamics of Institutional Change in the EU', special issue of the *Journal of European Public Policy* 10/6.

Rodden, J. (2005) 'Comparative Federalism and Decentralization: On Meaning and Measurement', *Comparative Politics* 36/4: 481–500.

Sapir, A., Aghion, P., Bertola, G. *et al.* (2004) *An Agenda for a Growing Europe: The Sapir Report* (Oxford: Oxford University Press).

Scharpf, F. W. (1988) 'The Joint-Decision Trap: Lessons from German Federalism and European Integration', *Public Administration* 66: 239–78.

—— (1999) *Governing Europe. Effective and Democratic?* (Oxford: Oxford University Press).

Shackleton, M. (1990) *Financing the European Community*, The Royal Institute of International Affairs (London: Pinter Publishers).

Stepan, A. (1999) 'Federalism and Democracy: Beyond the U.S. Model', *Journal of Democracy* 10/4: 19–33.

Streeck, W. and Thelen, K. (eds) (2005) *Beyond Continuity: Explorations in the Dynamics of Advanced Political Economies* (Oxford: Oxford University Press).

The Economist (2003) 'Snoring while a superstate emerges?', 8 May.

205

Chapter 10

The process of enlargement

Problems, interests, and norms

FRANK SCHIMMELFENNIG

Introduction

On 1 May 2004, ten new member states acceded to the European Union (EU). Besides Malta and the Republic of Cyprus, the group consists of eight formerly communist countries: the Baltic countries of Estonia, Latvia, and Lithuania, the Czech Republic, Hungary, Poland, Slovakia, and Slovenia. The eastern enlargement round has already been the biggest in the history of the Community, and it is not finished. Accession treaties with Bulgaria and Romania were signed on 25 April 2005; both countries plan to join the EU in 2007. The opening of accession talks with Croatia was slated for 2005 but still depends on the full cooperation of Croatia with the International War Crimes Tribunal in The Hague; and negotiations with Turkey are planned to begin in October 2005. Finally, the EU extended an open invitation to the remaining countries of the Balkans. At the conclusion of eastern enlargement, the EU might have more than doubled its membership to over 30 states. This huge expansion has far-reaching effects on the institutional set-up and central policies of the EU and has triggered tough negotiations on budget and institutional reforms. The accession countries, however, have arguably been affected even more strongly: EU accession conditionality has triggered a comprehensive 'Europeanisation' of the state and its policies.

This chapter first gives an overview of the political problems of enlargement for the EU and the accession countries – and of the theoretical challenges that it presents to

Table 10.1 Chronology of eastern enlargement

Country	Signing of association treaty	Membership application	Beginning of accession negotiations	Accession
Poland	16/12/1991	5/4/1994	31/3/1998	1/5/2004
Hungary	16/12/1991	31/3/1994	31/3/1998	1/5/2004
Slovakia	16/12/1991 (10/1993)[1]	27/6/1995	15/2/2000	1/5/2004
Czech Republic	16/12/1991 (10/1993)[1]	17/1/1996	31/3/1998	1/5/2004
Romania	1/2/1993	22/6/1995	15/2/2000	Possibly 2007
Bulgaria	8/3/1993	14/12/1995	15/2/2000	Possibly 2007
Estonia	12/6/1995	24/11/1995	31/3/1998	1/5/2004
Latvia	12/6/1995	13/10/1995	15/2/2000	1/5/2004
Lithuania	12/6/1995	8/12/1995	15/2/2000	1/5/2004
Slovenia	10/6/1996	10/6/1996	31/3/1998	1/5/2004
Macedonia	9/4/2001	22/3/2004		
Croatia	29/10/2001	21/2/2003		

1 After the dissolution of Czechoslovakia on 1 January 1993, the association agreements had to be renegotiated.

theorising European integration. It then offers an analysis of the various stages and processes of enlargement, from the association of the Central and Eastern European countries (CEECs) via the EU decisions on enlargement, the selection of candidates, and EU reform, to the accession negotiations and the impact of EU accession conditionality on the new member states. For a chronological overview of these stages, see table 10.1.

The analysis demonstrates the interplay of enlargement and Europeanisation as well as of interests, power, and norms. The grave problems of efficiency and distribution caused by enlargement account for the initial reticence of a majority of the member states and their procrastination over EU reforms. The rapid and pervasive adoption of EU rules in the accession countries can be attributed to the strong incentives of EU membership and the concomitant bargaining power of the Union. On the other hand, EU norms explain why enlargement came about in spite of initial scepticism and outstanding reforms, how EU candidates were selected among the CEECs, and why the new member states attained a few important concessions during the accession negotiations.

Political problems and theoretical challenges of EU enlargement

Any enlargement of an international organisation is fraught with specific costs but also offers potential benefits for member states old and new. Concerning the collective goods provided by the organisation, enlargement is likely to produce 'crowding costs' because additional members will want a share of them. In addition, enlargement increases decision and transaction costs: administrative costs rise, communication becomes more cumbersome, and expenses for translation and interpreting increase disproportionately. The greater heterogeneity of attitudes and preferences that comes with enlargement makes it more difficult to reach decisions, in particular under unanimity and qualified majority voting. Because of the large number of accession countries and their low level of socio-economic development (compared to the member states), the potential costs of eastern enlargement are particularly high (Schimmelfennig 2003: 55–62).

The incumbent EU member states benefit from an expanded internal market in general. It fully integrates a new market for western European exports and investments in their close proximity. In addition, the supply of cheaper resources and cheaper but qualified labour reduces costs and strengthens European competitiveness on the world market. However, these positive effects are relatively small and unevenly distributed among member states and their economic sectors. Moreover, it was expected that EU agriculture as well as the low-tech sectors of the textiles, leather and metalworking industries would be exposed to stiff competition from the CEECs. This concerns mostly the southern member states, which specialise in these industries (Baldwin *et al.* 1997: 138, 148; Hagen 1996: 6).

Approximately 80 per cent of the budget goes into agricultural and regional subsidies. As the CEECs are on average far more agricultural and poorer than the old member states, it was anticipated that the CEECs would become net recipients for the foreseeable future, that is, EU transfers will outweigh their contributions to the budget. In its Agenda 2000 document, the Commission calculated that, whereas eastern enlargement would increase the population of the EU by 29 per cent, GDP would grow by only 9 per cent. In sum, GDP per head would decrease by 16 per cent.[1] Because of their low levels of wealth and income, the new members could expect to receive the highest assistance from the structural funds for their entire territory – even at the time of writing, only Slovenia surpasses the threshold of 75 per cent of average EU GDP. Depending on the enlargement scenario, studies calculated that the Community budget would have to increase by 20 per cent to two-thirds under pre-enlargement policy rules (see, e.g., Baldwin *et al*. 1997: 157). Since the net contributors to the EU budget (such as Germany or the Netherlands) quickly ruled out expanding the budget to cover the costs of enlargement, policy reforms appeared inevitable. Such reforms, however, would necessarily reduce transfers to the former main beneficiaries of EU subsidies (Greece, Ireland, Portugal, Spain).

Finally, eastern enlargement leads to a considerable increase in decision and transaction costs. This is not only because of the high number of small new member states (including a high number of rare languages) but also because of the increased heterogeneity of preferences resulting from the specific transformation problems of the region. The new members would bring in problematic legacies such as ethno-nationalistic conflicts and authoritarian political traditions, move the EU closer to the troubled regions of the Balkans, the Community of Independent States, or the Middle East, and aggravate distribution problems because of the wider economic cleavages. It was clear early on that enlargement would have to be accompanied by institutional reform (above all an expansion of majority voting and a reduction in the number of commissioners per country) to reduce the risk of paralysis.

The accession countries faced huge challenges, too. On the one hand, they will profit from an (almost) unimpeded access to their most important foreign market and from an increased inflow of capital. Moreover, they will receive subsidies from the EU budget that help to cushion the painful economic adaptation and catching-up processes. And last but not least, they would be entitled to participate in EU decision-making and thereby increase the influence that they lacked as small and poor states in European politics. On the other hand, however, the EU is not just a free-trade zone that requires its members to tear down trade barriers but a community of law and a market-regulating organisation that obliges new members to adopt its rules. The candidates therefore had to transpose the oft-quoted '80,000 pages' of the *acquis communautaire* into domestic law and to create new or reform existing domestic administrations and procedures in line with EU prescriptions.

Finally, the central role of enlargement in the post-Cold War development of the EU poses a challenge for theories of European integration. First, enlargement – or the horizontal dimension of integration – has long been a neglected issue in the theory of European integration (Schimmelfennig and Sedelmeier 2002). Second, the fact that eastern enlargement occurred – and continues – in spite of the enormous political problems it creates for the EU, calls for an explanation. Intergovernmentalism faces the challenge of accounting for the process and outcome of enlargement as a result of the constellation of domestic and state interests and of power relations among member state governments as well as between member and candidate state governments. At first glance, enlargement appears to constitute a puzzle for intergovernmentalism because the high crowding and transaction costs seem to preclude a net positive utility for the member governments. If this impression is correct, then supranationalist theories need to explain enlargement either in terms of transnational societal interests and supranational entrepreneurship or as an identity- and norm-driven policy.[2]

From Cold War to Association

Institutionalised cooperation and political conditionality

Almost immediately after the beginnings of democratic transition in Eastern Europe, the European Community started to expand its relations with the CEECs and to assist the political and economic transformation. By as early as 1988 it had established diplomatic relations with its Eastern counterpart, the Council for Mutual Economic Assistance (CMEA), and concluded a first Trade and Cooperation Agreement with Hungary. Similar agreements followed with the other CEECs, including the Soviet Union (in December 1989). In 1989, the Commission also began to coordinate the economic assistance of the entire G24 group of western states and issued its Phare programme of economic and technical aid for Poland and Hungary. Later it was extended to further CEECs and complemented by a similar program for the successor countries of the Soviet Union (Tacis). Finally, in April 1991, the European Bank for Reconstruction and Development was founded to support the development of a private sector and a functioning market economy in the transformation countries.

The early negotiations and agreements between the EC and the CEECs already show a central feature of the entire enlargement process: political conditionality. In January 1989, the European Parliament demanded that 'reference to human rights should figure' in the Trade and Cooperation Agreements the EC was beginning to negotiate with the CEECs,[3] and in November, the European Council established that 'initiatives aimed at the countries of Eastern Europe as a whole are applicable only to those which re-establish freedom and democracy'.[4] After the dissolution of the Soviet Union, the Commission confirmed that 'negotiating ... new types of agreements has to be subject to political conditions' (respect for human rights and democratic freedoms, guarantees for minorities, and so on).[5] In May 1992 the Council agreed on a general 'human rights clause' to be added to all agreements with third states, which stipulated suspension in case of non-compliance. In November 1992 and July 1993, the EC extended this political conditionality to Phare and Tacis assistance.

Member state preferences

The CEECs, however, were not only interested in support but quickly demanded a membership perspective. This demand met with divergent member state preferences, which mainly reflected an unequal distribution of enlargement costs and benefits. First, eastern enlargement was contested as such. Whereas the 'drivers' advocated an early and firm commitment to Eastern enlargement, the 'brakemen' were reticent and tried to put off the decision. Second, member states debated the scope of eastern enlargement. Here, one group of countries pushed for a limited (first) round focusing on the central European states; others favoured an inclusive approach. Table 10.2 shows the distribution of preferences on these two issues (see Schimmelfennig 2001: 48–53).

The distribution of preferences largely corresponds with the geographical distance between the member states and the CEECs. Except for Greece and Italy, the drivers neighboured the CEECs, and with the exception of the UK, the more distant member states belonged to the brakemen. The countries of the 'central region' of the EU

Table 10.2 Member state enlargement preferences

	Limited enlargement	Inclusive enlargement
Drivers	Austria, Finland, Germany	Denmark, Sweden, UK
Brakemen	Belgium, Luxembourg, Netherlands	France, Greece, Ireland, Italy, Portugal, Spain

preferred a limited (first round of) enlargement, whereas the northern countries (except for Finland) and the southern countries favoured a more inclusive approach.

In general, international interdependence increases with geographical proximity. Member states on the eastern border of the Community are more sensitive to negative developments in the CEECs – such as economic crises, wars, migration, and environmental degradation – than the more remote members. For them, enlargement was an instrument to stabilise the CEECs and control the negative externalities of transformation. In addition, geographical proximity creates opportunities for economic gains from trade and investment, for instance, by reducing the costs of transport and communication. Member states close to the CEECs therefore stand to gain most from market integration. For these reasons, member states are also particularly interested in the accession of those states on which they border or which are in close proximity. This explains member state preferences on the scope of enlargement.

However, the unequal gains from controlling negative, and exploiting positive, interdependence do not fully account for the divergence. To explain why Greece and Italy, two neighbours of the CEECs, joined Ireland, Spain, and Portugal as brakemen, we need to include the trade and budgetary competition that was to affect the low-tech producers and net recipients among the member states most strongly. Finally, geopolitical interests had an influence. France, in particular, was concerned that the community balance of power would shift east and in favour of Germany, the most important economic partner of the CEECs. In addition, the Italian government feared that eastern enlargement would divert the EU's attention and funding from the Mediterranean region. In contrast, the strong and early British commitment to enlargement is generally attributed to the 'europhobia' of the Conservatives who regarded a territorial expansion of the Community as an obstacle to its further deepening or its dilution towards a free-trade area.

Association

The drivers represented not only a minority of member states but also wielded less bargaining power. Even for Germany, the greatest potential beneficiary of eastern enlargement, the CEECs were of far smaller economic and political importance than the brakemen states. Under these circumstances, the drivers had no attractive outside options and could not credibly threaten the brakemen with exit or alternative agreements. As a result, the Community only offered the CEECs association according to Art. 238 of the EC Treaty and explicitly refused to give them a membership perspective. The only concession the drivers and the CEECs achieved during the negotiations was a reference to future membership as 'their', but not the Community's 'final objective'.[6]

The first 'Europe Agreements' were concluded with the Czech Republic, Poland, and Hungary. The Baltic countries, Bulgaria, Romania, and Slovenia followed until the mid-1990s. A new round of association began in 1999 when, under the impression of the Kosovo conflict, the EU offered the countries of the western Balkans Stabilisation and Association Agreements (SAA). The first SAAs were signed with Croatia and Macedonia in 2001; negotiations with Albania started in early 2003.

The association agreements contained provisions on a political dialogue, the intensification of economic, financial, and cultural cooperation, and the adaptation of (market-related) legislation in the CEECs to EC law. The substantive core of the association agreements, however, was a progressive liberalisation of the movement of goods. For the EC member states, association constituted the most efficient design for EC–CEEC relations. On the one hand, it enabled the potential winners of enlargement to intensify their economic involvement in CEE markets. On the other hand, it protected the potential losers of enlargement against the costs of trade and budget competition by equipping them with 'anti-dumping' and 'safeguard' measures in those sectors (agriculture, textiles, coal, iron, and steel) in which they were particularly vulnerable to competition from the CEECs and by blocking the CEECs' access to the Community budget. Resistance by interest groups, especially in France, Portugal, and Spain, blocked further liberalisation and led negotiations repeatedly to the brink of breakdown. Yet despite constant complaints about the EC's failure to commit itself to the goal of enlargement and to provide a more generous market opening, the CEECs accepted the Europe Agreements because association was still preferable to a weaker or not institutionalised relationship with the EC.

The account of the early enlargement process generally corroborates the LI analysis of European integration as driven by preferences and power. First, the divergent member state preferences reflected variation in international interdependence and the distribution of enlargement benefits and costs and, second, the association outcome can be explained by the superior bargaining power of the brakemen within the EC and of the EC as a whole vis-à-vis the CEECs. But why did the Community finally commit itself to and prepare for the admission of CEECs as full members, even though the constellation of preferences and bargaining power did not substantially change during the 1990s? This is a major puzzle for LI.[7]

Enlargement decision-making

The decision to expand

The CEECs and the drivers regarded association only as a provisional solution. Since they did not have the material bargaining power to make the brakemen consent to enlargement, they mainly used normative pressure based on the collective identity and the core political principles of the Community. The institutionalised collective identity of the EU is that of a community of European, liberal-democratic states as stated in Article 6(1) of the Treaty on European Union – 'The Union is founded on the principles of liberty, democracy, respect for human rights and fundamental freedoms, and the rule of law …' – and reaffirmed in its membership rules: 'Any European state which respects the principles set out in Article 6(1) may apply to become a member of the Union' (Art. 46 TEU).

The main strategy of the proponents of enlargement consisted in constructing enlargement as an issue of identity, values and norms, and opposition to enlargement as a betrayal of the Community's principles, purpose and past promises (see Schimmelfennig 2001: 62–76). In a first step, the CEECs invoked the pan-European, liberal identity of the community and claimed to share this identity. According to this line of argument, the CEECs have traditionally shared the values and norms of European culture and civilisation, demonstrated this orientation in the revolution of 1989, and 'returned to Europe' after the Cold War period of artificial separation. Advocates then framed enlargement as an issue of the EU's identity, arguing that it ought not to be seen and decided from the vantage point of national interests and material cost–benefit calculations. They referred to the constitutive values and norms of the EU and the intentions of the founding fathers of the Community and demanded that the member states base their decisions on historical and political criteria and on the long-term collective goals of pan-European peace, stability and welfare. Finally, they accused the reticent EU member states of acting inconsistently and betraying the fundamental values and norms of their own community if they continued to privilege their individual economic or geopolitical interest and to procrastinate. They appealed to the 'bad historic conscience' of the member states by denouncing their reticence as a new 'Yalta' or 'Iron Curtain' and demanded to be treated according to the standards of earlier enlargement rounds – above all the overriding goal of democracy promotion in the southern enlargement of the 1980s.

The most systematic and formal attempt to rhetorically commit the Community to Eastern enlargement can be found in the Commission's report to the Lisbon summit in June 1992, entitled *Europe and the Challenge of Enlargement*. The Commission referred to the Community's vision of a pan-European liberal order as creating specific obligations in the current situation: 'The Community has never been a closed club, and cannot now refuse the historic challenge to assume its continental responsibilities and contribute to the development of a political and economic order for the whole of Europe.'[8] It was difficult for the brakemen to rebut these arguments without, at the same time, casting doubts on their own commitment to the institutionalised identity and fundamental norms of the EU. Consequently, they did not publicly reject Eastern enlargement for instrumental reasons. The fact that the Commission's report, which presented enlargement as inevitable, was attached without discussion to the Conclusions of the Presidency at Lisbon and 'hardly discussed by the Member States and certainly not disputed in the many hours of discussion and negotiation leading up to the' Copenhagen summit in June 1993 indicates the effectiveness of normative pressure for the 'silencing' of the brakemen (Mayhew 1998: 25–7).

In addition, this process was aided by some of the EU's formal institutional features. First, its proposal power allowed the Commission to frame the intergovernmental debate and to put the member states under pressure to make decisions. Second, the rotating Council presidency allowed the drivers to use their agenda-setting discretion in favour of enlargement. During the Danish presidency, the Copenhagen Council of June 1993 offered the CEECs a general membership perspective – under the condition that they develop stable democratic institutions, a functioning market economy, and the capacity to cope with competitive pressure in the internal market and adopt and implement the *acquis communautaire*. Moreover, the Community was to have achieved the capacity to absorb new members without endangering the momentum of European integration. During the German presidency, the Essen Council of December 1994 agreed on a pre-accession strategy. Third, the typical incrementalism of EU policy-making facilitated a programmatic commitment at a time when the concrete costs of enlargement would only have to be borne in the longer term.

The selection of candidates

After the member states had made the principled decision to expand to the East, the selection of candidates among the applicants was the next step in the enlargement process. The Commission gave its Opinions on the ten associated CEECs in July 1997 and proposed to open accession negotiations with half of them: the Czech Republic, Estonia, Hungary, Poland, and Slovenia. The European Council followed this proposal at its Luxembourg summit in December. As a 'consolation prize', the EU also opened the formal accession process (according to Art. 49 TEU) with the other five countries as well but did not yet enter into concrete negotiations.

According to the fundamental community norms and the political conditionality of the EU, the selection mainly followed political criteria of liberal-democratic consolidation. Table 10.3 ranks the CEECs according to the status of their relationship with the EU in 1997, 1999 and 2004 together with their Freedom House ratings, a widely used indicator of democratic consolidation. It shows, first, that – with the exception of Slovakia in 1997 and Macedonia in 2004 – the group of 'free' CEECs is congruent with the group of associated CEECs. Already at this medium stage of integration, democratic consolidation is strongly related with the strength of institutional relations.

Second, the more detailed figures for political rights and civil liberties reveal a distinction between the five CEECs that were invited in 1997 to accession talks and the other associated countries: all countries of the top group received the best rating for political rights (1) and the second best rating (2) for civil liberties, whereas Bulgaria, Latvia, Romania, and Slovakia scored only 2 for political rights and 2 or worse for civil liberties. Only the fact that Lithuania was not selected for concrete negotiations cannot be explained by these data. Moreover, the ratings for the invited countries match the ratings for current EU members. EU members are generally rated 1 for political rights and 1 or 2 for civil liberties.

In 1999, the EU decided to start accession negotiations with the remaining five associated CEECs. Again, the EU upheld the principle to negotiate only with fairly consolidated democracies – all new countries at the negotiating table were rated 'free' and three of them had improved their ratings as a result of changes in government and/or legislation. Apart from that, however, the criteria were less strict than in 1997. The key to explaining the more generous treatment of the remaining candidates is the Kosovo conflict (Skålnes 2005). First, the EU was under pressure to do more for stabilising the Balkans and to 'reward' Bulgaria and Romania for supporting the NATO intervention. In addition, this situation offered the drivers – in particular Germany, who held the presidency – an opportunity to establish a membership perspective for south-eastern Europe (Friis and Murphy 2000). Finally, the formal opening of the accession process in 1997 might have created an institutional momentum towards beginning concrete talks.

The two enlargement decisions of 2004 match this general pattern. Even though Croatia had been comparatively well developed and transformed economically, the political situation under the Tudjman regime blocked association and membership. Since

Table 10.3 Selection of CEECs for EU association and accession

Status	Country	1997 PR/CL[1]	1997 Freedom Index	1999 PR/CL	1999 Freedom Index	2004 PR/CL	2004 Freedom Index
EU membership	Czech Republic	1/2	Free	1/2	Free	1/2	Free
	Estonia	1/2	Free	1/2	Free	1/2	Free
	Hungary	1/2	Free	1/2	Free	1/2	Free
	Poland	1/2	Free	1/2	Free	1/2	Free
	Slovenia	1/2	Free	1/2	Free	1/1	Free
EU accession talks	Latvia	2/2	Free	1/2	Free	1/2	Free
	Lithuania	1/2	Free	1/2	Free	1/2	Free
	Slovakia	2/4	Partly free	2/2	Free	1/2	Free
EU association	Bulgaria	2/3	Free	2/3	Free	1/2	Free
	Romania	2/3	Free	2/2	Free	2/2	Free
no association	Croatia	4/4	Partly free	4/4	Partly free	2/2	Free
	Macedonia	4/3	Partly free	3/3	Partly free	3/3	Partly free
	Albania	4/4	Partly free	4/5	Partly free	3/3	Partly free
	Belarus	6/6	Not free	6/6	Not free	6/6	Not free
	Bosnia-Herzogovina	5/5	Partly free	5/5	Partly free	4/4	Partly free
	Moldova	3/4	Partly free	2/4	Partly free	3/4	Partly free
	Russia	3/4	Partly free	4/4	Partly free	5/5	Partly free
	Ukraine	3/4	Partly free	3/4	Partly free	4/4	Partly free
	Yugoslavia	6/6	Not free	6/6	Not free	3/2	Partly free

1   PR stands for 'political rights', CL for 'civil liberties'

2000, the ratings for Croatia have improved considerably. The same is true for Turkey. Although the accession of Turkey will probably create even more economic problems and heterogeneity for the EU than that of the CEECs, the Opinion of the Commission in October 2004 was predominantly based on the positive evaluation of the country's progress in liberal-democratic consolidation.

Preparing the EU for enlargement?

The Copenhagen criteria not only defined conditions for the candidates but also obliged the EU to prepare for enlargement by reforming its most expensive policies and its institutions and procedures. In 1996, the member states launched an Inter-governmental Conference (IGC) to tackle the institutional reforms. The resulting Treaty of Amsterdam (1998), however, referred the central problems (voting proce-dures in the Council and composition of the Commission) to yet another IGC. But the strongly contested Treaty of Nice (2000) also failed to go beyond the minimal requirement of re-weighting the votes in the Council for the enlarged EU. It did not include a 'big leap' toward majority voting, and it raised the quorum for majority deci-sions – instead of lowering it to facilitate decision-making. Furthermore, even though the member states will nominate only one Commissioner each in the future, they could not agree on reducing the Commission below the number of member states (probably 27 in 2007). It was immediately clear to the participants that the Nice Treaty, and the method of treaty revision through intergovernmental conferences in general, had failed to provide institutional efficiency for the enlarged Union. A new, 'constitutional' treaty was drafted by the European Convention in June 2003 but fell through at the Rome summit in December. The disagreement about voting weights in the Council was not removed before the new members joined in May 2004, and although the treaty was finally signed in Brussels in June 2004, ratification failed as a result of the negative French and Dutch referendums.

The reform of the most expensive EU policies was similarly troublesome. On the one hand, the net contributors firmly rejected an increase in the Community's budget ceiling of 1.24 per cent of EU Gross National Income to compensate for higher expenditures. On the other hand, the main beneficiaries of these policies blocked any reform that would have reduced their subsidies significantly. Consequently, the old member states could not agree on changing the rules for payments from the structural funds and assigned a fixed amount to the new members until the end of 2006. Regarding the CAP they decided to continue direct payments to their own farmers but exclude the new members. In the end, enlargement took place before the EU had completed its 'homework'. However, the painful reforms that the EU avoided for the time being will be back on the Agenda 2007 and are likely to lead to even more intense distributional conflict in the enlarged EU with its more pronounced economic cleavages and budgetary constraints.

In general, EU decision-making on Eastern enlargement corroborates the central constructivist supranationalist hypothesis about the expansion of international commu-nities: horizontal integration increases as outside states adopt their collective identity, values and norms. The identity of the EU as a pan-European liberal international community has shaped both the general decision to expand and the selection of candi-dates. The process, however, was one of social influence and normative pressure rather than persuasion and interest change. As expected by intergovernmentalism, the brakemen continued to be reluctant about enlargement and all member states fought for their own institutional and material advantage in the negotiations on EU reform. Reforms proved extremely difficult and the EU quickly fell behind schedule. That the decision to enlarge was made and maintained in spite of adverse constellations of prefer-ences and bargaining power and in the absence of reforms, can be attributed to path dependencies emphasised by rationalist supranationalism. The member states were 'rhetorically entrapped' by their past commitments and constrained by the incremental dynamic and the institutional momentum of the enlargement process.

Accession negotiations

The EU as a collective conducts its accession negotiations bilaterally with each individual applicant country. The concept of 'negotiations', however, suggests an openness that does not exist in the accession process. The substantive outcome of the negotiations is largely pre-determined by the special characteristic of the EU as a community of law: the applicants' adoption of the entire body of EU legislation and policies codified in the *acquis communautaire*. Accession negotiations then mainly consist in a process of rule transfer, 'screening' and 'reporting', in which the Commission explains the *acquis* to the applicants, assesses their deficits, and monitors their progress in adopting the *acquis*. The only true negotiations concern the possibility and length of 'transition periods' during which the application of EU rules in the new member states is suspended after accession. Thus, accession negotiations are apparently structured highly asymmetrically in favour of the member states. Yet the *acquis* binds the EU as well as the applicants. In principle, the incumbent members can require the applicants to adopt only those rules that they follow themselves, and they can restrict or suspend costly rights and expenditures only for a limited time period.

The *acquis* was subdivided into 31 chapters for the negotiations. After 'screening' was completed, negotiations began with the 'easy' chapters, which created no controversy and no demands for transition periods. The negotiations received new momentum in November 2000 when the Commission proposed a 'roadmap' for completing the negotiations until the end of 2002. This put the EU and the applicants under effective time pressure. At this time, the negotiations also reached those chapters that were more problematic because of their financial implications or domestic sensitivities.[9]

For instance, the environmental *acquis* could have meant a substantial financial burden for the candidate countries if they had had to meet the standards of the old members. It was considerably reduced, however, by excluding those standards that do not immediately affect the internal market (such as the quality of drinking water). The chapter on the free movement of persons was complicated by fears of uncontrolled and massive migration, in particular in the former border countries of Austria and Germany. Here the EU imposed a transition period of up to seven years on the candidate countries, during which the old members were allowed to restrict the free movement. In return, however, the Union felt obliged to accommodate domestic concerns of some of the CEECs and permit them to restrict the acquisition of land by foreigners for the same period of time. Finally, in the course of the negotiations on the agricultural chapter, the EU gave up its plan to exclude the new members from the 'direct payments' regime. Since the direct payments are part of the agricultural *acquis*, this plan stood on shaky legal grounds anyhow. Instead, direct payments to the farmers of the new members will rise steadily during a transition period of ten years.

On the whole, the EU and the CEECs agreed on 322 transition periods, most of them in agriculture, taxation, and environmental policy. The results were less unfavourable to the newcomers than expected given the highly asymmetrical bargaining power between old and new members. The *acquis* proved to be a stable bulwark against a permanent discrimination of the new members; transition periods in favour of the old members were compensated by those favouring the new members; and, finally, the old members accepted that no new member should become a net contributor to the EU budget. After the EU had made further financial concessions during the final negotiations in Copenhagen in December 2002 – above all to accommodate Poland, the biggest new member state – the accession treaties were signed in April 2003.

Conditionality and Europeanisation

Political conditionality and democratic consolidation

Political conditionality has had a decisive influence on the selection of candidate countries: the fundamental liberal principles of legitimate statehood constitute the most important filter for entry into the EU. But did it also have an impact on the outside countries themselves? Did it contribute to their democratic consolidation? Comparative analysis shows that the EU had the most significant impact in one specific group of transformation states – unconsolidated democracies with mixed party constellations – and that this impact depended on both a credible membership perspective and low domestic power costs. In contrast, EU political conditionality has been largely redundant in the forerunners of democratisation in the region and ineffective in the consolidated autocracies (Kelley 2004; Kubicek 2003; Schimmelfennig 2005; Schimmelfennig, Engert and Knobel 2003).

In the forerunner democracies, EU political conditionality has been largely redundant. Poland, the Czech Republic, Slovenia and Hungary had been well on the way towards democratic consolidation before the EU had made its decision to enlarge and set the political conditions for opening accession negotiations. In addition, the endogenous forces for liberal democracy in these countries were so dominant that they would most likely have continued on the path to democratic consolidation without political conditionality. In the forerunner countries, all major parties base their legitimacy claims and programmes on liberal reform and integration into the western organisations. Thus, the perceived costs of political adaptation are low and do not change after changes in government.

At the other extreme, EU conditionality was not strong enough to produce democratic change in the autocratic or authoritarian countries of the region (such as Belarus, Russia, Ukraine and Serbia under Milošević). For the ruling elites of these countries, the costs of political adaptation to EU conditions were always high because compliance would have affected their core practices of power preservation (for instance, control of the media, manipulation of elections, concentration of competences in the executive). Consequently, domestic power concerns clearly dominated the external incentives of European integration.

The impact of EU political conditionality has been most significant in those CEECs that were situated between these extremes. In the forerunner democracies, the EU furthered compliance with those rules that are not generally shared by liberal parties. In Central and Eastern Europe, this has mainly been the case with minority protection. Most visibly in the Baltic countries, accession conditionality strengthened moderate forces in the government and built up sufficient pressure for parliaments to pass contested minority legislation.

Most importantly, however, EU political conditionality has had a major impact in 'mixed countries' with both major liberal and anti-liberal parties, in which there is no elite consensus on liberal democratic reform and western integration. Liberal parties or coalitions have been able to come to power in these systems but did not exclusively shape their post-communist development. Either superficially reconstructed communist parties initiated (but also slowed down and distorted) democratic transition from above (such as in Romania). Or reform-adverse nationalists and populists benefited from the failure of reform-oriented parties to provide for economic recovery or efficient governance. In most of these countries, governmental authority has shifted more than once between the two camps.

First, EU accession conditionality helped to consolidate the liberal forces in the mixed countries. Even though the EU does not have a decisive influence on elections and the defeat of anti-liberal parties in Slovakia, Romania, Bulgaria, Croatia and Serbia between 1996 and 2000 is best explained by domestic factors, political conditionality motivated the often fragmented democratic opposition to join forces for the elections and, after their victory, to preserve coalition discipline. This is best observed in Slovakia, where an extremely heterogeneous multi-party coalition under Prime Minister Dzurinda survived until 2003, when accession was secured.

Second, when liberal parties were in government, the liberal domestic changes they institutionalised led to progress in EU integration, and the benefits of EU integration subsequently raised the stakes in democratic consolidation and increased the costs of any future reversal. Populist parties therefore adapted their political goals in order to preserve the achieved benefits of integration. After the major nationalist-authoritarian parties of Croatia (HDZ), Romania (PDSR) and Slovakia (HZDS) had been voted out of government, Romania and Slovakia started accession negotiations with the EU, and Croatia became an EU associate and applied for membership. During the same time, these parties modified their programmes and presented themselves as unequivocally pro-integration. When the PDSR and the HDZ were back in power in 2000 and 2003, they stayed the course of reform and integration. Thus, the lock-in effects of western integration create path-dependency across changes in government and, eventually, change the party constellation from mixed to liberal.

Acquis *conditionality and rule transfer*

Acquis conditionality takes centre stage during the accession negotiations between the EU and the applicant states. Whereas the success of political conditionality depended on both the credibility of the membership perspective and low domestic costs, and its impact was mainly felt in CEECs with mixed party constellations, the impact of *acquis* conditionality has been highly pervasive in all countries that passed the threshold of accession negotiations and covered not only basic political institutions but the whole range of EU policies.[10]

Studies in this area show that the key condition for the success of EU rule transfer is the high credibility of *acquis* conditionality. There was some adoption of *acquis* rules even before the EU's conditionality was spelled out, but it was patchy and selective. In addition, Central and Eastern European governments often adapted EU rules or mixed EU rules with other models. However, once a policy issue became subject of the accession negotiations and *acquis* conditionality, rule adoption increased dramatically and became a consistent feature across countries and issue areas. The massive benefits of EU membership being within close reach, the fulfilment of EU *acquis* conditions became the highest priority in CEEC policy-making and crowded out alternative models (such as rules of other international organisation or third countries like the USA) as well as domestic opposition and obstacles.

The importance of domestic power costs thus contrasts sharply with political conditionality. As *acquis* conditionality does not concern the political system and bases of political power as such, governments generally do not have to fear that the costs of rule adoption in individual policy areas will lead to a loss of office. Costs are thus unlikely to be prohibitive. Moreover, once a credible membership perspective has been established, adoption costs in individual policy areas are discounted against the (aggregate) benefits of membership, rather than just the benefits in this particular policy area. As a consequence, variation in adoption costs merely explains variation in the *speed* (not the fact) of rule adoption across issue areas and countries. Where those costs were high, governments tended to comply only in the final stage of the accession negotiations. But comply they did.

The pervasiveness of *acquis* conditionality, the sheer quantity of rules that had to be transposed and the enormous time pressure of the accession process made *acquis* transfer a highly technocratic process. On the part of the EU, it is the Commission bureaucracy that specifies, explicates, and monitors the demands on the applicant states. On the side of the accession countries, it negotiates with the chief negotiators and their teams, delegations of line ministries or even with inter-ministerial coordination units specifically created for the accession negotiations. Thus, the accession processes further contributed to the centralisation and strengthening of the executive; societal interest groups and parliaments were marginalised (Grabbe 2001: 1016–18; Bruszt and Stark 2003: 78). During the accession negotiations, the parliamentary agenda was primarily set from the outside. The applicant states introduced accelerated procedures for adopting EU rules and were under pressure to pass – and often rubber-stamp – the *acquis*-related legislation at high speed to provide for accession in time. The Hungarian parliament, for instance, did not even debate 152 out of 180 laws passed in June 1999, because they were part of the *acquis*.[11]

The technocratic tendencies of *acquis* transfer were strengthened by the implantation of the 'regulatory state' in the CEECs. The expansion of the regulatory state is a typical feature of the development of western democracies but even more characteristic for the political system of the EU (Majone 1996). It is the main purpose of the regulatory state to correct 'market failure' through regulation – in contrast with the politics of redistribution of the 'welfare state' and the politics of macro-economic stabilisation of the 'intervention state'. Correspondingly, the *acquis* transfer to the CEECs consisted predominantly in the transfer of organisations and rules for market regulation that had no roots there. Numerous regulatory policy areas such as environmental and consumer protection, product safety, regional policy and competition policy were either added to the portfolio of traditional policies or at least strongly expanded. At the same time, *acquis* conditionality led to a mushrooming of the technocratic agencies of the regulatory state: independent central banks, competition authorities, offices for environmental protection, transport and food safety agencies, and many more (Grzymala-Busse and Innes 2003: 70–1; Maniokas 2002).

Conclusion

Almost 15 years after the end of communism in Central and Eastern Europe, the first eight CEECs have become members of the EU – in spite of severe efficiency and distribution problems, stringent demands for rule adoption in the accession countries, widespread scepticism among the member states, and still outstanding reform tasks for the Union. The 'Europeanisation' of the applicants – the quick and comprehensive transfer of EU rules – was mainly produced by the high and credible incentives of EU membership. The difficult but finally successful way to enlargement, however, was paved by the pan-European, liberal-democratic identity and the concomitant enlargement norms, which could be used by the pro-enlargement coalition to legitimise eastern enlargement, put normative pressure on the sceptics, and keep accession on target despite high costs and delayed reform. Enlargement and Europeanisation proved interdependent and mutually reinforcing: while the democratic transformation and Europeanisation of the CEECs put pressure on the EU to expand, EU accession conditionality put pressure on the CEECs to reform themselves and adopt EU rules.

The main theories of European integration cover different aspects of the enlargement process. In general, intergovernmentalism is best at explaining the preferences and negotiating behaviour of the actors. First, the enlargement preferences of the member states and Central and Eastern European responses to EU conditionality varied with the distribution of enlargement benefits and costs. Second, negotiations on association, accession and internal reform as well as EU political and *acquis* conditionality were characterised by tough bargaining including threats to block or delay enlargement. Yet contrary to intergovernmentalist expectations, the actors with superior material bargaining power did not generally prevail in the internal EU or the EU–CEEC negotiations. Rather, they were constrained by fundamental community norms derived from the collective identity of the EU – emphasised by constructivist supranationalism – and by path-dependencies emphasised in rational-supranationalist accounts of European integration. Community norms defined the content of the conditions in EU political and *acquis* conditionality, provided legitimacy to the pro-enlargement coalition, and softened the EU-candidate asymmetry in the accession negotiations. There is no strong evidence, however, that community norms shaped and changed the specific enlargement and Europeanisation preferences of the political actors involved. Rather, they constrained their behaviour through path-dependencies. In the EU, past identity commitments, promises, and enlargement practices bound the opponents of the present enlargement and could be used by the drivers to rhetorically entrap them and to keep the enlargement process on track. In the candidate countries, progress in integration effectively locked in domestic reform and generated programmatic change in authoritarian parties. In sum, the analysis of the enlargement process supports the supranationalist assumption of the transformative powers of European integration and the claim that intergovernmental bargains are shaped and constrained by previously established EU norms, rules, and practices.

The massive enlargement of the EU that started in the 1990s is not over with the accession of ten new members in May 2004. On the one hand, and in addition to the successive integration of the Balkans, the question of the Turkish accession will remain at the top of the EU's integration agenda for the foreseeable future. In this case, we already see many features of the history of eastern enlargement repeating: the problems of efficiency and distribution, divergent member preferences, the power of past commitments and community norms and the beneficial effects of political conditionality on democratic consolidation in unstable and illiberal democracies. On the other hand, the accession and Europeanisation of the new member states has only come to a formal conclusion. EU politics will remain occupied with enlargement-driven policy and institutional reform, adapting to decision-making and policy-making with an enlarged and more heterogeneous membership, and promoting the implementation of the *acquis* in the new member states.

Notes

1   European Commission, *Agenda 2000*, DOC/97/7.
2   See Schimmelfennig and Rittberger, this volume, chapter 4. For a collection of theory-oriented analyses of EU enlargement, see Schimmelfennig and Sedelmeier (2005a).
3   *Agence Europe*, 20 January 1989.
4   *Agence Europe*, 22 November 1989.
5   *Agence Europe*, 27 February 1992.
6   Sedelmeier and Wallace (2000: 438). On the association negotiations in general, see Torreblanca (2001).
7   For an LI analysis of eastern enlargement negotiations, see Moravcsik and Vachudova (2003).
8   European Commission, *Europe and the Challenge of Enlargement* (Agence Europe, Europe Documents 1790, 1992). On the relevance of the 'responsibility' theme, see Sedelmeier (2000).
9   See Avery (2004) for a description of the accession negotiations.
10 The findings presented are based on a collaborative project on the Europeanisation of Central and Eastern Europe in a great variety of countries and issue-areas (Schimmelfennig and Sedelmeier 2005b).
11 *Magyar Nemzet*, 19 June 1999, quoted in Kopstein and Reilly (2000: 27).

References

Avery, G. (2004) 'The Enlargement Negotiations', in Fraser F. Cameron (ed.), *The Future of Europe: Integration and Enlargement* (London: Routledge).

Baldwin, R. E., Francois, J. F. and Portes, R. (1997) 'The Costs and Benefits of Eastern Enlargement: the Impact on the EU and Central Europe', *Economic Policy* 24: 125–76.

Bruszt, L. and Stark, D. (2003) 'Who Counts? Supranational Norms and Societal Needs', *East European Politics and Societies*, 17: 74–82.

Friis, L. and Murphy, A. (2000) '"Turbo-Charged Negotiations": The EU and the Stability Pact for South-Eastern Europe', *Journal of European Public Policy* 7: 767–86.

Grabbe, H. (2001) 'How Does Europeanization Affect CEE Governance? Conditionality, Diffusion and Diversity', *Journal of European Public Policy* 8: 1013–31.

Grzymala-Busse, A. and Innes, A. (2003) 'Great Expectations: The EU and Domestic Political Competition in East Central Europe', *East European Politics and Societies* 17: 64–73.

Hagen, J. von (1996) 'The Political Economy of Eastern Enlargement of the EU', in L. Ambrus-Lakatos and M. E. Schaffer (eds), *Coming to Terms with Accession* (London: CEPR and Institute for EastWest Studies).

Kelley, J. G. (2004) *Ethnic Politics in Europe: The Power of Norms and Incentives* (Princeton, NJ: Princeton University Press).

Kopstein, J. and Reilly, D. (2000) 'Geographic Diffusion and the Transformation of the Post-communist World', *World Politics* 53: 1–37.

Kubicek, P. J. (ed.) (2003) *The European Union and Democratization* (London: Routledge).

Majone, G. (1996) *Regulating Europe* (London: Routledge).

Maniokas, K. (2002) 'EU Enlargement and Europeanization: When a Patchwork Becomes a Blueprint. Summary', Mimeo.

Mayhew, A. (1998) *Recreating Europe: The European Union's Policy towards Central and Eastern Europe* (Cambridge: Cambridge University Press).

Moravcsik, A. and Vachudova, M. (2003) 'National Interests, State Power, EU Enlargement', *East European Politics and Societies* 17: 42–57.

Schimmelfennig, F. (2001) 'The Community Trap: Liberal Norms, Rhetorical Action, and the Eastern Enlargement of the European Union', *International Organization* 55: 47–80.

—— (2003) *The EU, NATO and the Integration of Europe. Rules and Rhetoric* (Cambridge: Cambridge University Press).

—— (2005) 'Strategic Calculation and International Socialization: Membership Incentives, Party Constellations, and Sustained Compliance in Central and Eastern Europe', *International Organization* 59: in print.

Schimmelfennig, F. and Sedelmeier, U. (2002) 'Theorizing EU Enlargement: Research Focus, Hypotheses, and the State of Research', *Journal of European Public Policy* 9: 500–28.

—— (eds) (2005a) *Theoretical Approaches to the Politics of EU Enlargement* (London: Routledge).

—— (eds) (2005b) *The Europeanization of Central and Eastern Europe* (Ithaca, NY: Cornell University Press).

Schimmelfennig, F., Engert, S. and Knobel, H. (2003) 'Cost, Commitment and Compliance: The Impact of EU Democratic Conditionality on Latvia, Slovakia and Turkey', *Journal of Common Market Studies*, 41: 495–518.

Sedelmeier, U. (2000) 'Eastern Enlargement: Risk, Rationality, and Role-Compliance', in M. Green Cowles and M. Smith (eds), *Risks, Reforms, Resistance and Revival* (Oxford: Oxford University Press).

Sedelmeier, U. and Wallace, H. (2000) 'Eastern Enlargement. Strategy or Second Thoughts?', in H. Wallace and W. Wallace (eds), *Policy-Making in the European Union*, 4th edn (Oxford: Oxford University Press).

Skålnes, Lars (2005) 'Geopolitics and the Eastern Enlargement of the European Union', in F. Schimmelfennig and U. Sedelmeier (eds.) *Theoretical Approaches to the Politics of EU Enlargement* (London: Routledge).

Torreblanca, J. I. (2001) *The Reuniting of Europe: Promises, Negotiations and Compromises* (Aldershot: Ashgate).

Part III

CHANNELS OF REPRESENTATION

Chapter 11

European elections and the European voter

MARK FRANKLIN

Introduction

Elections in a democracy are supposed to perform the functions of holding governments accountable and representing voters' interests, thus legitimising the exercise of power. Elections to the European Parliament fail to perform these functions. Since the Treaty of Union (often known as the Maastricht Treaty after the town where it was signed) came into force in November 1993, the European Parliament has had a role to play in selecting the President (and, more recently, the members) of the European Commission. Nevertheless, European elections do not set in motion a process of government formation in the same way as do national elections in the member states. Moreover, policies proposed by parties and candidates in European elections rarely have much European content. Instead they relate to the national political arena and are generally specific to particular countries. Parties use these elections as opportunities to test their standing with the public in terms of their domestic political agendas. But national governments do not stand or fall by European election results either, so the choices of voters have no immediately obvious repercussions on policy at either level. In the circumstances it is perhaps not surprising that many citizens of the European Union fail to take these elections seriously, and turnout is generally low – often even lower than at regional and local elections, which in all EU countries are less important than national elections. The low level of public participation in European elections in turn raises questions in some minds about the legitimacy of the European Union.

But the fact that European elections have no consequences for government formation at the national or European levels, and no readily discernible effect on the conduct of European affairs, does not mean that they have no effects. Indeed the very failure of European elections to legitimate the exercise of power in the EU has consequences for the future of the European Union, and European elections do have many consequences – most of them unanticipated and many of them unfortunate – for the politics of member states. They also determine the composition of the European Parliament (even if voters do not focus on this aspect of their votes) which in turn can have implications for policy-making, especially since the European Parliament acquired co-decision-making powers following the Treaty of Union and Treaty of Amsterdam.

In this chapter we will not concern ourselves with the consequences of European elections for policy since this would require a focus on EU policy-making rather than on EU elections. Instead we will describe some of the effects that European elections have had on the politics of member states, and evaluate their role in creating a 'crisis of legitimacy' for the European union. But first we need to describe the nature of these elections.

The European electoral process

Elections to the European Parliament (EP) were first conducted in the (then) nine members of the (then) European Economic Community in June 1979, and were repeated in June of every fifth year thereafter. Greece held its first European elections in 1981, adding its representatives to the Parliament already elected in 1979; Portugal and Spain did the same in 1987, adding their representatives to the Parliament of 1984–89; Austria, Finland and Sweden followed the same path in 1996, adding their representatives to the

Parliament of 1994–99. In 2004, for the first time, new member countries took part in a European Parliament election at the same time as established member countries, and twenty-five countries took part in those elections, sending their representatives to the Parliament of 2004–9. By 2004, therefore, ten countries had participated in six European elections, twelve countries had participated in five, fifteen countries had participated in three and ten countries had participated in one election – 89 elections altogether – enough, it might be thought, for us to be able to grasp the processes involved in the different countries and to reach some fairly firm conclusions about consequences.

It should be noted, however, that the election of 2004 was unique in a number of ways. Not only was it the first EP election at which newly admitted countries took part alongside established members. In addition there were more new countries than ever before, and in several of these countries voters have displayed behaviour at national elections that is not well understood. Our ability to explain their behaviour at European Parliament elections must therefore be considered to be quite preliminary.

While we can speak broadly of Europe-wide elections, there are significant variations in the way in which these elections are conducted in member states. Most strikingly, they are not all conducted on the same day. Some European countries traditionally go to the polls on Sundays while others have favoured Saturday or mid-week voting. The latest European elections were held on a Thursday in Britain and the Netherlands, on Friday in the Czech Republic and Ireland, on Saturday in the Czech Republic (two days of voting), Italy, Latvia and Malta, and on Sunday elsewhere. Although this difference in timing has potentially important implications (similar to the consequences of polls closing in California after outcomes have been announced in New York) – and in 2004 the Netherlands did announce provisional results soon after its polls closed, earning a rebuke from the European Commission – in fact it matters little because the contests are so different in different countries that the outcome in one country can hold little interest for those voting anywhere else. Another difference between countries is the electoral system employed. Except in the British Isles, list-system proportional representation has been universal since 1979, but in England, Scotland and Wales (until and including the election of 1994) plurality voting was used (first past the post, with single-member districts); while in Ireland and Northern Ireland a Single Transferable Vote system continues to be employed, similar to that used in Ireland in national elections (Northern Ireland uses the British system for national elections). Again these differences would have potential consequences for the nature of the representational process in the European Union if European elections contributed to any such process. As it is, far more important than these differences between countries are the differences between the system employed in any particular country for European elections and that employed for national elections in the same country.

As already mentioned, Northern Ireland (and now Britain too) has a quite different electoral system for European than for national elections. In other countries the system may be superficially similar in both types of election, but there are always differences in practice – sometimes quite subtle ones. Except in the Netherlands, which effectively has only a single constituency for national elections, the number of constituencies into which the electorate is divided is always fewer in European elections (78 in Britain until 1994, five in Italy, four in Ireland, two in Belgium, and one each in the remaining countries). In Germany and Italy the two-vote system used for national elections is changed in European elections to a single-vote system, with the same constituencies as are used for second votes in national elections. Fewer constituencies make it easier for a party to run candidates throughout the country, and this benefits smaller parties. On the other hand, except in countries such as Germany and Poland (which enforce the same 5 per cent threshold in European as in national elections), the number of votes required to get any candidate elected is greater in European elections (much greater in the Netherlands), which has the contrary effect – disadvantaging small parties. To the extent that small parties are advantaged or disadvantaged in European elections this can have important consequences for national politics if European elections themselves are taken as indicators of strength in the national political arena.

Although the European Parliament contains party 'groups' that sit together and cooperate in legislative matters, these groups are hardly relevant to the electoral process. In some countries the European Parliamentary group affiliation is mentioned on campaign literature (in Ireland, for example, Fine Gael campaigns as part of the social democratic People's Party of Europe) but this does not appear to be salient to voters. Transnational party activity was probably most extensive at the first elections in 1979, when EC funds were available for such activities, but voters appear to have paid little attention even then. There was little perception of the result of the election in transnational terms. Blumler and Fox, in their study of the 1979 European elections (1982) revealed that about 50 per cent of voters admitted they had no idea which party grouping had been most successful in Europe as a whole, and that even among voters who claimed to have some idea there was considerable diversity of opinion (cf. Marsh and Franklin 1996).

Only in Denmark are there parties that campaign specifically on European issues (one is against Danish membership in the EU and the other is against any further moves towards closer union), and European elections in Denmark do have a distinctively European flavour (Worre 1993; 1996); but this simply emphasises the lack of European flavour to these elections elsewhere. In other countries it is rare for a European issue to intrude on a European election campaign, although Franklin and Curtice (1996) have shown that in 1989 attitudes to the Social Charter had measurable consequences for the outcome of the election in Britain (Franklin and Curtice argue that the issue was 'domesticated' in terms of national political discourse). The same thing appears to have happened again in Britain in 1999, and this process might serve as a model for the way in which European issues could in time come to have more impact in other countries; but, to the extent that this happens, the consequences of European elections for domestic politics will become even more unpredictable than they are at present (see below).

European elections and the national political arena

The apparent lack of any distinctively European character to European elections led commentators to focus initially on the manner in which these elections reflect national political processes. Reif and Schmitt (1980) applied the term 'second-order national election' to stress the similarity between European elections and local and regional elections, where voting patterns also tend to reflect national political trends (see also Reif 1984; 1985). The most important characteristic of second-order national elections is that there is less at stake than in first-order elections. This is why turnout is expected to be lower. It is also why European election outcomes are expected to reflect the balance of political forces in the national political arena.

But this early focus on the way in which European elections reflect national political forces left a great deal unexplained. In particular, while turnout in European elections was everywhere lower than in national elections, there were also major differences between turnout in successive European elections held in the same country. Moreover, the connection between support for government parties in European and national elections is closer when European elections are compared to subsequent national elections than when they are compared to previous national elections (Marsh and Franklin 1996; Marsh 1998), suggesting that any causal connection might actually run the other way than was initially supposed.

Partly because of these findings, later research started to focus on how European elections affect the national political arena in member countries of the European Union. Most importantly, the very fact that these elections can be used as 'markers' for the standing of national parties in the national political arena gives them an importance as catalysts of change in that arena. It is well established that European electoral success played a role in the rise of the National Front in France and was important to the early success of the German Greens. Reif (1984) notes that government coalitions may be strained by adverse results, and gives illustrations. However, the nature of these effects and their importance depends on when the elections occur in the national electoral cycle (Oppenhuis *et al.* 1996).

Since European elections are held at the same time in all participating countries but national elections are not, it follows that European elections occur at different times relative to national elections in different countries (and in the same country at different European elections). Sometimes the European elections occur shortly after a national election, sometimes only after the elapse of a number of months or years, and sometimes they occur in the shadow of national elections that are known (or felt) to be imminent. Evidently the value of European elections as markers for what would happen in a national election held at the same time as (or instead of) the European election will depend on how soon a national election will be held. If a national election was recent, then the value of a European election outcome as a marker will be minimal: a better marker already exists in the shape of the recent national result. On the other hand, if some considerable time has elapsed since the most recent national election (and especially if another national election is imminent) then the importance of European elections as markers is evidently much greater. We will see that the position in the electoral cycle at which a European election occurs matters for the choices made by voters and for the consequences of the election for national politics, as well as for the level of turnout in the election itself.

Only in Denmark (and in Britain since 1999) can European elections not be employed as markers for the standing of national parties. In Denmark, this is because the two Eurosceptical parties in that country compete only in European elections. Because they receive a significant share of the vote, which is taken from other parties in proportions that are hard to compute with any accuracy, these elections do not have an outcome that is readily interpreted in national terms. Politicians and commentators in Denmark cannot easily tell what would have been the outcome of a national election held at the same time as (or instead of) the European election, and so Danish domestic politics are insulated from the consequences of European elections as nowhere else in the EU. Since the introduction of PR voting for EP elections in 1999, Britain is in a similar position, employing so different an electoral system for

European elections that the outcome is hard to interpret in national political terms, though this does not seem to have discouraged commentators from making the attempt.

European elections and the study of voting behaviour

Because European elections have no apparent European content (except in Denmark) and no consequences for policy-making in the European arena that are discernible to voters, the political behaviour displayed at European elections is the behaviour of individuals in relation to their national political arenas; but because national political power is not at issue in these elections, the national electoral processes we see are uncontaminated (with a few important exceptions) by the intrusion of political concerns that might dominate particular national elections. Consequently, European elections present themselves as unique laboratories for truly comparative studies of why people vote and why they vote the way they do.

The most important feature of this laboratory is that it permits us to measure the effects of contextual variables that are necessarily invariant in any particular national election. These contextual variables include the nature of the electoral system, whether compulsory voting is in effect, the timing of elections (weekend or weekday), and other institutional factors that are different in different countries of the European Union. They also include social and political factors that not only vary as between countries but can also change (perhaps slowly) over time even in particular countries. Such factors include educational level (the most widely validated influence determining the likelihood that individuals will vote), extent of unionisation (generally supposed to promote voting by social groups that would otherwise have low participation – see Verba *et al.* 1979; Parry *et al.* 1990), and the strength of linkages between social groups and political parties (class or cleavage voting, see Powell 1980; 1986). They also include the number of parties (one indicator of the adequacy of choices available), their distribution in terms of size (and hence their likelihood of wielding government power) and the extent to which citizens appear satisfied with the choices on offer (van der Eijk and Oppenhuis 1991; cf. Sartori 1994). Even more importantly, European elections, by falling at different times in the national political calendar, differ in their importance to voters for reasons explained above.

Over and above these contextual differences is one additional way in which European elections differ from each other: some of them occur concurrently with national elections (this happened twelve times between 1979 and 2004). Our ability to treat this circumstance as a contextual variable along with other contextual variables permits us to validate our analyses of the extent to which voters behave differently in European elections than they would have done in national elections.

The characteristics outlined above are quite numerous, but we have 89 elections conducted in different countries since 1979 that differ in terms of these variables – more elections than variables by a considerable margin, especially as it turns out that most of the listed factors have no influence on the outcomes of European elections. To the extent that these factors account for the different outcomes we observe, we will know that these outcomes are not the result of idiosyncratic peculiarities of individual countries but are simply the consequence of the political, social and institutional setting within which the elections are held. Indeed, it appears that the peculiarities of European elections can very largely be explained in such terms.

Turnout variations

One of the most evident differences between European and national elections has always been the low turnout recorded in European elections. Many commentators have suggested that low turnout indicates lack of legitimacy for the EC/EU, since citizens appear by their failure to vote to be withholding their support for European institutions. Table 11.1a shows that Britain and Denmark, the two most Eurosceptical among established members of the EU, have often been the countries with lowest turnout in European elections.

Indeed, two early studies of individual-level voting choice found a connection between attitudes to Europe and propensity to vote (Inglehart and Rabier 1989; Blumler and Fox 1982). Later studies, however, found this relationship to be spurious (Niedemeier 1990; van der Eijk and Schmitt 1991; Schmitt and Mannheimer 1991; Marsh and Franklin 1996) – the result of failing to control for other variables – and table 11.1 does show that turnout in the by no means Eurosceptical Netherlands has averaged even less than in Denmark. If individual-level analyses fail to find effects on turnout from attitudes to Europe, then presumably we should seek explanations for the low aggregate level of turnout in the Netherlands and Britain from among the contextual features of European elections listed earlier.

One additional contextual feature that we have not yet mentioned has been widely noted in the literature: the first European election ever held in each established member country (in 1996 in Austria, Finland and Sweden; in 1987 in Portugal and Spain; in 1981 in Greece; and in 1979 elsewhere) saw generally higher levels of turnout than later elections. The exceptions are the compulsory voting countries, Belgium, Italy, Greece and Luxemburg (where turnout was maintained at a high level in subsequent elections because of the compulsion to vote) together with Britain and Denmark, where turnout in the initial election was very low; but in ten other countries the inauguration of European elections evidently generated a level of interest that could not be sustained (the ten most recent members cannot be evaluated in these terms since they have not yet had the chance to vote in more than their inaugural European Parliament election). Indeed, apart from a temporary plateau from 1984 to 1989, the decline in turnout over the course of five European elections until 1999 appeared to have been continuous, fuelling concerns about a democratic deficit in the conduct of EU affairs.

These concerns were probably misplaced. There is certainly a democratic deficit in the governance of the European Union (van der Eijk, Franklin *et al.* 1996: ch. 21), and the low turnout in European elections is certainly due to the fact that European elections do not provide European voters with meaningful choices that would give them a real say in the future direction of European policy-making (van der Eijk, Franklin, *et al.* 1996: ch. 19). However, the decline in the average level of turnout across the EU as a whole in successive elections to the European Parliament was not a sign that this deficit was increasing. Rather it was primarily an artifact of the accession to the EU of new countries with characteristics that were different from those of the original member countries, and the evolution of these countries from first-time participants to seasoned (perhaps 'disil-

Table 11.1 Turnout (%) in European Parliament elections by country, 1979–2004[1]

	(a) Established EU members							(b) New members	
	Year of parliament						Average		Year
Country	1979[2]	1984[3]	1989	1994[4]	1999	2004	'79–'04	Country	2004
Austria[4]				67.7	49.4	42.4	53.2	Cyprus	71.2
Belgium[5]	90.4	92.2	90.7	90.7	91	90.8	91.0	Czechia	28.3
Denmark	47.8	52.4	47.2	52.9	50.5	47.9	49.8	Estonia	26.8
Finland[4]				60.3	31.4	39.4	43.7	Hungary	38.5
France	60.7	56.7	48.8	52.7	46.8	42.8	51.4	Latvia	41.3
Germany	65.7	56.8	62.3	60.0	45.2	43.0	55.5	Lithuania	48.4
Great Britain	32.2	32.6	36.2	36.1	24	38.8	33.3	Malta	82.4
Greece[2,5]	78.6	77.2	79.9	71.2	75.3	63.2	74.2	Poland	20.9
Ireland	63.6	47.6	68.3	44.0	50.2	58.8	55.4	Slovakia	17.0
Italy[5]	84.9	83.4	81.5	74.8	70.8	73.1	78.1	Slovenia	28.3
Luxembourg[5]	88.9	88.8	87.4	88.5	87.3	89.0	88.3		
Netherlands	57.8	50.6	47.2	35.6	30	39.3	43.4		
Portugal[3]		72.4	51.2	35.5	40	38.6	47.5		
Spain[3]		68.9	54.6	59.1	63	45.1	58.1		
Sweden[4]				41.6	38.8	37.8	39.4		
EU Average[1]	67.1	65.0	62.9	58.0	52.9	52.7	57.5		40.3
N	10	12	12	15	15	15	79		10

1 All countries weighted equally.
2 The first election for Greece was held in 1981.
3 The first elections for Spain and Portugal were held in 1987.
4 The first elections for Austria, Finland and Sweden were held in 1996.
5 Compulsory voting country (Italy only until 1993).

lusioned' would be a better word) members. In the 2004 elections, among established member countries, turnout was about the same as in 1999. The long decline in turnout among established member countries can most easily be explained in the context of an analysis of the determinants of turnout among these countries in European Parliament elections (we will consider the ten new member countries separately).

When countries are coded on the basis of contextual features, and these features are used to try to explain differences in turnout from country to country and election to election, one important variable is time until the next national election which, at the date of writing, is unknown for most members of the 2004 European Parliament. For these cases we have estimated the time to the next national election on the basis of the average from past electoral cycles. Over all elections held since direct elections to the European Parliament were inaugurated in 1979, our ability to explain the large variations in turnout shown in table 11.1 above is impressive. Table 11.2 reports the effects on turnout of those variables whose effects prove significant in multivariate perspective. Taken together, three variables explain 81 per cent of the country-to-country turnout variations, and come within 5 per cent of accounting for most of the 79 values of turnout recorded for established member countries in these elections. Only Britain and (more recently) Sweden show turnout that is always below what would have been expected on the basis of their characteristics (by averages of 13 and 11 per cent, respectively). At the other end of the scale, Spain has averaged 10 per cent more than expected. No other country's turnout diverges significantly (in the statistical sense) from what would be predicted on the basis of characteristics listed in table 11.2. So the variations in turnout among established member countries that we saw in table 11.1 can be largely explained by the divergent contexts within which European elections take place (for a more detailed assessment of the sources of turnout variation see Franklin *et al.* 1996; Franklin 2001). For countries that were new members in 2004, we are going to have to wait for the passage of at least one more EP election before being able to tell whether these countries respond to the same forces as established member countries. Their initial participation was generally far below the level for established member countries, with only Cyprus, Estonia, Lithuania and Malta registering average or higher than average turnout.

The most powerful predictors of turnout at European elections appear to be compulsory voting, the length of time yet to elapse before the next national election, and whether the election was the first election to the European Parliament ever held in the country concerned. Countries with compulsory voting on average see turnout that is 33 per cent higher than those in which voting is strictly voluntary; turnout is generally lower by about 2.8 per cent for each year that is still to elapse before the next national

Table 11.2 Effects on turnout of contextual factors, established members only[1]

Variable	b	SE	SIGF
(Constant)	52.9	2.4	.0001
Compulsory voting in country[2]	33.0	3.0	.0001
Years until next national election (where no compulsion)[3]	−2.8	0.8	.0001
First EP election held in country (where no compulsion)[3]	10.9	2.9	.0001
Adjusted variance explained	0.81		
N	79		

1   The data for this analysis are taken from the Established EU member portion of Table 11.1. Because it is generally recognised that Greece's turnout is underestimated, each of the figures for turnout in that country is increased by 6% in the dataset upon which Table 11.2 is based,

2   Coded 0 or 1 except in Italy after 1993, when its effect can be expected to have diminished in proportion to the share of the electorate new since 1993. There it is coded 0.875 in 1999 and 0.75 in 2004, as explained in Franklin (2001, 2004).

3   Compulsory voting countries coded 0 because the compulsion to vote should override this effect.

election (except for compulsory voting countries); and the first EP election in each country saw turnout higher by 10.9 per cent on average than later elections (except for compulsory voting countries).

It is well known that compulsory voting raises turnout. The surprise is to find it having so great an effect; but the reason is that turnout in EP elections would otherwise be very low. In low-turnout elections, compulsory voting shows its power to greatest advantage (Franklin 1999). This fact alone explains much of the decline in turnout over the twenty-five years of European Parliament elections, because the countries taking part in the elections of 2004 are very different countries from those that elected the 1979–84 parliament. In those first elections, almost half the countries taking part (four out of ten) did so under conditions of compulsory voting. Today there are only three countries with compulsory voting (Italy having abandoned compulsory voting in 1993), but these are now three out of twenty-five – only twelve percent. Because of the large effect of compulsory voting, this drop of 28 per cent in the proportion of countries with this characteristic would lead us to expect a drop of almost 10 per cent in turnout as a pure mathematical consequence (28 per cent of 33 per cent). Moreover, in elections to the Parliament of 1979–1984 six of the ten countries were eligible for the 10.9 per cent first-election turnout boost, whereas in 2004 none of the established member countries were taking part in an EP election for the very first time. These two effects cannot simply be added (because compulsory voting countries do not receive the first-time turnout boost), but together they go a long way towards accounting in a rather prosaic fashion for the overall decline in turnout since 1979.

Of course, table 11.1 shows that individual countries have seen big changes in turnout that cannot be accounted for by these two factors. From this perspective, more interesting is the 2.8 per cent per year effect of time until the next national election. As already mentioned, European elections gain a surrogate importance from their role as barometers of the standing of national parties. Evidently this role is more important as national elections approach; but again the surprise is to find so great an effect. In a country with five-year parliaments, position in the electoral cycle could make a 14 per cent difference to European election turnout (5 times 2.8 per cent). With four-year parliaments, position in the electoral cycle could make a 11 per cent difference. Given the largely random position of European elections within national election cycles (except for Luxemburg, which has always held both elections on the same day), this one factor explains much of the variation seen in table 11.1 from election to election within particular countries. Indeed the huge falls in turnout seen in Germany in 1999 and in the Netherlands in 1994 are quite understandable when one recalls that those particular EP elections were held shortly after national elections in those countries, whereas the previous European Parliament elections in both countries were held just before national elections. Indeed, in established member countries between 1979 and 1999, we would have expected a fall in turnout of 1.6 per cent (seven-twelfths of 2.8 per cent) in 1999 simply because of the fact that in that year, on average, EP elections were held seven months earlier in the electoral cycles of member countries than had been the case for earlier EP elections.

So while the fact of low turnout at European Parliament elections is a matter for some concern, the apparent decline in EP turnout is not. Indeed, when we correct for the factors listed in table 11.2, turnout actually appears to have increased after 1979 to a peak about 6 points higher in 1989 and then to have fallen off in 1994 – a fall that continued in 1999 to a point about level with the 1979 starting position. This movement might be random (the changes each year are not statistically significant) but it is possible that there are other things that move turnout, apart from the factors we have been discussing. If so, those other things appear to create fluctuating turnout levels rather than a steady decline (see Franklin 2001, 2004, for a more detailed discussion of these matters).

But even if turnout has remained pretty close to the level we should have expected, other analyses indicate that the extent to which turnout can be explained by contextual factors has declined. Until 1994, Sunday voting was a significant predictor of turnout, as was the proportionality of the electoral system; but when we include the elections of 1999 and 2004 these variables cease to discriminate significantly between higher and lower turnout countries. What seems to be happening is that, with the passage of time, those voters who do turn out at elections to the European Parliament are behaving in a manner that is less and less structured by their national political contexts. We will see further evidence of this when we look at the rate at which those who do vote support different parties than they would have done in a national election.

Results of European elections

The outcomes of European elections in terms of party choice differ much less from what would have occurred in concurrent national elections than does turnout. Nevertheless, some parties do gain and some parties do lose compared to what would have occurred had the elections been national elections – often by as much as 6 per cent of total votes. These gains and losses occur for two reasons. Some parties gain (lose) from the fact that they are more (less) successful in getting their normal supporters to the polls. The low turnout in European elections helps or hurts some more than others. Other parties gain (lose) because they are supported (abandoned) in European elections by voters who in national elections would have voted differently. For some parties these two processes cancel out, leaving them with about the same level of support that they would have enjoyed in national elections; for others the two processes reinforce each other, leading to quite dramatic divergences from national election outcomes. However, by far the greater of the two effects is the effect of people voting differently, which is generally more than twice as great as the turnout effect, and can involve more than 40 per cent of those voting (at the 1994 elections in France and Denmark, and at the 2004 election in Denmark and the Netherlands), as shown in table 11.3. Note, however, that this total amount of what has been called 'quasi-switching' (van der Eijk, Franklin *et al.* 1996) involves a great many contrary movements that cancel out in aggregate, leaving net effects of much lower magnitude (seldom more than 6 per cent, as already mentioned).

The consequence of this behaviour by voters is very different for different parties. To a large party, the loss of 6 per cent may be chastening but not disastrous. To a small party, the loss of 6 per cent could amount to decimation. Thus in 1989 the British Conservatives lost about 3 per cent compared to what they would have expected to get in a general election, while the Liberal Democrats lost some 4 per cent. But while to the Conservatives this was just a rather poor showing, to the Liberal Democrats it amounted to a virtual halving of the vote they would have received had the election been a national general election (Franklin and Curtice 1996). Meanwhile, the British

Table 11.3 Voting differently (%) in European Parliament elections by country[1]

Country	(a) Established EU members				Average	(b) New members	Year
	Year of parliament						
	1989	1994	1999	2004[1]	'89–'04	Country	2004[1]
Austria			13.4	19.4	11.4	Cyprus	11.4
Belgium	12.6	18.5	16.6		15.9	Czechia	14.1
Denmark	35.4	42.9	39.8	40.4	36.5	Estonia	25.4
Finland			17.7	13.2	12.2	Hungary	4.0
France	27.2	40.8	25.4	21.7	29.2	Latvia	34.2
Germany	11.8	14.2	16.9	10.9	11.8	Lithuania	32.7
Great Britain	13.0	16.0	22.3	25.2	15.4	Malta	
Greece	8.1	12.4	9.6	8.6	8.9	Poland	24.2
Ireland	28.7	23.8	32.3	28.7	31.5	Slovakia	52.9
Italy	19.7	20.7	32.0	29.8	23.6	Slovenia	17.8
Luxembourg	15.0	14.3	15.5		14.9		
Netherlands	12.4	19.6	13.9	41.3	15.3		
Portugal	9.7	12.7	7.5	17.7	11.8		
Spain	22.2	12.5	15.5	10.8	14.0		
Sweden			24.2	28.7	24.2		

1 At the time of writing, the necessary matching of European and National parties for the election of 2004 had not yet been finalised, so figures for 2004 are provisional and incomplete.

Green Party benefited by 6.6 per cent, virtually doubling the vote it would have received in a national election.

The example of the British Liberal Democrats notwithstanding, most losses in European elections are suffered by large parties and most gains are enjoyed by small parties. This appears not to be because of the desire of voters to punish government parties (opposition parties also lose if they are large) but purely because political power is not at stake in European elections. It turns out that (when political power seems to be at stake) an important influence on voting choice is party size: other things being equal, voters prefer to support a party that has a better chance of putting its policies into practice. Evidently this question is not at issue in a European election, and so large parties fail to get the bonus that they would have been accorded in a national election (van der Eijk, Franklin and Oppenhuis 1996) – a bonus that appears to be worth about 5 per cent of the vote to a party that enjoys the support of 40 per cent of the electorate. But while small parties gain in European elections compared to their performance in national elections, such gains are not apportioned evenly among small parties. Moreover, which particular small parties gain depends very largely on the location of the European elections in the domestic electoral cycle. Just as in the case of turnout, people behave differently when a national election is imminent.

The critical difference appears to be the attention paid to the outcome by politicians and commentators. We have indicated that, in the immediate aftermath of a national election, a European election outcome is of no great interest. A better marker of the standing of parties in the national arena already exists. These are also the elections in which the largest transfer of votes from large to small parties takes place, and the small parties that benefit are on the whole moderate parties of the centre. It is as though, freed from concerns about governing the country, voters in such elections could 'vote with the heart'. These are the elections in which voting is apparently most sincere, in contrast to national elections themselves, when voters 'vote with the head', taking into account the strategic situation in which large parties are more likely to get their policies enacted.

As the national electoral cycle advances, however, and the next national election comes closer, two things happen to affect the behaviour of voters should a European election take place. The first is that the marker set by the previous national election has become obsolete, so that party leaders and commentators look to the European election as a relevant measure of the standing of parties. The second is that, with the approach of a national election, party leaders are motivated to take account of any messages they receive from the electorate in order to improve their chances when the national election comes. This is the circumstance in which protest voting appears most prevalent, since this is when extreme parties do best. Clearly voters do not suppose that their votes will cause such parties to gain office; but they evidently hope that the parties they normally support will take note of the protest and adapt their policies accordingly. Borrowing a phrase from the lexicon of British football hooligans, we have called this behaviour 'voting with the boot' (van der Eijk, Franklin and Oppenhuis 1996). Votes for far right parties in France and Germany at European elections should be seen in this light, as should votes for Green parties in some countries (especially Britain).

The striking thing about these findings, both those relating to turnout and those relating to party choice, is the apparent sophistication of the voting act. In the shadow of a forthcoming national election up to 15 per cent more people will take the opportunity to give their parties a piece of their mind than in the immediate aftermath of a national election; and the message that is sent in such circumstances is quite different from the message sent at a national election or in the aftermath of one. At the individual level, the evidence of rationality is even greater (van der Eijk, Franklin et al. 1996).

Of more concern, however, is another manifestation of rationality. In elections to the European Parliament, voters are increasingly casting their votes without reference to features that would have governed their behaviour in national elections. The reason why electoral proportionality is supposed to affect turnout is because the incentive to vote is greater if voters are assured that their votes will not be wasted. Given that proportionality of the electoral system had, by 1999, ceased to discriminate significantly between low and high turnout countries, it seems voters are becoming aware that their votes in these elections have no value in the conventional sense. The same implication flows from the fact that, with some experience of EP elections behind them, voters are more likely to vote for different parties in European than in national elections. Though any trend is not marked, and our data for 2004 are incomplete, at least among established member countries experience of EP elections appears to have progressively liberated voters from their normal party loyalties when they vote in European Parliament elections. How quasi-switching evolves among new member countries will be of considerable interest in coming elections.

In itself such a liberation from party loyalties in EP elections would be no bad thing. Indeed, if it meant that voters were turning their attention to European matters at European elections then the change would be a good thing. In fact what seems more likely is that, over the course of their first few European Parliament elections, voters learn to take advantage of the opportunity to behave differently than at national elections, voting with heart or boot rather than with their heads, and making it problematic to interpret the results of European elections as markers for parties' standing in their national political arenas. To the extent that this misleads national party leaders into making poor policy choices, the perverse effects of European elections for national politics – the subject of the next section – can only increase.

Consequences for national politics

The consequences of European elections for national politics are of three kinds. In the first place national parties may be led to take various actions as a result of extrapolating the outcome to a national election situation. Sometimes a government party may be led to call an early national election, as in Spain in 1989, to capitalise on the popularity they see themselves enjoying (del Castillo 1996). Sometimes such a party may be led to adapt its policies, as in Germany in the same year (when a much harsher policy towards Eastern European migration was briefly adopted) in order to defuse the apparent appeal of an extreme party (Schmitt 1996). These reactions may or may not have the effect that the party intended, depending on how accurately the European election outcome reflected the true situation in the national political arena; but there will always be a tendency for miscalculations to occur in proportion to the extent of the interest taken in the European election outcome: to the extent that party leaders and commentators take notice, voters behave differently than they would have done had national power been truly at stake (which is different again from how they would have behaved had no one been paying attention).

This mismatch between the use of the indicator and the accuracy of the indicator might appear perverse, but it is a natural result of the different objectives and perceptions of voters and politicians. Because real national power is not at stake, voters expect no repercussions from voting one way rather than another; so, when politicians indicate that they are paying attention to the outcome, voters suddenly find themselves in an unaccustomed position of power. They can send a message of displeasure without the risk of electing a party that is untried or dangerous.

The second type of consequence is more insidious. European election outcomes differ from the outcomes that would occur in national elections for more reasons than that voters behave differently than politicians expect. Small parties are often advantaged for technical reasons as well, having to do with differences in the electoral system under which European elections are held. Yet their gains give them legitimacy that can be reflected in the next national election. For both these reasons a party system can progressively break down under the impact of successive European elections, as appears to be happening in France (Cayrol and Ysmal 1996) and perhaps also in Germany (Schmitt 1996).

The third type of consequence results more directly from the fact that European elections are not employed as opportunities to put forward or oppose policies related to the European arena. Keeping such policies off the national agenda seems to be a preoccupation of national politicians, for reasons too complex to be discussed here (see Franklin *et al*. 1996). Occasionally, however, such issues break through to become salient in national terms. When this happens, the results can be quite devastating for individual parties or leaders (such as Britain's Mrs Thatcher after 1989). European elections would be the proper venue for such matters to be discussed, if only such elections could be fought by different parties than fight national elections; but this only happens in Denmark. There, precisely because they are not fought by the same parties as fight national elections, European elections cannot be used as markers even while they can be used to give an airing to real European issues. Elsewhere, European elections constitute something of a sword of Damocles that national parties hang over their heads, apparently unknowingly, because of the potential that European issues have for splitting national parties into pro- and anti-European factions (Franklin *et al*. 1996; van der Eijk and Franklin 2004).

Decoupling European elections from the national political arena would remove this uncertainty, and would also mitigate the other two consequences summarised above, since all three arise from the use of these elections as markers for what would happen in national elections. Mitigating their effects on national politics would be good enough reason to reform the way in which European elections are conducted; but there are even better reasons when one considers these elections from a European perspective.

Consequences for the future of the European Union

Proper democratic representation and accountability are associated with the notion of free elections. However, in order for elections to fulfil these functions, a number of conditions must be met which are not necessarily provided by the simple institution of elections per se. The logic of democratic elections presupposes that the political verdict of electorates can be construed as emanating from the political preferences of voters – preferences that are relevant to the decision-making arena concerned. If this condition is met, elections can be considered simultaneously (1) to legitimise power allocated by the elections (and therefore also to legitimise policies which may be devised with this power), (2) to exert electoral control by holding officeholders accountable and (3) to represent groups of citizens and their interests in the political process (thus showing sensitivity to their concerns). In order for elections to function in these ways, electorates must have some awareness of the political stance and record, in the arena under consideration, of those who are contending for their votes (Franklin and van der Eijk 1996).

It is evident that these conditions are generally lacking in the present-day European Union. Voters have on the whole never been encouraged to develop preferences for different European policies that would permit them to choose among candidates and parties in a European election in such a way as to legitimate and control the exercise of power at the European level. Indeed, candidates and parties seldom put forward policies that differ in regard to Europe, and frequently do not put forward policies of any relevance at all to European matters. By failing to take the opportunity to present voters with meaningful choices, party leaders also miss the chance to educate them about European affairs. This failure is primarily due to the fact that the parties that select candidates and put forward policies at European elections are not European parties but national ones, and these parties generally treat European elections as opportunities to test their own relative popularity in the national arena. Naturally, national elections offer even less of a forum for discussion of European matters. So neither in their choice of national leaders who compose the Council of Ministers nor in their choice of Members of the European Parliament who hold the Commissioners accountable are voters given the opportunity to have any input into the conduct of European affairs. As Bogdanor once stated (1989: 214), 'Elections, if they are to be meaningful, must fundamentally allow for choice', but national party systems provide 'an artificial superstructure unable to articulate the wishes of the electorate'. There are reasons why politicians maintain this 'artificial superstructure' – reasons that may not be easily overcome (Franklin *et al*. 1996) – but the consequence is that input into the European decision-making process is restricted to individuals and groups who have non-electoral routes (for example interest group lobbying) for making their desires known.

This lack of proper democratic accountability and control in European affairs is a grave problem, potentially amounting to a crisis of legitimacy for the European Union. How this crisis will manifest itself cannot be anticipated, but the ratification process for the Treaty of European Union signalled a warning that should not have been ignored (Dinan 1994: 290–1).

Members of the European Parliament (as well as many professional observers of European integration) diagnose a democratic deficit in European representative institutions. To their eyes, this deficit often appears in terms of a lack of power on the part of the European Parliament to assert itself in relation to the Commission and (particularly) the Council of Ministers. In fact, it should be evident from a reading of this chapter that the democratic deficit felt by Members of the European Parliament actually results from European elections being fought primarily around national political concerns rather than European ones. It is true that the European Parliament lacks certain powers (in comparison with modern-day national parliaments); but what it lacks most is not power but a mandate to use that power in any particular manner. It lacks that mandate because of the way in which European elections are conducted. Lacking a succession of mandates to develop Europe in any particular way, the European Union and its predecessor entities were built by national governments with little input from their citizenry, on the basis of what has been called a 'permissive consensus' regarding successive moves towards European unity (Inglehart 1971).

The consequence of this permissive consensus has been to free national parties from the need to coherently address and articulate European policy concerns – often a difficult matter for parties whose origins lie in the aggregation of quite other sorts of interests and concerns. Instead of defending their participation in European regulatory decision-making on the grounds of fulfilling an electoral mandate, ruling parties have consistently defended such actions on the grounds that they have done their best to protect national interests, thus casting European politics as a zero-sum game between the member states and undermining efforts made by the same actors in other spheres to stress the positive-sum aspects of European integration. Sometimes, of course, their 'best' is not enough, and unpopular consequences seem to flow from European developments.

Governments are then tempted to blame 'Europe' for these consequences. But to the extent that governments succeed in this, they merely cause themselves to appear impotent to influence events in Brussels, displacing the crisis of legitimacy from the European to the national arena (Franklin and van der Eijk 1996).

This is particularly unfortunate in the light of recent evidence of public responsiveness to European policy-making (Franklin and Wlezien 1997). It seems that European voters are aware (even if unconsciously) of the amount of policy forthcoming from Brussels, and react against excessive legislation by reducing their support for 'more integration'. Unpublished research has shown that this relationship holds true not only over the EU as a whole but also in individual countries (Franklin and McGillivray 1999). By contrast, there is no evidence that European policy-makers are in the least responsive to these fluctuations in support by voters for 'more integration'. The opinions of voters track the productions of European policy-makers surprisingly closely, but there is absolutely no sign of corresponding variations in the volume of new EU policies that would demonstrate awareness by policy-makers of voters' concerns. The fact that European elections provide voters with no means for making their concerns known (other than through protest voting), or for compelling attention by policy-makers to these concerns, further threatens the legitimacy of European policy-making, and further enhances the possibility of repercussions at national elections

In these ways, the permissive consensus appears to be eroding, faster in some countries than in others. A variety of developments have increased the salience and visibility of European policies to individual citizens. In the absence of well-established alternatives regarding the substantive direction of such policies, leading to a debate within each country (or over Europe as a whole) regarding what type of European Union the people want to live in, criticism might well move from a focus on 'what Europe' to 'whether Europe'. This would yield unpredictable consequences for European political systems, as amply demonstrated as long ago as the early 1990s by the Danish and French referenda regarding the Maastricht treaty and Mr Major's difficulties with the British Conservative Party when that treaty came to be ratified. A similar dynamic was evident in Ireland where two referenda had to be held in order to ratify the Treaty of Nice, and in France and the Netherlands in 2005 when their electorates voted against the proposed EU Constitution. The same problem also puts into question the very future of the European project.

This is because of the possibility that the failure of governments to acquire mandates from voters for their support of 'more integration' could result instead, at some time in some country, in a mandate to withdraw that country from the EU. All that it would take would be the arrival on the political scene in that country of a political entrepreneur willing to capitalise on the pent-up frustrations engendered by decades of failure to educate and consult the voters of that country. Depending on which country this was, the consequence could be more or less fatal for Europe's more perfect union but, even if it was a peripheral country that withdrew, the example would likely have a contagious effect on political discourse in other countries, increasing the chances that a critical member might withdraw.

Commentators write as though a ratchet was at work with European unification, locking in all gains and preventing backsliding by any country. But the ratchet has only worked because of failure to give voters a say in the process of unification. True consultation would have greatly slowed the pace of unification and made the process more closely resemble the 'two steps forward, one step back' sequence common in other policy areas. But continued lack of consultation could ultimately be much more damaging to the European project.

The proper place for consultations of this kind would be in the context of European election campaigns, but European elections have never been used for such a purpose. Possible means of stimulating genuine policy debates at European elections were discussed at length in the final chapter of van der Eijk, Franklin *et al.* (1996); but the first step is to recognise the potentially disastrous consequences of a continued failure to conduct meaningful elections to the European Parliament.

References

Blumler, J. and Fox, A. (1982) *The European Voter: Popular Responses to the First European Community Elections* (London: Policy Studies Institute).

Bogdanor, V. (1989) 'Direct Elections, Representative Democracy and European Integration', *Electoral Studies* 8: 205–16.

Castillo, P. del (1996) 'Spain: A Dress Rehearsal', in C. van der Eijk, M. Franklin *et al.* (eds) *Choosing Europe? The European Electorate and National Politics in the Face of Union* (Ann Arbor: University of Michigan Press).

Cayrol, R. and Ysmal, C. (1996) 'France: The Midwife Came to Call', in C. van der Eijk, M. Franklin *et al.* (eds) *Choosing Europe? The European Electorate and National Politics in the Face of Union* (Ann Arbor: University of Michigan Press).

Dinan, D. (1994) *Ever Closer Union? An Introduction to the European Community* (London: Macmillan).

Eijk, C. van der and Franklin, M. (2004) 'Potential for Contestation on European Matters at National Elections in Europe', in G. Marks and M. Steenbergen (eds) *European Integration and Political Conflict.* (Cambridge: Cambridge University Press).

Eijk, C. van der and Oppenhuis, E. (1991) 'European Parties' Performance in Electoral Competition', *European Journal of Political Research* 19: 55–80.

Eijk, C. van der and Schmitt, H. (1991) 'The Role of the Eurobarometer in the Study of European Elections and the Development of Comparative Electoral Research', in K. Reif and R. Inglehart (eds), *Eurobarometer: The Dynamics of European Opinion* (London: Macmillan).

Eijk, C. van der, Franklin, M. and Oppenhuis, E. (1996) 'The Strategic Context: Voting Choice', in C. van der Eijk, M. Franklin *et al.* (eds) *Choosing Europe? The European Electorate and National Politics in the Face of Union* (Ann Arbor: University of Michigan Press).

Eijk, C. van der and Franklin, M., with Ackaert, J. *et al.* (1996) *Choosing Europe? The European Electorate and National Politics in the Face of Union* (Ann Arbor: University of Michigan Press).

Franklin, M. (1999) 'Electoral Engineering and Cross-National Turnout Differences: What Role for Compulsory Voting?' *British Journal of Political Science* 29: 205–16.

—— (2001) 'How Structural Factors Have Caused Turnout Decline at European Parliament Elections', *European Union Politics* 2: 309–28.

—— (2004) *Voter Turnout and the Dynamics of Electoral Competition in Established Democracies since 1945* (New York: Cambridge University Press).

Franklin, M. and Curtice, J. (1996) 'Britain: Opening Pandora's Box', in C. van der Eijk, M. Franklin *et al.* (eds) *Choosing Europe? The European Electorate and National Politics in the Face of Union* (Ann Arbor: University of Michigan Press).

Franklin, M. and van der Eijk, C. (1996) 'The Problem: Representation and Democracy in the European Union', in C. van der Eijk, M. Franklin *et al.* (eds) *Choosing Europe? The European*

Electorate and National Politics in the Face of Union (Ann Arbor: University of Michigan Press).

Franklin, M. and McGillivray, F. (1999) 'European Union Politics as a Multi-Level Game Against Voters', paper presented at the 1999 meeting of the American Political Science Association.

Franklin, M. and Wlezien, C. (1997) 'The Responsive Public: Issue Salience, Policy Change, and Preferences for European Unification', *Journal of Theoretical Politics* 9: 347–63.

Franklin, M., van der Eijk, C. and Marsh, M. (1996) 'Conclusions: The Electoral Connection and the Democratic Deficit', in C. van der Eijk, M. Franklin *et al.* (eds) *Choosing Europe? The European Electorate and National Politics in the Face of Union* (Ann Arbor: University of Michigan Press).

Franklin, M., van der Eijk, C. and Oppenhuis, E. (1995) 'The Motivational Basis of Turnout in European Elections, 1979–1994: The Case of Britain', in C. Rallings, D. Farrell, D. Broughton and D. Denver (eds), *British Elections and Parties Yearbook 1995* (London: Frank Cass).

—— (1996) 'The Systemic Context: Turnout', in C. van der Eijk, M. Franklin *et al.* (eds) *Choosing Europe? The European Electorate and National Politics in the Face of Union* (Ann Arbor: University of Michigan Press).

Inglehart, R. (1971) 'Public Opinion and European Integration', in L. Lindberg and S. Scheingold (eds), *European Integration* (Cambridge, MA: Harvard University Press).

Inglehart, R. and Rabier, J. (1989) 'Europe Elects a Parliament', *Government and Opposition* 14/4: 479–505.

Marsh, M. (1998) 'Testing the Second-Order Election Model after Four European Elections', *British Journal of Political Science* 28: 591–608.

Marsh, M. and Franklin, M. (1996) 'Understanding European Elections, 1979–1994', in C. van der Eijk, M. Franklin *et al.* (eds) *Choosing Europe? The European Electorate and National Politics in the Face of Union* (Ann Arbor: University of Michigan Press).

Niedemeier, O. (1990) 'Turnout in the European Elections', *Electoral Studies* 9/1: 45–50.

Oppenhuis, E., van der Eijk, C. and Franklin, M. (1996) 'The Party Context: Outcomes', in C. van der Eijk, M. Franklin *et al.* (eds) *Choosing Europe? The European Electorate and National Politics in the Face of Union* (Ann Arbor: University of Michigan Press).

Parry, G., Moiser, G. and Day, N. (1990) *Political Participation and Democracy in Britain* (Cambridge: Cambridge University Press).

Powell, B. (1980) 'Voter Turnout in Thirty Democracies: Partisan, Legal and Socio-Economic Influences' in R. Rose (ed.), *Electoral Participation: A Comparative Analysis* (Beverly Hills, CA: Sage).

—— (1986) 'American Voter Turnout in Comparative Perspective', *American Political Science Review* 80: 17–43.

Reif, K. (1984) 'National Electoral Cycles and European Elections', *Electoral Studies* 3/3: 244–55.

—— (1985) 'Ten Second-Order National Elections', in K. Reif (ed.), *Ten European Elections* (Aldershot: Gower).

Reif, K. and Schmitt, H. (1980) 'Nine Second-Order National Elections: A Conceptual Framework For The Analysis Of European Election Results', *European Journal of Political Research* 8/1: 3–44.

Sartori, G. (1994) *Comparative Constitutional Engineering: An Inquiry into Structures, Incentives, and Outcomes* (New York: New York University Press).

Schmitt, H. (1996) 'Germany: A Bored Electorate', in C. van der Eijk, M. Franklin *et al.* (eds) *Choosing Europe? The European Electorate and National Politics in the Face of Union* (Ann Arbor: University of Michigan Press).

Schmitt, H. and Mannheimer, R. (1991) 'About Voting and Non-voting in the European Elections of June 1989', *European Journal of Political Research* 19/1: 31–54.

Verba, S., Nie, N. and Kim, J. (1979) *Participation and Political Equality: A Seven Nation Comparison* (Cambridge: Cambridge University Press).

245

Worre, T. (1993) 'Denmark and the European Union', in B. Thomesen (ed.), *The Odd Man Out? Denmark and European Integration 1948–1992* (Odense: Odense University Press).

—— (1996) 'Denmark: Second Order Containment', in C. van der Eijk, M. Franklin *et al.* (eds) *Choosing Europe? The European Electorate and National Politics in the Face of Union* (Ann Arbor: University of Michigan Press).

Chapter 12

Interest groups and EU policy-making

Organisational logic and venue shopping

SONIA MAZEY AND JEREMY RICHARDSON

Introduction: three assumptions

Our central thesis is that once the EU began to develop into a significant venue or arena for public policy-making in Europe, a certain trajectory of institutionalised interaction between the EU and interest groups was likely. We base this prediction on three theoretical assumptions:

- First, bureaucracies have a tendency to construct stable and manageable relationships with interest groups in each policy domain as a means of securing some kind of 'negotiated order' or stable environment.
- Second, interest groups generally exhibit a preference for state bureaucracies as a venue for informing themselves about and influencing public policy.
- Third, interest groups will seek to exploit new opportunity structures or venues as a means of maximising their capacity to shape public policy to their own advantage.

We suggest that different types of actors have associated behavioural patterns – or at least exhibit *procedural ambitions* (Richardson and Jordan 1979) which condition and structure their behaviour in the real world. Moreover, as many of these procedural ambitions are deeply embedded in the political cultures of the majority of the member states, it should be no surprise to see the gradual emergence of a 'European policy style' emphasising group intermediation (Mazey and Richardson 1995: 337–59).

The European Commission as a bureaucracy: the art of strategic group politics

Our theoretical starting point is bureaucracy and the particular behavioural traits that modern bureaucracies exhibit. In his classic study of bureaucracies, Anthony Downs formulated many hypotheses concerning bureaucratic behaviour. Two of his central hypotheses are especially relevant to a discussion of Commission/group relations. He assumed *rational behaviour* on the part of bureaucrats – 'they act in the most efficient manner possible given their limited capabilities and the cost of information' (Downs 1967: 2). He also hypothesised that 'Every organization's social functions strongly influence its internal structure and behaviour, and vice versa' (1967: 2). If we apply these two hypotheses to the Commission (which certainly has limited resources and an especially great need for information from across the twenty-five member states), we can assume that it will structure itself in ways that facilitate efficient policy formulation – its 'social function' under the Treaty of Rome. We can also assume that it will adopt behavioural patterns that maximise its ability to interpret the external world so as to facilitate efficient policy formulation. If we regard the Commission as a relatively new or *adolescent* bureaucracy (Mazey and Richardson 1995), then another of Downs's observations seems valuable – namely that the 'generation of ... external support is particularly crucial for a new bureau'. He suggests that a new bureau's survival strategy includes continually demonstrating that its services are worthwhile to some group with influence over sufficient resources to keep it alive (Downs 1967: 7). Initially, the external sources of support are said to be 'weak, scattered and not accustomed to relations with the bureau. The latter must therefore rapidly organise so that its services become very valuable to the users' (Downs 1967: 7–8). Once the users of the bureau's services get used to the gains they secure from it 'and *have developed routinised relations with it*', the bureau then can rely on a degree of inertia to maintain the external support (Downs 1967: 8, emphasis added). This rather clientelistic relationship itself leads to *institutionalisation* in the form of rule-making, he predicts. Thus, 'many of the decisions of bureaux covered by *formalized rules* involve interactions with people outside the bureau' (Downs 1967: 60, emphasis added). In the case of the Commission, it has developed sets of informal and formal 'rules' which emphasise the key role that consultation with interest groups plays in policy-making. Thus, from what we know about bureaucracies generally, we might predict the emergence of 'normal' interest groups politics in the EU.

All of these hypotheses and observations seem to fit the Commission perfectly. It has acted rationally as a 'purposeful opportunist' (Klein and O'Higgins 1985; Cram 1994) in expanding its policy domains and creating new ones (extending its 'territoriality' in Downs's terms). It has also practised the art of 'strategic group politics' – the capacity of a policy-maker to 'regulate their interactions with outside constituencies in a way that fulfils their strategic objectives' (Peterson 1992: 612). In particular, it has recognised the utility of interest groups as sources of (a) information, (b) support and (c) legitimacy in its key policy-making roles. Finally, like all 'state' bureaucracies, it has recognised that *institutionalising* consultation (Mazey and Richardson 2001) with interests is a classic form of *risk reduction*. By seating the appropriate stakeholders at the appropriate seats, bureaucrats both reduce likely resistance to their policy proposals at other venues and avoid the blame for subsequent policy failures or fiascos (Henderson 1977). Moreover, in the context of the EU, the need to construct complex advocacy coalitions (Sabatier 1988, 1998) in favour of policy innovation is especially pressing for the Commission, which has the power to *propose* but not *dispose*. Faced with intense institutional competition for policy space, it has every incentive to seek, nurture and construct coalitions which can cross institutional boundaries in the complex EU policy process.

Interest groups: exploiting multiple venues and allocating resources rationally

From what we know about interest groups in Western democracies, we can expect them to seek to establish close relations with state bureaucracies and regulatory agencies. Interest groups are capable of allocating resources rationally as between possible lobbying targets – be they institutions (see Coen 1997, 1998; Bennett 1997, 1999; Bouwen 2002; Broscheid and Coen 2003, 2004: Lahusen 2003; Bouwen 2004a, 2004b) or individual legislators (Snyder 1991), or indeed the public at large (Beyers 2004). Empirical studies of interest groups often reveal marked preferences for the bureaucratic venue as a means of influencing public policy decisions. Within the EU, groups were quick to recognise the formal and informal powers of the Commission as an agenda-setter. Lobbying resources allocated to this early stage of EU agenda-setting are likely to produce bigger policy pay-offs than resources allocated to lobbying later in the policy process. Similarly, groups know that lobbying is not just about influencing or changing public policy – it is also about minimising their surprises. Hence, knowing what is going on may be just as important to an adaptive interest organisation as trying to influence what is going on. In that sense, participation is perfectly rational even if no policy pay-off results. Finally, the increasing technical content of policy and the 'unpacking' of broad policy problems into more manageable, low-salience, technical issues, so familiar in Western democracies, further increases the incentive for groups to form 'policy partnerships' with Commission bureaucrats in (preferably) closed policy-making structures. This process facilitates continuous trade-offs in a system of 'mutual exchange' (Jordan and Richardson 1982). In fact, the notion of mutual exchange is now part of the conventional wisdom of EU lobbying studies. For example, Bouwen has recently argued that 'the key to understanding the lobbying activities of business interests in the European institutions is to conceive of the relations between these private actors as an exchange relation between two interdependent organizations' (Bouwen 2004b). Groups and the Commission have an especially acute, mutual interest in trying to form stable policy communities and policy networks over time.

Making policy communities and networks work can be difficult, even at the national level (Richardson 2000). Many exogenous factors intervene – including new ideas or 'frames' (Schön and Rein 1994); the structure of institutions; the arrival of new interests in a policy area; and the sheer number of interests to be accommodated. The EU is a classic example of the appearance of a new opportunity structure (Kitschelt 1986) whose emergence has brought the possibility of a different stakeholder bias in terms of institutional power (Lindblom 1977; Dahl 1982; McAdam 1996). Thus, our third hypothesis, reflecting the work of social movement theorists and interest group analysts alike, is that interest groups will seek to exploit (and sometimes create) new opportunity structures, or venues, which they believe will maximise their chances of public policy pay-offs. The EU as a polity presents an American-style plethora of opportunity structures to which interest groups can go. The creation of the EU has, therefore, created a new opportunity for what Baumgartner and Jones term 'venue shopping' by national and cross-national interest group actors in Europe (not all of whom, of course, are 'European'). As Baumgartner and Jones suggest, political actors are capable of strategic action by employing a dual strategy as follows:

> On the one hand they try to control the prevailing image of the policy problem through the use of rhetoric, symbols and policy analysis. On the other hand, they try to alter the roster of participants who are involved in the issue by seeking out the most favourable venue for consideration of these issues.
>
> (Baumgartner and Jones 1991: 1045)

Although Baumgartner and Jones developed the 'venue shopping' thesis from their study of nuclear energy politics in the USA, its relevance to the EU is clear. It too is a system of multiple access points created by institutionalised multi-level governance. We believe that the creation of a maturing system of interest group intermediation at the European level has both transformed national policy-making systems and fundamentally changed the roster of actors who constitute the power elites in Europe.

This transformation is due to the simple fact that national governments have, for whatever reasons, ceded sovereignty over large areas of public policy-making to the EU level. Once public policy started to be made at the supranational level, groups were bound to allocate increasing amounts of lobbying resources to that level. There are, as Mahoney notes, both supply and demand factors at work in the creation of the EU lobbying system. She argues that scholars have tended to overlook the role of governments in influencing the behaviour of interest groups. Thus, 'the central governing body draws interests to it by increasing its attention to and control of certain policy areas' (Mahoney 2004, p440. Interestingly, Lahusen's study of commercial consultants in the EU (a sector about whose efficacy in terms of influence we ourselves have some doubts) also uses a demand and supply model to explain expansion. He argues (citing Richardson's adaptation of the garbage can model developed in this volume) that the sheer complexity of the EU's policy process leads to demands from clients for 'information brokers' such as commercial lobbying consultants (Lahusen 2003: 195) and that the commercial lobbyists, in turn, will seek out to supply this service to an ever widening range of interests (Lahusen 2003: 213).

Whether caused by supply or demand factors, the very involvement of interest groups in transnational settings, such as the EU, in turn contributed to a further reduction of national sovereignty, whether or not states (individually or collectively) agreed. In their study of transnational activists Keck and Sikkink argue that 'by thus blurring boundaries between a state's relations with its own nationals and the recourse both citizens and states have to the international systems, advocacy networks are helping to transform the practice of national sovereignty' (Keck and Sikkink 1998: 1–2). Though their study focuses on a particular type of transnational actor (such as environmental, human rights and women's groups), much the same conclusions could be reached by studying the behaviour of more conventional groups, such as firms (for example see Coen 1997, 1998; Broscheid and Coen 2003) in the EU. A central theme in the Keck and Sikkink thesis, and in ours, is the autonomy from states which transnational action can deliver to activists and interest groups. As Keck and Sikkink suggest, the 'two-level game' metaphor developed by Putnam (Putnam 1988) is useful in pointing out the role played by domestic interests in shaping national preferences. Putnam sees 'international relations as a two-way street, in which political entrepreneurs bring international influence to bear on domestic politics at the same time that domestic politics shapes their international positions' (Keck and Sikkink 1998: 4). This is precisely our argument in the case of the EU as an 'international system'. It is incredibly open and permeable to interest group lobbying compared with even the more pluralistic member states. The permeability of the Commission and other EU venues such as the European Parliament (EP) and European Court of Justice (ECJ) to interest groups weakens the ability of states to control and steer national interest groups and, indeed, to control their national policy agendas. Insofar as groups become 'activists beyond borders', to borrow Keck and Sikkink's terminology, they both weaken the power of states in the process of transnational governance and may become an independent source of integration.

The above argument presents a challenge to the intergovernmentalist position that 'the primary source of integration lies in the interests of the states themselves and the relative power that each brings to Brussels' (Moravcsik 1991: 75). More specifically, it is a challenge to the view that 'the unique institutional structure of the EC is acceptable to national governments only insofar as it strengthens, rather than weakens, their control over domestic affairs, permitting them to attain goals otherwise unachievable' (Moravcsik 1993: 507). The difference between our position and that of classic intergovernmentalists is that like Keck and Sikkink, we argue that interest groups can act independently of states and thereby help to shape international policy agendas and outcomes. Thus, we do not accept that 'above all, the primary political instrument by which individuals and groups in civil society seek to influence international negotiations is the nation-state, which acts externally as a unity and rational actor on behalf of its constituents' (Moravcsik 1998: 22). In summary, our thesis is that the national preference formation process is certainly 'shaped through contention among domestic political groups' (Moravcsik 1998: 22) as intergovernmentalists argue, but that domestic groups are also increasingly engaged *independently* at the supranational level and see that level as a venue where they can pursue their own goals.

This does not mean, of course, that all groups trying to influence EU public policy operate at the EU level. As Grossman notes, 'not all groups are equally well equipped to benefit from multi-level policy making' (Grossman 2004: 647). Even for those well informed and well-heeled interests such as multi-national companies, the national route will not be ignored. In fact, Grossman is a sceptic regarding the thesis that economic interests have played a decisive role in the path of European integration, arguing that integration 'continues to be a very political process in the sense that political institutions, such as elected governments and, to a lesser extent, European institutions, remain the central actors' (Grossman 2004: 650; see also Schneider and Baltz 2004). Nevertheless, Grossman acknowledges that even if groups do not play a key role in issues having major institutional implications, they may well play such a role in regulatory policy-making concerning their particular areas of economic activity. At a time when the new European Constitution is an issue of great political saliency, it is important to remember that European integration is not just about grand bargains and the high politics of history-making decisions. Increasingly, it is about technical regulations and soft law. At this level of policy-making interest groups may well be better informed on specific (and often very technical) policy issues and policy proposals than national governments and may sometimes be disinclined to share information with them.

The rational and independent exploitation of new EU structures by interest groups exists alongside a less tangible process of identification with the new Euro-level structures in which these interests participate – especially if the structures deliver valuable policy pay-offs. Transnational lobbying, particularly as it becomes institutionalised in the EU, can have longlasting effects on the perceptions and behaviours of actors. The newly created institutional structures can be constructed as 'meaningful objects of identification' (Breton 1995: 40). Following Breton's analysis, some kind of path dependency in the EU might therefore be postulated. Transnational organisation expands in virtually all domains. The expanding scope and diversity of players is accompanied by increased institutionalisation; the critical institutions are those established for collective decision-making, mobilisation of resources, circulation of information, coordination of activities and control of free-riders. The corresponding ideologies are those that legitimise particular institutional arrangements; the experience of interdependence in turn tends to generate a 'community fate' identity, a pragmatic solidarity (drawn from Breton 1995: 40–2). We see, therefore, a similar phenomenon in the European policy-making process and in the long-established traditions of national policy-making in Western Europe – namely a high degree of interest group integration into the policy process, based upon the twin 'logics' of organisation and negotiation. This development appears to take place at the two main levels in the European policy process – at the European level itself and within the existing national states. Indeed, the importance of Euro-lobbying at both of these levels (and at the regional level too for some issues) raises an important paradox – namely that the gradual shift in the locus of power to the European level in many policy sectors has caused both a proliferation of lobbying at the supranational level and an intensification of lobbying at the national level. Spence suggests that national officials who participate in the Euro-policy process are *'lobbied lobbyists'* – they are simultaneously subjected to influence and called upon to exercise it (Spence 1993: 48). Spence also highlights a central feature of the Euro-lobbying system. It is essentially a multi-arena, multi-level, decision-making system, in which all actors *necessarily* participate in a complex series of what Tsebelis termed 'nested games' (Tsebelis 1990). This makes it especially difficult to make reliable and robust generalisations about the distribution of power between the different policy actors or stakeholders in the EU policy process which can apply to both grand bargains and routinised policy-making. However, one comment seems to be well founded and based on solid empirical evidence: the number and range of interest groups active at the European level has increased enormously over the history of the EU. Thus, the EU now exhibits the same phenomenon as seen in the US which experienced a 37 per cent increase in registered lobbyists between 1997 and 1999 (Grossman and Helpman 2001: 6). It is to the trajectory of interest mobilization in the EU that we now turn.

The emergence of a European interest group system: from under-supply to over-supply of representation?

One of the earliest systematic studies of the emergence of a European interest group system was Kirchner's analysis of interest group formation at the EU level (Kirchner 1980a). This study cites Meynaud and Sidjanski's earlier study of European pressure groups, which found that many of these groupings established themselves at the Community level in response to the formation of a new centre of decision-making and as a result of advantages expected from Community action (Kirchner 1980a: 96–7). Sidjanski's study suggests that some of the groups were formed as the EEC's own institutions were created, others when it became clear that the EEC's regulatory powers could significantly affect different interests in society (Sidjanski 1970: 402). Sidjanski also noted a phenomenon common in all developed political systems – that public bureaucrats often assist the emergence and creation of groups, reflecting the functional 'logic' which we suggested earlier. If a European interest group system did not exist, the Commission would have to invent it as an essential building block of a European policy-making system. For example, Mazey notes that, since the late 1970s, 'the Commission has also fostered the development of transnational women's networks and set up European networks of "experts" to monitor and advise on various aspects of equality policy. This *constituency mobilisation strategy* is consistent with theories of bureaucratic expansion and neo-functionalist models of European integration' (Mazey 1995: 606, emphasis added). A similar phenomenon was identified by Cowles, who describes the role of the Commission in the setting up of the European Round Table (ERT), representing some of the largest companies within the EU. She records that 'the first list of potential industry members was drawn up in 1982 in the Commission's Berlaymont building by Volvo and Commission staff' (Cowles 1997: 504).

Kirchner notes that another phenomenon familiar from studies of national interest groups systems was evident in the early years of the Union – namely that groups beget more groups. Once one set of interests is mobilised and organised to influence decision-makers, those interests in society who have not yet organised will see the need to do so;

if they do not, they are leaving policy space exclusively occupied by rival interests. Interest group mobilisation is at least a means of 'risk avoidance' in the manner first suggested by David Truman in 1950. In an attempt to defend pluralism in the USA (surely, now the defining characteristic of the EU interest group system), he argued that over time interest group power would tend to reach some kind of equilibrium. This was partly because society was full of what he termed 'potential groups' which, when threatened by the successes of those interests already organised, would themselves become organised to defend their own objectives (Truman 1951: 31). Kirchner suggests that the mobilisation of trade unions at the European level is a classic example of this phenomenon. (Kirchner 1977: 28). A similar risk-avoidance 'insurance' strategy has been noted even for powerful multinational companies. McLaughlin and Jordan suggest that a 'negative incentive' is at work for firms when deciding whether or not to join the relevant European association for their industry. If a firm does not join, the Euro-association in question may produce 'unwelcome group decisions' (McLaughlin and Jordan 1993: 155). The danger of *not* participating in a European association is that the Commission (formally emphasising, as it does, the importance of Euro-associations in its consultation procedures) might take the Euro-association's view as the definitive view of the industry as a whole, to the detriment of the non-participating firm. These 'counterstrike' or risk-avoidance strategies go some way to explaining the seemingly endless increase in interest group mobilisation at the European level.

It would be quite wrong, however, to explain the emergence of a European interest group system solely in defensive terms. As Kirchner notes in the case of trade unions, there were also perceived positive benefits from European-level organisation. He suggests that one of the aims of the trade unions in mobilising at the Euro-level 'is to promote, at the European level, the interests which become increasingly difficult to achieve at the national level' (Kirchner 1980b: 132). Increasingly, this is a major motivation underpinning the continuation and further development of the EU interest group system, consistent with neo-functionalist theory, i.e. groups increasingly see positive benefits from Euro-level solutions. This is particularly the case for groups concerned with trans-frontier problems, such as environmental groups and even companies bearing heavy costs due to the proliferation of different national regulations. At a more theoretical level, Stone Sweet and Sandholtz posit a demand/supply model of European integration, similar to Deutsch's transaction theory (Stone Sweet and Sandholtz 1998; Deutsch 1957). They argue that the Community's rules for organisations favour 'economic actors with a stake in cross-border transactions (trade, investment, production, distribution). Rising levels of transnational exchange trigger processes that generate movement toward increased supranational governance' (Stone Sweet and Sandholtz 1998: 2). Essentially, transnational interests demand more Euro-level regulation as it facilitates efficient (and increased) transnational exchange, and European-level institutions are keen to supply more regulation. Indeed, Kirchner's data imply that the development of the EU and the development of the EU interest group system went hand in hand.

The story since 1980 has been one of rapid acceleration of Euro-interest group formation. By 1985, Butt Philip was reporting that 'almost five hundred Europe-wide pressure groups now devote their resources to influencing decisions taken by the EC' (Butt Philip 1985: 1). He predicted that 'we should not expect much increase in the number of such [Euro] groups in the future' (Butt Philip 1985: 88), but in 1986 Grote found rather more Euro-groups than Butt Philip had done the previous year – 654 in fact (Greenwood,

Grote and Ronit 1992: 1). By February 2000, the Secretary-General's list of non-profit making interest groups included some 800 groups. More recently, Mahoney's analysis of the so-called CONECCS dataset constructed by the Commission (see below, p. 357) identified some 700 civil society groups (Mahoney 2004: 445). The growth in other types of Euro-level representation seems to have been almost exponential. Back in 1992, the Commission estimated that there were no less than 3,000 'special interest groups of varying types in Brussels, with up to 10,000 employees working in the lobbying sector' (Commission 1992: 4). In addition, the Commission estimated that at that time, over 200 firms had direct representation in Brussels, and that approximately 100 lobbying consultancy firms were represented in Brussels. In 2003 Lahusen reported that the rate of formation of lobbying consultancy firms appeared to have slowed after the burst following the passage of the Single European Act of 1986, but that the sector was nevertheless continuing to expand by about 8–10 new organisations per year (Lahusen 2003: 197). It is difficult to gauge how reliable the data on numbers and types of groups really are, or, indeed, how meaningful the numbers are given that we do not know how *active* in the lobbying process groups and individuals are. Aspinwall and Greenwood (1998: 2) consider the Commission's figure to be something of an overestimate. Undoubtedly, many Euro-groups will be small-scale operations – mere 'listening posts' whose function is to simply gather information about funding opportunities or new EU-level policy initiatives. However, it is also possible to argue that the true size of the Brussels-level lobbying industry could actually be *higher* than the Commission's estimate, if the census were to include all those individuals who visit Brussels in order to lobby, but who are not based in Brussels. Our guess is that the number of people in this category runs into many thousands.

Data collected by Greenwood *et al.* (1999: 129) on the formation of Euro-associations show that two-thirds of their sample of Euro-associations were formed before 1980. Our hypothesis is that the rate of formation of new Euro-associations will in future be quite slow. Most significant interests in Europe have by now formed a Euro-association. In any case, Euro-associations are often regarded by EU policy-makers to be rather sluggish policy actors, due to their complex and slow internal decision-making processes. Also they are often under-resourced, especially in terms of the technical expertise which is often the currency of influence. Greenwood *et al.* report that 'over half (56% – 230) of all Euro groups have at least 3 employees' (Greenwood *et al.* 1999: 130). This leaves 44 per cent with fewer than 3 employees – hardly an indicator of a robust pillar on which the Commission (or European Parliament) could build a stable and manageable system of interest group intermediation. In practice, it is unusual to find examples of Commission officials relying solely on Euro-associations in the consultation process. Though Commission officials do consult Euro-assocations as a general rule, they also habitually go directly to the source of technical expertise on which the Euro-associations themselves usually draw in order to ensure that proposals are technically robust and that all the stakeholders have been mobilised. Whilst being in a Euro-association might be a cheap insurance policy, there is probably no substitute for having an office in Brussels if a group has an ongoing and long-term interest in European public policy. As Mahoney notes, having a Brussels office appears to be a key organisational characteristic influencing participation in the influential, official consultative committees (Mahoney 2004: 453).

Individual members of Euro-associations (such as national associations and individual firms) have increasingly spread their lobbying resources in a risk avoidance strategy.

Brussels might be a policy-making maze, but groups learn their way round it. They could not be corralled into working exclusively via Euro-groups even if the Commission wished it. For example, there appears to be a proliferation of ad hoc coalitions focusing on single-issue politics (Coen 1997; Pijnenburg 1998) and an increase in direct Euro-lobbying by firms (Coen 1997, 1998). The more complex the multi-venue Euro-policy game becomes, the greater the need for flexibility and manoeuvrability by interest groups if they are to create policy win situations. Concentrating resources on one type of (federal or confederal) organ of representation is a very risky strategy and likely to fail. Creating ad hoc coalitions, often between groups who might oppose each other on different issues, is a sensible strategy, particularly when multiple opportunity structures (each having a different institutional bias) present themselves. Rational action demands direct lobbying in multiple venues. The problem for both the Commission and the Euro-associations is that direct lobbying is not conducive to the creation of the type of intermediation on which a corporatist or neo-corporatist system could be built. Promiscuity, rather than monogamy, is the more rational interest group behaviour.

Promiscuity, institutionalisation, e-consultation, and venue shopping

The EU policy system – characterised by uncertain agendas, shifting networks and coalitions, and unstable procedural rules – encourages interest groups (and other actors) to behave promiscuously. However, all actors recognise that although promiscuity might be inevitable, it is a costly strategy. Hence there are attempts, especially by the Commission, to institutionalise promiscuity. The Commission has not only been a 'purposeful opportunist' in terms of policy expansion. It has also been opportunistic in creating new institutions as a means of locking diverse interests into the *ongoing* process of Europeanisation. It has been a strategic actor in constructing constellations of stakeholders concerned with each of the Commission's policy sectors. This construction process takes place both as a means for the Commission to create new Europeanised policy areas and, once established, for the long-term management of established European policies in an ongoing policy process (see Richardson in this volume). It is important to stress, however, that each institutional innovation is linked to a broad *organisational culture* which has become embedded in most parts of the Commission. This culture is clearly outlined in the Commission's 1992 definitive publication *An Open and Structured Dialogue* (Commission 1992) and further developed in publications subsequent to the Cardiff European Council of 15/16 June 1998. The latter document stressed the need to bring the Union nearer to its citizens by making it more transparent, more understandable and closer to everyday life. In practice, this has meant even greater emphasis on interest group accommodation by the Commission.

In its 1992 document the Commission had argued that it 'has always been an institution open to outside input. The Commission believes this process to be fundamental to the development of its policies. It is in the Commission's own interest to maintain open access since interest groups can provide the services with technical information and constructive advice' (Commission 1992: 1). Over time, the Commission has introduced a number of measures designed to increase openness and transparency, consistent with its embedded policy style. These include earlier publication of the Commission's legislative programme, a commitment to ensure that target groups are aware of new policy initiatives, and greater use of Green (consultative) Papers. Prior to 1990, the Commission appears to have published only four Green Papers; in the following eight years approximately fifty were published. The Commission's Report, *Better Lawmaking in 2003* (COM (2003) 770 Final) records that in that year it published five Green Papers and 142 Communications, as well as seventy-three Reports.

More recently, use of the internet has become an increasingly important characteristic of the Commission's group management strategy. In a sense, e-governance has arrived at least in the form of e-consultation! In April 2001, the Commission adopted a Communication on Interactive Policy Making (C(2001) 1014). The so-called IPM initiative involves the development of two internet-based mechanisms to assist the consultation processes: a feedback facility to allow existing networks to report to the Commission on a continuous basis; and an online consultation tool, designed to receive and store rapidly reactions to new initiatives. In 2003 the Commission conducted sixty internet consultations through 'Your Voice in Europe', the Commission's single access point for consultations. Consultations in 2004, under this initiative, included consultations on 'The Future of the Simple Pressure Vessels Directive', 'Strengthening the EU–US Economic Partnership', and 'The Green Paper on Defence Procurement'. As part of its policy on openness, contributions to open public consultations are also published on the internet at the Your Voice in Europe portal. Shortly after the internet consultation on the European Sustainable Development Strategy ended in October 2004, the Commission reported that it had received over 100 answers to its long questionnaire and nearly 700 answers to the online questionnaire.

The Commission has also created a web-based database of formal and structured consultative bodies in the field of civil society, the so-called CONECCS (Consultation, the European Commission and Civil Society). The database provides information on those Commission committees and other Commission frameworks through which civil society organisations are consulted in a formal or structured way and which are relatively permanent and meet at least once a year. The database does not hold information on committees composed solely of representatives of member states or expert groups which do not systematically include civil society organisations. Examples of Commission committees included on the database include the Advisory Committee on the Common Agricultural Policy and the Advisory Committee on Fisheries and Agriculture. Examples of other structured consultative bodies include Biodegradable Waste-NGOs and Industry, and the Satellite Action Plan Regulatory Working Group. For each group, the database lists its objectives, period of mandate, frequency of meetings, secretariat and chair of the body, as well as information on members and links to member organisations. This is a relatively recent development and sceptics might wonder how important these bodies really are in terms of influencing policy outcomes. Cynics might see these structures as 'sham consultation' designed to legitimise the Commission's policy-making roles rather than grant influence over public policy to groups. Some credence to this cynical view is lent by the fact that CONECCS does not include what the Commission calls 'open consultation procedures'. These often less visible consultation exercises include bilateral contacts and/or ad hoc consultations between the Commission and groups. Thus, the Commission's CONECCS data may well be just the tip of a rather large iceberg, with the bulk of 'real' consultation lying well and truly beyond the water line.

For many years the Commission has helped to fund public interest European lobbies such as the European Women's Lobby and the European Environmental Bureau. In an attempt to allay public fears about the EU's democratic deficit, the Commission has, since the early 1990s, redoubled its efforts to achieve a more balanced institutionalisation of interest group intermediation, mainly through the construction of a series of inclusive social networks such as the Social Policy Forum. As Mahoney suggests, this 'can be seen as an effort by the EU to promote wider civil society participation, working to lessen some of the endemic biases inherent in the patterns of mobilisation of different sectors of society' (Mahoney 2004: 446). As long ago as 1997, the Commission adopted a Communication, *Promoting the Role of Voluntary Organizations and Foundations in Europe,* which stressed the need for NGOs to be consulted more widely and more systematically. As the Commission noted in 2002 (COM(2002) 704), this initiative underlined its intention to 'reduce the risk of the policy-makers just listening to one side of the argument or of particular groups getting privileged access'. The increasing institutionalisation of NGO–Commission relations is also reflected in the considerable financial support that NGOs receive from the Commission. Some 2.65 MECU were set aside for funding environmental NGOs during the period 1998–2001 (OJL 354 of 30 December 1997). More generally, there is increasing emphasis on involving civil society organisations in the Commission's policy process, as highlighted in the Commission's White Paper on European Governance and again, in 2002 in COM (2002) 704. This stated 'the Commission particularly encourages a coherent approach to representation of civil society organisations at the European level … belonging to an association is another way for citizens to participate actively, in addition to involvement in political parties or through elections'. More recently the role of civil society groups within the EU policy process was enshrined in the new Constitution, provisionally adopted by European leaders in November 2004. The rejection of the Constitution by the Dutch and French in 2005 is likely to have no adverse effect on the status accorded to civil society groups. Indeed, we predict that the troubles over the Constitution will cause further emphasis to be placed on trying to involve the European citizenry more rather than less.

The Commission's need to demonstrate openness and transparency is paralleled by its need to mobilise a consensus in favour of technically sound and politically feasible policies. These potentially conflicting objectives are typically achieved through different institutional structures used at various stages of the policy-making process. Broadly speaking, the Commission employs two different strategies for involving groups in the policy process: large, open gatherings (including consultations via the internet as outlined above), and more restrictive committees, forums and a myriad of bilateral meetings. Though it is impossible to generalise about the relative importance of these two types of interest aggregation within the Commission, our own research suggests that there might be a pattern emerging. In the early stages of the policy process, consultative structures tend to be open and inclusive, bringing together all potential stakeholders in an open forum, seminar or conference. Generally speaking, the purpose of this form of consultation is to inform potential stakeholders, try out new ideas and obtain early feedback on proposals.

However, the subsequent formulation and implementation of detailed proposals usually takes place within the myriad formal and informal advisory committees and working parties in the Commission, which comprise group representatives and technical experts. Formal committees include so-called 'expert committees' composed of national officials and experts, who are nominated by government departments. In practice, however, these nominees tend to perceive their role as being that of technical experts rather than national government agents. Generally, the Commission *must* consult the relevant expert committee(s) during the policy formulation process (though it is under no obligation to respond to the advice offered by the experts). The more broadly based 'consultative committees' represent sectoral interests and are composed of representatives of Euro-associations and national groups. Though the Commission has a procedural ambition to deal primarily with the Euro-associations, the latter are not always able to provide the level of expertise (and cross-national knowledge) required. The raison d'être of all these committees is to advise the Commission on the technical details of its proposals. The importance of these committees in the policy process is considerable. Back in 1997 it was estimated that there were some 1,000 advisory committees involving some 50,000 representatives from national administrations and the private sector (Greenwood 1997: 41; see also Van Schendelen 1998). In addition, the Commission frequently sets up informal, high level groups or working parties to consider a specific problem.

In practice, it is possible to distinguish between rather open and 'thin' institutions such as very large conferences and seminars and the more restricted 'thick' institutions where only the key players are present. Coen, observing this trend with respect to business interests, refers to the emergence at the EU level of 'the creeping institutionalisation of forum style politics' (Coen 1999: 16). This process is described as the Commission acting as both policy entrepreneur and *political* entrepreneur in response to the further explosion of lobbying after the Maastricht Treaty. In short, the Commission uses institutional engineering in the service of political entrepreneurship. This policy style is itself a recipe for promiscuity in terms of relations between the Commission and interest groups. The more the Commission stresses openness and consultation, the more new groups will come to Brussels. The more groups there are in Brussels, the more groups will want to come to Brussels. The intensity and scope of lobbying has itself become a problem in need of regulation of some kind, and both the Commission and the EP have investigated this possibility (for a comprehensive review, see Greenwood 1997: 80–100; and Preston 1998: 222–32). In practice, the usual difficulties have arisen and it would be wrong to suggest that even a basic, legally based regulatory system has emerged. However, some very basic written rules exist, in the form of guidelines and voluntary codes of practice. In reality, these are supplementary to some rather important informal, but unwritten, rules and norms which facilitate exchange among individuals.

Controlling or over-regulating access is unlikely to be a strategy adopted by the Commission (or, indeed, by the Parliament); consulting as many stakeholders as possible is rational behaviour given the need to obtain the best information and knowledge. It is also a good way of avoiding the dangers of asymmetric information supplied by lobbyists. (For a discussion of lobbying and asymmetric information, see Potters and Van Windern 1992.) Even if the broadening of consultations produces no new (or usable) information, it does strengthen the Commission's position in inter-institutional battles. Sometimes the receipt of information can be as important as the information itself. Thus, as Potters and Van Windern suggest, 'it need not be the *content* of the message as such that transmits information, but merely the *fact* that a message has been received' (Potters and Van Windern 1992: 286). For example, when the Environment Council failed to adopt a Common Position on a text from the Council in December 1998, the Commissioner responsible complained that the delay was unnecessary as 'industry had been consulted all along'. This is, of course, the classic response that public bureaucrats make to elected politicians, essentially arguing that everyone who 'counts' has been consulted and who are you to upset the consensus which has been reached! As we suggested earlier, the functional logic for a bureaucracy to behave in this way is compelling. In addition, the Commission needs to get ever closer to groups as it knows that groups have access to other attractive EU venues. For example, the European Parliament has over time secured for itself a greater role in the EU via the series of grand bargains to which Moravcsik (1998) refers. As a result of this shift in the balance of power between EU institutions (and the continuing uncertainty of how the latest institutional bargain works in each particular case), the EP has moved up the rank order of lobbying targets, depending on the issue at hand.

It has been conventional wisdom to argue that the European Parliament is an inherently weak institution and therefore a relatively unattractive opportunity structure for interest groups. (Interestingly, similar remarks are often made about several EU member states' national parliaments.) Yet important qualifications to this analysis are needed. First, the EP has, for a very long time (and long before the recent increases in its powers), attracted a great deal of lobbying activity – so much so, in fact, that the question of regulating lobbying has been a key issue within the EP for several years. There are three obvious explanations for this apparent inconsistency. First, groups, as rational actors, recognise that the EU policy process demands a multi-track lobbying strategy – a 'belt and braces' approach to lobbying. Expressing a preference for one opportunity structure over another does not preclude some lobbying of less favoured structures. Second, it seems likely that the EP attracts a disproportionate amount of lobbying from certain types of groups (environmentalists, women, consumers, animal rights) who, historically, may not have enjoyed such easy access to the Commission and/or their national governments. Third, the EP's power in the EU policy process varies across policy sectors both because of the Treaties and because of the internal political dynamics of different policy sectors. Where there are effective EP committees, and legislative power is shared between the Council and the Parliament under co-decision-making procedures, lobbying the EP is likely to be more intense. The significant expansion of the EP's legislative role since 1986 has changed the calculation of the logic of influence by groups. As Kohler-Koch (1997) suggests, 'reflecting the new role of the EP as an important institution in the European decision-making process, the Parliamentarians are becoming a decisive target group for lobbyists, and lobbyists have to cope with the institutional structure, the procedures, and the policy style within the Parliament' (Kohler-Koch 1997: 10).

Indeed, Kohler-Koch's research suggests that interest groups and the Parliament can sometimes be effective 'advocacy coalitions' in the EU policy process, albeit sometimes coalitions of the weak. As she argues, changes in the Parliament's role, and in its relationship with groups, seem to be shifting the EP in the direction of a US Congress-type legislature. For example, there has been a proliferation of EP 'intergroups' (of which there are now approximately sixty) – informal meetings of MEPs to discuss policy issues. As one lobbyist has reported, intergroups such as the Pharmaceutical Intergroup are often the target of interest groups (Porter 1998: 4). Two other lobbyists have argued that the increased role for the EP has 'wrested power from other institutions of the EU and especially from closed negotiations between governments and officials in Brussels' and this development is 'good for commercial and other interests' (Earnshaw and Wood 1998: 10). Typically, the public hearings of the EP's committees attract the relevant stakeholders, all interested in pressing their view on the Parliament. As Bouwen and McCown note, 'since the Treaty of Maastricht, the co-decision power has provided the European Parliament with real veto power in the legislative process' (Bouwen and MCCown 2004: 4–5. The gradual increase in the EP's powers has, of course, further increased the complexity of the Brussels lobbying game. Few interests now dare risk leaving the parliamentary arena to their opponents and, hence, parliamentary hearings attract the full melange of stakeholders. Wessels has produced data showing that there are some 67,000 contacts between the EP and interest groups annually (Wessels 1999: 109). Following Kohler-Koch, he concludes that 'the more the EP becomes a veto-player, the more attention it receives' (Wessels 1999: 109). Similarly, Grant notes that business interests have realised that more attention needs to be paid to the EP, citing the example of the chemical industry's Euro-association, CEFIC, which appointed a full-time EP liaison officer in 1990 (Grant 2000: 118). In a more recent study, Bouwen finds the supply and demand model (in this case the demand and supply for 'access goods') useful for explaining interest group access to the EP. The access goods in question all relate to information: expert knowledge; information about the European encompassing interest (i.e. the needs of the particular policy sector under discussion at any time); and information about the domestic encompassing interest. His central thesis is that the crucial access good supplied to the EP by interest groups is not technical information (the access good that we stress for Commission/group relations) but the European encompassing interest. This access good provides MEPs with the European perspective which they need if an agreement is to be forged within the transnational groups in the EP (Bouwen 2004a: 476–80). In addition, in order to increase their chances of re-election, MEPs also need the third access good, namely information on national needs and preferences. Thus, both European and national associations gain access to the EP by supplying goods which the EP demands, albeit sometimes rather different goods to those demanded by the Commission.

The crucial attention that interest groups pay to the EP is a direct reflection of its power as an institution. Similarly, the ECJ's attractiveness as a venue relates to its position in the EU's institutional hierarchy. Here, again, we see the EU interest intermediation system exhibiting some familiar features. In those political systems which accord the judiciary a major role in the interpretation of legal and constitutional arrangements, recourse to the courts has long been a standard 'lobbying' strategy. In the EU, once the ECJ had acquired for itself a major role in the EU policy process it was inevitable that interest groups would devote more attention and resources to influencing Court rulings. As courts acquire power in the field of public policy so they present groups with a new option, namely a litigation strategy. The ECJ represents a perfect example of the 'venue shopping' theory of Baumgartner and Jones, cited earlier. When groups fail to gain satisfaction at the national level, the Commission, EP or Council of Ministers, they have the option – albeit a costly one – of trying to bring a case before the Court, or of persuading the Commission to bring a case before the Court.

Women's and environmental groups (and also trade unions) have been adept in securing favourable ECJ decisions which have been extremely important in prompting policy change. Mazey argues that the EU generally has been an important venue for women's groups and that the ECJ, in particular, has been a very important opportunity structure or venue in supporting the plight of working women and forcing national policy change (Mazey 1998: 136). In the environmental field, Cichowski has reached similar conclusions. She argues that the ECJ has played an important role in the creation of supranational norms which fuel the integration process, often in opposition to the preferences of member states. Private litigants (individuals and interest groups) have played an integral role in this process (Cichowski 1998). These interest groups are, of course, not exclusively environmental groups, but include business groups who, for example, seek to prevent 'tough' national environmental laws from being used to undermine the principles of free and unrestricted trade enshrined in the SEA. At a more general level, Stone Sweet and Brunell have portrayed the Court as a 'supplying' institution – supplying integrative decisions in response to the demands of transnational actors such as businesses and individuals who need European rules and those who are advantaged by European law and practices compared with national law and practices (Stone Sweet and Brunell 1998: 72). Dehousse also argues that the expansion of EU competence, particularly in the areas of environmental and social policies, has prompted much greater use of the ECJ by individuals and groups who perceive the ECJ as an ally (Dehousse 1998). Bouwen and McCown have analysed the conditions under which groups choose between litigation and lobbying strategies. The attraction of litigation (usually via the preliminary reference process under Art. 234 of the Treaties) is that the activist case law of the ECJ provides 'interest groups with potentially powerful legal tools for promoting policy change' (Bouwen and McCown 2004: 8). This strategy can bring about long-term policy change as 'interest groups that successfully litigate in order to shape EU policy, not only effect the removal on national rules, on the basis of EU law, but also typically shape the form of future legislation' (Bouwen and McCown 2004: 9; see also McCown, this volume, chapter 8). Their research suggests that the most successful litigation strategy is not to bring a single case to the courts but to bring multiple cases, either in sequence or simultaneously in order to take advantage of the ECJ's tendency towards precedent-based decision-making (see McCown, this volume, and Bouwen and McCown 2004: 11). Although litigation strategies are used effectively by interest groups, Bouwen and McCown nevertheless conclude that the bias is still in favour of lobbying 'because of the differential resource threshold between the two influence strategies' (Bouwen and McCown 2004: 15).

An intergovernmental theorist would argue that, in theory, the Council of Ministers should be the main European-level opportunity structure to be targeted by interest groups. Yet it is the least *directly* accessible of all EU institutions. As with Cabinets in Western democracies, lobbying has to be rather indirect. Nevertheless, as Hayes-Renshaw and Wallace suggest, although groups 'have no formalised relationship with the Council, their influencing efforts pervade the atmosphere in which the Council works' (Hayes-Renshaw and Wallace 1997: 22). There are three main channels of indirect lobbying of the Council. First, interest groups routinely lobby the national delegations in Brussels, i.e. those national officials who are members of the so-called Permanent Representations based in Brussels. These officials participate in the Council working groups, of which there are approximately 200 (Van Schendelen 1998: 6) and prepare the ground for meetings of the Committee of Permanent Representatives (Coreper) and the ministerial Councils. Where possible, these officials try to reach consensus and compromise between their respective national governments, leaving only the most contentious points to be resolved when the ambassadors meet in Coreper I and II (or, ultimately, the ministers in the Council meetings). As the national representatives (i.e. the ambassadors and deputy ambassadors to the EU) in Coreper play such a key role in the Council process (some 80 per cent of legislative proposals are adopted at Coreper level), national groups make sure that they lobby 'their' national officials, who (the interest groups hope) will then ensure that their views are represented in the Coreper meetings – hence the description of members of Coreper as the 'lobbied lobbyists' (Spence 1993: 48). Euro-groups and those national associations and firms who really understand the importance of intergovernmentalism in EU policy-making typically lobby a range of national delegations in Brussels – particularly of those member states who are known to hold strong positions on any given policy issue. In addition, it appears that 'explanatory material' from lobbyists is sometimes circulated within the Council Secretariat (Hayes-Renshaw and Wallace 1997: 22). Bouwen's comparative study of the business lobbying of EU institutions sheds some light on the lobbying of the Council. Thus, he finds that national associations and individual firms, rather than European associations, have the highest degree of access to the Council. Indeed, it appears that national associations have better access to the Council than to either the Parliament or the Commission (Bouwen 2004b: 358). He explains this bias by reference to his access goods theory (cited above). Basically, the Council needs information on information on the 'domestic encompassing interest', i.e. the aggregate needs and interests of a sector in the domestic markets (Bouwen 2004b: 358).

A second, common means of lobbying the Council is for interest groups to lobby members of the many Council working groups. Rather like Coreper, this form of institutionalised 'issue processing' presents opportunities for detailed, technical arguments to be presented and for national representatives to be won over. The working groups are one of the boiler-houses of European integration. Composed of national officials 'congregating in their thousands every working day in Brussels, they (constitute) the backbone of the European system of integration … they are performing the vital and frequently time-consuming technical groundwork for what will eventually become a piece of European legislation or policy' (Hayes-Renshaw and Wallace 1997: 98). For example, if a Council working group on vehicle pollution is meeting and contains a civil servant from the Swedish government, the civil servant will certainly have been lobbied by Volvo and Saab and will be fully aware of the ways in which the Swedish motor vehicle industry might be affected by any proposed EU legislation.

The third and most obvious means of influencing the Council is, of course, directly via national governments. Several authors see national governments as, in fact, the *main* opportunity structure for interest groups, not just as a means of influencing the Council but as the key opportunity structure through which groups can influence the EU policy process as a whole. For example, Grant has long been sceptical of the thesis that Brussels is the most effective lobbying arena (Grant 2000: 106–15). Similarly, Greenwood describes the 'national route' as the 'tried and tested ground for many organised interests' (Greenwood 1997: 32). Wessels also argues that 'a European route of interest intermediation is clearly not dominant' (Wessels 1999: 117). Bennett's survey data on the lobbying strategies of British business associations confirms this view of interest group behaviour. He found that the national route was the preferred Euro-lobbying strategy of the majority of associations (except federations). He, too, argues that this is perfectly rational: 'the preference for this route can be explained by its relative cheapness and its continuity of use of traditional channels of information and exchange that have developed from the period before European economic integration' (Bennett 1997: 85). More recently, writers such as Grossman and Schneider *et al.* have echoed 'the primacy of the national route' thesis. Indeed, Schneider *et al*. go so far as to suggest that the system is largely étatist and that groups are, therefore, generally weak in relation to national governments. Thus they conclude that 'although governments have to respect the interests of their stakeholders to some extent, they possess ample and largely uncontrolled discretion in EU affairs' (Schneider *et al*. 2004: 25). Clearly, the importance of national governments as an opportunity structure varies according to the policy issue, the type of interest group, the time, and the nature of the national government itself. The continued extension of qualified majority voting in the Council is likely to erode still further the traditional ties between interest groups and national governments and to force interests to develop strategies independent of 'their' governments. Even when an interest group and its national government are on the same side in a policy development debate (often not a reasonable assumption), the group cannot rely on its national government being able to deliver the desired policy objective under QMV. Moreover, as cross-sectoral trade-offs between member states are not uncommon in last-minute bargaining, a national government may choose to 'dump' an interest group in favour of some other policy goal.

Conclusion: the politics of uncertainty

In their analysis of the origins of the Single Market, Sandholtz and Zysman suggest that the 1992 movement was characterised by uncertainty – 'neither the pay-off from nor the preferences for any strategy were or are yet clear' (Sandholtz and Zysman 1989: 107). We conclude on this note of uncertainty. It is an affliction suffered by all players in the EU policy process. In such situations those policy actors possessing certain 'decisional' and 'attitudinal' attributes may have particular advantages in constructing 'win' situations in a series of nested games. Two such attributes might be, first, the development of a long-term view of Europe and its place in the globalisation process, and, second, an ability to change preferences readily in response to changing circumstances. At least *some* European interest groups appear to possess these attributes: for example the large multinational companies do take a European and global view; they may also have a more flexible decision-making process and preference-formation processes than, say, member states, or those interest groups exclusively 'anchored' in national interest group systems. As Heinz *et al*. argue in their study of US interest groups, 'interest representation involves learning. A group's understanding of its interests may change as a result of improved analysis or reflection on past experience' (Heinz *et al*. 1993: 392). Much more research is needed, but it seems reasonable to hypothesise that organisations such as multinationals and interest groups such as Greenpeace, Friends of the Earth (FOE) and World Wide Fund for Nature (WWF) are probably less constrained in their lobbying strategies and have more flexible preference-formation processes than, for example, governments. If, as Heinz *et al*. suggest, uncertainty begets uncertainty, it would be rational for all interest groups wishing to influence the European policy process to avoid becoming locked into any one set of relationships (e.g. with 'their' national government) or into just one 'advocacy coalition' (Sabatier 1988) or any one policy community or policy network.

Thus, we conclude by suggesting that lobbying in the EU is likely to remain pluralistic, unpredictable and to favour those actors who can mobilise ideas and knowledge in order to 'massage' the 'framing' of public policies, who can manage a series of multi-level and shifting coalitions, and who can reformulate their preferences rapidly and consistently with the long-term goals of their organisation. The practical reality of the EU interest group intermediation system is that more and more groups participate in more and more institutions of intermediation. However, we do not suggest that these institutions are necessarily stable or, indeed, neutral. All institutions have a bias and create winners and losers. The central paradox is that institutionalisation and promiscuity go hand in hand. In a sense, institutionalisation is an attempt to constrain promiscuity. The fact that there are so many different venues for group lobbying means that the EU is an inherently *disjointed* policy process. Deals done at one institutional site can be undone elsewhere. At best, therefore, we might see a process of serial institutionalisation of group intermediation in each EU venue, leaving problematic the ambition for joined-up governance in the European Union. Even more problematic, of course, is the question of who gains what, if anything, from this now dense process of group participation in the EU policy process. Clearly, participation does not necessarily equal the exercise of power over policy-making, but it is a necessary condition for the exercise of power. Whether the policy pay-offs from interest group participation in the EU policy process are high or low, we seem set to see more participation rather than less.

References

Aspinwall, M. and Greenwood, J. (1998) 'Conceptualising Collective Action in the European Union: An Introduction' in J. Greenwood and M. Aspinwall (eds), *Collective Action in the European Union: Interests and the New Politics of Associability* (London: Routledge).

Baumgartner, F. and Jones, B. (1991) 'Agenda Dynamics and Instability in American Politics', *Journal of Politics* 53/4: 1044–73.

Bennett, R. (1997) 'The Impact of European Integration on Business Associations: The UK Case', *West European Politics* 20/3: 6–90.

—— (1999) 'Business Routes of Influence in Brussels: Exploring the Choice of Direct Representation', *Political Studies* 47: 240–57.

Bouwen, P. (2004a) 'The Logic of Access to the European Parliament', *Journal of Common Market Studies* 42/3: 473–96.

—— (2004b) 'Exchange Access Good for Access. A Comparative Study of Business Lobbying in the EU Institutions', *European Journal of Political Research* 43/3: 337–69.

Bouwen, P. and McCown, M. (2004), 'Lobbying versus Litigation: Political and Legal Strategies of Interest Representation in the European Union'. Paper presented at the ECPR Standing Group on the European Union, Second Pan-European Conference on EU Politics, 24–26 June 2004, Bologna.

Breton, R. (1995) 'Identification in Transnational Communities', in K. Knop, S. Ostry, R. Simeon and K. Swinton (eds), *Rethinking Federalism: Citizens, Markets, and Governments in a Changing World* (Vancouver: University of British Columbia Press).

Broscheid, A. and Coen, D. (2003) 'Insider and Outsider Lobbying of the European Commission: an Informational Model of Forum Politics', *European Union Politics* 4/2: 165–90.

Butt Philip, A. (1985) *Pressure Groups in the European Community* (London: University Association for Contemporary European Studies (UACES)).

Cichowski, R. (1998) 'Constrained Court or Autonomous Policy-maker? The European Court of Justice and Integration', *Journal of European Public Policy* 5/3: 387–405.

Coen, D. (1997) 'The Evolution of the Large Firm as a Political Actor in the European Union', *Journal of European Public Policy* 4/1: 91–108.

Coen, D. (1998) 'The European Business Interest and the Nation-State: Large-Firm Lobbying in the European Union and Member States', *Journal of Public Policy* 18/1: 75–100.

Commission of the European Communities (1992) *An Open and Structured Dialogue*, SEC (1992) 2272 final (Brussels: European Commission).

—— (1997) *Promoting the Role of Voluntary Organisations and Foundations in Europe* (Luxembourg: Office for Official Publications of the European Communities (ISBN 92–828–1613–3)).

Cowles, M. Green (1997) 'Organizing Industrial Coalitions: A Challenge for the Future?, in H. Wallace and A. Young (eds), *Participation and Policy-Making in the European Union* (Oxford: Clarendon Press).

Cram, L. (1994) 'The European Commission as a Multi-Organisation: Social Policy and IT Policy in the EU', *Journal of European Public Policy* 1/1: 195–218.

Dahl, R. (1982) *Dilemmas of Pluralist Democracy* (London: Yale University Press).

Dehousse, R. (1998) *The European Court of Justice* (Basingstoke: Macmillan).

Deutsch, K. (1957) *Political Community at the International Level: Problems of Definition and Management* (Garden City, NY: Doubleday).

Downs, A. (1967) *Inside Bureaucracy* (Boston, MA: Little, Brown).

Earnshaw, D. and Wood, J. (1998) 'Winning in Brussels', The Public Affairs Newsletter, July.

Grant, W. (1989) *Pressure Groups, Politics and Democracy in Britain* (London: Philip Allen).

—— (2000) *Pressure Groups in British Politics* (Basingstoke: Macmillan).

Greenwood, J. (1997) *Representing Interests in the European Union* (Basingstoke: Macmillan).

Greenwood, J., Grote, J. and Ronit, K. (1992) 'Introduction: Organized Interests and the Transnational Dimension', in J. Greenwood, J. Grote and K. Ronit, *Organized Interests in the European Community* (London: Sage).

Greenwood, J., Strangward, L. and Stancich, L. (1999) 'The Capacities of Euro Groups in the Integration Process', *Political Studies* 47: 127–38.

Grossman, E. (2004), 'Bringing Politics back in: Rethinking the Role of Economic Interest Groups in European Integration', *Journal of European Public Policy* 11/4: 637–56.

Grossman, E. and Helpman, E. (2001) *Special Interest Politics* (Cambridge, MA: MIT Press).

Hayes-Renshaw, F. and Wallace, H. (1997) *The Council of Ministers* (London: Macmillan).

Heinz, J. P., Laumann, E. O., Nelson, R. L., Salisbury, R. H. (1993) *The Hollow Core: Private Interests in National Policy Making* (Cambridge, MA: Harvard University Press).

Henderson, P. E. (1977) 'Two British Errors: Their Probable Size and Some Possible Lessons', *Economic Papers* 29/2: 159–205.

Jordan, G. and Richardson, J. (1982) 'The British Policy Style or the Logic of Negotiation?', in J. Richardson (ed.), *Policy Styles in Western Europe* (London: George Allen and Unwin).

Keck, M. E, and Sikkink, K. (1998) *Activists Beyond Borders* (Ithaca, NY: Cornell University Press).

Kirchner, E. (1977) *Trade Unions as Pressure Groups in the European Community* (Farnborough: Saxon House).

—— (1980a) 'International Trade Union Collaboration and the Prospect for European Industrial Relations', *West European Politics* 3/1: 124–37.

—— (1980b) 'Interest Group Behaviour at the Community Level', in L. Hurwitz (ed.), *Contemporary Perspectives on European Integration* (London: Aldwich).

Kitschelt, H. P. (1986) 'Political Opportunity Structures and Political Protest: Anti-nuclear Movements in Four Democracies', *British Journal of Political Science* 16/1: 57–85.

Klein, R. and O'Higgins, M. (1985) 'Social Policy After Incrementalism', in R. Klein and M. O'Higgins (eds), *The Future of Welfare* (Oxford: Blackwell).

Kohler-Koch, B. (1997) 'Organised Interests in the EU and the European Parliament', paper presented to the International Political Science Association XVIII Congress, Seoul, 17–21 August 1997.

Lahusen, C. (2003), 'Moving into European Orbit: Commercial consultants in the European Union', *European Union Politics* 4/2: 191–218.

266

McAdam, D. (1996) 'Conceptual Origins, Current Problems, Future Directions', in D. McAdam, J. McCarthy and M. Zald (eds), *Comparative Perspectives on Social Movements: Political Opportunities, Mobilizing Structures, and Cultural Framings* (Cambridge: Cambridge University Press).

McAdam, D., McCarthy, J. and Zald, M. (1996) 'Introduction: Opportunities, Mobilizing Structures and Framing Processes: Towards a Synthetic, Comparative Perspective on Social Movements', in D. McAdam, J. McCarthy and M. Zald (eds), *Comparative Perspectives on Social Movements: Political Opportunities, Mobilizing Structures and Cultural Framings* (Cambridge: Cambridge University Press).

McLaughlin, A. and Jordan, G. (1993) 'The Rationality of Lobbying in Europe: Why are Euro-groups so Numerous and so Weak? Some Evidence from the Car Industry', in S. Mazey and J. Richardson (eds), *Lobbying in the EC* (Oxford: Oxford University Press).

Mahoney, C. (2004), 'The Power of Institutions: State and Interest Group Activity in the European Union', *European Union Politics* 5/4: 441–66.

Mazey, S. (1995) 'The Development of EU Equality Policies: Bureaucratic Expansion on Behalf of Woman?', *Public Administration* 73/4: 591–609.

—— (1998) 'The European Union and Women's Rights: From the Europeanisation of National Agendas to the Nationalisation of a European Agenda?', *Journal of European Public Policy* 5/1: 131–52.

Mazey, S. and Richardson, J. (eds) (1993) *Lobbying in the European Community* (Oxford: Oxford University Press).

—— (1995) 'Promiscuous Policymaking: The European Policy Style?', in C. Rhodes and S. Mazey (eds), *The State of the European Union, vol. 3: Building a European Polity?* (Boulder, CO: Lynne Rienner).

—— (1997) 'Policy Framing: Interest Groups and the Lead up to the 1996 Inter-Governmental Conference', *West European Politics* 20/3: 111–33.

—— (2001) 'Institutionalising Promiscuity: Commission/Interest Group Relations in the EU', in N. Fligstein, W. Sandholtz and A. Stone Sweet (eds), *The Institutionalisation of Europe* (Oxford: Oxford University Press).

Moravcsik, A. (1991) 'Negotiating the Single European Act: National Interests and Conventional Statecraft in the European Community', *International Organisation* 45: 19–56.

—— (1993) 'Preferences and Power in the European Community: A Liberal Intergovernmentalist Approach', *Journal of Common Market Studies* 31: 473–524.

—— (1998) *The Choice for Europe: Social Purpose and State Power from Messina to Maastricht* (London: UCL Press).

Peterson, M. A. (1992) 'The Presidency and Organized Interests: White House Patterns of Interest Group Liaison', *American Political Science Review* 86/3: 612–25.

Pijnenburg, B. (1998) 'EC Lobbying by ad hoc Coalitions: An Exploratory Case Study', *Journal of European Public Policy* 5/2: 303–21.

Porter, M. (1998) 'Intergroups and Interest Representation in the EU', *ELIR Newsletter* 4/1: 4–5.

Potters, J. and Van Windern, F. (1992) 'Lobbying and Asymmetric Information', *Public Choice* 74: 269–92.

Putnam, R. (1988) 'Diplomacy and the Logic of Two-level Games', *International Organisation* 42: 427–60.

Richardson, J. (ed.) (1982) *Policy Styles in Western Europe* (London: George Allen and Unwin).

—— (2000) 'Government, Interest Groups and Policy Change', *Political Studies* 48/5: 1006–25

Richardson, J. J. and Jordan, A. G. (1979) *Governing Under Pressure* (Oxford: Martin Robertson).

Sabatier, P. A. (1988) 'An Advocacy Coalition Framework of Policy Change and the Role of Policy-oriented Learning Therein', *Policy Sciences* 21: 129–68.

—— (1998) 'The Advocacy Coalition Framework: Revisions and Relevance for Europe, *Journal of European Public Policy* 5/1: 98–130.

Sandholtz, W. and Zysman, J. (1989) '1992: Recasting the European Bargain', *World Politics* 42/1: 95–128.

Van Schendelen, M. P. C. M. (1998) 'Prolegomena to EU Committees as Influential Policymakers', in M. P. C. M. Van Schendelen (ed.), *EU Committees as Influential Policymakers* (Aldershot: Ashgate).

Van Schendelen, R. (2002) *Machiavelli in Brussels* (Amsterdam: Amsterdam University Press).

Schneider, G. and Baltz, K. (2004), 'Paying the Piper, Calling the Tune: Interest Intermediation in the Pre-Negotiations of EU Legislation'. Paper presented at the Pan-European Conference of International Relations, The Hague, 9–11 September.

Schön, D. A. and Rein, M. (1994) *Frame Reflection: Toward the Resolution of Intractable Policy Controversies* (New York: Basic Books).

Sidjanski, D. (1970) 'Pressure Groups and the European Economic Community', in C. Cosgrove and K. Twitchett (eds), *The New International Actors: The United Nations and the European Economic Community* (London: Macmillan).

Snyder, J. M., Jr (1991) 'On Buying Legislators', *Economics and Politics* 3/2: 95–109.

Spence, D. (1993) 'The Role of the National Civil Service in European Lobbying: The British Case', in S. Mazey and J. Richardson (eds), *Lobbying in the European Community* (Oxford: Oxford University Press).

Stone Sweet, A. and Brunell, T. (1998) 'The European Court and the National Courts: A Statistical Analysis of Preliminary References, 1961–95', *Journal of European Public Policy* 5/1: 69–97.

Stone Sweet, A. and Sandholtz, W. (1998) 'Integration, Supranational Governance, and the Institutionalisation of the European Polity', in W. Sandholtz and A. Stone Sweet (eds), *European Integration and Supranational Governance* (Oxford: Oxford University Press).

Truman, D. (1951) *The Governmental Process: Political Interests and Public Opinion* (New York: Knopf).

Tsebelis, G. (1990) *Nested Games: Rational Choice in Comparative Politics* (Berkeley: University of California Press).

Wessels, B. (1999) 'European Parliament and Interest Groups', in R. Katz and B. Wessels (eds), *The European Parliament, the National Parliaments, and European Integration* (Oxford: Oxford University Press).

Chapter 13

Bypassing the nation-state?

Regions and the EU policy process

MICHAEL KEATING AND LIESBET HOOGHE

Introduction

European integration and regionalism have both altered the architecture of the Western European political order, creating new spaces above and below the nation-state. Their combined effects have created new forms of politics and a complex of three-level interactions. Much has been written on the Europe of the regions (Petschen 1993), which some observers think, or hope, will rival or even displace the Europe of states. Others have discerned new forms of 'multi-level governance' (Jachtenfuchs and Kohler-Koch 1995; Marks 1993; Marks, Hooghe and Blank 1996; Scharpf 1994, 1999) or third-level politics (Bullman 1994; Jeffrey 1996). In this chapter we examine the emergence of the region in the context of the state and of the European Union. Then we look at the links between regions and the EU and the influence of regions in EU policy-making. We find that, rather than a new and ordered territorial hierarchy, authority is diffused across multiple territorial levels. Policy-making continues to be centred primarily on the state, but national governments increasingly share decision-making with European and regional actors.

Regions and regionalism in Western Europe

The emergence of the region, like that of the EU itself, is a response to functional, political and institutional developments which have had varied impacts in different places. Functionalist analyses stress the links between territory and economic change and the rediscovery of the region as the motor of economic development (Storper 1997; Scott 1998). Together with the decline of national diversionary regional policies and planning, this has led to an emphasis on endogenous development and self-help and to increased competition among regions for investment, markets and technology (Keating 1998). This analysis is taken to extremes by observers like Ohmae (1995), who sees regions engaged in a struggle for economic advantage to the exclusion of all other policy considerations. In fact, regions are defined not merely by economics but also by culture and history, which define their boundaries and shape social relations within them. Regions are also the outcome of political leadership and competition. In some parts of Europe territory has become a significant political cleavage and regions have emerged as political spaces, sustaining a debate about the common interest and sustaining a distinct political agenda. Regions have also emerged as institutions, an intermediate level of government between states and municipalities, but taking very different forms, from the fully-fledged federalism of Germany, Belgium and Austria, to the weak, administrative regionalism of Italy and France. This has produced a heterogeneous pattern across Europe, according to whether the various meanings of the region coincide or not, and to the degree of institutionalisation of regional government. In some places, like Scotland or Catalonia, the economic, cultural and political regions (or rather stateless nations) coincide and are endowed with important institutions with legislative and administrative competences. Some of the other Spanish autonomous communities and many of the German *Länder* have a much weaker sense of political and cultural identity, although still possessing autonomous institutions. French regions were designed to suppress rather than encourage political and cultural identity and, like Italian regions, rarely constitute political spaces or a primary reference point for political debate. In some of the smaller states there are no elected regional governments and, at best, a system of functionally specific agencies for economic development. In some cases, the most important level for economic, social and political mobilisation is not the region but the city.

As a polity, the region has much in common with the EU itself. It is complex, patchily institutionalised and contested. Arenas and actors vary across policy areas and policy-making is organised through networks, which may be functionally or territorially based. As in Europe (Hooghe and Marks 1999), there is a constant struggle between those who see the region as primarily an economic entity, driven by competitive market considerations locked in a neo-mercantilist competition for economic advantage, and those who favour a stronger social dimension (Keating 1998). As in the European Union, concerns of economic competitiveness have usually trumped questions regarding the region as a basis for social solidarity. In a few regions, strong regional governments are able to impose coherence on the array of local actors and define a common territorial interest. In other regions, development coalitions have emerged to promote a vision of the region's place in European and global markets but without an overall social project. Yet other regions are a political no man's land, fought over by rival political and social interests, often with different territorial bases.

Regions and European integration

European integration has further enhanced the importance of regions, in the political and economic domains, and produced a new dynamic. In the economic domain, the opening of markets has produced a new territorial hierarchy. At one time, it was thought that integration would concentrate development in the central regions of the 'golden triangle' to produce a new centre–periphery cleavage, but it is clear now that matters are more complex. Some French economists replaced the analogy of the golden triangle with that of the 'blue banana' and others have favoured the analogy of the mosaic, with pockets of underdevelopment even in the booming regions. There is, however, a broad, if not universal, consensus that market integration is still likely to exacerbate territorial disparities (Keeble *et al.* 1988; Camagni 1992; Steinle 1992; Begg and Mayes 1993; Commission 1991, 1999). Unlike nation-states, the EU has no automatic compensation mechanism through fiscal equalisation and large universal spending programmes financed by general taxation (Mackay 1993). The needs of national competitiveness together with EU rules also prevent states from intervening to correct these disparities through diversionary policies. EU competition policy may disadvantage marginal regions, through preventing cross-subsidisation of communications services and opening public procurement. Other EU policies, including agriculture and research spending, also tend to benefit the more developed regions (Cheshire *et al.* 1991; Commission 1996). The single-market programme has further disarmed national governments, while economic and monetary union has removed their ability to manipulate exchange rates and interest rates or to run budget deficits, all instruments used for regional as well as national purposes.

Politically, European integration has also served to enhance the salience of regions. On the one side, European integration has had a *positive* mobilisation effect on regions. As economic regulation has shifted to the European Union, the functional argument against regional decentralisation has lost appeal. The European Union – not national states – regulates a single economic market, including setting interest and exchange rates, deciding on investment conditions, settling trade disputes, and internalising negative externalities. European market integration, then, has lowered the bar for regions desiring political autonomy by reducing the economic costs of decentralisation (Alesina and Spolaore 2003; Marks and Hooghe 2000.) But European integration has also mobilised regions *against* Europe. Competences transferred to the EU include matters in which regions have a direct interest. This not only removes power to Europe, it also serves to increase centralisation within states, since it is the member state governments who compose the Council of Ministers.

There have been two types of reaction at the regional level. A rejectionist regionalism opposes European integration, anxiously fearing a further loss of democratic control, more remote government or the triumph of market principles. This reaction was common in many regions in the 1970s, is still visible in Scandinavia, and has recently become more apparent in some core autonomist regions including the Flemish region (Vlaams Blok), Northern Italy (Northern League), and some German *Länder* (De Winter and Türsan 1998; De Winter and Gomez-Reino Cachafeiro 2002). A second type of regionalism seeks to use Europe as a source of political and economic resources, if necessary against the state itself. Most obviously this involves economic development issues, but Europe has also been seen as a source of support for minority cultures and languages threatened within large states (Cardús 1991; de Witte 1992). Hence regional interests have sought new mechanisms to get into the European policy game.

Europe has also provided a new arena for the expression of regional and minority nationalist aspirations. Some minority nationalist movements note that European integration has reduced the cost of national independence, and propose simply to join the list of member states; this is the case of the Scottish National Party and some Basque nationalists. Others want to replace the existing Union with a federation of regions and small nations, abolishing the existing states; this is the policy of the Welsh nationalist party Plaid Cymru and of many Basque nationalists. Others again are more pragmatic, seeing in Europe an arena in which their nationalist aspirations can be expressed and legitimised, while seeking to exert influence at whatever points are available. In its most advanced form, this takes the form of post-sovereignty arguments in which nationalists abandon the search for a nation-state in favour of the construction of a pluralist and multi-level Europe, often calling in older, pre-state traditions of authority to support them (Keating 2001).

European integration is ambivalent for regions. European integration signifies opportunity in that it opens up a 'second front' for regions to challenge the national state. European integration may also threaten deeply held regional values and fundamental territorial interests when it constrains local choice. The effect of European integration on regions has also changed over time: as European integration has deepened from market integration to political integration, opportunities for regional empowerment have turned out to be less than transformative and constraints on local choice more than symbolic. So the image of European integration is two-sided, and it is changing over time.

This affects regionalist politics in profound ways. Regionalist parties as a group have become decidedly less pro-European. Expert data on party positioning on European integration, which track parties at the time intervals of 1984, 1988, 1992, 1996, 1999 and 2002, provide a clear read on this: until 1996, support for European integration was higher among regionalists than among the average party family; from 1999, support has been lower. In 2002, the most recent data point available to us, their average score was

4.7 on a scale from 1 (strongly opposed) to 7 (strongly in favour), and this contrasts with an average for all party families of 5.6. Regionalists are now *less* pro-European than Christian democrats, socialists, liberals, conservatives and the greens. But there is great variation among regionalist parties. Compared to other party families, regionalists tend to hold more diverse views, and they are more likely to shift position over time. While some regionalist-autonomist parties, such as the Catalan CiU, the Scottish SNP, the Welsh Plaid Cymru and the Flemish Volksunie, have been consistently pro-European, others, such as the Irish Sinn Fein, the Basque Herri Batasuna and its successors, and the Flemish Bloc, have been consistently Eurosceptical, and yet others have switched over time, such as the Northern League (switch to Euroscepticism) or the Finnish SKF (switch to pro-European position). We hypothesise that these differences reflect the differential importance of opportunity and threat for particular regionalist parties.[1]

European integration and regionalism are Janus-faced phenomena. On the one hand, they appear to weaken the nation-state. On the other hand, they represent attempts to create new political arenas to try and recapture control over state functions. The shape of these arenas will condition the politics that is possible within them, hence a series of conflicts over the character of the European Union: the social versus the market vision; the unitary versus the federalist vision; and the role of regions. In the next section, we examine the channels by which regional interests have sought to influence Europe. Then we examine how the European Union has itself sought to use regions in pursuit of its own policy objectives. The result has been a dynamic interplay of interests at three levels, among regions, the EU and nation states. This has spawned a considerable literature examining the ways in which regions can influence policy in the EU (Balme 1996; Bullman 1994; Hooghe 1996; Jeffrey 1996; Jones and Keating 1995; Keating and Jones 1985; Le Galès and Lequesne 1997).

Channels of access

Formulating an interest

Regions, as emphasised above, are not merely actors but also political arenas, containing a plurality of interests. Their first problem in seeking access to European decision-making is formulating a regional interest. In some cases, such as the German *Länder*, the Belgian regions or the Austrian *Länder*, strong regional governments are able to formulate a regional interest, given legitimacy by democratic election. In others, such as the French regions, regional governments are institutionally weak and rivalled by powerful political figures rooted in the cities and departments as well as in a territorial bureaucracy of the central state. Some states have no regional governments at all.

A number of regions have a capacity to mobilise territorial lobbies encompassing both governmental and private actors. Despite the lack of elected institutions before 1999, Scotland has shown a consistent ability to mobilise a territorial lobby encompassing business, trade unions, municipal governments, religious and other social leaders, and the deconcentrated arms of the central bureaucracy itself (Midwinter *et al.* 1991). In the historical Spanish regions of Catalonia, the Basque Country and Galicia, regional governments are able to draw upon a sense of historical identity to legitimise a regional interest, though with varied results. In some French regions, powerful notables are able

273

to mobilise a lobby around themselves, despite the fragmentation of the system of political representation, with its three levels of subnational government. In England, there is no general level of regional governments and the capacity to organise lobbies within civil society is rather low. Italian regional governments have traditionally been institutionally weak, dominated by national political parties and poorly linked to civil society (Trigilia 1991); this has undermined their ability to formulate a regional interest.

There are some interests common to regions within the EU. These include institutional matters, the design of partnerships in policy implementation and the general principle of subsidiarity and its interpretation. There are also common interests in inter-regional cooperation and cross-border initiatives. Yet regions are also in competition with each other, to attract public funding and private investment, and to shape EU policies to suit their particular interests. So there is a constant tension between promotion of regionalism in general, and the pursuit of regions' individual concerns. Regions have a multiplicity of channels for the pursuit of these collective and individual matters, of varying efficacy depending on the subject to be pursued and the political context. There is not, nor can there be, a single mode of representation of 'regional' interests in the EU.

Access via the national government

The most important channel of influence is via national governments. Generally, the more effectively regional interests are integrated into the national policy-making system, the better they will be looked after in Brussels. The strongest mechanism is provided by Article 203, originally introduced in the Maastricht Treaty, which allows a state to be represented by a minister of a subnational government in the Council of Ministers. This clause, which stipulates that representatives must have ministerial status, was designed for federal states like Austria, Germany and Belgium or federalising ones like Spain and the UK, and not for countries with administrative regions like France. It does not, it must be emphasised, allow regions to represent themselves at the Council of Ministers. A regional minister appearing there represents the state, and there needs to be a prior agreement among the regions and the state as to what their interest is. The clause has been used in Germany, Belgium, Austria and the UK, but in rather different ways. In the German case, the *Länder* negotiate an agreement through the Bundesrat, and one of them then represents the common position. The Belgian regions, communities and federal government have laid down by special law detailed arrangements on federal–subnational representation and decision-making in Council of Ministers machinery. Each level represents the Belgian position and casts the vote in matters exclusively under its own jurisdiction, while both are involved in matters of joint competence, with one taking the lead. In contrast to the German collective approach, Belgian regions and communities minimise the need for prior agreement by taking turns in assuming the lead responsibility for the Councils on matters within their jurisdiction. The distinction between the collective and the individual approach rests upon fundamentally different premises. The German approach accepts that regions are the third level in a multi-layered European polity and that they are ultimately nested in a national arena. The Belgian approach minimises the national mould. Europe is seen as a polity with multiple actors at multiple levels who interact directly with European institutions on matters within their competencies. In the UK, the devolved administrations are allowed into the delegation to the Council of Ministers at the invitation of the central government, and must follow the overall UK line. This has allowed them considerable information and the status of insiders, but at the loss of a capacity publicly to take their own line, and has been possible only while both levels of government are dominated by the same political party. There is also provision for participation by Northern Ireland ministers, but the most interesting stipulation there is for cooperation with the Republic of Ireland on European matters.

Regions may also be involved in the process of treaty revision, to secure their own rights. As a condition of the ratification of the Maastricht Treaty in the Bundesrat, the *Länder* obtained a provision that the Bundesrat would have to approve all further transfers of sovereignty, even those that do not impinge on Länder competencies. In Belgium, treaty changes need the approval not only of the Senate, which is the federal chamber but, where regional competencies are involved, of each regional and community assembly separately.

Elsewhere, regions have only a consultative role in European matters. In Spain, the central government consults the autonomous communities through sectoral conferences, but the impact of these is uneven. In 1996, the Catalans and Basques secured the appointment of an observer from the autonomous communities in the Permanent Representation and participation in working groups. In 2004 the New Socialist government agreed to regional representation in the Council of Ministers. Italian regions have some input through the six-monthly meetings of the Standing Conference on State–Regional Relations.

France provides another model of influence via the national state, through its integrated bureaucracy which links local and national policy-making, and the cumulation of mandates, by which politicians may simultaneously hold national and local office. To some degree, this unitary system with territorial influence has been extended to the EU (Balme 1995) but it is uneven in its incidence. While the presence of local politicians in the national parliament provides a powerful institutional defence for the system of local government in France, there is no powerful lobby for the defence of these institutional interests in Europe.

Individual regional interests may also be projected through national governments by partisan links. This is particularly important in southern Europe. Successive Spanish governments in the 1990s and 2000s have needed the territorial parties in order to be invested by the Parliament and to govern. This provides access to national policy-making and thence to Europe. In Belgium too, regional interests have access to the federal government through party networks.

Direct access: subnational offices

Recent years have seen a spectacular growth in direct links with the EU. These take a variety of forms. Regional and local governments make frequent visits to Brussels to lobby Commission officials, and they often engage the services of consultants to help them make a case and find their way through the bureaucracy. Many have opened permanent offices in Brussels. In the fifteen years to 2000, the number of these grew from just two to 165 (Marks, Salk, Ray and Nielsen 1996; Marks, Haesly and Mbaye 2002). Stronger regions have their own offices. Thus one finds every German *Land*, all three Belgian regions and all Austrian *Länder* represented in Brussels along with most Spanish autonomous communities. In countries with a weaker regional tier, representation usually consists of a mixture of local and regional units. In France, most offices represent regions, but several *départements* also have offices. In the United Kingdom, local authorities, regional quangos, regional enterprise organisations, national local authority organisations, universities and elected regional assemblies fund offices representing individual local authorities, regional groupings of local authorities and a national local authority organisation, alongside offices representing the North of England, Northern Ireland, Scotland, and Wales. In unitary systems, such as the Netherlands and Scandinavia, local governments (or associations of local governments) predominate.

The status of these offices differs considerably. Some are public–private consortia concerned with economic issues, while others are political representatives of the regional government. Catalonia has maintained the public–private formula with the Patronat Català Pro-Europa, while the Basque government has chosen to establish a direct political presence. Scotland has both forms, Scotland Europa, founded in 1992 as a platform for Scottish interests, and Scotland House, the representative of the Scottish Executive; since 1999, they share the same roof. The legal status of the offices also differs according to domestic law. Spanish and Italian regions had to go to court to challenge national bans on opening Brussels offices and the French regions had to tread carefully around the constitution. The German federal government only recognised the *Länder* offices in 1993. Particular sensitivity is aroused by ventures across national borders; the Italian government long resisted a proposal for a joint office between the region of Alto-Adige and its Austrian neighbour Tyrol. On the other hand, cross-border joint lobbying in Brussels is specifically encouraged in the Northern Ireland peace agreements as a way of defusing conflict.

These offices are sometimes represented as forms of direct representation in EU decision-making, yet the Commission is tied by regulations in deciding on matters like the allocation of regional funds, while political decision-making is in the hands of the Council of Ministers and the European Parliament. Regions do try, and occasionally succeed, to influence European policy, but such influence is usually confined to narrowly circumscribed issues, and tends to be the privilege of the larger, politically autonomous, and resourceful regions. Most offices concentrate on the more subtle roles of information exchange, and of liaising. In the first place, they provide information to regions on upcoming policy initiatives, allowing them to lobby their national governments; and they provide information and regional viewpoints to Commission officials, who are otherwise dependent on national governments for information. In the second place, they serve a symbolic role in projecting regions and regional politicians in the European arena and presenting them as participants in the policy process. This liaising role allows regional politicians to take credit for EU initiatives and particularly for funding that they would have received in any case under existing regulations. The open bureaucracy of the Commission encourages lobbying, while the opacity of the political decision-making process and the funding regulations allows a whole variety of actors to take credit for the outcomes (Marks, Haesly and Mbaye 2002).

Regional lobbies are rarely powerful on their own in Brussels. Where they can work with a national government, they can achieve more. Thus the Spanish regions as well as the French regions regularly meet collectively with their respective national permanent representations to exchange information and discuss strategy. The Scottish and Welsh representatives are described as part of the 'UKREP family', closely tied to the British permanent representative. Regional lobbies may also be effective when linked with powerful sectoral interests, such as a major corporation based in the region, or a sector with links into the Commission directorates. The best examples are in Germany, where sectoral interests are often linked into the system of territorial government in the *Länder*.

European-wide lobbies

Several organisations lobby for regions as a whole at European level. The International Union of Local Authorities and the Council of Communes and Regions of Europe are both wider in scope than the Community and have been closely associated with the Council of Europe, which they persuaded to establish a Permanent Conference of Local and Regional Authorities in 1957. In 1986, they opened a joint office to deal with the EC. In 1985, the Council (later Assembly) of European Regions was launched, with 107 members including eleven Swiss cantons. It has pressed for involvement of regions in European decision-making, for the principle of subsidiarity, and for institutional changes. Other regional organisations seeking to influence policy-making in Brussels are the Conference of Peripheral Maritime Regions; the Association of European Frontier Regions; Working Group of Traditional Industrial Regions; and a number of transnational frontier organisations.

Consultative mechanisms: Committee of the Regions

The establishment of formal rights of consultation with the Community owed a great deal to the pressure of the European Parliament, which in the course of the reforms of the regional fund stressed the need for greater involvement of regions. In 1988, the Commission created a Consultative Council of Regional and Local Authorities with consultative rights over the formulation and implementation of regional policies as well as the regional implications of other Community policies. Its forty-two members were appointed by the Commission on the joint nomination of the Assembly of European Regions, the International Union of Local Authorities and the Council of Regions and Communes of Europe. The Maastricht Treaty replaced this with a stronger Committee of the Regions (CoR), which the Commission, the Council of Ministers and, since the Amsterdam Treaty, the Parliament are obliged to consult. It has the same status and powers as the Economic and Social Committee, with which it was initially organisationally linked, although its scope is slightly narrower. It can also issue opinions on its own initiative and forward these to the Commission and Council. More ardent regionalists had hoped for a regionally based second chamber of the European Parliament or even of the Council of Ministers; what they got was a great deal less. In addition to its purely consultative status, several factors weaken the Committee (Farrows and McCarthy 1997). Its membership is decided by national governments, some of which, like France, have exercised strong control, while others, including Belgium, German, Spain and the UK (for Scotland and Wales), have left the matter to regions themselves. National politics is also felt in the allocation of committee chairs and memberships and even the allocation of own-initiative opinions by national quotas. The committee includes not just regions but municipal representatives, with different institutional interests. The German *Länder*, who might be a powerful presence, have a more promising channel through their national government. Finally, the Committee has the task of representing regions as a whole, which may limit it to institutional matters where a common interest can be discerned, though even here the regional–local division may cause problems. In the early 2000s, tensions developed with the emergence of a group of strong 'regions with legislative powers' (RegLeg), who argued that their task in applying EU directives gave them a role analogous to national governments and different from that of municipalities and ordinary regions. They did not manage to convince CoR as a whole of their case but continue as an organised group, while still participating as individual regions within CoR.

The Convention on the Future of Europe

Regional interests had some hopes for the Convention on the Future of Europe, especially when the Laeken Declaration that launched it under the Belgian presidency contained some encouraging language. In the event, the regional theme was a minor one. CoR was given six observers rather than full members, although they were allowed to take part in the debates. The demand for a working group on sub-national government was refused and there was just one part of a plenary session on the issue. CoR itself was divided, between the legislative regions and the others, and between a group that wanted to entrench regional competences against Europe and another that wanted more Europe, following the Community method, but with a stronger regional role. It formulated a series of amendments to give more symbolic recognition of territorial pluralism, most of which were accepted, and achieved some extension of the fields in which it must be consulted. The major gain was a right for CoR to go to the Court of Justice where it thinks that subsidiarity principles have been violated, although this was not extended to individual regions as RegLeg wanted. More radical proposals were floated by some regions but did not even make the Convention agenda. So the Flemish government, along with the Catalan Convention on Europe, suggested that, where regions were representing the state in the Council of Ministers, the member state's votes could be split among them. The Basque government's proposal for an Associated State, which radically extended a proposal from French MEP Alain Lamassoure, that regions could be partners of the Union, did not feature in the debates, nor did that of the European Free Alliance for 'internal enlargement', giving stateless nations the possibility of becoming full members of the EU. The Convention demonstrated again that, in matters of constitutional reform, the member states are masters of the game and that regions must seek to work out a position in their own state before they can be effective in Europe.

The Commission and the regions

Traffic between regional interests and the EU is not one-way. The Commission has itself played an important role in mobilising regional interests, establishing new networks and creating a dialogue among regions, states and itself. The main stimulus for this has been the EU's regional policy, now subsumed under the structural funds. These now account for a third of the EU budget, less than agricultural spending but far more than any other item. Elsewhere (Hooghe and Keating 1994) we have explained the development of regional and structural policy as the product of converging logics. A policy logic, whose guardian is the Commission, combines with a political and distributive logic, located in the Council of Ministers and intergovernmental negotiations. The policy logic for EU regional policy is similar to that for national regional policies of the 1960s and 1970s. It is a mechanism for rectifying the territorial disparities produced by market integration and for achieving allocative efficiency; it is a social compensation for losers in the process of economic restructuring; and it is a device to legitimise the European project in regions where support might otherwise be lacking. The political logic is the need to redistribute resources among member states. Initially, this meant compensating Britain for its disproportionately large net contribution to the Community budget in the 1970s. Later, the policy was extended to compensate the southern European countries for the effects of the single market programme and EMU. These different logics produced conflicts between the Commission and member states from the inauguration of the European Regional Development Fund (ERDF) in 1975. In order to gain the consent of member states, the ERDF was divided into fixed national quotas; all regions that were eligible under national regional policies were eligible for ERDF funding. Funds were administered by national governments, who almost invariably refused to treat them as additional to national spending but rather as a reimbursement to themselves for their own regional policy spending. Consequently, the policy was a way of dressing up an interstate transfer mechanism as a European policy.

Over the years, the Commission has sought to increase its own influence over the framing and implementation of the policy, to convert it to a genuine instrument of regional policy, and to ensure that spending is additional to national spending programmes. From the late 1980s, it also sought to co-opt regional interests as partners in designing and implementing programmes. This has produced a three-level contest for control of the policy instrument, among the Commission, member states and regions themselves. In 1988, there was a major reform, again guided by both political and policy logics. The political logic was provided by the need to compensate the countries of southern Europe and Ireland for the adoption of the single market programme measures in the period to 1993. The policy logic was the Commission's desire to convert the ERDF and other structural funds into a genuine policy. The funds doubled and the three main ones, the ERDF, the European Social Fund (ESF) and the Guidance Section of the European Agricultural Guidance and Guarantee Fund (EAGGF) were brought together (Armstrong 1995). Community-wide objectives were laid down and for the first time, the Commission drew up its own map of eligible areas, using Community-wide criteria. Funds were disbursed only to projects within approved Community Support Frameworks (CSFs), apart from 9 per cent, which was reserved for Community Initiatives sponsored by the Commission. CSFs were negotiated between the Commission and member states, with the involvement of regions themselves. Additionality was laid down as a general principle, so that spending would be over and above national spending. The whole policy was guided by the notion of subsidiarity, with the greatest possible involvement of regional and local interests and the social partners in the world of business, labour and voluntary groups. The regulations prescribed an integrated approach to regional development: as this links spatial policy to technology, environmental policy, education, public procurement and competition policy, it was intended to bring regions into contact with a range of EU policies and directorates. The Commission, in line with contemporary thinking on development policy, also sought to move from infrastructure to human capital, productive investment and indigenous development. This too implies a more active and participative role for regional actors of various sorts.

279

These changes potentially paved the way for greater regional involvement in policy-making and for stronger direct links between the Commission and regional interests. To a significant extent, this has happened (Hooghe and Marks 2001). Those states without regional structures have been obliged to create them, or at least a substitute for them, in order to be eligible for funds. This is the case in Greece, Ireland and even Sweden. There has been a great deal of political mobilisation around the funds. Some English regions have even constituted lobbies in the absence of regional governments, in order to face the European challenge (Burch and Holliday 1993). The belief that there is a pot of gold in Brussels is one reason for the explosion of regional lobbying and offices in the EU capital. Regional actors have been brought into contact with Commission officials, and its thinking on development policy has diffused through the mechanism of partnership.

Yet the effect on territorial relations should not be overstated. For one thing, the Commission itself does not have a consistent definition of what a region is. Its NUTS table (Nomenclature of Territorial Units for Statistics) consists of five levels, each of which is an aggregation of national administrative units. Nor does it limit itself to regional authorities, however defined. Sometimes its initiatives involve municipal governments, others are aimed at the private sector or local action groups within civil society. The Commission's objective following its policy logic is to get programmes going, to spend the funds in the most effective way possible, and to involve whatever partners are appropriate for the task at hand.

National governments have also found their way back into the act and from the high point of 1988 there has been considerable re-nationalisation of the policy field. While the Commission has succeeded in concentrating funds on the neediest regions, it still has to make sure that everyone gets something in order to keep national governments on side. Even the new Nordic members, although net contributors to the EU budget, received a piece of the structural policy in 1995, through a new Objective 6 aimed at areas of sparse population. While there are officially no national quotas, there was an understanding that Britain, for example, would get a large share of the funds for industrial areas, while France would do well in the rural category. The map of eligible areas is negotiated between states and the Commission, a practice that was formalised in 1993.

The most recent reforms, for the period starting in 2006, are marked by the needs of enlargement, pressures for renationalisation, and budget constraints. Enlargement more than doubled the disparities between the 10 per cent most prosperous and the 10 per cent least prosperous areas, calling for massive transfers if the policy were to operate on the same lines as in the past. The British government and some German *Länder* took the opportunity to argue that EU regional policy should be restricted to the new member states, leaving them to manage their own programmes while limiting their contribution to the budget. The Commission's proposals adopted in 2004 did not go this far but provided for further concentration of funding, decentralisation to member states and a simplification of policy instruments. At the same time, however, it proposed to increase spending so that cohesion policy would overtake agriculture as the largest item in the budget (Giordano 2004). Seventy-eight per cent of the new allocation would go to a 'cohesion' objective, for regions with a gross domestic product less than 75 per cent of the average, in effect retaining the old Objective 1 category. Eighteen per cent would go to a competitiveness objective and not be restricted as to geographical coverage, The remainder would be for territorial cooperation, meaning cross-border programmes. The

Commission would adopt a lighter touch, especially where it is spending a small amount of money, as under the second objective. National frameworks would be negotiated between the Commission and member states, and national and regional programmes would be worked out within these (Commission, 2004).

The retreat from interventionist regional policy since 1988 reflects general political pressures to contain the role and power of the Commission. It also stems from a concern within the Commission that an active role was too costly in time and resources and ineffective in control; regional funds featured in the mismanagement scandals that erupted in the late 1990s (Hooghe 1998). So, while structural policy has stimulated increased regional activity, this has followed distinctly national lines. Where regional governments have a strong institutional position in the domestic arena, they have become important actors. Where they are weak domestically, states have largely retained their central role concerning links to the Commission and control of regional policy implementation. At one extreme are the Belgian regions, which deal directly with the Commission on the designation of eligible areas, the allocation of the funds, negotiation of the contracts and implementation. The German *Länder* are also deeply involved, through the mechanisms of cooperative federalism. Individual *Länder* participate in the design and implementation of CSFs, through the Joint Tasks Framework *Gemeinschaftsaufgabe* (Anderson 1992). At the other extreme are Ireland and Portugal, which lack an elected regional tier of government, as well as Greece, with an elected though extremely weak regional level. At the urging of the Commission, even in those inhospitable settings, local actors have become more involved, though the changes fall well short of undermining the state's gatekeeping role (Reese and Holmes 1995; Yannopoulos and Featherstone 1995). In France and the UK (outside Scotland and Wales) there has, paradoxically, been some increased centralisation since the 1988 reforms, as the structural funds have become financially significant and politically more salient (Balme 1995; Jones and Keating 1995).

Overall, the institutional machinery of partnership, oiled by a considerable budget, has strengthened features of multi-level governance (Ansell *et al.* 1997; Hooghe 1998). In a 1999 report, the Commission concludes that 'as an institution, the delivery system developed for the structural funds is characterised by multi-level governance, i.e. the Commission, national governments and regional and local authorities are formally autonomous, but there is a high level of shared responsibility at each stage of the decision-making process. The relationship between these is, accordingly, one of partnership and negotiation, rather than being a hierarchical one' (Commission 1999: 143). This challenges state-centric governance in that European institutions set general rules, regions participate in making decisions, and the three parties are in a relationship of mutual dependency rather than hierarchy. But this partnership has never applied evenly across all phases of decision-making. It has traditionally been strongest in the implementation stage of structural programming, but weak in the strategic planning stages. Successive reforms since 1993 have reduced the interventionist role of the Commission and given more scope to member states. With the new rules encouraging more partners (not only subnational authorities), greater adjustment to national practices, and greater separation of responsibilities, partnership rules may no longer provide regional authorities with an unconditional entitlement to participate in EU decision-making.

Enlargement

Regional issues featured quite prominently in the European debate in the accession countries of central and eastern Europe. In the early years of the process, the impression was given that, to be a modern European country, it was necessary to have regional government on the western model. As there is no western model, but a variety of types, this was a great simplification, but the idea persisted that regions of a critical 'European' scale are essential for economic competitiveness.

Another widespread belief was that regional government is needed in order to receive and manage Structural Funds (Hughes *et al.* 2003). There is no written record of the Commission having laid this down, but this impression seems to have been given by Commission officials and consultants, and taken up in domestic debates by those pressing for reform for their own reasons. Around 2000, the Commission clarified that the only formal requirement for the Structural Funds was that accession countries should have a level of administration at the NUTS2 level. It then proceeded, in what looks like a radical change of perspective, to lay down a highly centralised model for the planning and management of Structural Fund programmes. Its motive appears to have been worries about the lack of capacity at the regional level and of clientelism and corruption, together with the need to spend the Structural Fund allocation for the remainder of the programming period 2001–7 in the mere two years available after accession (Keating 2003). So the Commission pressed for as few sectoral and territorial programmes as possible, a single paying authority, and strong National Development Plans as the basis for the future Structural Fund programmes. A third of the funding was to be given through the Cohesion Fund, which does not have a regional dimension. In a further departure from its own practice, it has insisted that a large part of the funds should go to hard infrastructure rather than the 'soft' development measures, such as human capital and entrepreneurship, now favoured by regional policy in the west.

The result has been a de-linking of European policy from the domestic politics of regionalism in the new member states. Only Poland has a level of regional government corresponding to NUTS2 regions, and these do not control the Structural Funds. In the Czech Republic, the regions are too small and need to come together in consortia to form NUTS2 units. In Hungary, the planning regions are at NUTS2 level but are not elected governments. In a final twist, Commission officials have taken to justifying the model of centralised regional policy in the new member states by citing the experience of Ireland and Portugal, which enjoyed high rates of growth while running centralised development programmes – passing over the fact that at that time the Commission had been urging those countries to decentralise! The weakness of the regional tier in the new member states means that they are unlikely to be among the protagonists of a stronger regional presence. There are, for example, no regions with legislative powers among them.

Conclusion

Regionalism and European integration have changed the national state in important ways. It is difficult, however, to isolate these from other factors pointing in the same direction – the internationalisation of markets; capital mobility; the rise of transnational corporations; and neo-liberal ideology. Territorial politics in the European Union is complex. We have not seen the rise of a homogeneous regional tier of government in the EU. Instead, variety in forms of territorial mobilisation has persisted: historic nations; large provincial regions; units in federal or quasi-federal states; cities and city-regions. Regions also differ in their social and political constitution. In some cases, the region can be identified with a structure of government; in others, civil society or private groups are more important in defining and carrying forward a regional interest.

We have not seen the rise of a new territorial hierarchy. The national state has not been bypassed in favour of a Europe of the regions. The national state remains the primary actor in the EU. This does not mean, however, that policy-making in this field can be explained simply by interstate bargaining. The intergovernmental perspective on EU policy-making presents national politics as a closed, domestic game, where the national interest is formulated before being taken to the EU, where a second game commences, characterised by intergovernmental bargaining (Moravcsik 1993). In fact, national politics is penetrated by European influences, through law, bureaucratic contacts, political exchange, the role of the Commission in agenda-setting and, to a greater or lesser extent according to the state, through regional influences. So we are witnessing both a Europeanisation and a regionalisation of national policy-making.

The aspiration to see regions recognised as a 'third level' (Bullman 1994; Jeffrey 1996) within the EU has been partially satisfied. Both the institutionalisation of the regions and the interest of the Commission in an active and interventionist role peaked around the early 1990s, and since then there has been consolidation. Regions have continued to seek a role in Europe, but access and influence are unevenly distributed. The regions that are best equipped institutionally and that have the best access to their national governments are advantaged in the new setting. They also tend to be the most economically and technologically advanced. EU initiatives through the structural funds have attempted to offset these advantages for resource-rich regions by concentrating resources on the poorer regions and encouraging partnership and administrative modernisation, especially in southern Europe. As we have seen, these efforts have been partially successful. Furthermore, the practice of multi-level policy-making seems now entrenched in European policy-making: the previously dyadic relationship between European institutions and national governments has been transformed into a three-way one – among regions, national states and European actors. Keeping the 'second' relationship going enables each party in the triad to retain a degree of autonomy (Ansell *et al.* 1997). Regions, even in southern Europe, are unlikely to be blocked from access by their national governments.

A Union of twenty-five members contains vastly more territorial diversity than that for which the regional instruments and policies were designed in the 1980s and 1990s. Terrritorial disparities will continue to be a major concern for Europe and regional policy, in one form or another, will be a major spending priority. It still has an economic rationale, in helping poorer regions contribute to European and national competitiveness, a social role as one of the few real measures of solidarity at the EU level, and a political one, in showing the potential losers that there is something for them in the European project. Pressures from stronger regions for constitutional recognition and greater involvement in European policy-making will also persist. So both weak and strong regions will continue to press on the EU policy agenda.

Note

1   These data are extracted from three consecutive party expert surveys on European integration conducted by Leonard Ray (1999), Gary Marks and Marco Steenbergen (http://
www.unc.edu/~gwmarks), and the 2002 Chapel Hill expert survey. For further information
on the latter, please contact hooghe@unc.edu.

References

Alesina, A. and Spolaore, E. (2003) *The Optimal Size of Nations* (Cambridge, MA: MIT Press).
Anderson, J. (1992) 'Sceptical Reflections on a Europe of the Regions: Britain, Germany and the
ERDF', *Journal of Public Policy* 10/4: 417–47.
Ansell, C., Parsons, C. and Darden, K. (1997) 'Dual Networks in European Regional Development
Policy', *Journal of Common Market Studies* 35: 347–75.
Armstrong, W. H. (1995) 'The Role and Evolution of European Community Regional Policy', in B.
Jones and M. Keating (eds), *The European Union and the Regions* (Oxford: Clarendon).
Balme, R. (1995) 'French Regionalization and European Integration: Territorial Adaptation and
Change in a Unitary State', in B. Jones and M. Keating (eds), *The European Union and the
Regions* (Oxford: Clarendon).
—— (ed.) (1996) *Les politiques du néo-régionalisme* (Paris: Economica).
Begg, I. and Mayes, D. (1993) 'Cohesion, Convergence and Economic and Monetary Union in
Europe', *Regional Studies* 27/2: 149–65.
Bullman, U. (ed.) (1994) *Die Politik der dritten Ebene* (Baden-Baden: NOMOS).
Burch, M. and Holliday, I. (1993) 'Institutional Emergence: The Case of the North West Region of
England', *Regional Politics and Policy* 3/2: 29–50.
Camagni, R. (1992) 'Development Scenarios and Policy Guidelines for the Lagging Regions in the
1990s', *Regional Studies* 26/4: 361–74.
Cardús, S. (1991) 'Identidad cultural, legitimidad politica e interés económico', in *Construir
Europa*. (Catalunya, Madrid: Encuentro).
Cheshire, P., Camagni, R., Gaudemar, J.-P. and Cuadrado Roura, J. (1991) '1957 to 1992: Moving
toward a Europe of Regions and Regional Policy', in L. Rodwin and H. Sazanami (eds),
Industrial Change and Regional Economic Transformation: The Experience of Western Europe
(London: HarperCollins).
Commission of the European Communities (1991) *Les Régions dans les Années 90. Quatrième rapport
périodique sur la situation et l'évolution socio-économique des régions de la Communauté*
(Luxemburg: Office for Official Publications of the European Communities).
—— (1996) *First Report on Economic and Social Cohesion 1996*, preliminary edn (Luxemburg:
Office for Official Publications of the European Communities).
—— (1999) *Sixth Periodic Report on the Social and Economic Situation and Development of the
Regions of the EU* (Brussels: Commission of the European Communities).
—— (2004) Proposal for a Council Regulation laying down general provisions on the European
Regional Development Fund, the European Social Fund and the Cohesion Fund.
Farrows, M. and McCarthy, R. (1997) 'Opinion Formulation and Impact in the Committee of the
Regions', *Regional and Federal Studies* 7/1: 23–49.
Giordano, B. (2004) 'The Future of EU Regional Policy after 2006?', *Regions: The Newsletter of the
Regional Studies Association* 252: 19–22.
Hooghe, L. (ed.) (1996) *Cohesion Policy and European Integration: Building Multi-level Governance*
(Oxford: Oxford University Press).
—— (1998) 'EU Cohesion Policy and Competing Models of European Capitalism', *Journal of
Common Market Studies* 36/4: 457–77.

Hooghe, L. and Keating, M. (1994) 'The Politics of European Union Regional Policy', *Journal of European Public Policy* 1/3: 367–93.

Hooghe, L. and Marks, G. (1999) 'The Making of a Polity: The Struggle Over European Integration', in H. Kitschelt, P. Lange, G. Marks and J. Stephens (eds), *Continuity and Change in Contemporary Capitalism* (Cambridge: Cambridge University Press).

—— (2001) *Multilevel Governance and European Integration* (Lanham, MD: Rowman & Littlefield).

Hughes, J., Sasse, G. and Gordon, C. (2003), 'EU Enlargement, Europeanisation and the Dynamics of Regionalism in the CEECs', in M. Keating and J. Hughes (eds), *The Regional Challenge in Central and Eastern Europe: Territorial Restructuring and European Integration* (Brussels: Presses interuniversitaires européennes/Peter Lang).

Jachtenfuchs, M. and Kohler-Koch, B. (1995) 'Regieren im dynamischen Mehrebenensystem', in M. Jachtenfuchs and B. Kohler-Koch (eds), *Europäische Integration* (Opladen: Leske & Budrich).

Jeffrey, C. (1996) *The Regional Dimension of the European Union: Towards a Third Level in Europe?* (London: Frank Cass).

Jones, B. and Keating, M. (eds) (1995) *The European Union and the Regions* (Oxford: Clarendon).

Keating, M. (1998) *The New Regionalism in Western Europe: Territorial Restructuring and Political Change* (Aldershot: Edward Elgar).

—— (2001), *Plurinational Democracy: Stateless Nations in a Post-Sovereignty Era* (Oxford: Oxford University Press).

—— (2003), 'Regionalization in Central and Eastern Europe: The Diffusion of a Western Model?', in M. Keating and J. Hughes (eds), *The Regional Challenge in Central and Eastern Europe. Territorial Restructuring and European Integration* (Brussels: Presses interuniversitaires européennes/Peter Lang).

Keating, M. and Jones, B. (eds) (1985) *Regions in the European Community* (Oxford: Clarendon).

Keeble, D., Offord, J. and Walker, S. (1988) *Peripheral Regions in a Community of Twelve Member States* (Luxembourg: Office of Publications of the European Communities).

Le Galès, P. and Lequesne, C. (eds) (1997) *Les paradoxes des régions en Europe* (Paris: Editions La Découverte).

Mackay, R. R. (1993) 'A Europe of the Regions: A Role for Non-market Forces?', *Regional Studies* 27/5: 419–31.

Marks, G. (1993) 'Structural Policy and Multi-level Governance in the European Community', in A. Cafruny and G. Rosenthal (eds), *The State of the European Community: The Maastricht Debates and Beyond* (Boulder: University of Colorado Press).

Marks, G. and Hooghe, L. (2000) 'Optimality and Authority: A Critique of Neo-Classical Theory', *Journal of Common Market Studies* 38/5: 795–816.

Marks, G., Hooghe, L. and Blank, K. (1996) 'European Integration since the 1980s: State-Centric versus Multi-Level Governance', *Journal of Common Market Studies* 34/4: 341–78.

Marks, G., Salk, J., Ray, L. and Nielsen, F. (1996) 'Conflict, Cracks and Conflicts: Regional Mobilization in the European Union', *Comparative Political Studies* 29/2: 164–92.

Marks, G., Haesly, R. and Mbaye, H. A. D. (2002) 'What Do Regional Offices Think They are Doing in Brussels?', *Regional and Federal Studies* 12/3: 1–23.

Midwinter, A., Keating, M. and Mitchell, J. (1991) *Politics and Public Policy in Scotland* (London: Macmillan).

Moravcsik, A. (1993) 'Preferences and Power in the European Community: A Liberal Intergovernmentalist Approach', *Journal of Common Market Studies* 31/4: 473–524.

Ohmae, Kenichi (1995) *The End of the Nation State: The Rise of Regional Economies* (New York: Free Press).

Petschen, S. (1993) *La Europa de las regiones* (Barcelona: Generalitat de Catalunya).

Ray, L. (1999) 'Measuring Party Orientation Towards European Integration: Results from an Expert Survey', *European Journal of Political Research* 36: 283–306.

Reese, N. and Holmes, M. (1995) 'Regions within a Region: The Paradox of the Republic of Ireland', in B. Jones and M. Keating (eds), *The European Union and the Regions* (Oxford: Clarendon).

Scharpf, F. (1994) 'Community and Autonomy: Multi-Level Policy-Making in the European Union', *Journal of European Public Policy* 1/2: 219–42.

—— (1999) *Governing in Europe: Effective and Democratic?* (Oxford: Oxford University Press).

Scott, A. (1998) *Regions and the World Economy: The Coming Shape of Global Production, Competition, and Political Order* (Oxford: Oxford University Press).

Steinle, W. J. (1992) 'Regional Competitiveness and the Single European Market', *Regional Studies* 26/4: 307–18.

Storper, M. (1997) *The Regional World: Territorial Development in a Global Economy* (New York and London: Guildford).

Trigilia, C. (1991), 'The Paradox of the Region: Economic Regulation and the Representation of Interests', trans. Carl Levy, *Economy and Society* 20/3: 306–27.

De Winter, L. and Cachafeiro, M. G.-R. (2002) 'European integration and Ethnoregionalist parties', *Party Politics* 8/4: 483–503.

De Winter, L. and Türsan, H. (eds) (1998) *Regionalist Parties in Western Europe* (New York: Routledge).

de Witte, B. (1992) 'Surviving in Babel? Language Rights and European Integration', *Israel Yearbook on Human Rights* 21: 103–26.

Yannopoulos, G. and Featherstone, K. (1995) 'The European Community and Greece: Integration and the Challenge to Centralism', in B. Jones and M. Keating (eds), *The European Union and the Regions* (Oxford: Clarendon).

Part IV

A SUPRANATIONAL STATE?

Chapter 14

The EU as an international actor

MICHAEL SMITH

Introduction

From the beginning, the European Communities and now the EU have had to exist in a changing international context; indeed, many treatments of the history of European integration place great weight on the international dimension of both the foundation and the development of the phenomenon (Story 1993; Wallace 1990; Pinder 1991a; Dinan 2004). The EU, as will be shown in more detail later in this chapter, is also a major presence in the contemporary global arena. It is thus not surprising that there should have been consistent and growing attention to the international 'credentials' of the EC and then the EU.

To state this position, though, is to beg a central question. Although the EU is a major component of the contemporary world arena, just what is its status, role and impact? At one end of the spectrum, there are those who can discern a progression in the EU towards full-fledged international 'actorness', comparable to that of the national states that comprise the major concentrations of power in world politics. But such views have to wrestle with the inconvenient fact that the EU is not a 'state' in the accepted international meaning of the term, although it undoubtedly demonstrates some 'statelike' features. Notwithstanding its ability to act in the economic and diplomatic fields, the EU has been slow to develop a coherent security policy or even the beginnings of a European-level defence policy (Hill 1990, 1993, 1995; M. Smith 1994, 2005; Cameron 1999; Gnesotto 2004; Howorth 2005).

Thwarted in the search for an EU version of statehood, others have attempted to define the EU as a growing and increasingly structured 'presence' in the international arena, with its own forms of international behaviour and influence, and most significantly an important place in the foreign policies of other international actors, whether they be states or non-state groupings (Allen and Smith 1990, 1998). Thus, the EU cannot be avoided by national foreign policy-makers, nor can it be bypassed by international organisations such as the United Nations. This approach has its undoubted advantages, not least that of finessing the issue of statehood, but it also begs major questions. Perhaps most importantly, it raises the issue of relations between the EU's 'presence' and the persistence of the essentially national powers of the EU's member states themselves (Hill 1995; Manners and Whitman 2000).

Whatever the position taken on the EU's claims to 'actorness' or 'presence' in the international arena, the analyst must take into account two crucial aspects of the EU's international existence. First, the EU is not simply an 'actor' or a 'presence' but also a *process*: a set of complex institutions, roles and rules which structure the activities of the EU itself and those of other internationally significant groupings with which it comes into contact. Second, the EU as 'actor', 'presence' and process exists today in a world which has *changed* greatly, not to say fundamentally, since the foundation of the ECSC, the Treaty of Rome or even the Single European Act in the mid-1980s.

Since the late 1990s, it might be argued, a number of these pressures have converged to provide a new impetus for the development of the EU's international 'actorness'. Whilst the Treaty of Amsterdam (1997) was widely perceived to have fallen short of its aims in a number of areas, it did make some significant revisions to the CFSP. It gave the European Council responsibility for the framing of 'common strategies' to guide foreign ministers; it regularised the budgetary situation of CFSP; it established a Policy Planning Unit to provide the beginnings of an intelligence and planning capability; and it provided for the appointment of a 'high representative' to act as the figurehead for CFSP. These detailed changes were given new focus by the emergence during 1998 and 1999 of important new initiatives designed to formalise a 'defence policy' element in the CFSP, and by the drive by the British and French governments in particular to add strength to the EU's security and defence activities. By the time of the Treaty of Nice in 2000, the 'muscles' of an emerging EU defence policy were more clearly defined, and by 2003–4 these were employed in the EU's first coordinated military operations. At the same time, the production of the Constitutional Treaty from 2002 onwards led to further formalisation of both the foreign and the defence policy structures of the Union. The question remained, however, how far these initiatives would go and how much they would change the EU's operations in specific international arenas, in particular when the interests of the United States were engaged or when the coercive as opposed to persuasive use of military assets was at issue (Cameron 1999, chapters 8–9; Everts *et al*. 2004; Howorth 2000, 2005).

Two central questions thus act as the focus for this chapter. First, what is the evidence that the EU is moving towards full-fledged 'actorness' in the international arena, adding new focus and impact to its established presence and processes? Second, what role does the EU play in the new Europe and the new world of the twenty-first century, and how does that role reflect the unique status of the EU? On the basis of the discussion of these two areas, the chapter also attempts to project the possible future development of the EU's international role.

The structure of the chapter reflects the agenda set out above. First, it deals with the foundations, both institutional and political, of the EU's international role and impact. Second, it assesses the pattern of issues, interactions and relationships that constitute the substance of the EU's international life; and finally, it evaluates the models available to describe and explain the EU's international policy-making. The institutional focus is on developments up to and including the Treaty of Nice. In its conclusions, however, the chapter makes reference to the changes in international policy-making proposed in the Constitutional Treaty of 2004; although the prospects for ratification of the Constitutional Treaty at the time of writing this chapter were dramatically reduced by the French and Dutch 'noes' in their May 2005 referenda, the external policy proposals nonetheless provide an important guide to where future policies might head.

The foundations

As already noted, the EU derives much of its international role and impact from the foundations on which it is built. Perhaps the most obvious, yet also problematical of these foundations, is the EU's international 'weight'. In particular, the fact that the EU accounts for a large proportion of the world's economic activity, and is the world's champion trader, creates an inevitable focus on the extent to which and the ways in which the weight is translated into international outcomes. The difficulty, as Chris Hill has ably pointed out, is that there is a 'capability-expectations gap': to put it bluntly, the EU does not deliver consistently on the raw material given to it by the economic prosperity and muscle of the system it has developed. By implication, the conversion of muscle into meaningful action is deficient (Hill 1993, 1998). This theme will be developed further later in the chapter, but at this stage it leads directly into a discussion of the institutions and the politics of EU external policy-making.

The EU's international role rests explicitly on the constitutional base established in the treaties, but that base is neither comprehensive nor unambiguous. It is least unambiguous in the area of the Common Commercial Policy and the EU's international trade policies. Article 113 of the Treaty of Rome (now article 133 in the Consolidated Treaties) gave the European Economic Community the responsibility for conducting the trade relations of the Community with the rest of the world, and from it has grown a complex web of both institutions and relationships. In important ways, the CCP was inevitable given the establishment of the customs union and the Common External Tariff; the need to manage the external trade relations of the Community, and to conduct relations with international partners, was a logical outcome of the establishment of the customs union, and the acquisition of international competence was one of the first items on the Commission's agenda (M. Smith 2005).

During the 1950s, 1960s and 1970s, therefore, the EEC developed a complicated network of international agreements, and came to play an important role in the development of the world trading system. The Commission was recognised as the voice of the EEC in the conduct of international trade negotiations, and the enlargement of the Community during the 1970s further increased the range and scope of its international economic involvement. Another impact of the enlargement was the need to develop and implement a more comprehensive Community policy on international development assistance, and this led to the so-called Lomé system based on the Convention signed in 1975 and then later revisions. But this was a partial international role at best: the Community and the Commission had competence in trade negotiations, but even in this area there was a division of powers between the Commission and the Council of Ministers; when the Commission negotiated on international trade, it was on the basis of a mandate from the Council and with the close attention of what became known as the '113 Committee' of national trade officials. In the area of development policy there was even more of a 'mixed' system in which the views and resources of member states remained central. Although other aspects of international economic relations such as monetary policy and investment were in many respects crucial to the development of the Community, they were not the subject of Community-level policy-making. Even the establishment of the European Monetary System in the late 1970s did not extend Community competence fully into this area, since the system was effectively operated by the central banks of the member states (Tsoukalis 1997).

If the initial competence of the Community was limited in the field of international economic policy, it was almost non-existent in the field of what some would call 'real' foreign policy: the 'high politics' of diplomacy, defence and security. What emerged in this area during the 1970s was not a Community policy but a series of mechanisms through which the national foreign policies of the EC's members could be more closely coordinated. By the end of the 1970s, this had evolved into the framework known as European Political Cooperation (EPC), which effectively acted as a procedural device for the management of common interests. But the member states had not yielded any of their formal freedom of action to the Community, and they retained the right to pursue purely national policies at the same time as participating in the EPC mechanism (Allen et al. 1982; Hill 1983).

This meant that by the early 1980s, there was only a patchy and partial basis for the development of the EC's international role. There were areas of intense and continuous activity, for example in the conduct of trade policy and the implementation of the

Lomé Conventions; there were areas of intense but temporary activity, such as those centred on the energy crises of the 1970s or the issue of economic sanctions as Soviet–American tensions waxed and waned; but in many areas including the politics of national security, the national policy mechanisms of EC members remained almost untouched.

During the 1980s, however, there were important changes both in the international conditions and in the institutional base for EC international policy-making. At the international level, it became apparent more and more that the separation of 'economic' and 'political' or 'security' issues was artificial. Indeed, many of the most pressing international problems were intractable precisely because of the ways in which the economic, the political and the security elements were intertwined and interdependent. Not only this, but in the world political economy itself there was an increasing awareness of the issues arising from technological change and shifts in competitive advantage (Smith and Woolcock 1993; Stubbs and Underhill 2005).

At the Community level, one response to the latter development was the Single Market Programme. It is possible to see the Commission White Paper of 1985 and the subsequent legislative programme simply as a process dealing with the internal economic activity of the EC, but it was apparent to many from the outset that this was also a programme designed to enhance the international presence and impact of the EC and its economic groupings. This implied a major increase in the international activity of the Community, not only to ensure that the single market was effectively integrated with the international economic framework but also to defuse the often suspicious reactions of economic partners and rivals such as the United States or Japan (Redmond 1992; Hufbauer 1990; Ishikawa 1989; Woolcock and Hodges 1996; Smith and Woolcock 1993; Hocking and Smith 1997).

Alongside this, though, went crucial developments in the area of 'high politics', which gave the Community and its members both the incentive and some of the instruments to develop policy in new domains. One such development, already noted, was the linkage between economic and security aims in the world arena, at its most obvious in the use of economic sanctions against (for example) the Iranians, the USSR and South Africa. In these cases, however much the member states might have wished to act on a national basis, they could not do so effectively because of the concentration of commercial policy powers at the Community level (Pijpers et al. 1988; Allen and Pijpers 1984; Nuttall 1992).

Another set of significant international policy developments arose from the further evolution of EPC. During the 1980s, a process which remained resolutely intergovernmental was given further definition and a more formal institutional framework. The Single European Act for the first time created a treaty base – albeit an explicitly intergovernmental one – for the EPC mechanisms. It also formalised the 'troika' through which successive Council presidencies ensured continuity, and it established a permanent though small EPC secretariat. It even went so far as to introduce the word 'security' into the EPC framework, although there was a firm restriction to the 'political aspects' of security issues (Pijpers et al. 1988; Nuttall 1992).

By the late 1980s, then, the framework for EC international policy consisted effectively of two strands: the Community strand as applied through the CCP and its instruments (with the additional but related dimension of development policy), which was given added force by the external impact of the Single Market; and the intergovernmental strand as exemplified in Title III of the SEA and the EPC mechanisms. At the same time, there was an increasing consciousness of the artificiality of distinctions between 'high' and 'low' politics, or between economics and security. The lesson was borne in with unprecedented force by the events of 1989 in Europe, with the fall of the Berlin Wall and the subsequent more or less peaceful revolutions in central and Eastern European countries (Wallace 1990; Pinder 1991b; Allen and Smith 1991–92).

It was in this context that the Maastricht Treaty on European Union attacked the issues of the 'second pillar' or foreign and security policy. Indeed, it was because of this context that the EC's members felt the need to go beyond the limits of intergovernmental cooperation so far established and to develop new mechanisms for foreign policy coordination. Whilst the external commercial policy powers of the Community were hardly altered by the TEU, the provisions on a common foreign and security policy (CFSP) in the treaty broke new ground both in terms of substance and in terms of the organisational framework. The treaty declared the members' determination to establish a common foreign and security policy, which would lead in time to a common defence policy and even to a common defence (by implication, a military community to stand alongside the economic one in the framework of the Union). The existing Western European Union was defined as the defence arm of the Union, with provision for a growing together of the two organisations and a definitive review of their relations in the 1996 IGC (Norgaard et al. 1993; Rummel 1992; Forster and Wallace 1996; Regelsberger et al. 1997).

To support this set of aims and intentions, the TEU established new procedures. The Commission was given a (non-exclusive) right of initiative in the CFSP field, whilst the intergovernmental character of the framework was preserved by the guiding role of the European Council and the continued location of the primary operational responsibilities with the Council of Ministers. For the first time, voting procedures including majority voting were introduced to the domain of foreign policy, although there were strong safeguards for national positions. The common diplomatic positions generated by the EPC mechanism were supplemented by potential 'joint actions' within agreed limits, raising a number of issues about resourcing and the role of the Commission in implementing foreign policy decisions (Norgaard et al. 1993; Rummel 1992; Laursen and Vanhoonacker 1992; Regelsberger et al. 1997; Cameron 1999, chapters 2–4).

As noted earlier in the chapter, the Treaty of Amsterdam in many ways continued the processes set in motion by the TEU. Indeed, since the TEU only entered into force in late 1993, the CFSP provisions had had little time to develop before they were once again subject to review. In addition to the procedural innovations summarised earlier – 'common strategies', the budgetary provisions, the Planning Unit and the 'high representative' – Amsterdam also introduced general provisions for 'flexibility', and for an extension of Qualified Majority Voting (QMV), whereby those member states wishing to move more rapidly, or to take more muscular action, might hope not to be impeded by the others. The Treaty also introduced into the CFSP the so-called 'Petersberg tasks' relating to humanitarian intervention and peace-keeping activities, and foreshadowed the eventual absorption of the WEU into the Union. These measures were not insignificant; indeed, they could form a basis for creative exploitation of the potential in the CFSP, as long as the political will was to be found. But it is open to question whether in themselves they resolved the 'unstable compromise' hammered together at Maastricht in 1991 (Forster and Wallace 1996; Cameron 1999, chapter 5).

The Treaty of Nice in 2000 did little to alter the detailed provisions for CFSP, but as noted earlier it reflected in the provisions on Common Security and Defence Policy

(CSDP) the major steps undertaken since the Franco-British St Malo summit of 1998. As a result, the EU's institutional structure by 2004 showed significant changes with the introduction of what some described as a 'fourth pillar' dealing with the military aspects of the Union's external policies. The Western European Union, a previously independent European security organisation, had been effectively absorbed into the Union, and military uniforms were an increasingly salient feature of everyday life in the Brussels administration (Howorth 2000, 2005).

Later parts of the chapter will deal with the practical impact of these CFSP and CSDP provisions, but at this stage a review of the position reached in the TEU (and as modified at Amsterdam and Nice) is in order. Three interim conclusions are apparent. In the first place, the longstanding foundations of the EC's external policy powers in the field of trade and related areas continued to flourish, reinforced by the impact of the single market programme and the intensification of international economic interdependence. Second, the 'civilian power' of the Community had been supplemented through intergovernmental channels by the increasingly 'high politics' of EPC, then the CFSP and finally the CSDP. Not only this, but in a number of cases it had been demonstrated that the Community and its powers were essential to the successful pursuit of diplomatic objectives in the area of 'high politics'.

Finally, although this may appear to have been an inexorable advance towards the construction of an integrated Union foreign policy, and thus the achievement of full international 'actorness' on the part of the Union, there were a number of reasons to be cautious in making such judgements. The CFSP and CSDP remained intergovernmental, albeit much more effectively institutionalised than the original EPC framework. Member states might recognise the logic of fuller EU responsibilities for foreign policy, but certainly in the case of the major members they would be reluctant to give up the core elements of sovereignty and national security. And perhaps above all, the fluid and potentially dangerous situation in the 'new Europe' and the broader 'new world disorder' was always capable of placing severe strains on the coordination mechanisms available even under the TEU, Amsterdam and Nice. With this, it is appropriate to turn to the substance of EU international activities.

The substance of policy

In order to arrive at a more precise description of the EU's international connections, and to explore the ways in which they affect policy-making, this part of the chapter examines four aspects of the problem. First, it evaluates the *agendas* on which the EU's international activities are focused. Second, it identifies the *arenas* within which the EU is involved. Third, it looks at the *relationships* that are central to the EU's international existence. Finally, it reviews the *levels* at which EU actions are shaped and take place, and provides some brief examples of the implications of multi-level policy-making. Whilst these four aspects are separated here for analytical purposes, in reality they are often closely – indeed, inextricably – linked. The final section of the chapter will attempt to bring them together in an examination of modes of EU policy-making.

Agendas

The longest established agenda for action at the European level is that of trade and commercial relations, including development policies. As the EU has evolved, it has spawned an extensive set of international trade and aid agreements, which some have described as a 'pyramid of privilege'. The extent and complexity of this network reflect the centrality of the trade and aid agenda to the EU; after all, this was the original raison d'etre of the EEC, and the focus of the earliest common policy efforts of the Community in the international field. Thus today, the Union finds itself deeply and continuously engaged in international trade negotiations, either on a bilateral basis, or on an inter-regional basis, or in the context of the World Trade Organization. At the same time, it deals with less developed countries, particularly those of the African, Caribbean and Pacific grouping (ACP) in the framework of the Cotonou Agreement, which replaced the series of Lomé Conventions in 2000. During the 1990s and early 2000s, a novel trade and aid agenda emerged, centred on the development and stabilisation needs of what came to be called the enlarged EU's 'neighbourhood', including the former Soviet bloc and the Mediterranean (Edwards and Regelsberger 1990; Hine 1985; Pinder 1991b; Piening 1997; Dent 1997; Dannreuther 2004).

Trade, aid and commercial agreements are thus at the core of the EU's international agenda. As the growth of international interdependence and interpenetration has proceeded since the 1980s, this traditional focus has been joined by another: the links between markets and regulatory structures within and outside the EU. The Single Market Programme was launched in a different world from that of the Treaty of Rome or the CAP – a world in which the seemingly 'domestic' concerns of market regulation, standards-setting and competition policies were becoming the stuff of international politics through processes loosely termed 'globalisation'. As a result, the EC and then the EU have had to develop new structures and procedures to deal with such matters as public procurement, mergers and acquisitions, market access and environmental regulation at the international level (Woolcock 1992; Harrison 1994; Woolcock and Hodges 1996; Hocking and Smith 1997; M. Smith 1999; Young 2002).

The agenda for diplomacy, security and defence was for a long time separated from the more central economic and commercial EU agendas, but as time has gone on it has become increasingly difficult to maintain the distance between matters of economic welfare and matters of national or European security. The intertwining of these areas became especially apparent in the aftermath of the collapse of the USSR; not only had the geopolitical division of Europe disappeared, but so also had the functional division in the EU between civilian and security agendas (Laffan *et al*. 2000, chapter 3). No clearer example of this new logic could be found than in the events and processes surrounding the development of the 'European defence identity' after 1998. Whilst the formal institutionalisation process revolved around successive political 'summits', first between the British and the French at St Malo in the autumn of 1998, then in the European Councils of Cologne and Helsinki during 1999 and in the intergovernmental conference leading up to the Treaty of Nice, there was also a move during the same period to set up a European Aerospace and Defence corporation, to express the growing feeling that the EU's defence industries should consolidate and integrate. By 2004, there were active moves towards the establishment of a European arms procurement agency – the potential 'customer' for the products of a consolidated Union defence industrial complex (Howorth 2000, 2005).

Arenas

For many years, from the 1960s to the late 1980s, the EC's dominant arena of action, its main reference point for any sort of international identity, was the western system and in particular the economic structure built around the North Atlantic area (Allen and Smith 1991–2; Smith and Woolcock 1993; Story 1993). Just as the policy agenda for the EU has been transformed since the 1980s, so has the arena for its international actions. Whilst the long established institutional arrangements have not disappeared, they are implanted in a radically changed context, and have been joined by a number of novel arrangements reflecting the needs of the post-Cold War world. Many of these new arrangements reflect the linkages between agendas already noted: for example, the influence of the Organisation on Security and Cooperation in Europe with its focus on non-military as well as military aspects of security, or the role of the European Bank for Reconstruction and Development in the political and economic stabilisation of the 'new Europe'. The EU finds itself not only in a transformed world arena, but also in a newly-institutionalised and rapidly developing European order, and this is a challenge to international action (Allen and Smith 1991–2; Smith and Woolcock 1993; Carlsnaes and Smith 1994; Laffan *et al.* 2000; K. Smith 2003, 2005).

The challenge is complicated further by two sets of contradictions, which surround and penetrate the arenas for EU action. First, there is the coexistence of new and developing institutions with persistent disorder and conflict. This contradiction was first clearly seen in the conflicts that erupted in the former Yugoslavia during the 1990s. Although there was no shortage of institutions with roles and responsibilities, one of which was the EU itself, they were challenged and often defeated by the mercurial and combustible array of contending forces with an interest in chaos and destruction.

An arguably even more dramatic illustration of this problem came in the wake of the attack on the World Trade Center and the Pentagon in the USA on 11 September 2001. In many ways, this highlighted the fact that the EU had been insulated for a generation from the impact of global disorder; after '9/11', the intimate linkages between the EU's roles in the European order and the broader global disorder posed severe problems of management at the European level, spanning areas such as justice and home affairs, the developing European security and defence institutions and the engagement of NATO and other bodies in the 'war on terror'. The contradictions and tensions were underlined further by the US-led attack on Iraq in 2003, where both the European and many global institutions proved incapable of meeting the challenges (Peterson and Pollack 2003).

A second set of contradictions surrounds the EU's role in the world political economy, where the coexisting forces of globalisation and regionalisation have given rise to major policy dilemmas and problems of management. The result of these contradictions is a complex, multilayered and often apparently uncontrollable set of policy arenas, in which the EU is not the only body subject to challenge (Laffan *et al.* 2000, chapters 3–4). On issues such as the management of the global environment, the EU has solid credentials arising from its internal regulatory processes, but finds itself engaged in a global arena where there is a constant and ever more politicised tension between management through national authorities, regional bodies and multilateral or global institutions. Often also, these fluctuating tensions bring to the fore EU relationships with major trading and political partners.

Relationships

Certain relationships are central to the international policies of the EU, demanding continuous management and producing a series of interrelated challenges and opportunities. The most intense, highly developed and longest established is that with the USA. Together, the EU and the USA account for nearly half of the world economy, and their relationship is both extensive and rich. It is one from which both parties benefit considerably, and in which the balance of economic advantage is relatively even. Not only this, but the EU/US relationship is implanted in the broader security relationship expressed through NATO and other institutions (Smith and Woolcock 1993; Peterson 1996; Featherstone and Ginsberg 1996; Frellesen and Ginsberg 1994; Guay 1999; Pollack and Shaffer 2001).

Given the intensity of the interdependence between the two partners, it is not at all surprising that there will be a continuous flow of disputes between them, particularly in areas of important trade or financial competition. Thus the relationship in the 1990s and early 2000s was beset by disputes over agricultural trade, over the openness of the Single Market to US financial and other institutions, and over politically symbolic high-technology projects such as the European Airbus. Not only this but an emerging new agenda of disputes over such areas as genetically modified foods, competition policy and taxation regimes has created a new set of challenges in the new millennium. The point is that, whilst challenging, such issues are dealt with on the whole in the cooperative mode, with the intention of resolving differences and building new procedures. This aim was first expressed in the Transatlantic Declaration of November 1990, which spawned a set of specialist working groups and other forms of cooperation on significant issues (Frellesen and Ginsberg 1994). It was followed in the mid- and late 1990s by the New Transatlantic Agenda of 1995 and the Transatlantic Economic Partnership of 1998 (M. Smith 1998a; Pollack and Shaffer 2001).

The end of the Cold War put a new complexion on important aspects of EU/US relations. On the one hand, it found the EU anxious to develop new international roles in the development of the 'new Europe', often in areas where the US found it difficult to respond. On the other, it became apparent that the role of the EU in high politics and security had severe limitations; there were still areas in which and ways in which only the US had the capacity to act, particularly where this implied the rapid mobilisation of major military assets (as in former Yugoslavia and more recently in Afghanistan and Iraq). Although the Maastricht agreements established the CFSP, and recognised the growing linkage between the EU and the Western European Union in the evolution of security policy, this did not and could not make it the equal of the USA in theatres of active military conflict (Smith and Woolcock 1994; Allen and Smith 1998; Everts *et al.* 2004). As noted earlier in the chapter, from 1998 onwards there were apparently fundamental shifts in the EU's ability to muster a 'hard security' capability, with plans to set up a 60,000-strong EU Rapid Deployment Force and to enter actively into peace-keeping and peace-building operations. Significantly, the US government expressed reservations both about the feasibility and the appropriateness of this enterprise, reservations which for many were borne out by experience first in Kosovo during 1999 and later in the 'war on terror' and the attack on Iraq. In the first of these, NATO proved the only viable means of collective action, whilst in the second and third cases, the EU was to all intents and purposes bypassed both by the USA and by key EU member states such as the UK.

Notwithstanding the later evidence of the EU's capacity to manage or to contribute to the post-conflict stabilisation processes in Kosovo and Afghanistan, the record in such EU–US collisions was not a happy one (Peterson and Pollack 2003).

The relationship between the EU and the USA has thus been and will continue to be a central policy concern. Less comprehensive, but no less sensitive at times, has been the relationship with Japan, and alongside it those with China and the Asia-Pacific region. In the case of Japan, the texture of the relationship is primarily that of economic interdependence and economic competition, with the Japanese enjoying a considerable credit balance in the areas of trade and financial services. Thus, the EU has found itself dealing with the Japanese on a succession of more or less serious trade disputes, most notably in the areas of automobiles and consumer electronics. Although the early 1990s produced an EU/Japan Declaration modelled after the Transatlantic Declaration, the effective scope of collaboration between the two partners remained significantly less ambitious and intensive. Partly this is a reflection of history, partly it reflects the relative distance and lack of complementarity between the two entities; nonetheless, there is a growing need to organise the relations between the two (Gilson 2000).

With China, the EU during the 1990s and early 2000s experienced a rapidly growing relationship, but one bedevilled by trade disputes as the Chinese expanded their overseas trade, and by lingering tensions over human rights. The trajectory of the EU–China relationship, though, means that it has effectively supplanted that with Japan as the second most salient relationship in the EU's external relations, creating new institutional contacts such as those in the WTO but also creating a series of new bilateral economic challenges. At the same time, the EU has made significant efforts to establish inter-regional contacts with the countries of Southeast Asia, through agreements with the members of the Association of Southeast Asian Nations (ASEAN), and to bring together all of its Asia-Pacific partners in the Asia–Europe Meetings (ASEM), the first of which was held in 1996 (Smith 1998b; Maull *et al.* 1998; Dent 1999; Wiessala 2002). Parallel efforts have been made to increase and to institutionalise contacts with Latin America and Africa through a series of inter-regional conferences and networks aimed at promoting both economic transactions and political dialogue.

In respect of the 'new Europe', there have been two components to the EU's international activity since the early 1990s. On the one hand there was the need during the early 1990s to incorporate three new members – Finland, Sweden and Austria (see chapter 13). On the other hand, there was the establishment and intensification of relations with the countries of the former Soviet bloc, either on the basis of 'arm's length' relationships based on trade and assistance or (as in the case of the 'Visegrad countries') on the basis of increasingly close linkages and eventual membership of the Union itself (Pinder 1991b; Carlsnaes and Smith 1994; H. Wallace 1991; K. Smith 1999; Henderson 1999). The 'eastern enlargement' that took place during 2004, with the prospect of further new entrants as early as 2007, led to a further reorientation of both the economic and the political-security aspects of EU external policies, particularly as a result of the new 'geopolitics' and 'geoeconomics' implied by a shift to the east and to a common border with the former Soviet Union. Coupled with the continuing attention to the Mediterranean and the 'south', this was the key stimulus to the development of a new 'neighbourhood' policy during 2002–4 aimed at stabilising and managing the new neighbours who had no prospect of early membership in the Union – or in some cases, no realistic prospect at all (Dannreuther 2004).

For the EU's international activities and policies, the overall impact of these changes in agendas, arenas and relationships has been profound. Whilst the Cold War years were far from simple, they at least made it possible for EC leaders to focus on 'civilian' activities and to operate within a well-defined set of institutional and political arrangements. A combination of factors ranging from the Single Market Programme through the collapse of the USSR to the transformation of the global economy and the 'war on terror' has made redundant a number of the longstanding assumptions on which the EC's international role was founded. This has meant a series of unavoidable challenges both for EU policy-makers and for the EU's institutions (W. Wallace 1990; Keohane *et al.*1993; Story 1993; Laffan *et al.* 2000; Hill and Smith 2005).

Levels

Not the least of these challenges has been that of dealing with the implications of multi-level politics and diplomacy. The EU has found in a number of contexts that it has to reconcile its own – often limited – capacity to act with the needs and demands of international institutions, major political and trading partners, and not least its own member states and their governments. Two examples will suffice to demonstrate this set of inter-locking dilemmas.

First, in the area of traditional EC/EU action, there is the experience of the negotiations in the World Trade Organization, centred on the attempt to conclude the so-called Doha Development Round, which began in 2002 and continued at the time of writing of this chapter. Over an extended period, the EU had to project its trade policy competence into new areas, meeting competition and conflicting demands from the USA, developing countries and a range of agricultural interests. At the same time, the continued deepening of the Single Market strengthened key areas of EU international activity such as competition policy, radically changing and extending the perception of the EC as an international economic force. Not only this, but the divergent interests of EC members were underlined by the demands of the international negotiation process, and fed back into it often with widespread and potentially damaging implications (M. Smith 1999; Young 2002; de Burca and Scott 2002). Whilst this can be seen as a challenge mainly for policy-makers at the EU level, it is also a key example in the growth and problems of 'global governance' in the economic sphere.

A second and very different example is provided by the EU's involvement in the conflicts in former Yugoslavia – from the independence of Croatia and Slovenia in 1991, through the Bosnian conflict of 1992–5 to the Kosovo crisis of 1999. In this most dangerous series of post-Cold War European conflicts, the assumption at the outset was that the EU would have a special role and responsibility, not least because the USA proved unwilling to become directly engaged. A number of – often tragic – dilemmas ensued for the EU and its members. First, there was the problem of the recognition of Slovenia, Croatia and finally Bosnia-Herzegovina, in which the tensions between EU members were apparent throughout. Second, there was the problem of dealing with the escalation of the conflict, particularly in Bosnia – a conflict that exposed to the full the lack of military muscle behind the EU's position, and the overlapping concerns and competences of the UN, the EU and other organisations such as the CSCE. Third, there was the issue of stabilisation and the creation of safe areas for the ravaged population of Bosnia – a task to which the EU was in many respects peripheral, and in which the interaction of the UN and NATO came to play a central part. Whilst playing a dogged and persistent diplomatic role, backed up by economic sanctions, the EU inevitably found it difficult if not impossible to go beyond exhortation and indirect pressure (Nuttall 1994; Zucconi 1996). By the time the Kosovo crisis became acute in 1999, expectations of EU action were understandably modest, and indeed, the EU itself played no significant role in the military campaign. On the other hand, the Union was able to take a positive lead in post-war reconstruction, and mounted an important long-term initiative in the shape of the Stability Pact for the Balkans, which coupled short-term stabilisation measures with the long-term prospect of EU membership for some if not all of the region's regimes.

A third and in some respects even more challenging set of issues for the EU arose out of the 'war on terror' after the events of 11 September 2001, and the subsequent attack on Iraq. As noted earlier, this was a major challenge for the EU in terms of its policy competence, but it was also a challenge at a host of interrelated levels of policy and action. Within the EU there was the need to manage the impact of the 'war on terror' on policy areas as diverse as transportation and justice and home affairs; this intersected with the need to manage relationships between member states, which were often at odds, to manage transatlantic relations, to operate within the United Nations and other global institutions, and to link these activities with others in policy areas ranging from trade to military security and defence (Peterson and Pollack 2003).

The conclusion here is not that the EU succeeded or failed in either the GATT/WTO context or former Yugoslavia, or in the 'war on terror' and Iraq. The point is to show the ways in which since the early 1990s, the EU has been faced with profoundly challenging tasks in the international field. The evolution both of the world economy and of the post-Cold War international order created opportunities for a more expansive and ambitious EU role, but it also raised questions about the extent to which the EU policy process was capable of defining and pursuing appropriate and effective international action, and about the risks that were run in so doing (Allen and Smith 1991–2, 1998). Those questions are the starting point for the next section.

Modes of international policy-making in the EU

From the preceding discussion, it should be clear that the EU has important roles to play in the contemporary international arena. Chris Hill (1993, 1998) has identified both a number of functions the EC and the EU have played in the international system up to the late 1990s and a number of potential future roles or functions. In the past, the EC performed the roles of regional stabiliser in Western Europe; co-manager of world trade; a principal voice for the developed world in relations with the less developed countries; and provider of a second western voice in international diplomacy. For the future, Hill discerned in 1998 a number of conceivable roles: a replacement for the USSR in the global balance of power; a regional pacifier; a global intervenor; a mediator of conflicts; a bridge between the rich and the poor; and a joint supervisor of the world economy. But to list these past and possible future roles is to identify a central problem, which Hill has encapsulated in the notion of the 'capability-expectations gap' (see above): to put it simply, the EU can seem a desirable or logical actor in many international contexts, but this tells us nothing about its prospects of influence or effectiveness.

In this part of the chapter, it is suggested that one crucial element in the resolution of this problem is the study of *modes of EU international policy-making*. From the evidence produced so far, three such modes of policy can be identified and will be examined here (see White 2001 for a related classification):

- First, there is what can be termed *Community policy-making*: the development of the instruments and processes typical of the European Community and of its role in the world political economy.
- Second, there is what can be described as *Union policy-making*: the policy processes generated by the interaction of member governments and European institutions in the context of the Treaties and their practical application.
- Finally, there is the style of policy which can best be described as *negotiated order*: the response of both Community and Union to the multilayered political and economic environment in which they are implanted, and the outcome of the complex exchange relationships in which the member states and other actors are involved.

All three of these policy modes are affected and focused by a number of key dilemmas and assumptions, which have been ably evaluated by Hill and other analysts. They have to cope with the problem of *competence and consistency* within the EU, and the matching of institutional means to appropriate and agreed purposes. They must deal with the *intersection of economic, political and security issues* in the contemporary international arena. They confront the test of *multilayered policy-making and a multiplicity of policy actors* which is characteristic of the contemporary European and international milieu. And finally, they face the need to account for the *proliferation of institutions and instruments* which is equally central to the management of international policies in the new millennium.

Community policy-making

The longest established and most highly developed form of EU policy process in the international sphere is that of *Community policy-making*. This is the external policy mode encapsulated in the Common Commercial Policy and other parts of the Treaty of Rome dealing with the negotiation and conclusion of international agreements. The key elements of this policy mode are thus the concept of Community competence expressed through the Commission, and the development of policy instruments at the European level. They reach their highest point of development in the Community's role with respect to the GATT and the WTO, and in the use of policy instruments such as anti-dumping regulations. More recently, they have been extended into areas such as the international regulation of competition and the international coordination of policies in such areas as standards setting or public procurement; less certainly, they have also been extended into more contested areas such as international regulation of air transport and the environment. In many ways, as it can be seen from these examples, the policy style is an external expression of internal Community powers and concerns. As such, it forms the core of the Community's claims to international 'actorness'.

It might be thought that in this policy mode, the development of internal Community competence would inexorably be reflected in the extension of its exclusive international competence. In fact, and significantly for those who see the EU as an international actor in the making, there are distinct variations both in the coverage of the process and in the extent to which it can be halted or reversed. An example will illustrate the point. The negotiation and conclusion of international agreements by the Community through the Commission remains crucially dependent on agreement between the member states in the Council of Ministers. For GATT/WTO negotiations, they give the mandate to the Commission and it is they who finally conclude the agreements after the involvement of the European Parliament and the Commission. In the early 1990s, the Court of Justice concluded that even the trade policy powers of the Community exercised through the Commission were limited. To be specific, areas of trade negotiation going beyond traditional trade in goods were the joint responsibility of the Community and the member states (so-called 'mixed agreements'). The Court's opinion, delivered in November 1994, clearly implied a set of boundaries to the Common Commercial Policy which had not been suspected previously, and which led to a series of tensions in the policy-making process during the later 1990s (Smith and Woolcock 1999; Meunier and Nicolaidis 1999). These tensions were effectively resolved by the time the treaty of Nice was agreed in 2000, but it can be seen that as the internationalisation of successive areas of economic and related activities take place, there can still be 'boundary problems' raising the question of EU competence.

Union policy-making

Community policy-making is thus a crucial but incomplete model for the conduct of the EU's international business. Alongside it there has developed what is termed here *Union policy-making*. The keynote of this mode of policy-making is the intensive and continuous coordination of national policies, rather than the application of agreed common policies. Central to its development is the evolution of EPC and then the establishment of the CFSP and eventually the CSDP, but these are not the only examples. In this policy mode, the Commission is not the exclusive bearer of the Community mandate: rather, it is fully associated with the process and a vital source of information, advice and initiatives alongside increasingly 'Europeanised' national governments.

It is clear that this mode of international policy-making falls close to the intergovernmental mode of general EU policy-making. But there are important, not to say crucial, differences. In particular, the role of the Commission as an active and continuous participant, and a vital facilitator of action, is distinctive; indeed, in some areas such as the imposition of sanctions or the provision of humanitarian or technical assistance, the Commission and the Community can be the only possible implementers of policy.

One dramatic example of this came in the Bosnian conflict, where during 1994 the EU installed an administrator to run the city of Mostar. This 'pro-consul' had wide-ranging powers, including that of derogating from the Bosnian Constitution. Whilst the administrator was put in place through the CFSP, the infrastructure for the office and the financial resources were to an important extent provided through the Commission and the Community budget. A complex form of words expressed the equally complex reality: the policy was to be implemented by 'the member states of the EU working within the framework of the Union and in close association with the European Commission'. This appears to demonstrate that Union policy-making, far from marking a retreat to intergovernmentalism, marks a new departure and a creative way of bringing the various EU institutions and the member governments together. As noted above, the ways in which the EU operated during the Kosovo crisis of 1999 also raised the prospect of linkages between Union membership and regional stabilisation in a novel way. Other early joint actions in South Africa and in Russia (in each case primarily the monitoring of elections) were less dramatic but raised the same issues and possibilities; much later, the involvement of the Union in security and policing activities both in former Yugoslavia and elsewhere again demonstrated the complex management processes at work.

International policy as negotiated order

Such developments give support to a third mode of international policy-making in the EU; indeed, the three modes being examined here represent coexisting tendencies rather than competing and mutually exclusive models. Given the complex institutional relationships and processes of exchange between Community, member governments and other actors in the Union's international policy process, it could be argued that the EU in its international activities constitutes an evolving *negotiated order*. Within the administrative, institutional and political structures established over the life of the Community and the EU, there is a constant, rule-governed process of negotiation between actors which produces policy positions and international policy outcomes. Process is as important as outcome, and it is thus inappropriate to apply to the EU the concepts of statehood or foreign policy which are typical of conventional international relations models and approaches (Allen and Smith 1990; Smith 1994; Elgström and Smith 2000).

It is important to note that this perspective on the international policy process in the EU coincides with new patterns of analysis for the global arena more generally, which stress precisely the multi-level, institutionalised and rule-governed behaviour to which attention has been drawn in this chapter (Hocking and Smith 1997, chapters 1–2; Prakash and Hart 1999; Pollack and Shaffer 2001; Stubbs and Underhill 2005). In the more strictly EU context, such an approach leads in a number of directions. First, it draws attention to the ways in which 'Community policy-making' as outlined above is itself a focus for negotiation and exchange between a number of actors. To give but one example, the new Commission installed in 1999 – and its successor installed in 2004 – had within them at least six Commissioners with substantial international policy responsibilities, and the process of allocating these responsibilities had in each case been a source of considerable negotiation. The appointment of Chris Patten in 1999 as a kind of 'lead Commissioner' for external policies, and the development of consolidated coordination mechanisms not only between the Commissioners concerned but also between Patten and the 'high representative' for CFSP, Javier Solana, symbolised a major effort to ensure consistency among the various channels of EU external policy in conditions of complex policy-making.

A second feature of EU international policy-making which is captured by a 'negotiated order' focus is that in many cases the EU's international activities are undertaken in a multi-level negotiation context. The example of the Doha Development Round cited earlier in this chapter is perhaps the most significant recent instance of the ways in which negotiations within the WTO, within the Commission, within and between the EU institutions and the member states all came together to provide a potent mix of overlapping and often irreconcilable claims. There are, though, many other instances of such relationships: the EU/US partnership, the attempts through negotiation to consolidate the post-Cold War European order, the negotiations attending the accession of new members, the development of global environmental governance.

In this view, then, the EU's international positions and actions are both the product of an institutionalised negotiation process and frequently part of such a process in the international arena. As such, they epitomise many features of the changing world political economy in the twenty-first century, but they also focus them in a very distinctive way. A key area of policy analysis for the foreseeable future will be the ways in which this situation plays out for the enlarged EU, in particular in the context of the 'new Europe'.

Conclusion: towards an EU foreign policy?

This chapter started by examining briefly the debates which have centred on the EU's credentials as an international actor, and by suggesting the significance of the developments that have taken place in the EU's international involvement. Often, the debates and the significance are placed into the context of a broader debate about statehood, foreign policy and the EU's approximation to the conventional model of both. The argument in this chapter has tested both the substantive basis for claims about the EU's international significance and the broader conceptual claims made by those who foresee the emergence of a 'foreign policy' conducted by the Union or its representatives.

The general conclusions from the argument are threefold:

- First, the EC and now the EU have long-established and material foundations for their presence and impact in the international arena. These foundations are the reflection of the economic and political weight of the EU, of its institutional capacity and of the ways in which it has enlarged its tasks and roles in the changing world arena. But they are not monolithic, nor do they suppress the claims or the prerogatives of the member states. Indeed, as the EU has entered new areas of activity, it has occasionally seemed to reach the limits of its capacity to lay claim to the new territory on which it finds itself.
- Second, the substance of EU international policy betrays not only the value placed on the EU both by its members and by others as an international role-player, but also the limitations imposed by the ways in which the EU is constrained in its mobilisation of resources. Whilst this is particularly apparent in the area of international security and defence policy, there is no shortage of other examples to illustrate the 'capability-expectations gap' (or rather the multiple 'capability-expectations gaps') in the EU's international existence.
- Third, one way of taking further an appreciation of the distinctive nature of EU international policy is to focus on modes of policy-making. There is no single mode of such policy-making, and therein lies part of the unique character of the European construction. There are elements of 'Community policy-making', of 'Union policy-making' and of 'negotiated order' in all aspects of the EU's international policy. The challenge lies in interpreting the circumstances in which and the conditions in which they interact to produce distinctive mixes of policy.

As this chapter was written, debate continued about the ways in which the Constitutional Treaty agreed during the summer of 2004 would affect the conduct of the EU's international policies. In some respects, the Treaty could be seen as going further down the road towards a 'real' EU foreign policy, for example, by proposing the post of 'Foreign Minister' for the Union and thus bringing together several of the coexisting strands of institutional and policy responsibility explored in this chapter. In other respects, it could equally be argued that the proposals in the Treaty would have institutionalised the continuing role of the member states in running the EU's external policies and confirmed the 'negotiated' characteristics of the existing policy processes. The rejection of the Treaty in the French and Dutch referenda of May and June 2005 will not end discussion of these issues.

There is therefore no definitive answer to the question 'Does the EU have a foreign policy?'. Rather, there is a series of increasingly well-focused questions about the nature of EU international action and the foundations on which it is based, which constitute a major research agenda for the present and the future.

References

Allen, D. and Pijpers, A. (1984) *European Foreign Policy Making and the Arab-Israeli Dispute* (The Hague: Nijhoff).

Allen, D. and Smith, M. (1990) 'Western Europe's Presence in the Contemporary International Arena', *Review of International Studies* 16/1: 19–39.

—— (1991–92) 'The European Community in the New Europe: Bearing the Burden of Change', *International Journal* 47/1: 1–28.

—— (1998) 'The European Union's Security Presence: Barrier, Facilitator or Manager?' in C. Rhodes (ed.), *The European Union in the World Community* (Boulder, CO: Lynne Rienner).

Allen, D., Rummel, R. and Wessels, W. (1982) *European Political Cooperation: Towards a Foreign Policy for Western Europe?* (London: Butterworth).

De Burca, G. and Scott. J. (2001) *The European Union and the World Trade Organisation: Legal and Constitutional Issues* (Oxford: Hart Publishing).

Cameron, F. (1999) *The Foreign and Security Policy of the European Union: Past, Present and Future* (Sheffield: Sheffield Academic Press).

Carlsnaes, W. and Smith, S. (eds) (1994) *European Foreign Policy: The EC and Changing Perspectives in Europe* (London: Sage).

Dannreuther, R. (ed.) (2004) *European Union Foreign and Security Policy: Towards a Neighborhood Policy* (London: Routledge).

Dent, C. (1997) *The European Economy: The Global Context* (London: Routledge).

—— (1999) *The European Union and East Asia: An Economic Relationship* (London: Routledge).

Dinan, D. (2004) *Europe Recast: A History of European Union* (Boulder, CO: Lynne Rienner; Basingstoke, Palgrave-Macmillan).

Edwards, G. and Regelsberger, E. (eds.) (1990) *Europe's Global Links: The European Community and Inter-regional Cooperation* (London: Pinter).

Elgström, O. and Smith, M. (eds) (2000) 'Negotiation and Policy-Making in the European Union: Processes, System and Order', special issue of *Journal of European Public Policy* (December).

Everts, S., Freedman, L., Grant, C., Heisbourg, F., Keohane, D. and O'Hanlon, M. (2004) *A European Way of War* (London: Centre for European Reform).

Featherstone, K. and Ginsberg, R. (1996) *The United States and the European Community in the 1990s: Partners in Transition*, 2nd edn (London: Macmillan; New York: St Martin's Press).

Forster, A. and Wallace, W. (1996) 'Common Foreign and Security Policy: A New Policy or Just a New Name?' in H. Wallace and W. Wallace (eds), *Policy-Making in the European Union* (Oxford: Oxford University Press).

Frellesen, T. and Ginsberg, R. (1994) *EU–US Foreign Policy Cooperation in the 1990s: Elements of Partnership* (Brussels: Centre for European Policy Studies).

Gilson, J. (2000) *Japan and the European Union: A Partnership for the Twenty-First Century?* (Basingstoke: Macmillan).

Gnesotto, N. (ed.) (2004) *European Security and Defence Policy: the First Five Years (1999–2004).* (Paris: European Union Institute for Security Studies).

Guay, T. (1999) *The European Union and the United States: The Political Economy of a Relationship* (Sheffield: Sheffield Academic Press).

Harrison, G. (ed.) (1994) *Europe and the United States: Competition and Cooperation in the 1990s* (Armonk, NY: Sharpe).

Henderson, K. (ed.) (1999) *Back to Europe: Central and Eastern Europe and the European Union* (London: UCL Press).

Hill, C. (ed.) (1983) *National Foreign Policies and European Political Cooperation* (London: George Allen and Unwin).

—— (1990) 'European Foreign Policy: Power Bloc, Civilian Model – or Flop?' in R. Rummel (ed.), *The Evolution of an International Actor: Western Europe's New Assertiveness.* (Boulder, CO: Westview Press).

—— (1993) 'The Capability-expectations Gap, or Conceptualising Europe's International Role', *Journal of Common Market Studies* 31/3: 305–28.

—— (ed.) (1995) *The Actors in European Political Cooperation* (London: Routledge).

—— (1998) 'Closing the Capabilities-expectations Gap?' in J. Peterson and H. Sjursen (eds) *A Common Foreign Policy for Europe? Competing Visions of the CFSP* (London: Routledge).

Hill, C. and Smith, M. (eds) (2005) *The International Relations of the European Union* (Oxford: Oxford University Press).

Hine, R. (1985) *The Political Economy of European Trade* (Brighton: Harvester-Wheatsheaf).

Hocking, B. and Smith, M. (1997) *Beyond Foreign Economic Policy: The United States, the Single European Market and a Changing World Economy* (London: Cassell/Pinter).

Howorth, J. (2000) *European Integration and Defence: The Ultimate Challenge?* Chaillot Paper 43 (Paris: Institute for Security Studies of the WEU).

—— (2005) 'From Security to Defence' in C. Hill and M. Smith (eds) *The International Relations of the European Union* (Oxford: Oxford University Press).

Hufbauer, G. (ed.) (1990) *Europe 1992: An American Perspective* (Washington, DC: Brookings Institution).

Ishikawa, K. (1989) *Japan and the Challenge of Europe 1992* (London: Pinter).

Keohane, R., Nye, J. and Hoffmann, S. (eds.) (1993) *After the Cold War: International Institutions and State Strategies in Europe, 1989–1991* (Cambridge, MA: Harvard University Press).

Laffan, B., O'Donnell, R. and Smith, M. (2000) *Europe's Experimental Union: Rethinking Integration* (London: Routledge).

Laursen, F. and Vanhoonacker, S. (eds.) *The Intergovernmental Conference on Political Union: Institutional Reforms, New Policies and International Identity of the European Community* (Maastricht: European Institute of Public Administration).

Manners, I. and Whitman, R. (eds) (2000) *The Foreign Policies of European Union Member States* (Manchester: Manchester University Press).

Maull, H., Segal, G. and Wanandi, J. (eds) (1998) *Europe and the Asia-Pacific* (London: Routledge).

Meunier, S. and Nicolaidis, K. (1999) 'Who Speaks for Europe? The Delegation of Trade Authority in the EU', *Journal of Common Market Studies* 37/3: 477–502.

Norgaard, O., Pedersen, T. and Petersen, N. (eds.) (1993) *The European Community in World Politics* (London: Pinter).

Nuttall, S. (1992) *European Political Cooperation* (Oxford: Clarendon Press).

—— (1994) 'The EC and Yugoslavia – Deus Ex Machina or Machina Sine Deo?' in N. Nugent (ed.), *The European Union 1993: Annual Review of Activities* (Oxford: Blackwell).

307

Peterson, J. (1996) *Europe and America in the 1990s: Prospects for Partnership*, 2nd edn (London: Routledge).

Peterson, J. and Pollack, M. (2003) *Europe, America, Bush: Transatlantic Relations in the Twenty-first Century* (London: Routledge).

Piening, C. (1997) *Global Europe: The European Union in World Affairs* (Boulder, CO: Lynne Rienner).

Pijpers, A., Regelsberger, E. and Wessels, W. (eds.) (1988) *European Political Cooperation in the 1980s: A Common Foreign Policy for Western Europe?* (Dordrecht: Nijhoff).

Pinder, J. (1991a) *European Community: The Building of a Union* (Oxford: Oxford University Press).

—— (1991b) *The European Community and Eastern Europe* (London: Royal Institute of International Affairs/Pinter Publishers).

Pollack, M. and Shaffer, G. (eds) (2001) *Transatlantic Governance in the Global Economy* (Lanham, MD: Rowman & Littlefield).

Prakash, A. and Hart, J. (eds) (1999) *Globalisation and Governance* (London: Routledge).

Redmond, J. (ed.) (1992) *The External Relations of the European Community: The International Response to 1992* (London: Macmillan).

Regelsberger, E., de Schoutheete de Tervarent, P. and Wessels, W. (eds) (1997) *Foreign Policy of the European Union: from EPC to CFSP and Beyond* (Boulder, CO: Lynne Rienner).

Rummel, R. (ed.) (1992) *Toward Political Union: Planning a Common Foreign and Security Policy in the European Community* (Boulder, CO: Westview Press).

Smith, K. (1999) *The Making of EU Foreign Policy: The Case of Eastern Europe* (London: Macmillan).

—— (2003) *European Union Foreign Policy in a Changing World* (Cambridge: Polity Press).

—— (2005) 'Enlargement and European Order' in C. Hill and M. Smith (eds) *The International Relations of the European Union* (Oxford: Oxford University Press).

Smith, M. (1994) 'The European Union, Foreign Economic Policy and a Changing World Arena', *Journal of European Public Policy* 1/2: 283–302.

—— (1998a) 'Competitive Cooperation and EU-US Relations: Can the EU be a Strategic Partner for the US in the World Political Economy?', *Journal of European Public Policy* 5/4: 561–77.

—— (1998b) 'The European Union and the Asia-Pacific', in A. McGrew and C. Brook (eds), *Asia-Pacific in the New World Order* (London: Routledge).

—— (1999) 'The European Union' in B. Hocking and S. McGuire (eds), *Trade Politics: International, Domestic and Regional Perspectives* (London: Routledge).

—— (2005) 'The Commission and External Relations', in D. Spence (ed.), *The European Commission*, 3rd edn (London: John Harper Publishing).

Smith, M. and Woolcock, S. (1993) *The United States and the European Community in a Transformed World* (London: Royal Institute of International Affairs/Pinter Publishers).

—— (1994) 'Learning to Cooperate: the Clinton Administration and the European Union', *International Affairs* 70/3: 459–76.

—— (1999) 'European Commercial Policy: A Leadership Role in the New Millennium?' *European Foreign Affairs Review* 4/4: 439–62.

Story, J. (ed.) (1993) *The New Europe: Politics, Government and Society since 1945* (Oxford: Blackwell).

Stubbs, R. and Underhill, G. (eds) (2005) *Political Economy and the Changing Global Order*, 3rd edn (Toronto: Oxford University Press).

Tsoukalis, L. (1997) *The New European Economy Revisited* (Oxford: Oxford University Press).

Wallace, H. (ed.) (1991) *The Wider Western Europe: Reshaping the EC/EFTA relationship* (London: Royal Institute of International Affairs/Pinter Publishers).

Wallace, W. (1990) *The Transformation of Western Europe* (London: Royal Institute of International Affairs/Pinter Publishers).

White, B. (2001) *Understanding European Foreign Policy* (Basingstoke: Palgrave/Macmillan).

Wiessala, G. (2002) *The European Union and Asian Countries* (Sheffield: Sheffield Academic Press).

Woolcock, S. (1992) *Market Access Issues in EC/US Trade Relations: Trading Partners or Trading Blows?* (London: Royal Institute of International Affairs/Pinter Publishers).

Woolcock, S. and Hodges, M. (1996) 'EU Policy in the Uruguay Round' in H. Wallace and W. Wallace (eds), *Policy-Making in the European Union* (Oxford: Oxford University Press).

Young, A. (2002) *Extending European Cooperation: The European Union and the 'New' International Trade Agenda* (Manchester: Manchester University Press).

Zucconi, M. (1996) 'The European Union in the Former Yugoslavia' in A. Chayes and A. Chayes (eds), *Preventing Conflict in the Post-Communist World: Mobilizing International and Regional Organizations* (Washington, DC: Brookings Institution).

Chapter 15

European regulation

MARK THATCHER

Introduction

The EC's central policy activity is regulation rather than distribution or redistribution: its expenditure, revenues and staffing have remained small compared to those of national governments. In contrast, its regulatory role has grown rapidly between the 1980s and today, as part of a general trend towards the 'regulatory state' in Europe (cf. Majone 1996, Héritier and Thatcher 2002, Moran 2002). The EC has extended its activities into new policy areas and deepened its role in its existing policy domains. Aided by the doctrine of legal supremacy of Community law, it has become a prominent source of regulation.

The chapter examines the development of EC regulation.[1] It begins by mapping its expansion, which has been very diverse in forms and across policy domains. Many factors and actors are responsible for that expansion, and analysis is linked to wider debates about European integration. Hence the chapter puts forward three analytical 'models' or lenses to examine the growth of EC regulation: a neo-functionalist or 'top-down' model; an intergovernmental or delegation model; and a dynamic governance model. Thereafter, it considers an increasingly important topic, namely the impacts of EC regulation and 'Europeanisation', and concludes by discussing the limits of EC regulation.

EC regulation: forms and growth

Several different definitions of 'regulation' exist. Economists usually emphasise rules to correct market failures (cf. Gaitsos and Seabright 1989), whereas political scientists and sociologists have broader conceptions that include rules governing state activity and that can extend to all forms of social control and influence (Baldwin and Cave 1999: 2; cf. Wilks 1996; Majone 1996). Its 'central meaning' (Selznick 1985) is 'sustained and focused control by a public agency over activities that are valued by the community'. Control through regulation involves rules, although these can vary from formal legislation to informal norms.

EC regulation covers this spectrum. It includes Treaty Articles that define the competencies and policy domains of the EC, and secondary legislation – regulations, directives and decisions. Regulations, and some Treaty Articles and directives, are directly effective and hence can be used by litigants in national courts; in addition, the doctrine of 'indirect effect' allows EC law to influence national law. The EC also uses non-binding forms of regulation, often called 'soft law', which include recommendations, resolutions and declarations. Finally, the EC exercises regulatory influence by activities such as benchmarking, attempts to spread 'best practice', studies, conferences, and encouragement of reform. These can aid the development of European norms and standards of behaviour. They form a central part of the 'open method of coordination' promoted after 2000 by the Commission (Commission 2001, Regent 2003, de la Porte 2002).

EC regulatory activities have expanded far beyond those existing in 1958 in terms of legal competencies, legislation and policy fields. The EC's initial focus was on creating a free-trade area through removing barriers to trade ('negative integration'), in particular tariff barriers. Thereafter, EC action extended to non-tariff barriers to trade, from product standards to monopolies and restrictive rules on supply. The domains covered are mixed and numerous, ranging from telecommunications to financial services. However, whilst liberalisation measures are its most visible forms of regulation, the EC has not 'deregulated'.

On the contrary, it has engaged in considerable 're-regulation', corresponding to 'positive integration', setting rules governing competition and 'harmonisation' or minimal standards.

EC regulation covers focused, 'vertical' fields such as sectoral regulation for public utilities, agriculture, pharmaceuticals, financial services and professional services. However, it also takes 'horizontal' cross-sectoral forms – not just general competition policy but also increasingly social, consumer and environmental regulation. Numbers also indicate the expansion of EC regulation. In 1970, 20 directives and 46 regulations were passed; in 1980, the figures were 57 directives and 113 regulations; in 1999, there were 169 directives and 1316 regulations; in 2003, 121 directives and 837 regulations (Commission 1999, 2003).

Whilst the overall picture is of EC regulatory growth, the speed, timing and extent of EC regulation have varied across policy domains. The most detailed EC regulation has been in economic regulation, especially covering competition. Even here, however, there have been cross-sectoral differences – for example, telecommunications have seen more detailed and earlier regulation than postal services. In other fields, EC action has been more recent and remains less developed – for instance, food safety and labelling or privacy. Nevertheless, there are fewer and fewer areas of policy that lack an EC regulatory presence. Even sport is now subject to EC regulation (Parrish 2003).

The process of EC regulatory expansion has taken place through several related channels. Regulatory powers and competencies have been explicitly given to the EC by member states via Treaties as the EC's policy domains have been progressively extended (cf. Fligstein and McNichol 1998). Under the 1958 Treaty of Rome, the EC's core powers mostly concerned building a free-trade area – removing restrictions on the free movement of goods, persons, services and capital. The 1980s and 1990s saw member states provide further regulatory areas and powers to EC institutions via new Treaties. The Single European Act added explicit horizontal competencies, including the health and safety of workers, environmental protection, research and development, and economic and social cohesion. Crucially, it introduced qualified majority voting for certain fields; the most notable (under Article 95 [100A]) was used for the internal market programme ('1992'). The Maastricht Treaty provided further explicit policy fields for EC regulation, notably consumer protection, public health and education. It also included social regulations, albeit in a separate Social Protocol that applied to all member states except Britain. Moreover, it widened the scope of qualified majority voting to areas such as consumer protection, the environment and some parts of social policy. The 1997 Treaty of Amsterdam and the 2001 Treaty of Nice continued the expansion of EC competencies in social policy, the environment, employment and international negotiations, and also the extension of qualified majority voting.

The greatest direct source of increased EC regulation has been through programmes and secondary legislation (directives and regulations) agreed by the Council of Ministers and, in the 1990s, also the European Parliament. The most trumpeted extension, after the initial foundation of the EC, was the Internal Market Programme ('1992') (Commission 1985; Egan 2001; Armstrong and Bulmer 1998). This involved 300 legislative proposals to remove trade barriers within the EC through opening up markets, removing non-tariff barriers and setting EC standards. However, in many other fields, the expansion of EC regulation has taken place through gradual accretion over time – seen, for example, in social policy, environmental protection or employment. Passing secondary legislation has been made easier by the extension of qualified majority voting, and the volume of legislation rose sharply after the Single European Act (Fligstein and McNicol 1998).

Another, vital, source of EC regulatory expansion has been European Court of Justice decisions (cf. Stone Sweet and Caporaso 1998). An important example is Article 28 [30] which prohibits member states from introducing quantitative restrictions on imports from other member states or measures having 'equivalent effect'. The ECJ stated (in the Dassonville case of 1974: ECJ 1974) that 'all trading rules enacted by member states which are capable of hindering, actually or potentially, intra-Community trade' were covered by Article 28 [30]. It therefore greatly extended the ECJ's powers to strike down a host of national rules that, regardless of intention or even current effects, could reduce trade among member states.

Since the late 1990s, 'networks' of national regulatory agencies (NRAs) have increasingly been used by the EU. Important examples include competition, telecommunications, electricity and gas authorities (Wilks 2005; Eberlein 2004; cf. Geradin *et al.*2005). These are potentially significant in producing 'soft law' forms of regulation such as codes and norms. Equally, they may strengthen European epistemic regulatory communities and encourage cross-national policy learning and transfer. Thus they may represent a significant stimulus to new forms of governance whereby the EC regulates through coordination. However, behind the networks lies traditional 'hard law': the Commission has formal legal powers to oblige NRAs to notify it and other NRAs over measures that may affect trade among member states and to order the NRA to withdraw measures; examples include telecommunications and general competition authorities (European Parliament and Council 2002; Wilks 2005)

Explaining EC regulatory expansion

Many related factors have driven the expansion of EC regulatory activity: the interests and role of the Commission; the ECJ and the EC's legal framework; decisions by national governments; national regulatory inadequacies; interest groups and increased transnational trade; the dynamics of EC policy-making. Assessing the balance of importance among these factors, and especially the weight of supra-national actors (the Commission and ECJ), transnational trade and decisions by national governments, relates closely to general debates on European integration – particularly those between intergovernmentalism, neo-functionalism and more recent multi-level governance, policy transfer and delegation approaches (cf. Sandholtz and Stone Sweet 1998; Moravcsik 1993; Hooghe and Marks 2001; Eberlein and Kerwer 2004; Nicolaides 2004; Pollack 2003; Radaelli 2000; Bulmer and Padgett forthcoming). The relative importance of the different factors has also varied from one policy domain to another, due to variations in Commission powers and resources, ECJ case law, Treaty Articles, the position of national governments, exposure to transnational trade and interests and the extent of domestic regulatory inadequacies. No single approach or factor can explain EC regulatory growth. Instead, what is put forward below are three analytical 'models' or lenses, with empirical examples, which themselves relate to broader theoretical frameworks for analysing EC integration.

A neo-functionalist or 'top–down' model of EC regulatory growth

This model emphasises the roles of the EC Commission, ECJ and powerful interest groups, especially firms who engage in cross-border trade. It sees EC regulation as largely driven by these actors, often against the will of national governments.

A key starting point is Commission activism. The Commission has been a central actor in EC regulatory expansion, putting forward new ideas, pressing for action and proposing specific action. At times, it has launched headline-catching ambitious initiatives; the '1992 Programme' for the internal market was the most prominent example. More generally, however, it has taken a less public but perhaps more effective strategy involving incremental steps and persistence even in the face of inertia and opposition by member states. The Commission has tended to follow a long process of garnering support before acting – for example, holding conferences and workshops with experts and interested groups, issuing Green Papers, commissioning studies and seeking to accommodate different points of view. It has then made specific legislative proposals and been able to offer a direction for regulation, with opponents left facing considerable momentum and a well-developed agenda. Merger control illustrates Commission patience and persistence: discussion of empowering the Commission to vet large cross-border mergers began in 1973, and eventually led to the 1989 Merger Regulation which covered notification and approval of mergers (Cini and McGowan 1998). Similar stories of the Commission continuing its efforts until circumstances were propitious can be told in many other fields, such as the environment, occupational safety, social policy or gender discrimination (cf. Eichener 1997; Richardson 1994; Wendon 1998; Mazey 1995; Cichowski 2001).

The Commission has been able to utilise its legal monopoly over secondary legislative proposals, together with great influence as an 'agenda-setter' at the centre of many European networks (Peterson 1997; cf. Peters 1994). Within the Commission, different DGs compete with each other for prestige and territory, creating further pressures for action; for example, in the late 1980s, DGIV (the competition Directorate) was spurred into activity as its rival, DGIII (at that time, both industry and internal market), used the 1992 Programme to expand its role. Perhaps most important of all, the Commission has been able to wait, taking time to place new ideas of increased EC regulation in the European policy space, testing out the balance of forces, gradually creating a climate of opinion and coalition supportive of its ideas, refining those ideas to match the balance of forces and finally, making proposals at suitable times, or simply repeating them until accepted.

Yet the Commission has not been able to expand EC regulation on its own. A key ally has often been the ECJ, which has frequently supported the expansion of EC competencies and regulation, taking a broad view of the scope of EC powers and legislation. The ECJ's decisions that directives could be directly effective made passing such secondary legislation an attractive and relatively easy method of EC action, especially in combination with the doctrine of the supremacy of EC law. Moreover, the ECJ has offered wide interpretations of Treaty provisions and secondary legislation. Thus for example, in a series of cases under Article 119 (equal pay for equal work), and other directives on equal pay for work of equal value (Directive 75/119), equal treatment in employment (Directive 76/207), and equal treatment in social security matters (Directive 97/7), it took a broad view of payment and discrimination, so that it interpreted Article 119 to mean equal pay for work of equal value, found that discrimination could be indirect and included pensions and retirement ages, even though these had been excluded from the Directives (Stone Sweet and Caporaso 1998: 121–7; cf. Mazey 1995). The ECJ has played a key role in the expansion of many other areas of EC regulation, from competition policy to the environment (cf. Stone Sweet and Caparoso 1998; Stone Sweet, Sandholtz and Fligstein 2001; Weiler 1991; Bulmer 1998; Gerber 1994; Cichowski 1998).

ECJ rulings have not only strengthened EC regulatory capacities but have also created incentives for secondary legislation. The best-known example is the Cassis de Dijon case (ECJ 1979): the ECJ ruled that goods legally produced in one member state, according to its rules and regulations, could be sold in other member states. 'In the absence of common rules', it was for individual member states to set their own rules, but other member states could not impose national restrictions that hindered trade (being caught by Article 28 [30]) except under limited circumstances (set out in Article 30 [36], including for instance, public morality, public policy or health and safety). Such rulings put pressure on member states to pass EC secondary legislation, in order to avoid uncertainty and also to allow them to play a part in the detail of regulation rather than merely following judicial decisions (cf. Bulmer 1998). The jurisprudence of the Dassonville and Cassis cases produced great impetus for legislation to set standards, since otherwise member states would have to accept the standards of other member states, over which they had no control, and/or justify restrictions in a possible flood of court cases, causing uncertainty and damage to trade. These legal cases were followed by the Internal Market programme and the 'new approach' to harmonisation and standardisation in the 1980s whereby the EC set minimum standards rather than seeking to pursue full harmonisation, which had largely failed (Pelkmans 1987).

However, the ECJ is reliant on cases being brought before it, whilst the Commission is a small bureaucracy, dependent on other actors to provide it with information, expertise, political support and legitimacy. A neo-functionalist model underlines how interest groups such as firms, trade unions and pressure groups in areas such as the environment or gender equality have sought increased EC regulation. They have done so at the EC level, especially as the Brussels bureaucracy is remarkably permeable and open to lobbying (Mazey and Richardson 1993), and also at the national level. They have offered information to the Commission as part of their strategies of influencing EC regulation (Broscheid and Coen 2003). Frequently such activity has been linked to the growth of transnational trade, which has provided important incentives for EC integration (cf. Sandholtz and Stone Sweet 1998).

International firms (sometimes in conjunction with national associations and governments) have urged EC action to open up closed domestic markets and to establish a single set of predictable rules across the EC (Coen 1998). Thus, for example, companies such as BT and large City institutions, supported by the supposedly 'Eurosceptical' British governments of the 1980s and 1990s, urged EC measures to liberalise areas such as financial services, airlines or telecommunications (cf. Hayward 1995). Conversely, firms facing 'dumping' or 'unfairly' subsidised foreign competitors (industries such as consumer electronics, steel or coal) have sought EC protection. Equally, in international 'standards battles', European firms and policy-makers have turned to the EC to create Europe-wide standards in areas ranging from mobile communications to environmental requirements. Thus a neo-functionalist model analyses EC regulation as the product of a coalition or at least cooperation between the Commission, ECJ and interest groups that is sufficiently powerful to overcome resistance by national governments.

An intergovernmental or delegation model of EC regulation

An alternative model, however, sees EC regulation as desired and indeed intended by national governments. Far from having decisions imposed upon them, governments choose to delegate to the Commission and ECJ the resolution of problems such as lack of credible commitment, dealing with information asymmetries or aiding monitoring and compliance across nations (Pollack 2003). This model underlines that national governments have chosen to provide increasingly wide regulatory powers to the EC under successive Treaties. When faced with insistent opposition from a small minority (often Britain), governments have found ways to circumvent it – for example, through the Social Protocol to the Maastricht Treaty, signed by all member states except Britain. Moreover, governments have made passing secondary regulatory legislation easier by extending qualified majority voting and restricting the requirement of unanimity in the Council of Ministers in the Single European Act and later Treaties; hence individual member states have found themselves obliged to compromise and trade.

National governments have accepted initiatives to expand EC regulation. As early as 1962, they passed Regulation 17 (Council 1962), whereby the Commission implemented competition law, including acting against anti-competitive agreements and abuse of a dominant position and granting exemptions under Article 81 [85](3). Later, they welcomed the 1992 Programme and accepted EC directives for environmental protection in the 1970s and 1980s. Even in an area such as social policy, apparently far removed from ending barriers to trade, they accepted EC regulatory action (Rhodes 1995). At times, member states have used broad Articles to extend the EC's regulatory activities. In particular, Article 308 [235] operated as a 'catch-all' provision, since it allowed the EC action that is necessary to attain EC objectives but for which powers were not provided for explicitly in the Treaty; it was used to initiate EC regulation in several fields, including social security for migrants, the environment and equal treatment in employment. Later on, explicit Treaty Articles followed, in effect ratifying the EC's entry into new areas.

Telecommunications provides a good example of the 'partnership' between the Commission and national governments (Thatcher 2001). The latter had formal and informal institutional controls over the Commission that made it very sensitive to their preferences over the substance of telecommunications regulation. These controls were exercised through the participation of national governments at all stages of decision-making. Their impacts were seen in the nature of EU decision-making over telecommunications legislation, which was marked by incrementalist decision-making, compromises, linkages between policy choices to provide compensation for compromises, and legislation that allowed room for significant discretion in implementation at the national level. The Commission engaged in extensive consultation with governments and then made detailed proposals for EC directives that were largely accepted by national governments. Far from the Commission imposing EC regulation, it engaged in a partnership with national governments in which they agreed on expanded EC legislation.

Why should national governments accept or welcome increased EC regulation? Principal-agent models point to several reasons. First, national policy-makers may be faced with potential gains from coordination. These may arise from interdependence and 'regulatory externalities' in which the decisions of national regulators have effects on other EC member states; the clearest example is pollution, where discharges in one country affect other countries (for example, waste in the North Sea or air pollution in border areas). But whilst nation states may gain from cooperation, they face international prisoners' dilemmas (Gaitsos and Seabright 1989). Thus for instance, the benefits of regulatory decisions in one member state (for instance, higher pollution standards) may be negated by decisions in another, leaving the first with higher costs. Moreover, national regulators may also engage in strategic behaviour, whereby some or all of the costs of their decisions are borne by other nations; one example is member states' competition in increasing state subsidies to non-viable firms, negating their effects and using resources that could be better used for other purposes. Cross-national cooperation faces information and transaction costs, arising, for example, from cheating, enforcement, discretion, differing cultures and organisational barriers to trading national gains and losses across policy fields (cf. Majone 1996, ch. 4). EC regulation allows cooperation and coordination to capture externalities – for example by setting common rules for state aids, pollution or standards. It offers a mechanism to establish rules that member states can accept more easily in the knowledge that other member states are placed under the same rules, making cheating and gaining regulatory advantages more difficult. In other words, the EC acts as a credible supranational monitor, arbitrator and enforcer (Pollack 2003).

EC regulation may also enhance credible commitment by governments. Such commitment is important if governments, firms and investors rely on long-term policies being followed. For example, they may need to be reassured that competition policies will be enforced in practice or that standards will be followed before investing or implementing difficult policies such as reducing state aid or complying with expensive standards. Governments may wish to provide such reassurance, since it will lead to beneficial outcomes such as higher investment, but lack credibility to make promises because of short-term incentives, especially electoral ones. In contrast, the EC as a non-majoritarian supranational organisation offers greater credibility for long-term promises, lowering the costs of regulation (for example, enforcement costs) and increasing benefits (Majone 2000).

A third reason for governments to delegate regulation to the EC is blame-shifting. EC regulation can provide a good external reason decisions that face powerful domestic opposition, such as ending monopolies, reducing state aid, altering standards or privatisation to name but a few. These reforms may be desired for both EC and non-EC reasons, but be unpopular domestically. A general analysis is that national governments are able to engage in a 'two-level game' (Putnam 1988; Evans *et al.* 1993) whereby they pursue their domestic interests at the EC level, avoiding or reducing domestic obstacles to their policies.

A dynamic 'governance' model

The third model looks at how processes arising from interactions between the EC, national and international levels create pressures and incentives for an expansion of EU regulation. These processes can include regulatory competition, the growth of epistemic communities and cross-national policy transfer. The model is thus rather eclectic, encompassing several theoretical literatures, but the central common feature is that events at the EU level influence and are themselves influenced by events at the national and international levels, resulting in greater EC regulation.

Member states are frequently in competition with each other: they seek to 'export' their regulatory model to the EC level, as this provides domestic companies with competitive advantages and requires little national adaptation. In the EC, there are often important first-mover advantages, notably in defining problems and setting agendas (Peters 1994). At the same time, member states may seek to respond to the danger of regulatory competition by cooperation through the EU (cf. Holzinger and Knill 2004). In competition and cooperation, the Commission plays a key role as a gatekeeper, due to its position at the centre of many European networks and its monopoly over legislative proposals. Member states therefore have an incentive to act quickly and offer nationally advantageous ideas for EC regulation to the Commission, before other countries enter the field and offer their own agendas and suggestions. The Commission is unlikely to accept proposals that reduce its powers and competencies. The result is a dynamic towards increased EC regulation, based on member states suggesting EC action. Examples can be found in many policy areas, from pollution control to electricity regulation, as national policy-makers vie for the ear of the Commission and influence over EC regulatory development.

The interaction between negative and positive integration offers another dynamic that sustains EC regulatory growth. Attempts to end non-tariff barriers create strong forces for EC re-regulation, since national standards and norms can and often do operate as non-tariff barriers. Moreover, they raise the problem of standards: if no EC standards are set and if member states are obliged to allow entry of products regardless of domestic standards, there are dangers of 'races to the bottom', as firms in EC countries with lower and less costly standards enjoy competitive advantages leading to the progressive reduction of standards (Dehousse 1992). Moreover, as markets are opened up, firms seek certainty about standards in order to plan ahead and compete effectively. Hence the internal market and liberalisation of markets such as telecommunications have seen both the removal of non-tariff barriers to trade and the development of EC regulatory standards. These range from minimum standards to voluntary Europe-wide norms to compulsory harmonised standards in fields ranging from electronic equipment to environmental standards (cf. Holzinger and Knill 2004; Lenschow 2002).

A third process involves the EU encouraging policy learning, policy coordination and the development of European epistemic or policy communities. This may happen formally, notably through committees or the open method of coordination. However, it can also take place informally, as the EU encourages the development of cross-national networks. Such processes can alter policy preferences of member states, as well as their strategic calculations and their ability to link different policy areas and hence trade off gains and losses. The results can be seen in 'hard' regulation – i.e. the production of EC legislation; thus it is argued that the process of liberalising the electricity market saw modifications in national governments' preferences over competition (Eising 2002). However, such processes are most likely to have greatest initial effects through the production of EC norms and other 'softer' forms of law (cf. Bulmer and Padgett 2004). They may be seen in measures after 2000 to try to develop EC norms in politically sensitive areas such as employment and social exclusion (Regent 2003; de la Porte 2002; Lenschow 2002).

Europeanisation and EC regulation

Increasing attention is being paid to the effects of EC regulation at the national level – i.e. 'Europeanisation' (Green Cowles *et al.* 2001; Radaelli and Schmidt 2004). Assessing the impacts of EC regulation within member states is far from easy since they have varied both from one sector to another and across member states. At one extreme, in certain sectors there has been little EC regulation, and/or EC measures had already been introduced by some member states so that the EC was following rather than leading; in addition, EC rules may not have been implemented in practice, their impact being more apparent than real. Moreover, the EC has only been one force for regulatory change, as other factors such as globalisation have been at work (cf. V. Schmidt 2002). At the other extreme, EC regulation has caused major repercussions in markets, institutions and strategies in member states, with claims of a move towards a 'European regulatory state' (McGowan and Wallace 1996). Despite these problems in assessing the impacts of EC regulation, certain traits can be sketched.

A key impact has been on domestic institutional change. National markets have been opened to competition at least in terms of formal rules. The EC has contributed to ending legal monopolies lying at the heart of states, such as telecommunications, energy and railways. It has also aided the spread of independent regulatory authorities, has provided re-regulatory rules and sometimes has provided impetus for privatisation.

EC regulation has encouraged the internationalisation of European firms through cross-border mergers and takeovers aimed at becoming European-wide suppliers – from banking and insurance mergers to cars and pharmaceuticals. It has also aided the entry of foreign suppliers (European and subsidiaries of non-European firms) into previously closed national markets in sectors ranging from the utilities or financial services to manufactured goods. It has increased pressures on publicly-owned enterprises, which have lost many of their legal monopolies and found their privileged relationships with governments under scrutiny by the Commission, especially under state aid provisions (cf. Hayward 1995).

Some Europeanisation has occurred by imposition of EC regulation on member states. However, other processes seem to be more important. The EC has aided policy transfer, through policy learning and emulation. Thus for instance, the EC encouraged the spread of the 'British model' of regulating the electricity sector (complete liberalisation, regulated access to the transmission infrastructure, simple authorization of new capacity, legal separation of transmission and supply and independent sectoral regulators) although these features were not required by EC law (Padgett 2003). Even in telecommunications, where a detailed EC regulatory regime has developed, the main impacts have been to provide legitimation and explanation for national governments to pursue policies desired for non-EC reasons (Thatcher 2004; cf. Radaelli and Schmidt 2004). Thus, for instance, governments used EC regulation to justify the privatisation of Telecom Italia or France Télécom, which they sought for other reasons, notably raising money for budgets; even governments favouring public ownership, such as the Jospin government of 1997–2002, have argued that, 'reluctantly', they needed to privatise in order to meet EC pressures (Thatcher 1999).

Limits on EC regulation

In analysing EC regulation, it is too easy to lose sight of the real limits on its growth and significance: increased activity is only one indicator of importance and the expansion of EC regulation must be analysed in the context of its impact on member states. Closer examination reveals several factors that constrain the EC.

Veto points and the power of member states

There are many 'veto points' in the EC's decision-making processes that allow key actors, particularly member states, to block, hinder or delay EC regulation. Treaty amendments to provide the EC with new powers are slow and require approval by all member states. Passing secondary legislation, the key means of EC regulation, is now mostly covered by the co-decision procedure that gives powers to three actors (the Commission, Council and European Parliament), each with its own interests. The comitology process, a central method of moving from general principles and aims to specific EC requirements, involves national officials (cf. Vos 1997). The Commission itself is a collegial body, headed by the appointees of national governments (although the Amsterdam Treaty slightly strengthens the President). Regulatory decisions, including 'technical' ones in a highly juridicised environment such as the application of competition policy, must be approved by the College of Commissioners, leading to intense and often highly politicised battles (McGowan and Cini 1999). Individual Commissioners must therefore build alliances within the College and watch carefully the reactions of national governments.

The resources of the Commission

Although the scope of EC regulation and the amount of legislation have expanded, the Commission remains a small organisation with severely constrained material resources. It has very few staff and low expenditure, especially relative to national bureaucracies and large firms. Even DG Competition, responsible for policing and sometimes enforcing competition policy, has a tiny staff (approximately 400) relative to the breadth and importance of its tasks. Yet producing regulation is frequently difficult, and highly technical. The Commission therefore has to be very selective in where to attempt to regulate. Moreover, it relies heavily on other actors for information and expertise – including national governments and regulators, firms and interest groups. National officials play a key role in the preparation of legislative proposals (including through Coreper) and then, after directives have been passed, in fleshing out 'technical' matters through the comitology system. These 'committees' are composed of national and Commission officials. There were estimated to be at least 1,500 committees by the mid-1990s, of which 410 were 'comitology committees' established under secondary legislation to undertake a variety of advisory, managerial and rule-making functions in its application (Wessels 1998; Joerges and Vos 1999). Through these committees national officials are intimately involved in passing most EC regulatory legislation, in advising, managing and making detailed rules. In addition, Commission staffing is constantly a problem, and many officials in Brussels are in fact seconded national officials and experts.

Implementation

Closely linked to lack of Commission resources is the fact that most EC legislation is broad, and offers only a framework for decision-making within member states. Directives are only binding as to their objectives and not their means. Almost all implementation is undertaken by national regulators. Although EC regulation has been extended, few new EC regulatory agencies have been created. Bodies such as the European Agency for the Evaluation of Medicinal Products and the European Environment Agency are the exception rather than the rule, and they have limited powers, relying heavily on national bodies and with the Commission maintaining important final powers over their decisions (Dehousse 1997; Kelemen 2002).

These features make effective enforcement by the EC difficult. There can be considerable gaps between EC rules and their operation in practice. If member states oppose EC regulation and lose, they can be tempted to seek a 'second round' by resisting effective implementation. However, even when member states agree to EU legislation, they may fail to implement it, due not only to 'opposition through the backdoor', but also to administrative weaknesses, difficulties in interpreting it and linkage with other issues (Falkner *et al.* 2004). The Commission lacks resources to pursue all member states over implementation, even if it so wished. Moreover, infringement proceedings are slow and difficult. Private litigants within member states can play a part, but legal action is frequently financially costly, damaging to relationships with national actors and unlikely to offer swift results that may be required in fast-moving markets.

Existing national regulation and regulators

The decentralised nature of most EC regulation makes the national level very important for regulation in practice. Key decisions are still made within nation states, on matters such as ownership or the institutional structure of domestic regulators. National institutions such as public ownership or the existence and powers of independent agencies, influence decision-making (Thatcher 1999). Legally, the EC cannot require changes in ownership (under Article 295(222)). Yet ownership can affect the impact of EC regulation; for example, public ownership of commercial enterprises poses significant difficulties over matters such as distinguishing state aid and new capital injections and can create incentives for governments to favour state-owned companies. The EC has been unable to break up large oligopolistic or monopolistic suppliers: even in markets subject to considerable EC regulation, powerful national champions such as BT, France Télécom, Deutsche Telekom, British Airways, EdF, Lufthansa, continue to enjoy dominance in domestic telecommunications, electricity or airline markets. EC structural intervention has been largely confined to occasions of takeovers and mergers, and even on these, its requirements have been limited to the disposal of limited parts of businesses. Member states retain great freedom over the organisational features of national regulatory authorities, as EC requirements are often limited; hence, for instance, in utilities regulation EC directives typically demand that national regulatory authorities be organisationally separate from suppliers and that they must act fairly and transparently, but add little detail about decision-making procedures and processes and do not insist that they be independent of elected politicians.

EC regulation also leaves much room for national choices in features other than organisational structures, especially in re-regulation – for instance, over social obligations, tariffs or professional registration requirements (Héritier 2002). One reason is that re-regulation often depends on mutual recognition (of standards among member states), which is subject to minimum standards and exceptions, leaving much room for national discretion. Moreover, even when domestic markets such as road haulage or insurance have been liberalised following EC regulation, they have continued to be dominated by domestic firms (S. Schmidt 2002). The result is that even within policy fields with a fairly high degree of EC regulation such as the utilities or financial services, considerable national variations continue (Coen and Thatcher 1999; Eberlein 1999; Héritier and Thatcher 2002; Héritier 2001; Coen *et al.* 2002).

Interest groups

The EC is highly dependent on interest groups – to persuade national policy-makers to accept its regulation, for information, for expertise and for monitoring implementation and challenging non-compliance (if necessary through litigation). Its scope to regulate in the face of well-organised hostile interests is therefore limited. This holds true even in competition policy, where the Commission offers informal guidance and negotiates with firms to obtain agreements, and seeks to avoid lengthy legal proceedings that will take up time and resources; thus, for example, in 2003, 295 out of 319 cases opened by DG Competition under competition Treaty Articles (anti-trust and state monopolies – Articles 81, 82, 31 and 86) were closed through its 'informal procedures' (Commission 2004: 61).

International regulation

Since the 1990s, international regulation has expanded, notably the GATT and WTO. International trade negotiations may have strengthened EC regulation, as the Commission frequently represented the EC, member states were obliged to cooperate with it due to shared competencies and as the Community sought to maximise its influence by establishing common positions. However, EC regulation is now subject to the WTO and legislation and decisions that affect international trade are liable to challenge under WTO rules. As a result, much of EC regulation, from food health and safety rules to product standards or EC content requirements is open to attack; this process has already begun, often led by US multinationals and public officials, seen recently in disputes over genetically-modified food.

The legitimacy of EC regulation

EC regulation suffers from significant problems of legitimacy. Under the first pillar of the EU, the EC has supranational competencies, and hence can impose regulation on unwilling member states. Yet passing legislation is shared between the Commission, the Council of Ministers and the European Parliament, with the ECJ playing a crucial role. The constitutional basis of the EC is therefore hybrid between elected (directly or indirectly) and non-majoritarian bodies. EC decision-making procedures appear opaque – for example, debates within the Council and the Commission are not published, there is no overall code of conduct on how regulatory decisions should be made and the comitology system is closed and largely private. Lines of accountability are multiple and unclear, especially after the strengthening of the European Parliament's powers under the Maastricht and Amsterdam Treaties – the Commission answers to both it and the Council. Due to its limited resources and the power of national interests at all stages of regulation, the Commission's expertise, effectiveness and independence are open to severe questioning. Such problems rise rapidly to the surface whenever controversial decisions are taken that involve powerful national interests, as evidenced in the BSE crisis or regulation of state aid.

Conclusion

EC regulation has grown, expanding from removal of tariffs to dealing with non-tariff barriers and introducing Community re-regulatory standards and rules. It has spread across many sectors, from utilities to food. Its development has been the product of many factors: Commission activism, ECJ rulings, delegation by national governments, pressure by interest groups have all played a part. To create analytical simplicity and to link to broader claims about European integration, the chapter has offered three 'models' or lenses: a top-down view, in which the expansion of EC regulation has been led by the Commission and ECJ; a delegation model, in which national governments have chosen to delegate to the EC, and a dynamic framework, in which EC regulation is the result of processes arising from interactions between different levels of decision-making.

As EC regulation has increased, greater attention is being paid to its effects at the national level. This often reveals the limits of EC regulation and the continuing importance of the domestic arenas of member states. EC regulation has expanded but remains intimately intertwined with national politics.

Notes

1   References are to the European Community since almost all regulation discussed here falls under the EC pillar of the EU. The athor acknowledges the support of the New Governance project as part of the EU 6th Framework Programme (project CITI–CT–2004–506392).

References

Armstrong, K. and Bulmer, S. (1998) *Governance of the Single European Market* (Manchester: Manchester University Press).

Baldwin, R. and Cave, M. (1999) *Understanding Regulation* (Oxford: Oxford University Press).

Broscheid, A. and Coen, D. (2003) 'Insider and Outsider Lobbying of the European Commission', *European Union Politics* 4/2: 165–89.

Bulmer, S. J. (1998), 'New Institutionalism and the Governance of the Single European Market', *Journal of European Public Policy* 5/3: 365–86.

Bulmer, S. J. and Padgett, S. (forthcoming) 'Policy Transfer in the European Union: An Institutionalist Perspective', *British Journal of Political Science*.

Cichowski, R. (2001), 'Judicial Rulemaking and the Institutionalization of European Union Sex Equality Policy', in A. Stone Sweet, W. Sandholtz and N. Fligstein (eds), *The Institutionalization of Europe* (Oxford: Oxford University Press).

Coen, D. (1998) 'The European Business Interest and the Nation State: Large-firm Lobbying in the European Union and Member States', *Journal of Public Policy* 18/1: 75–100.

Coen, D. and Thatcher, M. (1999) 'Regulating European Utilities', *Current Politics and Economics of Europe* special issue 6/4.

Coen, D., Héritier, A. and Böllhoff, D. (2002) *Regulating the Utilities: Business and Regulator Perspectives in the UK and Germany* (Berlin: Anglo-German Foundation).

Commission of the European Communities (1985) *Completing the Internal Market: White Paper from the Commission to the European Council* (Luxembourg: Office for Official Publications of the European Communities).

—— (1999) Directory of Community Legislation in Force and Other Acts of the Community Institutions, *Official Journal* vol. II.

—— (2001) *European Governance: A White Paper*, COM(2001) 428 (Brussels: Commission of the European Communities).

—— (2003) *General Report on the Activity of the European Union 2003* (Brussels: Commission of the European Communities).

—— (2004) *European Union Competition Policy 2003* (Brussels: Commission of the European Communities).

Council of the European Communities (1962) *Council Regulation 17/62*, 1962 O.J. 204.

—— (1990) *Council Regulation 4064/89*, 1990 O.J. L257 14 (corrected version of 1989 O.J. L395 1).

Dehousse, R. (1992) 'Integration v. Regulation? On the Dynamics of Regulation in the European Community', *Journal of Common Market Studies* 30/4: 383–402.

—— (1997) 'Regulation by Networks in the European Community: the Role of European Agencies', *Journal of European Public Policy* 4/2: 246–61.

Eberlein, B. (1999) 'Configurations of Economic Regulation in the European Union: the Case of Electricity in Comparative Perspective', *Current Politics and Economics of Europe* 6/4: 31–51.

—— (2004) 'Formal and Informal Governance in Single Market Regulation', in T. Christiansen and S. Piattoni (eds), *Informal Governance in the EU* (Cheltenham: Edward Elgar).

Eberlein, B. and Kerwer, D. (2004) 'New Governance in the European Union: A Theoretical Perspective', *Journal of Common Market Studies* 42/1: 121–42.

ECJ (1974) Case 8/74, Procureur du Roi v. Dassonville [1974] ECR 837.

—— (1979) Case 120/78, Rewe [1979] ECR 649. [Cassis de Dijon].

—— (1987) Case 156/84 [1987] ECR 4487.

—— (1991) Case 202/88 French Republic v. Commission [1991] ECR I–1223.

—— (1992) Joined Cases C–271/90, C–281/90 and C–289/90 Spain, France, Belgium and Italy v. Commission [1992] ECR I–5833.

Egan, M. (2001) *Constructing a European Market* (Oxford: Oxford University Press).

Eichener, V. (1997) 'Effective European Problem-solving: Lessons from the Regulation of Occupational Safety and Environmental Protection', *Journal of European Public Policy* 4/4: 591–608.

Eising, R. (2002) 'Policy Learning in Embedded Negotiations: Explaining EU Electricity Liberalization', *International Organization* 56/1: 85–120.

European Parliament and Council (2002) Directive of the European Parliament and of the Council on a common regulatory framework for electronic communications of networks and services (Framework Directive) OJ L 108, 24.4.2002: 33.

Evans, P., Jacobson, H. and Putnam, R. (eds) (1993) *Double-Edged Diplomacy: International Bargaining and Domestic Politics* (Berkeley: University of California Press).

Falkner, G. and Hartlapp, M. (2004) 'Non-Compliance with EU Directives in the Member States', *West European Politics* 27/3: 452–73.

Falkner, G., Hartlapp, M., Leiber, S. and Treib, O. (2004) 'Non-compliance with EU Directives in the Member States', *West European Politics* 27/3: 452–73.

Fligstein, N. and McNichol, J. (1998) 'The Institutional Terrain of the European Union', in W. Sandholtz and A. Stone Sweet (eds), *European Integration and Supranational Governance* (Oxford: Oxford University Press).

Gaitsos, K. and Seabright, P. (1989) 'Regulation in the European Community', *Oxford Review of Economic Policy* 5/2: 37–60.

Geradin, D., Munoz, R. and Petit, N. (eds) (2005) *Regulatory Authorities in the EC: a New Paradigm for European Governance* (Aldershot: Edward Elgar).

325

Gerber, D. J. (1994) 'The Transformation of European Community Competition Law?', *Harvard International Law Review* 35/1: 97–147.

Green Cowles, M., Caporaso, J. and Risse, T. (eds) (2001), *Transforming Europe* (Ithaca, NY: Cornell University Press).

Hayward, J. E. S. (ed.) (1995) *Industrial Enterprise and European Integration* (Oxford: Oxford University Press).

Héritier, A. (2002) 'Public-interest Services Revisited', *Journal of European Public Policy* 9/6: 995–1019.

Héritier, A. and Thatcher, M. (eds) (2002), 'Regulatory Reform in Europe', *Journal of European Public Policy* special issue 9/6.

Héritier, A., Kerwer, D., Knill, C., Lehmkuhl, C., Teuscg, M., and Douillet, A.-C. (2001) *Differential Europe* (Lanham, MD: Rowman & Littlefield).

Holzinger, K. and Knill, C. (2004) 'Competition and Cooperation in Environmental Policy', *Journal of Public Policy* 24/1: 25–47.

Hooghe, L. and Marks, G. (2001) *Multi-level Governance and European Integration* (Lanham, MD: Rowman & Littlefield).

Joerges, C. and Vos, E. (eds) (1999) *EU Committees: Social Regulation, Law and Politics* (Oxford: Hart).

Kelemen, D. (2002) 'The Politics of "Eurocratic" Structure and the New European Agencies', *West European Politics* 25/4: 93–118.

Lenschow, A. (2002) 'New Regulatory Approaches to "Greening" EU Policies', *European Law Journal* 8/1: 19–37.

McGowan, F. and Wallace, H. (1996) 'Towards a European Regulatory State', *Journal of European Public Policy* 3/4: 560–76.

McGowan, L. and Cini, M. (1999) 'Discretion and Politicization in EU Competition Policy: The Case of Merger Control', *Governance* 12/2: 175–200.

Majone, G. (ed.) (1996) *Regulating Europe* (London: Routledge).

—— (2000) 'The Credibility Crisis of Community Regulation', *Journal of Common Market Studies* 38/2: 273–302.

Mazey, S. (1995) 'The Development of EU Equality Policies: Bureaucratic Expansion on Behalf of Women', *Public Administration* 73/4: 591–609.

Mazey, S. and Richardson, J. (eds) (1993) *Lobbying in the European Community* (Oxford: Oxford University Press).

Moran, M. (2002) 'Understanding the Regulatory State', *British Journal of Political Science* 32: 391–413

Moravcsik, A. (1993) 'Preferences and Power in the European Community: A Liberal Intergovernmentalist Approach', *Journal of Common Market Studies* 31/4: 473–524.

Nicolaides, P. (2004) 'The Political Economy of Multi-tiered Regulation in Europe', *Journal of Common Market Studies* 42/3: 599–618.

Padgett, S. (2003) 'Between Synthesis and Emulation: EU Policy Transfer in the Power Sector', *Journal of European Public Policy* 10/2: 227–45.

Parrish, R. (2003) 'The Politics of Sport Regulation in the European Union', *Journal of European Public Policy* 10/2: 246–62.

Pelkmans, J. (1987) 'The New Approach to Technical Harmonisation and Standardisation', *Journal of Common Market Studies* 25/3: 249–69.

Peters, B. G. (1994) 'Agenda-Setting in the European Community', *Journal of European Public Policy* 1/1: 9–26.

Peterson, J. (1997) 'States, Societies and the European Union', *West European Politics* 20/4: 1–23.

Pollack, M. (2003) *The Engines of European Integration* (Oxford: Oxford University Press).

Porte, C. de la (2002), 'Is the Open Method of Coordination Appropriate for Organising Activities at European Level in Sensitive Policy Areas?', *European Law Journal* 8/1: 38–58.

Putnam, R. D. (1988) 'Diplomacy and Domestic Politics: The Logic of Two-Level Games', *International Organization* 42/3: 427–60.

Radaelli, C. (2000) 'Policy Transfer in the European Union', *Governance* 13/1: 25–43.

Radaelli, C. and Schmidt, V. (eds) (2004) 'Europeanisation, Discourse and Policy Change', *West European Politics* special issue 27/2.

Regent, S. (2003) 'The Open Method of Coordination: A New Supranational Form of Governance?', *European Law Journal* 9/2: 190–214.

Rhodes, M. (1995) 'A Regulatory Conundrum: Industrial Relations and the Social Dimension', in S. Liebfried and P. Pierson (eds), *European Social Policy* (Washington, DC: Brookings).

Richardson, J. (1994) 'EU Water Policy: Uncertain Agendas, Shifting Networks and Complex Coalitions', *Environmental Politics* 3/4: 139–67.

Sandholtz, W. and Stone Sweet, A. (eds) (1998) *European Integration and Supranational Governance* (Oxford: Oxford University Press).

Scharpf, F. W. (1997) *Games Real Actors Play* (Boulder, CO: Westview Press).

Schmidt, S. (2002) 'The Impact of Mutual Recognition – Inbuilt Limits and Domestic Responses to the Single Market', *Journal of European Public Policy* 9/6: 935–53.

Schmidt, V. (2002) *The Futures of European Capitalism* (Oxford: Oxford University Press).

Selznick, P. (1985) 'Focusing Organizational Research on Regulation', in R. Noll (ed.) *Regulatory Policy and the Social Sciences* (Berkeley: University of California Press).

Stone Sweet, A. and Caporaso, J. A. (1998) 'From Free Trade to Supranational Polity: The European Court and Integration', in W. Sandholtz and A. Stone Sweet (eds) *European Integration and Supranational Governance* (Oxford: Oxford University Press).

Stone Sweet, A. Sandholtz, W. and Fligstein, N. (eds) (2001) *The Institutionalization of Europe* (Oxford: Oxford University Press).

Thatcher, M. (1999) *The Politics of Telecommunications* (Oxford: Oxford University Press).

—— (2001) 'The Commission and National Governments as Partners: EC Regulatory Expansion in Telecommunications 1979–2000', *Journal of European Public Policy* 8/4: 558–84.

—— (2004) 'Winners and Losers in Europeanization: Reforming the National Regulation of Telecommunications', *West European Politics* 27/2: 102–27.

Vos, E. (1997) 'The Rise of Committees', *European Law Journal* 3/3: 210–29.

Weiler, J. (1991) 'The Transformation of Europe', *Yale Law Journal* 100: 2403–83.

Wendon, B. (1998) 'The Commission as Image-venue Entrepreneur in EU Social Policy', *Journal of European Public Policy* 5/2: 339–53.

Wessels, W. (1998) 'Comitology: Fusion in Action. Politico-administrative Trends in the EU System', *Journal of European Public Policy* 5/2: 209–34.

Wilks, S. (1996) 'Regulatory Compliance and Capitalist Diversity in Europe', *Journal of European Public Policy* 3/4: 536–59.

—— (2005), 'Agency Escape: Decentralisation or Dominance of the European Commission in the Modernisation of Competition Policy?', *Governance* (Summer).

Chapter 16

European macroeconomic governance

Erik Jones

Introduction

Just over five years into its existence, the European macroeconomic policy framework is in crisis. Targets are missed, discipline is lost, performance is flagging, and volatility is on the rise. As a result, even some of the more sensible newspaper columnists and pundits are suggesting that Europe should throw whole parts of the system out and start again. Despite the rising tension, however, the European Union's (EU) framework for macroeconomic governance proves remarkably difficult to reform. Radical proposals are floated to great fanfare. However, they soon become watered down. And, once diluted, they are almost never fully implemented. To round it all off, popular recognition that Europe is just muddling through on the macroeconomic front deepens the sense of failure and strengthens the perception of crisis.

Muddling through is rarely a popular reaction to such a dramatic sequence of events. Sometimes it makes sense nevertheless. The argument in this chapter is that European macroeconomic governance is one of those cases. Although there are important failings in the European system, these tend to overshadow the even more important achievements that the European Union has made. Moreover, rectifying the system is best done through trial and error, not radical reform. To torture an aphorism, there is much more baby than bathwater in the European macroeconomic framework.

This argument constitutes an extension of the relationship between European integration and national idiosyncrasy that I analyse in my book on *The Politics of Economic and Monetary Union* (Jones 2002a). In that book, I challenge the conventional belief that the European single currency will founder on the differences between European member states. What I find is that the diversity of Europe constitutes both a weakness and a strength for the single currency: it can explain why monetary integration was so hard to bring about, but it can also explain why it will be hard to do away with. Recent developments in the European macroeconomic framework only strengthen that assessment. Europe has stumbled in reaction to different problems in different countries, but it has responded by making the macroeconomic framework more resilient in the face of such differences. The changes are incremental, to be sure. But the whole of the macroeconomic framework is more effective as a result.

This view of monetary integration contrasts with the mainstream – particularly in the United Kingdom. Writers like David McKay (1999) and Larry Siedentop (2001) make the strong claim that the decision to form a single currency was the founding act of a federal bargain that will ultimately lead to a centralisation of European economic authority. McKay (1999: 182–3) and Siedentop (2001: 231) are concerned that such centralisation will race ahead of popular support for political union. As a result, 'the people' will contest the political legitimacy of the emergent European superstate and so undermine the functioning of the monetary union. In my argument there is no federal bargain and no rush to form a European superstate. On the contrary, the single currency is the result of a very complex intergovernmental negotiation. The macroeconomic framework can only evolve incrementally because too many different national actors have effective veto power over proposals for reform. Once again, Europe is condemned to muddling through. And once again, muddling through might be the most appropriate way to move forward.

The chapter has four sections. The first describes the EU macroeconomic framework as set down in the Maastricht and Amsterdam Treaties, and as elaborated up through the

March 2000 European Council summit held at Lisbon. The next two sections explain why that framework was deficient and how it has evolved in response. The fourth section concludes with implications for the practice of macroeconomic governance in particular and for the progress of European integration as a whole.

Europe's macroeconomic framework

Macroeconomic policy became a central focus for European integration in the 1990s. The 1992 Maastricht Treaty started the process by announcing the goal of achieving an economic and monetary union by the end of the decade. The 1997 Amsterdam Treaty took matters further by broadening the ambit of macroeconomic concerns to include matters relating to employment as well as money. Post-Amsterdam, Article 2 of the Treaty Establishing the European Community (TEC) lists 'a high level of employment' and 'sustainable and non-inflationary growth' as important aspects of the 'task' of the European Community. Meanwhile, Article 4, paragraph 3, declares that the 'guiding principles' for European macroeconomic policy are: 'stable money, sound public finances and monetary conditions, and a sustainable balance of payments'.[1] There is nothing inherently wrong with bringing macroeconomic governance within the process of European integration. By the same token, it is hard to imagine who would object either to the stated goals or to underlying principles. The challenge is making it all work.

The European solution to the problem of macroeconomic governance is anything but straightforward. It touches on at least four different policy areas, including monetary policy, fiscal policy, market structures, and exchange rates. And it operates on four different levels – across the European Union as a whole, within those countries participating in the single currency (called the eurozone), at the member state level, and at the (subnational) regional level within the member states. Finally, not all policy areas operate at all levels of policy-making. Monetary policy is a matter for the eurozone and the member states but not the European Union as a whole. Fiscal policy and market structural policy are matters for the European Union, the member states, and the regions, but do not fall within the jurisdiction of eurozone institutions. And responsibility for the external value of the euro is ambiguous.

Monetary policy

There are two different sets of rules governing monetary policy within the EU – one for countries within the eurozone, and another for those outside. The countries in the eurozone have a common monetary policy that is managed by the Governing Council of the European System of Central Banks (ESCB) and presented by the president of the European Central Bank (ECB). The countries outside the eurozone have their own currencies and their own monetary policies, which are managed by their national central banks.

The rules governing the eurozone are unambiguous. Article 105, paragraph 1 of the TEC declares that 'the primary objective' of the common monetary policy is 'to maintain price stability'. Of course the same paragraph does mention the possibility that eurozone monetary policy will be used to 'support the general economic policies of the Community'. However the text is clear in qualifying that any such action should be 'without prejudice to the objective of price stability'. Moreover, paragraph 2 of Article 105 gives the

ESCB the power 'to define and implement the monetary policy of the Community' and Article 108 ensures that the ESCB will act without instruction 'from Community institutions or bodies, from any government of a Member State, or from any other body'. By implication, the Governing Council of the ESCB is the sole judge of what it should and should not do.

When it started operations, the ECB defined price stability according to two different monetary indicators – the historic growth of monetary liquidity (M3) and the expected rate of inflation over the medium term.[2] Moreover, it announced specific targets for both indicators. Liquidity growth should be measured against a 'reference value' of 4.5 per cent increase per annum and medium-term estimates should place the inflation rate below 2 per cent per annum. Where past liquidity growth or expected inflation are found to be relatively high, the Governing Council may see a threat to price stability and so respond by raising interest rates. And where liquidity growth and inflation are below target, the Governing Council may see no threat to price stability and so may lower interest rates in order to support or encourage the pace of economic activity in the eurozone. These interpretations are written with the conditional 'may' because the ECB refuses to give any precise mechanical formula for predicting monetary policy on the basis of economic data. Moreover, the ECB provides no guidance for when monetary policy might be used to support Community economic policies more generally beyond repeated assertions that the best macroeconomic support the ECB can offer to the Community as a whole is to maintain price stability within the eurozone (Trichet 2001: 10).

The rules governing the conduct of monetary policy for those countries outside the eurozone are less clear cut. The guiding principle of stable prices applies to all member states regardless of whether they join the single currency, but the notion that price stability is more important for monetary authorities than a high level of employment or sustainable growth is not explicit. With the exception of Denmark and Britain, countries outside the eurozone are also committed to the goal of joining the single currency, including efforts to make their national inflation rates converge on performance within the eurozone and to insulate their national central banks from political influence in the conduct of monetary policy.[3] Finally, all non-eurozone member states – including Denmark and Britain – have the obligation to 'treat [their] exchange-rate policy as a matter of common interest' in line with 'experience acquired in cooperation within the framework of the European Monetary System' (TEC Article 124, paragraph 1). The implication of this provision is to connect monetary policy in the non-eurozone countries to the single currency through the exchange rate between their national currency and the euro. Hence while the monetary rules for countries outside the eurozone are somewhat ambiguous, the effect is to extend the price-stability mandate of the eurozone out onto those countries that do not yet participate in the single currency.

Fiscal policy

The conduct of fiscal policy is subject to two rules and three procedures. The rules are to avoid excessive fiscal deficits and 'to respect the medium-term budgetary objective of close to balance or in surplus'.[4] The first rule is a legacy of the Maastricht convergence process that started in the early 1990s as part of the run-up to the formation of the single currency. The second derives from the 'Stability and Growth Pact' that was agreed just before the single currency was launched and when the member states adopted the

Amsterdam Treaty in 1997. These rules apply to all countries, whether or not they choose to join the single European currency. The rules also apply to subnational regions, at least insofar as regional governments have important fiscal responsibilities that could contribute to the overall level of national fiscal deficits or debts. Finally, these fiscal rules follow logically from the general principle of maintaining sound public finances. The point to note, however, is that these are rules only in the economic sense and not in the legal sense. They represent useful guidelines for policy-making but they are not enforceable per se.

Any enforcement operates through the procedures for policy coordination and not through the rules themselves. The member states introduced two procedures at Maastricht (1992) and a third at Amsterdam (1997). The Maastricht procedures are for the 'multilateral surveillance' of economic policy and for the elimination of excessive fiscal deficits (called the 'excessive deficit procedure'). The multilateral surveillance procedure serves the goal of making national economic policy in the common European interest. It requires all member states to participate in the elaboration of 'broad guidelines of the economic policies of the Member States and of the Community' – called the Broad Economic Policy Guidelines, or BEPGs. And it provides the means through which the Council of Ministers can monitor the implementation of recommendations made in the guidelines by the different member states. Such recommendations may help to avoid excessive deficits in the short term or they may promote fiscal balance over the medium term. All that matters is that the recommendations be made in the BEPGs. Finally, the procedure makes it possible for the Council of Ministers to reprimand member states that fail to do as they are recommended.

The excessive deficit procedure is more narrowly focused and does not apply to Great Britain (which negotiated an opt-out in a protocol attached to the Maastricht Treaty). This procedure builds on a specific definition of what constitutes an excessive deficit – defined as a ratio of actual or planned government deficit equal to 3 per cent of gross domestic product (GDP) or a ratio of government debt equal to 60 per cent of GDP. It also specifies which accounting measures to use and it requires the member states to provide relevant and accurate financial information about their own accounts. Finally, the procedure sets out the specific steps that need to be taken at each stage in the process from identifying to rectifying excessive deficits within the member states. These stages extend up to and include the possibility that the Council of Ministers would be able to levy fines against those countries that refuse to comply. Importantly, the procedure also includes a critical decision point or procedural firebreak – set out in Article 104, paragraph 10, of the TEC. Before that point, the usual European instruments for legal or procedural redress do not apply. Beyond it, the various parties to the excessive deficit procedure become legally responsible for their actions.

The two procedures set out in the Maastricht Treaty are both overlapping and open-ended. Either could be used to recommend changes to the fiscal policies of the member states and neither provides a clear chronology of which should be done or when. Therefore the Council of Ministers introduced two pieces of legislation as part of the Stability and Growth Pact at Amsterdam – one (1467/97) clarifying the time-frame for applying the excessive deficit procedure and the other (1466/97) making it possible for the Council of Ministers to issue an early warning in the event that it has sufficient evidence to believe that a member state would run afoul of the requirements for either the multilateral surveillance or the excessive deficit procedures. This 'early warning procedure' draws much of its force from the process of multilateral surveillance and so increases the likelihood that a member state will coordinate its fiscal policy under the threat of a formal reprimand long before approaching the firebreak in the excessive deficit procedure that could open the door to strong legal sanctions for non-compliance.

Market structures

The coordination of market structures in Europe is both unusual and important for overall macroeconomic performance. It is unusual insofar as few (if any) textbooks on macroeconomics pay much attention to market structures or to the process of market-structural reform. More often, these are considered matters for microeconomics and not for macroeconomics. Nevertheless, the inclusion of market-structural reform is important in Europe because of the way European politicians designed their economic and monetary union. From the start, economists noted that the eurozone benefits from few if any mechanisms to transfer resources from one part of Europe to another and it suffers from a predominantly restrictive notion of macroeconomic policy coordination. The fiscal rules described above make no provision for coordinating policy in any activist sense and so they offer little hope that Europe's policy-makers would be able to engineer a joint fiscal expansion to counter an economic downturn. Meanwhile, monetary policy is focused almost exclusively on price stability. Hence many economists questioned whether the single currency would be stable over the medium-to-long term or whether it would founder in reaction to a sharp downturn in macroeconomic performance either across the eurozone or within some important participating country.

The European response to such concerns has been to emphasise the importance of 'efficient local factor markets' – meaning the markets for capital and labour. This awkward piece of jargon covers a potential sleight of hand. When markets are 'efficient' in economic terms, they do a good job matching workers to jobs and capital to investment opportunities. Therefore, they do not exhibit any of the symptoms of inefficiency such as high unemployment or inadequate investment. Moreover, when the efficiency is 'local', markets can solve their own problems without sending workers abroad or becoming dependent upon foreign capital – which must be repaid with interest. These features are important in Europe because there is no desire to see workers migrate from one country to another and little likelihood that capital flows across Europe will effectively compensate for relative economic performance from one place to the next. Hence, locally efficient factor markets should be able to accommodate any downturn in macroeconomic activity whether it is specific to a given country or region or whether it is general to the European Union as a whole. Unfortunately, it takes only a brief glance at the data to reveal that such local efficiency does not exist in European markets in the real world. By implication, the success of European macroeconomic policy coordination is contingent upon the effectiveness of market-structural reform (Jones 1998).

The European framework for market-structural reform encompasses three 'processes', one 'strategy', and an underlying 'method'. The complexity of the framework derives from its piecemeal elaboration. The origins can be found in the decision to include a title on employment in the Amsterdam Treaty and to call for a special European Council summit on employment to be held during the Luxembourg presidency in the Autumn of 1997. The result was the introduction of the 'Luxembourg process' for encouraging the adoption of active labour market policies across the member states and for monitoring labour market performance through the European institutions. This was followed in June 1998 by the 'Cardiff process' for reforming the markets for goods and services and in June 1999 by the 'Cologne process' for involving the representatives of industry and labour (collectively referred to as the 'social partners') in a pattern of macroeconomic dialogue. These processes depend crucially on action taken at the member state level. However, they also create opportunities to deepen the involvement of the European Commission in monitoring member state performance and to broaden the scope of both the procedure for multilateral surveillance and the formulation of the broad economic policy guidelines as described above.

The special economic summit of the European Council held in Lisbon during March 2000 brought the three processes together. The Lisbon European Council established a new strategic goal, 'to become the most competitive and dynamic knowledge-based economy in the world' by 2010. It also outlined action in three areas, two of which focused on structural reform to enhance competitiveness and to modernise the European social model. The third makes reference to the importance of 'applying an appropriate macro-economic policy mix'.[5] Finally, the Lisbon Council outlined a new 'open method for coordination' that could be used to foster necessary reforms. This 'open method' is the real innovation in the strategy. Not only does it focus attention on the need for member states to learn from and support one another in the reform process, but it also recognises the inevitability that the problem of reform will be different from one market and one member state to the next (Hodson and Maher 2001; Jones 2001).

The Lisbon strategy also created a set timetable for the conduct of European macro-economic policy coordination as it takes place through the multilateral surveillance procedure and through the overlapping processes for market-structural reform. From 2000 onward, the European Council would meet to discuss economic policy in a special summit. There they would discuss both the progress made in past reform efforts and the action that should be taken under the forthcoming broad economic policy guidelines. The March summits could also be used to launch major economic initiatives, to recognise exceptional achievement, and to underscore the cost of failure.

Exchange rates

The rules governing exchange rate policy are most notable for their absence. Exchange rates between the member states have already been touched upon in the context of monetary policy. What matters here concerns relations between the single European currency and third countries. In practice, this means relations between the euro and the dollar. The presumption was always that an explicit exchange rate policy would not be necessary given the relative size of the eurozone and its limited exposure to the outside world. Where even some of Europe's larger countries such as France or Germany have an export-to-GDP ratio of between 20 and 30 per cent, the ratio for the eurozone as a whole is closer to 10 per cent. The eurozone is approximately as large as the United States and it experiences much the same level of vulnerability to the influence of exchange rates on overall levels of production. Therefore, so the argument runs, Europe should worry about movements in the dollar only as much as the United States worries about movements in the euro. By implication, exchange rate policy matters only as it impacts on domestic objectives or, in the European case, on the priority given to maintaining price stability (Jones 2002a: 123–41; Taylor 2004).

This logic is embedded in Article 111 of the TEC. Paragraph 1 suggests that the Council of Ministers could enter into a formal exchange rate arrangement with third countries but only after extensive consultation with other European institutions 'in an endeavor to reach a consensus consistent with the objective of price stability'. Absent a formal arrangement, paragraph 2 indicates that the Council could formulate general guidelines to limit exchange rate movements. Here too, however, 'these general orientations shall be without prejudice to the primary objective of the ESCB to maintain price stability'. In practice, such constraints make it unlikely that the eurozone would ever come up with an exchange rate policy to govern the relationship between the euro and the dollar.

Putting it all together

The European macroeconomic framework is complicated both in structure and in effect. It involves a range of different rules, procedures, processes and omissions. It plays out across different levels of government. And it depends upon a number of strong assumptions – the most important being about the efficiency of local factor markets and about the relative vulnerability of the eurozone to movements in the euro–dollar exchange rate. Nevertheless, it is intellectually coherent, it is broadly comprehensive, and – most important – it is politically acceptable. Moreover, it started out with unanticipated success.

During the first year after the single currency was launched, Europe's macroeconomic authorities benefited from strong growth, diminishing unemployment, and relatively stable macroeconomic conditions. The choice at Lisbon to strive to create the world's most dynamic and competitive knowledge-based economy by 2010 seemed hyperbolic, but only a little. Although Europe had been slow to adapt to the 'new economy' of the late 1990s, it looked ready for a much brighter future.

Europe's macroeconomic crisis

Looks can be deceiving and in economics they often are. Rather than heralding a future of 'sustainable and non-inflationary growth', the European macroeconomic framework has run into a number of obstacles. The point to note, however, is that the most important problems in the framework were unforeseen. Although complicated, Europe's various rules and procedures for macroeconomic governance succeeded in addressing (or avoiding) the problems they were meant to solve.

Where the European macroeconomic framework failed is in relation to the problems that no one seriously expected to encounter. The single currency was set to defend against rising prices and not falling prices. The fiscal rules were to safeguard against smaller or weaker countries and not against France and Germany. Market structural reforms were meant to shore up the economic and monetary union and not to become the centrepiece for macroeconomic governance. And the euro–dollar exchange rate was meant to be stable and not volatile. In any event, any impact of movements in the euro–dollar exchange rate on Europe was to be less and not more important.

The problem of falling prices was perhaps the greatest surprise of European monetary integration. The concern expressed during the run-up to monetary integration was that the single currency would not prove to be as stable as the currencies that it replaced, most notably the Deutschmark. Hence the ECB was careful to define an upper bound for price stability (the 2 per cent expectation over the medium term) but paid little attention to the need for a lower bound. A few commentators suggested that it would be more prudent to express price stability as a range rather than a ceiling (Buiter 1999). However, such concerns had little impact on ECB policy.

Little that happened during the early months of monetary integration displaced the threat of inflation as the central concern for the ECB. Nevertheless, political developments did begin to challenge the assumptions upon which monetary integration was founded. Specifically, the left-wing German Finance Minister, Oskar Lafontaine, challenged the legitimacy of a monetary policy that paid scant heed to the need to stimulate growth. At the time, growth across the eurozone was running almost a full percentage point ahead of growth within Germany. Lafontaine hoped that the ECB could be persuaded (cajoled) into lowering interest rates to stimulate growth further – and primarily in Germany's interest. As it happened, however, the ECB only lowered rates in April 1999 once Lafontaine resigned from office. This timing of events was intentional. The first ECB president, Wim Duisenberg, wanted to underscore that the ECB remained wedded to its price stability mandate and that it would not relax policy in a way that could bring the credibility of its commitment to fight inflation into doubt (Jones 2000: 252–5).

Growth accelerated in the eurozone toward the end of 1999 and continued to increase in 2000. Meanwhile price inflation began to accelerate as well. Hence the ECB decided to reverse its interest rate cut and to initiate a rapid monetary tightening. By October 2000, the main refinancing rate was 4.75 per cent as opposed to the 3.00 per cent set in January 1999.[6] The cycle then quickly reversed itself. In 2001, growth began to slow and yet inflation remained stubbornly high. In addition, the growth in monetary liquidity (M3) surged well beyond its reference value of 4.5 per cent – growing 8 per cent for the year as a whole. Hence while the ECB began to lower interest rates, its efforts to loosen monetary policy in 2001 were much slower than its efforts to tighten had been in 2000.

The ECB only moved more aggressively in the aftermath of the September 11 terrorist attack on the United States – lowering its main refinancing rate by half a percentage point soon after the attack and by another half a percentage point in November. Given the persistence of consumer price inflation and the fast pace of monetary growth, however, the ECB soon ran out of room to manoeuvre. Although the main refinancing rate remained positive at 3.25 per cent, the arguments for loosening monetary conditions further simply could not find support in the data. Hence from November 2001 to December 2002, the ECB held monetary policy constant. Meanwhile, economic conditions deteriorated sharply. The eurozone as a whole grew by just under 1 per cent in real terms. Germany did not grow at all. Moreover, prices in Germany actually started to fall. Although the year-on-year data for consumer price inflation showed an increase of 1.3 per cent, the monthly data for June, July and August of 2002 recorded straight declines.

The threat of falling prices in Germany presented a range of unexpected dilemmas for the ECB. First, the fall in German inflation rates implied a rise in the real interest rates confronting German borrowers. In turn, this rise in real interest rates risked depressing the German economy even further and so exacerbating the tendency toward deflation. Second, while German inflation for 2002 was 1.3 per cent on average, inflation elsewhere in the eurozone was sufficiently robust to push the average for the eurozone as a whole to 2.3 per cent. Since Germany is the largest economy in the eurozone, this high average implied a wide variation in inflation performance across the smaller member states – just under 5 per cent in Ireland and just under 4 per cent in Greece, Spain, Portugal, and the Netherlands. Third, liquidity growth remained well above the reference value – at 7 per cent rather than 4.5 per cent. Hence, not only did Europe have sufficient liquidity to accommodate growth but also economic actors were building up an excess of liquidity that could translate into inflation at some point in the future. Taken together, these factors pointed in different directions: the ECB should lower interest rates for Germany, but this might only fuel inflation elsewhere. Worse still, any loosening of monetary policy might have no effect on underlying growth rates and it might add to the growing excess of liquidity, which would increase the threat of sudden inflation in the future.

The ECB ultimately chose to continue with its strategy of cutting interest rates. Moreover, it did so despite the persistence of high eurozone inflation, fast liquidity growth, and the growing threat to future price stability represented by the overhang of excess liquidity. However, many commentators regarded this action as too little, too late. Such criticism was probably unfair. Although the rhetoric of the ECB remained wedded to its price stability mandate, the actions of monetary policy makers showed more flexibility (Allsopp and Artis 2003). The problem is that ECB action by itself was not enough to solve Europe's macroeconomic problems. Trying to jump-start the economy by lowering interest rates was – to borrow from the language of the Great Depression – a little like pushing on a string. Growth slowed to just one half of a percentage point across the eurozone for 2003. Meanwhile, the German economy contracted.

Defection

The poor performance of the German economy explains to a large extent the second major crisis in the European macroeconomic framework – the November 2003 defection of France and Germany from the excessive deficit procedure and the stability and growth pact. Like the ECB's price stability mandate, the fiscal rules in the European macroeconomic policy framework focused almost exclusively on the threat of inflation. These rules were both introduced and strengthened at the insistence of Germany. By implication, few if any observers gave much thought to the prospect that the rules would be used to constrain Germany itself.

The anti-inflation bias in the fiscal rules exists no matter what procedure is used to enforce them. Consider, for example, the reprimand issued to Ireland by the Council of Economics and Finance Ministers (ECOFIN Council) in February 2001. This action was taken under the multilateral surveillance procedure and the complaint was that Ireland failed to run a sufficiently large fiscal surplus. To put this into context, average real GDP growth in Ireland during the 1996–2000 period was near 10 per cent, compared to only 2.6 per cent for the eurozone as a whole. Hence in March 2000, the Irish government accepted recommendations within the BEPGs that it should increase its fiscal surplus in order to reduce the threat that the economy would overheat and so transmit inflation to the rest of the eurozone. By December 2000, however, the Irish Taoiseach (prime minister) moved legislation to reduce the surplus slightly as part of a pre-election budget. The ECOFIN Council viewed this action as a breach of the BEPGs and so issued a reprimand. As it turned out, the Irish government chose to ignore the reprimand and the general slowdown in the eurozone's economy made the matter moot by the year end. Nevertheless, the anti-inflationary bias in the fiscal framework remained predominant (Jones 2002b).

The irony in the Irish example is that while the slowdown in the eurozone's economy reduced the threat of Irish inflation, it exacerbated the problem of fiscal performance in Germany. German fiscal accounts fell from a surplus of 1.3 per cent of GDP in 2000 to a deficit of 3.7 per cent in 2002. In contrast to the Irish situation, however, the ECOFIN Council was slow to respond to the problem in Germany. When the Commission recommended that the German government be given an 'early warning' in February 2002, the Council instead chose to accept reassurances that the German government would act. By extension, the Council accepted similar assurances from Portugal. In the event, neither country was able to translate such reassurances into effective action (Jones 2003).

By the end of 2002, it was clear that the rules for fiscal policy coordination suffered from two different problems – one relating to fiscal accounting and the other related to fiscal performance. The accounting problem is straightforward. As European officials discovered to their dismay, the Portuguese government had grossly understated its fiscal deficits. Once the figures were corrected, it was obvious that Portugal should be instructed to undertake consolidations in line with the excessive deficit procedure. Hence the ECOFIN Council began to take official action against Portugal in November 2002. This accounting problem would resurface in 2004 with reference to Greece. The point to note in both cases, however, is that the governments were quick to recognise the error of their ways and eager to make amends (Hodson 2004).

The problem of fiscal performance is much more troublesome. When the ECOFIN Council initiated the excessive deficit procedure for Germany in January 2003, the German government promised again to rectify its fiscal position and yet failed to do so. Meanwhile, fiscal problems became manifest in France as well. The ECOFIN Council initiated the excessive deficit procedure against France in June 2003. However, the French government did not even indicate a willingness to act. For both of the eurozone's two largest economies, the fear was that efforts would have two consequences, both negative. First, fiscal consolidation would strengthen popular political opposition against already unpopular governments. Second, the effect of fiscal consolidation would be to slow down economic performance and so make matters even worse. During the summer months of 2003, both the French president and the German chancellor began to emphasise the importance of the word 'growth' in the stability and growth pact. Going into the autumn, their position only hardened.

The decisive moment came on 25 November 2003 when the ECOFIN Council met to consider whether both France and Germany should be moved beyond the firebreak in the excessive deficit procedure. A positive vote would not only make it possible for both countries to be subject to sanctions for their failure to comply with fiscal policy recommendations, but it would also create a legal obligation for the ECOFIN Council to act. When the votes were called, however, there was not a majority in favour. Many of the smaller countries voted in support of decisive action. The larger countries simply refused. The architects of the excessive deficit procedure had never planned for this possibility – any more than they had imagined that Germany would be the object of the procedure itself. As a result, when the majority failed to materialise the ECOFIN Council found itself without clear procedural recourse. The Council members cobbled together a decision to hold the excessive deficit procedure 'in abeyance' for France and Germany, essentially making much the same recommendations that had been put forward by the Commission but without the threat of sanction or other enforcement. Both the Commission and the ECB expressed their immediate dismay and the Commission even threatened to appeal the matter to the European Court of Justice (ECJ). However, neither institution had the power to reverse the course of events (Jones 2003).

Inertia

The explanation for the defection of France and Germany from the excessive deficit procedure lies not in their desire to run deficits per se, but in their inability to reduce them. Moreover, there is little reason to believe that either country will be able to grow their way out of this dilemma. As the European Commission has noted, and the ECOFIN Council has recognised, the deficits for both countries are structural and not cyclical in nature. They can be resolved only through market-structural reform. In this way, the success of the Lisbon strategy is essential to a resolution of the crisis in the Stability and Growth Pact.

The role of the Lisbon strategy in supporting the Stability and Growth Pact is the third unexpected development in the macroeconomic framework. Here it is useful to recall that fiscal consolidation is a prerequisite to membership in the single currency. Eurozone governments were expected already to have achieved most of the major structural adjustments to their fiscal accounts prior to joining. The processes culminating in the Lisbon strategy were conceived to improve market function, not to encourage further fiscal reform. Once it became clear that fiscal consolidation is an unending process, however, fiscal reform soon became attached to the Lisbon strategy and its attendant open method of coordination.

This expansion of the Lisbon strategy in the fiscal domain was mirrored elsewhere as well. Within only a few years of the March 2000 Lisbon summit, the range of policy areas addressed through the open method was staggering. Social scientists even began to question whether the open method could replace the more traditional 'community method' as the principal driver for European integration (Jones 2001, Borrás and Jacobsson 2004). Such academic inquiry invariably raised more questions than it could answer (Borrás and Greve 2004). Meanwhile, member state governments displayed a surprising eagerness to re-brand any number of public policy issues – from continuing education to social exclusion, pension reform to health care – as part of the Lisbon agenda.

The unexpected popularity of the Lisbon strategy was not met with unexpected success. While the open method provided a new instrument to deal with market-structural reform, it did not change the political dynamics that make such reforms so difficult to manage in the first place (Jones 2003). Meanwhile, the increasing complexity of the Lisbon agenda made matters worse and not better. Governments confronted an ever wider range of benchmarks and targets, they engaged in ever longer and more complicated discussions, and they generated ever more recommendations for future action. As a result, the sense of priority was overwhelmed and the momentum for reform fell off. By January 2004 it was clear that the Lisbon strategy would fall well short of its strategic objective to make Europe the world's most competitive and dynamic knowledge-based economy by 2010.

In its annual report on progress made in implementing the BEPGs, The European Commission recommended to the March 2004 European Council that the open method would have to be streamlined in order to salvage the Lisbon agenda. In particular, the Commission argued that the member states should focus on ways to improve implementation. The European Council responded in its presidency conclusions to the summit by setting wide parameters for the mid-term review of the Lisbon strategy. The European Council also called on former Dutch prime minister Wim Kok to lead a high level group in making an independent assessment on how the Lisbon strategy could be improved. Such bureaucratic manoeuvres are not obviously the stuff of crisis.[7] However, given the diffuse nature of the open method and the importance of market structural reform for all parts of the macroeconomic framework, even the risk that member states would abandon the Lisbon agenda as unworkable was major cause for concern.

Volatility

The problem of the exchange rates can be illustrated easily by poking fun at some of the expectations held prior to the formation of Europe's economic and monetary union. During the 1990s there were two widespread beliefs. The first was that the euro would appreciate soon after being launched as global economic actors – including central banks – took advantage of the new currency to diversify commodity pricing and asset portfolios. The second belief was that the external value of the euro would be dependent upon the effective functioning of the macroeconomic framework. If the ECB failed to deliver on price stability, if the member states failed to adhere to the Stability and Growth Pact, and if European market-structural reforms did not succeed in alleviating unemployment, then global economic actors would abandon the euro and the single currency would experience a sharp depreciation.

Both beliefs were sorely mistaken, at least insofar as relations between the euro and the dollar are concerned. The single currency launched into an accelerating free-fall. From January 1999 to September 2000, the euro declined from $1.17 to $0.87. For the next fifteen months, the single currency stabilised at around $0.90, dipping again to $0.87 in February 2002 – the same month that the ECOFIN Council declined the Commission's recommendation to give an early warning to Germany about poor fiscal performance. Thereafter, the euro began a period of sharp ascent. It reached parity with the dollar as the ECOFIN Council started the excessive deficit procedure against Portugal in November 2002. It gained a further 6 cents on the dollar the following January, as Germany entered into the excessive deficit procedure as well. And it returned to its launch rate in June 2003, the same month that the excessive deficit procedure was started for France. The single currency weakened slightly during the summer of 2003, but it returned to $1.17 when the ECOFIN Council met to consider sanctions against France and Germany for failing to meet their obligations under the stability and growth pact. Once the ECOFIN Council suspended the fiscal rules, the euro powered ahead to new highs against the dollar. By the end of 2004, the euro traded at $1.34 – with no clear end to the appreciation in sight.[8]

These sharp movements in the euro belied expectations in all senses – direction, speed, and magnitude. More important, the unexpected volatility in the euro–dollar exchange rate clearly alarmed European policy-makers more than their American counterparts. During the autumn of 2000, ECB president Wim Duisenberg complained that the weakness of the euro against the dollar was placing unwarranted upward pressure on prices in the eurozone. To stave off this potential source of inflation, Duisenberg called on US Treasury Secretary Lawrence Summers to intervene jointly against the dollar. Summers agreed to the intervention but undermined the outcome by stating that a strong dollar remained in the interests of the United States. Duisenberg then gave a disastrous interview to *The Times* of London in which he dismissed the suggestion of further central bank intervention in the currency markets. His comments only triggered another round of speculation against the euro and forced the ECB to act alone to stabilise the fall of the single currency (Jones 2002a: 136–8; Taylor 2004: 874).

The formation of the single currency was intended to insulate the European economy from the impact of exchange rate fluctuations. It was only a partial success. Intra-European exchange rates no longer fluctuate but exchange rates between the euro and the dollar remain volatile. Moreover, the economic impact of these exchange rates is at least potentially important. Duisenberg was correct to express concern that the fall in the euro would add to European inflation. Moreover, he had a clear responsibility to act given the price-stability mandate of the ECB. Things become more complicated after February 2002. As the euro appreciates against the dollar, the threat to inflation diminishes but the threat to growth increases. A stronger euro translates into higher European export prices in dollar markets and therefore lower cost-competitiveness. In turn, this drop in competitiveness constitutes a threat to growth – particularly for those countries, like Germany, that rely heavily on trade with the United States. The ECB has no clear mandate to support growth in one country and so no clear incentive to manage an appreciation of the euro against the dollar. The exchange rate component of the European macroeconomic framework remains notable for its absence.

Bad luck

It is tempting to argue that this crisis in the European macroeconomic framework constitutes some kind of perfect storm. However, such an assessment would be too kind. The European framework just ran into a patch of bad luck. This has happened many times during the process of European monetary integration. Indeed, 'bad luck' is part of the argument that is used most often to explain why the single currency was so hard to bring about (Jones 1998). Given its history, the architects and managers of the European macroeconomic framework should have planned more carefully for exactly these sorts of possibilities. The danger of overblowing the rhetoric around the Lisbon strategy was particularly easy to foresee. That they failed to do so creates the impression of incompetence.

That impression is only partly warranted. The macroeconomic framework is sound insofar as such things go. However it needs to be made more flexible to accommodate persistent differences across the member states. Moreover, the credibility of the framework should not be contingent upon the prior success of reform efforts at the member state level. If anything, the macroeconomic framework should support welfare state reforms rather than depend upon them.

Responding to the crisis

Responses to the crisis in macroeconomic governance have been muted and changes to the macroeconomic framework have been very slow in coming. A good example is the draft constitutional treaty that is now stalled in ratification and that was intended to replace the TEC. The point to note is that very little has changed, at least insofar as macroeconomic governance is concerned. The articles have different numbers, some of the provisions have been moved around in the text, and the Commission has a new power to address its opinions about the existence of excessive deficits directly to the member states (in Article III–76, paragraph 5), but the rest is almost word-for-word the same.

Nevertheless, there have been critical moments that set the trajectory for future responses. This section focuses on four such moments – one for each policy area. These include the May 2003 review of the conduct of monetary policy, the July 2004 ECJ decision about the Council's handling of the Stability and Growth Pact, the November 2004 Kok report on the future of the Lisbon Strategy, and the exchange rate controversies following the November 2003 changeover from Wim Duisenberg to Jean-Claude Trichet as ECB president.

Inflation targeting

In May 2003, the ECB announced the results of a comprehensive review of its monetary policy-making. At the same time, it introduced three important changes. First, price stability would be defined as expected inflation over the medium term of less than but close to 2 per cent. By implication, the ECB has accepted a more symmetrical inflation target with much greater concern both for the variation in inflation rates across different countries in the single currency and for the threat posed by deflation in one or more member states. Second, the ECB announced that it would no longer review the reference value for M3 growth on an annual basis although it would continue to pay attention to the role of liquidity growth in anticipating future threats to price stability. This represents a substantial weakening of one-half of the two pillar strategy for monetary policy-making and effectively concentrates attention on the medium-term inflation target. Third, the ECB has upgraded the importance of 'economic analysis' in assessing future price developments. In essence this means that the ECB will pay due attention to growth and employment in setting monetary policy.

These changes in the conduct of monetary policy do not subtract from the price stability mandate in any formal sense. Indeed, the ECB has been adamant both about protecting its own political independence and about the need to continue to focus on maintaining stable prices. However the May 2003 reforms should make it easier for monetary policy-makers to bring the rhetoric of policy-making more closely in line with the underlying practice. They also reflect a much greater appreciation on the part of monetary policy-makers for the differences in economic performance from one member state to the next. As a result, monetary policy-making should be more responsive to the types of challenges that the eurozone has faced so far.

Nevertheless, the weakness of monetary policy in the eurozone remains its dependence upon the successful performance in the rest of macroeconomic policy framework. When the reforms were announced, ECB president Wim Duisenberg again took the opportunity to underscore the importance of successful fiscal consolidation and market structural reform. There was nothing new in this assertion. Such statements appear in the opening statements of every press conference given by the ECB, they play a prominent role in ECB testimony before the European Parliament, and they are a recurrent refrain in the speeches given by ECB officials. More to the point, assertions about the need for fiscal consolidation and market-structural reform are justified.

Focus on stability

The November 2003 decision of the ECOFIN Council to hold the excessive deficit procedure in abeyance for France and Germany created two different problems for the Stability and Growth Pact. One of these problems is about whether the content of the pact is reasonable in economic terms. The larger countries clearly believed that the fiscal rules should not encourage fiscal consolidation at the expense of economic performance. However, since it is clear that these are rules only in the economic sense of being guidelines for action, this problem is essentially more of a technical nature than a political one. Hence, economists both in the Commission and in the member states are hard at work debating whether the rules should be changed or whether they should remain the same. On balance these discussions are leaning toward a slight change in the rules to emphasise the long-term stability of member states fiscal accounts over a too close monitoring of actual deficits. If adopted, the implication of such changes would be to add even greater emphasis to the need for welfare state reform.

The other problem raised by the November 2003 decision concerns who has the right to determine the reasonableness of the pact. This is a question about procedures and not about rules. But in the fiscal part of the European macroeconomic framework, procedure is where enforcement takes place. Hence on 13 January 2004, the European Commission appealed the decision of the ECOFIN Council to the European Court of Justice challenging that the Council had abused its authority in holding the excessive deficit procedure in abeyance. If successful in its petition, the Commission could weaken the importance of the procedural firebreak and so strengthen the legal force of the excessive deficit procedure at all levels. By implication, the Commission would gain considerable authority over the procedure by dint of its power to make recommendations at different stages in the process.

On 13 July, the ECJ issued a carefully balanced judgement. It upheld at least part of the Commission's petition and found that the ECOFIN Council did abuse its authority in managing the procedures. Moreover, the Court maintained that the Commission retains the right of initiative with respect to decisions relating to the excessive deficit procedure – essentially meaning that Commission recommendations cannot be set aside without justification. Nevertheless, the ECJ agreed that the ECOFIN Council is primarily responsible for the management of the Stability and Growth Pact, that it retains broad powers of discretion, and that it can even hold the excessive deficit procedure in abeyance in fact if not in law.[9]

The ECJ decision effectively ends the dissolution of fiscal policy coordination by preserving an important role for the European Commission. At the same time, the decision paves the way for a much more flexible interpretation and enforcement of fiscal rules. When the European Council voted to reform the rules for fiscal policy coordination in March 2005, it chose not to alter the language of the treaties. Instead, the Council introduced two innovations – one relating to the medium-term budgetary targets, the other relating to the excessive deficit procedure. Specifically, the Council made it possible for countries with low public debts or high growth potential to target a fiscal deficit over the medium term of up to 1 per cent of GDP. The Council also enumerated a list of conditions under which an excessive deficit could be discounted as temporary or exceptional. These reforms were more controversial than meaningful. Nevertheless, they did add flexibility into the process of fiscal coordination.

When this flexibility is added to the heightened concern for long-term stability on the technical side, it creates the possibility of a much less rigid and much more effective fiscal framework to be developed in the future. The reinterpreted Stability and Growth Pact will not solve all of the macroeconomic problems of the European Union and it will not even eliminate much of the tension observed between member states and between monetary and fiscal policy-makers in the eurozone. Nevertheless, it is a move in the right direction. And, once again, the focus is now on the importance of welfare state reform.

Lowering expectations

The review of progress under the Lisbon strategy represents the third leg in this pattern of incremental change in the macroeconomic framework. Taking its cue from the European Commission, the Kok Report argues that the problems besetting the Lisbon strategy are due to 'an overloaded agenda, poor co-ordination and conflicting priorities' (Kok 2004: 3). Therefore the key recommendation in the report is that the Lisbon strategy be streamlined to focus more intensively on the requirements for growth and employment. If accepted, this recommendation will help to bring the open method to focus on those areas of reform most needed to shore up the macroeconomic framework as a whole.

Behind this central recommendation, however, the Kok report makes substantial headway in deflating the rhetoric surrounding the Lisbon strategy while at the same time underscoring the stakes involved. Rather than insisting on the headline goal of becoming the world's most competitive and dynamic knowledge-based economy, the Kok report suggests that 'Lisbon is about Europe becoming ... among the best in the world'. The report also emphasises that 'at risk – in the medium to long run – is nothing less than the sustainability of the society Europe has built' (Kok 2004: 13). In this way, the Lisbon strategy is defensive and not offensive. It is about protecting the European social model and not imposing European competitiveness on world markets. Moreover, the measure of performance is not so much the achievement of success as the avoidance of failure. Where the original Lisbon declaration was full of promise, the Kok report (2004: 39) is bleak: 'Nothing less than the future prosperity of the European model is at stake.'

Talk policy

The image of a European Union beset by volatile world market forces fits well with the uncontrollable appreciation of the euro against the dollar. As mentioned above, this appreciation gathered considerable force after November 2003. That timing coincides not just with the crisis in the Stability and Growth Pact, but with the changeover in the ECB presidency from Wim Duisenberg to Jean-Claude Trichet. And, almost immediately upon assuming office, Trichet made clear his concern about the volatility in the euro–dollar exchange rate. He did not intervene in foreign currency markets and he did not even threaten to intervene. But he did not mince words either. In effect, his exchange rate policy is to try to calm the markets with words.

The words of the ECB president do not move markets. However they do help to prevent the offhand remarks of national politicians from creating confusion about who has control over exchange rate policy within the macroeconomic framework. What is clear from conversations with financial journalists is that Trichet leaves little doubt as to who is in charge. Hence when prominent members of the Italian and German governments began talking about the need for intervention during the autumn of 2004 market makers looked to the ECB president before reacting. In this way, Trichet has had a calming influence – damping down the volatility of the euro–dollar exchange rate if not always changing the direction in which it is moving. Such actions cannot repair the absence of an exchange rate policy altogether. But they can at least improve the perception that the single currency operates through a single voice.

The future of macroeconomic governance in Europe

The outcomes at each juncture in the crisis besetting the European macroeconomic framework have been incremental. The conduct of monetary policy remains focused on the need for price stability. Fiscal policy is still constrained by the Stability and Growth Pact and the excessive deficit procedure. The Lisbon strategy continues to depend upon the capacity of member states to reform domestic market structures. And the euro–dollar exchange rate has an important and uncontrollable influence on the European economy as a whole. When all this is taken into consideration, it is clear that Europe is muddling through the crisis.

Muddling through is nevertheless an appropriate response. To begin with, there is clear evidence that the European macroeconomic framework is adapting to accommodate persistent differences between the member states. The monetary rule affords a wider degree of variation in inflation performance without forcing any member state to experience an unnecessary deflation. The fiscal rules pay more attention to stability than to arbitrary reference values. The process of welfare state reform is becoming more supportive (even as the rhetoric is becoming less hyperbolic and more imperative). And the exchange rate policy is at least preventing the inevitable consequences of fluctuations in the euro–dollar exchange rate from resulting in more or sharper fluctuations and so from making matters worse (if not better).

More important, the incremental evolution of the macroeconomic framework builds upon an implicit acceptance of the accomplishments that European monetary integration has helped to bring about. Although there is some variation in inflation performance across member states, this is substantially less than the wide differences that existed before monetary integration took place. Fiscal reform may be faltering, but it is clearly more successful as a result of monetary integration than it was beforehand. The same is true of accounting irregularities. The excessive deficit procedure did not give rise to accounting gimmicks. If anything it made such gimmicks more difficult to use and easier to uncover. Finally, it would be difficult if not impossible to argue that Europe is somehow more vulnerable to the volatility of the dollar than it would be without the single currency. Hence, these three legs of the macroeconomic framework constitute a clear improvement on the status quo ante.

The only real debate lies in the area of welfare state reform. I argue above that the macroeconomic framework should facilitate reform rather than depend upon the success of reform efforts. That assertion rests on a false dichotomy. Clearly both aspects can be true at the same time. The European macroeconomic framework does facilitate welfare state and market-structural reform. But it is also dependent upon the success of reform efforts. Nevertheless, this two-way interaction is not a good reason to get rid of the macroeconomic framework as a whole. All that would succeed in doing is leave Europe with the problem of reform but without the support that stable macroeconomic conditions provide for reform efforts. The two-way interaction between macroeconomic governance and welfare state reform does not even justify a radical revision of the macroeconomic framework. Such a sweeping effort would be more likely to open a time-consuming and potentially unresolvable conflict between the member states than to result in some institutional *optimum optimorum*.

If welfare state reform is really the central issue for the future of European economic governance, then the best that policy-makers can offer on the macroeconomic front is to create European stability without constraining national flexibility. Despite the evidence of crisis, the European macroeconomic framework works to achieve that goal. Moreover, the various responses of European policy-makers to the crisis in macroeconomic policy coordination have been to increase the flexibility of the framework without prejudice to the goal of stability. Such actions may seem muted in comparison with the headlines generated by the crisis itself, but they are better than the alternative. Indeed, to the extent to which reforms succeed in making the macroeconomic framework more resilient in the face of persistent national differences, the responses in train constitute a step in the right direction.

This defence of incrementalism extends beyond the problem of welfare state reform to cover the macroeconomic framework as a whole. Muddling through in macroeconomic policy-making may be unpopular, but the radical alternatives would be much worse. Hence, while many criticise the constitution of Europe's economic and monetary union, few argue that the EU would be better off with no macroeconomic framework at all. Having given rise to the popular expectation that the European Union has an important role to play in providing for macroeconomic stability conducive to growth and employment, it would be difficult in the extreme to announce now that the member states are left to fend for themselves (Jones 2005). The creation of a single European economic superstate lies at the other end of the spectrum of choices on offer. Writers like McKay (1999) and Siedentop (2001) worry that the economic inadequacies of the existing macroeconomic framework will require further centralisation of authority at the European level. Moreover, they agree that Europe is politically unprepared for such a radical burst of federalism. McKay (1999: 183) concludes his analysis by insisting that 'the political conditions necessary to accommodate what could be substantial economic centralisation resulting from EMU are largely absent. Therein lies the danger to the viability of European monetary union.' Siedentop (2001: 231) is equally direct: 'Federalism is the right goal for Europe. But Europe is not yet ready for federalism.'

In an odd way, Europe is fortunate to be muddling through. Moreover, this fortune is by design and not accident. The member states created a common macroeconomic framework within which each could pursue its own national interest. This framework does not work perfectly for all member states, under all conditions, all the time. But the goal of promoting the national interest, like the goal of promoting an interest that is national, persists. The inevitability of incrementalism persists as well. So long as the member states remain united in their pursuit of self-interest, they remain condemned to path of piecemeal reform and muddling through. Such progress may not constitute an economic optimality. It makes sense nevertheless. The European Union has made important achievements in macroeconomic governance. It would be a tragedy to sacrifice these on the altar of ill-planned, undesired, or insupportable reform.

Notes

1 As mentioned in the introduction, this description focuses on the macroeconomic framework as laid down in the Maastricht and Amsterdam Treaties. Therefore, references to the TEC are to the post-Amsterdam consolidated version of the treaty which is available online, http://europa.eu.int.

2 Technically, monetary policy actions are taking by the Governing Council of the ESCB, which includes representatives of each of the member state central banks in the eurozone, plus the six members of the executive board of the ECB. In practice, monetary policy decisions are communicated by the president of the ECB or by its press office. Therefore, it is a convenient shorthand to ascribe responsibility for the monetary policy of the eurozone to the ECB rather than constantly repeating allusions to the Governing Council of the ESCB.

3 This obligation also applies to Sweden although that country has chosen not to participate in the single currency nonetheless.

4 This citation is from the Resolution of the European Council on the Stability and Growth Pact as adopted in June 1997 which is available online, http://europa.eu.int.

5 The citations are taken from the text of the Presidency Conclusions to the Lisbon European Council which are available online, http://europa.eu.int.

6 The data in this section comes from the European Central Bank's *Statistics Pocket Book* and from the European Commission's *AMECO* database. Both resources are available online, http://www.ecb.int and http://europa.eu.int.

7 Both the European Commission reports and the Presidency Conclusions to the March 2003 European Council summit are available online, http://europa.eu.int.

8 This exchange rate data is freely available for download from the website of the Dutch national bank, http://www.dnb.nl.

9 The text of the judgement can be found online, http://www.curia.eu.int.

References

Allsopp, C. and Artis, M. J. (2003) 'The Assessment: EMU, Four Years On', *Oxford Review of Economic Policy* 19/1: 1–29.

Borrás, S. and Greve B. (2004) 'Concluding Remarks: New Method or Just Cheap Talk?', *Journal of European Public Policy* 11/2: 329–36.

Borrás, S. and Jacobsson, K. (2004) 'The Open Method of Coordination and New Governance Patterns in the EU', *Journal of European Public Policy* 11/2: 185–208.

Buiter, W. (1999) 'Alice in Euroland', *Journal of Common Market Studies* 37/2: 181–209.

Hodson, D. (2004) 'Macroeconomic Coordination in the Euro Area: The Scope and Limits of the Open Method', *Journal of European Public Policy* 11:2: 231–48.

Hodson, D. and Maher, I. (2001) 'The Open Method as a New Form of Governance', *Journal of Common Market Studies* 39:4: 719–46.

Jones, E. (1998) 'Economic and Monetary Union: Playing with Money', in A. Moravcsik (ed.) *Centralization or Fragmentation? Europe Facing the Challenges of Deepening, Diversity, and Democracy* (New York: Council of Foreign Relations).

—— (2000) 'The Politics of Europe 1999: Spring Cleaning', *Industrial Relations Journal* 31/4: 247–60.

—— (2001) 'The Politics of Europe 2000: Unity *through* Diversity', *Industrial Relations Journal* 32/5: 362–79.

—— (2002a) *The Politics of Economic and Monetary Union: Integration and Idiosyncrasy* (Lanham, MD: Rowman & Littlefield).

—— (2002b) 'The Politics of Europe 2001: Adversity and Persistence', *Industrial Relations Journal* 33/5: 377–91.

—— (2003) 'The Politics of Europe 2002: Flexibility and Adjustment', *Industrial Relations Journal* 34/5: 363–78.

—— (2005) 'European Economic Governance: Forging an Integrated Agenda', *Briefing paper No. 05/02* (London: Chatham House, International Economics Program (February)).

Kok, W. (2004) 'Facing the Challenge: The Lisbon Strategy for Growth and Employment', Brussels: European Commission (November).

McKay, D. (1999) *Federalism and European Union: A Political Economy Perspective* (Oxford: Oxford University Press).

Siedentop, L. (2001) *Democracy in Europe* (New York: Columbia University Press).

Taylor, C. (2004) 'An Exchange-Rate Regime for the Euro', *Journal of European Public Policy* 11/5: 871–89.

Trichet, J.-C. (2001) 'The Euro after Two Years', *Journal of Common Market Studies* 39/1: 1–13.

Chapter 17

Implementation

C̲HRISTOPH̲ K̲NILL

Introduction

What happens to a European law or programme after its official passing at the European level? How do the formal transposition and the practical application of legal acts take shape at the national level? Which problems and deviations from the European objectives can be observed? At first glance, it could be assumed that questions like these are relatively trivial. Why should there be any problems in putting into practice an apparently well-devised measure that was accepted by the Council of Ministers? Political reality is more complex, however, as can be seen from the widespread implementation deficits that are generally observed regarding European policies. Research into policy implementation had already demonstrated in the 1970s and 1980s that even with national programmes, great deviations and shifts in objectives could occur during the execution phase. It is rarely the case that administrative agencies follow political guidelines unrestrictedly during implementation, and even if they do so, in some cases the results deviate remarkably from political expectations.

For instance, in a classic study on policy implementation, Pressman and Wildavsky (1973) analysed why a labour-market programme of the American federal state that had received broad political support was not duly implemented at the level of the constituent states. The subtitle of their book concisely summarises the central message of the analysis: 'How great expectations in Washington are dashed in Oakland; or, why it's amazing that federal programmes work at all ...'. Pressman and Wildavsky argued that the effective transposition of political programmes is an exception rather than the rule because they require the cooperation of a vast number of actors involved inside the implementation chain (including political decision-makers, responsible administrative agencies at different institutional levels as well as various societal interest groups and policy addressees) – all trying to influence the execution according to their interests.

The general finding that shifts in policy objectives and deviations from the original political intentions are frequently observed during the implementation stage can be expected to be of particular relevance when it comes to the implementation of EU policies. This arises primarily from the fact that in executing EU measures a vast number of actors at different institutional levels are involved. Additionally, the Commission, when monitoring, as the 'guardian of the treaties', the transposition of the Community law in the member states, possesses comparatively few resources to ensure the cooperation at all levels of the public and private actors participating in the implementation process. Consequently the EU can be seen from many perspectives to have a systematic implementation problem (Krislov *et al.* 1986; Mendrinou 1996; Snyder 1993; Tallberg 1999; Weiler 1988).

In view of this general assessment, it is the objective of this chapter to investigate the implementation of EU policies from an empirical and theoretical perspective. It proceeds as follows. In the first part, the institutional, political and empirical background with regard to the implementation of EU policies is presented. What are the institutional framework conditions that are relevant for the execution of European policies? How large is the European implementation deficit and which measures were adopted in order to reduce it? This stock-taking forms the basis for a subsequent theoretical interpretation and analysis of the empirical findings.

Implementation effectiveness of European policies: institutional framework, political background and empirical assessment

Considering the political and scientific discussion about the implementation of European policies, two aspects in particular appear rather striking. First, an explanation is needed for the fact that it is only since the mid-1980s that the implementation of EU policies has been perceived as a political problem. Second, existing studies point to fundamental problems with regard to the measurement of implementation deficits. In particular, empirical assessments can noticeably vary depending on the chosen scale. These issues will be considered after outlining the institutional framework within which the implementation of EU policies takes place.

Institutional framework

In the EU, there is a clear-cut distribution of competence concerning the implementation of common policies in its member states. Responsibility for the execution of the Community law generally lies with the member states (article 10 [ex-art. 5] TEC):

> Member States shall take all appropriate measures, whether general or particular, to ensure fulfilment of the obligations arising out of this Treaty or resulting from action taken by the institutions of the Community. They shall facilitate the achievement of the Community's tasks.

As the 'guardian of the treaties' the Commission is responsible for controlling the transposition and application of Community law in the member states. For ensuring the correct implementation of European measures, the Commission, in accordance with article 226 (ex-art. 169) TEC, can instruct an infringement procedure against member states that did not fulfil the commitments resulting from Community law. But before such a procedure is instructed, the Commission takes various formal and informal steps to warrant the proper transposition of the legal acts. In this respect, the following steps can be distinguished.

If the Commission believes that there is an infringement against Community law in a member state, it first takes up informal contacts with the competent national authorities in order to discuss the details and possible problems concerning the execution of the affected measure (Collins and Earnshaw 1992; Krämer 1996). Depending on the results of these informal discussions, the Commission can instruct the second step of the procedure, which consists of a reminder letter from the Commission to the member state (Holzinger 1994: 102; Jordan 1999: 74). In this way, the member state can be given the opportunity to clarify potential obscurities and problems within the implementation process and eliminate them if necessary. If a consensual solution cannot be found even at this level, the third step is for the Commission to give a reasoned opinion explaining to what extent the member state concerned has infringed the Community law. Following this the state will be given a time-limit within which the detected implementation deficits have to be redressed.

If the member state does not comply with the obligations resulting from the reasoned opinion within the given time-limit, the Commission can appeal to the European Court of Justice (ECJ). The Court finally decides whether a member state has infringed an

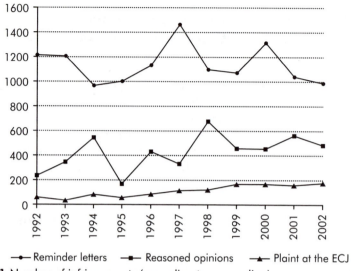

Figure 17.1 Number of infringements (according to proceeding)
Source: European Commission (1997, 2004)

obligation of the Treaty. The member state is then obliged to take the steps required by the judgment of the ECJ. But the EU has only humble sanctions at its disposal for compelling such obligations. The potential for sanctions has been somewhat widened, however, with the Maastricht Treaty, which allows for the imposition of fines on member states who do not fulfil obligations emerging from European law:

> Although the European Court of Justice can rule that member states are in breach of EU environmental law it has virtually no power to enforce its decisions, being, for instance, unable to send erring ministers to prison. There are member states who still have not complied with environmental rulings issued by the Court in the early 1990s.
>
> (Jordan 1999: 78)

Before the stage of appealing to the ECJ is reached, however, bilateral negotiations between the Commission and the member state in question will often take place, with the objective of finding a 'last minute' consensual solution. Correspondingly, as shown in figure 17.1, the number of commencements of proceedings before the ECJ is very low in relation to reminder letters and reasoned opinions:

> Even when formal proceedings are initiated, something like 80% are settled before they go to court. [...] Court cases tend to be long-winded, extremely complicated, stretch the Commission's meagre resources and endanger the goodwill of states. Decisions to take cases to the Court are not taken lightly; they must be sanctioned by the Commission's Legal Services and receive the support of the College of Commissioners. Being so political, recourse to court proceedings is therefore considered as a very last resort.
>
> (Jordan 1999: 81)

Table 17.1 Investigative criteria for the introduction of infringement proceedings

	Focus	Criteria
Formal transposition	Legal and administrative provisions for the transposition of European law into the national legal and administrative system	• Time frame (Commission notification) • Completeness • Correct integration into the regulative context
Practical transposition	National regulation practice (regulatory style, organisational and administrative structures)	• Correct application and adherence to legal guidelines

For instructing infringement proceedings, three constituent facts are to be distinguished: (1) the non-communication of transposition measures in the member states, (2) the incorrect or incomplete transposition and (3) the incorrect application of Community law. While the first two aspects refer to the formal transposition, the third factor relates to the practical application of the Community law.

With regard to formal transposition, the focus is on the respective legal and administrative provisions that have been created to incorporate into the national legal order the legal and institutional requirements resulting from European policies. In this context, effective implementation not only implies the timely and complete adaptation to European requirements, but also requires the corresponding integration of these rules into the existing regulatory context. When it comes to the practical transposition of European policies, the activities of implementers and policy addressees are at the centre of attention. To what extent did the legal modifications indeed result in corresponding adjustments in national regulation practice? Are the European requirements (e.g. threshold values, the foundation of new administrative agencies or the modification of existing administrative procedures) actually complied with (Knill and Lenschow 1999: 595; Weale *et al.* 2000: 297)?

Politicisation of implementation problems

Until the mid-1980s, problems of implementation of Community law played a minor role on the political agenda. The rather late politicisation of implementation deficits does not mean, however, that such deficits have been absent in the previous decades (Jordan 1999: 73). Rather, it has been in the interest of the Commission and member states to neglect problems in the implementation of Community law.

For a long time the Commission and member states concentrated their activities primarily on policy-making. The objectives of European integration were focused more on the formulation of Common policies and less on their implementation. On the side of the Commission, this orientation was favoured by its own institutional interests in expanding its political authority. In this situation, fortified interventions by the Commission in order to control and monitor the implementation effectiveness of EU policies would have endangered the political support of member states for the expanding political competence at the European level (Jordan 1999: 74). The Commission's position was broadly congruent with the objectives of member states, which were, for obvious reasons, hardly interested in exposing their respective problems and failures in the transposition of European policies.

This initial constellation of interests, which largely favoured the depoliticisation of implementation problems, changed from the mid-1980s onwards. Efficacy in implementing European policies became increasingly the focus of political and academic attention. First, the objective of completing the integration of the Common Market until 1992, as defined by the Single European Act (SEA), implied that questions about the effective transposition of Community law gained political significance (Weiler 1988). Beyond this, the increasing politicisation of implementation problems was facilitated by various judgements of the ECJ. In this context, the principles of supremacy and direct effect of Community law (which were not mentioned in the constituting treaties) have to be stressed in particular. Not only did the ECJ clarify that Community law is to be regarded as superior in case of a collision between European and national rules but at at the same time the Court stated that, independent of their national implementation, European legal acts are directly effective at the national level (Alter and Meunier-Aitsahalia 1994).

As a result of these developments, the implementation effectiveness of European policies became a central issue on the political agenda during the 1990s. However, the mere observation that the implementation of EU policies became an increasingly politicised issue does not allow us to draw conclusions on the actual size of the European implementation deficit. This question and related problems of measurement and assessment will be analysed in the following section.

Problems of measurement and data

Existing empirical data hardly allow for a comprehensive assessment of the implementation effectiveness of European policies. In the absence of alternative resources, comprehensive information on implementation across policies and member states can only be obtained from the data provided by the Commission. Of particular relevance in this respect are the annual reports on the application of Community law in member states that the Commission has published since 1984. Although the data provided in these reports are currently the only comprehensive source for judging the implementation effectiveness of European policies, they only allow reliable statements about general tendencies to a very limited extent (Macrory and Purdy 1997: 39), due to several problems in interpreting the data.

First, although there is an observable increase in the number of introduced infringement proceedings, opinions and reminder letters, it cannot be concluded that there has been a rise in implementation deficits. For instance, Jordan (1999: 81) stresses that 'the recent rise in complaints and infringement proceedings may simply reflect the Commission's determination to tighten up on enforcement rather than increasing lawlessness among member states'. From this perspective, the numerical increase in implementation deficits reflects the modified political priorities of the Commission rather than an actual increase in implementation problems.

A second problem refers to the fact that the data published by the Commission are partially inconsistent. For example, over the years the Commission has changed the basis for the collection and assignment of implementation failures (such as the amount of infringement proceedings). The same applies to the criteria of the allocation of individual measures to policy sectors, implying, for instance, that implementation deficits for directives restricting the use of chemicals in the agricultural industry have sometimes been allocated to agriculture and sometimes to the environmental sector. Frequent modifications of the basis for data collection severely restrict the opportunities to make valid statements with regard to the development of the European implementation deficit over time and across countries and policies (Börzel 2001: 810–11).

Third, data from the Commission are incomplete in various regards. On the one hand, the data only include those violations against Community law that the Commission has discovered itself or that have been drawn to its attention following complaints by domestic interest groups or citizens. On the other hand, the 'clearing quota' of the Commission concerning formal and practical implementation is unevenly distributed. So deficits of member states in the formal transposition of European requirements into national law can still be quite easily ascertained. However, when it comes to the practical application of the Community law the detection of implementation deficits is much more difficult. Because of its limited financial and personnel resources, the Commission has difficulty in monitoring and controlling the practical implementation of EU policies in member states, and must rely either on the information provided by national authorities or on complaints from other sources. As shown in table 17.2, the number of infringement proceedings originating from complaints is much higher than the cases detected by the Commission. The implementation statistics of the Commission therefore primarily refer to the problems of formal transposition, and do not sufficiently capture the probably more severe problems of practical application (Jordan 1999; Weale *et al*. 2000: 299).

A fourth difficulty results from the comparative interpretation of the Commission data. These data often reveal more about political and administrative differences between member states than about possible domestic differences in the quality of the implementation of Community law (Jordan 1999: 82; Krämer 2000: 143). Member states with a federal structure, for instance, typically have greater problems with formal implementation than do unitary states, since legal transposition generally entails comprehensive coordination requirements with the individual sub-states or regions that are responsible for the practical implementation (Toonen 1992).

Table 17.2 Origin of conjectural Treaty infringements

Year	Complaints	Cases detected by the Commission	Failure to notify	Total
1995	955	297	459	1711
1996	819	257	1079	2155
1997	957	261	760	1978
1998	1128	396	610	2134
1999	1305	288	677	2270
2000	1225	313	896	2434
2001	1300	272	607	2180
2002	1431	318	607	2356

Source: European Commission (1999, 2004)

Moreover, the number of implementation failures per member state can be strongly affected by existing administrative capacities for controlling and monitoring the enforcement of EU policies. Problems of practical implementation can be identified only if domestic administrations have sufficient resources to measure and control the compliance with European requirements. As a consequence, the implementation performance of member states with a low administrative capacity might be less successful than suggested by the Commission data. The implementation of the 1980 Drinking Water Directive, for example, seemed to be very successful in Spain at first glance, simply because the national water authorities had not distributed the technical equipment necessary to detect the small limit values for nitrates and pesticides as defined by the directive. In Germany, by contrast, where the necessary measurement technology was available, non-compliance with the strict European standards resulted in the Commission initiating infringement proceedings (Knill 2001: 153–4).

Empirical findings

Although there is as yet no solid data base that allows for a comprehensive assessment of the implementation effectiveness of EU policies, it is possible nevertheless to identify certain general patterns. These can be derived not only from a careful interpretation of Commission data but also from the results of various research projects on the implementation of EU policies in different policy fields (Börzel 2000; Collins and Earnshaw 1992; Jordan 1999; Knill and Lenschow 1999, 2000; Krämer 1996; Lübbe-Wolff 1996; Macrory 1992; Siedentopf and Ziller 1988). To be sure, these findings hardly provide a solid basis for answering the question whether the intensified politicisation of implementation deficits that has been observed since the mid-1980s correlates indeed with a real increase in implementation problems or whether it is just the result of a shift in political priorities and the perception of problems. Despite this, however, we are at least able to single out stable empirical trends.

A first pattern that is rather striking in this respect refers to the fact that the implementation effectiveness of EU policies varies strongly across policy sectors. Comparative data reveal that implementation problems are much more pronounced for policies directed at environmental protection, the integration of the Common market, consumer protection or social policy than is the case for other policy fields of the Community.

Second, and in contrast with the pattern observed across policy areas, differences in the implementation performance of member states are far less pronounced than one might have expected. In particular, the often stated hypothesis of the so-called 'Mediterranean syndrome', which expects that southern member states implement EU policies less effectively as a result of lacking administrative resources, is not confirmed (Börzel 2000). Rather, implementation deficits vary in a relatively unsystematic manner across countries, regardless of their geographic location (Knill and Lenschow 1999, 2000). This holds true, in particular, if implementation effectiveness is measured not only by focusing on the formal transpositions of EU policies but also by considering the dimension of practical application.

Third, different studies indicate that there is not necessarily a causal linkage between the implementation performance and the choice of policy instruments at the European level. This aspect has been identified especially in the field of environmental policy. EU

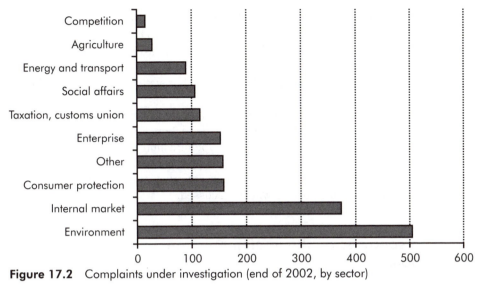

Figure 17.2 Complaints under investigation (end of 2002, by sector)
Source: European Commission 2004

environmental policy had traditionally relied on instruments associated with hierarchical intervention and command-and-control regulation. Typical of this approach were highly detailed legal rules and standards which left the member states comparatively little discretion during implementation. In many cases, EU policies not only defined detailed procedural rules but also specified substantive objectives in terms of content (such as emission or quality standards) that had to be complied with by the member states, regardless of potentially differing environmental conditions and problems at the domestic level. Notwithstanding the definition of ambitious and detailed policy requirements from the European level, however, the implementation deficit in the environmental policy field continuously increased.

In response to these problems, the Commission strongly promoted the development of so-called new instruments from the early 1990s onwards. New instruments were expected to improve the implementation effectiveness of environmental policy in basically two ways. First, they purportedly left member states more leeway to comply with EU requirements by taking account of domestic context conditions. In contrast to the detailed and substantive, standard-oriented 'old' instruments that were to be uniformly implemented regardless of the physical, economic or political context, new instruments focus on establishing basic procedures for improving environmental awareness and behaviour and set no concrete environmental targets. Second, new instruments also target the policy context directly and aim to change context factors in order to facilitate the formal and practical implementation of environmental policy in general. Here we can distinguish two strategies: the mobilisation of society through more transparent processes and participatory opportunities; and the provision of economic incentives for industrial self-regulation (Lenschow 1999; Knill and Lenschow 2000: 4; Mol *et al.* 2000).

Comparative research, however, shows that there is obviously no direct causal relationship between the choice of European policy instruments and implementation effectiveness. Instead, successes and failures vary across policies and countries, without indicating a direct causal linkage between instrument type and implementation performance. The formal and practical transposition of new instruments poses by no means fewer problems than it is the case for old instruments. These results are reported in comparative studies (Börzel 2000; Knill 1998; Knill and Lenschow 1998, 2000) as well as in different investigations that are restricted to individual policies or the implementation of EU environmental policy in the individual member states (Bouma 2000; Kimber 2000; Wright 2000).

Against the backdrop of these at first glance rather surprising findings two central questions arise that will be addressed in the following section. First, we will consider the factors that might account for why neither the type of country nor the type of policy instrument seems to have an impact on the implementation effectiveness of EU policies. Second, and closely related to the first aspect, alternative concepts to improve the implementation performance of EU policies will be discussed.

Theoretical perspectives on the implementation of European policies

Despite significant efforts during the 1970s and 1980s, when implementation research was a 'flourishing industry', theory-building remained comparatively underdeveloped. With the increasing number of case studies it became more and more apparent that, given the high variety, singularity and contingency of implementation results, the ambitious plans for developing comprehensive and general theoretical models had to be abandoned (cf. Mayntz 1983: 8; Windhoff-Héritier 1987: 88). Hence, the number of generally applicable concepts remained low. They included, for instance, the argument that the success of implementation is not only dependent on policy characteristics and contents but also on the preferences, capabilities and resources of subordinate administrative actors dealing with practical enforcement as well as societal actors addressed by the policy in question (Hanf and Downing 1982; Mayntz 1983). Without questioning the validity of these arguments, their limited degree of specification hardly allows for the development of testable hypotheses specifying the conditions under which we might expect more or less effective implementation. These theoretical deficits are further aggravated by the fact that the concept of implementation effectiveness is operationalised differently in the literature.

This general picture, however, does not mean that no specific theoretical approaches for the analysis of European implementation processes were developed. This is facilitated by the fact that analysing the implementation of EU policies – compared to the analysis of domestic policies – offers an important methodological advantage. We are able to investigate the implementation of policies whose requirements are identical for all member states in a cross-country comparison. Moreover, it can be analysed how different countries cope with different types of policies enacted at the EU level.

Different conceptions of effective implementation

To ascertain whether or not a measure was implemented successfully, it is crucially important how effective implementation is operationalised (Hill 1997). Generally, the potentially relevant concepts can be spread along two dimensions that refer to the analytical focus and the underlying perspective of research (see figure 17.3).

The first dimension refers to the distinction between policy outcomes and policy impacts. With a focus on policy impacts, effective implementation is already assumed, if the legal transposition and the practical application correspond to the objectives defined by the policy under investigation. Yet this does not consider whether and to what extent the objectives of a policy are actually achieved. Did the introduction of limits for automobile emissions, for instance, indeed lead to the intended improvement in air quality? Hence the focus on concrete outcomes implies a substantially more ambitious definition of effective implementation.

In addition to the distinction between outcomes and impacts, on a second dimension, two different research perspectives on the implementation process can be identified (Peters 1993), often referred to as 'top-down' and 'bottom-up' perspectives. When analysing the implementation of political programmes in a 'top-down' manner, implementation success is judged on the basis of a comparison between the intended and actually achieved outcomes. The degree of goal attainment serves as an indicator for the implementation success, and effective implementation implies a match between objectives and outcomes. If the objective of European legislation is, for instance, to set a certain standard for industrial emissions into the air, effective implementation is achieved as soon as the prescribed level is complied with throughout the Community.

This perspective is frequently grounded on a highly simplified model of political steering. Governments and legislators are assumed to have homogenous preferences, implying clear and unambiguous standards and guidelines for administrative authorities responsible for implementation and enforcement. From analysing potential implementation deficits, it becomes possible to draw conclusions about improving the design of future policies (concerning, for instance, policy objectives, the allocation of resources or the structures of the coordination and control of subordinate administrative agencies).

By contrast, the assessment of effective implementation viewed from a 'bottom-up' perspective is primarily process-oriented. Policy objectives and instruments are no longer defined as benchmarks to be reached; instead it is expected that they may undergo modifications during the process of policy implementation. Implementers should have flexibility and autonomy to adjust the policy in the light of particular local requirements, changes in the perception or constellation of policy problems, as well as new scientific evidence on causal relationships between means and ends. Hence, effective implementation is not measured by the attainment of a certain centrally defined objective but judged by the extent to which the perceived outcomes correspond with the preferences of the actors involved in the implementation process. The crucial question for evaluating implementation success is to what extent did a certain policy allow for processes of learning, capacity-building and support-building in order to address policy

Figure 17.3 Different conceptions of effective implementation

		Analytical Focus	
		Impact	Outcomes
Research Perspective	Target-oriented	1	2
	Process-oriented	3	4

Source: Weale et al. (2000: 45)

problems in a decentralised way consistent with the interests of the actors involved (Ingram and Schneider 1990).

This conception challenges the simplifying assumptions of the 'top-down' perspective and tries to take into account the complexity of implementation processes. Thus, it is emphasised that the formulation of clear-cut objectives often contrasts with the interests of politicians who have a preference for vague and ambiguous rather than clear-cut objectives in order to make an easy evaluation and detection of potential failures more difficult. In addition, the 'bottom-up' perspective takes account of the fact that implementation processes are rarely characterised by a clear delineation of competencies between the political and administrative actors involved at different institutional levels. Implementation more often implies complex interactions between public and private actors and organisations at the national, regional or local level, with potentially diverging interests, beliefs and perceptions with regard to the underlying policy problem. From this perspective, implementation is seen less as being based on hierarchically defined and controlled requirements and is understood more as a bargaining process between a great number of organisations and administrative agencies participating in the implementation process. Bargaining at the same time implies that during the implementation phase, initial policy objectives might undergo significant modifications.

With regard to the analysis of the implementation of European policies, in most cases, a target-oriented perspective is applied, evaluating implementation performance by comparing policy objectives and impacts (box 1 in figure 17.3). It asks to what extent the necessary legal and administrative conditions were created in order to meet the objectives of European measures. It is therefore the manner of the legal and practical implementation of European policies, rather than the evaluation of policy outcomes, which mostly serves as an indicator for assessing implementation effectiveness (Collins and Earnshaw 1992; Jordan 1999; Knill and Lenschow 1999; Weale *et al*. 2000). Although this perspective implies a somewhat restricted focus, it bears several analytical advantages.

First, conceptual problems (which are confronted with alternative definitions) are avoided. A focus on policy outcomes is analytically problematic as it obscures the actual link between policy instruments and their effects. Whether policy objectives are achieved or not depends on contingencies of the political, economic, and social policy context beside the deliberate choice of policy instruments. Hence, this perspective passes over important questions such as 'How do we know whether air water quality has improved as a result of European legislation rather than as the consequence of other factors completely independent from European developments, such as modified weather conditions, privatisation, or economic decline?'. It does not take into account that the success of policy implementation in terms of policy outcomes is not predictable given the scientific uncertainties and socio-economic complexities underlying a given problem constellation (Baier *et al*. 1990). The application of a process-oriented 'bottom-up' perspective, by contrast, remains characterised by the absence of a baseline for evaluating implementation results. It fails to offer a measuring rod for learning, capacity or support. When do these processes actually occur and work successfully? Moreover, and maybe even more significantly from the perspective of evaluating the impact of different policy instruments, this definition ignores the nature of the link between the (EU) policy and the local process of learning and problem-solving. After all, local processes could have entirely different origins. In order to assess whether an EU policy has had any impact on these local processes, we need to observe whether its 'instructions' – however open they might be – have been complied with (Knill and Lenschow 1999: 596).

Second, a focus on policy impacts (i.e. the formal and practical implementation of EU policies) provides the opportunity to compare implementation results even of widely different measures. By contrast, it would be problematic to measure and hence compare the contributions of different policies (e.g. the Directive for Free Access to Environmental Information, and the Large Combustion Plant Directive) with respect to their achievement of certain policy outcomes (such as air quality) (Knill and Lenschow 1999: 596). Against this background, a focus on the impacts of EU policies in the member states generally appears to be an appropriate measurement rod for judging their implementation effectiveness.

Theoretical ambiguity

The central analytical interest of implementation studies that focus on a comparison of policy objectives and impacts is placed in the factors that influence the extent to which formal and practical implementation actually corresponds with the aims defined in the policy. How can the implementation effectiveness be improved? Which instruments (e.g. old versus new instruments) are more appropriate in that respect?

Such considerations were, as mentioned above, of decisive relevance for the development of new instruments in EU environmental policy. The Commission in particular assumed that implementation effectiveness in that policy field could be notably improved by relying on less interventionist approaches. However, as empirical results indicate, the expectations of the Commission were not fulfilled. The implementation of new instruments did not prove to be more effective than the traditional interventionist approaches. How can this surprising result be explained?

A closer look at the theoretical arguments developed in implementation research quickly reveals that the new instruments, as they were promoted by the Commission, could by no means be regarded as a superior form of governance. Certainly there are to be found in the implementation literature many arguments that assume there will be fewer implementation problems with new instruments than with interventionist approaches. However, such arguments can hardly claim universal validity. Rather, a more detailed analysis reveals that implementation theory suffers from inconsistencies and ambiguities in its argumentation and hence in its implications for actual policy-making.

As a consequence, studies pointing to the advantages of new instruments and indicating the need to consider the specific context constellation in which a certain policy is implemented (Lipsky 1980; Berman 1980) cannot be regarded as representative of the whole field of implementation research. There are, for example, many studies that emphasise the need for classical forms of interventionist regulation, particularly because of the clear-cut objectives and requirements for implementation and enforcement that need to be complied with by both implementers and addressees (Krämer 2000; Lübbe-Wolf 1996). Between these two extremes, other analyses suggest a mix of interventionist and context-oriented elements as the perfect solution (cf. Sabatier 1986: 23–5) or advocate a contingent approach to the choice of policy instruments (Hanf and Scharpf 1978; Linder and Peters 1989; Ingram and Schneider 1990; Peters 1993).

The empirical richness of the implementation case studies of the 1980s, in particular, contributed to scholars increasingly shying away from seeking a universal model (Mayntz 1983; Windhoff-Héritier 1987). Instead the focus was on mid-level conclusions (e.g. on the appropriateness of certain policy instruments in light of distinctive policy problems and context characteristics), in the best case amounting to general contingency models.

But even these less abstract contingency models, identifying different problem constellations in which either old or new instruments are expected to be more successful, ended up contradicting one another. For instance, Ingram and Schneider (1990) argue that in constellations of low support for a policy, new instruments emphasising learning and support-building will lead to better implementation performance than detailed intervention. This view contrasts with an argument advanced by Cerych and Sabatier (1986), stating that clear and specific objectives might enhance learning by lower level agents because it produces obvious performance indicators.

Another example is the recommendation to apply new instruments in constellations characterised by high uncertainty and complexity in order to allow for sufficient flexibility to react to new developments in the light of specific context conditions and the generation of ideas useful for the further evolution of a policy (Ingram and Schneider 1990). Again, there are also good arguments to justify detailed intervention in such constellations. First, too much discretion for subordinate agents might imply that nothing happens at all (Lane 1995: 112; Lübbe-Wolff 1996). Second, even an interventionist policy that takes little account of the given complexity might succeed in stimulating learning processes by trial and error.

Such a list of the conflicting and contradictory advice that can be derived from implementation research can readily be added to. It illustrates the general ambiguity of implementation theory. Even attempts to classify contingencies, identifying particular problem or context constellations, fail to establish convincing causal linkages between policy choice and implementation effectiveness.

To come back to our example of EU environmental policy, regardless of the reasons that are eventually responsible for the shift in the use of policy instruments at the European level, implementation research does not provide a sufficient theoretical basis to justify such a step with regard to a more effective implementation. Obviously, there is no simple causal relation between policy instruments and implementation effectiveness.

Effective implementation as a problem of institutional adjustment

If the implementation success of European policies is neither dependent on country-specific factors nor influenced by the underlying instrument type, we have to look for alternative explanations to account for variance in implementation effectiveness across policies and countries. In this context, several more recent studies focus on institutional theories. The central argument underlying these approaches is that implementation performance of EU policies is not affected by the choice of instruments per se, but by the degree of institutional adjustment pressure resulting from EU policies for national arrangements (Duina 1997; Knill 1998, 2001; Knill and Lenschow 1998, 1999, 2000). The more European measures require domestic adaptations, the higher the probability will be that institutional inertia might have a negative impact on implementation effectiveness. This is not to say that the implementation of EU policies is inevitably ineffective, as soon as adjustments of national institutions are required. Rather, institutional theories suggest that the adaptability of national arrangements is subject to certain institutional limits.

The institutional perspective rests on two central assumptions that are outlined below before we consider their consequences for implementation effectiveness: (1) effective implementation is generally a question of effective institutional adaptation; and (2) the extent of institutional change is limited by the given institutional arrangements.

Effective institutional adaptation

Although EU policies are primarily directed at the specification of policy contents and instruments rather than institutional arrangements, it should not be overlooked that there is often a tight linkage between policy content and corresponding institutional implementation requirements. Therefore, decisions on instruments to a certain extent always entail decisions on corresponding institutional arrangements for their proper application. While being aware of the fact that the degree to which policy contents and institutional implications are coupled may vary from policy to policy and from sector to sector, it cannot be ignored that the growing importance of EU policies leaves its mark on domestic institutions. Consequently, implementation problems can be conceived as problems of institutional change (Knill and Lenschow 1999: 608–9).

The connection between instruments and institutions has long been acknowledged in the implementation literature. However, institutions were basically analysed from the perspective of adequate design. Analysts coming from the 'top-down' perspective developed optimal structural and organisational arrangements that would permit effective implementation of a certain policy (cf. Pressmann and Wildavsky 1973; Scharpf 1978). This thinking relies on the implicit assumption that national institutions would easily adapt to the suggested 'model' structure. Problems of institutional change were ignored. The 'bottom-up' perspective assumes a similar malleability of existing institutional factors. Here, analysts are interested in the impact of varying institutional designs on the skills, resources and capacities of relevant actors. They ask what is the perfect design that serves to equip the implementing authorities with sufficient financial, legal and personal resources.

Without denying the importance of adequate institutional design, such a perspective remains incomplete as long as it ignores the problems associated with the process of adjusting the existing institutional arrangements to the defined 'ideal' arrangements. It is in particular this latter aspect and to a lesser extent the knowledge of the correct institutional design that makes the implementation of European policies problematic.

Given institutional arrangements

This leads us to the second basic assumption of the institutionalist perspective: effective institutional adaptation to external requirements can only be expected within certain limits. It is one of the few generally accepted findings in the otherwise diverse institutionalist literature (Hall and Taylor 1996) that institutional change, whether required explicitly or implicitly, rarely takes place in a smooth and unproblematic way. Existing institutions 'matter' and they do so mainly by constraining the options for future changes and adaptations.

The emphasis on institutional stability and continuity is, however, not synonymous with a static understanding of institutional development. Rather, institutions find themselves in a virtually permanent process of adaptation to their environment. However, the scope of these adaptations is restricted by the structuring effects of existing institutional arrangements. Institutional change is hence often limited to aspects that do not question the very identity of an institution (March and Olsen 1989; Thelen and Steinmo 1992).

This abstract argument is of limited explanatory value, however, while we lack criteria with which to judge in which constellations EU requirements exceed the adaptation capacity of national institutions and where they do not. To cope with this problem, Knill and Lenschow (1998) suggest a distinction between three levels of adaptation pressure, each of them linked to different expectations with regard to implementation effectiveness. This distinction is based on the understanding that institutionally grown structures and routines prevent easy adaptation to exogenous pressure (DiMaggio and Powell 1991; March and Olsen 1989). Hence, domestic adaptation appears to be more likely in cases where European policies imply incremental rather than fundamental departures from existing arrangements at the domestic level.

The first scenario refers to constellations of low adaptation pressure. In this case, the institutional implications of EU policies are completely in line with domestic arrangements; i.e., no, or only marginal, changes are demanded. Implementation therefore is expected to be rather effective, as institutional adjustment requirements are very limited or completely absent.

In the second scenario of high adaptation pressure, by contrast, EU requirements exceed the adjustment capacities of national institutions. Ineffective implementation is the probable consequence. Such constellations can be expected when EU requirements are in contradiction with institutionally strongly entrenched elements of national regulatory arrangements (see Krasner 1988). This is the case, for instance, if EU policies require changes in domestic regulatory styles and structures that represent general patterns of national state, legal and administrative traditions and that are strongly rooted in a country's political, administrative and legal system.

The third scenario of moderate adaptation pressure refers to constellations in which European policies require substantive adjustments of domestic institutions, without, however, challenging well entrenched core patterns of the political, legal and administrative system. While in such cases there is a higher probability for an effective implementation of European policies, effective implementation, nevertheless, cannot be taken for granted. In contrast with the two other scenarios, in these cases a mere institutional perspective is not sufficient to develop hypotheses on the expected implementation performance (in terms of domestic institutional adjustments to EU requirements). To answer this question we have to complement our analysis with a second explanatory step which considers the particular interest constellation and institutional opportunity structures at the domestic level. To what extent is there sufficient domestic support for adjusting to EU requirements? To what extent have domestic actors who support regulatory change sufficient powers and resources to realise their interests? Institutional adaptation and hence effective implementation can only be expected if they are facilitated by favourable domestic conditions in that respect (Knill and Lenschow 1998; Knill and Lehmkuhl 2002).

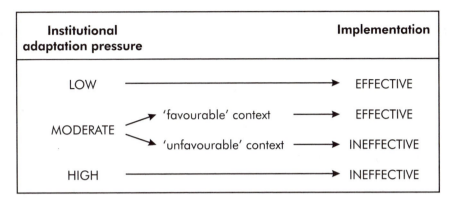

Figure 17.4 Institutional adaptation pressure and implementation effectiveness

Source: Knill and Lehmkuhl (2002)

Empirical illustration: the implementation of EU environmental policy in Britain, France and Germany

To illustrate these analytical considerations I draw on recent cross-national studies on the implementation of EU environmental policy (Knill and Lenschow 1998; Knill 2001). Similar arguments, however, are also advanced by other scholars investigating the implementation of European measures in the field of social policy (Duina 1997) or health and safety at work (Eichener 1996). The following examples refer to the implementation of three environmental policies which cover the regulatory variety of old and new instrument types in Britain, France and Germany.

The 1980 Drinking Water Directive is a good example of command-and-control regulation. The directive specifies quality standards for water intended for human consumption. These standards apply to a range of substances that may pose a threat to human health when present in certain levels of concentration in the water. The prescription of uniform and legally-binding standards assumes hierarchical structures of intervention and quite formal and legalistic patterns of administrative interest intermediation at the domestic level. The substantive standards defined in the directive are not negotiable and apply uniformly to all water providers. In view of these detailed specifications, national regulatory authorities have limited discretion and flexibility in implementing European legislation. In other words, there is a close link between policy content (uniform standards) and corresponding institutional arrangements for domestic compliance (formalist and legalist patterns of intervention).

The prescription of concrete regulatory arrangements for the domestic implementation of European requirements is not restricted to substantive measures, but can also be observed in policies with a merely procedural focus. In this context the Directive on the Freedom of Access to Environmental Information is a good case in point. Rather than defining substantive standards the directive aims to ensure free access to the information on the environment held by public authorities. It lays down the detailed conditions for making such information accessible, including appeals procedures against refusal or failure to provide information, charges for the provision of information, and exemptions from disclosure (Winter 1996). In view of these detailed procedural prescriptions, the directive has important implications on national patterns of administrative interest intermediation, namely by demanding a more open and transparent style of environmental regulation, with different societal interests having equal opportunities in access to administrative decision-making. In this way the scope for secretive and closed interaction patterns between regulatory authorities and the regulated industry, which may be observed in many member states, is significantly reduced.

Finally, the 1993 Environmental Management and Auditing Systems (EMAS) Regulation established a management tool to help European companies evaluate the environmental impact of their activities. Companies voluntarily adopt an environmental policy and conduct an environmental review. The environmental statement subsequently prepared by the company is validated by an officially appointed, independent and accredited environmental auditor. Although it leaves some leeway for domestic compliance, there is an implicit, clear shift in the regulation in favour of industrial self-regulation by the voluntary introduction of an environmental management system, as opposed to interventionist approaches. Instead, the state's role is to facilitate self-regulatory processes by providing and maintaining the institutional framework for the auditing process.

An investigation of the domestic responses to the institutional requirements of the three policies for Britain, France, and Germany reveals a great variety of implementation performance across both policies and countries, which is summarised in table 17.3 (cf. Knill and Lenschow 1998; Knill 2001).

When the explanatory framework developed above is applied, it becomes apparent that domestic responses in six of the nine cases can be explained already on the basis of the first explanatory step, which considers the institutional compatibility of European requirements and domestic arrangements. It is only for three cases, where change was potentially possible, that we have to additionally analyse the specific domestic interest constellations in order to understand the actual occurrence or non-occurrence of institutional adjustment.

Beginning with the perspective of institutional compatibility, four persistence cases (EMAS and information access in Britain, information access in France, and drinking water in Germany) can be explained by the fact that existing regulatory arrangements at the national level were already well in line with European requirements; there was hence no European pressure for domestic adjustment.

In the British EMAS case this can be explained by the fact that the domestic environmental management system served as a reference point for the subsequent European EMAS-Regulation. Turning to the information directive, both Britain and France had already established regulatory arrangements which corresponded with and partially went even beyond EU requirements. Hence, effective compliance was possible without any legal or practical changes. The same holds true for the German drinking water case, where the interventionist and formalist regulatory style implicit in the directive was well in line with the traditional approach in Germany (Héritier et al. 1996; Kimber 2000).

In the cases of access to information in Germany and drinking water in France, by contrast, domestic persistence emerged from the fact that European requirements clashed with core patterns of national administrative traditions which were strongly embedded institutionally. The institutional incompatibility of European and national arrangements was too great to allow for smooth regulatory adjustments. Instead, we observe strong resistance to change in both countries.

Table 17.3 Implementation effectiveness of environmental policies in Britain, France and Germany

Policy/Country	Britain	France	Germany
Drinking water	Effective	Ineffective	Effective
Information access	Effective	Effective	Ineffective
EMAS	Effective	Ineffective	Effective

In Germany the requirements of the Information Directive in favour of regulatory transparency and accountability did not correspond with the state and legal tradition, where public access to documents and information is only considered legitimate if the individual requesting it can show the 'direct effect' of the project or activity in question on the individual situation. This different notion of the role of the administration and the law in society has led to substantial implementation problems, and hence strong resistance to adjusting domestic arrangements in the light of European requirements (Winter 1996).

In a similar way the French implementation of the Drinking Water Directive was characterised by far-reaching resistance to adjusting the dominant regulatory practice, which provided regulatory authorities with considerable autonomy to define water quality standards on the basis of informal and consensual negotiations with water providers. This practice is institutionally entrenched in the strong integration of the so-called *grands corps*. Administrative coordination is achieved not so much by hierarchical means, as by the confidence with which the top ranks entrust the lower ranks (Montricher 1996). Against this background the formalist and legalist approach implicit in the European directive implied a fundamental challenge to French regulatory traditions.

It is only in three cases (EMAS in Germany and France, drinking water in Britain) that domestic adjustment could be considered as potentially possible from an institutional compatibility perspective; i.e. European legislation required substantive changes, albeit no challenges to core patterns of national administrative traditions. In these constellations the actual pattern of change or persistence cannot be inferred from a mere institutional compatibility perspective but must also take account of the specific policy context at the national level.

Thus the EMAS regulation did not challenge institutional core patterns in either Germany or in France. Although the regulation's emphasis on self-regulation and voluntary agreements clashed with the legalist and interventionist style of German environmental policy, they were nevertheless in line with the German tradition of corporatism (Benz and Goetz 1996). In France, too, the spirit of the regulation was basically in line with the French practice of voluntary agreements on industrial emission reductions and the use of economic incentives, notwithstanding the need to build up corresponding regulatory structures for administration of the system (Héritier *et al.* 1996).

Notwithstanding similar adjustment requirements, however, we observe different responses in the two countries, namely adjustment in Germany and resistance in France. Germany's smooth adaptation to European requirements can be traced to the fact that the domestic actor constellation was characterised by broad support for the regulation from both industrial and environmental organisations, partly because the legislation accorded with national debates on deregulation and administrative reforms. The strong support from industry, in particular, resulted from its expectation that future authorisation and inspection procedures might be 'slimmed' down for EMAS participants. In France, by contrast, there is considerable resistance to changing the existing regulatory practice as a consequence of the lack of support from industrial actors. Industry is concerned that information voluntarily provided within the context of EMAS might be used against it during authorisation and inspection procedures (Knill and Lenschow 1998).

In the British case of drinking water, the regulatory changes from industrial self-regulation towards a more interventionist regime associated with the privatisation of the water industry in 1989 had significantly reduced institutional incompatibilities between European and national arrangements. Although the reformed domestic regime was already congruent with the interventionist approach implied by the directive, certain adjustments were nevertheless necessary, in particular with regard to the formal and practical compliance with the legally binding standards prescribed by EU legislation. These remaining adjustments were facilitated by a favourable policy context. Privatisation meant that the economic costs of compliance with European standards no longer interfered with the government's objective of reducing public spending, as the costs for retrofitting existing plants had to be borne by private companies. Moreover, the regulatory regime set up in the context of privatisation strengthened the voice and influence of environmental and consumer groups, thereby providing new institutional access opportunities which favoured compliance with European objectives (Maloney and Richardson 1995).

In summary, this brief review of research findings illustrates that the implementation effectiveness of European policies can be understood on the basis of a two-step approach. As a first step we are able to evaluate the overall possibility of domestic adjustments, based on the institutional compatibility of European and domestic arrangements. Only if we need to investigate whether possible adjustments actually occur do we take an additional explanatory step and consider the underlying constellation of actors and opportunity structures.

Conclusions: how to improve the implementation of EU policies?

The empirical and theoretical analysis of the implementation of European policies suggests several conclusions which have to be taken into account when trying to improve the EU's implementation performance. First, empirical evidence shows that the implementation effectiveness of EU policies is difficult to explain fully by looking at country-specific factors. The formal transformation and practical application of Community law reveals no clear pattern of member states typically implementing EU policies either effectively or ineffectively. Rather the performance of each member state varies to a great extent from policy to policy and sector to sector.

Second, there is no direct link between the choice of European policy instruments and implementation effectiveness. The choice of instruments (old versus new) does not affect the implementation performance. This claim is supported by comparative implementation studies. At the same time, theoretical work on implementation is characterised by rather contradictory expectations with respect to the performance of different instrument types.

Third, in more recent studies on the implementation of EU policies, the institutional compatibility of EU requirements and national arrangements is emphasised as a more promising alternative in order to account for the highly varying implementation performance across policies and countries. The central argument is that the probability of deficient implementation increases with the extent to which EU policies require changes of strongly institutionalised domestic regulatory styles and structures. In this context, new instruments are not necessarily superior to old instruments. Both instrument types may demand a too high level of institutional adaptation in order to set in motion a process of problem-solving – instead, the policy may be resisted by its implementers and/or addressees.

Fourth, the institutional perspective suggests that in order to improve their implementation effectiveness, EU policy-makers face important challenges. On the one hand, imposing the 'ideal' policy design from the top while ignoring the potential impact of domestic institutions may significantly reduce the chance for effective problem-solving due to institutional resistance to adaptation. On the other hand, the design of policies in conformity with existing institutions may reduce the possibility to generate changes and solve problems. To overcome these problems, policy-makers have to develop policies that require something, but not too much, from member states. In other words, there exists a curvilinear relationship between the level of adaptation pressure implied in EU policies and the effectiveness of implementation (cf. Cerych and Sabatier 1986). Only if EU legislation fits into such 'bounded space for innovation' may it – be it old or new – contribute to problem-solving in the EU.

At the EU level, approaches that might be able to take these demands into account have been developed in recent years. They aim at minimising as far as possible the adaptation requirements for national institutions. In so doing, they combine relatively general substantive objectives (e.g. objectives for air quality) with procedural regulations demanding the publication and comparative assessment and monitoring of the implementation performance for each member state. In defining policy objectives that are as general as possible, the institutional adaptation costs shall be reduced to a minimum; simultaneously, political pressure through transparency and performance comparison shall be mobilised to improve the achievement of policy goals.

These new forms of governance become apparent in particular in the 'Open Method of Coordination' (OMC). While certain policy benchmarks are set for the Union, national responses are formulated independently and without the threat of formal sanctions. The EU merely provides a context and enabling structures for cooperation and learning among national policy-makers. The regulatory impact of this approach rests on dissemination of best practice and the provision of incentives (peer review) rather than legal obligation and control. Hence, the level of obligation to a regulatory centre is low and a wide range of policy strategies to achieve general EU targets could be chosen (de la Porte and Pochet 2002; Scott and Trubek 2002). At present the OMC is applied to domains like information society, research and development, enterprises, economic reforms, education, employment, social inclusion, health care and pensions – i.e. flanking policies for building the economic union with an emphasis on social cohesion. The concrete design of the OMC varies from policy field to policy field, some emphasising information exchange (e.g. pensions and health) others building up stronger adaptation pressure through cross-national and Commission peer reviews (e.g. employment and to a lesser extent also social inclusion).

However, even though these approaches are basically appropriate for avoiding the described problems of institutional adaptations, they are still of a limited relevance. This can be traced to the fact that in many cases voluntary and self-regulatory approaches do not provide for appropriate forms of steering for all policy problems (Héritier 2002; Holzinger *et al.* 2003). OMC constitutes a rather unsuitable approach, for instance, if the creation of a level playing field and hence harmonisation is one of the aims of the regulators. Such an aim would be best served through hierarchical regulatory standards. The same holds true if the decision-makers share a preference for predictable and reliable regulatory arrangements. The regulatory framework of OMC is likely to be too flexible, whereas hierarchical norms give clearly defined directions. By contrast, OMC could be the preferable option if the maintenance of national diversity is desirable or unchangeable. The same holds for constellations in which risk and insecurity are characterising the regulatory context with the effect that no clear and generally applicable regulatory solution is in supply.

Finally, it should be emphasised that different policy designs and governance approaches should not be interpreted as a panacea to overcome all problems causing implementation deficits in the EU. None of the discussed approaches will avoid the common practice of 'creative compliance' in the member states; this practice of avoiding the intention of a law without breaking the terms of the law, constitutes a common problem for all modes of regulation (cf. Cohn 2002; McBarnet and Whelan 1991). Moreover, it should not be overlooked that the design of a European policy is the result of often long-winded negotiations between the member states. As a result, policy proposals are often watered down (by making use of exception clauses or vague formulations) or enriched with elements that are in the interests of certain member states. Implementation deficits to a considerable degree are simply the result of inconsistent and ambiguous European policies. This basic deficit applies to all forms of European governance. The deliberate choice of European policy design therefore only allows for partial improvements of the implementation performance; the design of policies for effective implementation is constrained by the need to accommodate the diverse interests of the member states.

References

Alter, K. J. and Meunier-Aitsahalia, S. (1994) 'Judicial Politics in the European Community: European Integration and the Pathbreaking Cassis de Dijon Decision', *Comparative Political Studies* 26: 535–61.

Baier, V. E., March, J. G. and Sætren, H. (1990) 'Implementierung und Ungewißheit', in J. G. March (ed.), *Entwicklung und Organisation: Kritische und konstruktive Beiträge, Entwicklungen und Perspektiven* (Wiesbaden: Gabler).

Benz, A. and Goetz, K. H. (1996) *A New German Public Sector? Reform, Adaptation and Stability* (Dartmouth: Aldershot).

Berman, P. (1980) 'Thinking About Programmed and Adaptive Implementation: Matching Strategies to Situations', in H. Ingram and D. Mann (eds) *Why Policies Succeed or Fail* (London: Sage).

Börzel, T. A. (2000) 'Why There is no Southern Problem: On Environmental Leaders and Laggards in the EU', *Journal of European Public Policy* 7/1: 141–62.

—— (2001) 'Non-Compliance in the European Union: Pathology or Statistical Artefact?', *Journal of European Public Policy* 8/5: 803–24.

Bouma, J. J. (2000) 'Environmental Management Systems and Audits as Alternative Environ-mental Policy Instruments', in C. Knill and A. Lenschow (eds), *Implementing EU Environ-mental Policy: New Approaches to an Old Problem* (Manchester: Manchester University Press).

Cerych, L. and Sabatier, P. (1986) *Great Expectations and Mixed Preferences: The Implementation of European Higher Education Reforms* (Stoke on Trent: Trentham Books).

Cohn, M. (2002) 'Fuzzy Legality in Regulation: The Legislative Mandate Revisited', *Law and Policy* 23: 469–97.

Collins, K. and Earnshaw, D. (1992) 'The Implementation and Enforcement of European Commu-nity Environment Legislation', *Environmental Politics* 1/4: 213–49.

De la Porte, C. and Pochet, P. (2002) *Building Social Europe through the Open Method of Co-ordina-tion* (Brussels: P.I.E. – Peter Lang).

DiMaggio, P. J. and Powell, W. W. (1991) 'The Iron Cage Revisited: Institutionalized Isomorphism and Collective Rationality in Organizational Fields', in: P. J. DiMaggio and W. W. Powell (eds) *The New Institutionalism in Organizational Analysis* (Chicago: Chicago University Press).

Duina, F. (1997) 'Explaining Legal Implementation in the European Union', *International Journal of the Sociology of Law* 25: 155–79.

Eichener, V. (1996) 'Die Rückwirkungen der europäischen Integration auf nationale Politik-muster', in M. Jachtenfuchs and B. Kohler-Koch (eds) *Europäische Integration* (Opladen: Leske & Budrich).

Hall, P. A. and Taylor, R. C. (1996) *Political Science and the Three New Institutionalisms. MPIFG Discussion Paper 96/6* (Köln: Max-Planck-Instititut für Gesellschaftsforschung).

Hanf, K. and Downing, P. (1982) *International Comparisons in Implementing Pollution Laws* (Boston, MA: Kluwer-Nijhoff).

Hanf, K. and Scharpf, F. W. (1978) *Interorganizational Policy-making: Limits to Coordination and Central Control* (London: Sage).

Héritier, A. (2002) 'New Modes of Governance in Europe: Policy Making Without Legislating?' in A. Héritier (ed.), *The Provision of Common Goods: Governance across Multiple Arenas* (Boulder, CO: Rowman & Littlefield).

Héritier, A., Knill, C. and Mingers, S. (1996) *Ringing the Changes in Europe: Regulatory Competi-tion and the Transformation of the State* (Berlin: de Gruyter).

Hill, M. (1997) 'Implementation Theory', *Policy and Politics* 25: 375–85.

Holzinger, K. (1994) *Politik des kleinsten gemeinsamen Nenners? Umweltpolitische Entscheidungs-prozesse in der EG am Beispiel der Einführung des Katalysatorautos* (Berlin: Edition Sigma).

Holzinger, K., Knill, C. and Schäfer, A. (2003) 'Steuerungswandel in der europäischen Umwelt-politik?', in K. Holzinger, C. Knill and D. Lehmkuhl (eds), *Politische Steuerung im Wandel: Der Einfluss von Ideen und Problemstrukturen* (Opladen: Leske & Budrich).

Ingram, H. and Schneider, A. (1990) 'Improving Implementation Through Framing Smarter Stat-utes', *Journal of Public Policy* 10/1: 67–88.

Jordan, A. J. (1999) 'The Implementation of EU Environmental Policy: A Policy Problem Without a Political Solution?', *Environment and Planning C (Government and Policy)* 17/1: 69–90.

Kimber, C. (2000) 'Implementing European Environmental Policy and the Directive on Access to Environmental Information', in C. Knill and A. Lenschow (eds) *Implementing EU Environ-mental Policy: New Approaches to an Old Problem* (Manchester: Manchester University Press).

Knill, C. (1998) 'European Policies: The Impact of National Administrative Traditions on Euro-pean Policy Making', *Journal of Public Policy* 18/1: 1–28.

—— (2001) *The Europeanisation of National Administrations: Patterns of Institutional Change and Persistence* (Cambridge: Cambridge University Press).

Knill, C. and Lehmkuhl, D. (2002) 'The National Impact of EU Regulatory Policy: Three European-ization Mechanisms', *European Journal of Political Research* 41/2: 255–80.

Knill, C. and Lenschow, A., (1998 'Coping with Europe: the Impact of British and German Administration on the Implementation of EU Environmental Policy', *Journal of European Public Policy* 5/4: 595–614.

—— (1999) 'Neue Konzepte – alte Probleme? Die institutionellen Grenzen effektiver Implementation', *Politische Vierteljahresschrift* 40/4: 591–617.

—— (2000) *Implementing EU Environmental Policy: New Directions and Old Problems* (Manchester: Manchester University Press).

Krämer, L. (1996) 'Defizite im Vollzug des EG-Umweltrechts und ihre Ursachen', in G. Lübbe-Wolff (ed.), *Der Vollzug des europäischen Umweltrechts* (Berlin: Erich Schmidt Verlag).

—— (2000) *EC Environmental Law* (London: Sweet & Maxwell).

Krasner, S. D. (1988) 'Sovereignty: An Institutional Perspective', *Comparative Political Studies* 21/1: 66–94.

Krislov, S., Ehlermann, C.-D. and Weiler, J. (1986). 'The Political Organs and the Decision-Making Process in the United States and the European Community', in M. Cappelletti, M. Seccombe and J. Weiler (eds), *Integration Through Law, Methods, Tools and Institutions: Political Organs, Integration Techniques and Judicial Process* (Berlin: de Gruyter).

Lane, J.-E. (1995) *The Public Sector: Concepts, Models and Approaches* (London: Sage).

Lenschow, A. (1999) 'The Greening of the EU: the Common Agricultural Policy and the Structural Funds', *Environment and Planning C (Government and Policy)* 17/1: 91–108.

Linder, S. and Peters, B. G. (1989) 'Instruments of Government: Perceptions and Contexts', *Journal of Public Policy* 9/1: 35–58.

Lipsky, M. (1980) *Street-Level Bureaucracy* (New York: Russell Sage).

Lübbe-Wolff, G. (1996) 'Stand und Instrumente der Implementation des Umweltrechts in Deutschland', in G. Lübbe-Wolff (ed.), *Der Vollzug des europäischen Umweltrechts* (Berlin: Erich Schmidt Verlag).

McBarnet, D. and Whelan, C. (1991) 'The Elusive Spirit of the Law: Formalism and the Struggle of Legal Control', *Modern Law Review* 54: 848–73.

Macrory, R. (1992) 'The Enforcement of Community Environmental Laws: Critical Issues', *Common Market Law Review* 29: 347–369.

Macrory, R. and Purdy, R. (1997) 'The Enforcement of EC Environmental Law Against Member States', in J. Holder (ed.), *The Impact of EC Environmental Law in the UK* (Chichester: John Wiley and Sons).

Maloney, W. A. and Richardson, J. (1995) *Managing Policy Change in Britain: The Politics of Water* (Edinburgh: Edinburgh University Press).

March, J. G. and Olsen, J. P. (1989) *The New Institutionalism: Organizational Factors in Political Life* (New York: The Free Press).

Mayntz, R. (1983) *Implementation politischer Programme II* (Opladen: Westdeutscher Verlag).

Mendrinou, M. (1996) 'Non-Compliance and the European Commission's Role in Integration', *Journal of European Public Policy* 3/1: 1–22.

Mol, A., Lauber, V. and Liefferink, D. (2000) *The Voluntary Approach to Environmental Policy* (Oxford: Oxford University Press).

Montricher, N. de. (1996) 'France: In Search of Relevant Changes', in J. P. Olsen and B. G. Peters (eds), *Lessons from Experience. Experimental Learning and Administrative Reform in Eight European Democracies* (Oslo: Scandinavian University Press).

Peters, B. G. (1993) 'Alternative Modelle des Policy-Prozesses: Die Sicht "von unten" und die Sicht "von oben"', in A. Héritier (ed.), *Policy-Analyse: Kritik und Neuorientierung, PVS Sonderheft* 24: 289–306.

Pressman, J. and Wildavsky, A. (1973) *Implementation* (Berkeley: University of California Press).

Sabatier, P. A. (1986) 'Top-Down and Bottom-Up Approaches to Implementation Research', *Journal of Public Policy* 6: 21–48.

Scharpf, F. W. (1978) 'Interorganizational Policy Studies: Issues, Concepts, and Perspectives', in K. Hanf and F. W. Scharpf (eds) *Interorganizational Policy Making: Limits to Coordination and Central Control* (London: Sage).

Scott, J. and Trubek, D. M. (2002) 'Mind the Gap: Law and New Approaches to Governance in the European Union', *European Law Journal* 8/1: 1–18.

Siedentopf, H. and Ziller, J. (1988) *Making European Policies Work, The Implementation of Community Legislation in the Member States* (London: Sage).

Snyder, F. (1993) 'The Effectiveness of European Community Law: Institutions, Processes, Tools and Techniques', *Modern Law Review* 56: 19–54.

Tallberg, J. (1999) *Making States Comply: The European Commission, the European Court of Justice and the Enforcement of the Internal Market* (Lund: Studentliteratur).

Thelen, K. and Steinmo, S. (1992) 'Historical Institutionalism in Comparative Politics', in S. Steinmo, K. Thelen and F. Longstreth (eds.), *Structuring Politics: Historical Institutionalism in Comparative Analysis* (Cambridge: Cambridge University Press).

Toonen, T. A. J. (1992) 'Europe of the Administrations: The Challenges of '92 (and Beyond)', *Public Administration Review* 52/2: 108–15.

Weale, A. *et al.* (2000) *Environmental Governance in Europe* (Oxford/New York: Oxford University Press).

Weiler, J. (1988) 'The White Paper and the Application of Community Law', in R. Bieber, R. Dehousse, J. Pinder and J. H. H. Weiler (eds), *One European Market?* (Baden-Baden: Nomos).

Windhoff-Héritier, A. (1987) *Policy-Analyse: Eine Einführung* (Frankfurt: Campus).

Winter, G. (1996) 'Freedom of Environmental Information', in G. Winter (ed.), *European Environmental Law. A Comparative Perspective* (London: Aldershot).

Wright, R. (2000) 'Implementing Voluntary Policy Instruments: The Experience of the EU Ecolabel Award Scheme', in C. Knill and A. Lenschow (eds.), *Implementing EU Environmental Policy: New Approaches to an Old Problem* (Manchester: Manchester University Press).

Chapter 18

After the 'permissive consensus'

Still searching for democracy

Michael Newman

Introduction

European integration was constructed in the six original member states on the basis of a 'permissive consensus', with 'peace, prosperity and supranationalism' as its legitimating values and with little attempt to involve public or even parliamentary opinion in the process (Weiler 1994). While the underlying conditions for the success of this kind of governmental operation were increasingly eroded from the 1970s onwards, it was the ratification crisis over the Treaty of Maastricht in 1992–3 that finally brought matters to a head. For this demonstrated the possibility that new steps in the integration process regarded as desirable, or even essential, by political and economic elites could be threatened by a popular refusal to endorse them. This undoubtedly spurred the policy-makers to attempt to secure wider support by introducing a series of reforms. There is therefore no doubt that the European Parliament – the major focus of democracy within the institutional architecture – has gained significant new powers (see chapter 6). There have also been efforts to reinforce the legitimacy of the Union, both symbolically through the flag, anthem and passport, and more substantially through EU citizenship, the Charter of Fundamental Rights and the abortive Constitutional Treaty. Yet none of this has brought about any breakthrough. On the contrary, the situation in 2004–5 dramatically increased the continuing problems. While EU enlargement and the agreement of the European Council to endorse the Constitutional Treaty represented significant new steps in the integration project, the turnout in the European elections was lower than ever, with a substantial increase in the vote for populist, right-wing Eurosceptic parties. Furthermore, the Constitutional Treaty, designed in part to demonstrate the democratic credentials of the Union, was effectively abandoned in disarray in June 2005, following the 'no' votes in the French and Dutch referenda. The inescapable conclusion is that the EU has major democratic problems. Yet while most commentators are in agreement on this point, there is much less consensus about the nature of those problems or the ways in which they might be resolved.

This chapter does not pretend to offer a solution. Its aims are more modest: to provide a critical examination of some of the approaches that have been proposed and to suggest the directions in which progress might be made. However, it is first necessary to explain the assumptions about democracy that underlie the analysis.[1] In my view, normative issues about the nature, values and goals of democracy must remain paramount in any discussion, although these ideals must also take account of the lessons derived from historical experience. I believe that this means that such notions as freedom of information, opinion, expression and organisation, universal suffrage, a choice of political representatives, and a separation of powers are necessary in any complex society. However, democracy includes a cluster of *procedural* conditions and *substantive* values, and the relative importance of each of these is a matter of constant debate, with the commentator's priorities inevitably based in a particular ideological framework. My position on three perpetual tensions within the general concept of democracy is as follows. First, between *liberty* and *equality*, the emphasis here lies on greater equality. Secondly, between *elitist* and *participatory* forms of democracy, the stress here is on participation. And, thirdly, on the question of *exclusiveness* and *inclusiveness*, the view taken here is that a political system should be as inclusive as possible, valuing diversity. One further point is also relevant. I do not believe that the EU needs to replicate the institutional forms that have typified liberal-democracy within states or that it should try to secure legitimacy in the same way. However, it does require a form of democratic legitimacy that it has not yet attained if it is to escape from the impasse that currently besets it. The following discussion examines the various approaches to the problems of democracy from a perspective reflecting these normative values and assumptions.

The origins of the problems and traditional debates about solutions

The Treaty of Rome contained an interesting ambiguity. The signatories were members of governments, but the objective was to bring about ever closer union among *the peoples* of Europe. There was thus a clear assumption that the governments incorporated or represented the peoples. This was combined with a theory that held that the removal of economic barriers and concerted action on a competitive basis was the way to progress. The Treaty of Rome may therefore be viewed as a contract between governments to create a common market, with the Commission, the Court of Justice, and Community law as guarantors that the pledges would be honoured (Newman 1996). Certainly, the EEC included a parliamentary assembly, but as its members were nominated by the governments, this was no more than paying lip service to democratic principles. Furthermore, there was comparatively little discussion of the key decisions within the parliaments of the six and much less popular involvement. There was therefore weak authorisation for an innovation of historic importance and, to the extent that democracy and accountability operated, these were entirely on the basis of the domestic systems of the member states.

Yet it was during the 1950s and 1960s that the policy-making system was constructed on the basis of a common market on capitalist principles, with the European Court of Justice establishing the doctrines of direct effect and legal supremacy. This meant that there were increasing constraints on domestic autonomy, a particular kind of economic organisation was underpinned by supranational law, and a pattern of decision-making was introduced which strengthened governments in relation to those to whom they were theoretically accountable. Meanwhile the major economic interests developed effective ways of lobbying the Council and Commission, while less well resourced groups were generally unable to operate on this level. Yet parliaments and electorates still tended to view the interactions between the member states as traditional relations between states in the international system. Since the late 1970s, and still more, since the Maastricht ratification crisis, it is this view that has been called into question. Yet, in one form or another, the argument that democracy can operate only at the level of the state is highly resilient and continues to underlie many discussions about the problems of the EU.

State-centred views

The claim that the 'nation-state' is the only location for democracy has one key advantage over more complex notions of democratising the EU: the theory is easy to understand. The strongest claims about democracy and accountability operating through the electoral process are absorbed quite easily in early socialisation and political education. This provides a large part of the attraction for state-centred proposals for enhancing democracy and accountability. And this has particular relevance for states such as Britain and Sweden, which have had long traditions of liberal-democratic development, and political cultures emphasising their distinctiveness from 'Europe'. Nevertheless, it is necessary to distinguish between a *normative* perspective on the issues (often found in the so-called Eurosceptic view) and a more *analytical* perspective.

The normative position takes the territory of the 'nation-state' as the necessary location for liberal-democracy and opposes all aspects of the EU which demarcate it from a traditional international agreement between states. These are regarded as threatening to liberal-democracy within the state, and the solution is seen as the repatriation of policy until intergovernmentalism is restored (or, in more extreme versions, it could mean withdrawal from the EU). Typically, the demands have been an insistence on maintaining veto power in the Council, a weakening of the European Court of Justice, a strict limitation on EU competencies, governmental control over the Commission, and a rolling back of the power of the European Parliament. Currently such arguments are most commonly associated with the Right, and in a xenophobic form with the extreme Right, but historically they have just as frequently been emphasised by the Left. From this perspective, the case has been that, since the EU is a capitalist organisation, supranational integration reflects and strengthens the control of pro-capitalist forces over the labour movement and other social movements. In order to maintain the possibility of implementing more socialist policies, it has therefore been seen to be necessary to maintain looser forms of integration that allow for greater domestic autonomy at the level of the state. This line was, for example, often followed by the British Labour Party until the mid-1980s, and by the majority of Swedish Social Democrats in the referenda over membership in 1994 and entry into the euro in 2003. Rather surprisingly, it was also invoked by Laurent Fabius (a former middle-of-the-road Prime Minister), when putting himself at the head of an abortive campaign by the left-wing of the French Socialists for the party to vote against the Constitutional Treaty in a party referendum in December 2004. Both left- and right-wing aspects of the argument were subsequently used in the campaigns for a 'no' vote in France and the Netherlands.

Naturally, any normative case (against further integration and in favour of maintaining democratic accountability exclusively through the member states) must also be based on an analysis – or, in the case of populist Euroscepticism, a pseudo-analysis – of the existing distribution of power. In other words, the demand that power *ought* to be retained or restored to the state where it can be democratically controlled, is based on a claim that this is possible. However, a rather similar case may also be made on grounds that are purportedly solely analytical. In recent years the most cogent argument of this kind has been attempted by Andrew Moravcsik (2002).

Moravcsik's argument is based on the assumption that the EU has not changed, *in essence*, from the original entity created by the Treaty of Rome. To be sure, it has become far more complex and has taken on a range of additional powers and competencies. But this should not mislead observers into thinking that such developments constitute a *qualitative* change, for these policies have been agreed by governments engaged in a process of bargaining to promote their common and individual interests. Nor do any of the new policy areas – in particular, more extensive regional or social dimensions – fundamentally change the nature of the Union. These should be regarded as 'side-payments' – inducements for the governments of weaker economies to accept entry into a market in which many of their domestic constituents will be forced to bear substantial costs of adjustment. Moravcsik also argues that those who imply that vast amounts of policy are now controlled in 'Brussels' are exaggerating the significance of the spill-over effects of integration. Similarly, he seeks to correct the misconception (in his eyes) that the amount of regulation by the EU which evades democratic control and accountability through forms of delegated authority means that there is any special problem. This, he suggests, is merely a matter of *appearance* because it so happens that the areas of policy that have been entrusted to the EU are also those that are carried out by delegated authority within liberal-democratic states.

Some aspects of Moravcsik's arguments are valuable correctives to those who present the EU as a super-state, controlling every aspect of policy. He is also certainly right to emphasise the fact that the EU is a slow policy-making system based on the search for a high degree of consensus amongst the various elite actors who make the decisions. However, there are a number of flaws in his analysis. Having settled the issues to his own satisfaction, he asks 'Why then is there such public and scholarly concern about the democratic deficit?' and concludes that it is because most critics 'compare the EU to an ideal plebiscitary or parliamentary democracy, standing alone' (Moravcsik 2002: 621). His own method, he claims, is to compare the issues of widespread concern about the EU with the ways in which they are practised within existing democratic states. In fact, he simply compares the operation of a limited number of issues at the two levels without elaborating any concept of democracy. But if particular policies are insulated from democratic control at national level, it is hardly reassuring to find that this is also the case at EU level. Far from meaning that there *is* no democratic problem, this surely means that the problems are *compounded* because of the insulation of key policy areas from robust democratic control and accountability at both levels. Furthermore, while Moravcsik might not offer an explicit definition of democracy, many of his views are made apparent. It is therefore quite clear that he does not favour any mass involvement or participation in the questions that he regards as more appropriately controlled by those with technical expertise. He prefers the majority to remain 'rationally ignorant', rather than troubling themselves with matters with which they do not need to concern themselves. This in itself is an elitist version of democracy, but his arguments also reveal other ideological orientations. Social Democrats, he notes, have a specific concern about democracy: the alleged liberal economic bias of the EU. However, in Moravcsik's view this is a *positive* factor. Arguing that most EU states (or certainly the long-term members) have a bias to welfare, it is, he maintains, good that there is a countervailing tendency operating at EU level. Since those dependent on welfare – 'entrenched constituencies (the elderly, medical care consumers and the full-time unemployed)' – exert pressure on the member states to resist reform, the liberal orientation of the EU helps governments to withstand the pressures. For, according to Moravcsik: 'No responsible analyst believes that current individual social welfare entitlements can be maintained … In this context, the neo-liberal bias of the EU, if it exists, is justified by the social welfarist bias of current national policies' (2002: 618). His argument is in fact embedded in normative preferences in favour of international economic liberalism, but these are masked by an approach that appears to be solely analytical. His position is a defence of intergovernmentalism and neo-liberalism, imbued with an apparent nostalgia for the permissive consensus!

If some of Moravcsik's analytical insights into the limited degree of supranationalism should be taken into account in discussions of democracy and the EU, his argument remains unacceptable because of its elitism and its privileging of economic liberalism over the goal of equality.[2] The *explicitly* normative versions of state-centred views should, I believe, be rejected because the case for thoroughgoing repatriation of policies, let alone withdrawal from the EU, is now anachronistic for the following reasons. First, the extent of integration and interdependence is so advanced that the repatriation of policy to the member states could be secured only with massive disruption and destabilisation in Europe. Second, many of the forces of globalisation that undermine the domestic autonomy of all but the strongest states would operate whether or not the EU existed. Third, any state which attempted a repatriation of policies by itself would almost certainly suffer as a result of the greater potential punitive power of the other member states: at the very least, it would find that it needed the EU more than the EU needed it. Finally, there are some normative arguments against state-centred approaches, even when they are not based explicitly on extreme nationalism and xenophobia. The EU has created some positive forms of transnational politics in a multi-ethnic, multi-lingual environment and has the potential to go further in this respect. The repatriation of policies would set back this project and, given the vast practical, economic and political difficulties that would be involved, there is a strong probability that it would be accompanied by an intolerant nationalist rhetoric, whatever the original motivations for the strategy.

Federalist views

Since it has been argued for at least half a century that the European 'nation-state' is no longer viable as an autonomous location for democracy, some advocates of European integration have always accepted an argument at the other extreme. Because of the strength of the identification between a political system and the territorial state, many have found it compelling to view the EU as a kind of state, albeit of a highly decentralised and federal kind. Some have favoured the establishment of a United States of Europe on normative grounds, but others have also accepted such arguments as an apparently pragmatic response to the processes of globalisation and integration that have allegedly rendered the 'nation-state' obsolescent. Indeed it has often been suggested that the EU is already an embryonic federation, since it has a federal legal system, a single market (now reinforced by a single currency in most of its pre-2004 members), and supranational political institutions. On this argument, it appears to follow that the requirement is now to draw up an explicitly federal constitutional settlement, so that clear forms of democracy and accountability may be established.

Experts on the subject have demonstrated the diversity of federal systems and it has been argued very plausibly that the EU should be regarded as an 'embryonic federation' (McKay 2001; from a legal perspective, see also Weiler 1999). Yet its characteristics are so specific that it is difficult to see what is to be gained in analytical terms by defining it as federal. The governments, particularly of the larger and more powerful states, retain primacy in the policy-making process and exercise a range of powers in the domestic and external spheres which differ very considerably from those of regional governments within existing federal states. It is true that there is considerable variation in the relationships between the state and sub-state tiers of government in federations and that some sub-state tiers in particular countries exercise very considerable powers (Fitzmaurice 1996; McKay 2001). Nevertheless, federal systems have a hierarchical structure with the central state at the summit. In the EU, by contrast, the governments retain a vast array of domestic powers. Of perhaps still greater significance, the stronger member states remain important international actors and, despite the aspirations of the Common Foreign and Security Policy, the bilateral relationships of individual states (particularly with the USA) are often of greater significance than those between the member states. It is true that some states are more willing to cede new powers to the EU, but it is not clear how far even those that use the discourse of federalism would really be prepared to go in subordinating themselves to a powerful supranational body.

The reconstruction of liberal-democracy on a new territorial basis with a recognisable central government therefore seems highly unlikely for the foreseeable future. And because there is no transnational movement with significant support campaigning for federalism, there are *currently* democratic arguments against it (even if there would be no *prima facie* arguments against a federation that was open towards the rest of the world, inclusive in relation to all inhabitants, committed to egalitarianism and with sufficient decentralisation to permit high levels of participation). However, rejection of the federalist project does not mean rejection of all the arguments on which the call has been based. For it is true that EU law supersedes national law (in the way in which federal law 'trumps' state law in federal systems); and it is true that there is constant interaction between policy-makers at EU and member state levels (often including sub-state levels), and that an ever-increasing number of decisions are taken cooperatively rather than by the member states alone. Federalists have therefore been quite justified in suggesting both that there are democratic and accountability problems at EU level, and that some of the solutions must be sought in supranational and transnational terms.

Drawing from the institutional model of liberal democracy

An alternative way of applying the historical and conceptual model of liberal-democracy to the EU has been to assume that the *institutions* associated with the system within the state should play a similar role at EU level.

The European Parliament (EP) has been the central element in this assumption as it is the only body directly elected on European basis. Ever since the first direct election in 1979, the EP has therefore been seen (and has certainly seen itself) as the main vehicle for the democratisation of the EU and its powers have steadily increased. In general, MEPs have taken their role seriously and the Parliament has certainly become a far more important actor in the EU system as a whole. Nevertheless, there is room for considerable scepticism about the *extent* to which the EP has ameliorated the problems of democracy and accountability within the system, or can be expected to do so.

The first fundamental weakness in its position is its comparative remoteness from the concerns of its electorate, which is manifested both in the overwhelming salience of domestic issues in Euro-elections and in the constant decline in the turnout – from an average of 63 per cent in 1979 to 45.7 per cent in 2004.[3] While there are differences between the member states, it is generally the case that neither the EP itself, nor the MEPs, are firmly embedded in the political consciousness of the population as a whole. Given this, it is difficult to maintain that the Parliament is a strong expression of European democracy. Its second weakness is the relative obscurity of its role in relationship to *government* – that is, the fact that governments are not formed from it and cannot be forced out of office by it. The two weaknesses are probably inextricably connected: that is, the European electorate would take more note of the Parliament if it had the power to bring down the Council. However, even if true, this does not advance the argument since the EP will not be granted such power. This does not mean that the EP is impotent in relation to the Council, for it has used its powers effectively to enhance its role in decision-making. Indeed, the attempt to strengthen its position in an ongoing bargaining relationship with the Council and the Commission has probably been the Parliament's main preoccupation (Hoskyns and Lambert 2000). In recent years, the tendency has been for the Parliament to concentrate more on the Commission – something that has probably been welcomed by many of the governments. This was evident when the Parliament effectively forced the resignation of the Santer Commission in March 1999, and in its dramatic refusal to endorse Manuel José Barroso's Commission in November 2004. However, while these inter-institutional disputes were healthy in accentuating the role of the democratically elected body, they were never likely to bring cheering crowds onto the streets!

Another institutional approach has been to consider the possibilities of democratising the Commission. It was thus argued long ago that the EP did not have the potential to play the role ascribed to it but that the EU institutional system was much closer to the American model of liberal-democracy, in which there is a 'separation of institutions, a separation of persons and a separation of powers' and 'no one institution can control the others' (Bogdanor 1986). Following the analogy it was therefore suggested that the direct election of the Commissioners on alternative partisan programmes for the Community as a whole could stimulate popular interest in the system, promote a greater sense of division between 'government' and 'opposition' and provide the Commission with 'both a democratic base and a legitimacy which it presently lacks' (Bogdanor and Woodcock 1991). Such ideas have subsequently been advocated periodically (Decker 2002) and have a theoretical plausibility, but it is again highly unlikely that the governments will allow an alternative body, which has greater initiating power than the Parliament, to claim a democratic mandate that would be far more 'European' than its own. Nor would the EP want a new rival to challenge its democratic legitimacy. Nevertheless, the Treaties of Maastricht, Amsterdam and Nice have all strengthened the EP in relation to the appointment of the Commission, and it is likely that that both the nomination and accountability of the Commission will continue to be subject to bargaining between the Council and the Parliament. These incremental changes are helpful within the policy-making system. However, their democratic significance is limited because they remain imperceptible to the majority of the public. And, more generally, it seems that institutional 'tinkering', based on analogies with the liberal-democratic state model, is unlikely to address the fundamental issues.

Legitimacy and the 'nation-state' model

One way in which the Council and Commission have tended to react to the erosion of the 'permissive consensus' has been to seek legitimation through emulating the process of 'nation-state' construction. In other words, they have sought to counter democratic concerns by treating them as a crisis of *legitimacy* which might be reversed by enhancing the popularity of the Union (Beetham and Lord 1998). Some attempts to do so, like Jacques Delors' effort to construct a 'social dimension' to counterbalance the single market, resulted in some tangible benefits to ordinary people. But many of the initiatives have been largely symbolic efforts to recycle the rituals of national construction (Shore 2000).[4] A further development of this kind, with far greater potential importance, was the establishment of European Union citizenship, first introduced in the Maastricht Treaty. However, since a precondition for acquiring this status was citizenship in a member state, and the majority of the rights of EU citizens had already been acquired in earlier phases of the integration process, the innovation *in itself* was again largely symbolic.

The fundamental way in which the 'nation-state' has been the primary reference point has been in the claim that its legitimacy rests on a sense of common identity. Because of 'we-feelings' towards the rest of the population within the state we are, it is alleged, willing to accept 'our' state and its need for significant powers. However, the lessons drawn from this have not always been helpful in relation to the EU. The rather feeble attempt to construct a similar form of Union identity through symbols has largely failed. But this ineffectiveness can then lead to negative conclusions about the possibility of democratic legitimacy at Union level.

A range of thinkers have argued, from various perspectives, that the appropriate feelings towards peoples of the EU can never be sufficiently close to generate the notions of a 'community of destiny' that have underpinned democratic construction within the state. Some forms of this argument may rest on exclusivist ethnic definitions of the nation and will be resisted by all those who share the perspective underlying this chapter – that an inclusive approach to democracy must be adopted. However, others disavow this kind of ethnic nationalism, but still maintain that transnational forms of identification can never approach the 'thick' forms of identity that have, for example, permitted the establishment of welfare states and redistributive policies. Sometimes the argument is couched in terms of 'civic nationalism'(Miller 2000); sometimes it is claimed that the linguistic barriers and general sense of remoteness and complexity of the EU make it inconceivable that the solidarity that exists within nation-states can ever be constructed at a European level (Grimm 1995/7).[5] Furthermore, it may be argued that the wider, and more diverse the Union becomes, the looser and weaker the 'we-feelings' are likely to be.

Such arguments cannot be dismissed out of hand. There is, for example, considerable evidence that many people in Western Europe have far stronger sentiments of identity with countries such as Switzerland, Norway and Iceland (which remain outside the EU) than with some of the new member states, let alone with Turkey (*Eurobarometer* 2002: section 6.3). However, it is equally clear that such feelings are also part of the appeal of populist xenophobic parties – and this suggests that they should be *countered* rather than passively accepted as permanent. There is a further negative consequence of simply acquiescing in the impossibility of the EU achieving democratic legitimacy, for this can then be used to justify arguments that the EU itself must be evaluated from perspectives that either contain very weak forms of democracy or are hardly democratic at all. This has been a feature of many more recent contributions to the debate.

Weak forms of democratic evaluation

The EU as a regulatory framework

The 'nation-state', it has been argued, has high levels of welfare expenditure and elements of redistribution are acceptable because of a shared identity. From this perspective, it is concluded that the EU neither has the available funds nor the democratic legitimacy for these kinds of policies. Instead it is far more suited to *regulation* than *redistribution*, and the appropriate agency is that of an independent body of experts established by the EU to oversee tasks entrusted to it (Majone: 1996a).[6] Independence and accountability can be reconciled through various mechanisms, including statutory objectives for performance standards, reason-giving and transparency requirements facilitating judicial review and public participation, due process provisions to ensure fairness among the inevitable losers from regulatory decisions, and professionalism in order to withstand external interference and to reduce the risk of arbitrary use of agency discretion (ibid: 300, cited in Gustavsson 2000: 52). Indeed, Majone argues that this form of independence provides a stronger system of accountability than the conventional one, since it insulates the regulatory system from short-term political pressures and he thus envisages a future in which a 'web of networks of national and supranational regulatory institutions [are] held together by shared values and objectives, and by a common style of policy-making' (Majone 1996b: 276). Accountability in a regulatory system is thus recommended as a general approach in the EU. Since the European Central Bank (ECB) is an important example of such an agency, I will consider the general argument, with particular reference to monetary policy.

Although the approach stresses the specific characteristics of the EU, the argument is coupled with a critique of existing models of democracy at the level of the nation-state. In particular, it notes that governments have manipulated monetary policy for electoral advantage or to appease particular interest groups in society. Ensuring that the ECB is outside political control is therefore regarded as the best way of keeping it to its appointed tasks. However, this argument understates the politics of *any* form of economic policy and fails to appreciate the implications for democracy of the independence of the ECB and its current monetary guidelines. For the deflationary bias set out in Maastricht and the subsequent Stability and Growth Pact limits public expenditure, which in turn tends to reinforce the inequalities between areas and social groups; and the removal of levers of economic policy-making from the control of member states makes it far more difficult for them to counteract such tendencies. Moreover, the independence of the European Central Bank undermines any strong form of democratic authorisation or accountability for its policies at either domestic or EU levels (Gustavsson 1999; Lintner 2000; Grahl 2001). This led to an absurd position when France and Germany repeatedly failed to comply with the terms of the Stability and Growth Pact because of its negative domestic effects. When, in November 2003, they escaped the reprimands and warnings previously incurred by smaller states that had exceeded the expenditure limits, the Commission subsequently referred the matter to the Court of Justice as a breach of Community law (although it let the matter drop in December 2004). The resentment of the smaller states was quite understandable, but the real problem was the previous decision to exclude monetary policy from political control. And, more generally, the argument that independent agencies should be accountable for specific tasks entrusted to them because the EU is not an appropriate body for redistributive policies can have paradoxical consequences. If the decisions of the ECB may lead to regressive redistribution, this would suggest that the EU does not have the legitimacy for redistribution to *lessen* inequalities, but that no similar problems arise if its policies redistribute resources so as to *increase* them. Such conclusions are, in my view, unacceptable on democratic grounds. The fact that governments may have often abused monetary policy for political purposes, or that parliaments have generally been uninterested in the details of central banking decisions (Magnette 1999) are not justifications for effectively removing such areas of policy from traditional forms of democratic authorisation and accountability.

Policy-making by consensus and intra-elite accountability

A different argument for suggesting that traditional notions of democracy are inappropriate for the EU focuses more on the specific policy-making process at European level. This, it is claimed, is based on the construction of a *consensus*, while much conventional thinking about democracy (perhaps particularly in Britain) is based on assumptions of *conflict* (Lord 1998: 94–5). Such notions, it is argued, have little relevance for the policy-making process in the EU. The government–opposition dichotomy does not apply and there are very strong incentives for cooperative policy-making both within and between EU institutions. Votes take place only rarely within the Council and the main impact of qualified majority voting has been to facilitate the search for a consensus. Similarly, the need for the Parliament to secure an absolute majority of its component members to exploit its legislative role to full effect, has also encouraged the two biggest groupings (the Party of European Socialists and the European People's Party) to cooperate, rather than to compete (Hix and Lord 1997). Furthermore, the co-decision legislative system means that the Council, Commission and EP have powerful inducements to conciliate one another to ensure that agreement is reached on proposals. The same pressures are at work in the elaborate committee system in which national and EU officials, and the key interest groups whom they consult, translate outline proposals into detailed legal instruments. Finally, the conflict model, based upon alternative parties articulating opposing views in society as a whole, is also inappropriate because of the comparative weakness of the transnational parties and the continuing dominance of national political consciousness amongst party members and voters. All this means that the EU policy-making process is based on a constant search for consensus, with the result that the initial ideas for legislation are re-formulated and amended by this ongoing 'conversation' between all the actors within this elaborate process. This, it has been suggested, provides effective forms of accountability (Héritier 1997; Joerges and Neyer 1997).

This consensus system is certainly at work within the EU. But it does not follow that this form of policy-making, with an array of officials, politicians, and recognised interests scrutinising and amending proposals, is a substitute for more conventional notions of democracy and accountability. Moreover, the committee and comitology system remains singularly opaque (Rhinhard 1999; Armstrong 2000). Neither the manner of appointment to the committees, nor the ways in which they operate are transparent, and it is not clear that there are any clear channels for the control and scrutiny of their activities. As Chris Lord has put it:

> [T]he EU has developed an elaborate system of deliberation at *elite* level ... to include all kinds of actor types in mutual reflection and critiques. The Union is likewise characterized by often respectable levels of inter-elite accountability. As yet, however, the public is scarcely involved at all. At the risk of some frivolity, we might characterize it as democracy without the people ...
>
> (Lord 1998: 129)

But the exclusion of 'the people' obviously also excludes ideas that might undermine the elite consensus on which policy is currently based. Certainly, any major disturbance caused by intruders into the 'private conversation' could threaten to bring back the noisy conflicts which have more often characterised domestic politics. However, democracy necessitates the inclusion of discordant voices. Their current absence does not demonstrate that the EU policy process is inevitably different from that of the member states in this respect – only that these characteristics are the result of confining the system largely to privileged actors and interests.

Democratic 'outputs' and 'inputs'

A further reaction to concerns about democracy in relation to the EU has been to suggest that the problems can be resolved by greater a concentration on *outputs*. For example, Fritz Scharpf (1999) argues that full democratic legitimacy on the model of the nation-state is not possible. Drawing a distinction between 'input' and 'output' legitimacy, he suggests that the EU cannot secure 'input' legitimacy because this involves the traditional democratic notions of influencing policy through participation, voting, party activity and so on. However, it can achieve 'output' legitimacy through a democratisation of the beneficial effects of its activity in areas that the member states cannot attain by themselves – such as the legal regulation of market conditions across the Union as a whole, which themselves help to underpin social welfare policies. In other words, if the European electorate perceive the EU as providing added value to policies primarily operated at member state level, the EU can gain legitimacy through these additional outputs even if there is a very weak form of democratic legitimation on the input side.

This approach is helpful in several respects. First, it suggests that the EU can secure greater legitimacy through policies of democratic relevance, rather than through the barren route of emulating the nation-state through symbolic processes or institutional tinkering. Second, it recognises that allegiance to the EU can be *significant* even if it is relatively weak. For the implication of Scharpf's argument is that stronger forms of legitimacy are likely to remain at member state (and, no doubt, sub-state level) for the foreseeable future. However, the theory also assumes that there can be a bifurcation between democratic inputs and outputs and the suggestion that legitimacy can be based on outcomes alone is not persuasive (Beetham and Lord 1998; Lord 1998).

If outputs at EU level are dependent upon imperfect forms of democratic input within the member states and the bargaining between the governments of those states, the peoples of Europe are in a very weak position to exert pressure. And there is a further problem in concentrating on outputs alone. For the integrity and honesty of the governments of the member states cannot be relied upon: if EU policies appear popular with domestic electorates, governments are liable to take the credit themselves, but they will use the EU as a scapegoat for unpopular domestic strategies. It would therefore seem unlikely that adequate forms of legitimacy could be secured purely through outputs, and that the EU also needs to be shaped by democratic inputs if it is to further the goals of equality, participation and diversity. However, this is far easier to state than to envisage.

In principle there are various ways of improving the input side of EU democracy that do not replicate the institutional patterns of the states. The development of stronger transnational parties and civil society movements could help to construct new forms of horizontal solidarity across the Union, complementing and reinforcing the vertical pressures operating through the member states (Hix and Lord 1997; Bellamy 2001). From a different perspective, Heidrun Abromeit has argued that the current trend in the EU is towards greater centralisation, and that the attempt to build indirect democracy into the system has failed. She has therefore proposed the injection of direct democracy by developing the use of referendums which would provide a veto power against decisions taken at EU level (Abromeit 1998). The objectives of her proposals are to heighten popular involvement, ensure that policy is based on consent and to slow down the EU juggernaut. Such referendums would provide a form of participatory democracy, and their nature and frequency should help to counteract the well-known weaknesses of this form of direct democracy: in particular, manipulation by governments, or voters giving their opinions on quite different questions from those that they are asked. However, this proposal is explicitly justified on the basis of a *negative* approach through the establishment of a new participatory veto system. It therefore emphasises control and accountability rather than active participation in policy-making. Other authors have suggested that this might be strengthened by applying the insights of the theory of *deliberative democracy* to the EU (Bohman and Rehg 1997; Gerstenberg 1997; Hoskyns 2000a, 2000b; Benz 1999). This focuses on the manner in which decisions are taken, emphasising the inclusion of diverse voices and the whole range of interests affected by policy. Given that the EU policy-making system is already based on deliberation, the task is therefore seen as one of injecting new voices from civil society into the major deliberative forums, and far greater transparency about key processes such as the comitology system.

Both output and input legitimacy are necessary parts of the solution to the EU's democratic problems. However, it still takes a leap of faith to believe that the more radical proposals will be implemented or that, if implemented, they would have a transformative effect. Why then is it so difficult to envisage democracy in relation to the EU and are there any possibilities of a breakthrough? These questions will be addressed in the conclusion.

Towards enhanced democracy

Despite the reforms that have taken place, and increasingly sophisticated academic analyses, the problem of the EU's 'democratic deficits' still seems intractable. One reason is, I believe, that when thinking about the EU, we also need to recall the democratic malaise *within* states. In Western Europe the period since the 1980s has seen a rise in inequality, a decline in participation rates – at least through established political parties and trade unions – and a rise in xenophobia and racism. In former Soviet-controlled Eastern and East-Central Europe, these negative factors have been counter-balanced by the establishment of liberal-democracy. But there are also serious problems of poverty, inequality, social exclusion and discrimination. All this gives rise to a series of questions: how can participation be effected at EU level when there is a declining interest in politics within the member states? How can engagement in the EU be strengthened when allegiance to more traditional entities, such as trade unions, parties and parliaments is waning? It does not seem likely that an effective form of democracy can be built at EU level unless it has already been revitalised at lower levels. It is surely only if there is active political engagement within the localities and organisations of all kinds that the real pressure for the democratisation of the EU can emerge. And the extent of the EU dimension in domestic policy will become apparent to a wider sector of society only when there is more political activity and engagement so that the interconnections between the different levels and spheres are experienced and absorbed. In this sense the problem of democratising the EU is simply a particular aspect of the more general need to overcome the malaise affecting democracy as a whole. I would suggest that this will require a renewal of emphasis upon the value and goal of *equality*, anchored to appropriate social policies, and a form of politics that attempts to control the market rather than being controlled by it. All this would certainly require a reversal of EU priorities, but it is difficult to envisage this without prior changes in the politics of the most powerful member states.[7]

Yet the EU is also an actor that affects the domestic environments in which it is situated. It is helpful to view the Union as an entity which is simultaneously characterised by elements of fusion (Rometsch and Wessels 1996; Wessels 1997) and elements of separation (Chryssochoou 1998; Benz 1999). Given the continuing power of the member states, it is misleading simply to treat it as a polity characterised by 'multi-level governance' (Marks *et al.* 1996). Yet the extent of the interactions between the different levels of government and between transnational actors also makes it inappropriate to treat it as if any rigid demarcation between the EU and the states (or sub-state levels) was possible. This makes it far more difficult to conceptualise democracy than would be the case if either of the above characterisations – complete fusion or complete separation – was appropriate. There is a further complication: the fluidity of the contemporary world. Space and time have been compressed and there has been a fragmentation of traditional structures, solidarities and ideologies. However, this necessary recognition of complexity and flux can also go too far when it ignores the fundamental continuities in the situation – above all, the concentration of economic and political power amongst elite groups in society. While much has changed, much stays the same and, in my view, it is only possible to envisage democracy in relation to the EU by attempting to apply traditional concepts in this confusing situation. It is at least possible to indicate an approach based on the analysis in the previous sections and the ideas outlined in section 1.

First, I would suggest that the emphasis on institutional reform at EU level, which has so often dominated discussions of democracy and accountability, should play a subordinate role in the immediate future. This is not to say that further adjustments in the interinstitutional arrangements are unnecessary, but to argue that both experience and theory imply that they will not play a key role in enhancing democratisation at present (see also Mény 2003). Second, it appears impossible to privilege any one level – either in territorial or functional terms – in the attempt to enhance democratisation. This means that it is necessary simultaneously to seek democratic reforms at local, regional, national and transnational levels. This is partly because non-accountable forms of power, which are often interconnected, exist at all levels. If governments and major economic and financial interests operate both nationally and transnationally, countervailing democratic power also needs to operate on both levels. But it must be acknowledged that contradictions may result from democratic demands at different levels. Certainly, this will not always be the case. For example, both the EP and domestic parliaments have an interest in securing greater openness and transparency in the Council. Yet there can sometimes be tensions and clashes between those seeking stronger forms of democracy and accountability at the different levels and it is not possible (or even desirable) for those operating on one level always to take account of all the others.

Thirdly, it needs to be recognised that the EU is inherently contradictory and that this will permeate notions of democratisation. For example, the attempt to translate the values and goals of equality, participation and inclusion into a straightforward evaluation of the EU is fraught with difficulties. It would therefore be plausible to argue *both* of the following in relation to the EU:

(a) that it has reinforced inequalities through the creation of a competitive capitalist market that strengthens the position of the most powerful companies and interests; that it has made participation more difficult by creating an opaque and remote system with a highly complex and diffuse system of power; and that it has created an exclusive 'fortress' against the poor and dispossessed from developing countries;

and

(b) that it has led to far more advanced gender equality policies than would otherwise have been adopted by many of the states and that it is now promoting significant actions in relation to anti-racism and discrimination on the grounds of disability and age; that it has facilitated the development of transnational civil society organisations; and that it offers the beginnings of post-national citizenship in a multicultural, multi-ethnic Europe.

My own conclusions from these contradictions are that the EU cannot be regarded as either wholly negative or positive in relation to the perspective on democracy underpinning this chapter. It is both. However, this leads to a further question. If the EU is ever to secure democratic legitimation does it need to be *conceptualised* in a particular way?

It is helpful to recall that most states are legitimised in a variety of ways, even if democratic legitimation has become dominant. Some sectors of most electorates do not view the state as legitimate solely for democratic reasons and most governments consciously cultivate other appeals, including nationalism and tradition. It is not suggested that the EU should emulate this approach: indeed it was argued earlier that it has tried to do so with little success. However, the fact that legitimation is rarely promoted through a single claim has relevance for the EU. For it might mean that it may be *perceived* differently by the various actors and publics. For example, if the British government (and public) insist that it is an intergovernmental organisation, while the German government (and public) view it as a quasi-federation, does this matter as long as both work within it and regard it as important? Lord and Magnette (2004) recently implied that it did not, arguing that the EU's legitimation could even be enhanced by a diversity of perspectives about it. This is an important insight, but perhaps also a brave attempt to make a virtue of current reality. A single perspective is not possible or desirable, but it is difficult to envisage the EU as a site for vibrant democratic life unless it is viewed as at least potentially positive in this respect.

A tradition that argues that this is possible insists that the EU can be built upon forms of identity, even if they may not be so 'thick' as those that exist within states and nations. These could lie partly in the perception of the EU as a *political* actor operating at levels that are necessarily beyond the scope of the individual member states (see also Mayer and Palmowski 2004). This might be in terms of 'post-national citizenship' and the protection of human rights throughout the EU, and there have been some significant steps in this direction with EU citizenship, the incorporation of democracy as a condition of EU membership, and the signing of the Charter of Fundamental Rights. There is also evidence that the EU is widely perceived as an actor in defence, security and international policy, with the latest survey of opinion recording support of 78 per cent for a common defence and security policy and 69 per cent for a common foreign policy (*Eurobarometer* 2004).[8] Jacques Derrida and Jürgen Habermas suggested in May 2003, in an appeal for a 'Renewal of Europe' (simultaneously published in *Libération* and the *Frankfurter Allgemeinen Zeitung*), that the mass protests on the streets of Europe against the war in Iraq could provide the impetus for a breakthrough in the creation of a peaceful, cooperative post-national constellation. Instead, however, the EU manifested acute divisions over the alignment with the US, which have not yet been healed. Had the Derrida-Habermas scenario materialised, it would have had tremendous significance; but otherwise, while a conceptualisation of the EU as an actor in such areas as citizenship, rights and foreign and security policy could be important, there are also possible weaknesses. First, some of these still concentrate mainly on the 'output' side – albeit with links with potentially democratic inputs. Second, there are also dangers in *restricting* the EU to particular spheres: for example, by apparently confining its sphere to issues of political rights, it could be implied that its competence in social policy should be strictly limited. This brings us to the issue of a Constitution.

For several years, there has been discussion of the merits of a Constitution, with some of the most significant thinking on the subject associated with Jürgen Habermas (1995/1997; 2001), who has tackled the argument about democratic legitimacy head on. Against those who argue that only *nations* can be the communities of destiny on which democracies may be constructed, this approach suggests instead that communities are also constructed *politically* and through a particular kind of communication. Habermas himself has attached great importance to the drawing up a Constitution, arguing that this process could have a catalytic effect in the creation of a transnational public sphere. Others, who are equally committed to transnational (or post-national) forms of democracy, have been less convinced about the merits of Constitutions. For example, Joseph Weiler has argued that the EU has already developed a system of constitutional federation, based on the principle of constitutional tolerance that recognises that 'no matter how close the Union, it is to remain a union among distinct peoples, distinct political identities, distinct political communities' (Weiler 2001: 70, quoted in Bernal 2004: 19).[9] Weiler's concern was that a Constitution might jeopardise this fundamental principle, while others have argued that Constitutions generally freeze a temporary status quo, making it far more difficult to bring about change (Agnew 2002; Bellamy 2001). Whatever the merits of this debate, the 2004 Constitutional Treaty has an evident relevance.

The Convention on the Future of Europe that was to draft the treaty began its work in February 2002, under the Presidency of Giscard d'Estaing. Although he was keen to draw parallels with the Philadelphia Convention of 1787, there was little similarity between his Convention and those established in momentous historical situations when a new polity was constructed following a revolution, war or national liberation. There was little awareness of its work by most of the public; there was comparatively little involvement by civil society groups; and the gender and ethnic balance of the participants were quite unrepresentative of the peoples of the EU. The decision by Giscard d'Estaing that engagement with the public in the process was not feasible and that the aim was to make Europe more *understandable* was perhaps symptomatic of its weaknesses. Gisela Stuart MP (one of the two representatives of national parliaments on the Praesidium) also made the rather bitter, but pertinent, observation that 'not once in the sixteen months I spent on the Convention did representatives question whether deeper integration is what the people of Europe want, whether it serves their best interests or whether it provides the best basis for a sustainable structure for an expanding Union' (Stuart 2003, quoted in Smith 2004: 29–30). Moreover, the motives both for the Convention and the drawing up of a new Constitutional Treaty bore only a superficial similarity to the arguments of Habermas. Some no doubt saw it in the same symbolic terms as previous forms of legitimation, while others (including the British government) viewed it largely as a means of *limiting* the competencies of the Union. It is also highly questionable – particularly in retrospect – whether it was wise to include so much in the Constitution. Clearly, the left-wing campaign for a 'no' vote was fuelled by the fact that the capitalist system, currently operating on increasingly neo-liberal lines, was now given constitutional status. Constitutions are normally *political* documents and it would no doubt have been more sensible to have limited it in this way.

Despite these weaknesses, the Treaty that eventually emerged from the Convention and the subsequent processes of bargaining and negotiation between the governments could, *in principle*, have led to the kind of step-change that the proponents of legitimation through constitutional democratic construction have proposed. First, the Convention (even with all its defects) provided a visible focus for discussions about the future shape of the Union. Second, the Treaty incorporated some significant developments that went beyond the piecemeal tinkering of the past. Thus two authors, who are committed to the transformation of the EU into a multicultural union founded on basic rights and democratic decision-making procedures, regard the results of the Convention as a breakthrough, and have summarised the relevant changes (which remained in the final version of the Treaty) as follows:

1 The incorporation of the Charter of Fundamental Rights in the Constitution.
2 The recognition of the legal personality of the Union.
3 The elimination of the pillar structure.
4 The recognition of the supremacy of EU law.
5 Reduction and simplification of the instruments used in law-making and decision-making procedures, plus the introduction of a hierarchy of legal acts.
6 A delineation (though far from unambiguous) of the distribution of competences.
7 The generalisation of qualified majority voting in the Council and the designation of co-decision as the standard procedure, albeit subject to important exceptions.
8 Changes to the Council presidency.
9 A popular right of initiative.

(Eriksen and Fossum 2004: 449)[10]

Third, the Constitution provided a possibility for the EU to be regarded simultaneously as a Union of states *and* peoples, and thereby to secure a kind of complementary democratic legitimation that differed from that of the member states. However, it was never likely to achieve such results, at least in the short term, and it now appears destined to be buried in the dustbin of history

One reason for this is the fact that it coincided with an historical episode that had far greater contemporary importance and salience: the crisis over the Iraq war. Second, disputes over the weighting of votes within the Council, and the way in which the governments presented the issues, drew attention away from the democratic questions that were involved. Instead they tended to invoke nationalist arguments that fuelled Euroscepticism, rather than dispelling it. However, the inevitable abandonment of the Constitution after its decisive rejection by the French and Dutch electorates meant that the EU is likely to enter a new period of uncertainty. After so much effort had been invested in the Constitution, this defeat could further reduce the democratic legitimacy of the EU, creating mutual bitterness between the governments, and reinforcing divisions. Certainly, the summit on 16–17 July 2005, with its bitter recriminations, particularly between Chirac and Blair, indicated that this was the immediate result.

This might appear a a very negative conclusion but, from a different angle, the changes since the Maastricht Treaty may appear highly significant. When, in 1992–3, the ratification crisis manifested the end of the permissive consensus, the problem seemed to be to find a way of inserting forms of democracy into a framework that already existed. But the rapidity of change in the contemporary world means that analysis of existing forms of governance and proposals for reform must recognise the inadequacy of assumptions based on a static view (Lebessis and Paterson 1999; Bertrand *et al.* 1999). In the case of the EU, this led to a new preoccupation with statecraft in relation to the 'near abroad': helping to stabilise liberal-democratic capitalism in Central and East-Central Europe and, in 2004, absorbing ten new members. Nor will this process stop, with Bulgarian and Romanian membership already imminent, and many other states now joining the queue (although the crisis over the Constitution may well curtail this process, leading to bitter disappointment, particularly in Turkey). The question of how democracy should be conceptualised and enhanced in relation to the EU had implied a static situation in terms of membership, and even Habermas believed that the eventual size of the Union needed to be defined at the same time as a Constitution was devised (2001: 13). This has not happened, and in a world of flux and conflict, it might subsequently be acknowledged that the EU has not done so badly after all. Its gradual moves towards post-national democracy, with peaceful bargaining and negotiation amongst its ever more diverse states and peoples, have certainly not yet established a system of equality, participation and inclusiveness. Yet, in the words attributed to Galileo, after recanting his proposition that the earth moved round the sun, '*eppur si muove*' – 'but it does move'.

Notes

1 For a fuller version of this aspect of the argument, see Newman (2002).
2 Moravcsik criticises Fritz Scharpf, whom he views as the most sophisticated Social Democratic theorist, arguing that he is really concerned with domestic redistribution over transnational redistribution and that this benefits rich countries like Germany. However, this criticism would be more convincing if Moravcsik was himself proposing transnational redistribution.
3 It is true there is also declining turnout in national elections in most countries, but this has limited relevance. Declining electoral turnout suggests that there are major problems in

established liberal-democracies, but there is an important difference between the situation in such systems and the EU. For the EU has not established democratic credentials and the Euro-elections constitute the whole visible aspect of democracy.

4   Shore takes the emulation of nation-state construction very seriously, attributing considerable importance to the EU's efforts. For a different view, see Newman (2001)

5   For a useful exploration of such views (and several other positions), see Lacroix (2001)

6   Although Majone, the foremost theorist of this approach, has emphasised the distinctive characteristics of the EU, he has also argued that the tradition of regulation (rather than redistribution) has been embedded in the American system.

7   The development of democracy in both the EU and the member states, is also shaped by the nature of, and pressures from, the international political economy . For the sake of simplicity, these are not discussed here. For a very useful analysis, see Anderson (2002).

8   The UK was the only country out the twenty-five with less than 50 per cent in favour of a common foreign policy.

9   Bernal (2004) provides a very useful analysis of the differences between Habermas and Weiler.

10   Others are much less enthusiastic about the results. See, for example, Dinan (2004).

References

Abromeit, H. (1998) *Democracy in Europe: Legitimising Politics in a Non-State Polity* (New York/ Oxford: Berghan Books)

Agnew, J. (2002) 'The limits of federalism in transnational democracy: beyond the hegemony of the US model', in J. Anderson (ed.), *Transnational Democracy: Political Spaces and Border Crossings* (London: Routledge).

Anderson, J. (2002) 'Questions of democracy, territoriality and globalisation', in J. Anderson (ed.), *Transnational Democracy: Political Spaces and Border Crossing*s (London: Routledge).

Armstrong, K. (2000) *Regulation, Deregulation, Reregulation: The Paradoxes of European Governance* (London: Kogan Page).

Beetham, D. and Lord, C. (1998) *Legitimacy and the European Union* (London: Addison Wesley/ Longman).

Bellamy, R. (2001) 'The "Right to have Rights": Citizenship Practice and the Political Constitution of the EU', in R. Bellamy and A. Warleigh (eds), *Citizenship and Governance in the European Union* (London: Continuum).

Benz, A. (1999) 'Compounded Democracy and Multi-Level Governance in the EU', Paper presented at the conference of the IPSA Research Committee on European Unification, Brussels, 2–3 December 1999.

Bernal, A. (2004) 'On the "Paradox" of Constitutionalism and Democracy in the EU: The Case of the Convention on the Future of Europe', Paper for the Yale University Contemporary Politics Workshop, 20 February 2004.

Bertrand, G., Michalski, A. and Pench, L. (1999) *Scenarios Europe 2010: Five Possible Futures for Europe* (Brussels: European Commission (Forward Studies Unit)).

Bogdanor, V. (1986) 'The Future of the European Community: Two Models of Democracy', *Government and Opposition* 21/2: 161–76.

Bogdanor, V. and Woodcock, G. (1991) 'The European Community and Sovereignty', *Parliamentary Affairs* 44/4: 481–92.

Bohman, J. and Rehg, W. (eds) (1997) *Deliberative Democracy – Essays on Reason and Politics* (Cambridge, MA: MIT Press).

Chryssochoou, D. (1998) *Democracy in the European Union* (London/New York: Taurus).

Decker, F. (2002) 'Governance beyond the nation-state. Reflections on the democratic deficit of the European Union', *Journal of European Public Policy* 9/2: 256–72.

Dinan, D. (2004) 'Governance and Institutions: The Convention and the Intergovernmental Conference', *Journal of Common Market Studies* 42, Annual Review: 27–42.

Eriksen, E. O. and Fossum, J. E (2004) 'Europe in Search of Legitimacy: Strategies of Legitimation Assessed', *International Political Science Review* 25/4: 435–59

Eurobarometer 57 (2002) *Public Opinion in the European Union* (Brussels: European Commission).

Eurobarometer 62 (2004) *Public Opinion in the European Union* (Brussels: European Commission).

Fitzmaurice, J. (1996) *The Politics of Belgium: A Unique Federalism* (London: Hurst).

Gerstenberg, O. (1997) 'Law's Polyarchy: a Comment on Cohen and Sabel?', *European Law Journal* 3/4: 343–58.

Grahl, J. (2001) *European Monetary Union: Legitimacy, Development and Stability* (London: Kogan Page).

Grimm, D. (1995/1997) 'Does Europe Need a Constitution?', *European Law Journal* 1/3, republished in P. Gowan and P. Anderson (eds) (1997), *The Question of Europe* (London: Verso).

Gustavsson, S. (1999) 'Monetary Union without Fiscal Union: A Politically Sustainable Asymmetry?' Paper Presented at the Research Conference of the Nordic Political Science Association, Uppsala, 19–21 August.

—— (2000) 'Reconciling Suprastatism and Accountability: A View from Sweden', in C. Hoskyns and M. Newman (eds), *Democratizing the European Union: Issues for the Twenty-First Century* (Manchester: Manchester University Press).

Habermas, J. (1995/7) 'Remarks on Dieter Grimm's "Does Europe Need a Constitution?"', *European Law Journal* 1/3, republished in P. Gowan and P. Anderson (eds) (1997) *The Question of Europe* (London:Verso).

—— (2001) 'Why Europe Needs a Constitution', *New Left Review* 11.

Héritier, A. (1997) 'Policy-Making by Subterfuge: Interest Accommodation, Innovation and Substitute Democratic Legitimation in Europe. Perspectives from Distinctive Policy Areas', *Journal of European Public Policy* 4/2: 171–89.

Hix, S. and Lord, C. (1997) *Political Parties in the European Union* (Houndmills/London: Macmillan).

Hoskyns, C. (2000a) 'Democratizing the EU: Evidence and Argument' in C. Hoskyns and M. Newman (eds), *Democratizing the European Union: Issues for the Twenty-First Century* (Manchester: Manchester University Press).

—— (2000b) 'Deliberative Democracy and the European Union', Paper presented at the PSA Conference, London, 10–13 April.

Hoskyns, C. and Lambert, J. (2000) 'How Democratic is the European Parliament?' in C. Hoskyns and M. Newman (eds,) *Democratizing the European Union: Issues for the Twenty-First Century* (Manchester: Manchester University Press).

Joerges, C. and Neyer, J. (1997) 'Transforming Strategic Interaction into Deliberative Problem-Solving: European Comitology in the Foodstuffs Sector', *Journal of European Public Policy* 4/4: 609–25.

Lacroix, J. (2001) 'Constitutionalism, Democracy and Europe: Is a European political identity possible?', Paper for the 51st Political Studies Association, Manchester, 10–12 April.

Lebessis, N. and Paterson, J. (1999) *Improving the Effectiveness and Legitimacy of EU Governance: A Possible Reform Agenda for the Commission* (Brussels: European Commission (Forward Studies Unit)).

Lintner, V. (2000) 'Controlling EMU', in C. Hoskyns and M. Newman (eds), *Democratizing the European Union: Issues for the Twenty-First Century* (Manchester: Manchester University Press).

Lord, C. (1998) *Democracy in the European Union* (Sheffield: Sheffield Academic Press/UACES).

Lord, C. and Magnette, P. (2004) 'E Pluribus Unum? Creative Disagreement about Legitimacy in the EU', *Journal of Common Market Studies* 42/1: 183–202

McKay, D. (2001) *Designing Europe: Comparative Lessons from the Federal Experience* (Oxford: Oxford University Press).

Magnette, P. (1999) 'Can an Independent Organ be Held Accountable? The Emergent Parliamentary Control of the European Central Bank', Paper presented at the conference of the IPSA Research Committee on European Unification, Brussels, 2–3 December.

Majone, G. (1996a) 'Regulatory Legitimacy', in G. Majone (ed.) *Regulating Europe* (London: Routledge).

—— (1996b) 'A European Regulatory State?', in J. Richardson (ed.), *European Union: Power and Policy-Making* (London: Routledge).

Marks, G., Hooghe, L. and Blank, K. (1996) 'European Integration from the 1980s: State-Centric vs. Multi-Level Governance', *Journal of Common Market Studies* 34/3: 341–78.

Mayer, F. and Palmowski (2004) 'European Identities and the EU – The Ties that Bind the Peoples of Europe', *Journal of Common Market Studies*, 42/3.

Mény, Y. (2003) '*De la démocratie en Europe*: Old Concepts and New Challenges', *Journal of Common Market Studies*, 41/1: 1–13.

Moravcsik, A. (2002) 'In Defence of the "Democratic Deficit": Reassessing Legitimacy in the European Union', *Journal of Common Market Studies* 40/4: 603–24

Miller, D. (2000) *Citizenship and National Identity* (Cambridge: Polity Press).

Newman, M. (1996) *Democracy, Sovereignty and the European Union* (London: Hurst).

—— (2001) 'Allegiance, Legitimation, Democracy and the European Union', European University Institute: EUI Working Papers HEC No.2001/5.

—— (2002) 'Reconceptualising Democracy in the European Union' in J. Anderson (ed.) *Transnational Democracy: Political Spaces and Border Crossings* (London: Routledge).

Rhinhard, M. (1999) 'Governing in Committees: An Analysis of the Democratic Legitimacy of the European Union Committee System', Paper presented at the conference of the IPSA Research Committee on European Unification, Brussels, 2–3 December.

Rometsch, D. and Wessels, W. (eds) (1996) *The European Union and Member States: Towards Institutional Fusion* (Manchester: Manchester University Press).

Scharpf, F. (1999) *Governing in Europe: Effective and Democratic?* (Oxford: Oxford University Press).

Shore, C. (2000) *Building Europe: The Cultural Politics of European Integration* (London: Routledge).

Smith, R. (2004) 'Constitutionalising the European Union', *UACES European Studies On-Line Essays*; www.uaces.org

Stuart, G. (2003) *The Making of Europe's Constitution* (London: Fabian Society).

Weiler, J. (1994) 'Fin de siècle Europe', in R. Dehousse (ed.), *Europe After Maastricht: An Ever Closer Union?* (Munich: Beck).

—— (1999) *The Constitution of Europe* (Cambridge: Cambridge University Press).

—— (2001) 'Federalism Without Constitutionalism: Europe's *Sonderweg*', in K. Nicolaidis and R. Howse (eds), *The Federal Vision: Legitimacy and Levels of Governance in the United States and the European Union* (Oxford: Oxford University Press).

Wessels, W. (1997) 'An Ever Closer Fusion? A Dynamic Macropolitical View on Integration Processes', *Journal of Common Market Studies* 35/2: 267–99.

Index

Abromeit, H. 389
accession conditionality 208–9, 219–20, 222
accession countries 159, 208–10, 221–2, 282
accession negotiations 33, 207–9, 215, 218–23
accountability 68, 387; and democracy 378–94; and elections 241–2, 379; and European Commission 46, 110–16, 384; and European Parliament 129, 131, 383; and member states 379–82; and national parliaments 132–6; and regulation 386–7
actorness 97, 147, 160, 166
Adler, K. 14
advocacy coalition 7, 20, 22–3, 29, 35–7, 39, 43, 54, 120, 249, 260, 264, 268
agenda-setting 6–7, 21, 25, 29, 41–2, 48, 94, 123, 127, 131, 156–7, 160, 214, 249, 283, 326
Agnew, J. 392
Alesina, A. 191, 272
Allen, D. 290, 297, 301, 304
Allsop, C. 338
Almond, G. 4
Amsterdam Treaty 4, 36, 45–7, 114, 160, 165, 217, 277, 313; and CFSP 290, 294; and European Parliament 130, 323, 384; and macroeconomic policy 331–4; and weighted voting 151
Anderson, J. 281, 395
Ansell, C. 281, 283
Armstrong, K. 313, 387
Armstrong, N. 279
Artis, M. 338, 348
Aspinwall, M. 255

Baier, N. 362
Baldwin, R. 209, 210, 312
Baltz, K. 252
bargaining power 78–80, 82–4, 89, 189, 209, 212–13, 217–18, 222
bargaining theory 79, 80, 81

Barroso, Manuel 101, 104, 114, 116–17, 384
Baumgartner, F. 24, 250, 261
Bayer, N. 168
Beach, D. 164
Beetham, D. 384, 387
Begg, I. 271
Bellamy, R. 389, 392
benchmarking 7, 312
Bennett, R. 249, 263
Benz, A. 56, 129, 131, 139, 140, 389, 390
Bergman, T. 123
Berman, P. 363, 372
Bernal, A. 392
Bertrand, G. 394
best practice 34, 59, 66, 163, 312, 371
Beyers, J. 164, 249
Beyme, K. von 123
Blumler, J. 230, 233
Bogdanor, V. 242, 384
Bohman, J. 388
Bolton, P. 191
Bomberg, E. 58
Bouma, J, 360
Bouwen, P. 177, 249, 250, 261, 262, 263
Braun, D. 14
Brent, R. 100, 106
Breton, R. 252
Broscheid, A. 249, 251
Bruszt, L. 221
Bruter, M. 107
Bryce, J. 122
Buchanan, J. 190
Buitendijk, G. 111
Buiter, W. 337
Bullman, U. 269, 273, 282
Bulmer, S. 59, 64, 159, 313, 314, 316, 319
Burnham, J. 105
Burns, C. 112
Burns, T. 122
Busch, A. 14, 22, 59
Butt Philip, A. 254

399